Adaptive Web Services for Modular and Reusable Software Development:

Tactics and Solutions

Guadalupe Ortiz
University of Cádiz, Spain

Javier Cubo
University of Málaga, Spain

Information Science
REFERENCE

Managing Director:	Lindsay Johnston
Senior Editorial Director:	Heather A. Probst
Book Production Manager:	Jennifer Romanchak
Publishing Systems Analyst:	Adrienne Freeland
Managing Editor:	Joel Gamon
Development Editor:	Hannah Abelbeck
Assistant Acquisitions Editor:	Kayla Wolfe
Typesetter:	Travis Gundrum
Cover Design:	Nick Newcomer

Published in the United States of America by
Information Science Reference (an imprint of IGI Global)
701 E. Chocolate Avenue
Hershey PA 17033
Tel: 717-533-8845
Fax: 717-533-8661
E-mail: cust@igi-global.com
Web site: http://www.igi-global.com

Library of Congress Cataloging-in-Publication Data

Adaptive web services for modular and reusable software development: tactics and solutions / Guadalupe Ortiz and Javier Cubo, editors.
    p. cm.
  Includes bibliographical references and index.
  Summary: "The book comprises chapters that present tactics and solutions for modular and reusable software development in the field of adaptive Web services"--Provided by publisher.
  ISBN 978-1-4666-2089-6 (hardcover) -- ISBN 978-1-4666-2090-2 (ebook) -- ISBN 978-1-4666-2091-9 (print & perpetual access)
1. Web services. 2. Computer software--Reusability. 3. Component software 4. Computer software--Development. I. Ortiz, Guadalupe, 1977- II. Cubo, Javier, 1978-
  TK5105.88813.A365 2012
  006.7'8--dc23
                        2012013952

British Cataloguing in Publication Data
A Cataloguing in Publication record for this book is available from the British Library.

All work contributed to this book is new, previously-unpublished material. The views expressed in this book are those of the authors, but not necessarily of the publisher.

Table of Contents

Section 1
Contract-Based Adaptation and Interoperability

Section 2
Context-Aware Adaptation

Section 3
Adaptation for Composition

Section 4
Dynamic Adaptation

Section 5
Device-Based Future Internet Adaptation

Detailed Table of Contents

Section 1
Contract-Based Adaptation and Interoperability

During the service communication, different interoperability issues arise dynamically and continuously, which have to be detected and handled. Due to the black-box nature of the services in most cases it is impossible to modify services to adapt them. Therefore, they require a certain degree of adaptation by means of adaptation contracts in order to avoid interoperability problems during the composition. In this section, the following three chapters show the importance of the adaptation and propose tactics to tackle the interoperability issues in service-based systems in an automatic way.

This chapter proposes an Adaptive Enterprise Service Bus (ESB) Infrastructure which, based on the mediation capabilities provided by ESBs, can respond to adaptation requirements in service-based systems in an automatic and dynamic way at runtime. The chapter also specifies how the proposed solutions can be used to deal with concrete situations including response time degradation, services saturation and changes in services contracts.

In this chapter, author addresses interoperability from the perspective of both the consumer (compliance) and provider (conformance) services, and argues that compliance is a weaker requirement for service interoperability than conformance and should be the cornerstone to decrease coupling and to favor adaptability. This proposal uses structural interoperability, given that the lifecycles of distributed resources are decoupled. In addition, metrics to quantify adaptability based on similarity and decoupling are proposed.

Chapter 3

Mario Bravetti, University of Bologna, Italy & INRIA, France
Gianluigi Zavattaro, University of Bologna, Italy & INRIA, France

This chapter discusses the interplay between the notions of contract compliance, contract refinement and choreography conformance in the context of service oriented computing, by considering both synchronous and asynchronous communication. Service contracts are specified in a language independent way by means of finite labeled transition systems. Authors assume that a contract language has an operational semantics defined in terms of a labeled transition system, and they make a comparative analysis of synchronous and asynchronous communication.

Section 2
Context-Aware Adaptation

Context-awareness is the ability to detect and handle context changes in a system, by adapting its behaviour at run-time according to the changing conditions of the environment, as well as those of user preferences or privileges. One of the main features of context information is its dynamism. Thus, context-aware applications should support a high-level of adaptation in the values that define the context information. Adaptations may be as varied as the information related to the context, and as is presented in the two following chapters, it can be performed by using different techniques such as adaptation contracts or event processing.

Chapter 4

Javier Cubo, University of Málaga, Spain
Ernesto Pimentel, University of Málaga, Spain

In this chapter, authors present a framework to tackle reusing of software entities by means of context-aware discovery and adaptation processes in order to solve, as automatically as possible, mismatch cases which may be given at the different interoperability levels among service interfaces composing pervasive systems. The framework generates a mediating adaptor based on an adaptation contract.

Chapter 5

Guadalupe Ortiz, Quercus Software Engineering Group, Spain &
UCASE Software Engineering Group, Spain
Juan Boubeta-Puig, UCASE Software Engineering Group, Spain
Alfonso García de Prado, UCASE Software Engineering Group, Spain
Inmaculada Medina-Bulo, UCASE Software Engineering Group, Spain

This chapter proposes an architecture which utilizes complex event processing for detecting context events relevant to the services in question and an aspect-oriented adaptation, maintaining a loosely coupled service implementation as well as keeping its main functionality structure without adding any context-related intrusive code.

Section 3
Adaptation for Composition

Services are isolated pieces which can be reused and composed in order to provide more complex services. Sometimes the composition can be done straight from the original service. However, adaptation is required most of the times. Adaptation can be required when it is necessary to replace one service by another with the same functionality, or it may also be required when services do not correspond exactly to end-user needs and in these cases we need some mediation in order to achieve the right composition. The three chapters of this section present different solutions for enhancing the composition of service-based applications by means of technologies like autonomic computing, process mining, and Semantic Web.

Chapter 6

> *Valeria Cardellini, University of Roma "Tor Vergata," Italy*
> *Valerio Di Valerio, University of Roma "Tor Vergata," Italy*
> *Stefano Iannucci, University of Roma "Tor Vergata," Italy*
> *Francesco Lo Presti, University of Roma "Tor Vergata," Italy*

In this chapter, authors analyze how the MAPE-K (Monitor, Analyze, Plan, Execute, and Knowledge) reference model has been applied to design self-adaptive service-oriented systems. Although every phase is required in the realization of a control process, authors focus on the Plan phase because it is the core of the adaptation process. Specifically, they analyze how the service-oriented systems can self-adapt in order to satisfy some non-functional requirements. As a case study, authors present a framework, that realizes every phase of the MAPE-K model relying on a modular system architecture.

Chapter 7

> *Schahram Dustdar, Vienna University of Technology, Austria*
> *Philipp Leitner, Vienna University of Technology, Austria*
> *Franco Maria Nardini, ISTI-CNR, Pisa, Italy*
> *Fabrizio Silvestri, ISTI-CNR, Pisa, Italy*
> *Gabriele Tolomei, ISTI-CNR, Pisa, Italy*

This chapter focuses on process mining as a specific instance of the more general sequential pattern mining problem. Basically, the aim of this chapter is to detect frequent sequential patterns that might be presented in actual traces of service executions recorded in event logs. To this end, authors apply two sequential pattern mining algorithms to a real event log provided by the Vienna Runtime Environment for Service-oriented Computing (VRESCo). The obtained results show that the proposal enables to find services that are frequently invoked together within the same sequence (service recommendation).

In this chapter, authors discuss how standard service-oriented architectures have to evolve to tackle the above issues. They present a general architecture based on a shared spatial substrate mediating interactions of all the individual services of the pervasive computing system. Finally, authors show that this architecture can be implemented relying primarily on standard W3C Semantic Web technologies. A use case of adaptive pervasive displays for crowd steering applications is exploited as reference example.

Section 4
Dynamic Adaptation

Dynamic adaptation is an important issue to be addressed since rapid changes in software demand as well as runtime error or problems with runtime service availability may require the replacement of composite services dynamically, adapting them if necessary. In this section, each chapter describes a framework developed in order to tackle runtime adaptation on both service-based and real-time-constraints systems.

This chapter discusses limitations regarding the flexibility for the dynamic collaboration of the services involved in the process and introduces a framework for service collaboration that is suitable for cloud computing settings. The framework is based in techniques for coordination and service matching aim to achieve the dynamic service collaboration through matching goal-oriented service requests with providers that advertise their offerings dynamically.

Chapter 10

In this chapter, authors present Situation Action Networks, a new framework for modeling Service-Based Application adaptation triggered by interesting or critical situations. Situation Action Networks are tree-like hierarchical structures which enable goal decomposition into sub-goals and primitive actions in a recursive fashion which provides goal seeking execution plans, as a sequence of primitive actions. Situation Action Networks are dynamic and can evolve at runtime by using their inherent planning capabilities. Therefore, the framework is based on a goal model able to track at runtime the fulfillment of goals.

Fahad Bin Tariq, University of Paderborn, Germany

Sandeep Korrapati, University of Paderborn, Germany

This chapter presents an approach to tackle the issue of runtime adaptation on computationally constrained systems with real-time constraints. Authors focus on systems with only a single general purpose processor, with the responsibility to run the system and application software. They introduce a framework towards this aim, followed by the architecture and a case study.

Section 5
Device-Based Future Internet Adaptation

Device adaptation has become fashionable lately due to the huge and ever increasing use of devices such as mobiles or sensor nodes at present and the Future Internet. For example, users wish to access the same services whether they are using a desktop PC or a mobile device, and therefore these services need to be adapted. Thus, device-based Future Internet applications will have to support the interoperability between many diverse stakeholders by governing the convergence and life-cycle of things and contents coming from heterogeneous devices. The following three chapters present tactics and ideas for addressing adaptive device-based future internet applications.

Achilleas P. Achilleos, University of Cyprus, Cyprus

Kun Yang, University of Essex, UK

George A. Papadopoulos, University of Cyprus, Cyprus

In this chapter, authors propose a Model-Driven Web Service oriented approach, which allows designing and automatically generating mobile and desktop-based clients that are able to invoke ubiquitously Web Services from different devices. This is further enabled via the Web Services Description Language that allows generating the required proxy classes, which support the communication with platform-specific clients. The applicability and efficiency of the approach is demonstrated via the design and development of a device-aware Web Service prototype.

Valérie Monfort, SOIE, Tunisia

Sihem Cherif, SOIE, Tunisia

Rym Chaabani, ISIG, Tunisia

This chapter shows how authors extend Android to make it adaptable and interoperable. They also present how we communicate between different heterogeneous context-aware platforms as WComp and OpenORB by using Android and Web Services. The usefulness of the proposed approach is demonstrated through a concrete case study.

In this chapter, authors analyze and justify the need for the transition from adaptive Web services and service-based applications to adap¬tive Future Internet (FI) applications. Based on two real-world use cases from multimedia and logistics, they examine where current solutions fall short to properly address the adaptive needs of FI applications. Authors also propose future research challenges that should be considered in adaptive FI applications.

Foreword

Do you also always carry your mobile device? Do you use it everywhere, i.e. in the street, while travelling and at your workplace? Do you want to explicitly handle specific environment characteristics which are all different depending on where you are: For example, there usually is better connectivity at your workplace or at home than during travel, security aspects change accordingly, sometime you access your own, well-defined service environment, sometime you want to detect new services in unknown territory etc. But, of course, regardless of where and for what you use it, your device shall always function "right" in order to take advantage of whatever the specific environment has to offer (as, e.g., connectivity, compute power, service diversity, security, fun, etc.). What that basically means is, that your mobile device has to always "adapt" flexibly and appropriately to the specific characteristics of such respective environments.

In a bit more abstract terms: Most of today's software applications are distributed in one way or the other, and many of them are executed in heterogeneous and often dynamically changing environments – with examples ranging from relatively small and static multi-processor systems (such as in car electronics) up to open world-wide service co-operations in e-business or (just to mention another set of applications) highly dynamic multi-player games, for example. And for all such environments we need appropriate system software support.

Such a distributed system infrastructure (i.e. middleware) has to be generic (i.e. standardized) in order to provide the basis for state-of- the art software development for such applications. In addition, current distributed systems rely heavily on the paradigm of a Service-oriented Architecture (SOA) – with Web Services (WS) as its most prominent realization. Therefore, in the best of all worlds of open, service-oriented distributed systems, the "right" set of services is available when- and wherever needed and services can, in addition, be combined freely and flexibly – regardless of where, how and by whom they are realized, managed, and provided. So, new services can always be composed out of existing ones with as little effort and security problems as possible.

Reality, however, is still different and further challenges arise – just to name a few: appropriate services for such compositions may have to be "discovered" first and their respective interfaces as well as their behavior have to be uniquely identified; then, services which do not "fit" exactly, may have to be "adapted" and then (dynamically) combined in order to realize co-operative applications in various ways – dependent on, e.g., the underlying application pattern (e.g. by choreography or by orchestration); appropriate "agreements" on service-level characteristics have to be reached between co-operation partners; and, especially in pervasive and dynamic environments, sets of available services that change dynamically together with any context changes have to be taken care of.

So, at least service interfaces (esp. interface definitions) as well as co-operation patterns have to be agreed upon in order to make such co-operations possible in heterogeneous distributed environments. Some of the related standardization issues are addressed by corresponding WS*-standards and middleware platforms – although with standards mostly limited to a syntactical level. Some further ideas, e.g. on semantic extension, exist – but many of them still have to prove their relevance in practice.

The ultimate goal of software to support such applications is to be able to adapt to many heterogeneity and/or environment changes – ideally automatically and flexibly in ways as required by heterogeneous distributed service-oriented applications in dynamically changing environments.

Motivated by these challenges and related problems, this book addresses many issues of improving software development for such applications in a platform independent and loosely coupled manner – in order to realize modular and adaptive distributed service-oriented systems with great flexibility and easy to fulfill maintenance requirements. In this sense, advanced distributed applications should be self-contained, self-descriptive and self-adaptive as well as able to locate, access, and invoke related services and compose them freely, flexibly and context-dependently from any point of a distributed application environment. In addition, service compositions as well as service adaptations should be implemented in ways which preserve the loosely coupled nature of Web Services and which allow for implementation's integration in the whole service lifecycle.

Rather attractive and practice-relevant partial solutions which address many of these challenges exist already and are referenced in this book. Accordingly, state-or-the-art research results are described and discussed – ranging from "context adaptation" (i.e. context-aware services) over "device adaptation" (i.e. service adaptation to specific device characteristics) and "user preference adaptation" (i.e. service adaptation to the specific needs of mobile users in the web), software-as-a service etc. up to "adaptation for composition" (i.e. ways to make – independently developed – services ready for dynamic composition) and support for service mediation.

In summary, this book provides a compound collection of the most representative approaches in current research which tackle the different faces of Web Service adaptation for (e.g.) software engineers, from senior and young researchers at the academia to research and development groups in industry.

Winfried Lamersdorf
University of Hamburg, Germany March 2012

Winfried Lamersdorf *is a full Professor in the Informatics Department of Hamburg University since 1991, former department head as well as deputy head for research, and head of the "Distributed and Information Systems" research unit with specific responsibilities in the area of "Distributed Systems," and also a (founding) board member of the Hamburg Informatics Technology Transfer Institute HITeC e.V. After his PhD in Computer Science in 1985, he spent a year at the University of Maryland, USA, in collaboration with the National Institute of Standards and Technology (NIST). From 1983 to 1990 he was scientific staff member at the IBM Scientific and European Networking Centre(s) in Heidelberg working in the area of open distributed applications, with some 10 years of additional experiences in international standardization in that area. He has lead and conducted several research projects – e.g. several with the German national research fund (DFG), the European Commission (in FP 5, 6, and 7), the German ministry for education and research (BMBF), as well as with a number of industry partners (as, e.g., IBM, HP etc.). He has (co-) authored and edited numerous scientific papers as well as several books. In 2004 and 2008 he was scientific workshop co-chair and in 2006 program co-chair of the ICSOC conferences in Amsterdam (NL), Chicago (USA), and Sydney (AUS). Since 2008 he is also participating in the EU funded international Network of Excellence project in the area of Software Systems and Services (S-Cube).*

Preface

Web services provide a successful way to communicate distributed applications, in a platform independent and loosely coupled manner, providing systems with great flexibility and easier maintenance. In this sense, they are modular applications, which are self-descriptive and can be published, located and invoked from any point on the network. However, even though there are good procedures for the design, development, and management of Web services, there are scopes in which Web service adaptation is required. Service adaptations should be implemented appropriately, so that the loosely coupled nature of Web services is maintained, as well as allowing the implementation's integration in the whole service lifecycle.

The main aim of this publication is to collect and compile the most representative approaches in current research which tackle the different faces of Web service adaptation. In this regard, readers are able to acquire a panoramic overview of proposed tactics and existing solutions for service adaptation in different development scopes. In this sense, the book has a twofold purpose, not only as background reading on service adaptation, but also as a reference book in the search for adaptation solutions to service software engineering problems.

Therefore the book's target has been to compile high quality approaches on the different aspects of service adaptation in order to cover the wide spectrum of challenges which emerge in this area under different scenarios.

The target audience of this book covers a wide spectrum of software engineers, from senior and young researchers at the academia to research and development divisions at industry.

The interest of the book for academics is evident: researchers, assistants and professors seek novel and open research fields such as service adaptation; this book will offer this community the chance of having, the most relevant recent literature on the topic in question in a single publication, benefitting from gratifying reading which will provide them both with extensive knowledge of the state of the art of service adaptation as well as on open issues for further research.

On the other hand, industry always keeps an eye on the latest research results, especially on such a dynamic topic as software engineering and moreover on service engineering development. Research divisions from the top ten software industries spend considerable resources on service-related research. Therefore, this book will also be useful for this purpose, not only for them to be aware of what the research in the area is moving towards, but also to let them attempt to include new development ideas in the coming industry software tools.

CHAPTER DESCRIPTION

The book is made up of fourteen chapters which present tactics and solutions for modular and reusable software development in the field of adaptive Web services. These chapters are distributed into five sections: contract-based adaptation and interoperability, context-aware adaptation, adaptation for composition, dynamic adaptation, and device-based future internet adaptation.

Section 1 opens the book with three chapters that show the importance of adaptation and propose tactics to tackle the interoperability issues in service-based systems in an automatic way.

Chapter 1 proposes and specifies an Adaptive Enterprise Service Bus (ESB) Infrastructure which, based on the mediation capabilities provided by ESBs, allows addressing adaptation requirements in service-based systems in an automatic and dynamic way at runtime. The proposed adaptive infrastructure is based on messaging and integration patterns commonly supported in ESB products, so it provides a generic solution which is likely to be applied and implemented in most of these products. It also follows the key ideas of the S-Cube project (http://www.s-cube-network.eu/), exposing adaptation and monitoring capabilities, which can be used by overarching solutions, and leveraging some of its frameworks. This aims to be a step forward in developing dynamic and automatic adaptation capabilities in service-based systems which run over an ESB infrastructure.

Chapter 2 argues that the service-oriented paradigm is a good solution to achieve distributed interoperability, without impairing the capacity of adapting applications to cater for constantly evolving requirements. This goal depends on minimizing coupling between services, so that an adaptation of a service has the lowest possible impact on other services. Therefore, the objective of this chapter is to use structural interoperability and to propose metrics to quantify adaptability based on similarity and decoupling. Thus, this chapter claims to be a contribution to improve the quality of distributed applications and to make their development, maintenance and adaptation an easier task.

Chapter 3 addresses the definition of suitable notions for contract refinement and choreography conformance for services that communicate either synchronously or asynchronously through message queues. Service contracts are specified in a language independent way by means of finite labeled transition systems. This allows the definition of choreography projections in structured operational semantics, which determines that the use of choreography projection is an important step in order to define an appropriate notion of conformance. The notion of service contract presented in this chapter deals only with functional requirements and does not take into accounts non-functional aspects like those related to Service Level Agreement. As regards future research, this chapter proposes to investigate aspects like response time, frequency of client's invocations, and other quantitative requirements.

Section 2 focuses on context-aware adaptation, where systems must adapt their behaviour at run-time according to the changing conditions, which is tackled in two chapters by using adaptation contracts and event processing.

Chapter 4 presents a framework in order to address the discovery, composition and adaptation processes of pre-existing services by taking context information into account. The main goal of this chapter is to solve, as automatically as possible, mismatch cases which may be given at the different interoperability levels among service interfaces in the field of mobile and pervasive systems. Thus, the framework generates a mediating adaptor based on an adaptation contract obtained by means of a semantic-based matching, which at the same time is generated during the discovery process. This chapter plans future research directions such as tackling dynamic reconfiguration of services or addressing non-functional requirements at the service level.

Chapter 5 describes an envisaged architecture for context-aware Web services, where context is continuously monitored by a Complex Event Processing engine and service adaptation to context is done through a non-intrusive aspect-oriented implementation. Therefore, this chapter proposes to adapt Web services in multiple scenarios, doing the adaptation in the service-side, thus saving client resources. Aspect-oriented code for adaptation implementation allows the maintenance of the original main functionality service code completely encapsulated and separate from the adaptation code, facilitating not only maintenance of future changes due to new adaptation requirements, but also dynamic adaptations.

Section 3 is made up of three chapters which present different solutions for enhancing the composition of service-based applications by means of technologies like autonomic computing, process mining, and semantic Web.

Chapter 6 tackles the adaptive management of service composition by analyzing how service-oriented systems can self-adapt in order to satisfy non-functional requirements. To do that, the chapter introduces the MAPE-K (Monitor, Analyze, Plan, Execute, and Knowledge) reference model applied to design self-adaptive service-oriented systems. The main focus of the chapter is the Plan phase, since it is the core of the adaptation process. Through a case study, the chapter demonstrates how it is possible to improve the Quality of Service of a service-oriented architecture application that operates in a highly varying execution environment, where component services continuously appear and disappear.

Chapter 7 concerns the application of data mining techniques to a real-life service event log collected by the Vienna Runtime Environment for Service-oriented Computing (VRESCo). The aim of this chapter is to analyze the historical events stored on VRESCo in order to discover software services that are frequently invoked and composed together, i.e., process mining. Two sequential pattern mining algorithms are applied to a real event log provided by VRESCo, with results that show the capability of the approach proposed to find services that are frequently invoked together within the same sequence.

Chapter 8 presents a framework for pervasive service ecosystems, meant to overcome the limitations of standard service-oriented architecture when dealing with situated and adaptive pervasive computing systems, along with an implementation schema based on standard W3C technologies for the Semantic Web, and an application case of crowd steering by public/private displays. Some future works planned are to provide a formal operational model or to develop a methodology for the development of ecosystems, following the AOSE (agent-oriented software engineering) paradigm.

Section 4 tackles the dynamic adaptation issue, where three chapters describe three different frameworks developed to tackle runtime adaptation on both service-based and real-time-constrained systems.

Chapter 9 discusses limitations regarding the dynamic collaboration flexibility of the services involved in the process and introduced a framework for service collaboration that is suitable for cloud computing settings. The chapter also introduces a framework based in techniques for coordination and service matching to achieve dynamic service collaboration through matching goal-oriented service requests with providers that advertise their offerings dynamically. The framework may deal with a large number of providers and requesters working concurrently, which demonstrates the suitability of the approach for large multi-user service coordination environments such as cloud computing.

Chapter 10 presents a new framework for modeling service-based application adaptation triggered by interesting or critical situations based on Situation Action Networks (SAN). SANs are dynamic and can evolve at runtime by using their inherent planning capabilities. Therefore, the framework is based on a goal model able to track the fulfillment of goals at runtime. The future plans of this chapter include among others the experimentation with search and selection mechanisms that will enable SANs to take advantage of the abstract actions and action pools and support abstraction-based adaptation.

Chapter 11 deals the dynamic adaptation issue from a point of view of the increasing complexity of embedded systems, which are designed to have long life cycles. Thus, this chapter presents an approach to tackle the issue of runtime adaptation on computationally constrained systems, such as embedded systems composed by a set of components, services, or resources, with real-time constraints. The approach focuses on systems with only a single general purpose processor, with the responsibility to run the system and application software. In order to illustrate the framework, its architecture and a case study are described.

Section 5 presents tactics and ideas, in the three last chapters of the book, for addressing adaptive device-based future internet applications, so supporting the interoperability between diverse stakeholders and contents coming from heterogeneous devices.

Chapter 12 proposes a model-driven framework that automates the development of device-aware Web services. This approach allows modelling graphical user interfaces using the notation of the Presentation Modelling Language (PML), whereas the key contribution refers to the transformation of PML models to functional code targeting different platforms encountered on mobile and stationary devices. The chapter considers the preferences of the user when adapting the Web service as a future extension.

Chapter 13 presents how we communicate between different heterogeneous context-aware platforms by using Android and Web services. The main goal is to extend Android to make it adaptable and interoperable. The usefulness of the proposed approach is demonstrated through a concrete case study. As regards future research, this chapter plans to develop a concrete system with context adaption plate forms and data bases in Software-as-a-Service and Cloud environments, and to assess performances of such approach improving it from a security viewpoint.

Chapter 14 finalizes the book by analyzing the opportunities and challenges of adaptive Future Internet (FI) applications. Thus, this chapter discusses the need of rethinking and designing FI applications taking into account aspects beyond the ones considered by current adaptive Web services and service-based applications. There are many questions to be answered, and for each question new ones emerge. Despite all the uncertainties surrounding FI applications, there is at least one certain and incontestable fact: FI applications will have to be engineered explicitly considering adaptation aspects and will have to dynamically adapt to an unprecedented level of changes that may occur during runtime.

IMPACT FOR THE FIELD OF ADAPTIVE WEB SERVICES

Service adaptation is a hot topic with many emergent research proposals which to date have not had wide broadcasting, in spite of being worthy of consideration.

This book has been written to facilitate novice readers the understanding of the main issues solved in the proposals as well as providing enough detail in order to hold expert interest.

Chapters along the book provide good quality proposals from both novel and well-established proposals, with solid base and a thorough description of the adaptation problem they deal with and how they tackle it. Challenges and open issues for future work are also an important part of chapter contents, which can encourage prospective interested researchers to work on this relevant area of knowledge.

The editors hope this book will be a helpful reference and inspiring source for research and development activities of software engineers in the field of adaptive Web services at both the academia and the industry.

Guadalupe Ortiz
University of Cádiz, Spain

Javier Cubo
University of Málaga, Spain

Acknowledgment

The editors want to specially thank the authors for their contributions to this book, as well as to the editorial advisory board and peer reviewers for their on-time and fruitful reviews. Some selected papers of the International Workshop on Adaptive Services for the Future Internet (WAS4FI 2011) have been extended to be published as chapters in this book: we would like to thank WAS4FI authors and programme committee for their contributions and reviews, respectively. Winfried Lamersdorf deserves also a special mention and acknowledgment for writing the foreword, which perfectly fits with the ideas presented in this book. Their support has significantly contributed to the success of this book.

Guadalupe Ortiz acknowledges the support from Spanish Ministry of Science and Innovation (MICINN) and FEDER (TIN2008-02985).

Javier Cubo acknowledges the support from Spanish Ministry of Science and Innovation (MICINN) and FEDER (TIN2008-05932) and Andalusian Government (P11-TIC-7659).

Guadalupe Ortiz
University of Cádiz, Spain

Javier Cubo
University of Málaga, Spain

Section 1
Contract–Based Adaptation and Interoperability

Chapter 1
Adaptive ESB Infrastructure for Service Based Systems

Laura González
Instituto de Computación, Facultad de Ingeniería, Universidad de la República, Uruguay

Raúl Ruggia
Instituto de Computación, Facultad de Ingeniería, Universidad de la República, Uruguay

ABSTRACT

Service-based systems increasingly need adaptation capabilities to agilely respond to unexpected changes in their business or execution environment. Although service orientation constitutes a promising approach to achieve this goal, current methods and technologies do not fully support automatic and dynamic adaptation at runtime. In turn, the Enterprise Service Bus (ESB), one of the preferred middleware technologies to support the development of service-based systems, provides several built-in mediation capabilities (e.g. message transformation), which can be used to perform adaptation actions. However, the configuration of these capabilities cannot usually be performed at runtime. This chapter proposes an Adaptive ESB Infrastructure which, based on the mediation capabilities provided by ESBs, can respond to adaptation requirements in service-based systems in an automatic and dynamic way at runtime. The chapter also specifies how the proposed solutions can be used to deal with concrete situations including response time degradation, services saturation, and changes in services contracts.

INTRODUCTION

As service-based systems operate in an increasingly dynamic world, they need adaptation capabilities to behave correctly despite unexpected changes in their business or execution environment. These issues becomes especially relevant in large scale service-based systems (e.g. e-government systems), where their massively distribution introduces numerous challenges in terms of performance, availability, reliability and security, among others.

DOI: 10.4018/978-1-4666-2089-6.ch001

Although service orientation constitutes a promising approach for building software systems which can agilely adapt to different situations, current methods and technologies do not fully support automatic and dynamic adaptation at runtime. (Di Nitto, Ghezzi, Andreas Metzger, Mike Papazoglou, & Klaus Pohl, 2008)

In the context of the S-Cube project, adaptation in service-based systems has been recognized as a crosscutting issue across their different layers (i.e. the infrastructure layer, the composition layer and the business layer). The project is adopting a comprehensive approach to leverage the adaptation capabilities within each layer to provide overarching solutions. This aims to avoid, for example, conflicting adaptation actions across these layers. Additionally, the S-Cube project has specified an integrated Adaptation and Monitoring Framework, which generalizes and broadens the state of the art in adaptation in service-based systems. The framework specifies an overall adaptation process and defines key logical elements including monitoring mechanisms, monitored events, adaptation requirements, adaptation strategies and adaptation mechanisms. (M. Papazoglou, K. Pohl, Parkin, & A. Metzger, 2010)

In turn, Enterprise Service Buses (ESBs) are widely recognized as a mainstream middleware to support the service infrastructure layer of service-based systems. ESBs provide a middle integration layer, with reusable integration and communication logic, which helps to address mismatches between services regarding communication protocols, message formats, and Quality of Service (QoS), among others. Furthermore, propositions like the Internet Service Bus (Ferguson, 2010) aim to apply these technologies in internet scale service-based systems.

Within an ESB-based platform, rather than interacting directly services communicate by sending messages through the ESB. Messages are usually processed by mediation flows which apply them different mediation operations (e.g. transformations). Mediation flows implement the integration and communication logic, and they are the means by which the ESB can ensure that services can connect successfully (Hérault, Thomas, & Fourier, 2005) (Michael Papazoglou, 2007). These mediation capabilities also provide the means to agilely react to different kinds of changes. For example, if a service modifies its location or its functional interface, an integration expert can configure a routing or a transformation in the ESB, respectively, to make these changes transparent to clients. However nowadays, the implementation (or configuration) of these mediation capabilities is usually performed in static and manual ways, which restricts the rapid responsiveness of the systems.

This chapter proposes and specifies an Adaptive ESB Infrastructure which, based on the mediation capabilities provided by ESBs, allows addressing adaptation requirements in service-based systems in an automatic and dynamic way at runtime. The general idea to achieve adaptation at runtime is to intercept all ESB messages and, if an adaptation is required for the invoked service, drive them through adaptation flows. These flows include all the mediations steps (e.g. message transformation) required to carry out a specific adaptation strategy (e.g. invoke an equivalent service). In particular, the chapter focuses on services implemented through the Web Services technology and on adaptation requirements triggered by response time degradation, services saturation and changes in services contracts.

The proposed adaptive infrastructure is based on messaging and integration patterns commonly supported in ESB products, so it provides a generic solution which is likely to be applied and implemented in most of these products. It also follows the key ideas of the S-Cube project, exposing adaptation and monitoring capabilities, which can be used by overarching solutions, and leveraging some of its frameworks (e.g. the Adaptation and Monitoring Framework).

This chapter is organized as follows. Next section provides background on ESB and the S-

Cube project, and it presents related work. Then the Adaptive ESB Infrastructure is presented, describing its overall approach, presenting its logical architecture and specifying its main elements and decision mechanisms. After that, the chapter describes how the proposed solution can be used to deal with different situations including response time degradation, services saturation and changes in services contracts. Then, some implementation details are described. Finally, future research directions and conclusions are presented.

BACKGROUND

This section provides background on ESB and on the monitoring and adaptation vision within the S-Cube project. Additionally, it presents related work regarding adaptation within an ESB infrastructure.

Enterprise Service Bus

An Enterprise Service Bus (ESB) is a standards-based integration platform that combines messaging, Web Services, data transformation, and intelligent routing to reliably connect and coordinate the interaction of diverse applications with transactional integrity (Chappell, 2004).

It provides a middle integration layer with reusable integration and communication logic, which alleviates disparity problems between applications running on heterogeneous platforms, using diverse data formats and communicating through different protocols. The ESB is designed to provide interoperability between applications, services and other components via standard-based adapters and interfaces. (Michael Papazoglou, 2007)

Main Capabilities

Although the capabilities provided by ESB products can vary according to the specific provider,

they usually include message transformation, intermediate routing, mechanisms to implement mediation flows and monitoring capabilities. (Davis, 2009)(Rademakers & Dirksen, 2008)

Message transformation capabilities allow the communication between applications that use different data formats or data models. In particular, given the widely use of XML as a message format in service-based systems, most ESB product support XSLT to specify transformations.

Intermediate routing is the capability that allows the ESB to determine, at runtime, the destination of a message according to different factors. The content-based routing determines the message destination according to its content (Chappell, 2004). The load-balancing routing *(Jongtaveesataporn & Takada, 2010)* determines the message destination according to a load-balancing strategy (e.g. Round Robin). Finally, the itinerary-based routing determines the message destination according to an itinerary which is included in the message itself (Chappell, 2004).

Mediation flows (also known as mediations, mediation chains or micro-flows) specify a sequence of mediation operations (e.g. message transformation, routing) to execute over the messages. ESB products usually provide capabilities to specify and execute mediation flows.

Finally, most ESB products also include various monitoring capabilities which provide information regarding, for example, services response time and the amount of messages processed by the services (Yuan, S. W. Choi, & Soo Dong Kim, 2008).

ESB Connectivity Patterns

Through the experience gained in many real life implementations, in (Wylie & Peter Lambros, 2009) the authors present a set of patterns which encapsulate the connectivity or mediation logic between a set of applications or services. From an overall integration architecture perspective, they identify six categories of patterns.

Figure 1. Service virtualization patterns

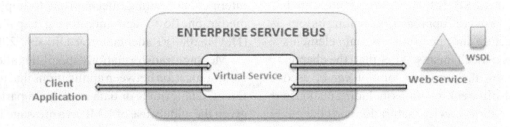

Service virtualization patterns take an existing service and deploy a new virtual service in the ESB. These patterns introduce a point of mediation in the ESB which can be used to route, transform or normalize requests, among others. Figure 1 graphically presents this category of patterns.

Service enablement patterns address the problem of providing a service-oriented interface to functionality which does not have one. These patterns allow leveraging existing assets which might be implemented using diverse technologies across the enterprise.

Gateway patterns are used to apply a common set of mediations to all incoming and/or outgoing messages. For example, a security gateway might perform authentication, authorization or audit operations. After that, the request can be routed to the target service or to further mediations. Figure 2 graphically presents this category of patterns.

Message-based integration patterns are used to build and deploy infrastructure level message-based applications. Functionally, in some regards they correspond to the service virtualization pat-

terns. However, they take a more producer-to-consumer approach instead of the provider-to-consumer approach typically taken in a service-oriented architecture (SOA).

Finally, file processing patterns deal with providing a managed execution environment for the processing of local or remote files through the ESB, and event-driven integration patterns deal with distribution of events in real time and integration with Complex Event Processing (CEP) engines.

The S-Cube Project

The Network of Excellence on Software Services and Systems (S-Cube) performs cross-discipline research to develop solutions for research challenges of next generation service-based systems. Research in S-Cube is organized around the S-Cube research framework which is presented (Andreas Metzger & Klaus Pohl, 2009).

The key elements of the framework comprise the three traditional SOA layers (i.e. service infrastructure (SI), service composition and

Figure 2. Gateway patterns

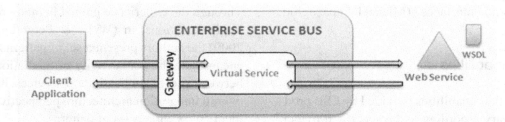

coordination (SCC), and business process management (BPM)) and three more elements which cover crosscutting issues throughout these layers (i.e. Service Adaptation and Monitoring (SAM), Service Quality Definition, Negotiation and Assurance (SQDNA) and Service Engineering and Design (SED)).

Specifically, the SI layer supports describing, publishing and discovering services, along with primitives for service communication. In addition, the SAM element deals with the cross-layer monitoring of service-based systems and its continuous adaptation.

The overall approach of the S-Cube framework is that the traditional layers offer capabilities (e.g. design, monitoring, adaptation) that can be exploited by the other elements of the framework, to define overarching principles and methodologies for addressing the identified crosscutting issues. (M. Papazoglou et al., 2010)

In the context of the SAM activities, an integrated Adaptation and Monitoring (A&M) Framework has been defined. As presented in (M. Papazoglou et al., 2010), the framework provides a high level view of the key logical elements needed for adaptation in SOA and the dependencies among them. The framework identifies Monitoring Mechanisms, Monitored Events, Adaptation Requirements, Adaptation Strategies and Adaptation Mechanisms.

Monitoring Mechanisms refer to any mechanism to check if the actual situation corresponds to the expected one. They are used to detect Monitored Events, which represent the fact that there is a difference with respect to the expected system state, functionality or environment. Monitored Events trigger Adaptation Requirements which represent the need of changing the underlying system, in order to remove the differences between the actual situation and the expected one. Finally, Adaptation Strategies define the possible ways to achieve these requirements and they are realized by Adaptation Mechanisms.

Besides these key elements, the relationships between them determine a general adaptation process where: (i) the relevant information is collected using the available monitoring mechanisms; (ii) critical events are detected; (iii) the need for an adaptation is identified; (iv) a suitable way to realize the adaptation is identified (i.e. an adaptation strategy is selected); (v) the adaptation is performed using the available adaptation mechanisms.

Although, the A&M Framework describes a standard sensing / planning / actuating control chain, its significance is in the very broad meaning of the different concepts, allowing a very general integration of a wide range of mechanisms, techniques and methodologies.

Adaptation within an ESB Infrastructure

As stated before, ESBs provide various mediation capabilities which can be used to build mediation flows in order to facilitate the integration and communication between services. However, although these capabilities can be use to address different adaptation requirements, current ESB products usually support applying these mediation capabilities in a static and manual way, which restricts the rapid responsiveness of the systems. This limitation has been identified by various authors which propose leveraging ESB capabilities in a more dynamic and automatic way, to deal with different adaptation requirements.

ESB routing capabilities have been addressed in several proposals in order to enable a more dynamic routing. Dynamic routing usually refers to the fact that the possible paths that a message can follow in the ESB are not known at design time. In (Ziyaeva, E. Choi, & Min, 2008), the authors define a mechanism to route messages based on different factors including services availability. Likewise, in (Bai, Xie, B. Chen, & Xiao, 2007) the authors propose selecting services taking into account the results gathered by a testing mechanism which measures different Quality of Service (QoS) factors, like response time. In (B. Wu, S. Liu, & L. Wu, 2008), the authors propose a dynamic and reliable routing mechanism which selects, at runtime, a list of possible target services to which route a particular request. If the routing to a service fails, the service is marked as inactive so it is not selected anymore as a possible target service. Finally, in (Jongtaveesataporn & Takada, 2010) the limitation of the static configuration of load-balancing ESB mechanisms is identified. The authors propose solutions to select services at runtime applying different load-balancing strategies, like round-robin and least-loaded.

Other work focuses on adapting services in the ESB, according to the client, user preferences and other characteristics which constitute the context in which the service-based application is executed. In (S. H Chang, La, Bae, Jeon, & S. D Kim, 2007) the authors propose a mechanism that allows selecting, at runtime, the services to be used when executing a WS-BPEL process. In this case, the services which compose the process are invoked through the ESB which, using a set of internal components, intercepts the invocations, selects the most suitable service according to the context and routes the invocation to that service. Eventually, a transformation is performed over the messages if the selected service is not fully compliant with the interface of the invoked service. On the other side, in (La, Bae, S. Chang, & S. Kim, 2007) a set of methods for adapting services within an ESB, according to their clients, are proposed. The authors identify four types of variability (workflow variability, composition variability, interface variability and logic variability) and they propose mechanisms, which are based on the ESB capabilities, to address them.

In (Kwei-Jay Lin, Panahi, & Y. Zhang, 2007) (Panahi et al., 2008)(Zou, Pavlovski, & Wang, 2008)(K. J Lin & S. H Chang, 2009) the authors propose a platform which provides the required infrastructure to continuously monitoring the services which compose business processes, and

dynamically adapt them performing reconfigurations in the processes at runtime. Given the characteristics of the required platform, the authors base its implementation in an ESB product, more precisely Mule ESB.

Finally, in (Masternak et al., 2010) the authors propose an Adaptive ESB as part of an Adaptive SOA platform (K. Zielinski et al., 2011). The Adaptive ESB focuses on adapting service compositions selecting, at runtime, the services invoked by them. Services selection is based on past invocations and QoS values.

Although these proposals address the problems of dynamic and automatic adaptation within the ESB, they use a limited number of ESB mediation capabilities and the structure of the mediation flows a message can follow is determine at design time. Additionally, most of these proposals only focus on dealing with a family of adaptation requirements, for instance regarding QoS.

In turn, the solution proposed in this chapter makes use of a more complete set of mediation capabilities and can be extended with other ones. It also enable, unlike other existing proposals, to select at runtime the concrete mediation flow a message can follow. This allows applying different strategies when a problem is detected (e.g. regarding response time). Moreover, the solution proposed in this chapter aims to provide a general framework to deal with different adaptation requirements. It is also important to note, that this work is largely compatible with existing proposals and various valuable ideas were taken from previous work including the routing table proposed in (Bai et al., 2007) and the dynamic mediation capabilities (e.g. dynamic wire tap) proposed in (B. Wu et al., 2008).

ADAPTIVE ESB INFRASTRUCTURE

The Adaptive ESB Infrastructure is an ESB-based platform with the ability to address adaptation requirements in service-based systems, by means of

Figure 3. General context

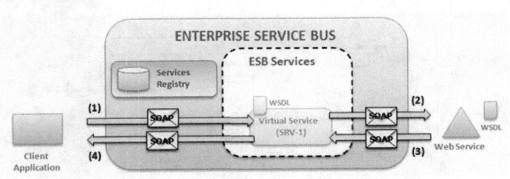

selecting, implementing and applying adaptation strategies, which are built using ESB mediation capabilities, in an automatic and dynamic way at runtime. A first proposal of this adaptive infrastructure was presented in (González & Ruggia, 2010).

This section presents a general description of this infrastructure, its logical architecture, a specification of some of its elements and how the main monitoring and adaptation decisions are taken within the infrastructure.

General Description

The proposed solution assumes, as a general context, a SOA where services are provided through an ESB infrastructure, following the Service Virtualization pattern described in the previous section. Figure 3 presents this general context, where client applications invoke external services through Virtual Services deployed in the ESB.

External services and Virtual Services are based on the Web Services technology. More precisely, they are described using WSDL and they can be invoked sending SOAP messages over HTTP. ESB Services, in particular Virtual Services, are identified by logical names and they are registered in the ESB Services Registry.

The proposed solution handles, in an ESB-based infrastructure, the concepts and the overall adaptation process defined within the S-Cube Adaptation and Monitoring Framework. In par-

ticular, the Adaptive ESB Infrastructure has the goal of addressing Virtual Services adaptation requirements, which correspond to known issues that may occur in a SOA (e.g. Quality of Service degradation). In turn, adaptation mechanisms map to ESB mediation capabilities (e.g. transformation and routing) and adaptation strategies aim to represent general approaches (e.g. invoke an equivalent service) that cope with the Virtual Services requirements using the available ESB adaptation mechanisms.

Given that it is assumed that there is not any control over the service providers and consumers infrastructure, adaptation actions are only performed within the ESB infrastructure. The general idea to achieve adaptation at runtime is to intercept all ESB messages and, if an adaptation is required for the invoked Virtual Service, drive them through a mediation flow. This flow, called adaptation flow, includes all the mediations steps (e.g. message transformation) required to carry out a specific adaptation strategy (e.g. invoke an equivalent service). Messages are intercepted by means of an adaptation gateway, following the gateway pattern described in the previous section.

Adaptation flows are composed of ESB Services and they are built at runtime in a dynamic and automatic way when an adaptation requirement is detected. Additionally, they are attached to ESB messages, following the itinerary-based routing pattern. ESB Services can be Virtual Services

Figure 4. Adaptation within the ESB

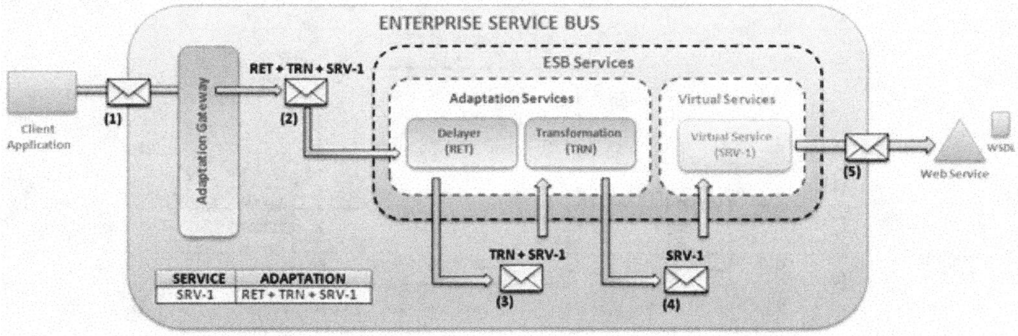

or Adaptation Services. The latter ones are ESB Services which, using one of the ESB adaptation mechanisms, perform an adaptation action (e.g. a message transformation).

Figure 4 presents an example aiming to describe the overall operation of the adaptive infrastructure. In this example, a client application invokes the service SRV-1 for which an adaptation requirement was detected. This requirement is addressed within the platform using an adaptation strategy implemented through and adaptation flow consisting of:

- An adaptation service using a delayer mechanism (it delays message delivery for a given time. interval).
- An adaptation service using a transformation mechanism
- A virtual service.

In this way, after the client application sends a message to invoke the service (1), the message is intercepted by the Adaptation Gateway and, given that there is an adaptation requirement for the service SRV-1, an adaptation flow is attached to the message (2). Then, the message is routed to the first step in the flow (RET), which processes the message and routes it to the next step (TRN). This step also processes the message and routes it to the next step (SRV-1), which finally invokes the external Web Service.

The Adaptive ESB Infrastructure also implements the decision mechanisms which allow detecting monitored events, triggering adaptation requirements, selecting adaptation strategies and implementing these strategies using the available adaptation mechanisms. In particular, in order to implement adaptation strategies in a dynamic and automatic way, each adaptation strategy handled by the infrastructure has a generic mediation flow associated. This flow specifies the general structure of the adaptation flow which implements the strategy.

Given the lack of a standard or uniform way to specify mediation flows among ESB products, the proposed solution uses YAWL (Yet Another Workflow Language) (Hofstede, Aalst, Adams, & Russell, 2009) which provides a product-agnostic way to specify these flows. An adaptation flow is represented as a YAWL Net in which each task correspond to the execution of a Virtual Service or an Adaptation Service. The tasks flows represent the possible paths a message can follow. The JOIN and SPLIT behavior of each task is determine by the number of input and output messages of the adaptation mechanism. Additionally, in order to graphically represent mediation flows, images are used to decorate the tasks of YAWL nets. For example, Figure 5 shows a YAWL net which specifies the general structure of the mediation flow associated with the adaptation strategy implemented in Figure 4.

Figure 5. Generic mediation flow using YAWL

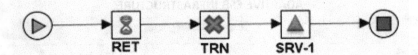

Generic mediation flows can be configured in different ways and can lead to various concrete adaptation flow. For instance, a mediation flow which implements the strategy "invoke an equivalent service" leads to different mediation flows, one for each equivalent service. In this way, the implementation of a given adaptation strategy within the platform consists in the configuration of the different components of its generic mediation flow and the selection of the most suitable concrete flow according to the given situation.

Logical Architecture

This section presents the logical architecture of the Adaptive ESB Infrastructure, describing its components and their main interactions.

Components

The Adaptive ESB Infrastructure extends an ESB with:

- Internal components, which enable the dynamic and automatic adaptation at runtime within the ESB.
- An Adaptation and Monitoring Engine, which supports the decision mechanisms within the adaptive infrastructure.

Figure 6 presents the logical architecture of the Adaptive ESB Infrastructure which consists of a Monitoring and Adaptation Engine, new components within the ESB infrastructure (Adaptation Gateway, Adaptation Services, Adaptation Manager, Monitoring Manager, Capabilities Manager

and Service Requirements Manager) and some other components which are usually included in ESB products (Services Registry, Monitoring Mechanisms and Adaptation Mechanisms). Additionally, the main interactions and information flows among these components are presented.

Monitoring Mechanisms provide monitoring functionalities and, in general, they are natively included in ESB products. They provide different kind of information, for example, regarding services response time and services availability. Additionally, these functionalities can usually be extended as presented in (Yuan et al., 2008).

The Monitoring Manager is an internal component which has the responsibility to calculate the values of the properties monitored by the infrastructure (e.g. average response time of services and number of service invocations within a time interval) and send them to the Monitoring and Adaptation Engine. It has the responsibility to:

- Know which properties must be monitored.
- Know how to calculate their values based on the data obtained from the monitoring mechanisms.
- Interact with the monitoring mechanisms to obtain data from them.
- Send the values of the monitored properties to the Adaptation and Monitoring Engine.

As stated before, Adaptation Mechanisms map to ESB mediation capabilities (e.g. message transformation) and they can be used to perform adaptation actions within the ESB.

The Adaptation Manager has the responsibility to manage (i.e. receive, store, return and delete)

Figure 6. Logical components of the adaptive ESB infrastructure

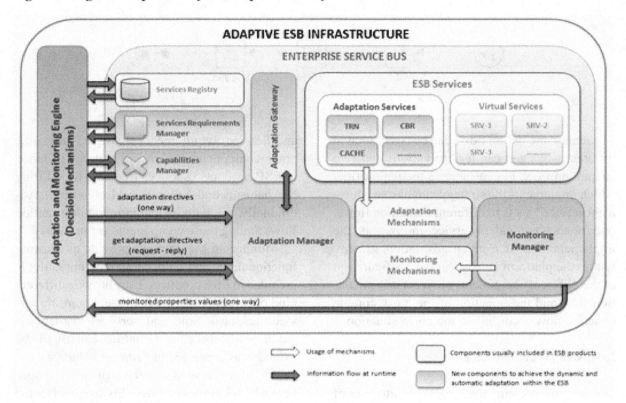

adaptation directives for the Virtual Services. Adaptation directives are specified through adaptation flows and they can have an expiration time.

ESB Services can be either Virtual Services or Adaptation Services. Virtual Services are ESB services which access external Web Services. Adaptation Services are services which execute an adaptation action using one of the ESB adaptation mechanisms. These Adaptation Services are generic in the sense that their behavior is not fully specified at design time, but it depends on run time information which is included in the messages. For instance, an Adaptation Service that performs message transformations executes different transformation logics every time it processes a message. Moreover, the specific transformation logic for each message is included in the message itself.

The Services Registry is the component which has the responsibility to manage the information of the services which are registered within the ESB infrastructure. It allows registering services, associating and querying their metadata, searching for services and finding equivalent services. Additionally, it manages the transformation logic to take input and output messages, for each one of the services operations, from and to a canonical data model. This allows invoking equivalent services even if they use different data models.

The Adaptation Gateway has the responsibility to intercept the messages which are sent through the ESB, interact with the Adaptation Manager to check if an adaptation is required for a given service and, in this case, attach the corresponding adaptation flow to the message and send it to the first step in the flow.

The Service Requirements Manager has the responsibility to manage service requirements, regarding for example, QoS. These requirements, along with the monitored information, allow detecting situations (monitored events) that might generate an adaptation requirement. Service requirements can be specified using monitored properties and services metadata. They have the following general form: "property – operator – value", where value can be a single value (e.g. an integer value) or the value of one of the metadata handled by the infrastructure. For example, the requirement "average-response-time < 800 ms" specifies that the average response time for the given service must not exceed eight hundred milliseconds.

The Capability Manager has the responsibility to manage the monitoring and adaptation capabilities provided by the ESB infrastructure and to make available the required information so that other components (e.g. the Adaptation and Monitoring Engine) can use them. In particular, this component provides information regarding the properties which are monitored by the infrastructure and the available adaptation mechanisms.

The Adaptation and Monitoring Engine has the responsibility to receive the monitored information from the Monitoring Manager, to take the adaptation and monitoring decisions within the infrastructure and to send these decisions to the Adaptation Manager. The main decisions this engine has to take are:

- Detecting when a monitoring event occurs for a given service.
- Deciding when an adaptation requirement has to be generated for a given service.
- Selecting the most appropriate strategy to deal with the requirement.
- Implementing this strategy with the adaptation mechanisms that are available in the ESB.

These four decisions correspond to the four connections between the conceptual elements of the S-Cube Monitoring and Adaptation Framework.

The Adaptation and Monitoring Engine is logically placed outside the ESB given that it is considered a crosscutting component throughout the different SOA layers. This vision aims to allow that this engine can interact with other SOA components (e.g. a WS-BPEL engine) with the goal of building overarching solutions to deal with adaptation in service-based systems.

Main Interactions

Two of the main interactions between the previous components are the sending of the monitored properties values and the sending of adaptation directives.

As previously described, the Monitoring Manager has the responsibility to calculate the values of the monitored properties and send them the Adaptation and Monitoring Engine. To this end, it has to interact with the different adaptation mechanisms within the ESB. Figure 7 presents a sequence diagram describing this process where, in this case, the Monitoring Manager interacts with one monitoring mechanism and it sends the properties values to the Adaptation and Monitoring Engine. Alternatively, the Monitoring Manager could interact with more than one monitoring mechanism.

On the other side, when the value of a monitored property changes an adaptation requirement could be triggered. In this situation, the adaptive infrastructure has to respond creating and applying adaptation directives. Figure 8 presents a sequence diagram in which the Adaptation and Monitoring Engine receive the value of a monitored property and, if an adaptation requirement is detected, it interacts with different components to build and finally send an adaptation directive to the Adaptation Manager.

Alternatively, if an adaptation requirement is not detected, adaptation directives are not created. Moreover, if an adaptation requirement is detected, but there is not any suitable adaptation

Figure 7. Sending monitored properties values

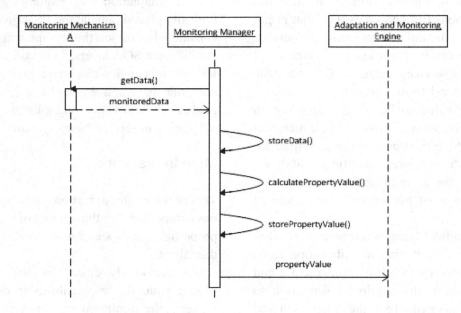

directive to deal with it, an alert is generated (e.g. an email to the administrators).

Infrastructure Specification

This section specifies in a more concrete way various elements of the Adaptive ESB Infrastructure. These elements are then used to specify some of the decision mechanisms. The complete specification of the adaptive infrastructure can be found in (González, 2011).

The Adaptive ESB Infrastructure is a triple: <ESB-Services, Services-Registry, Adaptation-Monitoring-Framework>, where:

- ESB-Services is the set of ESB Services registered in the infrastructure.
- Services-Registry is composed of elements which provides mechanisms that allows discovering services and managing their metadata.
- Adaptation-Monitoring-Framework is composed of elements that enable the adaptation and monitoring within the infrastructure.

Adaptation-Monitoring-Framework is a triple <Monitoring-Elements, Adaptation-Elements, Decision-Mechanisms>, where:

- Monitoring-Elements are the elements which enable the monitoring activities within the infrastructure, in particular:
  - Monitoring-Mechanisms is the set of monitoring mechanisms supported by the infrastructure.
  - Monitored-Properties is the set of properties monitored within the infrastructure.
  - Monitored-Events is the set of monitored events supported by the infrastructure.
- Adaptation-Elements are the elements which enable the adaptation activities within the infrastructure, in particular:
  - Adaptation-Requirements is the set of adaptation requirements supported by the infrastructure.
  - Adaptation-Strategies is the set of adaptation strategies supported by the infrastructure.

Figure 8. Sending adaptation directives

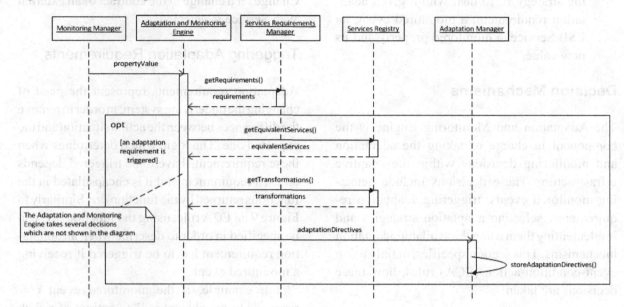

- ○ Adaptation-Mechanisms is the set of adaptation mechanisms supported by the infrastructure.
- Decision-Mechanisms are the elements which enable to take the monitoring and adaptation decisions within the infrastructure, for instance, selecting an adaptation strategy.

Decision-Mechanisms is a quintuple: <Monitored-Events-Rules, Adaptation-Requirement-Rules, Adaptation-Strategies-Rules, Strategies-Implementation-Rules, Strategies-Directives>, where:

- Monitored-Events-Rules (*mer*) is a function that for each monitored event M returns a function (mer_M). Each function mer_M returns true if the conditions are set to detect the event M, given an ESB Service, a monitored property and its new value. Otherwise, it returns false.
- Adaptation-Requirement-Rules (*arr*) is a function that for each adaptation requirement R returns a function (arr_R). Each

function arr_R returns true if the conditions are set to trigger the adaptation requirement R, given a monitored event, an ESB Service, a monitored property and its new value. Otherwise, it returns false.

- Adaptation-Strategies-Rules (*asr*) is a function that for each adaptation strategy E returns a function (asr_E). Each function asr_E returns true if the strategy E is suitable to deal with a given adaptation requirement, a monitored event, an ESB Service, a monitored property and its new value. Otherwise, it returns false.
- Strategies-Implementation-Rules (*sir*) is a function that for each adaptation strategy E returns a function (sir_E). Each function sir_E returns true if the strategy E can be implemented to deal with a given adaptation requirement, a monitored event, an ESB Service, a monitored property and its new value. Otherwise, it returns false.
- Strategies-Directives (*sd*) is a function that for each adaptation strategy E returns a function (sd_E). Each function sd_E returns all the possible adaptation directives, using

the strategy E, to deal with a given adaptation requirement, a monitored event, an ESB Service, a monitored property and its new value.

Decision Mechanisms

The Adaptation and Monitoring Engine is the component in charge of taking the adaptation and monitoring decisions within the adaptive infrastructure. These decisions include detecting monitored events, triggering adaptation requirements, selecting adaptation strategies and implementing them using the available adaptation mechanisms. This section specifies, mainly using event-condition-action (ECA) rules, how these decisions are taken.

Detecting Monitored Events

Monitored events represent the fact that there is a difference with respect to the expected system state, functionality or environment. The logic to detect these events depends on each event and it is encapsulated in the functions returned by the function *mer*. Figure 9 presents an ECA rule which specifies, in a general way, how monitored events are detected.

For example, the Adaptation and Monitoring Engine could trigger an event named "Contract Change" if a change in the contract of an external Web Service is detected.

Triggering Adaptation Requirements

Adaptation requirements represent the need of changing the underlying system, in order to remove the differences between the actual situation and the expected one. The logic which determines when these requirements have to be triggered depends on each requirement and it is encapsulated in the functions returned by the function *arr*. Similarly to Figure 9 an ECA rule, using the function *arr*, can be specified in order to describe when an adaptation requirement has to be triggered if receiving a monitored event.

For example, if the monitored event corresponds to the change in the contract of a Web Service, the Adaptation and Monitoring Engine can trigger an adaptation requirement named "Handle Incompatible Contract Change", if the change is detected to be incompatible with the previous version.

Selecting Adaptation Strategies

Adaptation Strategies define the possible ways to achieve adaptation requirements. Therefore, when detecting an adaptation requirement, decision mechanisms are required to determine the possible strategies to achieve it. The logic to determine this

Figure 9. ECA rule detecting monitored events

```
Event:
      New value v for the monitored property p for the service s.
Condition:
      ∃ m ∈ Monitored-Events / (mer(m))(s, p, v)
Action:
      ∀m ∈ Monitored-Events / (mer(m))(s, p, v):
            Create event "Monitored Event m for service s, property p and new
      value v".
```

Figure 10. ECA rule generating adaptation directives

```
Event:
        Adaptation requirement r for monitored event m, service s, property p and
        new value v.
Condition:
        ∃ e ∈ Adaptation-Strategies /
                (asr(e))(r, m, s, p, v) ∧ (sir(e))(r, m, s, p, v)
Action:
        Create adaptation directive d /
                d = getBestAdaptationDirective(r, m, s, p, v)
```

depends on each strategy and it is encapsulated in the functions returned by the function *asr*.

Additionally, even though a given strategy could be suitable to deal with an adaptation requirement, this strategy could not be able to be implemented with the available resources. For example, the strategy "invoke an equivalent service" can only be implemented if there are equivalent services. In this way, decision mechanisms to determine if a strategy can be implemented with the available recourses are also needed. This logic is encapsulated in the functions returned by the function *sir*.

Figure 10 presents an ECA rule which specifies, in a general way, how the generation of an adaptation directive is decided.

The function getBestAdaptationDirective is a function which returns the best adaptation directive for the given requirement, service and current situation. In this way, an adaptation directive is generated only if there is a suitable adaptation strategy and this strategy can be implemented with the available resources. Otherwise, an alert is generated.

Figure 11. Creating adaptation directives

```
Adaptation-Directive getBestAdaptationDirective(Adaptation-Requirement r,
                                                Monitored-Event m, ESB-Service s,
                                                Monitored-Property p, Value v){

        possible-strategies = {e / e ∈ Adaptation-Strategies ∧
                        (asr(e))(r, m, s, p, v) ∧ (sir(e))(r, m, s, p, v)};
        directives = ∅;
        for each e in possible-strategies do {
                directives = (sd(e))(r, m, s, p, v) ∪ directives;}
        return getBestDirective(directives);
}
```

Implementing Adaptation Strategies

As stated before, each supported adaptation strategy has a generic mediation flow associated. This flow specifies the general structure of the adaptation flow which implements the strategy. In this way, the implementation of a strategy within the platform consists in the configuration of the generic mediation flow associated with it (which can lead to various concrete flows) and the selection of the most suitable concrete flow given the current state of the platform.

Figure 11 presents how the best adaptation directive is selected from the suitable adaptation strategies to deal with a given adaptation requirement.

The function getBestDirective is a ranking function that given a set of adaptation directives returns the best one according to the current state of the platform.

ADDRESSING CONCRETE ADAPTATION REQUIREMENTS

This section describes how the Adaptive ESB Infrastructure can be used to deal with concrete adaptation requirements. In particular, the section focuses on handling response time degradation, services saturation and changes in services contracts. Some issues presented in this section were already analyzed and discussed in (González & Ruggia, 2011a) (González & Ruggia, 2011b).

Adaptation Mechanisms

Adaptation mechanisms are needed to implement the suitable adaptation strategies to deal with concrete adaptation requirements. As stated before, adaptation mechanisms within the proposed adaptive infrastructure correspond to ESB mediation capabilities. In order to identify, describe and provide a graphical representation for these

mechanisms various sources were reviewed and analyzed. In particular,

- The Enterprise Integration Patterns (EIP) described in (Hohpe & Woolf, 2003).
- Previous work which identifies ESB mediation patterns (Schmidt, Hutchison, P. Lambros, & Phippen, 2005) (Wylie & Peter Lambros, 2009)(Erl, 2009)(Hérault et al., 2005) (Hutchison, Schmidt, Wolfson, & Stockton, 2005)(Yan Fang et al., 2006).
- The proposal in (Thorsten Scheibler & Frank Leymann, 2008)(T. Scheibler, Mietzner, & F. Leymann, 2008) which aims to build a platform to execute EIPs in a Software as a Service context.
- The Guaraná project (Frantz, n.d.) (Sleiman, Sultán, Frantz, & Corchuelo, n.d.) which, among other goals, aims to build a Domain Specific Language to specify integration projects.
- The mediation functionalities provided in various ESB products, in particular, JBossESB, IBM WebSphere Process Server, Biztalk ESB Toolkit and other products like Apache Camel.

As in (Thorsten Scheibler & Frank Leymann, 2008), adaptation mechanisms are described giving a general overview of their features and specifying the additional characteristics to fully describe their behavior.

The transformation mechanism deals with the runtime transformation of messages. It receives one message and returns another one, transformed according to a given transformation logic. Some examples of transformation types are data model transformation, data format transformation, content filter and content enrichment. The characteristic to fully determine its behavior is the transformation logic.

The routing mechanism dynamically determines the message path according to different factors. It can be configured to have many target services, but only one is activated for a given message. The characteristics to fully determine its behavior are the list of target services and a routing logic. Some examples of this mechanism are content-based routing and load-balancing routing.

The recipient list mechanism distributes a message to multiple services. In this way, this mechanism receives one message and returns multiple messages. To completely specify the behavior of this mechanism, the list of target services must be specified.

The aggregator mechanism receives multiple messages containing an identifier in order to determine which ones are related. When a given set of messages is complete, a single message is returned consolidating the content of all the related messages. It requires the specification of two characteristics: a completion condition and an aggregation algorithm. The completion condition (e.g. "Wait for All", "Time Out", "First Bet") is used to determine when a given set of messages is complete. The aggregation algorithm (e.g. "Select the best answer", "Condense data") specifies how the messages content is combined to produce a single message.

The cache mechanism receives a request message and returns another message, which was previously stored and returned as a response for the given request. The additional required characteristic for this mechanism is the life time of the stored response messages.

Finally, the delayer mechanism receives a message and delays its delivery for a given time interval. The additional characteristic to be specified for this mechanism is the delay time.

Table 1 summarizes the described adaptation mechanisms and provides a graphical representation for them.

Dealing with Response Time Degradation

Response time degradation is a major concern in service-based systems. The massively distribu-

Table 1. Summary of adaptation mechanisms

Adaptation Mechanism	Graphical Representation	Additional Characteristics
Transformation		Transformation Logic
Routing		Routing Logic, List of Possible Target Service
Recipient List		List of Target Services
Aggregator		Completion Condition, Aggregation Algorithm
Cache		Life Time
Delayer		Delay Time

tion of these systems, the widely use of XML as message format (which involves packaging and parsing tasks) and the mediation operations that a message can undergo are some of the reasons which can cause a considerable overhead in the interactions among services. (Yan Fang et al., 2006)

Detecting Response Time Degradation

Generally, services response times are monitored by the native monitoring mechanisms included in ESB products. Response time degradation for a service can be detected using monitored information (i.e. monitored properties) and the service requirements.

For example, the property "daily average response time" (the average response time in the last twenty-four hours) can be monitored. To calculate its value, the Monitoring Manager can interact with the native ESB monitoring mechanisms, to get the response time values of the service invocations

Figure 12. Detecting response time degradation

```
boolean merE(ESB-Service s, Monitored-Property p, Value v) {
     if (p == "daily average response time"){
          for each r ∈ service-requirements(s) /
                    (r.property == "daily average response time" ∧
                    r.operator == "<") do {
                          if v >= r.value return true;
                    }
               }
     }
     return false;
}
```

within the last twenty-four hours and calculate their average value.

Additionally, a service requirement has to be set in order to specify the acceptable values for this property. For example, a requirement can specify that the "daily average response time" cannot be equal or greater than nine hundred milliseconds (i.e. "daily-average-response-time" < 900ms).

In this way, the adaptive infrastructure has all the required information to detect the monitored event "response time degradation". Figure 12 presents a possible implementation of the function mer_E for this monitored event, which returns true when the value of the monitored property "daily

average response time" is greater or equal to a maximum value specified in a service requirement.

Note that in this case $mer_E = mer$("response time degradation").

Triggering the Requirement to Reduce Response Time

Response time degradation can trigger, for a given service, an adaptation requirement called "reduce response time". In this case, it is assumed that this adaptation requirement is always triggered when detecting the monitored event "response time degradation". This means, as shown in Figure 13, that the function arr_R for this requirement will

Figure 13. Triggering the requirement to reduce response time

```
boolean rraR(Monitored-Event m, ESB-Service s, Monitored-Property p,
          Value v) {
     if (m=="response time degradation"){
          return true;
     }
     return false;
}
```

Figure 14. Invoke equivalent service

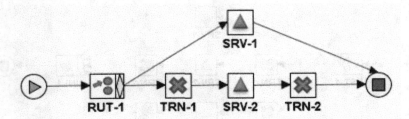

always return true when receiving the "response time degradation" event.

Note that in this case $rra_R = rra$("reduce response time").

Selecting and Implementing Adaptation Strategies

In order to address the previous adaptation requirement, an adaptation strategy has to be selected and implemented. In (González & Ruggia, 2011b) three possible adaptation strategies were identified and described to deal with this requirement: invoke an equivalent service, use previously stored information and distribute service requests to equivalent services.

The strategy "invoke an equivalent service" consists in invoking an equivalent service, with a lower response time than the service for which the requirement was triggered. Figure 14 presents a possible implementation of this strategy using the routing and transformation mechanisms.

When a message is sent to the ESB to invoke a service with a response time problem, the message is first processed by a routing mechanism which, according to different factors (e.g. invoked operation), can route the message to the invoked service (task SRV-1) or to an equivalent service (task SRV-2). If the equivalent service has a different technical interface, transformations have to be performed in order to transform the request message or the response message, to comply with the request expected by the service, or the response expected by the client, respectively. However, given that the required time to perform the transformations can have a considerable impact in the response time perceived by clients, this time has to be considered when selecting this strategy.

In order to implement this strategy, the adaptive infrastructure has to take the generic adaptation flow presented in Figure 14 and configure it with concrete values. In particular, equivalent services can be obtained from the Services Registry. Additionally, given that the adaptive infrastructure handles a canonical data model, it has all the information (i.e. transformation logics) to perform the required transformations.

Note that this configuration process can lead to various concrete adaptation flows, one for each equivalent service. Additionally, in order to be able

Figure 15. Use previously stored information

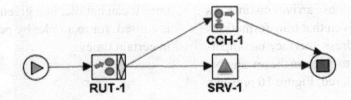

19

Figure 16. Distribute request to equivalent services

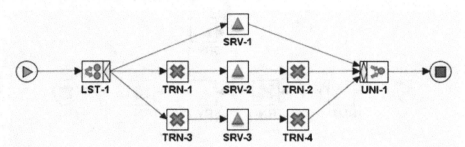

to implement and apply this strategy for a given service at least one equivalent service has to be registered in the ESB infrastructure.

On the other side, the strategy "use previously stored information" consists in using information previously sent and stored from other invocations as the response for a given request. In this way, a client application receives a response without invoking the target service. Figure 15 presents a possible implementation of this strategy using the routing and cache mechanisms.

Similar to the previous strategy, messages are first processed by a routing mechanism which, according to different factors, can route the message to the invoked service (task SRV-1) or to the cache service (task CCH-1).

The implementation of this strategy does not require major configurations. However, in order to be able to implement and apply this strategy for a given service, the service has to only return data, that is, this strategy is not applicable for services which perform, for example, update operations.

Finally, the strategy "distribute request to equivalent services" consists in sending a request to a set of equivalent services, including the service for which the problem was detected, and return the response which arrives first. In this way, there is more chance that a response arrives on time. As previously discussed, given that transformations might be required to address interface incompatibilities, the time needed to perform these transformations has to be considered. Figure 16 presents

a possible implementation of this strategy using the recipient list, transformation and aggregator mechanisms.

In order to implement this strategy, the generic adaptation flow presented in Figure 16 has to be configured with concrete values. In particular, the completion condition for the aggregator mechanism is "First Bet", and the aggregation algorithm for this mechanism is "Select the best (first) answer". As stated before, equivalent services can be obtained from the Services Registry and the transformation logic to perform the transformations is also available within the infrastructure.

Note that this configuration process can lead to various concrete adaptation flows, one for each possible sub-set of equivalent services. Additionally, in order to be able to implement and apply this strategy for a given service at least one equivalent service has to be registered in the ESB infrastructure.

Dealing with Service Saturation

Services saturation is another major concern in service-based systems. This situation occurs when a service receives more requests than the ones it can handle, in a given time interval. This is caused, for example, by peaks of transactions in certain times.

Detecting Service Saturation

Service requests (invocations) are also usually monitored in ESB products, so services saturation can be detected using this information and services requirements.

For example, the property "invocations per minute" (the amount of service invocations in a minute) can be monitored. To calculate its value, the Monitoring Manager can interact with the native ESB monitoring mechanisms, to get the information regarding service invocations and calculate the number of invocations performed per minute.

Additionally, a service requirement has to be set in order to specify the acceptable values for this property. For example, a requirement can specify that the "invocations per minute" property cannot be equal or greater than fifty (i.e. "invocations per minute" < 50).

In this way, the adaptive infrastructure has all the required information to detect the monitored event "service saturation".

Triggering the Requirement to Reduce Service Saturation

The service saturation event can trigger the requirement "reduce service saturation" (i.e. reduce the requests that a service receive in a given time interval). In this case, it is assumed that this ad-aptation requirement is always triggered when detecting the monitored event "service saturation". This means that the function arr_R for this requirement will always return true when receiving the "service saturation" event.

Selecting and Implementing Adaptation Strategies

In order to address the previous adaptation requirement, an adaptation strategy has to be selected and implemented. In (González & Ruggia, 2011b) three possible adaptation strategies were identified and described to deal with this requirement: load balancing, defer service requests and use previously stored information.

The load balancing strategy consists in balancing service requests among the service and a set of equivalent services using, for example, a round-robin strategy. Figure 17 presents a possible implementation of this strategy using the routing and transformation mechanisms.

Messages are first processed by a routing mechanism which, according to a load-balancing strategy, routes the message to the invoked service (task SRV-1) or to one of the equivalent services (tasks SRV-2 and SRV-3). Again, given that transformations might be required, the time needed to perform these transformations has to be considered when selecting this strategy.

Figure 17. Load balancing

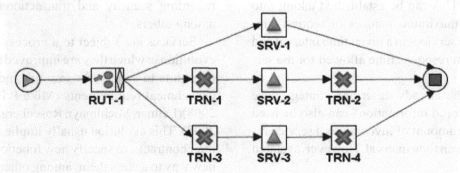

Figure 18. Defer service requests

In order to implement this strategy, the generic adaptation flow presented in Figure 17 has to be configured with concrete values. In particular, the load balancing strategy has to be set in the routing mechanism. As stated before, equivalent services can be obtained from the Services Registry and the transformation logic to perform the transformations is also available within the infrastructure.

Note that this configuration process can lead to various concrete adaptation flows, one for each possible sub-set of equivalent services. Additionally, in order to be able to implement and apply this strategy for a given service at least one equivalent service has to be registered in the ESB infrastructure.

On the other side, the "defer service requests" strategy consists in deferring the delivery of service requests with the goal of reducing the amount of invocations a service receives in a given time interval. This strategy has a clear impact in the response time perceived by client applications, so this is something to be considered when selecting and implementing this strategy. Figure 17 presents a possible implementation of this strategy using the delayer mechanism.

The implementation of this strategy consists in configuring the delay time in the delayer mechanism. This can be established taking into account the maximum number of request supported by the services in a given time interval and the maximum response time allowed for the service.

Finally, the already described strategy "use previously stored information" can also be used to reduce the amount of invocations a service receives in a given time interval. However, as stated before, this strategy is suitable just for services which only return data.

Dealing with Changes in Services Contracts

A service contract is composed of one or more published documents that describe the service. The fundamental parts of a service contract are the documents that express its technical interface. This interface establishes an Application Programming Interface (API) through which the service offers its functionalities. (Erl et al., 2008)

When services are implemented using the Web Services technology, their contracts usually include WSDL definitions, XML Schema definitions and WS-Policy definitions. WSDL definitions allow specifying the operations provided by the services, the message format to interact with the services and the location where the services can be accessed. XML Schema definitions allow specifying a detailed message structure defining which elements and attributes are allowed, in which order they have to be included and their possible data types. Finally, WS-Policy definitions allow extending the previous definitions to specify advanced characteristics or requirements regarding security and transactional behavior, among others.

Services are subject to a process of constant evolution in which they are improved and adapted over time to satisfy, for example, new business or technical requirements (Mike P Papazoglou, 2008)(Leitner, Michlmayr, Rosenberg, & Dustdar, 2008). This evolution usually implies changes in their contracts, to specify new functionalities or a new way to access them, among others. A change in a service contract is backward-compatible when the new version of the contract continues to support client programs designed to work with the old version; otherwise, the change is backward-incompatible (Erl et al., 2008). It is unreasonable to assume that every time a service changes in an incompatible way, all its clients will rapidly adapt to the change (Fang et al., 2007). In turn, an incompatible change can impact several client applications not allowing them to perform its work.

Various authors (Mike P Papazoglou, 2008) (Leitner et al., 2008) (Erl et al., 2008) identify the types of changes in a service contract and analyze their compatibility. For example, adding an operation and adding and optional parameter in an operation are considered to be compatible changes. However, renaming, or deleting, an operation are considered to be incompatible changes.

In this work, an incompatible change can be a manageable change or a non-manageable change. An incompatible change is manageable if it is possible to perform mediation operations, over the interchanged messages between clients and the service, so that it is possible to continue invoking the operation that changed. Otherwise, the incompatible change is non-manageable. For example, renaming an operation in the WSDL definitions is an incompatible change. The operation name is usually included in SOAP messages so that the Web Services framework can know which operation is being invoked. Therefore, if an operation is renamed and client applications continue specifying the old name, the Web Service framework will throw an exception notifying that the specified operation does not exist. However, this kind of change can be managed given that SOAP messages can be intercepted and transformed changing the elements which have a reference to the operation name. In this way, renaming an operation is a manageable change. Other examples of manageable changes are renaming parameters, deleting parameters, changing the order of parameters and some types of changes in the Message Exchange Pattern (MEP) specified in the service (for example, from request-reply to one-way). On the other side, an example of a non-manageable incompatible change is deleting an operation, given that it is not possible to apply mediation operations so that the same operation can be invoked.

Figure 19. Detecting a contract change

```
boolean merE(ESB-Service s, Monitored-Property p, Value v) {
      if (p == "service contract"){
            for each r ∈ service-requirements(s) /
                  (r.property == "service-contract" ∧
                  r.operator == "=") do {
                        // r.value correspond to the stored service contract
                        if v <> r.value return true;
                  }
            }
      }
      return false;
}
```

Detecting a Contract Change

Web Services contracts are usually publically published, so they can be monitored inspecting the documents which include the WSDL, XML Schema and WS-Policy definitions. A contract change can be detected if the infrastructure store the contracts, as service metadata, and periodically monitor the property "service contract" (the published service contract) and compare it with the stored metadata.

Additionally, a service requirement has to be set in order to specify that the monitored property "service contract" has to be equal to the one stored as metadata in the infrastructure (i.e. "service contract" = *metadata*("service-contract")).

In this way, the adaptive infrastructure has all the required information to detect the monitored event "service contract change." Figure 19 presents a possible implementation of the function mer_E for this monitored event, which returns true when the value of the monitored property "service contract" is not equal to the service contract stored as metadata in the infrastructure.

Note that in this case mer_E = *mer*("service contract change").

Triggering the Requirement to Handle an Incompatible Change

When a change in a service contract is not compatible, this monitored event can trigger the adaptation requirement "handle incompatible contract change". This means, as shown in Figure 20, that the function arr_R for this requirement returns true when receiving the "service contract change" event and the change is not compatible.

Note that in this case rra_R = *rra*("handle incompatible contract change").

Selecting and Implementing Adaptation Strategies

In order to address the previous adaptation requirement, an adaptation strategy has to be selected and implemented. In (González & Ruggia, 2011a) three possible adaptation strategies were identified and described to deal with this requirement: invoke an equivalent service, use previously stored information and modify request / response messages.

As presented before, the "invoke an equivalent service" strategy consists in invoking an equivalent service. In this case, it can be used to handle both types of incompatible changes. A possible implementation of this strategy, using the routing and transformation mechanisms, was already presented in Figure 14.

Figure 20. Triggering the requirement to handle an incompatible change

```
boolean rraR(Monitored-Event m, ESB-Service s, Monitored-Property p,
          Value v) {
     if (m=="service contract change"){
          if (not is-compatible((metadata(s, "service contract")),v)){
               return true;}
     }
     return false;
}
```

Figure 21. Modify request / response messages

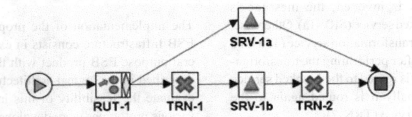

In this case, when a message is sent to the ESB to invoke a service whose contract has changed, the message is first processed by a routing mechanism. This mechanism performs a content-based routing according to the name of the invoked operation (usually included in SOAP messages). More concretely, the message is routed to an equivalent service only if an operation with changes is invoked.

On the other side, the strategy "use previously stored information" can also be used to handle both types of incompatible changes. A possible implementation of this strategy, using the routing and cache mechanisms, was already presented in Figure 15.

Similar to the previous strategy, messages are first processed by a routing mechanism which performs a content-based routing according to the

name of the invoked operation. If an operation with changes is invoked the message is routed to the cache service (CCH-1). Otherwise, the message is routed to the invoked service (SRV-1). As stated before, this strategy is suitable just for services which only return data.

Finally, the "modify request / response messages" consists in modifying the request and/or response messages interchanged between clients and services, and it can be used only for manageable incompatible changes. Figure 21 presents a possible implementation of this strategy using the transformation and routing mechanisms. Note that tasks SRV-1a and SRV-1b represent an invocation to the same service.

Similar to the previous strategy, messages are first processed by a routing mechanism which performs a content-based routing according to the

Figure 22. XSLT script to rename the element "citizenData" to "getCitizen"

```
<xsl:template match="node() | @*">
    <xsl:copy>
        <xsl:apply-templates select="@* | node()"/>
    </xsl:copy>
</xsl:template>

<xsl:template match="ns2:citizenData">
    <xsl:element name="ns2:getCitizen">
        <xsl:apply-templates/>
    </xsl:element>
</xsl:template>
```

name of the invoked operation. If an operation without changes is invoked, the message is routed to the invoked service (SRV-1a). Otherwise, it is routed to the transformation service (TRN-1). In this last case, after performing the transformation, the message is routed to the invoked service (SRV-1b) and finally it is routed again to the transformation service (TRN-2).

Note that the transformation mechanism is used to modify the request and / or response message, to comply with the new technical interface of the service. For example, Figure 22 presents an XSLT script which modifies a SOAP message renaming the element "citizenData" to "getCitizen", with the goal of handling a change in the name of the operation "citizenData".

Summary

Figure 23 presents a summary of the different monitoring and adaptation elements described in this section, in the context of the S-Cube Adaptation and Monitoring Framework.

IMPLEMENTATION

The implementation of the proposed Adaptive ESB Infrastructure consists in extending a general purpose ESB product with the components described in the logical architecture. In order to evaluate the feasibility of this implementation, various prototypes were developed. This section presents different alternatives to implement these components and describes how the prototypes were developed with the product JBossESB (*JBossESB*, 2010).

Virtual Services

The implementation of Virtual Services requires a way to consume external Web Services and to expose them as Web Services through the ESB. Given that these capabilities are provided by most ESB products, the implementation of Virtual Services should not present major problems.

In particular, the JBossESB product provides a direct way to implement Virtual Services through the SOAPProxy component, which exposes an

Figure 23. Summary of adaptation and monitoring elements

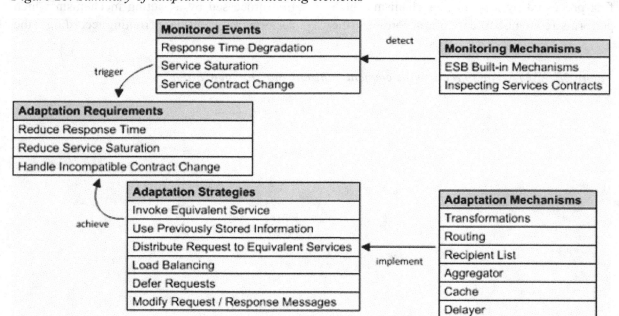

external Web Service through the ESB. Therefore, the developed prototype was based in this component to implement Virtual Services.

Adaptation Services

The implementation of Adaptation Services requires counting with the different adaptation mechanisms (e.g. routing), a way to build ESB services based on these mechanisms and a way to execute these services through an itinerary.

Regarding adaptation mechanisms, their support can substantially vary among ESB products. Considering the adaptation mechanisms used in this chapter, the transformation and routing mechanisms are usually supported in most ESB products. Additionally, the recipient list and aggregator mechanisms are also widely supported. However, the cache and delayer mechanism are not usually included, at least in a native way, in ESB products. In this way, their implementation would usually require an ad-hoc solution. In particular, JBossESB natively supports the transformation, routing, recipient list and aggregator mechanisms. Moreover, the cache mechanism was successfully implemented (Vergara & Beceiro, 2010) following the guidelines presented in (Yan Fang et al., 2006).

With respect to creating ESB services based on the previous mechanisms, ESB products usually support this capability. In particular, the developed prototypes rely on the mechanism provided by JBossESB which consists of creating ESB Services as action pipelines, in which each action can perform a mediation operation (e.g. a message transformation).

Finally, the capability to execute services through an itinerary attached to the messages is not always supported in ESB products. For instance, the BizTalk ESB Toolkit (*BizTalk ESB Toolkit*, 2010) provides this functionality out-of-the-box, but JBossESB does not natively include it. However, an initial solution was prototyped in JBossESB by implementing each Adaptation Service using two actions: the first one executes

the mediation operation over the message, and the second one routes the message to the next step in the itinerary.

Adaptation Gateway

The Adaptation Gateway has to intercept all messages sent to the ESB for invoking Virtual Services. There are different alternatives to implement this component in an ESB-based infrastructure. For example, many ESB products provide built-in mechanisms that allow intercepting the messages going in or out the ESB (e.g. filters and interceptors). Additionally, the Adaptation Gateway can be implemented as an ESB Service which constitutes a single entry point to the ESB for all the services invocations. The advantage of this solution is that it is generic enough to be implemented in most ESB products.

In particular, the Adaptation Gateway in the JBossESB product was implemented using this last approach. The standard WS-Addressing was used to specify the service to be invoked through the single entry point.

Adaptation and Monitoring Engine

The Adaptation and Monitoring Engine has to be able to receive monitored data from the Monitoring Manager, to send adaptation directives to the Adaptation Manager and to take the different adaptation and monitored decisions required by the adaptive infrastructure. Given these characteristics, it seems suitable to implement this component using Complex Event Processing (CEP) engines.

The JBoss platform provides the Drools Fusion (*Drools Fusion*, 2010) product as a CEP engine. In particular, a prototype was developed using this product (Simon, 2010) in which the engine receives different events with information regarding services. In particular, this information includes response times, services contracts and the result (ERROR or OK) of services invocations. Based on this information, different complex events are detected like changes in services contracts and the degradation of response times.

Summary

The implemented prototypes enabled to evaluate the functional feasibility of using a general purpose ESB to implement the proposed approach. Although some key functions (e.g. the cache mechanism) are not usually provided by these products, implementing them was also feasible. As the used features are mostly implemented in ESB products, these results are also applicable to other ones. However, the implementation complexity of the solution will depend on the functionalities provided by the specific product and its general architecture.

Concerning performance and workload, current prototypes do not enable to analyze these aspects and are part of ongoing work. Nevertheless, decision mechanisms would be executed in a specific component (i.e. the Adaptation and Monitoring Engine) devoted to perform an efficient event and rule processing.

FUTURE RESEARCH DIRECTIONS

This work is currently being extended by specifying and prototyping different strategies as well as by improving the overall dynamic approach.

Future work would consist in specifying and prototyping other adaptation strategies to deal with QoS degradation, services saturation and changes in services contracts. In particular, other quality factors will be addressed like availability and interoperability. Additionally, other types of contract changes regarding, for example, security or transactional requirements will be considered. This last issue poses several challenges given that these advanced requirements can also restrict the number of adaptation strategies to deal with a

given situation. For instance, if a service requires signed or encrypted information, the strategy "modify request / response messages" might not be an option anymore.

Two key aspects to further develop are the management of adaptation directives and the extension of adaptation to the different SOA layers (e.g. to the service composition and coordination layer). While the first includes aspects like enhancing strategies for selecting adaptation directives, the second addresses the issues of developing consistent adaptation mechanisms for all layers in the architecture.

In addition, other topics that require further exploration concern the application of REST-based protocols and the potentials and limits of general purpose ESB products to carry out service integration in the Web.

Finally, experimentation constitutes another working axe aiming to evaluate implementation and critical operational aspects, for example processing time of the adaptation directives. A detailed analysis of performance and overhead impacts would include the exploration of emerging tools for processing rules and events in the context of ESBs.

CONCLUSION

Although service-based systems increasingly require adaptation features, current mainstream techniques and products still lack of comprehensive and automatic mechanisms to respond to unexpected changes. While SOA provide the foundations of flexible service binding and ESBs enable to carry out a large number of mediation capabilities, they assume manual operations when changes occur and they do not include automatic and self-managed mechanisms.

This motivates using adaptive platforms, which provide much more sophisticated capabilities to achieve automatic changes on the middleware layer (e.g. an ESB). This chapter addressed these issues by presenting an approach based on an Adaptive ESB Infrastructure.

The approach leverages ESBs mediation capabilities to dynamically and automatically create adaptation flows through which a message is routed in order to perform the required adaptations. Given that the approach is based on commonly supported ESB patterns, it is likely to be applied in most ESB products. However, the implementation complexity of the solution depends on the functionalities provided by the specific product and its general architecture.

The approach has several advantages. Firstly, mediation flows provide a high level mechanism to specify the adaptation strategies. Second, as ESB platforms possess a number of features to address adaptation requirements, they provide the means to implement a variety of adaptation mechanisms in a mainstream infrastructure layer. Finally, the here presented approach is based on the key ideas developed by the S-Cube project, which provides a consistent framework to carry out dynamic adaptability across the different SOA layers.

Globally, the proposed Adaptive ESB Infrastructure, as it is based on a single framework and platform, enables to address a large range of adaptability requirements by combining the different provided adaptability mechanisms.

Experimental results have shown the feasibility of this approach, although a number of research aspects remain to be addressed. The implementation complexity of the solution depends on the functionalities provided by the specific product and its general architecture. Current prototypes are implemented using the JBossESB product; however, as the proposal is based on commonly supported ESB patterns, it is likely to be applied in most ESB products.

The main contributions of this work consist of the definition and specification of mechanisms to address automatic adaptability in service-based systems by applying a general purpose middleware platform. In addition, as the specification is based on mediation flows that abstract general purpose ESB operations, it enables a wide application. This aims to be a step forward in developing dynamic and automatic adaptation capabilities in service-based systems which run over an ESB infrastructure.

REFERENCES

Bai, X., Xie, J., Chen, B., & Xiao, S. (2007). DRESR: Dynamic routing in enterprise service bus. In *IEEE International Conference on E-Business Engineering,* (pp. 528-531). Los Alamitos, CA: IEEE Computer Society. Retrieved from http://doi.ieeecomputersociety.org/10.1109/ICEBE.2007.102

Chang, S. H., La, H. J., Bae, J. S., Jeon, W. Y., & Kim, S. D. (2007). Design of a dynamic composition handler for ESB-based services. In *IEEE International Conference on e-Business Engineering, ICEBE 2007* (pp. 287–294).

Chappell, D. (2004). *Enterprise service bus: Theory in practice*. O'Reilly Media.

Davis, J. (2009). *Open source SOA* (1st ed.). Manning Publications.

Di Nitto, E., Ghezzi, C., Metzger, A., Papazoglou, M., & Pohl, K. (2008). A journey to highly dynamic, self-adaptive service-based applications. *Automated Software Engineering, 15,* 313–341. doi:10.1007/s10515-008-0032-x

Drools Fusion. (2010). Retrieved from http://www.jboss.org/drools/drools-fusion.html

Erl, T. (2009). *SOA design patterns* (1st ed.). Prentice Hall PTR.

Erl, T., Karmarkar, A., Walmsley, P., Haas, H., Yalcinalp, L. U., & Liu, K. (2008). *Web service contract design and versioning for SOA* (1st ed.). Prentice Hall.

Fang, R., Chen, Y., Fong, L., Lam, L., Frank, D., Vignola, C., & Du, N. (2007). A version-aware approach for web service client application. In *10th IFIP/IEEE International Symposium on Integrated Network Management, IM'07* (pp. 401–409).

Ferguson, D. (2010). *The internet service bus. On the Move to Meaningful Internet Systems 2007: CoopIS* (p. 5). DOA, ODBASE, GADA, and IS.

Frantz, R. Z. (n.d.). *Guaraná DSL*. Retrieved June 26, 2011, from http://www.tdg-seville.info/rzfrantz/Guaran%C3%A1+DSL

González, L. (2011, October 18). *Plataforma ESB adaptativa para sistemas basados en servicios* (Master's Thesis). PEDECIBA Informática | Instituto de Computación – Facultad de Ingeniería – Universidad de la República.

González, L., & Ruggia, R. (2010). Towards dynamic adaptation within an ESB-based service infrastructure layer. In *Proceedings of the 3rd International Workshop on Monitoring, Adaptation and Beyond, MONA '10* (pp. 40–47). New York, NY: ACM. doi:10.1145/1929566.1929572

González, L., & Ruggia, R. (2011a). *Addressing the dynamics of services contracts through an adaptive ESB infrastructure*. Presented at the 1st International Workshop on Adaptive Services for the Future Internet, Poznan-Poland.

González, L., & Ruggia, R. (2011b). *Addressing QoS issues in service based systems through an adaptive ESB infrastructure*. Presented at the 6th Middleware for Service Oriented Computing Workshop, Lisboa-Portugal.

Hérault, C., Thomas, G., & Fourier, U. J. (2005). Mediation and enterprise service bus: A position paper. *Proceedings of the First International Workshop on Mediation in Semantic Web Services*. Retrieved from http://citeseerx.ist.psu.edu/viewdoc/summary?doi=10.1.1.142.7416

Hofstede, A. H. M. T., Aalst, W. M. P. V. D., Adams, M., & Russell, N. (2009). *Modern business process automation: YAWL and its support environment* (1st ed.). Springer.

Hohpe, G., & Woolf, B. (2003). *Enterprise integration patterns: Designing, building, and deploying messaging solutions*. Addison-Wesley Professional.

Hutchison, B., Schmidt, M., Wolfson, D., & Stockton, M. (2005, July 26). *SOA programming model for implementing Web services, Part 4: An introduction to the IBM enterprise service bus*. CT316. Retrieved June 26, 2011, from http://www.ibm.com/developerworks/library/ws-soa-progmodel4/

JBoss Community. (2010). *JBossESB*. Retrieved from http://www.jboss.org/jbossesb/

Jongtaveesataporn, A., & Takada, S. (2010). Enhancing enterprise service bus capability for load balancing. *WSEAS Transactions on Computers, 9*, 299–308.

La, H., Bae, J., Chang, S., & Kim, S. (2007). Practical methods for adapting services using enterprise service bus. *Proceedings of the 7ᵗʰ International Conference on Web Engineering*, (pp. 53–58).

Leitner, P., Michlmayr, A., Rosenberg, F., & Dustdar, S. (2008). End-to-end versioning support for Web services. In *2008 IEEE International Conference on Services Computing* (pp. 59-66). Honolulu, HI, USA. doi:10.1109/SCC.2008.21

Lin, K., Panahi, M., & Zhang, Y. (2007). The design of an intelligent accountability architecture. In *Proceedings of the IEEE International Conference on e-Business Engineering, ICEBE '07* (pp. 157–164). Washington, DC: IEEE Computer Society. Retrieved from http://dx.doi.org/10.1109/ICEBE.2007.145

Lin, K. J., & Chang, S. H. (2009). A service accountability framework for QoS service management and engineering. *Information Systems and e-Business Management, 7*(4), 429–446.

Masternak, T., Psiuk, M., Radziszowski, D., Szydlo, T., Szymacha, R., Zielinski, K., & Zmuda, D. (2010). ESB-modern SOA infrastructure. In Ambroszkiewicz, S. (Ed.), *SOA infrastructure tools: Concepts and methods*. Poznan University of Economics Press.

Metzger, A., & Pohl, K. (2009). Towards the next generation of service-based systems: The S-Cube research framework. In *Advanced Information. Systems Engineering*, 11–16. Retrieved from http://dx.doi.org/10.1007/978-3-642-02144-2_6

Microsoft. (2010). *BizTalk ESB toolkit*. Retrieved from http://msdn.microsoft.com/en-us/biztalk/dd876606

Panahi, M., & Lin, K. 0001, Y. Z., Chang, S., Zhang, J., & Varela, L. (2008). The LLAMA middleware support for accountable service-oriented architecture. In *ICSOC* (pp. 180-194).

Papazoglou, M. (2007). *Web services: Principles and technology* (1st ed.). Prentice Hall.

Papazoglou, M., Pohl, K., Parkin, M., & Metzger, A. (2010). *Service research challenges and solutions for the future internet: Towards mechanisms and methods for engineering, managing, and adapting service-based systems* (*Vol. 6500*). New York, NY: Springer-Verlag Inc.

Papazoglou, M. P. (2008). The challenges of service evolution. In *Proceedings of the 20th International Conference on Advanced Information Systems Engineering, CAiSE '08* (pp. 1–15). Berlin, Germany: Springer-Verlag. Retrieved from http://dx.doi.org/10.1007/978-3-540-69534-9_1

Rademakers, T., & Dirksen, J. (2008). *Open-source ESBs in action: Example implementations in mule and service mix* (1st ed.). Manning Publications.

Scheibler, T., & Leymann, F. (2008). A framework for executable enterprise application integration patterns. In *Enterprise Interoperability III* (pp. 485-497). Retrieved from http://dx.doi.org/10.1007/978-1-84800-221-0_38

Scheibler, T., Mietzner, R., & Leymann, F. (2008). EAI as a service - Combining the power of executable EAI patterns and SaaS. In *12th International IEEE Enterprise Distributed Object Computing Conference, EDOC '08.* (pp. 107-116). doi:10.1109/EDOC.2008.21

Schmidt, M., Hutchison, B., Lambros, P., & Phippen, R. (2005). The enterprise service bus: Making service-oriented architecture real. *IBM Systems Journal, 44*(4), 781–797. doi:10.1147/sj.444.0781

Simon, R. (2010). JBoss drools fusion. *Módulo de Taller - InCo - FING - UdelaR*. Retrieved August 7, 2011, from http://www.fing.edu.uy/~lauragon/tesis/mt-2010-drools-fusion.pdf

Sleiman, H. A., Sultán, A. W., Frantz, R. Z., & Corchuelo, R. (n.d.). *Towards automatic code generation for EAI solutions using DSL tools*.

Vergara, S., & Beceiro, J. (2010). Acceso a datos y servicios de la Web a través de un ESB. *Reporte Taller de Sistemas de Información 3 - InCo - FING - UdelaR*. Retrieved August 7, 2011, from http://www.fing.edu.uy/~lauragon/tesis/tsi3-2010-web-esb.pdf

Wu, B., Liu, S., & Wu, L. (2008). Dynamic reliable service routing in enterprise service bus. In *Proceedings of the 2008 IEEE Asia-Pacific Services Computing Conference* (pp. 349–354). Washington, DC: IEEE Computer Society. doi:10.1109/APSCC.2008.145

Wylie, H., & Lambros, P. (2009, March 10). *Enterprise connectivity patterns: Implementing integration solutions with IBM's enterprise service bus products.* CT316. Retrieved August 28, 2010, from http://www.ibm.com/developerworks/library/ws-enterpriseconnectivitypatterns/index.html

Yan Fang, R., Ru, F., Zhong, T., Eoin, L., Harini, S., Banks, T., & He, L. (2006, May 30). *Cache mediation pattern specification: An overview.* CT316. Retrieved July 21, 2010, from http://www.ibm.com/developerworks/webservices/library/ws-soa-cachemed/

Yuan, H., Choi, S. W., & Kim, S. D. (2008). A practical monitoring framework for ESB-based services. In *Proceedings of the 2008 IEEE Congress on Services Part II* (pp. 49–56). Washington, DC: IEEE Computer Society. doi:10.1109/SERVICES-2.2008.5

Zielinski, K., Szydło, T., Szymacha, R., Kosinski, J., Kosinska, J., Jarzab, M., & Mickiewicza, A. (2011). Adaptive SOA solution stack. *IEEE Transactions on Services Computing, 99*(1).

Ziyaeva, G., Choi, E., & Min, D. (2008). Content-based intelligent routing and message processing in enterprise service bus. In *International Conference on Hybrid Information Technology,* (pp. 245-249). Los Alamitos, CA: IEEE Computer Society. Retrieved from http://doi.ieeecomputersociety.org/10.1109/ICHIT.2008.267

Zou, J., Pavlovski, C. J., & Wang, Y. (2008). A disclosure framework for service accountability in SOA. In *IEEE International Conference on e-Business Engineering, ICEBE'08* (pp. 437–442).

KEY TERMS AND DEFINITIONS

Enterprise Service Bus (ESB): An Enterprise Service Bus is an integration middleware that acts as an integration layer for connecting applications and other services throughout an enterprise computing infrastructure.

Message Routing: It is the capability to route messages according to different factors (e.g. message content).

Message Transformation: It is the capability to transform messages, according to a transformation logic.

Middleware Adaptation: It is the capability of middleware platforms to automatically adapt to changes in the execution context.

Quality of Service (QoS): QoS comprises service execution properties like performance and availability.

Service Based Systems (SBSs): SBSs are software systems that follow a Service Oriented Architecture.

Service Contract: It is a set of documents specifying the functional and non-functional characteristics of a service.

Chapter 2
Structural Interoperability as a Basis for Service Adaptability

José C. Delgado
Instituto Superior Técnico, Technical University of Lisbon, Portugal

ABSTRACT

Web Services appeared essentially as an interoperability solution and REST as a closer match to the semantics of protocols such as HTTP. Clearly influenced by the original browsing goals of the Web, these technologies are not native solutions to the service-oriented paradigm, exhibit limitations to interoperability, and behavior has to be implemented in a separate language. Web Services offer a WSDL document to describe them, but assume that complex data use the same schema in both interacting services, which increases their coupling. This chapter discusses interoperability, from the perspective of both the consumer (compliance) and provider (conformance) services, and it argues that compliance is a weaker requirement for service interoperability than conformance and should be the cornerstone to decrease coupling and to favor adaptability. Structural interoperability is used, given that the lifecycles of distributed resources are decoupled. Metrics to quantify adaptability, based on similarity and decoupling, are proposed.

INTRODUCTION

The complexity and changeability of software have long been a huge challenge for software developers, affecting not only applications but also virtually all aspects of computer science, such as formats, protocols, languages, platforms, techniques and standards. It seems that change and adaptation are really the only constant things.

The object-oriented paradigm appeared as a solution to these issues, by structuring the programs according to some principles that tend

DOI: 10.4018/978-1-4666-2089-6.ch002

to limit the impact of a change, affecting fewer objects, and to increase the adaptability, allowing resources to be adapted, even without the source code (Meyer, 2000):

- **The Least Semantic Gap Principle:** The entities in the problem and solution spaces should have a one to one mapping, by modeling each problem entity with a solution entity, with both state and related behavior;

- **The Information Hiding Principle:** There must be a clear separation between interface (syntax and semantics) and its implementation. This reduces the change propagation effect. A change in one resource affects those that use it only if its interface is affected;

- **The Substitution Principle:** An object X should be able to be used with its own implementation wherever an object Y is expected, as long as X conforms to Y, a form of polymorphism;

- **The Non-Duplication of Information Principle:** Objects with similar features (state or behavior) should factor them and share a common definition, usually implemented by inheritance, instead of duplicating it;

- **The Open-Closed Principle:** An object should be closed, so that it can be used, but at the same time open, so that it can be changed. Actually, this is a corollary of the two previous principles and it means that it is possible to tune up objects by redefining operations, even if the source code is not available.

Unfortunately, most of the advantages of the object-oriented paradigm, namely information sharing (inheritance, in practice) and polymorphism, stem from the fact that the lifecycles of the objects are coupled, either at compile or link time, which is not the case for services, in SOA and cloud environments. These are loosely coupled

Figure 1. Basic service adaptability scenario

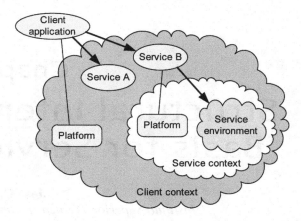

and evolve independently, but need nonetheless to interoperate. As one service changes, those that use it must adapt to maintain interoperability.

Figure 1 illustrates the possibilities of service adaptability. A client application can invoke several services. Its context consists of the platform that executes it, which can be a device such as a server, a laptop, a tablet or a smart phone, and the services available to it. Each service needs a platform to execute it and its environment is the set of services that it can invoke. For simplicity, the platform and environment is shown for service B only. The client application can also be a service, available to other applications.

The need for adaptation, either at design/compile time or at runtime, can arise in situations such as:

- Context awareness (Hong, Suh & Kim, 2009), both for applications and services, which involves two main slants:
  - Platform awareness, according to the platform's characteristics and capabilities, either from the local application or service or the services they invoke (Ortiz & Prado, 2009).
  - Environment awareness, in which the set of services available can vary ac-

cording to location or access rights, for example.

- Service changes, in which the client also needs to be changed to continue to use that service.

In this chapter, we focus on the latter issue. Our goal is to reduce the need to adapt a client as a result of changes in a service that it invokes, while maintaining interoperability, by relaxing the usual demand that both client and service use the same WSDL. We content that they only need to be compatible, as described below, and not the same. This allows for more leeway on part of the service to accommodate changes than the usual schema sharing mechanism of XML.

Basically, what we want to be able to do is:

- To invoke a service with a client generated with the WSDL of another service.
- To create a new service and invoke it with a client previously generated with another WSDL.

One of the basic problems with Web Services is that they constitute mainly an application integration mechanism and not a complete service-oriented programming solution. In particular, behavior needs to be provided by a separate programming language. The typical Web Service usage pattern is to obtain the WSDL of a service, generate a stub from it and compile and link it with the client application. Once this is done, the client is bound to that particular service. WSDL files go as far as specifying the URL of the service's endpoint, making them location specific. This static setting can be a disadvantage in more dynamic scenarios, such as mobile computing (Papageorgiou *et al*, 2009).

The Web, initially a mere distributed hypermedia document system for human access, evolved into a global Web of Services (Tolk, 2006), in which the interacting parties are both humans and computer applications and content is increas-

ingly dynamic, generated on the fly according to some database and business logic. Web Services embodied a major technological evolution, with the transition from the client-server to the service paradigm, but they have been built on top of a text document technology, XML, in which:

- Both sender and receiver must use the same schema, in a symmetric approach that mismatches the inherent asymmetric nature of the client-service relationship.
- The actual behavior code must be implemented by a separate mechanism, either a general programming language or an orchestration language such as BPEL (Juric and Pant, 2008).
- The notion of schema matching is used only for service discovery, not for message exchange, and is based on similarity, not on actual compatibility.

These characteristics and limitations have led to complex systems, including the WS-* stack, which has spurred a movement toward simpler architectures, namely RESTful applications (Fielding, 2000) with JSON (Zyp, 2010) as data format.

This chapter proposes the notion of structural interoperability, including both the notions of conformance (Läufer, Baumgartner and Russo, 2000) and compliance (Kokash & Arbab, 2009), as a solution to extend the principles of object-oriented computing to the distributed systems realm, at the same time that decoupling of the lifecycles of distributed services is not hampered.

The main problems at stake here, and which solution constitutes our goal, are:

- Service distribution and interoperability, as a support platform for higher level applications such as user interaction and enterprise integration. Although interoperability can be considered at several levels (Mykkänen & Tuomainen, 2008), this chapter goes only as far as to consider data and service interoperability levels.

- Ease of adaptability and maintainability, crucial for the enterprise agility that is so important in this fast paced world, by using an application driven model while trying to avoid technology imposed features and restrictions.

This chapter is structured as follows. We start by describing our underlying model of resources and services, which will be used throughout the chapter. Next, we establish the notion of structural interoperability, based on compliance and conformance, presenting an example for the case of Web Services. Finally, we show how this can improve the adaptability of services, deriving metrics to assess it.

BACKGROUND

The service-oriented paradigm (Earl, 2007) has been introduced as a solution to distributed application interoperability, in a more flexible way than classical object interoperability, based on RPC (Remote Procedure Call), such as Java-RMI or CORBA (Bolton, 2001).

Service interoperability (Athanasopoulos, Tsalgatidou & Pantazoglou, 2006) implies that interaction occurs according to the assumptions and expectations of the involved services. This involves several levels (Mykkänen & Tuomainen, 2008), such as communication protocol, message structure, data format, service syntax, semantics and composition (Khadka *et al*, 2011) and even non-functional and social aspects (Loutas, Peristeras & Tarabanis, 2011). This is an area of active research, with interoperability levels above interface syntax still largely dependent on manual or semi-automated work from programmers and architects.

However, achieving interoperability is not enough. Systems change constantly (Ross, Rhodes & Hastings, 2008), which means that the main challenge is to achieve interoperability with minimal coupling to better support system adaptability (Pautasso & Wilde, 2009). Coupling is known to be an indicator of how well service-oriented systems, distributed in nature, can be maintained (Perepletchikov, Ryan, Frampton & Tari, 2007), even when considering service choreographies (Oliva, Hatori, Leite & Gerosa, 2011). Separation of concerns and of policies (Tomas, Hmida & Monfort, 2006), as well as structural conformance (Kim and Shen, 2007), are important issues in this respect.

Data interoperability has largely followed the XML style, given the HTML momentum and in spite of verbosity and parsing inefficiency. The ability to self-describe data with a schema is one of XML's strongest points, albeit a great source of complexity. JSON is a simpler data format, but that is also very popular in browser-based applications since it is based on a subset of JavaScript and thus a natural format for client-side processing. There is now a proposal for a JSON data schema (Zyp, 2010).

In terms of behavior interoperability, the world is now divided into two main camps: service-oriented (Papazoglou, Traverso, Dustdar & Leymann, 2008) and resource-oriented (Overdick, 2007) architectures (SOA and ROA).

SOA, which in practice means Web Services, emphasizes behavior (albeit limited to interfaces, with state and structure hidden in the implementation). ROA follows the REST principles (Fielding, 2000) and emphasizes structure and state, by exposing inner resources (with interaction and application state separated and stored in the client and server, respectively, and behavior hidden in the dynamically changing structure and in the implementation of individual resources). Web Services are technologically more complex, but their model is a closer match to real world resources. REST is simpler and finer grained, but leans towards some restrictions (such as interaction statelessness) and is lower level (higher semantic gap between application concepts and REST resources), which for general, business-like applications means more effort to model, develop and adapt. Nevertheless, it constitutes a relevant candidate for service design and implementation (Pautasso, Zimmermann and Leymann, 2008), albeit it deals with a different mindset, architecture and granularity level, with adaptation oriented towards reorganizing resource state structure instead of adapting service functionality (Taylor, Medvidovic & Oreizy, 2009).

THE RELATIONSHIP BETWEEN RESOURCES, SERVICES, AND PROCESSES

This section presents the underlying model that we use throughout the chapter, making the distinction between resources and services and allowing us to encompass both Web Services and RESTful applications.

An application can usually be decomposed into components, or modules, made out of code and/or data, which cooperate to achieve that application's goals. Since we are aiming at SOA and cloud environments, in which decoupling, interoperability and distribution are key factors, we use a more general concept as a building block, the resource.

It is also our goal to seamlessly introduce people and their activities into the model. We should bear in mind that, if the user does not know specifically where an application resides in a cloud, the application does not know where the user is, either. From the perspective of both, the other is somewhere in the cloud. This has implications, namely in terms of security, privacy and interactivity (Delgado, 2012).

Our basic model can be briefly described in the following way:

- A resource is anything of any nature (material, virtual, conceptual, noun, action, and so on) that embodies a meaningful, complete and discrete concept, which makes sense by itself and can be distinguished from, although interact with, other resources.

- A resource can be atomic, an indivisible whole, or structured, recursively made of other resources, its components, with respect to which it performs the role of container. Each component can only have one direct container, yielding a strong composition model, in a tree shaped resource structure.

- The interior of a resource is the set of that resource and of all its components. The exterior is the set of all other existing resources.

- Each resource has at least one property, such as physical coordinates, name, IP address or URI, which allows to uniquely identifying it among all existing resources. A reference to a resource R_x is a resource that implements that property, allowing direct interaction with R_x, without having to follow the tree shaped container hierarchy (in fact, transforming the tree into a directed graph).

- Resources are created in a decentralized way, with no central resource factory, using some form of replication, and follow a lifecycle such as the one depicted in Figure 3. This ends by its destruction and is independent of other resources' lifecycle, except its containers. Structured resources have a mechanism to create and destroy its components. Destroying one resource implies destroying all the resources in its interior.

- Resources can migrate (move) from one container to another, changing the system's structure. This may involve a change in the resource's lifecycle (Figure 3), evolving to a migration stage, after which it is moved and then evolved to an operational stage at the new container.

- Resources can have state, either immutable or changeable. The state of a structured resource is recursively the set of the states, if any, of the components in its interior.

- Resources interact exclusively by sending stimuli to each other. There can be no direct access to the state of a resource from its exterior, either to read or to change it. A resource R_X can only send stimuli to its direct components and resources accessible by travelling the tree hierarchy upwards from R_X. A stimulus sent to a reference is automatically forwarded to the referenced resource.

- A stimulus is a resource, created in the interior of one resource, the sender, and migrated to the interior of another, the receiver, where it generates a reaction. Reactions can be of any sort, such as changing the resource's state, creating further resources, deleting existing resources, sending stimuli to other resources (including the sender and the receiver) or just plain ignoring. The concrete reaction does not depend on the sender, only on the stimulus and on the receiver and its state. However, the sender may also be affected, if the receiver reacts back by sending a stimulus back to the sender.

- Resources control their boundary, what from its interior is accessible from its exterior. This means that some of its components and reactions can be private, while the others are public.

- If two interacting resources, R_X and R_Y, are not in direct contact, they can use an intermediate resource, a channel, with which both are in direct contact and through which the stimulus migrates (that is the reaction of the channel when it receives the stimulus). The channel can be a structured resource, to cater for routing.

This model poses almost no restrictions on resources. A resource can be anything, such as a person or a computer application, and stimuli can even be analog and time unbounded. In practical terms and limiting our model to the computer science domain, we discretize and constrain this model in the following way:

- Only digital resources of finite size are considered. Analog resources are discretized and humans are represented by software resources that model their roles in the system and the resources that they use as interfaces. Other types of physical resources, such as trucks, are also modeled by software resources, if and as needed.

- There is a set of predefined resources, atomic and structured. New resources can only be created by replicating and/or composing existing resources, predefined or not.

- The lifecycle of a resource is discretized into a finite number of stages, of which Figure 3 represents a simplified example. In each stage, a resource can have a different digital representation, which can only have a finite number of different states. Whenever a change needs to be made, this lifecycle loops back, to start a new version, and the current one gets finalized, or it can coexist with the new one. The farther back the loop, the more profound the change is. Strategic evaluation can determine that this resource is no longer worthwhile and all existing versions are eliminated.

- Migration of a resource from one container R_X to another R_Y, a relevant issue in cloud computing, involves changing the representation of the resource to a passive form, such as a byte stream, destroying the resource at R_X, sending the byte stream to R_Y and creating a new component in R_Y from that byte stream. This corresponds to the migration loop in Figure 3. Cold start migration is usually called deployment.

- Stimuli become messages of finite size. Time unbounded streams can be modeled as a sequence of messages.
- The number of possible reactions of a resource to messages is discretized and modeled by a finite number of operations. Each operation knows only how to react to a limited set of messages.
- Reception of a message by a resource causes the execution of an operation that knows how to react to it. The mechanism that determines this capability is left unspecified at this level. A policy needs to be drawn up on what to do in case a message is received by a resource for which there is no such operation.
- Each operation is modeled by a finite number of actions.
- Channel transmission time is non-zero, but bounded (if a given time is exceeded, a fault may be assumed). This does not preclude starting to process an incoming message before fully receiving it.

On top of this model, we can derive the notions of service and process:

- A service is a set of logically related operations a resource. In other words, it is a facet of that resource that makes sense in terms of modeling the envisaged system. A service is pure behavior, albeit the implementation of concrete operations may depend on state, which needs a resource and eventually its components to be implemented. In most cases, only one service will be defined for each resource but, in other cases, usually more complex, it makes sense to organize the full set of the resource's operations into several services. Note that a service should be defined in terms of reactions to messages (an external view) and not in terms of state transitions or activity flows (an internal view). Nevertheless, given the boundary control by the resource, the set of services available to the resource itself contains the set of services available to the resources in its exterior.
- A resource R_X that sends a message to a resource R_Y is in fact invoking a service of R_Y, as long as the operation which that message stimulates belongs to that service, in what constitutes a service transaction between these two resources and in which the resources R_X and R_Y perform the role of service consumer and service provider, respectively. A service transaction can entail other service transactions, as part of the chain reaction to the message on part of the service provider.
- A process is a graph of all service transactions that are allowed to occur, starting with a service transaction initiated at some resource R_X and ending with a final service transaction, which neither reacts back nor initiates new service transactions. The process corresponds to a use case of resource R_X and usually involves other resources as service transactions flow.

In summary, resources entail structure, state and behavior. Services refer only to behavior, without implying a specific implementation. Processes are a view on the sequencing and flow of behavior along services, which are implemented by resources. This is a model inspired in real life, applicable not only to computer science but also to humans, themselves resources, and any other type of resources.

For physical resources, the strong composition model is the most adequate. No two resources can share the same physical space and every object is located inside another. Moving an object from one box to another is actually a migration as described above.

Figure 2. An example of resources, services and processes: (a) – Resources with services; (b) – Process view of a flow of service invocations

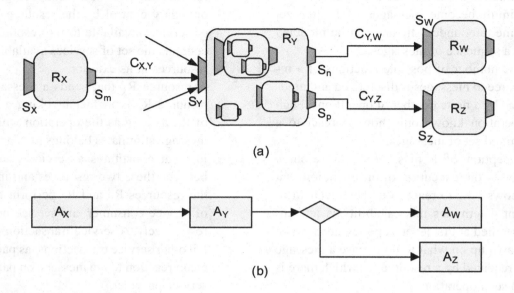

In terms of services, the society metaphor is the most familiar to us. Some resource (person or organization) executes an activity as a request and on behalf of another. Actually, service transactions constitute the foundations of our society. Each resource, from the outside, constitutes a black box that we deal with only by indirect means, by sending it a message. And each person, organization, and so on, can offer a different service, usually called role.

Figure 2 depicts an example of such a model. R_X, R_Y, R_W and R_Z are resources. R_Y exemplifies resource structure. Its interior reveals three resources, of which one is also structured, with two resources inside, in which relationships were omitted for simplicity. S_X, S_Y, S_W and S_Z are services offered by R_X, R_Y, R_W and R_Z, respectively, and its operations are graphically represented by the trapezoid on the left side of each resource. Only one is represented, but any combination of operations can be used to define a service. Structured resources, such as R_Y, can offer both behavior, in the form of services, and structure, in the form of internal resources accessible from its exterior.

The operations of a service are implemented by a resource through a set of actions, including sending a message to another service. In this example, an operation in S_X invokes S_Y, which in turn invokes S_W and S_Z. This flow of invocation of operations, and of the execution of individual actions within each operation, forms a process, exemplified by Figure 2b.

The three main concepts, resources, services and processes, lead to three main architectural styles grasped by the market and industry, according to the main concept that guides system modeling:

- **Process-Oriented Architectures (Van Der Aalst, 1999):** This is the classical approach to isolated or loosely integrated information systems, before the advent of XML-based electronic services.
- **Service-Oriented Architectures, or SOA (Earl, 2005):** Albeit not necessarily so, current implementations of SOA usually resort to Web Services and do not follow a pure service-oriented style, since basic

functionality is modeled by services but these need to be orchestrated and choreographed by processes (Barros, Dumas & Oaks, 2006), using a language such as BPEL. Nevertheless, services are the innovative factor.

- **Resource-Oriented Architectures, or ROA (Overdick, 2007):** In this style, everything is modeled as a resource, including behavior components. Structure and state become the dominant factors and each resource's service is reduced to a CRUD style (create, read, update and delete) with hypermedia links, following REST principles enunciated by Fielding (2000). The behavior complexity of SOA is traded for structure and state complexity. At a lower level than SOA, REST has some significant advantages for client-server web applications with many clients. Services and processes are secondary concepts, used mainly as modeling, intermediate steps (Laitkorpi, Selonen & Systa, 2009).

It is important to acknowledge that any active system, involving some form of activity execution, includes all the concepts defined in the previous section. After all, these are general concepts, stemming from system analysis (problem space) and not from system design (architectural solution space). Which emphasis is given to each of them and to what degree they are combined yields the architectural style of the system.

We say that two resources are distributed, relatively to each other, if their lifecycles are not interdependent. This precludes a component and its container, such as R_Y in Figure 2a, from being distributed, since the component depends on what happens to the container. In particular, a component cannot survive its container and migration of a container implies migrating all its components as well. The only way for a resource to interact with another, in a distributed way, is to have a reference to it. Resource distribution is a concept that has nothing to do with geographical separation.

In this context, the notion of a server is that of a top-level resource that has resources (applications) as its components and that most likely will also include a directory resource, with a list of references to these applications. By definition, servers are distributed, in relation to each other, but are connected to a channel (the Internet) and possess references (URIs) to the servers they want to interact with.

In the same way, an application is a structure of resources, implements one or more services and has a global identifier, built from the server's URI and the resource path within that server. Applications are distributed in relation to the others, but not to the server, and can migrate from server to server, albeit changing its URI.

For applications to interact:

- Their identifiers need to have global visibility, which URIs provide.
- Messages must have the concept of addressability.
- Servers must have a dispatch behavior, analyzing messages to find the application addressed and forwarding the message to it.

All this is consistent with today's vision of the Web, including REST and Web Service based applications, but note that we haven't restricted the communication protocol to HTTP or some other similar protocol. Only a transport level protocol is needed.

INTEROPERABILITY

This section addresses the problem of resource interoperability. Typing cannot simply be based on type names and dealt with by the compiler, since the environment is distributed and resources have separate lifecycles. We propose structural typing, based on:

- A set of primitive resources.
- A set of structuring mechanisms universally known.
- The notions of structural conformance and compliance.

The case of Web Services is analyzed as an example.

Conformance and Compliance

Resource connectivity is not enough. Interacting resources must also have interoperability, which essentially means that, if the resource R_X in Figure 2a sends a message to R_Y, which answers back, then:

1. The message sent by R_X must be in accordance with what R_Y expects and is able to deal with.
2. The corresponding reaction of R_Y and eventual side effects must be in accordance with the expectations of R_X, which was the objective a sending a message to R_Y in the first place.
3. The answer from R_Y to R_X, also a message, must be in accordance with what R_X expects and is able to deal with.

This three step interaction, which forms a service transaction, is a simplified version of a more general transaction pattern, which contemplates other variants, including asynchrony and cancelling the request during step 2 (Dietz, 2006). Here, we will only tackle its basic aspects, regarding interoperability and only in what steps 1 and 3 are concerned. Semantics interoperability (Khadka *et al*, 2011), corresponding to step 2, is harder to verify, is usually left to the programmer and is outside the scope of this chapter.

Interoperability is based on the notion of contract, which lays down the rights and obligations of the role of each participating partner. Multiparty contracts are known in the service realm as choreographies (Bravetti & Zavattaro, 2009). Any service fulfilling a role in a choreography must conform to that role, which means that it cannot claim more rights than the role grants and that it must fulfill at least all the obligations that the role requires. Choreography conformance is the basis for finding and selecting services to fulfill the roles of that choreography.

Any service choreography can be decomposed into individual service transactions, single interactions between a consumer and a provider, as described above. Since a service transaction is the simplest form of choreography, we build our case at the level of the service transaction. A choreography is satisfied if all the services conform to all the transactions they participate in.

The notion of conformance (Black et al., 1987) is fundamental even if only the interface is verified. Informally, conformance translates to compatibility, in the sense that a resource R_M conforms to a resource R_N if it can replace R_N where R_N is expected, implementing a service that fulfills the role expected from R_N in the choreography.

Conformance checking is meant to be performed on a message by message basis, to decide whether a resource knows how to cope with each incoming message. This can be done at runtime or at resource design time, in which case there must be a mechanism to detect that an invoked service has changed since the service invoking it has been designed and deployed. In other words, a message sent from one resource to another can be either unchecked, with validity checked at runtime by the receiver, or checked, in which case the resource that sends the message must have a description of what it thinks the invoked service in the receiver looks like.

This does not preclude the need of checking at the receiver, but can enable optimizations. For instance, a service may give its clients not only its description but also a sparse, non-repeatable token, such as a pseudorandom number, which the clients send with their messages to that service. If the service changes the token each time it is changed, a token mismatch automatically forces runtime conformance checking, until the consumer service updates its description and token of the provider service.

The description of a service, as seen by the service that invokes it, is represented graphically in Figure 2a by the smaller trapezoid on the right side of each resource. For example, S_m is the description of S_Y that is relevant to S_X, assuming that messages are sent to S_Y in the execution of an operation of S_X. The same can be said of S_n and S_p with respect to S_W and S_Z, respectively. If resources are implemented in a compiled language, S_m can be used as a partial description of what R_X thinks S_Y is.

We say relevant because in fact a service does not need to know all the operations of the services it invokes, but only those that it actually invokes. The others can even change without affecting S_X, as long as they have no impact on the operations that S_X invokes. This means that, if S_X invokes only some operations of S_Y but not all, what needs to conform to S_X is S'_Y, which is a service formed only by this subset of the operations of S_Y, and not the full S_Y. Therefore, this allows the usage of a weaker requirement in the implementation of S_X.

In the example Figure 2a, S_m is this potentially reduced version of S_Y and, since it includes a subset of the operations of S_Y, it is conformed by it (S_Y conforms to S_m). The S_m relationship to S_Y is designated compliance (S_m complies with S_Y). This means that S_m satisfies all the requirements of S_Y and that S_Y fulfills all the obligations towards S_m. However, S_m is not an actual service. It is only the view that S_X has of S_Y. Therefore, the relationship should be between S_X and S_Y. We then say that S_X complies with S_Y, which is represented in Figure 2a as $C_{X,Y}$. The same can be said about the relationship between S_n and S_W ($C_{Y,W}$) and S_p and S_Z ($C_{Y,Z}$).

Interoperability Relationships

Conformance and compliance are like the two faces of a coin (interoperability, in this case):

- Conformance to a role reflects the obligations of a choreography participant to be able to provide (implement) that role, whereas compliance with a role reflects the obligations of a choreography participant to be able to consume (use) that role.
- Conformance is an AND-interoperability, which means that the conforming service must support all the features of the service it conforms to. Compliance is an OR-interoperability, which means that the compliant service chooses which features to use of the service it complies with.

The concept of compliance as described here is consistent with the notion of regulatory compliance (Elgammal, Turetken, van den Heuvel & Papazoglou, 2011), in which a system compliant with a standard or norm uses and obeys its directives and requirements but does not take its form and cannot replace it.

Conformance and compliance are always present in any interaction and can be defined at various levels, including:

- **Resource to Resource:** In assignments and when transferring parameters and results of operations.
- **Operation to Operation:** Invocation of one operation by another.
- **Operation to Resource:** Access to a resource or to a component of a structured resource by a statement.
- **Service to Service:** Considering the complete set of operations of each service;
- **Service to Choreography Contract:** Considering the specification of the services and their interactions.

- **Choreography Contract to Choreography Contract:** Whether one contract can be replaced by another.

Usually, a concrete scenario involves a mix of these levels. For instance, invoking one operation by another also involves conformance and compliance between resources, when passing parameters and result. The complete treatment of this subject is outside the scope of this chapter. We outline only the first two cases, in the next section.

It is easy to note that both conformance and compliance are asymmetric relationships. In the example of Figure 2a, S_X complies with S_Y, assuming that S_m is a version of S_Y with fewer operations than S_Y, but S_Y needs not comply with S_X, although nothing prevents it. In the same manner, S_Y conforms to S_X but S_X will most likely not conform to S_Y, because an operation in S_Y but not in S_m could eventually be invoked, although nothing prevents S_X from offering that operation. This asymmetry stems from the fact that service usage is asymmetric, with different roles for the intervening services.

This also raises the issue of what should come first when modeling and designing: conformance or compliance. Should a consumer comply with an already existing provider, adapting to the provider's interface requirements, or should a provider conform to a role previously specified by a choreography? Given the discoverable nature usually attributed to the service paradigm, many authors tend to opt for the second option (Diaz & Rodriguez, 2009), in a polymorphic setting. Given a role in a choreography, any discovered service that is found to be conformant to that role can be used to fulfill that role. But, given the variability of software services, in particular if non-functional aspects are considered, how many services can we expect to conform to an independently specified role? A more realistic scenario, even in a distributed context, states that designing a system is a combination of top-down and bottom-up strategies, in which the expectations of the system have to be matched against and mapped onto already existing subsystems and the services they offer, with new services needed when there is no match or mapping. This means that conformance (bottom-up) and compliance (top-down) have to be dealt with together, in an overall strategy that constitutes the art and science of programming.

But the polymorphism idea is very interesting. In fact, it constitutes one of the major achievements of object-oriented programming. Consider again Figure 2a. S_m is all that S_X needs to know about S_Y. In fact, S_X does not even need to know that it is invoking S_Y. Any service that S_m complies with can be invoked by S_X in this blind manner. This is the compliance view of the choreography polymorphism, or consumer view, in this case of S_X. If the choreography specifies S_Y as one of its roles, then the conformance view of polymorphism says that any service that conforms to S_Y can fulfill that role. In other words, the service fulfilling a role can be replaced as a whole, affecting all other services using that role. In contrast, the compliance view of polymorphism says that S_X can replace S_Y by another that just conforms to S_m, independently of all others that use S_Y, which constitutes a weaker requirement and favors decoupling and distributed adaptability, which in turn can make versioning and adaptation of a service an easier matter.

However, S_m does not exist, since it is never specified as service on its own right, so it has no name and can only be inferred from the usage of S_Y by S_X, probably extracted from the role of S_X in the choreography. This means that we have two major problems to solve:

- How can we specify compliance-based service polymorphism, i.e., the set of services that can replace S_Y from the point of view of S_X?
- Services are just interfaces and cannot exist without resources, so we need to extend

the concept and support compliance-based resource polymorphism, i.e., make a partial assignment to a structured resource, using only a subset of its components.

Structural Interoperability

To see the importance of compliance in distributed systems, consider these two fundamental aspects of object-oriented programming:

- Polymorphism is based on conformance, not compliance. After an assignment statement such as k=m, in which k and m are variables containing references to instances of classes K and M, respectively, a subsequent usage of k, such as invoking a method or accessing a field, will in fact use m, as if it were k, which it replaces completely. In other words, class M must conform to class K, so that m can replace k. This is ensured by subtyping, usually implemented by inheritance and involves all the features of K, which M must support, even if the user of k (now m) invoked only one of its features, the only one that M would really need to support. This is a greater coupling that actually needed. Also, replacing the entire k by m is made easy by the reference semantics of common object-oriented languages. This means pointers, in practice, and for many languages garbage collection, but these are problematic in distributed, decoupled systems.
- Conformance (replacement) and compliance (usage) checking is done by using the names of the classes of the objects and inheritance relationships, which means in practice that the lifecycles of two interacting objects, such as the object calling a method and the owner of that method, have a strong coupling, implying synchronized changes, which is unacceptable in a distributed context.

The focal point of distributed systems is achieving interoperability and decoupling simultaneously. These are conflicting goals which Web Services and RESTful applications try to conciliate, with some limitations pointed out below.

Our solution to these problems, which extend and bridge these technologies, involves structural interoperability, which can be described essentially as follows:

- Checking conformance and compliance between two loosely coupled, distributed entities is done not by comparing the name of their type names but by inspecting them in greater detail, feature by feature, including structure. This leads to the notions of structural conformance (Läufer, Baumgartner & Russo, 2000; Kim & Shen, 2007) and structural compliance. Predefined resources have predefined interoperability rules and structured resources are recursively checked, component by component, until predefined resources are reached or a mismatch is found. These rules may allow component order to be different, as long as these components have some identifiable designation, such as name or a tag, such as those found in XML. XML has some form of structural matching, since unknown or irrelevant tags can be ignored by a XML processor, but there is no notion of conformance or compliance. Interoperability in XML is achieved by using the same schema in the producer and consumer of a document. This should not be confused with schema matching (Jeong, Lee, Cho & Lee, 2008), which measures similarity among schemas as a tool to ease the design stages of an integration of heterogeneous systems or to discover services.
- This involves not only services and their operations, but resources as well, including those passed as parameters to operations. Structural compliance implies partial

structural assignments and copy semantics. This means that, in an assignment k=m (including parameter passing), only the components in m that have a correspondence in k are actually assigned. The others in k stay unaffected and those in m with no correspondence in k are ignored. Assignments require only compliance, not conformance, and are made by copy, component by component, recursively, which is consistent with the distributed context.

- Resource compliance can be further controlled by using mandatory compliance. A resource can state those components that are mandatory in case of assignment. In the k=m example, these must be necessarily present in m so that it is compliant with k, whereas an optional component in k may not have a corresponding component in m, in which case the component in k is unaffected. If an optional component of k is present in m, it gets assigned, replacing the previous corresponding component value in k.

- All this assumes the existence of a universal set of predefined resource types and a universal structuring mechanism, which is accepted by all interacting parties and constitutes the basis of interoperability. All non-predefined resources are structured and support arbitrarily complex data interoperability. Predefined resources have predefined conformance and compliance rules. For conformance or compliance checking, structured resources are recursively checked, component by component, until predefined resources are reached and checked or a mismatch is found in conformance or compliance, respectively.

Conformance and compliance can be checked at design/compile time or at runtime. The first option leads to more efficient code and relies on the existence of a local definition of the service to invoke, which can be compiled and/or linked together with the invoking service. In the example of Figure 2a, if S_m is available as a definition, S_X can generate the messages sent to S_Y even without having access to S_Y or knowing which is the actual service behind S_m. This is compliance polymorphism at compile time, with compliance checked by the compiler. If neither S_m nor S_Y are available as definitions to S_X, then messages can be sent unchecked and verified at the receiver, at runtime.

We briefly outline the compliance rules between two resources, invoked when one variable m, containing a structured resource, is assigned to a variable k that contains another structured resource (k=m). An assignment does not need to entail an assignment statement and can simply correspond to the passing of a parameter to an operation or of a result from it. We consider that operations receive at most one resource as parameter and return at most one resource as result, but this can be a structured resource;

These rules are recursive because they reflect the recursive nature of the structure of resources and operations and, naturally, depend on the language used to describe the resources:

- If resources are atomic, primitive compliance rules apply. For example, an integer complies with a float, but not with a Boolean.
- If resources are structured, resource m complies with resource k if:
    - All the component resources of m satisfy the structural rules of k and each component in m that has a corresponding component in k complies with that component. The structural correspondence depends on component names, position and/or order. For example, consider the sequence, all and choice composing mechanisms of XML.

○ For each operation op_m in m that has a corresponding operation op_k in k, the parameter of op_m complies with the parameter of op_k and the result of op_m conforms to the result of op_k.

Conformance and Compliance with Web Services and REST

This section analyzes the support given by the two most common technologies to this interoperability model.

The REST style (Fielding, 2000) entails a much simpler model than Web Services, in which basically all resources provide a service with the same set of operations, although parameters, result and semantics can differ. Unlike Web Services, the emphasis is on structure and resources, rather than on behavior and services. In a sense, they explore the other side of the model that we have described in this chapter.

In RESTful applications, conformance, compliance and polymorphism are almost universal. Any resource can use and replace any other resource at any time, as long as the syntax of the protocol, such as HTTP, is correct. This is a consequence of the universal syntactic interface of resources and leads to a simplicity and flexibility that has spurred the popularity of the REST style.

However, these apparent advantages with respect to Web Services can be deceiving:

- Structured data still need structuring rules. This is particularly valid for results, since in practice HTTP is used and parameters are normally URL encoded. Either XML or JSON (Zyp, 2010) can be used, although the latter is very popular in REST because of its simplicity. Nevertheless, data are not full resources because they include only data. Structural interoperability, as discussed above, is not supported.
- The data level interoperability is buried into the code, since the data must be parsed

and processed. The semantic gap between the problem and the REST resources is higher than with Web Services, obscuring coupling between resources and imposing a greater burden on the programmer. That is why RESTful applications are usually simpler in terms of semantics. More complex interactions, such as those found in enterprise level applications, in which choreographies, conformance, compliance and polymorphism have greater emphasis, are less adequate to this style.

Web Services define their own interface and are described by WSDL documents. These correspond to S_m, S_w and S_z in Figure 2a. However, these are the descriptions of the whole services, which means that, with Web Services, compliance and conformance must target the same service specification. In other words, Web Services do not explicitly exploit the weaker requirement of compliance and therefore exhibit a higher level of coupling than needed.

By the same token, service replacement, such as in a choreography, is based on conformance. A service can only be replaced by another that fully supports the operations of the former, even those that no service invokes. There is also no message based polymorphism. Service replacement is a configuration issue that can happen at runtime, but at a much slower pace than messages occur.

Web Services have no structure, only behavior (operations). This means that there is no structural interoperability, either on the conformance or on the compliance side.

There is structure on the data passed as parameters and results, though, but with one important limitation. Except for predefined data types, both the client and provider should use the same schema, which is a strong coupling dependency. There is no message level schema conformance or compliance. Comparing schemas is done only for matching in service discovery (Jeong, Lee, Cho &

Lee, 2008), but once services are configured the conformance and compliance are fixed.

Nothing prevents a Web Service from accepting a SOAP message produced by a client generated for another Web Service. Message schema validation is usually done for security purposes only (Jensen, Meyer, Somorovsky & Schwenk, 2011). However, this is at risk of the client.

Our goal is to be able to do this in a managed way, by using the algorithm of the previous section to check whether a given client can safely invoke a given Web Service. This refers to the interface only and does not check the semantics of the operations invoked. Programs 1 and 2 illustrate this.

Program 1 contains a fragment of a WSDL file, showing only the relevant parts for the interface. It contains only one operation, to keep it simple. It receives the identification of an employee of a company (his name and company unit he belongs to) and returns his telephone numbers, up to three.

Program 1. A fragment of the WSDL of a Web service

```
<types>
        <xsd:schema xmlns:xsd="http://www.w3.org/2001/XMLSchema"
                    targetNamespace="http://example.com/schema/ex1"
                    xmlns="http://example.com/schema/ex1"
                    elementFormDefault="qualified">
            <xsd:element name="employeeSpec" type="EmployeeSpec"/>
            <xsd:element name="telInfo" type="TelInfo"/>
            <xsd:complexType name="EmployeeSpec">
                <xsd:sequence>
                    <xsd:element name="Name" type="xsd:string"
                                 minOccurs="1" maxOccurs="2"/>
                    <xsd:element name="Unit" type="xsd:string"
                                 minOccurs="0" maxOccurs="2"/>
                </xsd:sequence>
            </xsd:complexType>
            <xsd:complexType name="TelInfo">
                <xsd:sequence>
                    <xsd:element name="Telephone" type="xsd:string"
                                 minOccurs="0" maxOccurs="3"/>
                </xsd:sequence>
            </xsd:complexType>
        </xsd:schema>
</types>
<interface name="Employee_1">
        <operation name="getEmployeeInfo"
                        pattern="http://www.w3.org/2006/01/wsdl/in-out">
            <input messageLabel="In" element="ex1:employeeSpec"/>
            <output messageLabel="Out" element="ex1:telInfo"/>
        </operation>
</interface>
```

The name can be one or two strings, so that names and surnames can be separated if required, and the unit is optional but supports two strings so that department and branch, for example, can be specified.

Program 2 is a fragment of the WSDL of another Web Service, different from Program 1 but with some commonalities. Its operation provides the same functionality and has the same name. It

also obtains information on the employee, but now both name and unit are required and the information returned can include any number of telephone numbers and email addresses.

The usual way to invoke these services would be to generate two different clients, one for each service. However, by looking at both the WSDL fragments, we can notice that:

Program 2. A fragment of the WSDL of another Web service

```
<types>
        <xsd:schema xmlns:xsd="http://www.w3.org/2001/XMLSchema"
                    targetNamespace="http://example.com/schema/ex2"
                    xmlns="http://example.com/schema/ex2"
                    elementFormDefault="qualified">
                <xsd:element name="employee" type="Employee"/>
                <xsd:element name="employeeInfo" type="EmployeeInfo"/>
                <xsd:complexType name="Employee">
                        <xsd:sequence>
                                <xsd:element name="Name" type="xsd:string"
                                <xsd:element name="Unit" type="xsd:string"
                        </xsd:sequence>
                </xsd:complexType>
        </xsd:schema>
                <xsd:complexType name="EmployeeInfo">
                        <xsd:sequence>
                                <xsd:choice minOccurs="0" maxOccurs="unbounded">
                                        <xsd:element name="Telephone" type="xsd:string"
                                        <xsd:element name="Email" type="xsd:string"
                                </xsd:choice>
                        </xsd:sequence>
                </xsd:complexType>
        </xsd:schema>
</types>
<interface name="Employee_2">
        <operation name="getEmployeeInfo"
                        pattern="http://www.w3.org/2006/01/wsdl/in-out">
                <input messageLabel="In" element="ex2:employee"/>
                <output messageLabel="Out" element="ex2:employeeInfo"/>
        </operation>
</interface>
```

- The In element of the operation in Program 2, of type Employee, complies with the In element of the operation in Program 1, of type EmployeeSpec. In other words, supplying a Name and Unit with one string each is within the requirements of the operation in Program 1.
- The Out element of the operation in Program 2, of type EmployeeInfo, conforms to the Out element of the operation in Program 1, of type TelInfo. This means that it can take all the values that TelInfo can take.

The conclusion is that, although the services are different, a client generated to invoke the service in Program 1 can also be used, without changes, to invoke the service in Program 2, as long as both getEmployeeInfo operations are semantically consistent.

This is a form of distributed polymorphism, supported not by subtyping implemented by inheritance, as normally happens in object-oriented languages, but by structural interoperability, which means compliance when invoking operations and conformance when they provide the answer.

The need to have operations and their In and Out elements with the same names, so that the compliance and conformance apply, seems to contradict the claim that both services do not have their lifecycles tightly coupled. They really need to be related, at least in their goals, otherwise invoking one with a client generated for the other will not work, but they do not need to be compiled or linked together, and clients can be shared. In addition, XML substitution groups can be used to improve the matching between names or name mappings can be specified.

Checking structural interoperability between two WSDL files can be useful in situations such as:

- A Web Service changed its WSDL. Is the old WSDL structurally interoperable with the new one? This question corresponds to asking whether the WSDL can be replaced by the new one without changing the clients and without changing their service contracts.
- Given several Web Services, can one specific client access them all? In other words, is the WSDL that was used to generate that client structurally interoperable with the WSDLs of those services?
- A client was generated to access a Web Service with a given WSDL that is not interoperable with another Web Service that we want to access with this client. However, the client uses only a subset of the available operations. Is the WSDL corresponding to that subset interoperable with the service we want to access?

This is different from trying to structurally compare XML schemas (Formica, 2007; Rajesh & Srivatsa, 2010), which is typically done to find candidate services to invoke, the ones that have the closest match to specific requirements.

Structural comparison, to check compliance and conformance according to the rules enunciated in the previous section, can be done by using regular expression types (Hosoya & Pierce, 2002), using the method described by Chen and Chen (2008).

Since Web Services have only operations, not components, structural interoperability between two WSDLs depends on:

- The operation names, which must match.
- Compliance between the corresponding parameters.
- Conformance between the corresponding results.

The rules to do this stem directly from the XML schema rules. Without being exhaustive, Table 1 illustrates this with some XML types and the types that comply with and conform to each of them.

Table 1. Examples of compliance and conformance between XML types

Type	Types that comply with it	Types that conform to it
xsd:int	xsd:short, xsd:byte	xsd:long, xsd:float
xsd:float	xsd:long, xsd:int, xsd:decimal	xsd:double
Any simple type, with or without restrictions	Same simple type, with restrictions (limits inside the restriction limits of the simple type)	Same simple type, with restrictions (limits that completely include the restriction limits of the simple type)
Complex sequence	Complex sequence with same elements, same order, with cardinality limits within the corresponding ones in the complied type	Complex sequence with same elements, same order, with cardinality limits that completely include the corresponding ones in the conformed type
Complex all	Complex sequence or complex all, which includes at least the same elements, in any order	Complex all with same elements, but in any order
Complex choice	Complex choice, made out of a subset of the choices	Complex choice, made out of a superset of the choices

ADAPTABILITY

Now we use structural interoperability as a basis for service adaptability, deriving a model and metrics to assess its impact.

Adaptability Scenarios

Consider again Figure 2a, as a typical service interaction scenario, in which S_X is the client, S_Y is the provider and S_W and S_Z are outsourcers of S_Y, helping it fulfilling its role with respect to its client, S_X. S_Y can also be invoked by other client services. Just the arrows are represented, for simplicity.

Now let us suppose there is some evolution in the system and a service mismatch occurs somewhere. The same situation occurs if the system is still being designed and clients and providers are not fully interoperable yet. There can be:

- A compliance mismatch, due to a client that has changed and is not invoking its provider correctly anymore.
- A conformance mismatch, due to a provider that has been changed and is no longer fully supporting its previous features.

Naturally, the client says that the provider is not conformant to what it expects and the provider says that the client is not compliant with what it requires.

In any case, one or the other needs to be adapted, so that interoperability is possible. We use Figure 2a as the archetype of a service interaction pattern, in which we make three roles explicit:

- The consumer (S_X), or client.
- The provider (S_Y).
- The provider's context (S_W and S_Z).

We center our view on the provider, knowing that this pattern can be panned over the service architecture of the system, repeating the reasoning with changed roles, since any service can be both a consumer and a provider. For example, S_Y is part of the provider's context of S_X and S_Y is a consumer of S_W.

Several provider adaptability scenarios are possible, including:

- **Context-Awareness:** The provider is able to deal with several contexts, such as mobile versus fixed platform, type of device that implements the service (Ortiz & Prado, 2009) and type of location determination method, while maintaining conformance and therefore compliance from consumers;

- **Co-Production:** The provider, during the execution of a request from the consumer, invokes the consumer as a callback so that the consumer can participate in the execution of that request. This involves inverting the direction of conformance and compliance and, together with flexibility, support the personalization of the provider;

- **Evolution:** The provider changes as a result of new specifications, which can impair conformance to the previous specification and compliance from its clients;

- **Mediation:** An adapter service is inserted between the consumer and the provider, with the objective of offering the consumer conformance to what it expects and the provider compliance with what it requires. This can be a solution to problems caused by a change that breaks interoperability, a legacy migration or a custom arrangement to cater for a specific consumer.

To understand how structural interoperability can impact the way services are adapted, we need to derive a simple adaptability model.

Metrics of Adaptability

An adaptation of a service is a set of changes made to that service to establish conformance with a given specification. This implicitly assumes that the system already exists and the changes made correspond to a solution to bridge the differences between the previous and the new specification of the system. This can involve a higher cost than building the system from scratch from existing components.

Services are indissociable from the resources that implement them, and an adaptation of a service is in fact an adaptation of the underlying resource. Since services are the face of interac-

tion, however, we continue to refer to services, but we mean resources that implement services.

Adaptations can occur in any of the stages of the lifecycle of a service. Figure 3 illustrates an example such a lifecycle, with loops corresponding to iterations of the service during its life. More complete and detailed lifecycles are used in actual development projects, such as the one of RUP (Rational Unified Process) (Kruchten, 2003).

The more profound an adaptation is, the closer to strategy reformulation we need to get. Each adaptation gives birth to a new version of the service, with the current one finalized, and the service can even be terminated if deemed no longer worthwhile. The deployment phase contemplates the possibility of service migration, which can be seen as an adaptation to a new server location.

Given the recursive nature of resources, Figure 3 applies from the service of a small component of an application (typically, anything that can be compiled separately) up to the service of the whole application itself.

Adaptations occurred during the operation stage are usually automatic and correspond to service adaptiveness, which expresses the capability of a service to adapt automatically along time, within the limits of the flexibility of the operation stage.

Note that adaptiveness and adaptability are different concepts. The latter expresses how easily a service can suffer a given adaptation at a given stage in its lifecycle. As a metric, a value of 0 in adaptability means that the service cannot be adapted and is unable to conform to the intended specification, due to some limitation, and a value of 1 means that the cost of adaptation is zero. It depends essentially on two factors, defined quantitatively below:

- The forward decoupling D_F, the decoupling between the service and its context as a provider, i.e., the services it uses. We

Figure 3. An example of a service's lifecycle, with changeability loops

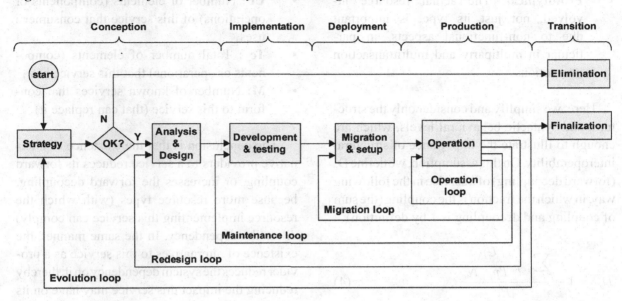

use decoupling instead of coupling to reflect our goal.

- The similarity S between the service specification before and after the adaptation.

Adaptability A is directly proportional to these two factors:

$$A = D_F \cdot S \tag{1}$$

This does not depend on which services use the service being adapted and reflects only the ability (can it be adapted?) and the cost/effort to adapt the service. The complementary adaptation question (may it be adapted?) is included in the changeability property C, defined as:

$$C = D_B \cdot D_F \cdot S \tag{2}$$

or

$$C = D_B \cdot A \tag{3}$$

in which D_B is the backward decoupling between the service being adapted and its consumers and expresses the impact of the adaptation of the service. All these factors vary between 0 and 1. Any low value becomes dominant and imposes a low value on the changeability, which translates to a bad service architecture.

Flexibility in a given stage of the lifecycle can be measured by the range of adaptations that can be made without having to backtrack to the previous stage. What is commonly called flexibility is actually the flexibility of the operation stage, which normally corresponds to variability available to consumers on request, or parameterization.

How can coupling and decoupling be quantified? A complete treatment of this issue must involve resources, not just services, because implementation is also involved, not just interface, and can be defined at various levels:

- **Structural**: Access to another resource's components.
- **Behavioral**: Syntactical interface of operations, semantics and interaction protocol, including asynchronous messages.

- **Prototypical**: The actual resource involved, not just its type, is important due to non-functional aspects, in particular in multiparty and multitransaction interactions.

Here, we simplify and consider only the structural and syntactic behavioral levels, which are enough to illustrate the importance of structural interoperability. On this assumption, we define D_F (forward decoupling) of a service in the following way, in which the fraction is the coupling (the sum of coupling and decoupling is 1 by definition):

$$D_F = 1 - \frac{\sum_{i \in P} \frac{Up_i}{Tp_i \cdot N_i}}{|P|} \qquad (4)$$

where

- **P:** Set of providers that this service uses
- **Up_i:** Number of elements (components or operations) that this service uses in provider i
- **Tp_i:** Total number of elements (components or operations) that provider i has
- **N_i:** Number of providers this service complies with in all uses of elements of provider i by this service (that can replace provider i in what this service is concerned)

In the same manner, we define D_B (backward decoupling) of a service in the following way:

$$D_B = 1 - \frac{\sum_{i \in C} \frac{Uc_i}{Tc \cdot M}}{|C|} \qquad (5)$$

where

- **C:** Set of consumers that use service

- **Uc_i:** Number of elements (components or operations) of this service that consumer i uses
- **Tc :** Total number of elements (components or operations) that this service has
- **M:** Number of known services that conform to this service (that can replace it)

The conclusion is that the existence of alternative providers to a service reduces its forward coupling, or increases the forward decoupling, because more resource types (with which the resource implementing this service can comply) dilute the dependency. In the same manner, the existence of alternatives to this service as a provider reduces the system dependency on it, thereby reducing the impact this service may have on its potential consumers.

The lifecycle of each service and of the system as a whole should be oriented towards achieving the required interoperability with the minimal coupling possible, which is essential to minimize the adaptation costs.

Finally, similarity between a resource after adaptation and its previous specification is defined as:

$$S = \begin{cases} 0 & \textit{changed atomic component} \\ 1 & \textit{unchanged atomic component} \\ \dfrac{\sum_{i \in C} S_i}{|C|} & \textit{structured component} \\ \dfrac{S_p + S_r}{2} & \textit{operation} \end{cases} \qquad (6)$$

where

- **C :** Set of components of this resource
- **S_i :** Similarity of component i (recursively)
- **S_p :** Similarity of the parameter of this operation
- **S_r :** Similarity of the result of this operation

Support for the Adaptability Scenarios

With this model in mind, the adaptability scenarios referred to previously can be implemented with structural interoperability (conformance and compliance) in the following way, in which the adaptable service is the provider in the consumer-provider-context service interaction pattern, described above:

- **Context-Awareness:** This is achieved by conformance in the provider's context. Each context (platform or device) has to provide an implementation of a context service, which differs from context to context, that the adaptable service invokes. All the implementations must conform to what the service expects.
- **Co-Production:** There are two ways to achieve this:
  - The consumer sends to the adaptable service a reference to a resource (the one implementing the consumer resource, or another) that implements a service which the adaptable service must comply with and which it invokes during the execution of the request. The net effect is that the request is partially executed by the adaptable service and the rest by the consumer or by some other resource that it designates. An example of this scenario is the browserver, a set of a browser and a server, working in tight cooperation (Delgado, 2012). This is intended to replace a simple browser as the web access device, albeit compatible with it, as the basic unit of interaction of a person with the web. The main difference is that, thanks to the server, it can host services and turn the user into a first class citizen in the web of services. For example,

it can host services that provide access to private information or personal preferences. These services can be invoked by the adaptable service and constitute a way to adapt it for personalization.
  - The consumer sends to the adaptable service a resource (the message itself) that includes a service that the adaptable service must comply with and which it invokes during the execution of the request. This corresponds to embedding code in the message and needs to be supported by sandboxing measures. The effect is an active parameterization of the adaptable service, by supplying code to process the request. Each message can parameterize the adaptable service in a different way.
- **Evolution:** There is no solution here. If a consumer is affected by a change in its provider, interoperability is affected. However, the advantage of considering compliance instead of conformance is that less features are at stake and the probability of affecting a consumer is lower.
- **Mediation:** This is the universal solution (an adapter to bridge two incompatible services), which does not require changing any of them. Again, the use of compliance reduces the requirements on the adapter down to what is really needed.

FUTURE RESEARCH DIRECTIONS

Our main lines of research in the near future are the following:

- The implementation of a language that fully implements the resource model described in this chapter, therefore encompassing both Web Services and REST approaches. This is not XML based and truly implements a structured resource paradigm, instead of relying on text structures such as those stemming from the original Web.

- Improvement of the compliance algorithm.
- The browserver and its potential of applicability. This corresponds to the client with execution capacity identified by Erenkrantz, Gorlick, Suryanarayana and Taylor (2007), by using true service-oriented technology, not Ajax (Holdener III, 2008). Since it entails a true change in user-level interaction, from a client-server to a peer model, it can introduce significant changes in areas such as workflow, authentication and application personalization, with direct implications in user-level service adaptability.

CONCLUSION

Our view is that the service-oriented paradigm is the best solution to achieve distributed interoperability, at the same time that the capacity of adapting applications, to cater for constantly evolving requirements, is not impaired. This goal depends on minimizing coupling between services, so that an adaptation of a service has the lowest possible impact on other services.

REST is too low level to act on this respect. Although seemingly decoupled, resources are in fact rather interdependent, because the internal structure of resources is exposed and much of the functionality depends on analyzing the contents of operation results. Furthermore, operations are invoked on resources with parameters in HTTP encoding and results are returned in structured data structures, creating a data paradigm mismatch.

Web Services are much closer to a true service-oriented system, but cannot execute functionality directly (a programming language is needed) and suffer from the basic tenet of XML interop-

erability, which is symmetric (using the same schema in both sides) rather than the asymmetric relationship between services. Web Services were conceived more as an interoperability harness that an instantiation of a true service-oriented system.

We have presented a structural interoperability model, based on partial compliance and conformance, by which:

- A client generated for a Web Service can also use another, as long as the client complies with both.
- A Web Service can replace another, as long as it conforms to it.

We have also presented adaptability metrics that show that structural interoperability increases adaptability. We hope that it constitutes a small contribution to improve the quality of distributed applications and to make their development, maintenance and adaptation an easier task.

REFERENCES

Athanasopoulos, G., Tsalgatidou, A., & Pantazoglou, M. (2006). Interoperability among heterogeneous services. In *International Conference on Services Computing* (pp. 174-181). IEEE Computer Society Press.

Barros, A., Dumas, M., & Oaks, P. (2006). Standards for Web service choreography and orchestration: Status and perspectives. In Bussler, C. (Eds.), *Business Process Management Workshops* (*Vol. 3812*, pp. 61–74). Lecture Notes in Computer Science Berlin, Germany: Springer-Verlag.

Black, A. (1987). Distribution and abstract types in Emerald. *IEEE Transactions on Software Engineering, 13*(1), 65–76.

Bolton, F. (2001). *Pure Corba*. SAMS Publishing.

Bravetti, M., & Zavattaro, G. (2009). A theory of contracts for strong service compliance. *Journal of Mathematical Structures in Computer Science, 19*(3), 601–638.

Chen, L., & Chen, H. (2008). Efficient type checking for a subclass of regular expression types. In *International Conference for Young Computer Scientists* (pp. 1647-1652). IEEE Computer Society Press.

Delgado, J. (2012). Bridging provider-centric and user-centric social networks. In Cruz-Cunha, M. (Eds.), *Handbook of research on business social networking: Organizational, managerial, and technological dimensions* (pp. 63–83). Hershey, PA: IGI Global.

Diaz, G., & Rodriguez, I. (2009). Automatically deriving choreography-conforming systems of services. In *IEEE international Conference on Services Computing* (pp. 9-16). IEEE Computer Society Press.

Dietz, J. (2006). *Enterprise ontology: Theory and methodology*. Berlin, Germany: Springer-Verlag.

Earl, T. (2005). *Service-oriented architecture: Concepts, technology, and design*. Upper Saddle River, NJ: Prentice Hall PTR.

Earl, T. (2007). *SOA: Principles of service design*. Upper Saddle River, NJ: Prentice Hall PTR.

Elgammal, A., Turetken, O., van den Heuvel, W., & Papazoglou, M. (2011). On the formal specification of regulatory compliance: A comparative analysis. In Maximilien, E. (Eds.), *Service-Oriented Computing* (*Vol. 6568*, pp. 27–38). Lecture Notes in Computer Science Berlin, Germany: Springer.

Erenkrantz, J., Gorlick, M., Suryanarayana, G., & Taylor, R. (2007). From representations to computations: The evolution of web architectures. In *6th Joint Meeting of the European Software Engineering Conference and the ACM SIGSOFT Symposium on the Foundations of Software Engineering* (pp. 255-264). ACM Press.

Fielding, R. (2000). *Architectural styles and the design of network-based software architectures*. Unpublished doctoral dissertation, University of California at Irvine, Irvine, California.

Formica, A. (2007). Similarity of XML-schema elements: A structural and information content approach. *The Computer Journal, 51*(2), 240–254.

Heckel, R. (2008). Architectural transformations: From legacy to three-tier and services. *Software Evolution, 2008*, 139–170.

Holdener, A. III. (2008). *Ajax: The definitive guide*. Sebastopol, CA: O'Reilly Media, Inc.

Hong, J., Suh, E., & Kim, S. (2009). Context-aware systems: A literature review and classification. *Expert Systems with Applications, 36*, 8509–8522.

Hosoya, H., & Pierce, B. (2002). Regular expression pattern matching for XML. *Journal of Functional Programming, 13*(6), 961–1004.

Jensen, M., Meyer, C., Somorovsky, J., & Schwenk, J. (2011). On the effectiveness of XML schema validation for countering XML signature wrapping attacks. In *InteRNational Workshop on Securing Services on the Cloud* (pp. 7–13). IEEE Computer Society Press.

Jeong, B., Lee, D., Cho, H., & Lee, J. (2008). A novel method for measuring semantic similarity for XML schema matching. *Expert Systems with Applications, 34*, 1651–1658.

Juric, M., & Pant, K. (2008). *Business process driven SOA using BPMN and BPEL: From business process modeling to orchestration and service oriented architecture*. Birmingham, UK: Packt Publishing.

Khadka, R. (2011). Model-driven development of service compositions for enterprise interoperability. In van Sinderen, M., & Johnson, P. (Eds.), *Lecture Notes in Business Information Processing, 76* (pp. 177–190). Berlin, Germany: Springer.

Kim, D., & Shen, W. (2007). An approach to evaluating structural pattern conformance of UML models. In *ACM Symposium on Applied Computing* (pp. 1404-1408). ACM Press.

Kokash, N., & Arbab, F. (2009). Formal behavioral modeling and compliance analysis for service-oriented systems. In Boer, F., Bonsangue, M., & Madelaine, E. (Eds.), *Formal Methods for Components and Objects* (Vol. *5751*, pp. 21–41). Lecture Notes In Computer Science Berlin, Germany: Springer-Verlag.

Kruchten, P. (2003). *The rational unified process: An introduction*. New York, NY: Addison Wesley.

Laitkorpi, M., Selonen, P., & Systa, T. (2009). Towards a model-driven process for designing Restful Web services. In *IEEE International Conference on Web Services* (pp. 173-180). IEEE Computer Society Press.

Läufer, K., Baumgartner, G., & Russo, V. (2000). Safe structural conformance for Java. *The Computer Journal*, *43*(6), 469–481.

Loutas, N., Peristeras, V., & Tarabanis, K. (2011). Towards a reference service model for the Web of services. *Data & Knowledge Engineering*, *70*, 753–774.

Meyer, B. (2000). *Object-oriented software construction* (2nd ed.). Upper Saddle River, NJ: Prentice Hall.

Mykkänen, J., & Tuomainen, M. (2008). An evaluation and selection framework for interoperability standards. *Information and Software Technology*, *50*, 176–197.

Oliva, G., Hatori, F., Leite, L., & Gerosa, M. (2011). *Web services choreographies adaptation: A systematic review*. Technical Report No: RT-MAC-2011-02. Retrieved October 30, 2011, from http://hal.inria.fr/inria-00585829/

Ortiz, G., & Prado, A. (2009). Adapting Web services for multiple devices: A model-driven, aspect-oriented approach. In *World Conference on Services* (pp. 754-761). IEEE Computer Society Press.

Overdick, H. (2007). The resource-oriented architecture. In *IEEE Congress on Services* (pp. 340-347). IEEE Computer Society Press.

Papageorgiou, A., et al. (2009). Bridging the gaps towards structured mobile SOA. In *InteRNational Conference on Advances in Mobile Computing & Multimedia* (pp. 288-294). ACM Press.

Papazoglou, P., Traverso, P., Dustdar, S., & Leymann, F. (2008). Service-oriented computing: A research roadmap. *International Journal of Cooperative Information Systems*, *17*(2), 223–255.

Pautasso, C., & Wilde, E. (2009). Why is the web loosely coupled? A multi-faceted metric for service design. In *International Conference on World Wide Web* (pp. 911-920). ACM Press.

Pautasso, C., Zimmermann, O., & Leymann, F. (2008). Restful web services vs. "big'" web services: Making the right architectural decision. In *InteRNational Conference on World Wide Web* (pp. 805-814). ACM Press.

Perepletchikov, M., Ryan, C., Frampton, K., & Tari, Z. (2007). Coupling metrics for predicting maintainability in service-oriented designs. In *Australian Software Engineering Conference* (pp. 329-340). IEEE Computer Society Press.

Rajesh, A., & Srivatsa, S. (2010). XML schema matching – Using structural information. *International Journal of Computer Applications*, *8*(2), 34–41.

Ross, A., Rhodes, D., & Hastings, D. (2008). Defining changeability: Reconciling flexibility, adaptability, scalability, modifiability, and robustness for maintaining system lifecycle value. *Systems Engineering*, *11*(3), 246–262.

Taylor, R., Medvidovic, N., & Oreizy, P. (2009). Architectural styles for runtime software adaptation. In *Joint Working IEEE/IFIP Conference on Software Architecture* (pp. 171-180). IEEE Computer Society Press.

Tolk, A. (2006). What comes after the Semantic Web - PADS implications for the dynamic Web. In *20th Workshop on Principles of Advanced and Distributed Simulation* (pp. 55-62). IEEE Computer Society Press.

Tomas, R., Hmida, M., & Monfort, V. (2006). Concrete solutions for web services adaptability using policies and aspects. *International Journal of Cooperative Information Systems*, *15*(3), 415–438.

van der Aalst, W. (1999). Process-oriented architectures for electronic commerce and inter-organizational workflow. *Information Systems*, *24*(8), 639–671.

Zyp, K. (Ed.). (2010). *A JSON media type for describing the structure and meaning of JSON documents*. Internet Engineering Task Force. Retrieved October 30, 2011, from http://tools.ietf.org/html/draft-zyp-json-schema-03

KEY TERMS AND DEFINITIONS

Adaptability: Property of a resource that expresses how easily a resource can suffer an adaptation at a given stage in its lifecycle. As a metric, a value of 0 in adaptability means that the service cannot be adapted and is unable to conform to the intended specification, due to some limitation, and a value of 1 means that the cost of adaptation is zero.

Compliance: Property between two services, consumer and provider, which expresses that the consumer fulfills all the requirements to invoke the provider. A consumer must comply with the provider, otherwise an error may occur.

Conformance: Property between service *A* and another *B* (*A* conforms to *B*) that indicates that *A* implements all the features of *B* required to allow it to replace *B* in its role in some service choreography.

Decoupling: Property between two resources, which expresses to what degree a change in one affects the other. As a metric, a value of 0 means they are completely independent (any change in one has no effect on the other) and a value of 1 means complete dependency (any change in one will have an effect on the other, eventually breaking interoperability).

Resource: An entity of any nature (material, virtual, conceptual, noun, action, and so on) that embodies a meaningful, complete and discrete concept, which makes sense by itself and can be distinguished from, although interact with, other entities.

Service Choreography: Contract between several services, which establishes how they cooperate to achieve some common goal.

Service: A set of related functionalities that define a meaningful concept in a resource interaction context.

Structural Interoperability: Property between resources which asserts their typed compatibility for interaction, based on their structure and structural interoperability of their components, checked recursively until primitive resources are reached.

Structural Similarity: Property between two resources, including the same resource before and after an adaptation, which expresses how similar they are, by comparing the structural similarity of their components, measured recursively until primitive resources are reached.

Chapter 3
Service Discovery and Composition Based on Contracts and Choreographic Descriptions

Mario Bravetti
University of Bologna, Italy & INRIA, France

Gianluigi Zavattaro
University of Bologna, Italy & INRIA, France

ABSTRACT

The authors discuss the interplay between the notions of contract compliance, contract refinement, and choreography conformance in the context of service oriented computing, by considering both synchronous and asynchronous communication. Service contracts are specified in a language independent way by means of finite labeled transition systems. In this way, the theory is general and foundational as the authors abstract away from the syntax of contracts and simply assume that a contract language has an operational semantics defined in terms of a labeled transition system. The chapter makes a comparative analysis of synchronous and asynchronous communication. Concerning the latter, a realistic scenario is considered in which services are endowed with queues used to store the received messages. In the simpler context of synchronous communication, the authors are able to resort to the theory of fair testing to provide decidability results.

DOI: 10.4018/978-1-4666-2089-6.ch003

INTRODUCTION

In the context of Service Oriented Computing (SOC) the problem of the specification of service composition is addressed using two main approaches: service *orchestration* and service *choreography*. According to the first approach, the activities of the composed services are coordinated by a specific component, called the orchestrator, that is responsible for invoking the composed services and collect their responses. Several languages have been proposed for programming orchestrators such as WS-BPEL (OASIS, 2007). As far as choreography languages are concerned, the two main representatives are WS-CDL (W3C, 2005) and BPEL4Chor (Decker, Kopp, Leymann & Weske, 2007). Differently from orchestration languages, choreography languages admit the direct interaction among the combined services without the mediation of the orchestrator. In WS-CDL, the basic activity is the interaction between a sender and a receiver, while according to the BPEL4Chor approach a choreography is obtained as the parallel composition of processes that independently execute send and receive activities.

Given an orchestrator (resp. a choreography), one of the main challenges for the SOC community is the definition of appropriate mechanisms for the (semi)automatic retrieval of services that, once combined with the orchestrator (resp. once reciprocally combined), are guaranteed to implement a correct service composition. The currently investigated approach for solving this problem is to associate to each available service a behavioral description that describes the externally observable message-passing behavior of the service itself. In the literature, this description is known with the name of *behavioral signature* (Rajamani & Rehof, 2002), *contract* (Fournet, Hoare, Rajamani & Rehof, 2004), or in the specific SOC area, *service contract* (Carpineti, Castagna, Laneve & Padovani, 2006) (Bravetti & Zavattaro, 2007b) (Laneve & Padovani, 2007) (Castagna, Padovani & Gesbert, 2008). Assuming that services expose

their contract, the above problem can be rephrased as follows: given an orchestrator (resp. a choreography) and a set of service contracts, check whether the services exposing the given contracts can be safely combined with the orchestrator (resp. safely reciprocally combined). The proposed theories of contracts solve this problem by formalizing the following notions: *contract compliance* (if a set of contracts is compliant then the corresponding services can be safely combined), *contract refinement* (if a service exposes a refinement of the contract of another service then the former is a safe substitute for the latter), and *choreography conformance* (if the contract of a service is conformant with a given role of a choreography then the service can be used to implement that role in any implementation of the choreography).

In this chapter we summarize the main results reported in Bravetti & Zavattaro (2007a) and Bravetti & Zavattaro (2009) about two theories for contract compliance, contract refinement, and choreography conformance. In Bravetti & Zavattaro (2007a) synchronous communication is considered, while in Bravetti & Zavattaro (2009) asynchronous communication is modeled by considering a more realistic scenario in which contracts are endowed with queues used to store the received messages. The main novelty of this chapter is the uniform presentation of the two theories. In fact, in Bravetti & Zavattaro (2007a) contracts are represented as terms of a specific process algebra thus the obtained results apply only to this specific language. On the contrary, in Bravetti & Zavattaro (2009) contracts are specified in a language independent way by means of finite labeled transition systems. In this chapter we adopt the second approach for both the theories thus obtaining more general and foundational results that can be applied to any contract language which has an operational semantics defined in terms of a labeled transition system.

The uniform presentation of the synchronus and asynchronous cases also allows us to better appreciate the impact of the addition of queues to the developed theories.

As far as the notion of contract compliance is concerned, for instance, we have that the following client and service are compliant under asynchronous communication while this is not the case in theories for synchronous communication (Carpineti, Castagna, Laneve & Padovani, 2006) (Bravetti & Zavattaro, 2007a) (Laneve & Padovani, 2007) (Castagna, Gesbert & Padovani, 2008):

$$Client = invoke(a); invoke(b)$$
$$Server = receive(b); receive(a)$$

In fact, the presence of queues allows the client to perform the invoke operation in a different order w.r.t. the receive order of the server.

As far as the notion of contract refinement is concerned, the main difference is that in the presence of queues the refinement can be done independently. That is, given a set of compliant contracts $C_1, \cdots, C_n$, each contract C_i can be replaced by any refinement C_i', and the overall system obtained by composition of $C_1', \cdots, C_n'$ is still compliant. In general, in a synchronous setting, independent refinement is not possible (Carpineti, Castagna, Laneve & Padovani, 2006). As an example, consider the two following service behaviors:

$$
\begin{aligned}
Printer &= receive(docToPrint) \\
PrinterFax &= receive(docToPrint) + \\
& \quad receive(docToFax); \\
& \quad invoke(faxReceipt)
\end{aligned}
$$

where + denotes a choice among alternative operations, and the two following client behaviors:

$$
\begin{aligned}
PrintClient &= invoke(docToPrint) \\
PrintFaxClient &= invoke(docToPrint) + \\
& \quad invoke(docToFax); \\
& \quad invoke(faxNum); \\
& \quad receive(faxReceipt)
\end{aligned}
$$

Printer and *PrintClient* can be safely combined. The composition is still correct even if we replace either *Printer* with *PrinterFax* or *PrintClient* with *PrintFaxClient*, but it turns out to be incorrect if we apply both replacements (due to the deadlock caused by "invoke(faxNum)"). For this reason we have that in a synchronous setting *PrinterFax* and *PrintFaxClient* cannot be considered valid refinements of *Printer* and *PrintClient*, respectively. On the contrary, we will prove that, with message queue based communication, due to the asymmetric treatment of inputs and outputs, at least one of the two refinements (*PrinterFax* refining $a_{r \to s}^-$) turns out to be valid. In general we will get a theory where refinements can add alternative behaviours guarded by new inputs (but not outputs). We will also show that a similar refinement scenario can be obtained also in the synchronous case by imposing constraints on the structure of contracts.

More precisely, message queue based communication decouples the send event (corresponding to the introduction of one message in a queue) from the receive event (corresponding to its consumption from the queue). Due to this decoupling, we propose a new interpretation of the semantics of a WS-CDL choreography language in which the two events are modeled by two distinct transitions labeled with a send and a receive label, respectively. Another novelty of our approach with respect to other work is that the choice of representing contracts by means of labeled transition systems allows us to define choreography projections in structured operational semantics. Notice that, in the synchronous case, the definition of such a projection is a contribution of this chapter (it was not included in Bravetti & Zavattaro (2007a)). As described below, the use of choreography projection is an important step in order to define an appropriate notion of conformance.

Conformance is an important notion to be used to retrieve services that, once combined, correctly implement a given choreography. Formally, we propose to define conformance as the maximal relation among contracts (ranged over by C), roles (ranged over by r), and choreographies (ranged over by H) written $C \lhd_r H$ such that, given a choreography H with roles $r_1, \cdots, r_n$ and a set of contracts $C_1, \cdots, C_n$ for which $C_1 \lhd_{r_1} H, \cdots, C_n \lhd_{r_n} H$, we have that the composition of $C_1, \cdots, C_n$ is a correct implementation of H. We show that, unfortunately, there exists no such maximal relation both under the synchronous and the asynchronous cases. The proof of this negative result is more complex for asynchronous communication because, due to the presence of message queues, we have to find out a more subtle counter-example. We partially alleviate this negative result showing that we can define a conformance notion with the above properties as follows: C is conformant to the role r of the choreography H if C is a refinement of the contract obtained by projecting the choreography H to the role r.

Due to space limitations, the proofs of our results are not included in this chapter but they can be found in Bravetti & Zavattaro (2006) and Bravetti & Zavattaro (2008).

Structure of the Chapter

The chapter is structured as follows.

In the second section we present our theory of contracts. We first present the formalization of contracts as finite labelled transitions systems and their syntactic representation as terms of a simple process calculus. Then we introduce the output persistence property that we impose on sinchronously communicating contracts to solve the problem discussed above with the printer example. Finally, we define the notion of service contract composition under synchronous and asynchronous communication, respectively.

In the third section we investigate the problem of service contract refinement. We first introduce our notion of correct composition of contracts, and then we define our refinement as the maximal subcontract relation that allows to refine independently the contracts in a composition by preserving its correctness. In the remainder of the section we discuss a sound characterization of this subcontract relation as a variant of the should testing pre-order (Rensink & Vogler, 2007).

In the fourth section we consider a simple language for choreographies. We first present its semantics under both synchronous and asynchronous communication. Then we present how to extract from a choreography contracts that are canonical representations of its participants These canonical representatives are then used in two ways: the first one is for checking whether a choreography is well formed, the second one is for verifying whether a service with a given service contract could correctly play a given role in a choreography.

The chapter ends with two sections, one dedicated to related work and another one that reports some concluding remarks.

THE THEORY OF CONTRACTS

Contracts

Contracts are defined as labeled transition systems over located action names, representing operations at a certain location over the network.

Definition (Finite connected LTS): A finite connected labeled transition system (LTS) with termination states is a tuple $\Im = (S, T, L, \rightarrow, s_0)$ where S is a finite set of states, $T \subseteq S$ is a set of states representing successful termination, L is a set of labels, the transition relation $\rightarrow$ is a finite subset of $S \times L \times S$, $s_0 \in S$ and it holds that every state in S is reachable (according to $\rightarrow$ from s_0).

Note that non-termination states may have no outgoing transitions: in this case they represent internal failures or deadlocks.

We assume a denumerable set of action names N, ranged over by $a, b, c, \ldots$ and a denumerable set Loc of location names, ranged over by $l, l', l_1, \cdots$. The set $N_{loc} = \{a_l \mid a \in N, l \in Loc\}$ is the set of located action names. We use $\tau \notin N$ to denote an internal (unsynchronizable) action.

Definition (Contract): A contract is a finite connected LTS with termination states $(S, T, L, \rightarrow, s_0)$, where $L = \{a, \bar{a_l}, \tau \mid a \in N, l \in Loc\}$, i.e. labels are either a receive (input) on some operation $a \in N$ or an invoke (output) directed to some operation $a \in N$ at some location l.

In the following we introduce a process algebraic representation for contracts by using a basic process algebra with prefixes over $\{a, \bar{a_l}, \tau \mid a \in N, l \in Loc\}$ and we show that from the LTS denoting a contract we can derive a process algebraic term whose behavior is the same as that of the LTS. The process algebra is a simple extension of basic CCS (Milner, 1989) with successful termination denoted by 1: this new term is necessary in order to have two kinds of states without outgoing transitions, those that are successfully terminating (that we denote with the process 1) and those that are not (denoted with the traditional null process 0).

Definition (Contract Syntax): We consider a denumerable set of contract variables Var ranged over by X, Y, $\cdots$. The syntax of contracts is defined by the following grammar

$$C \quad ::= \quad \mathbf{0} \quad | \quad \mathbf{1} \quad | \quad \alpha.C \quad | $$
$$\qquad\qquad C + C \quad | \quad X \quad | \quad recX.C$$
$$\alpha \quad ::= \quad \tau \quad | \quad a \quad | \quad \bar{a_l}$$

where $recX.\_$ is a binder for the process variable X denoting recursive definition of processes. The set of the contracts C in which all process variables are bound, i.e. C is a closed term, is denoted by P_{con}.

Besides the already commented recursion operator, we consider the standard prefix $\alpha.\_$ (with possible prefixes τ, a, and $\bar{a_l}$ denoting internal, input, and output action, respectively) and choice $\_ + \_$ operators. In the following we will omit trailing $\mathbf{1}$ when writing contracts.

The structured operational semantics of contracts is defined in terms of a transition system labeled over $L = \{a, \bar{a_l}, \tau, \mid a \in N, l \in Loc\}$ and a termination predicate $\sqrt{}$ over states obtained by the rules in Figure 1 (plus symmetric rule for choice).

Note that we use the notation $C\{recX.C \mathbin{/} X\}$ to denote syntactic replacement of free occurrences of variable X in C with the same contract C (where, as usual, α-conversion is applied to avoid the possible captures of variable names). The rules for the operational semantics are standard; we simply comment the actual meaning of the termination predicate $\sqrt{}$. Informally, a contract C satisfies the predicate if it is the successfully terminating terms $\mathbf{1}$ or it is a more complex term in which there is at least one $\mathbf{1}$ that does not occur inside a prefixed term $\alpha.C$.

We have that the semantics of a contract $C \in P_{con}$ gives rise to a finite connected LTS with termination states $(S, T, L, \rightarrow, C)$ where $L = \{a, \bar{a_l}, \tau, \mid a \in N, l \in Loc\}$ and: S is the set of states reachable from C, T is the subset of S of the states for which the predicate $\sqrt{}$ is true and $\rightarrow$ includes only transitions between states of S. Note that the fact that such a LTS is finite (i.e. finite-state and finitely branching) is a well-

Figure 1. Semantic rules for contracts (symmetric rules omitted)

$$1\sqrt{} \qquad\qquad \alpha.C \xrightarrow{\alpha} C$$

$$\frac{C \xrightarrow{\alpha} C'}{C+D \xrightarrow{\alpha} C'} \qquad\qquad \frac{C\sqrt{}}{C+D\sqrt{}}$$

$$\frac{C\{recX.C/X\} \xrightarrow{\alpha} C'}{recX.C \xrightarrow{\alpha} C'} \qquad\qquad \frac{C\{recX.C/X\}\sqrt{}}{recX.C\sqrt{}}$$

known fact for basic CCS (Milner, 1989) (and obviously the additional presence of successful termination does not change this fact).

Definition (Equation Set): A set of process algebraic equations is denoted by $\theta = \{X_i = C_i \mid 0 \leq i \leq n-1\}$, where n is the number of equation in the set, X_i are process variables, and C_i are contract terms (possibly including free process variables). The process algebraic equations θ is closed if only process variables X_i, with $0 \leq i \leq n-1$, occur free in the bodies C_j, with $0 \leq j \leq n-1$, of the equations in the set.

Let $\Im = (S, T, L, \rightarrow, s_0)$ be a contract. A contract term $C \in P_{con}$ is obtained from $\Im$ as follows:

- Supposed $S = \{s_0, ..., s_{n-1}\}$ (i.e. any given numbering on the states S), we first obtain from $\Im$ a finite closed set of equations $\theta = \{X_i = C_i \mid 0 \leq i \leq n-1\}$ as follows. Denoted by m_i the number of transitions outgoing from s_i, by α_j^i the label of the $j-th$ transition outgoing from s_i (for any given numbering on the transitions outgoing from s_i), with $j \leq m_i$, and by

$s_{succ_j^i}$ its target state, we take $C_i = \sum_{j \leq m_i} \alpha_j^i.X_{succ_j^i} + \{1\}$, where $\mathbf{1}$ is present only if $s_i \in T$ and an empty sum is assumed to yield $\mathbf{0}$.

- We then obtain, from the closed set of equations $\theta = \{X_i = C_i \mid 0 \leq i \leq n-1\}$, a closed contract term C by induction on the number of equations. The base case is $n = 1$: in this case we have that C is $recX_0.C_0$. In the inductive case we have that C is inductively defined as the term obtained from the equation set $\{X_i = C_i' \mid 0 \leq i \leq n-2\}$, where $C_i' = C_i\{recX_{n-1}.C_{n-1} / X_{n-1}\}$.

We now present an example of process algebraic representation for a looping contract. Consider a contract $\Im = (S, T, L, \rightarrow, s_0)$ with three states s_0, s_1 and s_2 such that s_0 reaches s_1 with an a transition, s_1 reaches s_2 with a b transition and s_2 reaches s_0 with a c transition. According to the procedure above we get the three equations $X_0 = a.X_1 + 1$, $X_1 = b.X_2$ and $X_2 = c.X_0$. Thus the process algebraic representation for $\Im$ would turn out to be: $recX_0.((a.b.c.X_0) + 1)$, where we omit recursion operators $recX_i$ such that X_i does not occur in their scope.

Definition (LTS Homomorphism): A homomorphism from a finite connected LTS $\Im = (S, T, L, \rightarrow, s_0)$ to a finite connected LTS with finite states $\Im' = (S', T', L, \rightarrow', s_0')$ is a function f from S to S' such that: $f(s_0) = s_0'$ and for all $s \in S$ we have $\{(l, s') \mid f(s) \overset{l}{\rightarrow}' s'\} = \{(l, f(s')) \mid s \overset{l}{\rightarrow} s'\}$, i.e. the set of transitions performable by $f(s)$ is the same as the set of transitions performable by s when f-images of the target states are considered, and $s \in T$ if and only if $f(s) \in T'$.

Note that, if f is a homomorphism between finite connected LTSes with finite states then f is surjective: this because all states reachable by $f(s_0)$ must be f-images of states reachable from s_0.

Proposition (Contract and Contract Terms):

Let $\Im = (S, T, L, \rightarrow, s_0)$ be a contract and $C \in P_{con}$ be a contract term obtained from $\Im$. There exists a (surjective) homomorphism from the semantics of C to $\Im$ itself.

We now present a simple example of a contract describing an authentication service that repeatedly performs two kinds of task: (i) the authentication of clients by receiving their username and password, and (ii) the request to an external account service for update of the list of the registered users:

$$recX.(username.password.(\overline{accepted}_{client}.X + \overline{failed}_{client}.X) + \overline{updateAccounts}_{accountServer}. newAccounts.X)$$

The contract indicates a repeated choice between the two possible tasks. The first task is activated by the reception of an invocation on *username*: after, a *password* should be received

and then two possible answers are sent back to the *client*: either *accepted* or *failed*. The second task is activated by sending a request for update to the *accountServer*: after, the *newAccounts* are received.

Output Persistence Property

In the introduction we have already discussed (by means of the printer example) that under synchronous communication independent refinement is not possible. One of the motivations for this negative result is the perfect symmetry between output and input actions in a purely synchronous setting. Nevertheless, we consider a restricted setting for synchronously communicating contracts in which output actions cannot be avoided when one program decides to execute them. We now formally define such property, that we call *output persistence*, then we justify the decision to restrict to output persistent contracts (at least when we consider sychronous communication).

In the remainder of the chapter we use the following notations: $C \overset{\lambda}{\rightarrow}$ to mean that there exists C' such that $C \overset{\lambda}{\rightarrow} C'$ and, given a string of labels $w \in L^*$, that is $w = \lambda_1 \lambda_2 \cdots \lambda_{n-1} \lambda_n$ (possibly empty, i.e., $w = \varepsilon$), we use $C \overset{w}{\rightarrow} C'$ to denote the sequence of transitions $C \overset{\lambda_1}{\rightarrow} C_1 \overset{\lambda_2}{\rightarrow} \cdots \overset{\lambda_{n-1}}{\rightarrow} C_{n-1} \overset{\lambda_n}{\rightarrow} C'$ (in case of $w = \varepsilon$ we have $C' = C$, i.e., $C \overset{\varepsilon}{\rightarrow} C$).

Definition (Output Persistence): Let $C \in P_{con}$ be a contract. It is output persistent if given $C \overset{w}{\rightarrow} C'$ with $C' \overset{\overline{a_l}}{\rightarrow}$ then: $C' \overset{\checkmark}{\rightarrow}$ does not hold and if $C' \overset{\alpha}{\rightarrow} C''$ with $\alpha \neq \overline{a_l}$ then also $C'' \overset{\overline{a_l}}{\rightarrow}$.

The output persistence property states that once a contract decides to execute an output, its actual execution is mandatory in order to successfully complete the execution of the contract. This property typically hold in languages for the description of service behaviours or for service orchestrations (see e.g. WS-BPEL) in which output actions cannot be used as guards in external choices (see e.g. the pick operator of WS-BPEL which is an external choice guarded on input actions). In these languages, when a process instance or an internal thread decides to execute an output actions, it will have to complete such action before successful completion.

In the context of process algebra with parallel composition a syntactical characterization that guarantees output persistence can be found in Bravetti & Zavattaro (2007a). The idea is to require that every output prefix (i.e. the term $\overline{a_l}.P$) is preceded by an internal τ prefix (i.e. the above term always occurs in the larger term $\tau.\overline{a_l}.P$).

Consider now the previous example of the authentication server. The contract is not output persistent as in its initial state the output action on *updateAccounts* is possible, while it is no longer executable after the execution of the input action *username*. The same problem also holds for the choice among the outputs on *accepted* and *failed*. We can simply add a τ action before the output actions in order to obtain an output persistent contract:

$$Authentication =$$
$$recX.(username.password.(\tau.\overline{accepted}_{client}.X$$
$$+\tau.\overline{failed}_{client}.X)$$
$$+\tau.\overline{updateAccounts}_{accountServer}.newAccounts.X)$$

This new contract is significantly different with respect to the previous one: the choice to perform the second task (i.e. the request to update the accounts) is now internal and does not require a synchronization with the *accountServer*, which is contacted after the decision has been taken. Also the choice of the output action on either *accepted* or *failed* is now internal.

The actual impact of output persistence (in turn coming from the asymmetric treatment of

inputs and outputs) in our theory is the existence of maximal independent refinement. This statement will be made precise by means of a counterexample that we postpone because we first need to formalize contract compositions as well as the notion of correct composition.

We now formalize a direct consequence of output persistence that we will use in the following.

Proposition (Output Persistence Until Termination): Let $C \in P_{con}$ be an output persistent contract such that $C \xrightarrow{w} C' \xrightarrow{\overline{a_l}}$. If $C' \xrightarrow{w'} C''$ and $C'' \xrightarrow{\checkmark}$ then the string w' must include $\overline{a_l}$.

In the remainder, when we consider synchronous communcation, we will restrict to output persistent contracts, namely, when we use P_{con} in synchronous contract compositions, we denote the set of output persistent contracts. Note that, it is meaningful to do this because any derivative of an output persistent contract is again an output persistent contract (as it can be immediately inferred from the Definition of output persistence) and homomorphism preserves output persistence (two homomorphic contracts are either both output persistent or no one is).

Synchronous Contract Composition

In the following we make use of the following set including the denotations of located input and output actions: $A_{loc} = N_{loc} \cup \{\overline{a_l} \mid a_l \in N_{loc}\}$.

Definition (Synchronous Systems): The syntax of synchronous systems (synchronous contract compositions) is defined by the following grammar

$$P ::= [C]_l \quad | \quad P \,|\, P \quad | \quad P \setminus L$$

where $L \subseteq A_{loc}$.

A contract located at location l is denoted with $[C]_l$. Located contracts can be combined in parallel with the operator $P \,|\, P$. The operator $P \setminus L$

denotes restriction: note that differently from classical process algebras like CCS, we can distinctly restrict on input and output actions. This is useful in a setting like ours in which, under the output persistence assumption, input and output actions are no longer perfectly symmetric actions. Nevertheless, the traditional restriction operator acting on names instead of input/output actions can be written with our operator by restricting both input and output actions on the considered name: namely $P \setminus a = P \setminus \{a_l, \overline{a_l}\}$.

Definition (Well-Formed Systems): A system P is well-formed if:

1. Every contract subterm $[C]_l$ occurs in P at a different location l.
2. No output action with destination l is syntactically included inside a contract subterm occurring in P at the same location l, i.e. actions $\underline{a}_l$ cannot occur inside a subterm $[C]_l$ of P.

As in the following we will consider only well-formed systems, they will be denoted simply with P, and we will call them just systems.

We now present a contract system in which we combine the previously discussed *Authentication* contract, that we locate at location *authServer*, with a *client* and an *accountServer* that perform, respectively, the actions complementary to the two tasks of the authentication server:

$$[Authentication]_{authServer} \|$$
$$[\overline{username}_{authServer}.\overline{password}_{authServer}.$$
$$(accepted + failed)]_{client} \|$$
$$[\overline{updateAccounts.newAccounts}_{authServer}]_{accountServer}$$

Given a system P, we use $loc(P)$ to denote the subset of Loc of the locations of contracts syntactically occurring inside P: e.g. $loc([C]_{l_1} \mid [C']_{l_2}) = \{l_1, l_2\}$.

Also the operational semantics of systems is defined in terms of a labeled transition system and a termination predicate $\sqrt{}$. The labels, denoted with λ, λ', $\cdots$, are taken from the set $\{a_s, \overline{a}_{rs}, a_{r \to s}, \tau \mid a \in N; r, s \in Loc\}$, where: a_s denotes a potential input by a receiver that is at location s, $\overline{a}_{rs}$ denotes a potential output where the sender is at location r and the receiver is at location s, $a_{r \to s}$ denotes a synchronization (that actually took place) where the sender is at location r and the receiver is at location s, and τ denotes a move performed internally by one contract in the system.

The operational semantics and the termination predicate of systems is defined by the rules in Figure 2 plus symmetric rules.

Asynchronous Contract Composition

There are two differences between synchronous and asynchronous contract systems: in the asyn-

Figure 2. Semantic rules for synchronous contract compositions (symmetric rules omitted)

$$\frac{C \xrightarrow{a} C'}{[C]_s \xrightarrow{a_s} [C']_s} \qquad \frac{C \xrightarrow{\overline{a}_s} C'}{[C]_r \xrightarrow{\overline{a}_{rs}} [C']_r} \qquad \frac{P \xrightarrow{\lambda} P'}{P\|Q \xrightarrow{\lambda} P'\|Q}$$

$$\frac{P \xrightarrow{a_s} P' \quad Q \xrightarrow{\overline{a}_{rs}} Q'}{P\|Q \xrightarrow{a_{r \to s}} P'\|Q'} \qquad \frac{C\sqrt{}}{[C]_l\sqrt{}} \qquad \frac{P\sqrt{} \quad Q\sqrt{}}{P\|Q\sqrt{}} \qquad \frac{P\sqrt{}}{P \setminus L\sqrt{}} \qquad \frac{P \xrightarrow{\lambda} P' \quad \lambda \notin L}{P \setminus L \xrightarrow{\lambda} P' \setminus L}$$

chronous setting located contracts are equipped with an input message queue and the restriction operator does not distinguish between input and output actions (this is no longer necessary as in the asynchronous case we do not make the output persistence assumption).

Definition (Asynchronous Systems): The syntax of asynchronous systems is defined by the following grammar

$$P ::= [C,Q]_l \mid P \mid P \mid P \setminus L$$
$$Q ::= \varepsilon \mid a^l :: Q$$

where $L \subseteq N_{loc}$.

The restriction operator $\_ \setminus L$ is now a binder for the names in located actions. Formally, if a_l is in L, then L binds a in any action a occurring in the contract located at l and in any action $\bar{a}_l$.

The terms in the syntactic category Q denote message queues. They are lists of messages, each one denoted with a^l where a is the action name and l is the location of the sender. We use ε to denote the empty message queue. Trailing ε are usually left implicit, and we use $::$ also as an operator over the syntax: if Q and Q' are ε-terminated queues, according to the syntax above, then $Q :: Q'$ means appending the two queues into a single ε-terminated list. Therefore, if Q is a queue, then $\varepsilon :: Q$, $Q :: \varepsilon$, and Q are syntactically equal.

Also for asynchronous systems we consider the very same notion of well-formedness considered in the synchronous case, that guarantees that two distinct contracts cannot be located at the same location l and no contract can perform an output action directed to its own location.

In the following, when we talk about asynchronous contract systems, we will use the shorthand $[C]_l$ to stand for $[C,\varepsilon]_l$.

Also the operational semantics of systems is defined in terms of a labeled transition system. The labels, denoted also in this case with λ,

λ', $\cdots$, are now taken from the set $\{a_{rs}, \bar{a}_{rs}, a^+_{r \to s}, a^-_{r \to s}, \tau \mid a \in N; r, s \in Loc\}$, where: a_{rs} denotes a potential input by a queue where the sender is at location r and the receiver queue is at location s, $\bar{a}_{rs}$ denotes a potential output where the sender is at location r and the receiver queue is at location s, $a^+_{r \to s}$ denotes an insertion in the queue (that actually took place) where the sender is at location r and the receiver queue is at location s, $a^-_{r \to s}$ denotes an extraction from the queue (that actually took place) where the sender (that originally sent the message) is at location r and the receiver queue is at location s, and τ denotes a move performed internally by one contract in the system. We use α-renaming of names bound by the restriction operator $\_ \setminus L$; namely, we write $P \equiv_\alpha Q$ if P is α-convertible into Q (or vice-versa), i.e. if Q can be obtained from P by turning subterms $P' \setminus L$ of P into subterms $Q' \setminus L'$ by renaming of located names a_l of L into located names $ren(a)_l$ (yielding L' with the same cardinality) and by correspondingly replacing: (i) each input-related syntactical occurrence of a with $ren(a)$ inside the unique subterm $[C,Q]_l$ of P', if it exists (more precisely occurrences of $a^{l'}$ inside Q are renamed into $ren(a)^{l'}$, independently of the location l', and a input prefixes inside C are renamed into $ren(a)$ input prefixes), and (ii) each syntactical occurrence of $\bar{a}_l$ inside P' with $\overline{ren(a)}_l$ (obviously a renaming is only allowed if it does not generate a name that is already present as a free name in association with the same location).

The rules in the Figure 3 (plus symmetric rules) define the transition system and the termination predicate ($\sqrt{}$) for asynchronous systems. In Figure 3 we assume that $a^l \in Q$ holds true if and only if a^l syntactically occurs inside Q.

As an example consider the following system:

Figure 3. Semantic rules for contract compositions (symmetric rules omitted)

$$[C, \mathcal{Q}]_s \xrightarrow{a_{rs}} [C, \mathcal{Q} :: a^r]_s \qquad \frac{C \xrightarrow{\bar{a}_s} C'}{[C, \mathcal{Q}]_r \xrightarrow{\bar{a}_{rs}} [C', \mathcal{Q}]_r} \qquad \frac{P \xrightarrow{a_{rs}} P' \quad Q \xrightarrow{\bar{a}_{rs}} Q'}{P \| Q \xrightarrow{a^+_{r \to s}} P' \| Q'}$$

$$\frac{C \xrightarrow{\tau} C'}{[C, \mathcal{Q}]_l \xrightarrow{\tau} [C', \mathcal{Q}]_l} \qquad \frac{C \checkmark}{[C, \epsilon]_l \checkmark} \qquad \frac{P \xrightarrow{\lambda} P'}{P \| Q \xrightarrow{\lambda} P' \| Q} \qquad \frac{P \checkmark \quad Q \checkmark}{P \| Q \checkmark}$$

$$\frac{P \xrightarrow{\lambda} P' \quad \text{if } \lambda = a_{rs}, \bar{a}_{rs} \text{ then } a_s \notin L}{P \backslash L \xrightarrow{\lambda} P' \backslash L} \qquad \frac{P \checkmark}{P \backslash L \checkmark}$$

$$\frac{P \equiv_\alpha P' \quad P' \xrightarrow{\lambda} Q}{P \xrightarrow{\lambda} Q} \qquad \frac{C \xrightarrow{a} C' \quad \text{if } b^l \in \mathcal{Q} \text{ then } b \neq a}{[C, \mathcal{Q} :: a^r :: \mathcal{Q}']_s \xrightarrow{a_{r \to s}} [C', \mathcal{Q} :: \mathcal{Q}']_s}$$

$[\bar{a}_r . \bar{b}_r]_s \| [b.a]_r$

In two transitions, representing the execution of the two invoke operations, the system evolves to the following:

$[\mathbf{1}]_s \| [b.a, a^s :: b^s]_r$

The receiver is now ready to consume the two messages stored in the message queue, thus reaching (after two transitions) the system:

$[\mathbf{1}]_s \| [\mathbf{1}]_r$

Notice that the two messages are consumed in the opposite order of reception.

CONTRACT REFINEMENT

We now move to the study of a notion of independent contract refinement that preserves correct composition of contracts for both synchronous and asynchronous communication.

In the following, and in the rest of the chapter, we will present definitions and results that hold, unless stated differently, for both the synchronous and asynchronous case in an uniform way (by, e.g., considering sets of labels that include labels of both synchronous and asynchronous systems).

Correct Contract Composition

We now define the notion of correct composition of contracts. Intuitively, a system composed of contracts is correct if all possible computations may guarantee completion; this means that the system is both deadlock and livelock free (there could be an infinite computation, but given any possible prefix of this infinite computation, it can be extended to reach a successfully completed computation).

Definition (Correct contract Composition): A system P is a correct contract composition, denoted $P\downarrow$, if for every P' such that $P \xrightarrow{w} P'$, with:

$$w \in \{a^+_{r \to s}, a^-_{r \to s}, a_{r \to s}, \tau \mid a \in N; r, s \in Loc\}^*,$$

there exists P'' such that $P' \xrightarrow{w'} P''$, with $w \in \{a^+_{r \to s}, a^-_{r \to s}, a_{r \to s}, \tau \mid a \in N; r, s \in Loc\}^*$, and $P'' \checkmark$.

It is interesting to observe that in the asynchronous case a correct contract composition, when all contracts successfully terminate, it is ensured that all the sent messages have been actually received. In fact, by definition of the termination predicate $\checkmark$ for contract compositions, a system is terminated only if all message queues are empty. Note also that, obviously, contracts that form correct contract compositions still form correct contract compositions if they are replaced by homomorphic ones.

We complete this subsection presenting a simple example of contract composition that is correct (both in the synchronous and asynchronous case):

$$[\overline{a}_{l_3}]_{l_1} \mid [\overline{b}_{l_3}]_{l_2} \mid [a.b]_{l_3}$$

composed by three contracts, the first one and the second one that send respectively the message a and b to the third one, and this last contract that consumes the two messages.

As another example of contract composition consider the system:

$$[\overline{b}_{l_3}.\overline{a}_{l_3}]_{l_1} \mid [a.b]_{l_3}$$

In this case the composition is correct only under asynchronous communication as the two different orders between the emission and the consumption of the messages is not problematic thanks to the presence of the message queue on location l_3.

As another example, consider the system composed of the *authServer*, the *client*, and the *accountServer* defined above. For simplicity we assume synchronous communication, even if the discussion is valid also under asynchronous communication. The above system is surely not correct because the *Authentication* contract is unable to perform the final $\checkmark$ transition. This problem can be solved by extending the *Authentication* contract with a third task consisting of its successful completion:

$$recX.(username.password.(\tau.\overline{accepted}_{client}.X +$$
$$\tau.\overline{failed}_{client}.X) +$$
$$\tau.updateAccounts_{accountServer}.newAccounts.X +$$
$$\mathbf{1})$$

It is interesting to note that even after replacing the *Authentication* contract with this new version, the contract composition is not yet correct. This follows from the fact that the *Authentication* contract can internally decide to activate invoke the update task twice while the contract of the *accountServer* is able to reply only once. This problem can be solved by replacing the contract of the *accountServer* with the following recursive one:

$$recX.(updateAccounts.\overline{newAccounts}_{authServer}.X$$
$$+ \mathbf{1})$$

After replacement of the *accountServer* contract with this last one, it is easy to see that the contract composition turns out to be correct: the system can always successfully complete after having performed (in every possible order) one authentication task and an arbitrary number of update tasks. A version in which also the authentication task can be performed arbitrarily many times before can be obtained by replacing the client contract with the following:

$$recX.(\overline{username}_{authServer}.\overline{password}_{authServer}.$$
$$(accepted.X + failed.X) + \mathbf{1})$$

Independent Subcontracts

In this Section we introduce our theory of contracts. The basic idea is to have a notion of refinement of contracts such that, given a system composed of the contracts $C_1, \cdots, C_n$, we can replace each contract C_i by one of its refinements $C_{i'}$ without breaking the correctness of the system.

This notion of refinement is useful when considering the problem of service discovery. Given the specification of a contract composition (composed of the so called "initial contracts"), the actual services to be composed are discovered independently sending queries to registries. It could be the case that services with a contract which exactly correspond to the "initial contracts" are not available; in this case, it is fundamental to also accept different contracts that could be replaced without affecting the overall correctness of the system.

Some simple examples of refinement follow. Consider the correct system $[C_1]_{l_1} \mid [C_2]_{l_2}$ with

$$C_1 = a + b \qquad C_2 = \tau.\bar{a}_{l_1} + \tau.\bar{b}_{l_1}$$

We can replace C_1 with $C'_1 = a + b + c$ or C_2 with $C'_2 = \bar{a}_{l_1}$ without breaking the correctness of the system. This example shows a first important intuition: a contract could be replaced with another one that has more external nondeterminism and/or less internal nondeterminism.

Consider now the correct system $[D_1]_{l_1} \mid [D_2]_{l_2}$ with

$$D_1 = a + b + c \qquad D_2 = \tau.\bar{a}_{l_1} + \tau.\bar{b}_{l_1}$$

where we can refine D_1 with $D'_1 = a + b + d$. Clearly, this refinement does not hold in general because we could have another correct system

$$D_1 = a + b + c \qquad D'_2 = \tau.\bar{a}_{l_1} + \tau.\bar{b}_{l_1} + \tau.\bar{c}_{l_1}$$

where such a refinement does not hold. In this sense we aim for a refinement relation that allow us to refine contracts, e.g. D_1, independently from the other contracts (and their refinements) that form a correct system.

We are now ready to define the notion of subcontract pre-order. Given a contract $C \in P_{con}$, we use $oloc(C)$ to denote the subset of Loc of the locations of the destinations of all the output actions occurring inside C.

With $P \overset{\tau^*}{\rightarrow} P'$ we denote the existence of a (possibly empty) sequence of τ-labeled transitions starting from the system P and leading to P'. Given the sequence of labels $w = \lambda_1 \cdots \lambda_n$, we write $P \overset{w}{\Rightarrow} P'$ if there exist $P_1, \cdots, P_m$ such that $P \overset{\tau^*}{\rightarrow} P_1 \overset{\lambda_1}{\rightarrow} P_2 \overset{\tau^*}{\rightarrow} \cdots \overset{\tau^*}{\rightarrow} P_{m-1} \overset{\lambda_n}{\rightarrow} P_m \overset{\tau^*}{\rightarrow} P'$.

Definition (Independent Subcontract Pre-Order): A pre-order $\leq$ over P_{con} is an independent subcontract pre-order if, for any $n \geq 1$, contracts $C_1, \ldots, C_n \in P_{con}$ and $C'_1, \doteq, C'_n \in P_{con}$ such that $\forall i.C'_i \leq C_i$, and distinguished location names $l_1, \ldots, l_n \in Loc$ such that

$$\forall i.oloc(C_i) \cup oloc(C'_i) \subseteq \{l_j \mid 1 \leq j \leq n \wedge j \neq i\}$$

we have $([C_1]_{l_1} \mid \ldots \mid [C_n]_{l_n}) \Downarrow$ implies

- $([C'_1]_{l_1} \parallel \doteq \parallel [C'_n]_{l_n}) \Downarrow$.
- $\forall w \in \{a^+_{r \to s}, a^-_{r \to s}, a_{r \to s} \mid a \in N; r, s \in Loc\}^*$.

if $\exists P' : ([C'_1]_{l_1} \parallel \doteq \parallel [C'_n]_{l_n}) \overset{w}{\Rightarrow} P' \wedge P' \surd$ then

$$\exists P'' : ([C_1]_{l_1} \parallel \doteq \parallel [C_n]_{l_n}) \overset{w}{\Rightarrow} P'' \wedge P'' \surd$$

An independent subcontract pre-order formalizes the possibility to replace in a correct contract composition every contract with one of its subcontract, with the guarantee that the new system is still correct and it does not introduce any new behaviour (namely, it does not introduce new contract communications).

In Bravetti & Zavattaro (2007b) it is shown that under synchronous communication, in the absence of the output persistence assumption, it could happen that given two independent subcontract pre-orders, their union is no longer an independent subcontract pre-order. In other words, there exists no maximal independent subcontract pre-order. This negative result is proved in Bravetti & Zavattaro (2007b) by considering a counter-example similar to the printer example we have discussed in the Introduction. On the contrary, under asynchronous communication, and also in the synchronous case under the assumption of output persistence, we will have that the maximal independent subcontract pre-order exists.

We will show that such maximal relation can be achieved by defining a more coarse form of refinement in which, given any system composed of a set of contracts, refinement is applied to one contract only (thus leaving the other unchanged). We call this form of refinement *singular subcontract pre-order*. Intuitively a pre-order $\leq$ over P_{con} is a singular subcontract pre-order whenever the correctness of systems is preserved by refining just one of the contracts. More precisely, for any $n \geq 1$, contracts $C_1,...,C_n \in P_{con}$, $1 \leq i \leq n, C_{i'} \in P_{con}$ such that $C'_i \leq C_i$, and distinguished location names $l_1,...,l_n \in Loc$ such that $\forall k \neq i.l_k \notin oloc(C_k)$ and $l_i \notin oloc(C_i) \cup oloc(C'_i)$, we require that $([C_1]_{l_1} \mid ... \mid [C_i]_{l_i} \mid ... \mid [C_n]_{l_n}) \Downarrow$ implies that the statement in the definition of independent subcontract pre-order holds for $([C_1]_{l_1} \parallel \doteq \parallel [C'_i]_{l_i} \parallel \doteq \parallel [C_n]_{l_n})$. By exploiting commutativity and associativity of parallel composition we can group the contracts which are not being refined and get the following cleaner definition. We let P_{conpar} denote the set of systems of

the form $[C_1]_{l_1} \mid ... \mid [C_n]_{l_n}$, with $C_i \in P_{con}$, for all $i \in \{1,...,n\}$.

Definition (Singular Subcontract Pre-Order): A pre-order $\leq$ over P_{con} is a singular subcontract pre-order if, for any $C, C' \in P_{con}$ such that $C' \leq C$, $l \in Loc$ and $P \in P_{conpar}$ such that $l \notin loc(P)$ and $oloc(C) \cup oloc(C') \subseteq loc(P)$, we have $([C]_l \mid P) \Downarrow$ implies

- $([C']_l \mid P) \Downarrow$.
- $\forall w \in \{a^+_{r \to s}, a^-_{r \to s}, a_{r \to s} \mid a \in N; r, s \in Loc\}^*$.

if $\exists P' : ([C']_l \mid P) \overset{w}{\Rightarrow} P' \wedge P' \sqrt{}$ then

$\exists P'' : ([C]_l \mid P) \overset{w}{\Rightarrow} P'' \wedge P'' \sqrt{}$

We now show that extending possible contexts with an external restriction does not change the notion of singular subcontract pre-order. We let $P_{conpres}$ denote the set of systems of the form $([C_1]_{l_1} \mid ... \mid [C_n]_{l_n}) \setminus L$, with $C_i \in P_{con}$ for all $i \in \{1,...,n\}$ (and $L \subseteq A_{loc}$ in the synchronous case, or $L \subseteq N_{loc}$ in the asynchronous one).

Proposition (Extension to Contexts with Restriction): Let $\leq$ be a singular subcontract pre-order. For any $C, C' \in P_{con}$ such that $C' \leq C$, $l \in Loc$ and $P \in P_{conpres}$ such that $l \notin loc(P)$ and $oloc(C) \cup oloc(C') \subseteq loc(P)$, we have that $([C]_l \mid P) \Downarrow$ implies

- $([C']_l \mid P) \Downarrow$.
- $\forall w \in \{a^+_{r \to s}, a^-_{r \to s}, a_{r \to s} \mid a \in N; r, s \in Loc\}^*$.

if $\exists P' : ([C']_l \mid P) \Rightarrow P' \wedge P' \sqrt{}$ then

$\exists P'' : ([C]_l \mid P) \overset{w}{\Rightarrow} P'' \wedge P'' \sqrt{}$

From the simple structure of their definition we can easily deduce that singular subcontract pre-orders have maximum, i.e. there exists a singular subcontract pre-order that includes all the other singular subcontract pre-orders.

Definition (Subcontract Relation): A contract C' is a subcontract of a contract C denoted $C' \preceq C$, if and only if for all $l \in Loc$ and $P \in P_{conpar}$ such that $l \notin loc(P)$ and $oloc(C) \cup oloc(C') \subseteq loc(P)$, we have that $([C]_l \mid P)\Downarrow$ implies

- $([C']_l \mid P)\Downarrow$.
- $\forall w \in \{a_{r \to s}^+, a_{r \to s}^-, a_{r \to s} \mid$
  $a \in N; r, s \in Loc\}^*$.

if $\exists P' : ([C']_l \mid P) \overset{w}{\Rightarrow} P' \wedge P'\sqrt{}$ then

$\exists P'' : ([C]_l \mid\mid P) \overset{w}{\Rightarrow} P'' \wedge P''\sqrt{}$

It is trivial to verify that the pre-order $\preceq$ is a singular subcontract pre-order and is the maximum of all the singular subcontract pre-orders.

In order to prove the existence of the maximal independent subcontract pre-order, we show the following result.

Theorem (Equivalence of Independent and Singular Subcontract Preorders): A pre-order $\leq$ is an independent subcontract pre-order if and only if it is a singular subcontract pre-order.

We can, therefore, conclude that there exists a maximal independent subcontract pre-order and it corresponds to the subcontract relation $\preceq$.

Input-Output Knowledge Independence

One of the peculiarities of our theory of refinement, is that we consider the possibility of relying on some knowledge about the "initial contracts", in particular, the input and output actions that occur in them. A very important consequence of this knowledge, is that we have the guarantee that a contract can be refined by another one that performs additional external input actions on names that do not occur in the initial contracts. For instance, the contract a can be refined by $a + b$ if we know that b is not among the possible outputs of the other initial contracts.

For instance, consider again the example

$$D_1 = a + b + c \qquad D_2' = \tau.\bar{a}_{l_1} + \tau.\bar{b}_{l_1} + \tau.\bar{c}_{l_1}$$

where the refinement of D_1 with $D_1' = a + b + d$ does not hold. This example shows that refinement is influenced by the potential actions that could be executed by the other contracts in the system. Indeed, D_1' is not a correct substitute for D_1 because D_2' has the possibility to produce $\bar{c}$.

Based on this intuition, we parameterize our notion of subcontract relation $C' \leq_{I,O} C$ on the set I of inputs, and the set O of outputs, that could be potentially executed by the other contracts in the system. We will see that $D_{1'} \preceq_{N_{loc}, N_{loc} - \{c_{l_1}, d_{l_1}\}} D_1$ but it does not hold that $D_{1'} \preceq_{N_{loc}, N_{loc}} D_1$.

In the following we will show that allowing the subcontract relation to depend on the knowledge about input and output actions of other initial contracts does not change the relation as long as the allowed inputs (outputs) for the other contracts include the outputs (inputs, repectively) of the refined contract. As a consequence of this fact we will show that input on new types (operations) can be freely added in refined contracts.

Given a set of located action names $I \subseteq N_{loc}$, we denote: with $\bar{I} = \{\bar{a}_l \mid a_l \in I\}$ the set of output actions performable on those names and with $I_l = \{a \mid a_l \in I\}$ the set of action names with associated location l.

Definition (Input and Output Sets): Given a contract $C \in P_{con}$, we define $I(C)$ (resp. $O(C)$) as the subset of N (resp. N_{loc}) of the potential input (resp. output) actions of C. Formally, we define $I(C)$ as follows ($O(C)$ is defined similarly):

$$I(\mathbf{0}) = I(\mathbf{1}) = I(X) = \varnothing$$
$$I(C + C') = I(C) \cup I(C')$$

$$I(a.C) = \{a\} \cup I(C)$$
$$I(\bar{a}_l.C) = I(\tau.C) = I(recX.C) = I(C)$$

Given a system $P \in P_{conpres}$, we define $I(P)$ (resp. $O(P)$) as the subset of N_{loc} of the potential input (resp. output) actions of P. Formally, we define $I(P)$ as follows ($O(P)$ is defined similarly):

$$I([C]_l) = \{a_l \mid a \in I(C)\}$$
$$I(P \mid P') = I(P) \cup I(P')$$
$$I(P \setminus L) = I(P) - L$$

In the following we let $P_{conpres,I,O}$, with $I, O \subseteq N_{loc}$, denote the subset of systems of $P_{conpres}$ such that $I(P) \subseteq I$ and $O(P) \subseteq O$.

Definition (Input-Output Subcontract Relation): A contract C' is a subcontract of a contract C with respect to a set of input located names $I \subseteq N_{loc}$ and output located names $O \subseteq N_{loc}$, denoted $C' \preceq_{I,O} C$, if and only if for all $l \in Loc$ and $P \in P_{conpres,I,O}$ such that $l \notin loc(P)$ and $oloc(C) \cup oloc(C') \subseteq loc(P)$, we have $([C]_l \mid P)\Downarrow$ implies

- $([C']_l \mid P)\Downarrow$
- $\forall w \in \{a^+_{r \to s}, a^-_{r \to s}, a_{r \to s} \mid a \in N; r, s \in Loc\}^*$.

if $\exists P' : ([C']_l \mid P) \overset{w}{\Rightarrow} P' \wedge P'\sqrt{}$ then $\exists P'' : ([C]_l \mid P) \overset{w}{\Rightarrow} P'' \wedge P''\sqrt{}$

Due to the proposition about extension to contexts with restriction, we have $\preceq = \preceq_{N_{loc},N_{loc}}$. The following proposition states an intuitive contravariant property: given $\preceq_{I',O'}$, and the greater sets I and O (i.e. $I' \subseteq I$ and $O' \subseteq O$) we obtain a smaller pre-order $\preceq_{I,O}$ (i.e. $\preceq_{I,O} \subseteq \preceq_{I',O'}$). This follows from the fact that extending the sets of input and output actions means considering a greater set of discriminating contexts.

Proposition (Extension of Context Sets): Let $C, C' \in P_{con}$ be two contracts, $I, I' \subseteq N_{loc}$ be two sets of input located names such that $I' \subseteq I$ and $O, O' \subseteq N_{loc}$ be two sets of output located names such that $O' \subseteq O$. We have:

$$C' \preceq_{I,O} C \quad \Rightarrow \quad C' \preceq_{I',O'} C$$

The following lemma, that will be used to characterize the subcontract relation, states that a subcontract is still a subcontract even if we modify it, so to consider only the inputs and outputs already occurring in the supercontract.

Lemma (Subcontract Restriction): Let $C, C' \in P_{con}$ be contracts and $I, O \subseteq N_{loc}$ be sets of located names. We have that both the following hold

$$C' \preceq_{I,O} C \Rightarrow$$
$$C'\{0 \mathbin{/} \alpha.C'' \mid \alpha \in I(C') - I(C)\} \preceq_{I,O} C$$
$$C' \preceq_{I,O} C \Rightarrow$$
$$C'\{T \mathbin{/} \alpha.C'' \mid \alpha \in \overline{O(C') - O(C)}\} \preceq_{I,O} C$$

where T is: 0 in the synchronous case, $\tau.0$ in the asynchronous case.

A fundamental result depending on the queue based communication (for the asynchronous case)/output persistence (in the synchronous case) is reported in the following proposition. It states that if we substitute a contract with one of its subcontract, the latter cannot activate outputs that were not included in the potential outputs of the supercontract (and similarly for the system considered as context).

Proposition (Output Activation): Let $C, C' \in P_{con}$ be contracts and $I, O \subseteq N_{loc}$ be sets of located names. Let $l \in Loc$ and $P \in P_{conpres,I,O}$, $l \notin loc(P)$ and $oloc(C) \cup oloc(C') \subseteq loc(P)$ be such that $([C]_l \mid P)\Downarrow$. We have that both the following hold: If $([C'\{T \mathbin{/} \alpha.C'' \mid \alpha \in \overline{O(C') - O(C)}\}]_l \mid P)\Downarrow$ then

$$([C']_l \mid P) \xrightarrow{w} ([C'_{der}, Q]_l \mid P_{der}) \wedge w \in \{$$
$$a_{r \to s}^+, a_{r \to s}^-, a_{r \to s}, \tau \mid a \in N; r, s \in Loc\}^* \Rightarrow$$
$$\neg \exists a_{l'} \in O(C') - O(C).C'_{der} \xrightarrow{\overline{a_{l'}}}$$

If $([C'\{0 \; / \; \alpha.C'' \mid \alpha \in I(C') - I(C)\}]_l \mid P)\!\!\downarrow$ then

$$([C']_l \mid P) \xrightarrow{w} ([C'_{der}, Q]_l \mid P_{der}) \wedge w \in \{$$
$$a_{r \to s}^+, a_{r \to s}^-, a_{r \to s}, \tau \mid a \in N; r, s \in Loc\}^* \Rightarrow$$
$$\neg \exists a \in I(C') - I(C), r \in loc(P).P_{der} \xrightarrow{\overline{a_{rl}}}$$

where the queue Q is absent in the synchronous case and T is: 0 in the synchronous case, $\tau.0$ in the asynchronous one.

The following propositions permit to conclude that the set of potential inputs and outputs of the other contracts in the system is an information that does not influence the subcontract relation.

Proposition (Input Independence): Let $C \in P_{con}$ be a contract, $O \subseteq N_{loc}$ be a set of located output names and $I, I' \subseteq N_{loc}$ be two sets of located input names such that $O(C) \subseteq I, I'$. We have that for every contract $C' \in P_{con}$,

$$C' \preceq_{I,O} C \quad \Leftrightarrow \quad C' \preceq_{I',O} C$$

Proposition (Output Independence): Let $C \in P_{con}$ be a contract, $O, O' \subseteq N_{loc}$ be two sets of located output names such that for every $l \in Loc$ we have $I(C) \subseteq O_l, O'_l$, and $I \subseteq N_{loc}$ be a set of located input names. We have that for every contract $C' \in P_{con}$,

$$C' \preceq_{I,O} C \quad \Leftrightarrow \quad C' \preceq_{I,O'} C$$

We finally show that the subcontract relation $\preceq$ allows input on new types (and unreachable outputs on new types) to be added in refined contracts. The result, that uses the lemma about subcontract restriction, is a direct consequence, in the case of inputs, of the fact that $C' \preceq_{N_{loc}, \bigcup_{l \in Loc} I([C]_l)} C$ if and only if $C' \preceq C$, i.e. it exploits the results above about independence from knowledge of types used by other initial contracts. In the case of output, we similarly use the fact that $C' \preceq_{O(C), N_{loc}} C$ if and only if $C' \preceq C$.

Theorem (Subcontracts with Additional Inputs and Outputs): Let $C, C' \in P_{con}$ be contracts. Both the following hold

$$C'\{0 \; / \; \alpha.C'' \mid \alpha \in I(C') - I(C)\} \preceq C \quad \Leftrightarrow \quad C' \preceq C$$
$$C'\{T \; / \; \alpha.C'' \mid \alpha \in \overline{O(C') - O(C)}\} \preceq C \quad \Leftrightarrow \quad C' \preceq C$$

where T is: 0 in the synchronous case, $\tau.0$ in the asynchronous case.

Resorting to Should Testing

The remainder of this section is devoted to the definition of an actual procedure for determining that two contracts are in subcontract relation. This is achieved resorting to the theory of *should-testing* (Rensink & Vogler, 2007).

In the following we denote with $\preceq_{test}$ the *should-testing* pre-order defined in Rensink & Vogler (2007) where we consider the set of actions used by terms as being:

$$\{a, \overline{a}, a_l, \overline{a_l}, \tau, \sqrt{} \mid a \in N, l \in Loc\}$$

(i.e. we consider located and unlocated input and output actions and $\sqrt{}$ is included in the set of actions of terms under testing as any other action). Here we consider λ to range over such a set of actions. We denote here with $\sqrt{}'$ the special action for the success of the test (denoted by $\sqrt{}$ in Rensink & Vogler (2007))

In order to resort to the theory defined in Rensink & Vogler (2007), we define a normal form for contracts of our calculus that corresponds to terms of the language in Rensink & Vogler (2007). The normal form of the contract C (denoted with $NF(C)$) is defined as follows, by using the operator $rec_X\theta$ (defined in Rensink & Vogler (2007)) that represents the value of X in the solution of the minimum fixpoint of the finite set of equations θ,

$$NF(C) = rec_{X_1}\theta \quad \textit{where } \theta \textit{ is the set of equations}$$
$$X_i = \sum_j \lambda_{i,j}; X_{der(i,j)}$$

where, assuming to enumerate the states in the labeled transition system of C starting from X_1, each variable X_i corresponds to the i-th state of the labeled transition system of C, $\lambda_{i,j}$ is the label of the j-th outgoing transition from X_i, and $der(i,j)$ is the index of the state reached with the j-th outgoing transition from X_i. We assume empty sums to be equal to $\mathbf{0}$, i.e. if there are no outgoing transitions from X_i, we have $X_i = \mathbf{0}$.

Theorem (Resorting to Should Testing): Let $C, C' \in P_{con}$ be two contracts. We have

$$NF(C'\{\mathbf{0}\,/\,\alpha.C'' \mid \alpha \in I(C') - I(C)\}) \preceq_{test}$$
$$NF(C) \Rightarrow C' \preceq C$$

In Bravetti & Zavattaro (2007a) counter-examples can be found, that prove that the opposite implication

$$C' \preceq C \Rightarrow NF(C'\{\mathbf{0}\,/\,\alpha.C'' \mid \alpha \in I(C') - I(C)\}) \preceq_{test} NF(C)$$

does not hold in general.

CONTRACT-BASED CHOREOGRAPHY CONFORMANCE

We now introduce a choreography language similar to those already presented in Busi, Gorrieri, Guidi, Lucchi & Zavattaro (2005), Carbone,

Honda & Yoshida (2005) and Bravetti & Zavattaro (2007a).

Definition (Choreographies): Let *Operations*, ranged over by $a, b, c, \cdots$ and *Roles*, ranged over by $r, s, t, \cdots$, be two countable sets of operation and role names, respectively. The set of *Choreographies*, ranged over by $H, L, \cdots$ is defined by the following grammar:

$$H ::= \quad a_{r \to s} \quad | \quad H + H \quad | \quad H; H \quad |$$
$$H \mid H \quad | \quad H^*$$

The invocations $a_{r \to s}$ (where we assume $r \neq s$) means that role r invokes the operation a provided by the role s. The other operators are choice $\_ + \_$, sequential $\_;\_$, parallel $\_ \mid \_$, and repetition $\_^*$.

Before presenting the formal definition of the semantics, we present an example of a choreographic description of our running example about the client, the authentication server, and the account server. In the last version of the example we have considered two possible conversations (one between the client and the authentication server, and another one between the authentication and the account servers) that could be repeated in interleaving an arbitrary amount of time. This corresponds to a repetitive choreography (obtained by using the operator $\_^*$) composed of two sub-choreographies (composed by using the choice operator $\_ + \_$) representing the two possible conversations, respectively:

$$((username_{client \to authServer}; password_{client \to authServer};$$
$$(accepted_{authServer \to client} + failed_{authServer \to client}) +$$
$$(updateAccounts_{authServer \to accountServer};$$
$$newAccounts_{accountServer \to authServer}))^*$$

We now present the operational semantics assuming synchronous communication. The formal definition considers the two auxiliary terms $\mathbf{1}$, and $\mathbf{0}$ and is given in Figure 4, where we take η to range over the set of labels:

Figure 4. Semantic rules for synchronous choreographies (symmetric rules omitted)

$$a_{r \to s} \xrightarrow{a_{r \to s}} 1 \qquad 1\surd \qquad H^* \surd$$

$$\frac{H \xrightarrow{\eta} H'}{H+L \xrightarrow{\eta} H'} \qquad \frac{H\surd}{H+L\surd} \qquad \frac{H \xrightarrow{\eta} H'}{H;L \xrightarrow{\eta} H';L} \qquad \frac{H\surd \quad L \xrightarrow{\eta} L'}{H;L \xrightarrow{\eta} L'}$$

$$\frac{H\surd \quad L\surd}{H|L\surd} \qquad \frac{H\surd \quad L\surd}{H;L\surd} \qquad \frac{H \xrightarrow{\eta} H'}{H|L \xrightarrow{\eta} H'|L} \qquad \frac{H \xrightarrow{\eta} H'}{H^* \xrightarrow{\eta} H';H^*}$$

$$\{a_{r \to s} \mid a \in Operations; r, s \in Roles\}$$

and the termination predicate $\surd$. The rules in Figure 4 are rather standard for process calculi with sequential composition and without synchronization; in fact, parallel composition simply allows for the interleaving of the actions executed by the operands.

If we consider asynchronous communication, we need to distinguish between the send and the receive events. For this reason we consider two distinct labels, one for the send event and one for the receive event, thus obtaining the following set $\{a^+_{r \to s}, a^-_{r \to s} \mid a \in Operations; r, s \in Roles\}$. Moreover, in the definition of the operational semantics we consider the auxiliary terms $a^-_{r \to s}$, used to model the fact that an asynchronous interaction has been activated (by performing the send event) but not yet completed (by performing the corresponding receive event). The formal definition is like the one presented in Figure 4

where the first rule is replaced by the two rule in Figure 5.

Choreographies are especially useful to describe the protocols of interactions within a group of collaborating services, nevertheless, even if choreography languages represent a simple and intuitive approach for the description of the message exchange among services, they are not yet very popular in the context of service oriented computing. The main problem to their diffusion is that it is not trivial to relate the high level choreography description with the actual implementation of the specified system realised as composition of services that are usually loosely coupled, independently developed by different companies, and autonomous. More precisely, the difficult task is, given a choreography, to lookup available services that, once combined, are ensured to behave according to the given choreography.

In order to formally investigate this problem, we define a mechanism to extract from a chore-

Figure 5. Alternative semantic rules for asynchronous choreographies

$$a_{r \to s} \xrightarrow{a^+_{r \to s}} a^-_{r \to s} \qquad a^-_{r \to s} \xrightarrow{a^-_{r \to s}} 1$$

ography the description of the behavior of a given role. Formally, for each role i, we define a labeled transition system with transitions $\xrightarrow{\eta}_i$ (see the rules in Figure 6) and termination predicate $\sqrt{}_i$ representing the behavior of the role i.

We first consider the synchronous case. Synchronous contracts should satisfy the output persistence property. As already discussed, output persistence characterizes that class of contracts in which output actions, once they are ready to be executed, must be performed before successful completion. In order to guarantee that the contracts extracted from a choreography obey to the output persistence property, we put an internal action before the output prefix that represents the internal decision to perform such an output operation. Technically speaking, we use an auxiliary term $a_{r \to s}^{\sim}$ that represents the fact that the role r has decided to perform the output action a by performing its internal action.

In the following, given a choreography H and one of its role i, with $[\![H]\!]_i$ we denote the contract term obtained from the labeled transition system $\xrightarrow{\eta}_i$.

The projection in the asynchronous case is defined as in Figure 6, with the difference that it is no longer necessary to guarantee output persistence. Hence, the first two rules are replaced by the simpler rule in Figure 7.

For instance, consider the choreography of our running example we presented above and, for simplicity, synchronous communication. The projection on the *accountServer* role would yield the contract corresponding to the term:

$$updateAccounts.recX.(\tau.\overline{newAccounts}_{authServer}.$$
$$(updateAccounts.X + 1) + 1)$$

The projection on the *client* role would instead produce:

$$\tau.recX.(\overline{username}_{authServer}.\tau.\overline{password}_{authServer}.$$
$$(accepted.(\tau.X + 1) + failed.(\tau.X + 1))) + 1$$

Finally, the projection on the *authServer* role would produce:

Figure 6. Projection on the role i of a synchronous choreography (symmetric rules omitted)

$$a_{r \to s} \xrightarrow{\tau}_r a_{r \to s}^{\sim} \qquad a_{r \to s}^{\sim} \xrightarrow{\overline{a}_s}_r \mathbf{1} \qquad a_{r \to s} \xrightarrow{a}_s \mathbf{1}$$

$$a_{r \to s} \sqrt{}_i \text{ if } i \neq r, s \qquad \mathbf{1}\sqrt{}_i \qquad H^*\sqrt{}_i$$

$$\frac{H \xrightarrow{\eta}_i H'}{H + L \xrightarrow{\eta}_i H'} \qquad \frac{H\sqrt{}_i}{H + L\sqrt{}_i} \qquad \frac{H \xrightarrow{\eta}_i H'}{H;L \xrightarrow{\eta}_i H';L} \qquad \frac{H\sqrt{}_i \quad L \xrightarrow{\eta}_i L'}{H;L \xrightarrow{\eta}_i L'}$$

$$\frac{H\sqrt{}_i \quad L\sqrt{}_i}{H|L\sqrt{}_i} \qquad \frac{H\sqrt{}_i \quad L\sqrt{}_i}{H;L\sqrt{}_i} \qquad \frac{H \xrightarrow{\eta}_i H'}{H|L \xrightarrow{\eta}_i H'|L} \qquad \frac{H \xrightarrow{\eta}_i H'}{H^* \xrightarrow{\eta}_i H';H^*}$$

Figure 7. Alternative projection rule for asynchronous choreography

$$a_{r \to s} \xrightarrow{\overline{a_s}}_r \mathbf{1}$$

$$username.password.(\tau.\overline{accepted}_{client}.C +$$
$$\tau.\overline{failed}_{client}.C) +$$
$$\tau.\overline{updateAccounts}_{accountServer} \cdot$$
$$newAccounts.C + \mathbf{1})$$

with C being the term

$$recX.(username.password.(\tau.\overline{accepted}_{client}.X$$
$$+ \tau.\overline{failed}_{client}.X) +$$
$$\tau.\overline{updateAccounts}_{accountServer} \cdot$$
$$newAccounts.X + \mathbf{1})$$

Notice that with respect to the contracts for the *accountServer*, *client* and *authServer* presented in the section about contract refinements, the contracts obtained by projection differ for: presence of initial "unfolded parts" of loops and states with a single outgoing transition (i.e. a transition not involved in a choice) turned into states with a single τ transition followed by the formerly outgoing transition.

It is immediate to observe that, since these kind of modifications obviously do not affect neither the termination capabilities nor the set of weak traces performed by the *accountServer*, *client* and *authServer*, the three contracts presented in the section about contract refinement are equivalent, according to the notion of subcontract relation (i.e the relation $\preceq$ holds in both directions), to the three contracts above obtained by projection.

We now move to the discussion about how to exploit the choreography and the contract calculus in order to define a procedure that checks whether a service exposing a specific contract C can play the role r within a given choreography.

First of all we need to uniform the choreography and the contract calculus. From a syntactical viewpoint, we have to map the operation names used for choreographies with the names used for contracts assuming $Operations = N$. We do the same also for the role names that are mapped into the location names, i.e., $Roles = Loc$. Taken these assumptions, we have that the labels of the operational semantics of the choreography calculus are a subset of the labels of the operational semantics of contract systems, i.e. $a_{r \to s}$ in the synchronous case, $a_{r \to s}^+$ and $a_{r \to s}^-$ in the asynchronous one.

We are now ready to formalize the notion of correct implementation of a choreography. Intuitively, a system implements a choreography if it is a correct composition of contracts and all of its conversations (i.e. the possible sequences of message exchanges), are admitted by the choreography. The definition applies to both the synchronous and asynchronous case (by considering all the labels $a_{r \to s}$, $a_{r \to s}^+$ and $a_{r \to s}^-$).

Definition (Choreography Implementation): Given the choreography H and the system P, we say that P implements H (written $P \propto H$) if

- P is a correct contract composition.
- Given a sequence w of labels of the kind $a_{r \to s}$, $a_{r \to s}^+$ and $a_{r \to s}^-$, if $P \stackrel{w}{\Rightarrow} P'$ and $P' \sqrt{}$ then there exists H' such that $H \stackrel{w}{\to} H'$ and $H' \sqrt{}$.

Note that it is not necessary for an implementation to include all possible conversations admitted by a choreography. As an example, consider the choreography

$reserve_{client \to server}; (accept_{server \to client} +$
$reject_{server \to client})$.

We can think of implementing it, both in the synchronous and the asynchronous cases, with the following system

$[\overline{reserve}_{server} . (accept + reject)]_{client} \mid$
$[\overline{reserve.accept}_{client}]_{server}$

where the server is always ready to accept the client's request.

Other possible implementations, which instead produce all possible conversations, are

$[\tau.\overline{reserve}_{server} . (accept + reject)]_{client} \mid$
$[reserve.(\tau.\overline{accept} + \tau.\overline{reject})_{client}]_{server}$,

that is the implementation obtained by projection in the synchronous case, and

$[\tau.\overline{reserve}_{server} . (accept + reject + retry)]_{client} \mid$
$[reserve.(\tau.\overline{accept} + \tau.\overline{reject})_{client}]_{server}$.

As another example, consider the coreography of our running example about the *accountServer*, the *client* and the *authServer*. It is immediate to observe that, in the synchronous case, both the system composed by the three contracts presented in the section about contract refinements and the system composed by the three contracts obtained by projection constitute an implementation of such a coreography.

It is interesting to also observe that given a choreography H, the system obtained by composing its projections is not ensured to be an implementation of H. For instance, consider the choreography $a_{r \to s}; b_{t \to u}$. The system obtained by projection (in the synchronous case) is $[\tau.\overline{a}_s]_r \mid [a]_s \mid [\tau.\overline{b}_u]_t \mid [b]_u$. Even if this is a correct composition of contracts, it is not an implementa-

tion of H because it comprises the conversation $b_{t \to u} a_{r \to s}$ which is not admitted by H.

The problem is not in the definition of the projection, but in the fact that the above choreography cannot be implemented preserving the message exchanges specified by the choreography. In fact, in order to guarantee that the communication between t and u is executed after the communication between r and s, it is necessary to add a further message exchange (for instance between s and r) which is not considered in the choreography. We restrict our interest to well formed choreographies.

Definition (Well Formed Choreography): A choreography H, defined on the roles $r_1, \cdots, r_n$, is *well formed* if $[[[H]]_{r_1}]_{r_1} \mid \cdots \mid [[[H]]_{r_n}]_{r_n} \propto H$

The choreography:

$reserve_{client \to server}; (accept_{server \to client} +$
$reject_{server \to client})$

considered before is well formed both in the synchronous and asynchronous cases: in the synchronous case we already observed that the projection constitutes an implementation (the asynchronous case is analogous apart that τ prefixes are not included). Similarly, the choreography of our running example is well formed in the synchronous case.

Notice that, in the synchronous case, well formedness is decidable. In fact, given a choreography H, it is sufficient to take the corresponding system P obtained by projection, then consider P and H as finite state automata, and finally check whether the language of the first automaton is included in the language of the second one. Note that terms H can be seen as finite state automata thanks to the fact that their infinite behaviours are defined using Kleene-star repetitions instead of general recursion.

As another example we consider the choreography $a_{l_1 \to l_3}; b_{l_2 \to l_3}$ which has the following projection (in the asynchronous case) $[\overline{a}l_3]_{l_1} \| [\overline{b}l_3]_{l_2} \| [a.b]_{l_3}$.

Such a choreography is not well formed in that, among the possible traces of the projection, we have $a_{l_3}^+ b_{l_3}^+ a_{l_3}^- b_{l_3}^-$ which is not a correct trace for the above choreography. This example is of interest because it shows that some interesting contract systems are not specifiable as choreographies. This follows from the fact that we have adopted the same approach of WS-CDL that exploits synchronizations as its basic activity. In order to model at a choreographic level the above contract system, we should separate also in the syntax (and not only in the semantics) the send from the receive actions. For instance, we could consider two distinct basic terms $a_{r \to s}^+$ and $a_{r \to s}^-$ for send and receive actions, respectively, and describe the above system with the choreography $a_{l_1 \to l_3}^+ \mid b_{l_2 \to l_3}^+ \mid a_{l_1 \to l_3}^- ; b_{l_2 \to l_3}^-$.

We are now in place for the definition of the relation $C \lhd_r H$ indicating whether the contract C can play the role r in the choreography H.

Definition (Conformance Relation): Given a well formed choreography H with roles $r_1, \cdots, r_n$, a relation among contracts, roles r of H and H, denoted with $C \lhd_r H$, is a *conformance relation* if, for every r_i with $1 \leq i \leq n$, there exists at least a contract C_i such that $C_i \lhd_{r_i} H$ and it holds that:

if $C_1 \lhd_{r_1} H, \cdots, C_n \lhd_{r_n} H$ then

$[C_1]_{r_1} \mid \cdots \mid [C_n]_{r_n} \propto H$

Differently from the subcontract pre-orders defined on contracts in the previous section, there exists no maximal conformance relation. As far as the synchronous case is concerned, consider the choreography $H = a_{r \to s} \mid b_{r \to s}$. We could have two different conformance relations $\lhd_H^1$ and $\lhd_H^2$, the first one including

$$(\bar{a}_s.\bar{b}_s + \bar{b}_s.\bar{a}_s) \lhd_r^1 H \qquad (\tau.a.b + \tau.b.a) \lhd_s^1 H$$

and the second one including

$$(\tau.\bar{a}_s.\bar{b}_s + \tau.\bar{b}_s.\bar{a}_s) \lhd_r^2 H \qquad (a.b + b.a) \lhd_s^2 H$$

It is easy to see that it is not possible to have a conformance relation that comprises the union of the two relations $\lhd_H^1$ and $\lhd_H^2$. In fact, the system

$$[\tau.\bar{a}_s.\bar{b}_s + \tau.\bar{b}_s.\bar{a}_s]_r \mid [\tau.a.b + \tau.b.a]_s$$

is not a correct composition because the two contracts may internally select two incompatible orderings for the execution of the two message exchanges (and in this case they stuck).

The counter-example does not work in the asynchronous case because, due to the presence of the message queue, the ordering of emission decided by the sender could be different from the order of consumption decided by the receiver. Nevertheless, a more subtle counter-example exists also for the asynchronous case. Consider the choreography $H = a_{r \to s} \mid b_{s \to r}$. We could have two different conformance relations, the first one $\lhd^1$ including

$$\bar{a}_s.b + b.\bar{a}_s \lhd_r^1 H \qquad a.\bar{b}_r \lhd_s^1 H$$

and the second one $\lhd^2$ including

$$b.\bar{a}_s \lhd_r^2 H \qquad a.\bar{b}_r + \bar{b}_r.a \lhd_r^2 H$$

It is easy to see that it is not possible to have a conformance relation that comprises the union of the two relations $\lhd^1$ and $\lhd^2$. In fact, the system $[b.\bar{a}_s]_r \mid [a.\bar{b}_r]_s$ is not a correct composition because the two contracts are both blocked for a never incoming message.

The remainder of the section is dedicated to the definition of a mechanism that, by exploiting the choreography projection and the notion of contract refinement previously defined, permits to characterize an interesting conformance relation. This relation is called *consonance*.

Definition (Consonance): We say that the contract C is *consonant* with the role r of the well formed choreography H (written $C \otimes^r H$) if $C \preceq [\![H]\!]_r$ where $\preceq$ is the relation introduced in the Definition of subcontract relation.

Theorem (Consonance as a Comformance Relation): Given a well formed choreography H, we have that the consonance relation $C \otimes^r H$ is a conformance relation.

In the previous section we have presented a testing-like characterization, of the subcontract relation for the synchronous case. This characterization can be used also here to obtain a sound characterization of consonance (at least for synchronously communicating choreographies).

Definition (Testing Consonance): We say that the contract C is *testing consonant* with the role r of the well formed choreography H (written $C \otimes^r_{test} H$) if

$$NF(C\{\mathbf{0} \, / \, \alpha.C' \mid \alpha \in I(C) - I([\![H]\!]_r)\}) \preceq_{test} NF([\![H]\!]_r)$$

where $\preceq_{test}$ is the should-testing pre-order.

Theorem (Consonance Characterization): Given a well formed choreography H, its role r, and a contract C, we have that if $C \otimes^r_{test} H$ then also $C \otimes^r H$ holds.

Consider again the case of our running example about the *accountServer*, the *client* and the *authServer*. It is immediate to observe that the three contracts presented in the section about contract refinement are testing consonant (hence consonant) with the corresponding roles of the choreography presented for the running example: they are in should-testing pre-order with the corresponding projections for the same reasons explained before, i.e. they differ just for introduction of unfolding of loops and τ transitions in front of transitions non involved in choices.

RELATED WORK

As already described in the introduction the present chapter reports the main results in Bravetti & Zavattaro (2007a) and Bravetti & Zavattaro (2009) about two theories (the former for synchronous communication and the latter for asychronous communication) about contract compliance, contract refinement, and choreography conformance. The main contribution of this chapter is the uniform presentation of the two theories. In Bravetti & Zavattaro (2007a) we considered a rather specific language for contracts, while in this chapter we adopt also for the synchronous case the language independent approach introduced for the first time in Bravetti & Zavattaro (2009). This also required the definition of a new technique for projecting choreographies in the synchronous case. Such a technique extracts from the choreography syntax the transition system corresponding to the contract of a given participant. The obtained transition system includes an internal action before every output operation in order to guarantee that the projected contract satisfies the output persistence property (required by our notion of contracts in the synchronous case). Finally, this chapter contains less technical details with respect to the previous publications and it includes more explaining examples and a novel running case study used to clarify the approach and the results.

In the introduction we have already commented similar contract theories available in the literature (Carpineti, Castagna, Laneve & Padovani, 2006) (Laneve & Padovani, 2007)(Castagna, Gesbert & Padovani, 2008) developed for synchronous communication. Similar ideas were already considered also in Fournet, Hoare, Rajamani & Rehof (2004) where the notion of *stuck-free* conformance is introduced. We now comment two contract theories for asynchronous communication, one by Rajamani & Rehof (2002) and another one by van der Aalst, Lohman, Massuthe, Stahl & Wolf (2010). In Rajamani & Rehof (2002) a conformance relation is defined in a bisimulation-like style introducing an ad-hoc treatment of internal and external choices that are included in the calculus as two distinct operators. We try somehow to be more general, avoiding the introduction of two distinct choice operators and by defining our refinement notion indirectly as the maximal contract substitution relation that preserves system correctness. In van der Aalst, Lohman, Massuthe, Stahl & Wolf (2010) the same approach for formalizing compliance and refinement that we have presented in Bravetti & Zavattaro (2007a) has been applied to service systems specified using open Workflow Nets (a special class of Petri nets) that communicate asynchronously. As in our works, they prove that contract refinement can be done independently. Moreover, they present an actual way for checking refinement that work assuming that contracts do not contain cycles. As a future work, we plan to investigate whether their decidability technique can be applied also in our different context in which message queues preserve the order of messages.

The notion of contract compliance used in this chapter has been adopted also in Padovani (2011) where fair subtyping for multiparty session types is investigated. A remarkable contribution of Padovani (2011) is the definition of an efficient procedure for deciding fair refinement which works for nondeterministic sequential processes consisting of internal choices of outputs and external choices of input.

We now comment on the testing theories developed for process calculi starting from the seminal work by De Nicola & Hennessy (1984). A careful comparison between the testing approach and our contract theory for synchronous communication can be found in Bravetti & Zavattaro (2007b) (where we resort to fair testing (Rensink & Vogler, 2007), a variant of De Nicola-Hennessy must testing for fair systems, to define an actual procedure to check contract refinement). The same comments apply also to the CSP failure refinement (Hoare, 1985) as it is well known that the must testing pre-order and the CSP failure refinement

coincide (at least for finitely branching processes without divergences) (De Nicola, 1987). Another interesting comparison between service contract refinement and testing pre-orders can be found in Laneve & Padovani (2007). As far as must testing for asynchronous communication is concerned, it has been investigated for asynchronous CCS in Castellani & Hennessy (1998) and Boreale, De Nicola & Pugliese (2002). An interesting law holding in that papers is that an input, immediately followed by the output of the same message, is equivalent to do nothing. This does not hold in our context. In fact, a receiver of a message cannot re-emit the read message because it is not possible for a service to introduce a message in its own message queue.

We would also to report about related work on the study of services communicating via asynchronous mechanisms and their conversations. In particular, in Fu, Bultan & Su (2005) the authors present a technique to establish satisfaction of a given property on service conversations from the specifications of the involved services and in Fu, Bultan & Su (2004) the authors study, given a specification of possible conversations, whether there exists or not a set of services realizing them. The problem of realizability of global choreographic specifications has been investigated also in more recent papers. For instance, in Basu, Bultan & Ouderni (2012) it is presented a procedure capable to verify whether a choreography, expressed as a transition system, can be implemented as a parallel composition of asynchronously communicating contracts by preserving the order of send events. The procedure is based on the verification of two conditions. The first one checks whether the observable behaviour of the choreography does not change when moving from a synchronous to an asynchronous semantics with buffers of capacity 1: this condition was already proposed in Basu & Bultan (2011) as a criterion to guarantee synchronizability, that is the observational equivalence between the synchronous and the asynchronous semantics of a choreography. The second one is a temporal property of the system: for every reachable configuration in which there is one message in one buffer, there exists a subsequent reachable configuration in which such message is consumed.

We finally observe that the relationship that we impose between choregraphies and their implementation under the asynchronous case is similar to the *disjoint* connectedness assumption proposed in Lanese, Guidi, Montesi & Zavattaro (2008). In that paper, several observational criteria are considered for the formalization of the relationship between choreographies and their implementation as parallel composition of contracts. One criterion corresponds to our synchronous case. For asynchronous communication, several criteria are considered: one observes only the send event, one considers only the receive event, one observe both events, and finally the *disjoint* criterion requires that two subsequent interactions do not overlap. The absence of overlap between subsequent interactions is guaranteed also under our approach as we require trace preservation, and in the traces of a choreography like $a_{l_1 \to l_3}; b_{l_2 \to l_3}$ the send event of the latter interaction always occurs after the receive event of the former.

CONCLUSION

We have addressed the problem of the definition of suitable notions of contract refinement and choreography conformance for services that communicate either synchronously, or asynchronously through message queues. We have attacked this problem by exploiting the following approach. In order to be language independent we have defined contracts as labeled transition systems. Then we have defined contract compositions for both the synchronous and the asynchronous cases, and we have formalized the notion of correct contract composition. This allowed us to define a notion of subcontract relation as the maximal refinement preserving correctness. We have in-

vestigated the relation induced by this definition under both synchronous and asynchronous communication; in particular, in the synchronous case, we have presented a characterization in terms of the should-testing pre-order (Rensink & Vogler, 2007). After, we have presented a choreography language equipped with both a sychronous and an asynchronous semantics. In both cases we have defined a technique to extract (by means of projection) the expected behaviour of each participant. By combining projection and contract refinement, we have finally defined a conformance relation that formalizes the possibility for one contract to correctly implement a specific role within a given choreography.

Concerning the subcontract relation in the asynchronous case, it is worth noting that differently from the synchronous case we do not present an actual way for deciding compliance, refinement, and conformance. This follows from the fact that the presence of message queues make a contract system possibly infinite. In fact, even if contracts are finite state, a contract could repeatedly emit the same message thus introducing an unbounded amount of messages in a queue. Contract systems can be limited to be finite in (at least) two possible ways, either considering bounded buffers or avoiding cycles in contracts.

As already discussed, in Bravetti & Zavattaro (2007a) and Bravetti & Zavattaro (2009) we proposed for the first time the approach to the formalization of service contracts and choreographies reported in this chapter. It is worth noting that the ideas reported in those papers had an impact on the research community as several subsequent papers adopted the same, or similar, approaches. For instance, to the best of our knowledge, Bravetti & Zavattaro (2007a) proposed for the first time in the context of service composition a fair notion of correctness which has been subsequently adopted in van der Aalst, Lohmann, Massuthe, Stahl & Wolf (2010) and Padovani (2011). Also the exploitation of trace semantics to formalize the correspondence between a choreography and a service composition has been used in several subsequent work. In Castagna, Dezani-Ciancaglini & Padovani (2011), where an asynchronous model of communication similar to ours is considered, a multiparty session (corresponding to an abstract description of a service composition) is considered as a correct implementation of a global type (corresponding to a choregraphy) if its traces are included in the traces of the global type, and for every trace of the global type the multiparty session exhibits at least one trace which is the same up to reordering. It is worth noting that differently from our approach, in Castagna, Dezani-Ciancaglini & Padovani (2011) only the receiving events are observed, while our trace asychronous semantics observe both the send and the receive events. In Zongyan, Xiangpeng, Chao & Hongli (2007) a process calculus for choreography, a process calculus for service contracts, and a corresponding projection are presented which are similar to those we proposed in Bravetti & Zavattaro (2007a). In addition, they study the problem of how to amend a choreography which is not well formed by adding centralized points of synchronization. This problem has been more recently studied also in Salaun, Bultan & Roohi (2011) where additional communications are added instead of central points of synchronization.

As a final remark, we comment that our notion of service contract deals only with functional requirements and does not take into accounts nonfunctional aspects like those related to Service Level Agreement. We plan to investigate aspects like response time, frequency of client's invocations, and other quantitative requirements in future work. To this aim, we plan to take advantage of previous work done in the area of quantitative calculi for service oriented computing like CC-pi (Buscemi & Montanari, 2011), an extension of both the pi-calculus and concurrent constraint programming, or Stochastic COWS (Prandi & Quaglia, 2007), a stochastic extension of the "Calculus for Orchestration of Web Services" (Lapadula, Pugliese & Tiezzi, 2007).

REFERENCES

W3C. (2005). *Web services choreography description language*. Retrieved from http://www.w3.org/TR/2005/CR-ws-cdl-10-20051109/

Basu, S., & Bultan, T. (2011). Choreography conformance via synchronizability. In *WWW'11* (pp. 795-804). ACM Press.

Basu, S., Bultan, T., & Ouderni, M. (2012). Deciding choreography realizability. In *POPL'12* (pp. 191-202). ACM Press.

Boreale, M., De Nicola, R., & Pugliese, R. (2002). Trace and testing equivalence on asynchronous processes. *Information and Computation, 172*(2), 139–164.

Bravetti, M., & Zavattaro, G. (2006). *Towards a unifying theory for choreography conformance and contract compliance*. Technical report. Retrieved from http://cs.unibo.it/~bravetti/html/techreports.

Bravetti, M., & Zavattaro, G. (2007a). Towards a unifying theory for choreography conformance and contract compliance. In *SC'06, volume 4829 of LNCS*, (pp. 34-50).

Bravetti, M., & Zavattaro, G. (2007b). Contract based multi-party service composition. In *FSEN'07, volume 4767 of LNCS*, (pp. 207-222).

Bravetti, M., & Zavattaro, G. (2007c). A theory for strong service compliance. In *Coordination'07, volume 4467 of LNCS*, (pp. 96-112).

Bravetti, M., & Zavattaro, G. (2008). *Contract compliance and choreography conformance in the presence of message queues*. Technical report. Retrieved from http://cs.unibo.it/~bravetti/html/techreports

Bravetti, M., & Zavattaro, G. (2009). Contract compliance and choreography conformance in the presence of message queues. *Proceedings WS-FM'08, volume 5387 of LNCS*, (pp. 37-54).

Buscemi, M. G., & Montanari, U. (2011). QoS negotiation in service composition. *Journal of Logic and Algebraic Programming, 80*(1), 13–24.

Busi, N., Gorrieri, R., Guidi, C., Lucchi, R., & Zavattaro, G. (2005). Choreography and orchestration: A synergic approach for system design. In *ICSOC'05, volume 3826 of LNCS*, (pp. 228-240).

Carbone, M., Honda, K., & Yoshida, N. (2007). Structured communication-centred programming for web services. In *ESOP'07, volume 4421 of LNCS*, (pp. 2-17).

Carpineti, S., Castagna, G., Laneve, C., & Padovani, L. (2006). A formal account of contracts for Web services. In *WS-FM'06, volume 4184 of LNCS*, (pp. 148-162).

Castagna, G., Dezani-Ciancaglini, M., & Padovani, L. (2011). On global types and multi-party sessions. In *FMOODS/FORTE'11, volume 6722 of LNCS*, (pp. 1-28).

Castagna, G., Gesbert, N., & Padovani, L. (2008). A theory of contracts for web services. In *POPL'08*, (pp. 261-272). ACM Press.

Castellani, I., & Hennessy, M. (1998). Testing theories for asynchronous languages. In *FSTTCS'98, volume 1530 of LNCS*, (pp. 90-101).

De Nicola, R. (1887). Extensional equivalences for transition systems. *Acta Informatica, 24*(2), 211–237.

De Nicola, R., & Hennessy, M. (1984). Testing equivalences for processes. *Theoretical Computer Science, 34*, 83–133.

Decker, G., Kopp, O., Leymann, F., & Weske, M. (2007). BPEL4Chor: Extending BPEL for modeling choreographies. In *IEEE 2007 International Conference on Web Services (ICWS)*. IEEE Computer Society.

Fournet, C., Hoare, C. A. R., Rajamani, S. K., & Rehof, J. (2004). Stuck-free conformance. In *CAV'04, volume 3114 of LNCS*, (pp. 242-254).

Fu, X., Bultan, T., & Su, J. (2004). Conversation protocols: A formalism for specification and verification of reactive electronic services. *Theoretical Computer Science, 328*(1-2), 19–37.

Fu, X., Bultan, T., & Su, J. (2005). Synchronizability of conversations among Web services. *IEEE Transactions on Software Engineering, 31*(12), 1042–1055.

Hoare, T. (1985). *Communicating sequential processes*. Prentice-Hall.

Lanese, I., Guidi, C., Montesi, F., & Zavattaro, G. (2008). Bridging the gap between interaction- and process-oriented choreographies. In *SEFM'08*, (pp. 323-332).

Laneve, C., & Padovani, L. (2007). The must preorder revisited - An algebraic theory for web services contracts. In *Concur'07*. In *LNCS* (*Vol. 4703*, pp. 212–225). Springer.

Lapadula, A., Pugliese, R., & Tiezzi, F. (2007). Calculus for orchestration of web services. In *ESOP'07, volume 4421 of LNCS*, (pp. 33-47).

Milner, R. (1989). *Communication and concurrency*. Prentice-Hall.

OASIS. (2007). *Web services business process execution language version 2.0*. Retrieved from http://docs.oasis-open.org/wsbpel/2.0/wsbpel-v2.0.pdf

Padovani, L. (2011). Fair subtyping for multi-party session types. In *Coordination'11*. In *LNCS* (*Vol. 6721*, pp. 127–141). Springer.

Prandi, D., & Quaglia, P. (2007). Stochastic COWS. In *ICSOC'07, volume 4749 of LNCS*, (pp. 245-256).

Rajamani, S. K., & Rehof, J. (2002). Conformance checking for models of asynchronous message passing software. In *CAV'02, volume 2404 of LNCS*, (pp. 166-179).

Rensink, A., & Vogler, W. (2007). Fair testing. *Information and Computation*, 205(2), 125–198.

Salaun, G., Bultan, T., & Roohi, N. (2011). Realizability of choreographies using process algebra encodings. *IEEE Transactions on Services Computing*, 99, 1.

van der Aalst, W. M. P., Lohmann, N., Massuthe, P., Stahl, C., & Wolf, K. (2010). Multiparty contracts: Agreeing and implementing interorganizaitonal processes. *The Computer Journal*, 53(1), 90–106.

Zongyan, Q., Xiangpeng, Z., Chao, C., & Hongli, Y. (2007). Towards the theoretical foundation of choreography. In *WWW'07*, (pp. 973–982). ACM Press.

Section 2
Context–Aware Adaptation

Chapter 4
Reusing Services through Context–Aware Discovery and Adaptation in Pervasive Systems

Javier Cubo
University of Málaga, Spain

Ernesto Pimentel
University of Málaga, Spain

ABSTRACT

Reusing of software entities, such as components or services, to develop software systems has matured in recent years. However, it has not become standard practice yet, since using pre-existing software requires the selection, composition, adaptation, and evolution of prefabricated software parts. Recent research approaches have independently tackled the discovery, composition, or adaptation processes. On the one hand, the discovery process aims at discovering the most suitable services for a request. On the other hand, the adaptation process solves, as automatically as possible, mismatch cases which may be given at the different interoperability levels among interfaces by generating a mediating adaptor based on an adaptation contract. In this chapter, the authors present the DAMASCo framework, which focuses on composing services in mobile and pervasive systems accessed through their public interfaces, by means of context-aware discovery and adaptation. DAMASCo has been implemented and evaluated on several examples.

INTRODUCTION

The increased usage of mobile and portable devices has given rise over the last few years to a new market of mobile and pervasive applications (Wang et al., 2007). These applications may be executed on either mobile computers (laptops, notebooks, tablet PCs, etc.), or wireless hand-held devices (PDAs -Personal Digital Assistants-, smart phones, etc.), or embedded systems (on-board computer, household appliances, intelligent buildings, etc.), or even on sensors or RFID tags. Their main goal is to provide connectivity and services at all time, adapting and monitoring when required

DOI: 10.4018/978-1-4666-2089-6.ch004

and improving the user experience. These systems are different to traditional distributed computing systems. On the one hand, a mobile system is able to change location allowing the communication via mobile devices. This results in some new problems which need to be resolved (connectivity, bandwidth, local resources, etc.). On the other hand, a pervasive application attempts to create an ambient intelligence environment to make the computing part of it and its enabling technologies essentially transparent.

Context-aware computing (Dargie, 2009) covers all the topics related to the building of systems which are sensitive to their context (location, identity, time and activity), by adapting their behaviour at run-time according to the changing conditions of the environment, as well as those of user preferences or privileges (Schilit el al., 1994). Such computing is incorporated into mobile and pervasive systems, with the inclusion of certain context-awareness features. One of the main features of context information is its dynamism. Thus, context-aware applications should support a high-level of adaptation in the values that define the context information. Adaptations may be as varied as the information related to the context. For example, a context-aware mobile device which detects that the user is in a meeting might vibrate instead of sounding. An application running on a PDA could adjust the level of screen brightness according to ambient light. An application that requires a server could make a cache of data to address the connection loss related to the wireless networks.

Developing real-world mobile and pervasive systems taking into account all the aforementioned concerns is extremely complex and error-prone. Therefore, it is essential to determine an effective methodology to develop software. In order to reduce efforts and costs, context-aware systems may be developed using existing Commercial-Off-The-Shelf (COTS) components or (Web) services, since reusability is considered one of the main concerns in software engineering that determines the quality of software. In contrast to the traditional approach in which software systems are implemented from scratch, COTS and services can be developed by different vendors using different languages and different computer platforms. Although the reuse of software has matured and has overcome the previously mentioned problems, it has not become standard practice yet, since reusing components or services requires the selection, composition, adaptation and evolution of prefabricated software parts. Component-Based Software Engineering (CBSE) (Szyperski, 2003), also known as Component-Based Software Development (CBSD), and Service-Oriented Architecture (SOA) (Erl, 2005) promote software reuse by selecting and assembling pre-existing software entities (COTS and services, respectively). Thus, these software development paradigms allow building fully working systems as efficient as possible in order to improve the level of software reusability.

While composing services, issues related to faults or changes arise dynamically and continuously, and they have to be detected and handled. These issues can be: (i) mismatch problems, (ii) requirement and configuration changes, (iii) network and remote system failures, and (iv) internal service errors. In this chapter, we focus mainly on avoiding mismatches. A proposal as an initial attempt to solve the third and fourth type of problems can be found in (Cubo et al., 2010; Cubo et al., 2011). Unfortunately, in most cases it is impossible to modify services in order to adapt them, since their internal implementation cannot be inspected or modified. Thus, due to the black-box nature of the services that compose the mobile and pervasive systems, they must be equipped with external interfaces giving information about service functionality. In particular, the interfaces of the constituent services of a system do not always fit one another and some features of these services may change at run-time, therefore they require a certain degree of adaptation in order to avoid mismatching during the composition. Mismatches may appear at different interoperability levels (signature, behavioural, quality of service and semantic or conceptual). Recent research approaches (Baresi et al., 2009; Brogi and Popescu, 2006; Inverardi & Tivoli, 2003; Nezhad et al., 2007; Sheng et al., 2009; Spanoudakis et al., 2007) have tackled independently the discovery, composition or adaptation processes focusing on different interoperability levels, and generating adaptors to solve mismatches. However, these works do not consider all the levels together.

Using context-aware, semantic-based, and adaptation based on model transformation, the main goals of this work focus on discovering and adapting context-aware services and components in pervasive systems. In order to achieve these goals, this chapter presents DAMASCo, a framework for **D**iscovery, **A**daptation and **M**onitoring of Context-**A**ware **S**ervices and **Co**mponents. DAMASCo also uses dependency analysis (Cubo et al., 2010) and error recovery (Cubo et al., 2011) mechanisms in order to address the service monitoring, but this is out of scope of this chapter. DAMASCo combines efforts to address the four interoperability levels together, modelling services and components with interfaces constituted by context and semantic information, a signature, and a behavioural description. We advocate the extension of traditional signature level interfaces with context information (service level), protocol descriptions maintaining conditions (behavioural level), and semantic representation instead of a syntactic one (semantic level). Hence, we propose software adaptation mechanisms to generate adaptation contracts automatically, which consider all the possible mismatch situations solved in our service discovery process. Therefore, we can generate a whole adaptor service that addresses all the interoperability levels, by considering not only the signature and behaviour levels of the services, but also the quality of service and semantic levels. Furthermore, most of the approaches dedicated to model-based composition and adaptation are independent of the implementation framework, and few of them relate with existing programming

languages and platforms, such as Common Object Request Broker Architecture (CORBA) (Gaspari and Zavattaro, 1999), Component Object Model (COM) / Distributed COM (DCOM) (Inverardi and Tivoli, 2003), Business Process Execution Language (BPEL) (Brogi and Popescu, 2006), and Service Component Architecture (SCA) (Nezhad et al., 2007). In this chapter, we illustrate the need to support the variability of the adaptation process in context-aware pervasive systems through a real-world case study, where software entities (components or services) are implemented using the platform Windows Workflow Foundation (WF) (Scribner, 2007) developed by Microsoft. It belongs to the .NET Framework 3.5 and is supported by Visual Studio 2008, interacting with Windows Communication Foundation (WCF) (Sharp, 2007) to define component and service interfaces. We have focused on WF because it is a useful and interesting alternative to BPEL, supporting behavioural descriptions of components and services using workflows (business processes), that has not been studied yet for this purpose. Nevertheless, we have also validated our proposal using BPEL. In addition, WF is increasingly prevalent in the software engineering community, and as a long term purpose, we want our proposal to benefit the largest number of people possible, who use the .NET Framework in private companies around the world.

We apply a model transformation process to extract transition systems specified in our interface model from WF services. These specifications are used to discover the most suitable services with respect to a client's request, and tackle verification, composition and adaptation. Then, we generate an adaptor specification, which is transformed into its corresponding WF adaptor service with the purpose of interacting with all the WF services of the system, thereby avoiding mismatch problems. Therefore, our model transformation process, according to the Model-Driven Architecture (MDA)[1], takes a source model (BPEL or WF) and produces a target model (in our case transition systems), and vice versa. Our whole process consists of a set of steps which have been implemented as a set of tools constituting the DAMASCo framework, which is integrated in the toolbox ITACA (Cámara et al., 2009). ITACA (Integrated Toolbox for the Automatic Composition and Adaptation of Web Services) is a toolbox under implementation at the Software Engineering Group of the University of Málaga (GISUM) for the automatic composition and adaptation of services accessed through their behavioural interfaces. The toolbox fully covers a generative adaptation process which goes from behavioural model extraction from existing service interface descriptions, to the final adaptor implementation.

The rest of the chapter is structured as follows. Section Background describes a background and compares our approach to related works to illustrate the need of our proposal. In Section Context-Aware Discovery and Adaptation our whole proposal is described in detail. Section Evaluation and Discussion shows the benefits of our approach by evaluating and validating it in several examples. Finally, in Sections Future Research Directions and Conclusions, we end the chapter with future works and conclusions of this work.

BACKGROUND

This section provides a background to the different software development paradigms, languages and models used in DAMASCo. Furthermore, while we present this background we emphasise the main contributions of DAMASCo when compared to current research efforts that address the problems tackled in our framework, specifically with respect to discovery and adaptation of context-aware services. We first give foundations and benefits of using the software development paradigms CBSE and SOA, and introduce the WF platform. Then, we describe a background and related work related to semantic-based context-aware service

discovery, composition and adaptation based on model transformation.

CBSE and SOA Paradigms

DAMASCo focuses on semantic-based discovery and adaptation related to context-aware mobile and pervasive systems, where devices and applications dynamically find and use components and services from their environment. These systems constitute enterprise applications, which are increasingly being developed using COTS components or Web services. On the one hand, COTS component middleware can be checked out from a component repository, and assembled into a target software system. Component middleware encapsulates sets of services in order to provide reusable building blocks that can be used to develop enterprise applications more rapidly and robustly than those built entirely from scratch. There are many examples of COTS component middleware, such as CORBA[2], COM and DCOM (Microsoft, 2010), Sun Microsystem's JavaBeans and Enterprise JavaBeans (J2EE)(Sun Microsystems, 2003), and emerging Web Services middleware, such as .NET (Microsoft, 2009). On the other hand, the goal of SOA is to achieve loose coupling among interacting services. Software components in SOA are services based on standard protocols, which are not just encapsulation of some code from the lower layer of application. A service is a software asset of distinctive functional meaning that encapsulates a high-level business concept including contract, interfaces, implementation, business logic and data. Oriented Object Programming (OOP) (Meyer, 1998), and Aspect-Oriented Software Development (AOSD) (Filman et al., 2004) have no corresponding elements for repositories, since they deal with the relationship between objects and with aspects of concern rather than modules of software code, respectively. In SOA, service repository provides facilities to discover services and acquires all the information needed in the use of the service, as well as additional information to service contract like location, availability, Quality of Service (QoS), provider information, constraints and so on. Moreover, it is necessary to enable long term benefits and reuse. Service Bus is used to connect all participants of a SOA. In computing, an Enterprise Service Bus (ESB) (Chappel, 2004) provides foundational services for more complex architectures via an event-driven and standards-based messaging engine, and generally provides an abstraction layer on top of an implementation of an enterprise messaging system which in turn allows integration architects to exploit the value of messaging without writing code. ESB does not implement a SOA but provides the features with which one may be implemented. Although ESB is commonly believed to not be necessarily web-services based, most ESB providers now build ESBs to incorporate SOA principles and increase their sales, *e.g.*, BPEL (Andrews et al., 2005). Based on these issues, we can determine CBSE and SOA as the most appropriate software development paradigms to address the reusing of software entities in context-aware and pervasive systems. Considering that services are a kind of software component, we assume our framework deals with components as services. Therefore, we focus on SOA to detail the set of principles of governing concepts used during phases of systems development and integration, and provided by this

approach. Figure 1 (a) depicts the reference model of SOA. Service-oriented applications are addressing traditional software engineering problems, such as distribution, requirements, specification, composition, verification, monitoring, adaptation and evolution, since many software applications are developed as services for possible use through standard interfaces and messaging protocols. Services can be integrated or used by particular users, who should be able to easily add, remove or adapt services to their needs.

Moreover, different organizations may develop, deploy, and evolve services exposed to different uses. A faithful specification of service functional and non-functional properties must be made available for other parties who may search for and discover them. Systems, implemented as composite service (interfaces), must be designed to fulfill requirements that very often evolve continuously, requiring adaptation in the solution. Furthermore, such systems depend on their combined services, which, in turn, may evolve autonomously. SOA provides a mature and scalable solution to solve these issues by reducing their complexity. For all these reasons, SOA is a new paradigm to take into consideration in self-adaptive systems. One way to implement SOA is using: Web Services Description Languages (WSDL)[3] for describing and locating services, Simple Object Access Protocol (SOAP)[4] for com-

Figure 1. Service-Oriented Architecture (SOA): (a) reference model, and (b) a basic SOA with a service consumer and a service provider interacting

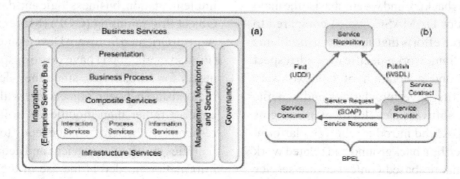

munication, Universal Description, Discovery and Integration (UDDI)[5] for service registry and discovery, and BPEL for service orchestration. Figure 1 (b) illustrates a basic service-oriented architecture. Service repository is a directory of available services which makes services easily accessible for multiple reuses. The service consumer sends a service request message to a service provider. This service provider returns a response message to the service consumer. The request and subsequent response connections are defined in services. It is obvious that SOA foundations are necessary and beneficial to the industry. However, SOA needs to be more agile and easy to model service applications. Modelling techniques, designing architectures, and implementing tools to support adaptation and evolution of the dynamic architectural aspects in these systems represent new challenges in this research field, by overcoming the limitations of existing Architectural Description Languages (ADLs) (López et al., 2008) with respect to capture the business aspects of service-oriented systems (Fiadeiro and Lopes, 2010). So far, it is difficult for business experts to model and verify their business processes. To address this, we use a model-based service-oriented architecture approach that makes the design, development, and deployment of processes more agile. Figure 2 shows the SOA layered architecture using model-based techniques

(based on IBM's SOA Solution Stack, S3 (Arsanjani et al., 2007)).

We use a model-based methodology because it is the unification of initiatives that aim to improve software development by employing high-level, domain specific, models in the implementation, integration, maintenance, and testing of software systems. This technique refers to architecture and application development driven by models that capture designs at various levels of abstraction being our model transformation process independent of the implementation. Model transformation provides a systematic and uniform view of incremental software development, making it easier to express and reason about adaptation and evolution. Since models tend to be represented using a graphical notation, MDA involves using visual-modeling languages. We adopt an expressive and user-friendly graphical notation based on transition systems, which reduces the complexity of modelling services and components, and may be represented by using the meta-model and UML profile for SOA, SoaML[6].

Windows Workflow Foundation for SOA

Windows Workflow Foundation (WF) is the programming model, engine and tools for quickly building workflow enabled applications on

Figure 2. A SOA layered architecture using model-based techniques

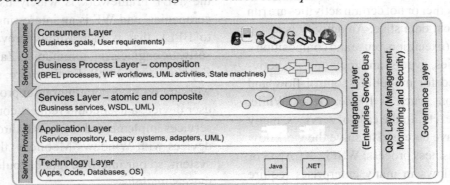

Windows (developed by Microsoft). It belongs to the .NET Framework 3.5 and is supported by Visual Studio 2008, interacting with Windows Communication Foundation (WCF) to define component and service interfaces. This section presents concepts used in WF, such as *workflow* and *activity*. A workflow is a set of activities stored as a model that describes a real-world process (software implementation of business process or logic). It is a way of describing the order of execution, and defines dependent relationships between different pieces. The main values of a workflow are: (i) transparency, (ii) flexibility, and (iii) extensibility. In addition, a workflow can be represented by means of a graph, like a flowchart, a state diagram or based on rules. WF is made up of an execution engine, rules engine, a number of activities, a number of supporting run-time services, and a designer allowing developers to design their graphical workflows on Visual Studio (Graphical debugger). The engine is designed building the workflow either as code constructs or in a declarative fashion using XAML, or even both. The engine allows alteration of the executing workflow at run-time. Figure 3 presents the WF architecture.

WF supports multiple workflow-authoring styles, such as sequential, state machine, and data-driven. The sequential style is straightforward and useful for repetitive, predictable operations that are always the same. The state machine workflow style consists of a set of event-driven states. The data-driven style relies on data to determine whether or not certain activities are run based on a local data state. An activity is a step in a workflow (execution, reuse and composition). It has properties, events, and methods. An activity is designed for modelling control flow and communications, such as IfElse, Delay, While, Send, Receive, etc. In the case of services, many approaches have emerged to solve the workflow problem or business process: WSFL, XLANG or BPEL. Workflows in many enterprises require the integration of non-serviceable legacy applica-

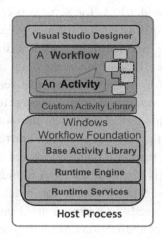

Figure 3. A Windows workflow foundation (WF) architecture

tions or even non-system human tasks, which fall beyond the scope of BPEL or any other orchestration technique applicable to SOA. With the purpose of solving this emerges WF. In WF the nature of a workflow lends itself to span across many different levels or software components, and allows the definition of workflows using any .NET-targeted language, allowing users to create workflows with previously known languages.

Therefore, for DAMASCo we have chosen WF because this platform supports behavioural descriptions of components and services using workflows (business processes). The WF platform makes the implementation of services easier thanks to its workflow-based graphical support and the automation of the code generation. In addition, the .NET Framework is widely used in many companies, and WF is an interesting alternative to BPEL that is increasingly prevalent in the software engineering community (Zapletal, 2008; Zapletal et al., 2009). Furthermore, since we are working on incorporating our approach inside a user device, a user could request components or services implemented using WF through mobile devices with Windows Mobile as the operating system, so our interface model could be used in these situations.

Semantic-Based Context-Aware Discovery

Service discovery can be defined as the ability to find out the most suitable services for a client's request, but it can become a complex task. When developing mobile and pervasive systems, it is desirable to provide semantic representation instead of only a syntactic one in order to find the most appropriate services for a specific request. In such a way, one could take advantage of this kind of discovery process in order to address most of the mismatch situations related to the four interoperability (signature, protocol, service and semantic) levels. In this section, we present the current semantic mechanisms to consider and manage the semantic representation of services, and we compare them to our proposal.

The integration of services in context-aware systems requires powerful meta-scheme, matching mechanisms supported by higher level abstractions, such as meta-models. Currently, there are different XML-based workflow platforms (Andrews et al., 2005; Scribner, 2007), but the dominant use of XML as a meta-data markup language makes the semantics of the processes ambiguous. In L platforms, the current service technology, XML-based SOA via SOAP, WSD and UDDI, only supports queries based on keywords and category. This may bring about low-precision results, as it is neither able to discover semantic capabilities of services nor be adapted to a changing environment without human intervention. However, different context and semantic information is used in real-world services to improve their features. Context-awareness enables a new class of applications in mobile and pervasive computing, providing the most relevant information to users, and capable of adapting to their situation and preferences (Schilit et al., 1994). Context information plays an important role in pervasive systems to control the scope of change, since it can help users to find nearby services, to decide the best service to use (according to the location,

connectivity, bandwidth, local resources, etc.), to control reaction of systems depending on certain situations, to find people with similar interests, and so on. Thus, a system using context information can reduce human effort in human-computer interaction. Therefore, it is essential to consider context information in the discovery of services deployed as part of mobile and pervasive applications. However, current programming technology offers only very weak support for developing context-aware applications, and new research is urgently needed to develop innovative Context-Oriented Programming (COP) mechanisms (Nierstrasz et al., 2009).

Furthermore, service discovery mechanisms need to overcome the heterogeneity of applications and devices, and provide services with compatible capabilities to user requirements. One of the main challenges in CBSE and SOA is to provide semantic representation instead of only a syntactic one. There are different languages that focus on Semantic Web technologies, Web Ontology Language for Services (OWL-S)[7], Web Services Modeling Ontology (WSMO) (Lausen et al., 2006), METEOR-S (Patil et al., 2004), or Semantic Annotations for WSDL and XML Schema (SAWSDL)[8]. W3C recommends the use of OWL-S to capture the semantic description of services. OWL-S is built on the Ontology Web Language (OWL)[9], which proposes a formal representation of a set of concepts within a domain by capturing the relationships between those concepts. This is called an ontology and is expressed in a machine-readable format that enables software entities (services, components, and so on) to understand and grasps the concepts within the domain. OWL is currently the de facto standard for constructing ontologies. Hence, operation profiles of a signature refer to OWL-S concepts with their arguments and their associated semantics. By using OWL-S ontologies, the matching process can perform inferences on the hierarchy of the ontologies leading to the recognition of semantic matches despite their syntactic differences. An ontology consists of classes, relationships and attributes, and provides a shared and common understanding of a particular domain. Figure 4 depicts a fragment of a vehicle ontology. Classes CAR and TRUCK are subclasses of VEHICLE (*i.e.*, VEHICLE subsumes CAR and TRUCK). Relationships can be defined as that AUDI A8 is a successor of AUDI A6.

Related Work: Service Discovery

Service discovery is one of the major challenges in service-oriented computing, thus many attempts are currently being studied. Service discovery mechanisms need to overcome the heterogeneity of applications and devices, and provide services with compatible capabilities to the user requirements.

Ideally, these capabilities should be selected on the basis of the signature, behavioural, service and semantic levels considering context information. To the best of our knowledge, the current efforts deal with these levels separately, except (Spanoudakis, 2007) which supports service discovery based on structural and behavioural service models, as well as quality constraints and contextual information. Compared to our framework, in (Spanoudakis, 2007), the authors do not consider a domain ontology for the signature matching, but they are compared by using a sub-graph isomorphism algorithm which the authors have developed. In addition, they convert BPEL service specifications in state machines used to check whether the behaviour of these services match with each other. We define a context-aware service model based on transition systems that is able to represent not only BPEL specifications, but also business processes defined in other industrial platforms, such as WF workflows. Furthermore, our context-aware service discovery process considers context information and performs semantic matchmaking based on ontologies by comparing context information, operation names, arguments and types, and protocol compatibility in order to select the most suitable services. Using context-

Figure 4. A fragment of a vehicle ontology

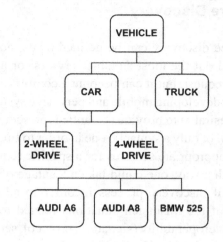

aware information, the topics related to the building of systems which are sensitive to their context is covered. In addition, the advantage of using protocol compatibility is that the services selected not only match at the signature and semantic levels, but also at the behavioural level. We also take advantage of the result of the discovery process to obtain automatically a set of correspondences from the interfaces corresponding to the services involved in an interaction.

A few approaches have been proposed to address protocol compatibility in service discovery. Hameurlain (Hameurlain, 2007) proposes a framework where are defined relations of compatibility and substitutability of component protocols depending on the context (environment) by means of Petri nets. In (Wang and Krishnan, 2006), the authors introduce a Simple Component Interface Language (SCIL) in order to implement a framework that supports semantic description and selection of components by checking their behavioural compatibility. Han *et al.* (Han et al., 2008) proposes a discovery process based on semantic and business process matchmaking. Compared to these works, the whole discovery process which will be presented in our approach, combines all the efforts: improves (Hameurlain, 2007) by adding semantic matching techniques, and (Wang and Krishnan, 2006; Han et al., 2008) by taking context information into account.

On the other hand, a major effort in service discovery is being promoted by the Web Service technologies, which aim at enriching service descriptions with semantic and behavioural information by using ontologies. Many semantic matchmaking algorithms, focusing on the matching of operation names and parameters, have been proposed based on the service profile and the service model of METEOR-S, WSMO or OWL-S to compose services (Aggarwal et al., 2004; Benatallah et al., 2003; Broens et al. 2004; Brogi et al., 2008; Keller et al., 2005; Klusch et al., 2006; Li and Horrocks, 2003; Mokhtar et al., 2006; Paolucci, 2002). These works consider neither context information in the semantic matching nor the service behaviour, except (Brogi et al., 2008) that is capable of suggesting parts of additional services as the existing ones cannot satisfy a query.

Summing up the comparison with the previously described service discovery proposals, DAMASCo goes further by tackling the four interoperability levels. That comes from our discovery process, which finds the most appropriate compatible service interfaces according to their context information, semantic matching at the signature level by using matching patterns defined in (Paolucci, 2002), and behavioural compatibility based on the deadlock-freeness notion. In addition, the candidate service interfaces are ranked according to the semantic matching.

Context-Oriented Composition and Adaptation

Once services have been discovered, it is necessary to determine that the services are free of inconsistences in order to compose them correctly. Component and service composition is one of the most powerful instruments of CBSE and SOA, respectively. It allows third parties to sell their software components and developers to reuse existing ones by selecting and assembling

them in order to build a complete software system. In a traditional distributed application or in a classic Web environment, in which statically all the requests are served in the same way, the composition is straightforward. The introduction of Web-enabled hand-held devices has created the need of a more context-oriented composition in which the produced response is based on the knowledge of certain contextual information on the requesting client.

Browsers running on hand-held devices transmit contextual information by adding them in the header of their HTTP requests. They usually do this by implicitly inferring certain information directly from the device and encoding them in a custom format which may not be interpreted correctly by the invoked service. For instance, consider a request to the inbox of Google Mail[10] performed on a Nokia N95 using two different browsers: Safari and OperaMini. The back-end of Google Mail tries to contextualise the response for the requesting but the client misunderstands the request from OperaMini and responds by transmitting the default front-end, which is too large to be rendered on a mobile phone and also requires more time to be received due to its larger size. Figure 5 shows the responses of both browsers. On the left, the query submitted by Safari was contextualized correctly for a mobile phone; on the right, the back-end responded wrongly to the same query performed using OperaMini. The requests performed by Safari and OperaMini only differ in their headers, in which both browsers have included contextual information (parameters), with the idea that the Web Service would use them correctly.

If multiple services are contextualising their response using different contexts, for instance, using the keyboard layout or the browser language, the response may be inconsistent. It can also happen that two services require two different parameters but they call them by the same name. Their composition needs to distinguish between them by introducing an extra layer of complexity and

Figure 5. A fragment of a vehicle ontology

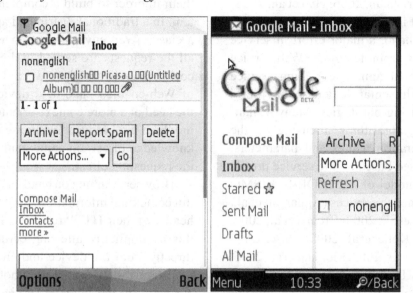

overhead to avoid inconsistencies. Therefore, before performing the process of context-aware service composition, it is necessary to check each individual service of the system to verify that these services are free of inconsistencies due to the contextual nature of the system. Taking into consideration the previous arguments, the services must be validated against a set of properties, such as determinism, state liveness, inter-communication liveness (related to request/response interactions), and non-blocking states.

Once services are checked, they can be composed. However, as we have previously mentioned, while composing services, different issues related to faults or changes arise dynamically. Therefore, adaptation techniques are required in these cases. The need to automate these adaptation tasks has driven the development of Software Adaptation (Canal et al., 2006). This discipline covers all the topics related to the management of communication between entities. It is characterised by highly dynamic runtime procedures that occur as devices and applications move from network to network, modifying or extending their behaviour, and enhancing the flexibility and maintainability

of systems. Software adaptation promotes the use of software adaptors. These are software entities capable of enabling components or services with mismatching problems to interoperate. They are automatically built from an abstract description of how mismatching can be solved, i.e., an "interface mapping" (Dumas et al., 2006) or an "adaptation contract" (Bracciali et al., 2005), which is based on the description of service interfaces. Specifically, in current mobile and pervasive systems, services are everywhere. These can be just accessed and used to fulfill basic requirements, or be composed with other services in order to build bigger systems which aim at working out complex tasks. In order to ease their reuse and enable their automatic composition, services must be equipped with rich interfaces enabling external access to their functionality. Several interoperability levels can be distinguished in interface description languages (i.e., signature, protocol, quality of service, and semantic). Composition of services is seldom achieved seamlessly because mismatch may occur at any of the different interoperability levels and must be solved. Software adaptation is the only way to compose non-intrusively black-

Figure 6. A simple example of adaptation

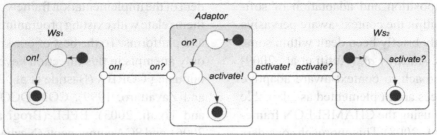

box components or services with mismatching interfaces by automatically generating mediating adaptor services or components that address all the interoperability levels. They would be obtained by means of adaptation contracts which consider all the possible mismatch situations detected in the service discovery process. An adaptor is a third-party service that is in charge of coordinating all the components or services involved in the system with respect to a set of interactions defined in a contract. Consequently, all the services communicate through the adaptor as illustrated in Figure 6, where a service Ws_1 wants to activate a Ws_2. The contract for this simple example is given by the vector $<ws_1: on!, ws_2: activate?>$. We emphasize that the adaptor interacts with the services using the same name of messages but the reversed directions, *e.g.* communication between *on!* in ws_1 and *on?* in the adaptor. Furthermore, the adaptor always starts a set of interactions formalised in a vector by the receptions (*on?*), and next handles the emissions (*activate!*).

Related Work: Service Composition and Adaptation

Deriving adaptors is a complicated task since, in order to avoid undesirable behaviours, the different behavioural constraints of the composition must be respected, and the correct execution order of the messages exchanged must be preserved while mismatch situations are corrected.

So far, many adaptation approaches have assumed interfaces described by signatures (operation names and types) and behaviours (interaction protocols). Describing protocol in service interfaces is essential because erroneous executions or deadlock situations may occur if the designer does not consider them while building the composite service. We compare our framework DAMASCo with related works in software composition and adaptation, especially those which focus on reusing components or services and on tackling the interoperability issues which exist at the different levels of component interaction. We also present works based on model transformation, thereby relating their approaches to existing programming languages and platforms.

First, related to the consideration of context changes in the composition and adaptation, context-aware computing is concerned with the design and implementation of applications which are able to modify their functionality depending on changing conditions of the environment and the user. Many authors have studied context-aware computing, and have built pervasive applications (Autili et al., 2009; Mokhtar et al., 2006; Nicoara and Alonso, 2005) to demonstrate the usefulness of this technology. There have even been significant achievements in the architectural support of context-aware applications (Chen et al., 2003; Salber et al., 1999). Ben Mokhtar *et al.* (Mokhtar et al., 2006) is an interesting proposal in this field. However, their approach does not consider the behavioural compatibility, so deadlock-freeness cannot be checked. However, at the behavioural level, the composition and adaptation of software entities within the context-aware pervasive systems has only briefly been dealt within some of these works. Autili *et al.* (Autili et al., 2009) present an approach to context-aware adaptive services. Services are implemented as adaptable components by using the CHAMELEON framework (Autili et al., 2008). This approach considers context information at design time, but the context changes at run-time are not evaluated.

DAMASCo proposes a model based on transition systems, extended with value passing, context and semantic information and conditions, which has not yet been studied in previous works (Cubo et al., 2007). We consider context changes not only at design-time, but also at run-time. That comes from the execution of the operational semantics of our service model that allows the continuous evaluation at run-time of dynamic context attributes. In addition, in our framework, the sending of context information is user-independent, as are the services which have to infer that information from the HTTP header of the SOAP message.

Second, most of the many approaches tackle model-based adaptation at signature and behavioural levels, and aim at generating adaptors which are used to solve mismatch in a non-intrusive way (Allen and Garlan, 1997; Autili et al., 2007; Bastide et al., 2000, Brogi and Popescu, 2006; Canal, 2008; Gaspari and Zavattaro, 1999; Inverardi and Tivoli, 2003, Nezhad et al., 2007; Yellin and Strom, 1997). Compared to these proposals, DAMASCo matches different name messages using correspondences of our adaptation contract, which is useful within context-aware systems. These approaches do not use any mapping language for the adaptor specification, so the adaptor is restricted to possible non-deadlocking behaviours (Inverardi and Tivoli, 2003). The notation we have proposed allows us to deal with possibly realistic and complex adaptation scenarios and it is possible to address behavioural adaptation.

Finally, most of these approaches are independent of the implementation framework, and few of them relate with existing programming languages and platforms. To the best of our knowledge, the only attempts in this direction have been carried out using CORBA (Bastide et al., 2000; Gaspari and Zavattaro, 1999), COM/DCOM (Inverardi and Tivoli, 2003), BPEL (Brogi and Popescu, 2006), and SCA components (Nezhad et al., 2007). Bastide et al. (Bastide et al., 2000) show that the OMG's style to specify services in CORBA does not guarantee interoperable and substitutable implementations. Gaspari and Zavattaro (Gaspari and Zavattaro, 1999) illustrate how CORBA models for requesting invocation can be mapped into a message passing architecture using the base of a process algebra. The work presented by Brogi and Popescu (Brogi and Popescu, 2006) outlines a methodology for the automated generation of adaptors capable of solving behavioural mismatch between BPEL processes. They use YAWL workflow (van der Aalst et al., 2005) as an intermediate language, and once the adaptor workflow is generated, they use lock analysis techniques to check if a full adaptor has been generated or only a partial one (some interaction scenarios cannot be resolved). Our adaptation approach may reorder messages in between services when required (Cubo et al., 2007). This ability is needed to ensure a correct interaction when communicating entities have messages which are not ordered as required. Inverardi and Tivoli (Inverardi and Tivoli, 2003) tackle the automatic synthesis of connectors in COM/DCOM environments, by guaranteeing deadlock-free interactions among components. Compared to this proposal, we may match different name messages using our correspondences, which is very useful within context-aware systems. In addition, this approach does not use any mapping language for the adaptor specification, so restricts the adaptor to possible non-deadlocking. Finally, Benatallah et al. (Nezhad et al., 2007) present techniques, as well as a tool providing semi-automated support for identification and resolution of mismatch between service interfaces and protocols, and generate adaptation behavioural specifications. They deal with data, and base on SCA architecture implementing the services and the generated adapter as SCA components.

In general, in comparison to the aforementioned works, we focus on modelling the behavioural composition, not only preventing mismatch problems, but also taking into account context changes and semantic matching in order to control states of inconsistence and to relate message names even when their signatures do not match. DAMASCo performs this solution, by generating a set of correspondences among the services of an interaction, which will be used as adaptation contract from which a third-party adaptor can be generated.

CONTEXT-AWARE DISCOVERY AND ADAPTATION

Service discovery and adaptation are two relevant paradigms in systems developed by assembling reusable software services accessed through their public interfaces. In this section, we present the discovery and adaptation processes of DAMASCo in order to compose reusing software entities, solving the possible mismatches or incompatibilities.

Motivating Example: On-Line Booking System

To illustrate our proposal, we describe an On-line Booking System (OBS) consisting of clients and a service repository. Clients can perform different requests; they can book a restaurant and/or a taxi by means of either a mobile device, a personal computer or a laptop. We assume the service repository contains components named Restaurant, Restaurant Database (or simply RestDB) and Taxi.

Figure 7 shows the interaction between the Client and the different Services offered by the system.

To facilitate the comprehension, we assume the Service repository contains services named Restaurant, which includes a RestDB (a restaurant database), and Taxi. Therefore, the Restaurant service is made up of two interfaces, i.e., Restaurant and RestDB service interfaces, which really can be handled as independent services. When a user executes several requests simultaneously or a reasonable number of users make requests concurrently, instances of the requested components are generated for each request. The system considers the context information given by the client, which is not sent explicitly, since components infer it from the client request (through the HTTP header of SOAP messages (Cubo et al., 2009)).

On the one hand, the Restaurant component can receive a client request to find restaurants close to a particular address, taking into account the context information related to the client privileges. We assume the system accepts two client profiles which defines the client privileges: (i) "VIP" refers to clients with a certain priority (memberships paying a fee to access to the system), or (ii) "Guest", i.e., regular clients. Depending on the privileges of a particular client, the list of restaurants returned will be different. Once the client knows the restaurants in the vicinity of that address, he/she can book one of them. The Restaurant component uses the Restaurant Database (RestDB) component to check whether the selected restaurant has a table available for a given date and a number of persons. After these interactions, the Restaurant component may receive a booking message and send an acknowledgement back. On the other hand, the Taxi component receives a client request to book a taxi, with a destination address and the context information related to the client location and his/her privileges (both inferred from the client request). The client will book a taxi only if the price does not exceed a limit amount, and he/she can either pay on reservation or later on. In the

Figure 7. On-line booking system (OBS)

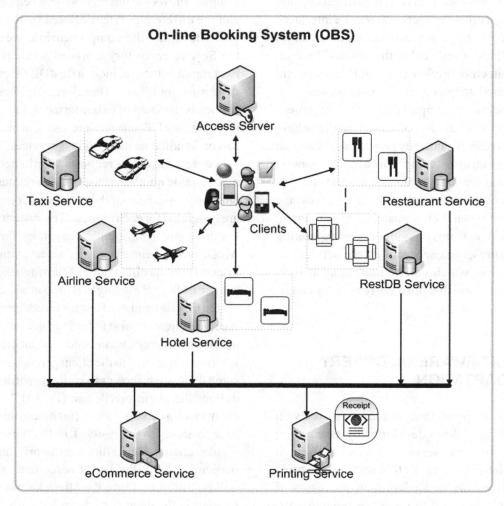

case where the client pays the taxi immediately, the Taxi component will send a receipt in the correct format depending on the context information corresponding to the client device (mobile or PC/laptop), and the client language.

This case study corresponds to a context-aware pervasive system in which the client location and profile can change at run-time. Depending on such variations, the system must adapt to work correctly in any situation. For the sake of comprehension, in the remainder of this article we focus on a single session which corresponds to the connection and use of the system by one client. An example

handling any number of sessions can be derived from our simplified version, generating instances of the requested components.

DAMASCo Architecture

We focus on avoiding mismatches related to the four interoperability levels. Based on CBSE, SOA and software adaptation, we combine efforts to tackle these levels together. We model services with interfaces constituted by context and semantic information, signatures, and protocol descriptions. We advocate the extension of traditional signature

Figure 8. DAMASCo architecture

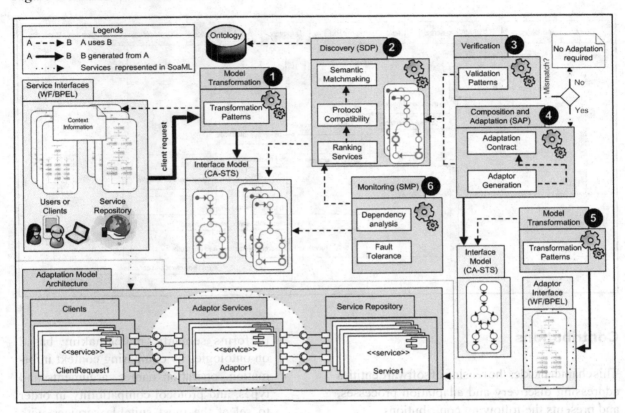

level interfaces with context information (signature and service levels), protocol descriptions with conditions (behavioural level), and semantic representation instead of only a syntactic one (semantic level). We also address the third and fourth type of errors related to dynamic faults by applying fault tolerance, although this is not described in this chapter (it is out of scope).

Our whole process consists of a set of processes constituting the DAMASCo architecture (Cubo and Pimentel, 2011), as shown in Figure 8 (detailed below). We focus on systems composed of a service repository, users (clients requesting services)[11], and a shared domain ontology.

The different elements of DAMASCo architecture have been implemented in Python as a set of tools which constitute a framework. We use throughout this section an on-line booking system as running example, consisting of clients and a service repository. Clients can perform different requests: book a restaurant, a taxi, a flight, and so on. This case study corresponds to a context-aware pervasive system in which certain context information related to the client (location, privileges, device or language) can change at runtime. Depending on such variations, the system must adapt to work correctly in any situation. Since our approach focuses on solving this kind of mismatch and/or fault situations, it is very appropriate to use our framework in order to work correctly this system. Let us consider a client performs a taxi request. Figure 9 details the process at an architectural point of view, so it depicts how after (a) services have been registered, the framework's elements interact when (b) the client performs the request from either a mobile device (PDA or smartphone) or a laptop, being executed the full process.

Figure 9. Dynamics of the DAMASCo framework

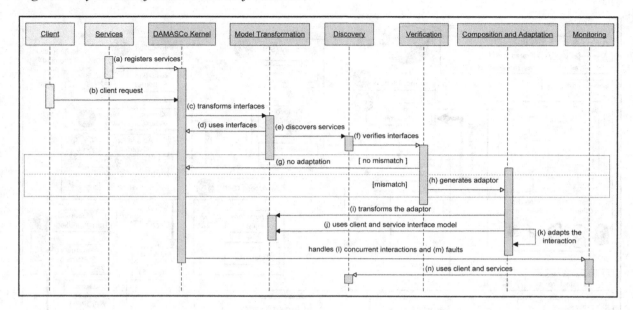

Contributions

This chapter tackles the reusing of software entities addressing discovery and adaptation processes, and presents the following contributions:

1. We define an interface model based on extended transition systems by considering context information and semantic representation, and supporting conditions to control the execution of the service protocols according to certain changes at run-time. Users can execute several requests simultaneously (concurrent interactions), and the services can be instantiated several times.

2. We propose a model transformation approach that extracts transition systems from service interfaces implemented in existing programming languages and platforms, and vice versa. This is done because of the capability of representing specifications of real-world services defined in different industrial platforms of our interface model.

3. We develop a service discovery process, which considers context information and

performs semantic matchmaking based on ontologies by comparing context information, operation names, arguments and types, and protocol compatibility in order to select the most suitable services with respect to a client's request. Using context-aware information, the topics related to the building of systems which are sensitive to their context is covered. In addition, the advantage of using protocol compatibility is that the services selected not only match at signature, service and semantic levels, but also at behavioural level. Our process may determine if an adaptation is necessary or not considering the four interoperability levels, and it generates correspondence sets among service interfaces involved in the interaction, which will be used in the composition and adaptation process as an adaptation contract.

4. We use verification techniques to validate if the client and the services are free of inconsistencies (with respect to a set of properties) by means of symbolic model checking.

5. We design a service composition and adaptation process, which automatically obtains the

adaptation contract from the correspondence sets and the synchronous product generated in the discovery process. An adaptor service can be generated considering not only the signature and behaviour levels of the services, but also some issues of the quality of service (context-aware information) and semantic (relationships between concepts of a ontology) levels. Therefore, our proposal generates an adaptor addressing all the interoperability levels.

Modeling Context-Aware Services

Different automata-based (de Alfaro and Henzinger, 2001) or Petri net-based (Luo et al., 2006) models, process algebras, such as CSS (Milner, 1980), or transition systems like Labelled Transition System (LTS) (Magee et al., 1999), can be used to describe behavioural interfaces. We chose transition systems to specify services in mobile and pervasive systems, because they are simple, especially suited to favour user-friendliness, and to make the graphical specification of interfaces possible, by providing a good level of abstraction to tackle discovery, verification, composition, or adaptation issues (Canal et al., 2008; Foster et al., 2006; Xu et al., 2004), which are the main goals of DAMASCo. As we already discussed throughout Section Background, in mobile and pervasive systems, it is essential to consider context information in the discovery and composition of services deployed as part of mobile and pervasive applications, since using a non-contextual approach, message correspondences are fixed, which means that any client's request is always associated to the same target message. However, current transition systems, such as LTS, Symbolic Transition System (STS) (Canal et al., 2008), Symbolic Transition System (STG) (Hennessy and Lin, 1995), do not offer support for capturing and handling context information. Therefore, a new model is needed to describe correctly this kind of systems.

In order to overcome this limitation, we have defined a new interface model, called Context-Aware Symbolic Transition System (CA-STS), based on STG, considering value passing, maintaining guards as boolean expressions, and taking context information into account. In this new extended model, conditions allow the control of the execution of the service protocols according to certain changes at run-time, by specifying how applications should react (*e.g.*, to context changes). Furthermore, we can model concurrent executions in the client side (several requests simultaneously) without the user having to continuously send the new context values, since automatically the system will infer them and return changing results according to the context changes. In addition, taking advantage of using the new model that supports a whole signature (context information, operation names, arguments and types), we specify not only syntactic information of services, but also semantic descriptions in order to compare elements of the signature with respect to their semantic matching. Therefore, the CA-STS model combines efforts to tackle the mismatch situations at the signature, behavioural and semantic levels, and even to address the service level by means of context information (non-functional property).

Service Interface Model

In our approach, a system consists of context-aware clients and services. We assume that client and service interfaces are specified using context profiles, signatures and protocols. Context profiles define information which may change according to the client preferences and service environment. Signatures correspond to operations profiles. Protocols are represented using transition systems. CA-STS client and services can interact according to the operational semantics we will define below.

A *context* is defined as *"the information that can be used to characterize the situation of an entity. An entity is a person, place, or object that is considered relevant to the interaction between a user and an application including the user and the application themselves"* (Dey and Abowd, 2000). Context information can be represented in different ways and can be classified in four main categories (Kouadri and Hirsbrunner 2003; Schilit et al 1994): (i) user context: role, preferences, language, calendar, social situation or privileges, (ii) device/computing context: network connectivity, device capabilities or server load, (iii) time context: current time, day, year, month or season, and (iv) physical context: location, weather or temperature. For our purpose, we only need a simple representation where contexts in both clients and services are defined by *context attributes* with associated values. In addition, we differentiate between static context attributes (*e.g.*, role, preferences, day, ...), and dynamic ones (*e.g.*, network connectivity, current time, location, privileges, temperature, ...). Dynamic attributes can change continuously at run-time, so they have to be dynamically evaluated during the service composition. Finally, both clients and services are characterized by public (*e.g.*, weather, temperature, season, ...), and private (*e.g.*, personal data, bandwidth, local resources, ...) context attributes. Thus, we represent and gather the service context information by using a *context profile*.

Definition 1 (Context Profile): A Context Profile is a set of tuples (CA;CV;CK;CT), where: CA is a context attribute (or simply context) with its corresponding value CV, CK determines if CA is static or dynamic, and CT indicates if CA is public or private.

For instance, *(priv, Guest, dynamic, public)*, indicate that *priv* is a public and dynamic context which corresponds to user privileges with *Guest* as value.

Definition 2 (Signature): A Signature Σ is a set of operation profiles. This set is a disjoint union of provided and required operations. An operation profile is the name of an operation, together with its (input/output) argument types (possibly empty), and its return types (possibly empty):

$$op: ti_1 * \ldots * ti_n \rightarrow to_1 * \ldots * to_m$$

Provided operations implement the functionality of the service and are thus offered to other services in the environment for invocation, whereas required operations are those that the services need to invoke in order to fulfill its purpose.

A *protocol* is represented using a STG, considering value passing, maintaining guards as boolean expressions, and taking context information into account, *i.e.*, the CA-STS model. Conditions specify how applications should react (*e.g.*, to context changes). We take advantage of using ontologies described in a specific domain to capture and manage the semantic information of the services in a system by comparing concepts, such as context information, operation names, arguments and types. In such a way, we can determine the relationship among the different concepts that belong to that domain. Let us introduce the notion of variable, expression, and label required by our CA-STS protocol. We consider two kinds of variables, those representing regular variables and those corresponding to context attributes (named context variables). In order to distinguish between them, we will mark the context variables with the symbol "~" over the specific variable. Context variables may be static or dynamic. Our model handles the static context variables as regular variables, since they are not changing dynamically. An expression is defined as a variable or a term constructed with a function symbol f (an identifier) applied to a sequence of expressions, $i \in f(F_1; \ldots; F_n)$, F_i being expressions.

Definition 3 (CA-STS label): A label corresponding to a transition of a CA-STS is either an internal action (tau) or a tuple (B;M;D;F) representing an event, where: B is a condition (represented by a boolean expression and used to manage both conditional choices and context changes), M is the operation name, D is the direction of operations (! and ? represent emission and reception, respectively), and F is a list of expressions if the operation corresponds to an emission, or a list of variables if the operation is a reception (in both cases including regular variables/terms or context variables/values).

Definition 4 (CA-STS Protocol): A Context-Aware Symbolic Transition System (CA-STS) Protocol is a tuple (A; S; I; Fc; T), where: A is an alphabet which corresponds to the set of CA-STS labels associated to transitions (set of events), S is a set of states, I $\in$ S is the initial state, Fc $\leq$ S are correct final states (only final states free of deadlocks are considered), and T $\leq$ S × A × S is the transition function whose elements (s1; a; s2) $\in$ T are usually denoted by $S_1 \xrightarrow{a} S_2$.

Finally, CA-STS interface is constituted by a tuple *(CP; SI; P)*, where: *CP* is a context profile, and *SI* is the signature of the CA-STS protocol *P*. At the user level, client and service interfaces can be specified by using:

- Context information into XML files for context profiles. Here, we assume context information is inferred by means of the client's requests (HTTP header of SOAP messages), in such a way that as a change occurs the new value of the context attribute is automatically sent to the corresponding service.
- IDL and WSDL descriptions are respectively used in component-based frameworks (*e.g.*, .NET or J2EE) and in service-oriented platforms (*e.g.*, BPEL or WF) for signatures. Specifically, in WSDL, services are defined as collection of ports. A port includes the set of operation profiles supported. In addition, each operation may contain a specific set of input and output messages carrying the arguments and return values of the operation, respectively.
- Business processes defined in industrial platforms, such as abstract BPEL or abstractions of WF workflows (Cubo et al., 2007b), for protocols. We also consider

processes (clients and services) implemented as business processes which provide the WSDL and protocol descriptions.

Figure 10 shows the interface model obtention from service platforms, as we will explain further. In our model, both client and services consist of a set of interfaces, since we assume they have several protocols with their corresponding signatures, and a context profile for each one. For instance, in our case study related to OBS (previously presented), a client may perform two different requests. Hence, as depicted in Figure 19, the client consists of two interfaces: one for the Client-Restaurant request *CR = (CPCR; SICR; PCR)* (left side) and the other one for the Client-Taxi request *CT = (CPCT ; SICT ; PCT)* (right side). In the Client-Restaurant request, *CPCR* refers to the context information related to the privileges of the user (dynamic context attribute, *priv*), SICR is formed by all the operation profiles, such as *CR: lcr$_1$ = searchRest!address: string; priv: Tpriv* (*CR* may be used as an identifier for Client-Restaurant request interface), and *PCR* is the protocol which indicates the behaviour of the CA-STS. For example, *lcr$_1$* (label identifier) means that a client with the context information related to privileges *priv* issues an emission looking for a restaurant in a specific *address* (data term), and then this client receives a list of restaurants (regular variable) close to that address *CR: lcr$_2$ = getList?list: Tlist*, and so on. It is worth mentioning we assume the context attribute *priv* is implicitly inferred from the HTTP header of SOAP message, which makes our system more independent, since the user does not have to provide such context information. Initial and final states are depicted in CA-STSs using bullet arrows and hollow states, respectively.

Our proposal is suitable for synchronous systems where clients interact with composite service interfaces (client/server model), such as mobile systems. We adopt a synchronous and binary communication model (as it will be explained in

Figure 10. Interface model obtention from service platforms

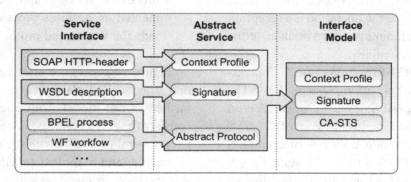

the next section). Clients can execute several protocols simultaneously, *i.e.*, concurrent interactions. Client and service protocols can be instantiated several times.

Model Transformation Process

To perform the service discovery, composition and adaptation, we first need to define a textual notation to abstract and formalise services implemented in a specific platform, which in this case is the WF platform. Second, we define our model transformation process.

Abstraction of WF Workflows: To illustrate the motivating example, we use a representative kernel of the WF activities, namely `Code`, `Terminate`, `Receive`, `Send`, `Sequence`, `IfElse`, `While`, and `Listen` with `EventDriven` activities, that are general enough to describe any service. In Table 1, we formalise the textual grammar defined for the WF activities considered in DAMASCo, which abstracts several implementation details. Our grammar considers as input textual workflows (defined in XML files) corresponding to the graphical description of the WF workflows, with WF activities *A*, where *Id* are service identifiers, *Op* are operations (activity names), I, I_i (inputs), O, O_i (outputs) are parameters of activities, and C, C_i are boolean conditions.

The WF platform is capable of developing workflows in different scenarios, from simple sequential ones to realistic and complex state machine-based workflows involving human interaction. The programming languages available in the platform are Visual Basic and C#. Our examples have been implemented in C#.

Example - Case Study OBS: The client and services described in the case study have been implemented in the WF platform as WF workflows.

We present here part of that implementation in order to illustrate the abstraction of those WF workflows. Thus, we have designed WF workflows for the Client-Restaurant and Client-Taxi requests, and for the Restaurant, RestDB and Taxi service interfaces.

On one hand, our model assumes context information is inferred by means of the client's requests, *i.e.*, from the HTTP header of SOAP messages. Figure 11 shows the basic structure of the corresponding SOAP message.

On the other hand, WF provides a WSDL description for each WF workflow. For instance, RestDB receives a request for information about the availability of tables for a specific restaurant, date and number of people, and responds to them with a boolean that indicates whether there is a table available or not. The specification of the single operation of the RestDB interface, given as a WSDL description (Figure 12), corresponds to the following signature:

Table 1. Grammar for the abstract notation of WF workflow activities

$$
\begin{array}{lll}
\mathcal{A} ::= & \text{Code} & \textit{executes a chunk of code} \\
| & \text{Terminate} & \textit{ends a workflow's execution} \\
| & \text{Receive}(Id,Op[,O,I_1,\ldots,I_n]) & \textit{receives a msg from a component/service} \\
| & \text{Send}(Id,Op[,O_1,\ldots,O_n,I]) & \textit{sends a msg from a component/service} \\
| & \text{Sequence}(\mathcal{A}_1,\mathcal{A}_2) & \textit{executes first } \mathcal{A}_1 \textit{ and then } \mathcal{A}_2 \\
| & \text{IfElse}((C_1,\mathcal{A}_1),\ldots,(C_n,\mathcal{A}_n),\mathcal{A}_{n+1}) & \textit{executes } \mathcal{A}_i \textit{ if } C_i \textit{ is true, } \mathcal{A}_{n+1} \textit{ otherwise} \\
| & \text{While}(C,\mathcal{A}) & \textit{executes } \mathcal{A} \textit{ while } C \textit{ is true} \\
| & \text{Listen}(E_1,\ldots,E_n) & \textit{fires one of the } E_i \textit{ branches} \\
E ::= & \text{EventDriven}(\text{Receive}(Id,Op[,I_i]),\mathcal{A}) & \textit{executes } \mathcal{A} \textit{ when } Id \textit{ is received}
\end{array}
$$

Figure 11. SOAP-based XML message for the client-restaurant request

```xml
<?xml version="1.0"?>
<soap-env:Envelope xmlns:env="http://www.w3.org/2003/05/soap-envelope">
 <soap-env:Header>
  <m:searchRest>
   <m:priv>VIP</m:priv>
  </m:searchRest>
 </soap-env:Header>
 <soap-env:Body>
  ...
  <soap-env:Fault>
   ...
  </soap-env:Fault>
 </soap-env:Body>
</soap-env:Envelope>
```

```
checksendAvailability: dateTime *
string * int → bool
```

For the sake of simplicity, in Figures 13 and 14 only the WF workflows that represent the behaviour of the Client-Restaurant request, and the Restaurant and RestDB service interfaces, respectively, are shown.

The Client-Taxi request and the Taxi service interfaces have been also implemented in WF, and the business processes corresponding to them are similar to those which are depicted here.

In the WF workflows, the message names prefixed with send and receive, such as send *searchRest* and receive *getList*, represent a Send and a Receive activity, respectively. Those prefixed with code (*e.g.*, code *getList*), correspond to the execution of C# code (Code activity). The while exit book label denotes that

the client will enter in a loop (While activity) where the ifElse exit book label indicates that the client will exit if the branch condition ifElseBranch exit is true (*[list==null]*, where the restaurant list is empty), or he/she will begin the booking of a restaurant if the branch condition ifElseBranch book is true (*[list!=null]*). Conditions defined in the IfElse construct are mutually exclusive, and we assume that a limited range of their values has been previously defined for each condition. In the booking process, the client will receive either an abort (receive *abort* message), because of the unavailability of tables in the selected restaurant or an acknowledgement of the booking (receive *ack*). This is controlled by means of the Listen activity listen abort *ack* with two EventDriven activities, eventDriven *abort* and eventDriven *ack*. The activities terminate *exit* and terminate *ack* corresponding to

Figure 12. WSDL description for the RestDB service interface

```xml
<?xml version="1.0" encoding="utf-8"?>
<wsdl:definitions xmlns:soap="http://schemas.xmlsoap.org/wsdl/soap/"
targetNamespace="http://tempuri.org/">
  <wsdl:types>
    <s:schema elementFormDefault="qualified" targetNamespace="http://tempuri.org/">
      <s:element name="checksendAvailability">
        <s:complexType>
          <s:sequence>
            <s:element name="date" type="s:DateTime" />
            <s:element name="rest" type="s:String" />
            <s:element name="nbpers" type="s:Int32" />
          </s:sequence>
        </s:complexType>
      </s:element>
      <s:element name="checksendAvailabilityResponse">
        <s:complexType>
          <s:sequence>
            <s:element name="tables" type="s:Boolean" />
          </s:sequence>
        </s:complexType>
      </s:element>
    </s:schema>
  </wsdl:types>
  <wsdl:message name="checksendAvailabilitySoapIn">
    <wsdl:part name="parameters" element="tns:checksendAvailability" />
  </wsdl:message>
  <wsdl:message name="checksendAvailabilitySoapOut">
    <wsdl:part name="parameters" element="tns:checksendAvailabilityResponse" />
  </wsdl:message>
  <wsdl:portType name="RestDBSoap">
    <wsdl:operation name="checksendAvailability">
      <wsdl:input message="tns:checksendAvailabilitySoapIn" />
      <wsdl:output message="tns:checksendAvailabilitySoapOut" />
    </wsdl:operation>
  </wsdl:portType>
  <wsdl:binding name="RestDBSoap" type="tns:RestDBSoap">
    <soap:binding transport="http://schemas.xmlsoap.org/soap/http" />
    <wsdl:operation name="checksendAvailability">
      <soap:operation soapAction="http://tempuri.org/checksendAvailability" />
      <wsdl:input>
        <soap:body use="literal" />
      </wsdl:input>
      <wsdl:output>
        <soap:body use="literal" />
      </wsdl:output>
    </wsdl:operation>
  </wsdl:binding>
  <wsdl:service name="RestDB">
    <wsdl:port name="RestDBSoap" binding="tns:RestDBSoap">
      <soap:address location="http://localhost:1935/WFRestDB/RestDB.asmx" />
    </wsdl:port>
  </wsdl:service>
</wsdl:definitions>
```

Figure 13. WF workflow corresponding to the client-restaurant request

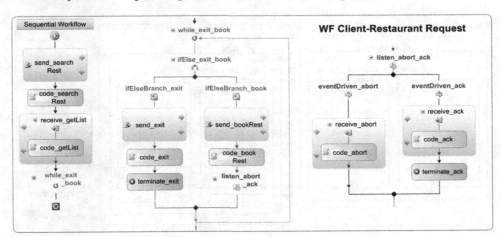

Figure 14. WF workflows corresponding to the restaurant and RestDB service interfaces

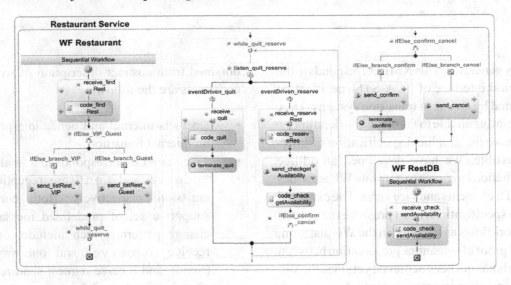

a `Terminate` activity, conclude the client session. Figure 15 shows a simplified WF workflow specification for the RestDB service interface.

To illustrate our textual notation, we focus on a part of the WF workflow corresponding to the Client-Restaurant request in Exhibit 1, which includes different WF constructs.

Extracting CA-STSs from WF Services: CA-STSs are used as an abstraction to focus on behavioural composition issues by describing service interfaces in a standard notation. As it was shown

in the process shown in Figure 8, these CA-STSs are automatically generated from the WF services.

For each WF service, our model transformation process parses the three XML files corresponding to its context information (remember that we assume this information is extracted implicitly from the HTTP header of SOAP messages), WSDL description, and WF workflow. A new XML file containing the information about its context profile, signature, and CA-STS protocol is auto-

Figure 15. XML based on the WF workflow description for the RestDB service interface

```
<SequentialWorkflowActivity x:Class="Restaurant.WFRestDB" x:Name="WFRestDB">
        <ns0:ReceiveActivity.WorkflowServiceAttributes>
                <ns0:WorkflowServiceAttributes Name="WFRestDB"/>
        </ns0:ReceiveActivity.WorkflowServiceAttributes>
        <ns0:ReceiveActivity x:Name="receive_checksendAvailability"
                CanCreateInstance="True">
                <ns0:ReceiveActivity.ServiceOperationInfo>
                        <ns0:OperationInfo Name="checksendAvailability"
                        ContractName="IRestDB">
                                <ns0:OperationInfo.Parameters>
                                        <ns0:OperationParameterInfo Attributes="Out"
                                        ParameterType="{x:Type p9:Boolean}"
                                        Name="(ReturnValue)" />
                                        <ns0:OperationParameterInfo Attributes="In"
                                        ParameterType="{x:Type p9:DateTime}" Name="date"/>
                                        <ns0:OperationParameterInfo Attributes="In"
                                        ParameterType="{x:Type p9:String}" Name="rest"/>
                                        <ns0:OperationParameterInfo Attributes="In"
                                        ParameterType="{x:Type p9:Int32}" Name="nbpers"/>
                                </ns0:OperationInfo.Parameters>
                        </ns0:OperationInfo>
                </ns0:ReceiveActivity.ServiceOperationInfo>
                <CodeActivity x:Name="code_checksendAvailability"
                        ExecuteCode="codeActivity1_ExecuteCode" />
        </ns0:ReceiveActivity>
</SequentialWorkflowActivity>
```

matically generated. This XML corresponds to the behavioural interface of a CA-STS specification represented by means of transition systems. They are especially suitable to favour user-friendliness, and to make the graphical specification of interfaces possible. We have developed an ad-hoc transformation language to translate WF activities in CA-STS elements and vice versa. The extracted CA-STS specifications must preserve the semantics of workflows as encoded in the WF platform. A formal proof of semantics preservation between both levels has not been achieved yet since the WF formal semantics is not rigorously documented. We plan to check this preservation when a more formal documentation of the WF activities will be released. Meanwhile, our encoding has been deduced from our experiments using the WF platform. The main ideas of the CA-STS specification obtained from abstract description of workflow constructs are the following:

- `Code` is internal and hence interpreted as an internal transition.
- `Terminate` corresponds to a final state.
- `Receive` and `Send` are reception and emission, respectively. Both constructs support a set of predefined message exchange pattern, which include: one-way receive (`Receive`) and one-way send (`Send`), and receive request-send response (`Receive`) and send request-receive reply (`Send`);
- `Sequence` is translated to preserve the order of the involved activities. Final states of the first activity are linked to the initial state of the second one.

Exhibit 1.

```
Sequence(...,Listen(EventDriven(Receive(receive_abort, abort),Code),
        EventDriven(Receive(receive_ack, ack) ,Sequence(Code,Terminate))))
```

- `IfElse` corresponds to an internal choice. This corresponds to as many transitions as there are branches in the `IfElse` construct (even the else). Each of these transitions lead to the initial state of the corresponding activity.
- `While` is translated as a looping behaviour, where the condition determines the choice between termination or loop.
- `Listen` corresponds to an external choice. This corresponds to as many outgoing transitions as there are branches in the `Listen` construct. These transitions are labelled with receptions corresponding to each of the messages that can be received and target the initial state of the related activity.

In addition, initial and final states in the CA-STS come respectively from the initial and final states that appear in the workflow. There is a single initial state that corresponds to the beginning of the workflow. Final states correspond either to a `Terminate` or to the end of the workflow, so several final states may appear in the CA-STS because several branches in the workflow may lead to a final state. The previously mentioned message exchange patterns supported by the `Receive` and `Send` constructs are predefined in WF in order to capture different behaviours in a business processes, as follows:

- One-way receive: the `Receive` activity receives a message without responding to the emitter (*e.g.*, `receive` *ack* of WF Client-Restaurant request presented in Figure 13).
- `Receive` request-send response: after a message is received and processed by the `Receive` activity, a response is sent back to the emitter (*e.g.*, receive *checksendAvailability* of WF RestDB service interface shown in Figure 14).

- One-way send: `Send` activity sends a message but does not expect a response from the receptor (*e.g.*, send exit of WF Client-Restaurant request in Figure 13).
- `Send` request-receive reply: `Send` activity sends a message and waits until a response is received from the receptor (*e.g.*, send *checkgetAvailability* of WF Restaurant service interface depicted in Figure 14).

Using the ideas presented above, we have implemented this process in a prototype tool, called WF2CASTS, following the patterns of our model transformation process presented in Figure 16.

Once the CA-STS is constructed, *tau* transitions (τ) corresponding to internal actions, such as assignments or write to console, are removed, since they do not affect the CA-STS's behaviour. Note that we use two representations for a correct final state. In addition, our transformation process for both `Receive` and `Send` activities, considers two different patterns corresponding to the message exchange patterns in WF: one-way receive or receive request send response for `Receive`; and one-way send or send request-receive reply for `Send`. Consequently, we have to support both kind of message exchange patterns when `Receive` and `Send` activities appear inside `Listen` and `IfElse` constructs, respectively. The latter one usually includes `Send` activities, but as can be seen in Figure 16, a branch can also execute other kind of WF activity.

Next, we make use of our case study to illustrate this transformation process.

Example - Case Study OBS: We apply the model transformation process to the WF services implemented for the case study, in order to obtain the corresponding CA-STS specifications. In Figure 17 the XML description of the interface of RestDB is presented. It can be observed that XML-based interface contains its context profile, which in this case is empty, its signature, and a description of its CA-STS protocol including labels, states and transitions. It is worth noting that labels on

Figure 16. Patterns of our model transformation process from WF workflow activities abstraction to CA-STS protocol elements abstraction and vice versa

WF workflow activities abstraction	CA-STS protocol elements abstraction
(start)	● → (S0)
Code	Internal actions such as assignments or write to console $\quad \xrightarrow{\tau}$ (S1)
▣ or Terminate	(Sn) or $\xrightarrow{FINAL}$ (Sn)
$Receive(Id, Op[, O, I_1, \ldots, I_n)$	(S0) $\xrightarrow{Op?[I_1,\ldots,I_n]}$ (S1) or (S0) $\xrightarrow{Op?[I_1,\ldots,I_n]}$ (S1) $\xrightarrow{Op!O}$ (S2)
$Send(Id, Op[, O_1, \ldots, O_n], I)$	(S0) $\xrightarrow{Op![O_1,\ldots,O_n]}$ (S1) or (S0) $\xrightarrow{Op![O_1,\ldots,O_n]}$ (S1) $\xrightarrow{Op?I}$ (S2)
$Sequence(A_1, A_2)$	$A_1.A_2$
$IfElse((C_1, Send(Id_1, Op_1[, O_i, I_1])), \ldots, (C_n, A_n), Send(Id_{n+1}, Op_{n+1}[, O_k, I_{n+1}]))$	(S0) $\xrightarrow{[C_1]Op_1![O_i]}$ (S1) $[\xrightarrow{Op_1?I_1}$ (S2) $]$ ... $\xrightarrow{[C_n]A_n}$ (S1) $\xrightarrow{Op_{n+1}![O_k]}$ (S1) $[\xrightarrow{Op_{n+1}?I_{n+1}}$ (S2) $]$
$While(C, A)$	(S0) $\xrightarrow{[C]A}$ ...
$Listen(EventDriven(Receive(Id_1, Op_1[, O_1, I_1]), A_1), \ldots, EventDriven(Receive(Id_n, Op_n[, O_n, I_j]), A_n))$	(S0) $\xrightarrow{Op_1?[I_i]}$ (S1) $[\xrightarrow{Op_1!O_1}$ (S2) $]$ ... $\xrightarrow{Op_n?[I_i]}$ (S1) $[\xrightarrow{Op_n!O_n}$ (S2) $]$

the CA-STS and operation names can be related through the name attribute included in labels.

We also show an excerpt of the XML description corresponding to the Client-Restaurant request (Figure 18) in order to illustrate the context information and conditions (marked in bold). Note that, in the signature and protocol, data term and regular variables (including their argument types) are identified by using the label dataItem, whereas context attributes and variables (as well as their argument types) are labelled with contextItem.

Finally, by applying our transformation process, we obtain the CA-STS protocols from the implemented WF workflows. Thus, Figures 19 and 20 show all the CA-STS protocols corresponding to the Client and Services of the case study (OBS), respectively.

It is worth noting that WF activities send *checkgetAvailability* and receive *checksendAvailability* corresponding to WF Restaurant and RestDB presented in Figure 14 respectively refer to a send request-receive reply (Send activity) and a receive request-send response (Receive activity) pattern. Therefore, as shown in Figure 20, both have been translated in a CA-STS operation with two CA-STS labels each by using our transformation process, *i.e.*, *checkAvailability!* and *getAvailability?* (CA-STS Restaurant protocol R) for send *checkgetAvailability*, and *checkAvailability?* and s*endAvailability!* (CA-STS RestDB protocol RD) for receive *checksendAvailability*. In addition, note that in the CA-STS protocols, we have removed the prefixes used in the WF activities (*e.g.*, send and receive), because they are not necessary anymore, since the activities are already translated for their cor-

Figure 17. CA-STS-based XML description for the RestDB service interface

```
<?xml version="1.0" ?>
<interface name="RestDB">
        <contextprofile>
        </contextprofile>
        <signatures>
                <signature name="checksendAvailability">
                        <inputs>
                                <dataItem name="dateTime"/>
                                <dataItem name="string"/>
                                <dataItem name="int"/>
                        </inputs>
                        <outputs>
                                <dataItem name="bool"/>
                        </outputs>
                </signature>
        </signatures>
        <protocol>
                <labels>
                        <label id="checkAvailability_REC" name="checksendAvailability"
                                                        type="IN">
                                <dataItem name="date"/>
                                <dataItem name="rest"/>
                                <dataItem name="nbpers"/>
                        </label>
                        <label id="sendAvailability_EM" name="checksendAvailability"
                                                        type="OUT">
                                <dataItem name="tables"/>
                        </label>
                </labels>
                <states>
                        <state id="rd_0" initial="True" final="True"/>
                        <state id="rd_1"/>
                </states>
                <transitions>
                        <transition label="checkAvailability_REC" source="rd_0"
                                                        target="rd_1"/>
                        <transition label="sendAvailability_EM" source="rd_1"
                                                        target="rd_0"/>
                </transitions>
        </protocol>
</interface>
```

responding CA-STS protocol elements (*e.g.*, *!* and *?*, respectively).

Our interface model is capable of storing and managing context attributes and variables. For instance, in the Client-Restaurant request, *CPCR* refers to the context information related to the privileges of the user (dynamic context attribute, *prĩv*). Therefore, when we have an operation profile including that context attribute, such as *CR:*

$lcr_1 = searchRest!address: string; prĩv: Tpriv$, our model assumes that *prĩv* is implicitly inferred from the HTTP header of SOAP message, so that the user does not have to provide such context information. Our model also takes the dynamic changes of the context attributes into account. In this way, the result which our services return for a client's request, could continuously and dynamically change according to the context changes. On

Figure 18. CA-STS-based XML description for the RestDB service interface

```xml
<?xml version="1.0" ?>
<interface name="ClientRest">
        <contextprofile>
                <context CA="priv" CV="Guest" CK="dynamic" CT="public"/>
        </contextprofile>
        <signatures>
                <signature name="searchRest">
                        <inputs>
                        </inputs>
                        <outputs>
                                <dataItem name="string"/>
                                <contextItem name="Tpriv"/>
                        </outputs>
                </signature>
                ...
                <signature name="bookRest">
                        <inputs>
                        </inputs>
                        <outputs>
                                <dataItem name="string"/>
                                <dataItem name="dateTime"/>
                                <dataItem name="int"/>
                        </outputs>
                </signature>
                ...
        </signatures>
        <protocol>
                <labels>
                        <label id="searchRest_EM" name="searchRest" type="OUT">
                                <dataItem name="address"/>
                                <contextItem name="priv"/>
                        </label>
                        ...
                        <label id="bookRest_EM" cond="list!=null" name="bookRest"
                                                        type="OUT">
                                <dataItem name="rest"/>
                                <dataItem name="date"/>
                                <dataItem name="nbpers"/>
                        </label>
                        ...
                        <label id="exit_EM" cond="list==null" name="exit" type="OUT"/>
                </labels>
                <states>
                        <state id="cr_0" initial="True"/>
                        ...
                        <state id="cr_4" final="True"/>
                </states>
                <transitions>
                        <transition label="searchRest_EM" source="cr_0" target="cr_1"/>
                        ...
                        <transition label="bookRest_EM" source="cr_2" target="cr_3"/>
                        ...
                        <transition label="exit_EM" source="cr_2" target="cr_4"/>
                </transitions>
        </protocol>
</interface>
```

Figure 19. CA-STS specifications of the OBS client interfaces with their context profiles, signatures and CA-STS protocols

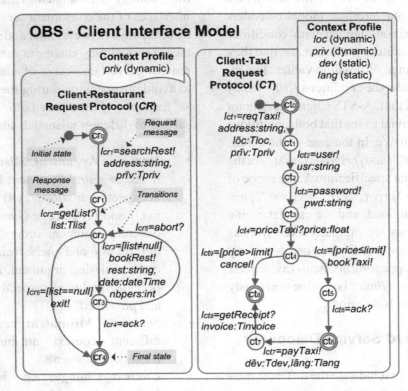

Figure 20. CA-STS specifications of the OBS service interfaces with their context profiles, signatures and CA-STS protocols

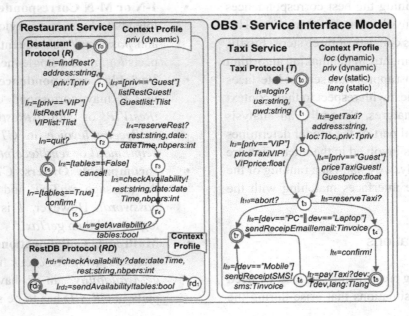

the other hand, our CA-STS protocols maintain conditions appearing in WF While and ifElse constructs, since our interface model considers them. Thus, transitions tagged with conditions must ensure their mutual exclusion and that they control the full range of possible values. For instance, if we consider the conditions *[list==null]* and *[list!=null]* of the CA-STS Client-Restaurant request *CR*, it is trivial to see that both conditions are mutually exclusive. In the case of the conditions *[priv=="VIP"]* and *[priv=="Guest"]* of the CA-STS Restaurant specification *R*, the range of values of the type *Tpriv* (*{"VIP", "Guest"}*) has been previously defined, and we can determine that both conditions are mutually exclusive, as well. As regards the conditions *[price=<limit]* and *[price>limit]* appearing in Client-Taxi request *CT*, we assume that *"limit"* is a value previously defined (e.g., 50 or 100 (euros)).

Semantic-Based Service Discovery

In this section, we first indicate the different mismatch problems which can arise during the composition of pre-existing services. Then, we propose a service discovery process in order to solve automatically the mismatch situations previously detected by obtaining the best correspondences among services involved in the interaction. This discovery process consists of three steps. Firstly, we introduce a semantic matchmaking algorithm that selects the most appropriate service interfaces for a client's request with respect to their context profiles and signatures. Secondly, an analysis of the behavioural part of the model determines whether protocols involved in the interaction are compatible. Lastly, we establish a ranking of the candidate service interfaces matching with the client's request.

Mismatch Situations

Before composing pre-existing services, we need to detect all the situations that arise during the interaction that may lead to an erroneous execution, namely a mismatch. This is because the interfaces of the constituent services of a system do not always fit one another and some features of these services may change at run-time, therefore requiring a certain degree of adaptation in order to avoid mismatching during the composition.

Example - Case Study OBS: Our scenario is subject to different mismatch situations:

- **Name or Argument Mismatch:** e.g., (i) message *searchRest!* sent by *CR*, when *R* is expecting *findRest?*; (ii) argument *price* in *CT* and *VIPprice* or *Guestprice* in *T*; (iii) different argument orders in *checkAvailability!* in *R* and *checkAvailability?* in *RD*; or (iv) missing argument, *login?* in *T* expects *usr* and *pwd*, respectively from *user!* and *password!* in *CT*.

- **Semantic Mismatch:** corresponding to different context attributes, operation names or arguments.

- **Context Change:** e.g., in *CT* contexts *loc* and *priv* can change dynamically. Our model handles these situations by simulating the environment's dynamic update according to the context changes.

- **1-N or M-N Correspondences:** while *CT* intends to login to a service sending *user!* and *password!* subsequently, whilst *T* expects *login?* as a single message.

- **Variable Correspondences:** e.g., *getList?* in *CR* may correspond either with *listRestVIP!* or with *listRestGuest!* in *R*; or *getReceipt?invoice* in *CT* with *sendReceiptEmail!* or *sendReceiptSMS!sms* in *T*.

- **Incompatible Orders:** *CT* first executes the message *reqTaxi!* and then *user!* and *password!*. However, *T* is expecting first *login?* and then *getTaxi?*.

- **Multipart Collaborations:** e.g., if *CR* interacts with *R*, *checkAvailability!* and *getAvailability?* in *R* have no counterparts in *CR*. *RD* has to be selected to con-

Exhibit 2. Algorithm 1

Algorithm 1 *service_discovery: discovers the most suitable interface(s) for a request*

---

inputs a CA-STS requester $I_r = (CP_r, SI_r, P_r)$, a CA-STS repository S_{rep}, an ontology Ont
output a ranked list of service interfaces IDM_{rank}
1:   $S_{av} := available\_services(S_{rep})$ // available services
2:   **for all** S_p in S_{av} **do**
3:      $IMT_{sempro} := []$ // interfaces matching
4:      **for all** I_p in S_p **do**
5:         $IMT_{sem} := semantic\_matchmaking(I_r, I_p, Ont)$
6:         **if** $IMT_{sem} \neq []$ **then**
7:            $IMT_{pro} := protocol\_compatibility(P_r, IMT_{sem}, Ont)$
8:            **if** $IMT_{pro} \neq []$ **then**
9:               $IMT_{sempro} := IMT_{sempro} \cup IMT_{pro})$ // adds the interface
10:             **end if**
11:          **end if**
12:      **end for**
13: **end for**
14: $IDM_{ranking} := rank\_interface(IMT_{semprot})$
15: **return** $IDM_{ranking}$ // ranking service interfaces' list

---

nect with *R*, with *checkAvailability?* and *sendAvailability!*.

Service Discovery Process

Our discovery process solves mismatch in three steps (Exhibit 2). First, a semantic matchmaking algorithm selects (in a similar way to UDDI, but considering semantic) the most appropriate interfaces for a client's request with respect to their context profiles and signatures. Second, an behavioural analysis determines whether protocols are compatible. Finally, we establish a ranking of the candidate interfaces.

Function *available_services* returns an available service list; semantic matchmaking, protocol compatibility, and rank interface are described below. Functions *semantic_matchmaking, protocol_compatibility*, are respectively presented in Algorithms 2 and 3. Note that we use concepts such as degree of match (relationship in between concepts, such as operation names, context attributes or arguments, in an ontology), and matching tuple set (best correspondences among operation profiles of services interacting). Because of comprehension reasons, these concepts will

also be explained in further detail in Definitions 5 and 6, respectively.

Example - Case Study OBS: Let us consider our corresponding case study. CA-STS interfaces were already presented in Figures 19 and 20. The service discovery process (Algorithm 1) is executed individually for each client's request: restaurant and taxi. For both requests, we consider the algorithm detects Restaurant, RestDB and Taxi as available service interfaces (running in the system).

Semantic Matchmaking: Both context attributes and operation profiles refer to OWL-S concepts with their associated semantics. The goal is to measure their semantic matching. The semantics of OWL-S descriptions allow the definition of a ranking function which distinguishes multiple degrees of match between two OWL-S concepts. We choose the notions of degree of match introduced in (Paolucci et. al, 2002) to define the semantic matchmaking based on ontologies.

Definition 5 (Degree of Match): Being cr and cp either two context attributes, two operation names, two arguments (input/output), or two return types, that belong to a requester and provider

Exhibit 3.

$$
degree\_match(c_r, c_p, Ont) = \begin{cases} \texttt{exact} & if \ (c_r = c_p \lor c_r \ subclass \ of \ c_p) \ in \ Ont \\ \texttt{plugIn} & if \ (c_p \ subsumes \ c_r) \ in \ Ont \\ \texttt{subsume} & if \ (c_r \ subsumes \ c_p) \ in \ Ont \\ \texttt{fail} & otherwise \end{cases}
$$

interface, respectively, we define their degree of match within an ontology Ont in Exhibit 3:

The order of matchmaking patterns is the following: 1) `exact`, 2) `plugin` since the concept of the provided service can be used in place of the one that is expected by the requester, 3) `subsume`, which indicates that the requirements of the requester are only partially satisfied, and 4) `fail` representing an unacceptable result. This order is determined by the function $\sqsupset$ that compares two degrees of match: exact $\sqsupset$ plugIn $\sqsupset$ subsume $\sqsupset$ fail. In order to calculate the average of the degrees of match, we discretise each degree of match to a numeric value to obtain the average among several degrees of match corresponding to several correspondences between messages. Then, this average value is transformed in its respective degree of match. In the semantic matchmaking we use *matching tuples* to store pairs of operation profiles with degrees of match.

Definition 6 (Matching Tuple): A matching tuple is defined as a tuple (opr, opp, DMop): opr and opp are operation profiles, and DMop is their degree of match.

Exhibit 4 consists of checking the matching of signatures, by considering their context information, operation names, arguments and types. It returns the candidate service interfaces to satisfy the client's request, as well as their corresponding matching tuple sets which represent the degree of match between the client interface and each of the service interfaces, at the signature and semantic levels (line 3), and even service (context-awareness, line 2). At protocol level it identifies

behavioural mismatch which will be solved in the protocol compatibility algorithm (lines 4-7).

Functions *context_profile_matching* and *signature_matching_compute* calculate the semantic matching between two context profiles and two signatures, respectively; *correspondence_label* labels with "*" the operation appearing in more than one counterpart; and *check_open_port* checks whether any provider's operation has no counterpart (open port labelled with "_").

Example - Case Study OBS: We apply the semantic process to our scenario. Figure 21 gives the shared domain ontology related to the on-line booking system. We present the classes used in our scenario with their relationships. These classes represent concepts which may be either a context attribute, an operation name, or an argument. This ontology has been generated graphically using Protégé 4.0.2[12].

First, for the Client-Restaurant request *CR*, Restaurant *R* and Taxi *T* service interfaces are selected, since both include the context attribute *priv* (see Exhibit 5). RestDB *RD* service interface is also selected, because its context profile is empty and the semantic matching process needs to know more information about it. Our algorithm determines that only the signature of *R* matches semantically the *CR* one. A matching tuple set for interaction *CR − R* is built (labels lcr_1, lr_1, etc., are represented in Figures 19 and 20, respectively).

This set indicates that, *e.g.*, in the first matching tuple, the degree of match for the operation profiles lcr_1 and lr_1 with respect to the ontology is `exact`. This is calculated as follows: (i) the

Exhibit 4. Algorithm 2

Algorithm 2 *semantic_matchmaking: returns interfaces satisfying a matching*

---

input a CA-STS requester $I_r = (CP_r, SI_r, P_r)$, a CA-STS provider $I_p = (CP_p, SI_p, P_p)$, Ont
output a list of interfaces with their matching tuple sets IMT_{sem}
1:   $IMT_{sem} := []$ // candidate service interfaces
2:   **if** $context\_profile\_matching(CP_r, CP_p, Ont)$ **then**
3:     $SM_{op}, MT_{op} := signature\_matching(S_r, SI_p, Ont)$ // matching
4:     **if** SM_{op} **then**
5:       $MT_{op} = correspondence\_label(MT_{op})$ // labels all the 1-N/N-M or variable correspondences
6:       $MT_{op} = check\_open\_port(SI_p, MT_{op})$ // checks if any operation in provider interface has no counterpart in requester interface (open port)
7:       $IMT_{sem} := IMT_{sem} \cup (I_p, MT_{op})$ // interface added to the list
8:     **end if**
9:   **end if**
10: **return** IMT_{sem} // a list of candidate interfaces with their matching tuple sets

---

Exhibit 5.

$$MT_{op_{CR,R}} = \{(l_{cr_1}, l_{r_1}, \text{exact}), (*l_{cr_2}, l_{r_2}, \text{subsume}), (*l_{cr_2}, l_{r_3}, \text{subsume}), \\ (l_{cr_3}, l_{r_4}, \text{exact}), (l_{cr_4}, l_{r_7}, \text{subsume}), (l_{cr_5}, l_{r_8}, \text{exact}), \\ (l_{cr_6}, l_{r_9}, \text{exact}), (\_, l_{r_5}, \_), (\_, l_{r_6}, \_)\}$$

Exhibit 6.

$$MT_{op_{R,RD}} = \{(l_{r_5}, l_{rd_1}, \text{exact}), (l_{r_6}, l_{rd_2}, \text{exact})\}$$

degree of match of the operation names *searchRest* and *findRest* is exact, (ii) the average of the degree of match between their arguments and return types is exact, and (iii) the degree of match for that matching tuple is the average between both degrees of match, *i.e.*, exact. This process is performed for the combination of lcr_1 with all the operation profiles of R whose directions are reversed (binding of emissions and receptions) to the direction of lcr_1, and the matching process determines that the best one is lr_1. Then, the process is executed for each operation profile in CR obtaining the rest of the matching tuples. Operations may have several (variable) correspondences, e.g., lcr_2 matches lr_2 or lr_3 according

to the value of the context attribute *priv*. In order to identify this mismatch, our process labels with "*" the label lcr_2. Furthermore, the operation profiles lr_5 and lr_6 in R have no counterparts in CR (multipart collaborations). Hence, interfaces connecting those operation profiles have to be discovered. The process selects RD, with the matching tuple in Exhibit 6.

Then, Algorithm 2 returns the interfaces replying the request CR, *i.e.*, the composite interface R-RD, with the matching tuple sets $MTop_{CR,R}$ and $MTop_{R,RD}$. The same procedure is performed to obtain the matching tuple set for the Client-Taxi request CT. Thus, our algorithm establishes cor-

Figure 21. On-line booking system ontology generated using Protégé 4.0.2

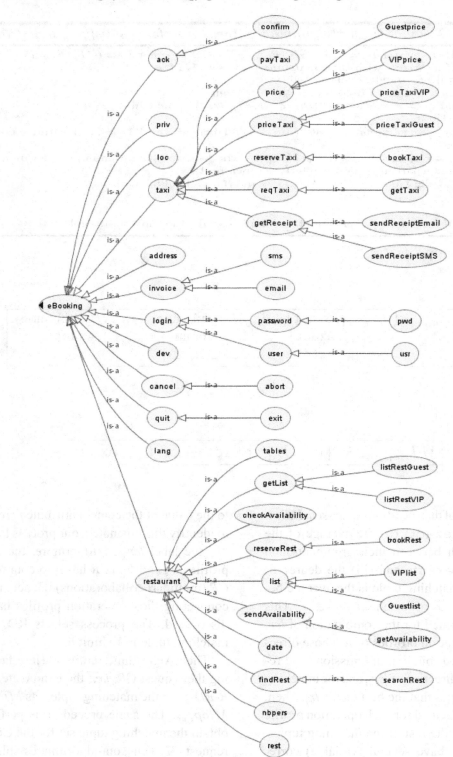

Exhibit 7.

$$
\begin{aligned}
MT_{op_{CT,T}} = \{ & (l_{ct_1}, l_{t_2}, \text{subsume}), (l_{ct_2}, *l_{t_1}, \text{exact}), (l_{ct_3}, *l_{t_1}, \text{exact}), \\
& (*l_{ct_4}, l_{t_3}, \text{subsume}), (*l_{ct_4}, l_{t_4}, \text{subsume}), (l_{ct_5}, l_{t_5}, \text{exact}), \\
& (l_{ct_6}, l_{t_6}, \text{subsume}), (l_{ct_7}, l_{t_7}, \text{exact}), (*l_{ct_8}, l_{t_8}, \text{subsume}), \\
& (*l_{ct_8}, l_{t_9}, \text{subsume}), (l_{ct_9}, l_{t_{10}}, \text{subsume}) \}
\end{aligned}
$$

respondences between *CT* and the Taxi interface *T*, with the matching tuple in Exhibit 7.

Here, our process also labels operation profiles with 1-N correspondences: *login?* (lt_1) which has two correspondences, with *user!* (lct_2) and *password!* (lct_3), has been labelled with "*". Algorithm 2 returns the interface *T* as the best candidate to reply the request *CT*, with $MTop_{CT,T}$. In addition, it is worth mentioning that incompatible orders are detected in this step and solved in the next one. Thus, $MTop_{CT,T}$, *reqTaxi!* (lct_1) corresponds with *getTaxi?* (lt_2), and then *user!* and *password!* are counterparts of *login?*.

Protocol Compatibility: The previous algorithm detects mismatch cases related to the signature, service and semantic levels, and identifies some behavioural mismatch. However, this is not enough to ensure the service compatibility, since the presence of incompatibilities in service interactions may result in a deadlocking execution of two services (Canal et. al, 2008). Therefore, we define a process which automatically finds out compatible service interfaces, and rules out the non-compatible ones, which reduces the time required to determine the compatibility between protocols during the discovery process. There exists different notions of compatibility in synchronous communication, such as opposite behaviours, unspecified reception, and deadlock-freeness (Bordeaux et. al, 2004). We have chosen the deadlock-freeness notion to illustrate our proposal, but other definitions could also be used. This compatibility definition guarantees that all the interactions between two services are performed in a satisfactory way, leading to a correct final state. Next, we present how this protocol compatibility notion is verified. First, the synchronous product of CA-STSs is computed. Then, we check whether the product is deadlock-free. The result of the synchronous product of several CA-STSs is a new CA-STS that contains all the interactions among the involved services.

Definition 7 (CA-STS Synchronous Product): The Synchronous Product of n CA-STSs Pi = (Ai, Si, Ii, Fi, Ti), i in {1, . . ., n}, with respect to a shared domain ontology Ont, and being given a matching tuple set MTop, is the CA-STS P1|| . . . ||Pn = (A, S, I, F, T) (see Exhibit 8)

All the mismatch situations related to 1-N or N-M correspondences, variable correspondences, incompatible orders, or multipart collaborations were already detected in the previous step and now they are solved in the computation of the synchronous product. Our CA-STS synchronous product will only consider those protocols which were selected in the semantic matchmaking, and checks problems which might arise at run-time because of the control over the conditions, computing a correct product free of these behavioural mismatch. In order to check mismatch detected in Algorithm 2, different functions are executed in the computation of the synchronous product. Thus, operation matching computes the matching between two operations; correspondence markup determines if an operation in a matching tuple is markup with the symbol "_" (1-N/N-M or variable correspondences); reordering label labels with "#" an operation profile as a counterpart executed in order to reorder messages (when an incompatible order is detected); count executed checks

Exhibit 8.

- $A = A_1 \times \ldots \times A_n$, $S = S_1 \times \ldots \times S_n$, $I = (I_1, \ldots, I_n)$, $F = F_1 \times \ldots \times F_n$, and
- T is defined as follows: $\forall (s_1, \ldots, s_n) \in S$, $\forall i, j \in \{1, \ldots, n\}$, $i < j$ such that $(s_i, a_i, s'_i) \in T_i$, $(s_j, a_j, s'_j) \in T_j$, where $a_i = [b_i] m_i d_i e_i$, $a_j = [b_j] m_j d_j e_j$:
  - if $operation\_matching(a_i, a_j, Ont) \neq$ **fail**:
    $(coor\_markup, corr\_number, MT_{op}) := correspondence\_markup(a_i, a_j, MT_{op}))$:
    - $((s_1, \ldots, s_n), (a_j), (s_1, \ldots, s'_j, \ldots, s_n)) \in T$ if $([b_j] = \varepsilon)$ and $(coor_markup == $ **true**$)$ and $((corr\_number \geq 1)$,
    - $((s_1, \ldots, s_n), (a_i, a_j), (s_1, \ldots, s'_j, \ldots, s_n)) \in T$ if $([b_j] \neq \varepsilon)$ and $(coor_markup == $ **true**$)$ and $(corr\_number \geq 1)$,
    - $((s_1, \ldots, s_n), (a_i, a_j), (s_1, \ldots, s'_i, \ldots, s'_j, \ldots, s_n)) \in T$ otherwise
  - otherwise $((s_1, \ldots, s_n), a_i, (s_1, \ldots, s'_i, \ldots, s_n)) \in T$: if $((count_executed(a_i, MT_{op}) == $ **false**$)$ such that: $MT_{op} := reordering\_label(a_i, MT_{op}))$ or $(count_executed(a_i, MT_{op}) == $ **true**$)$ or $(open_port(a_i, MT_{op}) == $ **true**$)$

---

if the counterpart of an specific operation profile was already executed; and open port checks if the operation does not have counterpart. We formalise the deadlock mismatch notion for a CA-STS, and our protocol compatibility checks for the absence of deadlocks in the synchronous product.

Definition 8 (Deadlock Mismatch): A CA-STS protocol P = (A, S, I, F, T) presents a deadlock mismatch, if there is a state s ∈ S such that s ∉ F and there are no outgoing transitions from *s: s* ∈ $S \wedge s \notin F c \wedge \nexists l \in A, s' \in S.(s, l, s') \in T'$, being such state s denoted by dead (s).

Definition 9 (Deadlock-freeness Compatibility): Given a matching tuple set MTop, n CA-STS protocols P1, P2, ..., Pn are deadlock-free compatible or protocol compatible, if their synchronous product P1||P2||...||Pn, considering the matching tuple set MTop, is free of deadlock mismatch.

Exhibit 9 takes a CA-STS client and a candidate CA-STS service interface with its matching tuple set as input, and returns a list made up of that CASTS service interface and its matching tuple set (interface selected in line 6) if both protocols are compatible according to the Definition 9 (line 5), or empty otherwise (interface discarded).

Example - Case Study OBS: We have to check the compatibility in the services interaction cor-responding to the two different client's requests in the On-line Booking System. In order to illustrate our protocol compatibility process, we first focus on the interaction between the Client-Restaurant request *CR* and the composite service interface Restaurant *R* with RestDB *RD*. Thus, our process generates the synchronous product for the interaction between those protocols. As can be observed in Figure 22, there is no any deadlock mismatch in the synchronous product corresponding to the communication of *CR* with *R-RD*, i.e., in *CR||R||RD*, since the behavioural mismatch were already detected during the semantic matchmaking algorithm and controlled in the CA-STS synchronous product. Therefore, our process determines that those three protocols are deadlock-free compatible.

In the same way, we perform the checking for the Client-Taxi request *CT*, which interacts with the Taxi *T* service. Figure 23 shows that the synchronous product *CT||T* is free of deadlock mismatch. Therefore, we can conclude that the interaction between both protocols is compatible.

Ranking Service Interfaces: The ranking process only takes into account those service interfaces whose protocols are deadlock-free compatible. The final list of selected service interfaces

Exhibit 9. Algorithm 3

Algorithm 3 *protocol_compatibility: determines if two protocols are compatible*

input a CA-STS client P_c, a CA-STS service with its matching set $IMT_{sem} = (I_{sem}, MT_{op})$, Ont
output a list with interface and its matching tuple set or empty $IMT_{semprot}$
1: $IMT_{semprot} := []$ // by default the list is empty
2: $I_{sem} := get\_interface(IMT_{sem})$ // gets the interface of IMT_{sem}
3: $P_{sem} := get\_protocol(I_{sem})$ // gets the protocol of I_{sem}
4: $MT_{op} := get\_matching\_tuple(IMT_{sem})$ // gets the matching tuple
5: **if** $protocol\_compatible(P_c, P_{sem}, MT_{op})$ **then**
6:     $IMT_{semprot} := IMT_{semprot} \cup (I_{sem}, MT_{op})$ // interface selected
7: **end if**
8: **return** $IMT_{semprot}$ // a list empty or not (if protocol compatible)

Figure 22. Deadlock-free CA-STS synchronous product of Client-Restaurant request protocol CR and the composite interaction of the restaurant R and RestDB RD protocols

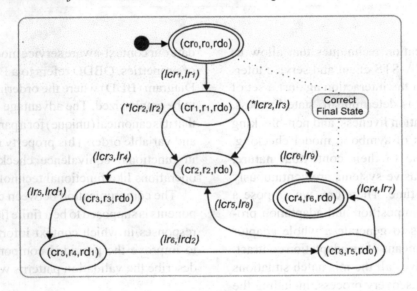

is ranked according to the degree of semantic matching of their signatures. For each service interface, our process rank interface computes the average for all their degrees of match with their corresponding numeric values. The average calculated is compared with the averages of the other service interfaces, by generating a new ranking with the service interfaces ordered on the basis of these averages.

Example - Case Study OBS: In our scenario, ranking of the selected service interfaces is not needed, because *CR* only match semantically with the composite service interface *R-RD*; and *CT* with the service interface *T*.

Context-Aware Composition and Adaptation

In the previous section, we presented a service discovery process that found out the service interfaces best replying a client's request. This process addressed the mismatch situations raised while composing pre-existing services at the four interoperability levels. Next, this section, first

Figure 23. Deadlock-free synchronous product of CT with T

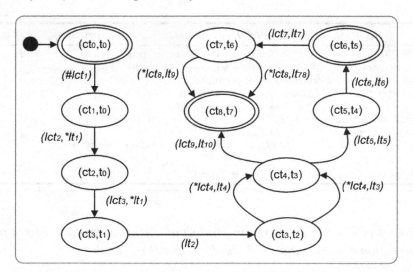

describes verification techniques that allow us to validate the CA-STS client and service interfaces involved in the interaction against a set of properties, such as determinism, state liveness, inter-communication liveness, and non-blocking states, by means of symbolic model checking. Furthermore, due to their contextual nature, mobile and pervasive systems are continuously changing at run-time. Therefore, we propose a context-aware composition and adaptation process, which aims to generate a whole adaptor specification by means of an adaptation contract. This contract solves all the mismatch situations detected in our discovery process, including the continuous dynamic context changes.

Verification of the Interface Model

Before performing the composition and adaptation process, we need to validate each CA-STS to assure they are free of inconsistences. This is required because of the inclusion of context information and conditions in our component interface model. We make use of symbolic model checking, specifically we have chosen Ordered Binary Diagram (ODBB) (Bryant, 1986) to vali-

date our context-aware service model against a set of properties. OBDD refers to a Binary Decision Diagram (BDD) where the ordering aspects need to be emphasized. The advantage of an OBDD is that it is canonical (unique) for a particular function and variable order. This property makes it useful in functional equivalence checking and other operations like functional technology mapping.

The communication between client and components is supposed to be a finite flow of requests/responses in which context information is used to improve the provided component. Next, we describe the validation patterns we consider:

- **Determinism:** In each state in which the computation can follow different paths, conditions on those multiple requests/responses must be mutually exclusive. If two conditions would be satisfiable simultaneously then the result would be non-deterministic and the result will depend on the implementation and not on the context value itself.

- **State Liveness:** If in a state context values are used to select the next request/response, at least one combination of values of those contexts must lead to a transition. It requires that at least one outbound transition is enabled for each state (with the exception of the final state).

- **Determinism:** Request/response liveness: if a request/response is conditioned by a certain value of the context, that condition must be satisfiable. It guarantees that all the specified transitions will be satisfiable for at least one combination of context values. A condition like *[priv=="VIP" && priv=="Guest"]* will never be satisfied and the corresponding transition will never be executed.

- **Non-Blocking States:** Irrespective of the values of the context variables, communication should always reach a final state. The absence of non-blocking states guarantees that independently from the values of the context, it should be possible to continue the communication avoiding deadlocks.

These properties are verified for the CA-STS protocols related to client and components. Once CA-STS adaptor is generated (next Sections), we could apply our OBDD verification model as well. However, it will not be needed, since the verification model assures that the properties are preserved in the composition of the CA-STSs already validated, *i.e.*, in the CA-STS adaptor. To validate these properties, we have designed an OBDD representation of our CA-STS protocols. We selects OBDD because it has been shown that in many circumstances OBDDs offer a compact way to represent and manipulate Boolean functions. Our idea here is to show how states and labels can be represented by means of conjunctions of Boolean variables, and transition relations can be encoded by means of Boolean formulae, which are manipulated using OBDDs. We have implemented a set of OBDD-based algorithms (Cubo et al. 2009) to verify the set of properties. CASTS2OBDD is a prototype tool that implements those algorithms by representing CA-STS protocols by means of OBDD.

Example - Case Study OBS: Our verification model determined our client and components are free of inconsistencies with respect to the validation patterns considered. This process is not obvious at a first analysis, but the verification mechanisms we apply can check automatically the set of properties previously defined. For instance, if we consider the CA-STS protocols corresponding to the Client-restaurant request CR, Restaurant R and RestDB RD, the verification of those properties required less than 1 second for all those CA-STSs. We employed up to 7 Boolean BDD variables (*i.e.*, 3 for CR, 3 for R, and 1 for RD) to encode our scenario, corresponding to a model of size 27. Notice that the properties presented above could not be checked using a standard model checker, because of the use of conditions over transitions and because our requirements reason about these conditions over transitions. Indeed, a standard model checkers only allows to reason about (sequences of) states by means of temporal formulae.

Composition and Adaptation

Following composition and adaptation processes presented in Figure 8, once we have checked that the client and services of the system are free of inconsistencies or faults, such as determinism or blocking states, we can compose them. First, we need to generate an adaptation contract that gives a mapping among the service events by avoiding mismatch problems. Using this contract, we can obtain a third-party adaptor service that coordinates the service interaction, which will be implemented as a WF service in order to be deployed with the WF client and services.

Moreover, apart from solving mismatch and inconsistent problems, we want composition and adaptation to distinguish between the available contexts when translating the messages among services. Using a non-contextual approach, message correspondences are fixed, which means that any client's request is always associated to the same target message. This prevents changes in these connections being taken into account, and motivates the need for new capabilities that our context-aware composition and adaptation approach provides in order to achieve message translation depending on contexts. These situations, *i.e.*, context changes, were also detected in our discovery process, and therefore they will be considered in our adaptation contract.

Adaptation Contract: A first goal of the contract is to define a mapping between events in the services. Thus, an adaptation contract is built as a set of correspondences between messages of the services involved. We define a notation based on vectors expressing correspondences between service messages, and on transition systems to specify the evolution of every service depending on certain conditions, such as context changes. These interactions are formalized through synchronisation vectors (Arnold, 1994). Hence, a synchronisation vector denotes a communication between several services. They allow messages with different names and even a different number of operations to be synchronised. Each event (or label) appearing in one vector is executed by one service, and the overall result corresponds to a global synchronisation among all the involved services. A vector may involve any number of services. In addition, a vector does not require interactions on the same names of events as it is the case in process algebra for instance.

Definition 11 (Synchronisation Vector): A synchronisation vector (or vector for short) for a set of services $Wsi = (Ai; Si; Ii; Fci; Ti)$, $i \in \{1...n\}$, is a tuple $<l_1,...,l_n>$ with $l_i \in A \{\varepsilon\}$, ε meaning that a service does not participate in a synchronisation.

To identify service operations in a vector, their names are prefixed by the service identifier. Hence, in a vector, all the services which do not participate in an interaction may be removed to simplify the notation, *e.g.*, $<ws_1:req1!; ws_2: \varepsilon; ws_3:rep2?>$ will be written as $<ws_1:req1!; ws_3:rep2?>$. Furthermore, in some situations it is essential to apply explicitly a specific order between vectors to avoid mismatch situations. Hence, we use as abstract notation to generate an LTS with vectors on transitions. This LTS is used as a guide in the application order of interactions denoted by those vectors. Therefore, an adaptation contract will be made up of vectors executed in a specific order.

Definition 12 (Adaptation Contract): An adaptation contract for a set of services Wsi, $i \in 1,...,n$, is defined as a couple $(Vws_i; Vlts)$ where: (see Exhibit 10)

Our adaptation process can automatically generate an adaptation contract from the matching tuple sets and the synchronous product obtained in our discovery process, solving the existing mismatch cases in the interaction between client and services.

On the one hand, the set of vectors, Vws_i, that establishes the correspondences between service events, is generated by using both the matching tuple set corresponding to the matching between operation profiles of services involved in an interaction, and the extra information given for the markup synchronous product (such as, the reordering of messages labelled with they symbol "#"). On the other hand, the vector LTS indicating the execution order of the vectors, $Vlts$, is generated automatically from the CA-STS synchronous product, since the product gives all the interactions between the involved services computed. Therefore, our adaptation contract addresses all the mismatch situations related to the four interoperability levels, which were previously detected during the discovery process. This is achieved because using vectors to express bindings between services establishes correspondences between messages with different names or arguments, to express 1-N or N-M or variable correspondences, handle context changes, reorder messages and simultaneously adapt multiple services. As regards to the vector LTS, it has the advantage of automatically indicating the execution order. Even, in some situations, it could be modified to enable

Exhibit 10.

- V_{Ws_i} is a set of vectors for services Ws_i, and

- V_{lts} is a vector LTS that indicates the order of interactions of the vectors V_{Ws_i}, such that:

  - an LTS (Labelled Transition System) is a tuple (A, S, I, Fc, T) where: A is an alphabet (set of events), S is a set of states, $I \in S$ is the initial state, $Fc \subseteq S$ are correct final states, and $T \subseteq S \times A \times S$ is the transition function whose elements $(s_1, a, s_2) \in T$ are usually denoted by $s_1 \xrightarrow{a} s_2$.

the developer to ignore those correspondences non-required in the composition.

Next, we use our case study in order to present the automatic generation of their adaptation contracts, by using the matching tuple sets and synchronous products generated for each interaction.

Example - Case Study OBS: Let us focus on Client-Restaurant request. The adaptation contract is specified by a set of synchronous vectors, and a vector LTS. Synchronous vectors are automatically obtained from the matching tuple sets ($MTop_{CR;R}$ and $MTop_{R;RD}$), which indicate the best matching between the interfaces corresponding to the Client-Restaurant and the composite service interface Restaurant and RestDB.

The vector LTS is generated from the synchronous product, which specifies the order of execution of the vectors which ensures a correct execution free of deadlock situations. The adaptation contract of the interaction between CR and the composite service interface R and RD is made up of the vectors $Vws_i \in \{CR;R;RD\}$, presented below (please refer Figures 19 and 20 to identify the operations), and the vector LTS $Vlts\{CR;R;RD\}$, depicted in Figure 24. As we consider value passing protocol and data exchanged by means of messages, we need to resolve conflicts at this level. To do this, we relate the exchanged data parameters of the messages correctly binding their names when required using placeholders. Considering the Client-Restaurant request CR,

e.g., we need to bind the parameter *list:Tlist* in CR with *VIPlist:Tlist* and *Guestlist:Tlist* in R. Thus, we will have, *getList?LIS* in CR related to *[PRV=="VIP"]listRestVIP?LIS* or *[PRV=="Guest"]listRestGuest?LIS* in R, with *LIS* as placeholder. In the same way, we use placeholders in conditions, thereby *PRV* used in the previous conditions comes from the placeholder used in the message *searchRest!ADR,PRV (see Exhibit 11)*. Note that we use label identifiers (such as *CR* for the Client-Restaurant request).

For the Client-Taxi request CT we can obtain the corresponding adaptation contract following the same procedure (see Exhibit 12). Then, the adaptation contract for the interaction between CT and T is made up of vectors $Vws_i \in \{CT;T\}$, and its vector LTS $Vlts\{CT;T\}$, shown in Figure 25.

Our example shows that in our adaptation process, we can generate adaptation contracts which address all the possible mismatch situations, related to the signature, semantic, protocol and service levels, including the continuous context changes at run-time.

Next, we describe the generation of a CA-STS adaptor in order to connect correctly client and services.

Adaptor Generation: From a set of interfaces (client and services), and an adaptation contract, an adaptor service can be generated as either a central adaptor (centralized view) (Mateescu et al.,

Figure 24. Vector LTS, Vlts{CR;R;RD}, indicating the order of the interaction between the client-restaurant request and the composite service interface restaurant and RestDB in OBS

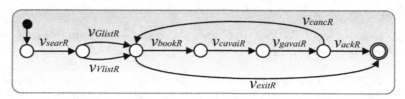

Exhibit 11.

$$
\begin{aligned}
V_{Ws_{i \in \{CR,R,RD\}}} = \\
\{v_{searR} &= \langle CR : searchRest!ADR, PRV; R : findRest?ADR, PRV \rangle, \\
v_{GlistR} &= \langle CR : getList?LIS; \\
& \quad R : [PRV == \text{``}VIP\text{''}]listRestVIP!LIS \rangle, \\
v_{VlistR} &= \langle CR : getList?LIS; \\
& \quad R : [PRV == \text{``}Guest\text{''}]listRestGuest!LIS \rangle, \\
v_{bookR} &= \langle CR : [LIS \neq null]bookRest!RES, DAT, NBP; \\
& \quad R : reserveRest?RES, DAT, NBP \rangle, \\
v_{ackR} &= \langle CR : ack?; R : [TAB == True]confirm! \rangle, \\
v_{cancR} &= \langle CR : abort?; R : [TAB == False]cancel! \rangle, \\
v_{exitR} &= \langle CR : [LIS == null]exit!; R : quit? \rangle, \\
v_{cavaiR} &= \langle R : checkAvailability!RES, DAT, NBP; \\
& \quad RD : checkAvailability?DAT, RES, NBP \rangle, \\
v_{gavaiR} &= \langle R : getAvailability?TAB; RD : sendAvailability!TAB \rangle \}
\end{aligned}
$$

Exhibit 12.

$$
\begin{aligned}
V_{Ws_{i \in \{CT,T\}}} = \\
\{v_{reqT} &= \langle CT : reqTaxi!ADR, LOC, PRV \rangle, \\
v_{userT} &= \langle CT : user!USR; T : login?USR, PWD \rangle, \\
v_{pwdT} &= \langle CT : password!PWD; T : login?USR, PWD \rangle, \\
v_{getT} &= \langle T : getTaxi?ADR, LOC, PRV \rangle, \\
v_{VpriT} &= \langle CT : priceTaxi?PRI; \\
& \quad T : [PRV == \text{``}VIP\text{''}]priceTaxiVIP!PRI \rangle, \\
v_{GpriT} &= \langle CT : priceTaxi?PRI; \\
& \quad T : [PRV == \text{`}Guest\text{''}]priceTaxiGuest!PRI \rangle, \\
v_{bookT} &= \langle CT : [PRI \leq limit]bookTaxi!; T : reserveTaxi? \rangle, \\
v_{ackT} &= \langle CT : ack?; T : confirm! \rangle, \\
v_{payT} &= \langle CT : payTaxi!DEV, LAN; T : payTaxi?DEV, LAN \rangle, \\
v_{receE} &= \langle CT : getReceipt?INV; T : [DEV == \text{``}PC\text{''} \\
& \quad ||DEV == \text{``}Laptop\text{''}]sendReceiptEmail!INV \rangle, \\
v_{receS} &= \langle CT : getReceipt?INV; \\
& \quad T : [DEV == \text{``}Mobile\text{''}]sendReceiptSMS!INV \rangle, \\
v_{cancT} &= \langle CT : [PRI > limit]cancel!; T : abort? \rangle \}
\end{aligned}
$$

Figure 25. Vector LTS, Vlts{CT;T}, indicating the order of the interaction between the client-taxi request and taxi service interface in OBS

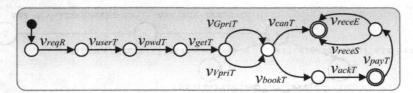

2008), or a set of adaptation wrappers (distributed view) (Salaün, 2008) to distribute the adaptation. Since our model considers context information and conditions, we need to keep them in the adaptor service. However, once we have generated the adaptation contract which defines the possible correspondences between operations of services, all contexts (not only static contexts but also dynamic ones) can be handled as data terms or regular variables and conditions need not be evaluated during the adaptor generation. Therefore, our process can use techniques presented in (Mateescu et al., 2008) in order to obtain a central CA-STS adaptor specification. This adaptor service will be deployed on a single machine together with the CA-STS client and services involved in the interaction, since the adaptor acts as a third-party service that is in charge of coordinating the client and services with respect to a set of interactions defined in the adaptation contract. Consequently, client and services communicate through the adaptor, which is able to compensate mismatch problems by making the required connections as specified in the contract. Client, service and adaptor protocols interact according to the operational semantics presented in our previous work (Cubo et al., 2010). Furthermore, an improvement of our approach with respect to other previous works (Canal et al., 2008; Cubo et al., 2009; Mateescu et al., 2008), is that our composition process manages the continuous and dynamic changes of context, thereby the user has not to indicate explicitly when a change occurs, by handling the synchronous communication, evaluating even the context changes, and simulating the dynamic up-

date of the environment according to the context changes at run-time.

Example - Case Study OBS: Following with the Client-Restaurant request of the On-line Booking System, Figure 26 shows the CA-STS adaptor for the interaction between *CR* and the composite service interface *R* with *RD*.

Note that message directions are reversed because all messages corresponding to the Client-Restaurant *CR* request and the Restaurant *R* and RestDB *RD* service interfaces will go through the adaptor. This latter has to synchronize with these messages using complementary directions, *e.g.*, communication between *searchRest!* in *CR* and *findRest?* in the adaptor. In addition, the adaptor starts the interaction with the reception searchRest?, corresponding to the emission *searchRest!* in *CR*, and next handles the emission *findRest!*. This way of how the adaptor synchronises with the services, is performed for all the correspondences in vectors. It is worth mentioning that the set of properties defined previously are preserved in the composition, so the CA-STS adaptor is free of inconsistencies. In the same way, we can also generate a CA-STS adaptor for communication between the Client-Taxi request *CT* and Taxi *T* service, which is depicted in Figure 27.

Figure 28 shows how a part of the composition corresponding to Client-Taxi request and Taxi service interface is synchronised through the adaptor by connecting parameters by means of placeholders. Specifically, the adaptation process synchronises the adaptor with the service interfaces by means of the same name of messages but using reversed directions. In addition, the

Figure 26. Adaptor CA-STS specification for the interaction between client-restaurant request and the composite service interface restaurant with RestDB

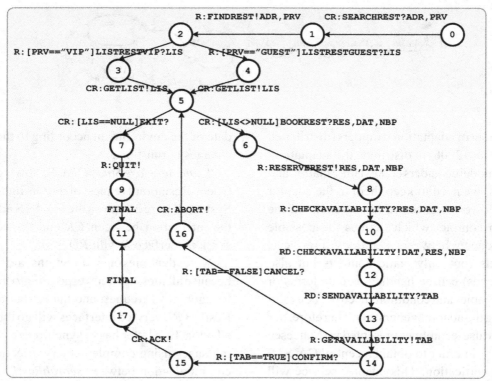

adaptation process always starts a set of correspondences formalised in a vector by the receptions, and next handles the emissions, since it would be meaningless to send something that has not been received yet. It can also be observed how the synchronisation solves behaviour mismatch such as 1-N correspondence (*user!* and *password!* with *login?*), variable correspondence *[priv == "VIP"]priceTaxiVIP!* or *[priv=="Guest"]priceTaxiGuest!* with *priceTaxi?*) and incompatible order (sequence *reqTaxi!*, *user!* and *login!* With respect to *login?* and *getTaxi?*). Furthermore, our process can control dynamic context changes. Thus, we assume the dynamic context attribute *prĩv* corresponding to the client privileges is *"Guest"* when the request of a taxi is issued. Then, that attribute changes to *"VIP"* at run-time before the request is received. During the composition, our process captures and

handles that dynamic context change, and then, the rule DYN simulates the dynamic update of the environment according to the context changes at run-time. The process carries on the execution by the branch corresponding to *"VIP"*, as is observed in Figure 28. Note we only use a data environment to keep track of the values of the messages of different CA-STSs, since there are no collisions in the names of variables, which correspond to placeholders in vectors.

During execution, on one hand, the data environment E may be updated upon reception of messages with data arguments. For instance, in the reception of the data term address and the context attributes *loc* and *priv* in the adaptor side, coming with message *reqTaxi!* from the Client-Taxi request, the environment E is updated associating their placeholder names (*ADR*, *LOC* and *PRV*, respectively) appearing in the definition

Figure 27. Adaptor CA-STS specification for the interaction between client-taxi request and taxi service interface

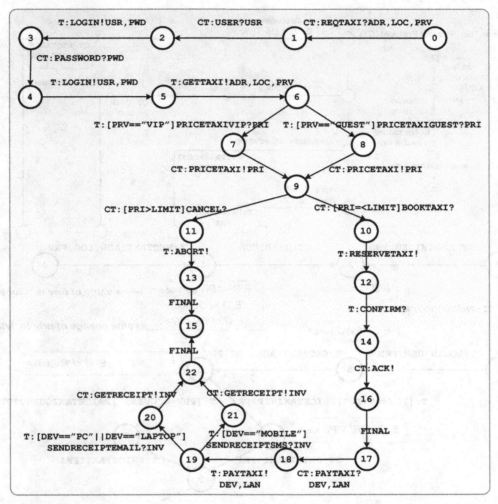

of the vector *vreqT* of the adaptation contract of the interaction between Client-Taxi request and Taxi service interface. On the other hand, *E* can be updated dynamically because of any context change, as occurs when the context variable *priv* changes from *"Guest"* to *"VIP"* (*E →d E'*). Figure 29 shows the sequence diagram between Client-Taxi request and the Taxi service interface by means of the corresponding Adaptor.

Finally, in order to complete our whole process presented in Figure 8, we apply our model transformation process to refine the CA-STS adaptor

with respect to a specific platform. Specifically, we generate a WF service from the CA-STS adaptor. This WF service represents the WF adaptor, which will be deployed to allow the correct connection of client and services.

Obtaining WF Adaptor from CA-STS Adaptor: Our interface model (CA-STS specifications) can take into account some kind of behaviours (interleavings) that cannot be implemented in executable languages (e.g., WF or BPEL). In order to make platform-independent adaptor implementable with respect to a specific platform, some filters are used

Figure 28. Synchronised composition between client-taxi request and the taxi service interface by means of the corresponding adaptor

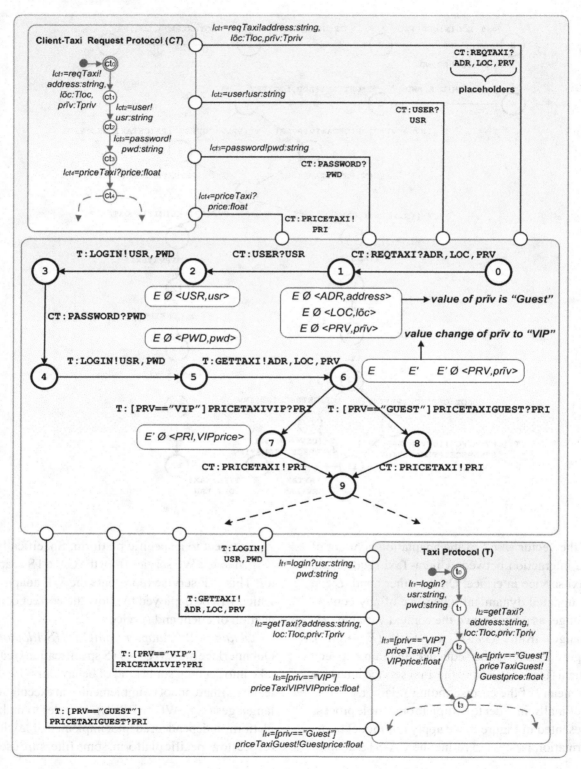

Figure 29. Sequence diagram between client-taxi request and the taxi service interface by means of the corresponding adaptor

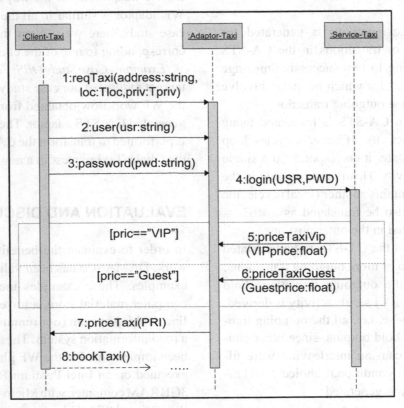

with the purpose of pruning parts of the CA-STS corresponding to these interleavings keeping only the executable paths. In particular, to implement an adaptor interface model (CA-STS adaptor) as an adaptor service (WF adaptor), we proceed in three steps: (i) filtering the interleaving cases that cannot be implemented (e.g., several emissions and receptions outgoing from a same state), (ii) checking that the pruning does not affect the correct functionality, and (iii) encoding the filtered model into the corresponding implementation language (in our case WF) using our transformation process. Once we have performed the two first steps manually and visually, we need to implement the corresponding WF adaptor following the guidelines presented below, and the patterns of our model transformation process presented in Figure 16.

First, the initial state of the CA-STS is encoded as the initial state of the WF workflow. Final states are encoded as Terminate activities. The transformation process derives step by step parts of the abstract workflow by focusing on one state of the CA-STS after the other. Next, we distinguish the translation of transitions corresponding to message activities (Receive, Send), and the generation of structuring activities (Sequence, While, IfElse, Listen).

Let us start with messages, considering the two different patterns corresponding to the message exchange supported by the Receive and Send:

- A transition labelled with one reception is translated into a Receive activity
- A transition labelled with one emission corresponds to a Send activity.

Now, we focus on the encoding of the CA-STS structuring within the workflow:

- A `Sequence` activity is generated for a sequence of transitions in the CA-STS corresponding to two successive message activities, and for which no states involve more than one outgoing transition.

- A cycle in a CA-STS is translated using a `While` activity. If several cycles loop on a same state, it corresponds to a single `While` activity. However if a cycle in the CA-STS contains another (local) cycle, the latter will also be translated as a `While` activity nested in the outermost one.

- If the state of the CA-STS to be translated involves two or more outgoing transitions:
  - If all the outgoing transitions hold inputs, a `Listen` activity is derived.
  - Otherwise, i.e., all the outgoing transitions hold outputs, since other situations causing interleaving were filtered, a conditional choice `IfElse` activity is generated.

We consider that a `While` construct always has priority over `IfElse` and `Listen`. Thus, when our process finds a pattern which can be transformed into `While` and `Listen` at the same time, we first apply the `While` pattern and second the `Listen` one.

The parsing process that computes the transformation from a CA-STS adaptor to a WF adaptor service, CASTS2WF, considers the guideline previously described. In addition, it uses a state machine pattern based on the transformation process from CA-STS protocol elements to WF workflow activities.

Finally, all the fragments of C# code required will be added by hand whilst refining the abstract workflow into a real WF workflow. These fragments include addresses of WF service interfaces to be specified in invocations in the WF adaptor. Therefore, to deploy our adapted system, we have

first to indicate the correct interface addresses into the WF adaptor. Since the way of generating the WF adaptor is similar in all the scenarios of our case study, here we present the WF workflow corresponding to one of the client's request.

Example - Case Study OBS: For the Client-Restaurant request of our case study, Figure 30 gives the WF workflow obtained from our previously generated CA-STS adaptor. The same procedure is performed to transform the CA-STS adaptor of the Client-Taxi request in a new WF workflow.

EVALUATION AND DISCUSSION

In order to evaluate the benefits of our framework, DAMASCo has been validated on several examples. These examples include an on-line computer material store, a travel agency, an on-line booking system (our running example), and a road information system. These scenarios have been implemented in the WF platform by us and executed on an Intel Pentium(R)D CPU 3GHz, 3GB RAM computer, with Microsoft Windows XP Professional SP2. This represents an initial stage, checking our whole framework, but the main goal of our approach is to support industrial systems by directly validating pre-existing applications in the real-world. We have evaluated the experimental results in two separate parts: discovery and adaptation processes, and monitoring process.

We have validated the full discovery process and the adaptation contract generation in two case studies: an on-line booking system (the one used throughout this chapter), and a road information system. For each case study, we have executed a client's request, and we have also studied three different versions for each, which are organised according to increasing size and complexity with respect to the number of interfaces involved, as well as the overall size of protocols as a total number of states and transitions. Table 2 shows the experimental results (CPU load and execution

Figure 30. WF workflow corresponding to the adaptor service interface that communicates CR with the composite service interface R with RD

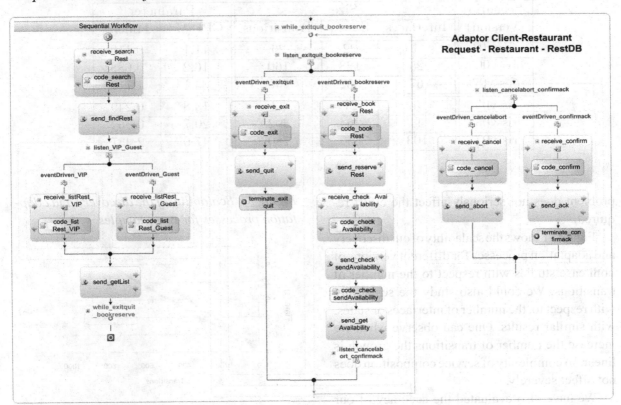

time) corresponding to different versions of two case studies.

On the one hand, for the on-line booking system (OBS), we have checked the discovery process and the generation of the adaptation contract for the Client-Restaurant request with a service repository containing: (i) the three interfaces corresponding to the Restaurant, RestDB and Taxi service interfaces (Figure 20), (obs-v004), (ii) those three interfaces plus 21 other interfaces related to book/buy a flight, a hotel room, a cinema, or a theater ticket, and so on, (obs-v005), and (iii) the three interfaces plus 63 more protocols, (obs-v07). These two latter tests have been performed to check the scalability of our framework, and thereby illustrate that the complexity of the problem does not seriously affect the effort required and the accuracy of our process as can be appreciated in the results shown in Table 2. In fact, the execution time shows a linear dependency related to the number of transitions. Therefore, our approach turned out to be cost-effective, and with respect to the concepts compared and execution time, it was more efficient than other semantic mechanisms, such as the one used in the WordNet::Similarity package[13]. In addition, using this package, only English terms defined in its data base can be compared. In our approach, one can define a specific domain ontology and use it without any restrictions comparing ontology concepts by means of matching patterns. On the other hand, for the road information system (RIS), the discovery and adaptation have been applied to a Client-Museum request. In the same way as the on-line booking system, the complexity of the

Table 2. Experimental results of the discovery and adaptation processes

Scenario (Version)	Size			Parameter	
	Interfaces	States	Transitions	CPU(%)	Time(s)
obs-v04	4	22	26	11,1	0,110
obs-v005	25	128	160	16,2	0,688
obs-v07	67	352	440	34,1	1,719
ris-v05	5	27	33	13,8	0,249
ris-v06	44	264	302	20,7	0,954
ris-v07	103	650	780	47,6	2,437

problem does not seriously affect the effort required.

Figure 31 shows the scalability of our discovery and adaptation processes for different versions of both case studies with respect to the number of transitions. We could also study the scalability with respect to. the number of interfaces or states, with similar results. One can observe when we increase the number of transitions the growth is linear, so complexity of service composition does not affect severely.

We have also evaluated the accuracy of our discovery process with precision, recall and F1 measures (Klusch, 2006) for different requests on the scenarios presented in Table 1. Precision is a measure of exactness, whereas recall is a measure of completeness, and F1 is the harmonic mean of precision and recall that combines both, and the values range for these three measures is between 0 and 1. For all requests that we performed, the results of precision and recall were equal 1, which shows our discovery process has 100% precision and recall, and the score F1 is always 1. These results prove the importance of the context-awareness, semantic matching and protocol compatibility mechanisms used in our process in order to discover services and generate a whole adaptation contract. In addition, we have validated the CA-STS interfaces corresponding to both case studies against a set of properties, by using our OBDD representation. The verification

Figure 31. Scalability of the discovery and adaptation processes for two examples

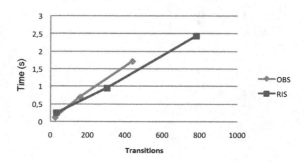

of those properties required less than 2 seconds for all the CA-STSs of each case study.

Our proposal shows a remarkable improvement over existing approaches related to discovery and adaptation processes when composing pre-existing software entities. The main goal of reusing software is to solve the mismatch situations at the four interoperability levels, which is achieved in this work. Nevertheless, our approach has some known limitations. DAMASCo supports synchronous systems, so we can not simulate asynchronous systems with our model. It would be necessary to perform new research studies to extend our proposal and take asynchronous communication into account. We have developed an ad-hoc transformation language to translate WF activities in CA-STS elements and vice versa. The extracted CA-STS specifications must preserve the semantics of workflows as encoded in the WF platform. However, a formal proof of semantics preservation between both levels has not been achieved yet since the WF formal semantics is not rigorously documented. We plan to check this preservation when a more formal documentation of the WF activities will be released. Meanwhile, our encoding has been deduced from our experiments using the WF platform. With respect to the discovery process, although ontologies represent certain advantages to discover services, and even though our approach could adopt other mechanisms different from ontologies preserving the relevance of our approach, such as Natural Language Processing (NLP)[14] or heuristic-based methodologies (Burton-Jones et. al, 2003), our process depends on the construction of shared domain ontologies, and there is no service market existing today which produces ontologies in a standard way.

FUTURE RESEARCH DIRECTIONS

We are currently extending our framework to open systems by tackling dynamic reconfiguration of services, by handling the addition or elimination of both services and requirements (such as context information), and fully solving other problems arisen in the context-aware service composition, such as exception or connection loss.

As regards future work, we plan to address other non-functional requirements at the service level, such as temporal requirements or security, in addition to context information, as well as more semantic capabilities of the service interfaces considering the full power of the Web Semantic technologies, which includes automated Web Service discovery, execution, composition and interoperation.

We also plan to design the model transformation process as a meta-model underlying in MDA,

as well as to perform formal demonstrations to determine the correction and completeness of this process. Other aspects of further research in the long-term could be: (i) to study the use of more powerful techniques, such as Multi Criteria Decision Making Methods (MCDM) (Idrissi et. al, 2010), to rank the services discovered, instead of the "average" and "round" of the degrees of match, (ii) to define *context ontologies* (Bouquet et. al, 2004) to be used in our framework, with the purpose of making context explicit for each concept of a domain ontology, and (iii) to incorporate our prototype tool inside a user device in order to support concurrency in real-world applications running on mobile devices.

CONCLUSION

We have illustrated the need to support the modelling, discovery and variability of the adaptation process according to the dynamic aspects of component and services in context-aware mobile and pervasive systems. Recent research approaches have tackled independently the discovery, composition and adaptation processes. DAMASCo framework has been presented as a novel solution which combines efforts to address all those issues through model transformations of real-world applications. More precisely, we have defined techniques to check semantic matching and protocol compatibility in order to find the service interfaces that better correspond to the client's needs. The candidate service interfaces are ranked in basis to the average values of their degrees of match. Mediating adaptors are generated by using the adaptation contracts previously defined in the discovery process. This chapter presents the DAMASCo architecture. We have validated our framework on several examples, and we have shown it is scalable, efficient and accurate.

REFERENCES

Aggarwal, R., Verma, K., Miller, J., & Milnor, W. (2004). Constraint driven web service composition in METEOR-S. In *Proceedings of SCC'04*, (pp. 23–30). IEEE Computer Society.

Allen, A., & Garlan, D. (1997). A formal basis for architectural connection. *ACM Transactions on Software Engineering and Methodology*, 6(3), 213–249.

Andrews, T., et al. (2005). *Business process execution language for web services (WSBPEL)*. BEA Systems, IBM, Microsoft, SAP AG, and Siebel Systems, 2005.

Arnold, A. (1994). *Finite transition systems. International Series in Computer Science.* Prentice-Hall.

Arsanjani, A., Zhang, L.-J., Ellis, M., Allam, A., & Channabasavaiah, K. (2007). S3: A service-oriented reference architecture. *IEEE IT Professional*, 9, 10–17.

Autili, M., Benedetto, P. D., & Inverardi, P. (2009). Context-aware adaptive services: The PLASTIC approach. In *Proceedings of FASE'09, volume 5503 of Lecture Notes in Computer Science*, (pp. 124–139). Springer.

Autili, M., Benedetto, P. D., Inverardi, P., & Mancinelli, F. (2008). *Chameleon Project*. SEA group.

Autili, M., Inverardi, P., Navarra, A., & Tivoli, M. (2007). SYNTHESIS: A tool for automatically assembling correct and distributed component-based systems. In *Proceedings of ICSE, 07*, 784–787.

Baresi, L., Guinea, S., Pistore, M., & Trainotti, M. (2009). Dynamo + Astro: An integrated approach for BPEL monitoring. In *Proceedings of ICWS, 09*, 230–237.

Bastide, R., Sy, O., Navarre, D., & Palanque, P. A. (2000). A formal specification of the CORBA event service. In *Proceedings of FMOODS, 00*, 371–396.

Benatallah, B., Hacid, M., Rey, C., & Toumani, F. (2003). Request rewriting-based web service discovery. In *Proceedings of ISWC'03, volume 2870 of Lecture Notes in Computer Science*, (pp. 242–257). Springer.

Bordeaux, L., Salaun, G., Berardi, D., & Mecella, M. (2004). When are two Web services compatible? In *Proceedings of TES'04, volume 3324 of Lecture Notes in Computer Science*, (pp. 15–28). Springer.

Bouquet, P., Giunchiglia, F., van Harmelen, F., Serafini, L., & Stuckenschmidt, H. (2004). Contextualizing ontologies. *Journal of Web Semantics*, 1(4), 325–343.

Bracciali, A., Brogi, A., & Canal, C. (2005). A formal approach to component adaptation. *Journal of Systems and Software*, 74(1), 45–54.

Broens, T., Pokraev, S., van Sinderen, M., Koolwaaij, J., & Costa, P. (2004). Context-aware, ontology-based service discovery. In *Proceedings of EUSAI'04, volume 3295 of Lecture Notes in Computer Science*, (pp. 72–83). Springer.

Brogi, A., Corfini, S., & Popescu, R. (2008). Semantics-based composition-oriented discovery of Web services. *ACM Transactions on Internet Technology*, 8(4), 19:1– 19:39.

Brogi, A., & Popescu, R. (2006). Automated generation of BPEL adapters. In *Proceedings of ICSOC'06, volume 4294 of Lecture Notes in Computer Science*, (pp. 27–39). Springer.

Bryant, R. (1986). Graph-based algorithms for Boolean function manipulation. *IEEE Transactions on Computers*, 35(8), 677–691.

Burton-Jones, A., Storey, V., Sugumaran, V., & Purao, S. (2003). A heuristic-based methodology for semantic augmentation of user queries on the Web. In *Proceedings of ER'03, volume 2813 of Lecture Notes in Computer Science*, (pp. 476–489). Springer.

Cámara, J., Martín, J., Salaün, G., Cubo, J., Ouederni, M., Canal, C., & Pimentel, E. (2009). ITACA: An integrated toolbox for the automatic composition and adaptation of web services. In *Proceedings of ICSE, 09*, 627–630.

Canal, C., Murillo, J., & Poizat, P. (2006). Software adaptation. *L'Objet Special Issue on Coordination and Adaptation Techniques for Software Entities, 12*(1), 9–31.

Canal, C., Poizat, P., & Salaün, G. (2008). Model-based adaptation of behavioural mismatching components. *IEEE Transactions on Software Engineering, 34*(4), 546–563.

Chappel, D. A. (2004). *Enterprise service bus*. O'Reilly, 2004.

Chen, H., Finin, T., & Joshi, A. (2003). An intelligent broker for context-aware systems. In *Proceedings of UbiComp, 03*, 183–184.

Cubo, J., Canal, C., & Pimentel, E. (2011). Model-based dependable composition of self-adaptive systems. *Informatica, 35*, 51–62.

Cubo, J., & Pimentel, E. (2011). DAMASCo: A framework for the automatic composition of component-based and service-oriented architectures. In *Proceedings of ECSA'11, volume 6903 of Lecture Notes in Computer Science*, (pp. 388–404). Springer.

Cubo, J., Pimentel, E., Salaün, G., & Canal, C. (2010). Handling data-based concurrency in context-aware service protocols. In *Proceedings of FOCLASA'10, volume 30 of Electronic Proceeding in Theoretical Computer Science*, (pp. 62–77).

Cubo, J., Salaün, G., Cámara, J., Canal, C., & Pimentel, E. (2007). Context-based adaptation of component behavioural interfaces. In *Proceedings of COORDINATION'07, volume 4467 of Lecture Notes in Computer Science*, (pp. 305–323). Springer.

Cubo, J., Salaün, G., Canal, C., Pimentel, E., & Poizat, P. (2007b). A model-based approach to the verification and adaptation of WF/.NET components. In *Proceedings of FACS'07, volume 215 of Electronic Notes in Theoretical Computer Science*, (pp. 39–55). Elsevier.

Cubo, J., Sama, M., Raimondi, F., & Rosenblum, D. (2009). A model to design and verify context-aware adaptive service composition. In *Proceedings of SCC'09*, (pp. 184–191). IEEE Computer Society.

Dargie, W. (Ed.). (2009). *Context-aware computing and self-managing systems*. CRC Press.

de Alfaro, L., & Henzinger, T. A. (2001). Interface automata. In *Proceedings of ESEC/FSE'01*, (pp. 109–120). ACM Press.

Dey, A., & Abowd, G. (2000). Towards a better understanding of context and context-awareness. In *Proceedings of Workshop on the What, Who, Where, When and How of Context-Awareness*, (pp. 304–307).

Dumas, M., Spork, M., & Wang, K. (2006). Adapt or perish: Algebra and visual notation for service interface adaptation. In *Proceedings of BPM'06, volume 4102 of Lecture Notes in Computer Science*, (pp. 65–80). Springer.

Erl, T. (2005). *Service-oriented architecture (SOA): Concepts, technology, and design*. Prentice Hall.

Fiadeiro, J. L., & Lopes, A. (2010). A model for dynamic reconfiguration in service-oriented architectures. In *Proceedings of ECSA'10, volume 6285 of Lecture Notes in Computer Science*, (pp. 70–85). Springer.

Filman, R. E., Elrad, T., Clarke, S., & Aksit, M. (2004). *Aspect-oriented software development*. Addison-Wesley.

Foster, H., Uchitel, S., & Kramer, J. (2006). LTSA-WS: A tool for model-based verification of web service compositions and choreography. In *Proceedings of ICSE, 06*, 771–774.

Fu, X., Bultan, T., & Su, J. (2004). Analysis of interacting BPEL web services. In *Proceedings of WWW, 04*, 621–630.

Gaspari, M., & Zavattaro, G. (1999). A process algebraic specification of the new asynchronous CORBA messaging service. In *Proceedings of ECOOP'99, volume 1628 of Lecture Notes in Computer Science*, (pp. 495–518).

Hameurlain, N. (2007). Flexible behavioural compatibility and substitutability for component protocols: A formal specification. In *Proceedings of SEFM, 07*, 391–400.

Han, W., Shi, X., & Chen, R. (2008). Process-context aware matchmaking for web service composition. *Journal of Network and Computer Applications, 31*(4), 559–576.

Hennessy, M., & Lin, H. (1995). Symbolic bisimulations. *Theoretical Computer Science, 138*(2), 353–389.

Idrissi, Y. E. B. E., Ajhoun, R., & Idrissi, M. J. (2010). Multicriteria-based decision for services discovery and selection. *Smart Innovation. Systems and Technologies, 6*, 41–51.

Inverardi, P., & Tivoli, M. (2003). Deadlock-free software architectures for COM/DCOM applications. *Journal of Systems and Software, 65*(3), 173–183.

Keller, U., Lara, R., Lausen, H., Polleres, A., & Fensel, D. (2005). Automatic location of services. In *Proceedings of ESWC'05, volume 3532 of Lecture Notes in Computer Science*, (pp. 1–16). Springer.

Klusch, M., Fries, B., & Sycara, K. (2006). Automated Semantic Web service discovery with OWLS-MX. In *Proceedings of AAMAS, 06*, 915–922.

Kouadri, S., & Hirsbrunner, B. (2003). Towards a context-based service composition framework. In. *Proceedings of ICWS, 03*, 42–45.

Lausen, H., Polleres, A., & Roman, D. (2006). *Web service modeling ontology (WSMO)*. W3C Member Submission.

Li, L., & Horrocks, I. (2003). A software framework for matchmaking based on Semantic Web technology. In *Proceedings of WWW, 03*, 331–339.

López, M., Qayyum, Z., Cuesta, C. E., Marcos, E., & Oquendo, F. (2008). Representing service-oriented architectural models using pi-AD. In *Proceedings of ECSA'08, volume 5292 of Lecture Notes in Computer Science*, (pp. 273–280). Springer.

Luo, N., Yan, J., Liu, M., & Yang, S. (2006). Towards context-aware composition of Web services. In *Proceedings of GCC'06*, (pp. 494–499). IEEE Computer Society.

Magee, J., Kramer, J., & Giannakopoulou, D. (1999). Behaviour analysis of software architectures. In *Proceedings of WICSA, 99*, 35–49.

Mateescu, R., Poizat, P., & Salaün, G. (2008). Adaptation of service protocols using process algebra and on-the-fly reduction techniques. In *Proceedings of ICSOC'08, volume 5364 of Lecture Notes in Computer Science*, (pp. 84–99). Springer.

Meyer, B. (1988). *Object-oriented software construction*. Prentice-Hall, 1988.

Microsoft. (2009). *The. NET framework*. Microsoft Corporation. Retrieved September 23, 2010, from http://www.microsoft.com/net

Microsoft. (2010). *COM: Component object model*. Microsoft Corporation. Retrieved October 10, 2011, from http://www.microsoft.com/com

Milner, R. (1980). Lecture Notes in Computer Science: *Vol. 2. Calculus of communicating systems*. Springer.

Mokhtar, S., Fournier, D., Georgantas, N., & Issarny, V. (2006). Context-aware service composition in pervasive computing environments. In *Proceedings of RISE'05, volume 3943 of Lecture Notes in Computer Science*, (pp. 129–144). Springer.

Nezhad, H. R. M., Benatallah, B., Martens, A., Curbera, F., & Casati, F. (2007). Semi-automated adaptation of service interactions. In *Proceedings of WWW'07*. ACM Press.

Nicoara, A., & Alonso, G. (2005). *PROSE - A middleware platform for dynamic adaptation*. Demo presented at AOSD'05.

Nierstrasz, O., Denker, M., & Renggli, L. (2009). Model-centric, context-aware software adaptation. In *Software Engineering for Self-Adaptive Systems*. In *Lecture Notes in Computer Science* (*Vol. 5525*, pp. 28–145). Springer.

Paolucci, M., Kawamura, T., Payne, T., & Sycara, K. (2002). Semantic matching of Web services capabilities. In *Proceedings of ISWC'02, volume 2342 of Lecture Notes in Computer Science*, (pp. 333–347). Springer.

Patil, A., Oundhakar, S., Sheth, A., & Verma, K. (2004). METEOR-S Web service annotation framework. In *Proceedings of WWW, 04*, 553–562.

Salaün, G. (2008). Generation of service wrapper protocols from choreography specifications. In *Proceedings of SEFM, 08*, 313–322.

Salber, D., Dey, A., & Abowd, G. (1999). The context toolkit: Aiding the development of context-enabled applications. In *Proceedings of CHI'99*, (pp. 434–441). ACM Press.

Schilit, B., Adams, N., & Want, R. (1994). Context-aware computing applications. In *Proceedings of WMCSA, 94*, 85–90.

Schilit, B., Adams, N., & Want, R. (1994). Context-aware computing applications. In *Proceedings of WMCSA, 94*, 85–90.

Scribner, K. (2007). *Microsoft Windows workflow foundation: Step by step*. Microsoft Press.

Sharp, J. (2007). *Microsoft Windows communication foundation: Step by step*. Microsoft Press.

Sheng, Q., Benatallah, B., Maamar, Z., Dumas, M., & Ngu, A. H. (2009). Configurable composition and adaptive provisioning of Web services. *IEEE Transactions on Services Computing, 2*(1), 34–49.

Spanoudakis, G., Mahbub, K., & Zisman, A. (2007). A platform for context aware runtime Web service discovery. In *Proceedings of ICWS, 07*, 233–240.

Sun Microsystems. (2003). *Java 2 platform enterprise edition specification*, v1.4. Final release, 11/24/03, Nov.

van der Aalst, W., & ter Hofstede, A. (2005). YAWL: Yet another workflow language. *Information Systems, 30*(4), 245–275.

Wang, L., & Krishnan, P. (2006). A framework for checking behavioral compatibility for component selection. In *Proceedings of ASWEC, 06*, 49–60.

Wang, Z., Elbaum, S., & Rosenblum, D. S. (2007). Automated generation of context-aware tests. *Proceedings of ICSE, 07*, 406–415.

Yellin, D. M., & Strom, D. E. (1997). Protocol specifications and components adaptors. *ACM Transactions on Programming Languages and Systems, 19*(2), 292–333.

Zapletal, M. (2008). Deriving business service interfaces in windows workflow from UMM transactions. In *Proceedings of ICSOC '08, volume 5364 of Lecture Notes in Computer Science*, (pp. 498–504). Springer.

Zapletal, M., van der Aalst, W., Russell, N., Liegl, P., & Werthner, H. (2009). An analysis of Windows workflow's control-flow expressiveness. In *Proceedings of ECOWS*, *09*, 200–209.

KEY TERMS AND DEFINITIONS

Adaptation Contract: Is a mapping gives between the service events by avoiding interoperability problems during the composition.

Behaviour or Protocol: Interaction protocols of a business process (such as a service).

Business Process Execution Language (BPEL): Is an OASIS standard executable language for specifying actions within business processes with web services.

Commercial-Off-The-Shelf (COTS): Describes ready-made products that can easily be obtained.

Context-Aware Computing: Covers all the topics related to the building of systems which are sensitive to their context (location, identity, time and activity), by adapting their behaviour at run-time according to the changing conditions.

Enterprise Service Bus (ESB): Is a software architecture model used to facilitate interaction and communication between service-oriented applications.

Service-Oriented Architecture (SOA): Is a set of principles and methodologies for designing and developing software in the form of interoperable services.

Signature: operation names and types of a component or service.

Simple Object Access Protocol (SOAP): Is a protocol specification for exchanging structured information in the implementation of Web Services in computer networks.

Symbolic Transition System (STS): Is a as a Labelled Transition System (LTS) augmented with state variables, guards and functions on transitions.

Semantic Web Technologies: Examples, Web Ontology Language for Services (OWL-S), Web Services Modeling Ontology (WSMO), METEOR-S, or Semantic Annotations for WSDL and XML Schema (SAWSDL).

Web Services Description Languages (WSDL): Is an XML-based language that is used for describing the functionality offered by a Web service.

Web Services: Is a method of communication between two electronic devices over the web (internet).

Windows Workflow Foundation (WF): Is a Microsoft technology that provides an API, an in-process workflow engine, and a rehostable designer to implement long-running business processes (components or services) as workflows within .NET applications.

ENDNOTES

[1] http://www.omg.org/mda/. Accessed on 10 October 2011.

[2] http://www.corba.org/. Accessed on 10 October 2011.

[3] http://www.w3.org/TR/wsdl. Accessed on 10 October 2011.

[4] http://www.w3.org/TR/soap/. Accessed on 10 October 2011.

[5] http://uddi.xml.org/. Accessed on 10 October 2011.

[6] http://www.omg.org/spec/SoaML/. Accessed on 10 October 2011.

[7] http://www.w3.org/Submission/OWL-S. Accessed on 10 October 2011.

[8] http://www.w3.org/TR/sawsdl. Accessed on 10 October 2011.

9   http://www.w3.org/TR/owl2-overview/. Accessed on 10 October 2011.

10   http://mail.google.com/. Accessed on 10 October 2011.

11   We distinguish clients and services, although both refer to components or services.

12   http://protege.stanford.edu/. Accessed on 10 October 2011.

13   http://wn-similarity.sourceforge.net/. Accessed on 10 October 2011.

14   http://www.w3.org/TR/nl-spec/. Accessed on 10 October 2011.

Chapter 5
Towards Event–Driven Context–Aware Web Services[1]

Guadalupe Ortiz
*Quercus Software Engineering Group, Spain &
UCASE Software Engineering Group, Spain*

Alfonso García de Prado
UCASE Software Engineering Group, Spain

Juan Boubeta-Puig
UCASE Software Engineering Group, Spain

Inmaculada Medina-Bulo
UCASE Software Engineering Group, Spain

ABSTRACT

Web services provide a successful way to communicate distributed applications, in a platform-independent and loosely coupled manner. Even though there are examples of good practice for the design, development, and management of web services, getting services to be context-aware is still under investigation. Current proposals require communication with an external context server or manager, slowing down service performance. In this work, the authors propose an architecture which utilizes complex event processing for detecting context events relevant to the services in question and an aspect-oriented adaptation, maintaining a loosely coupled service implementation as well as keeping its main functionality structure without adding any context-related intrusive code.

INTRODUCTION

In recent years, Service-Oriented Architectures (SOAs) have emerged as an efficient solution for the implementation of systems in which modularity and communication among third parties are key factors. This fact has led to the increasing development of distributed applications composed of reusable and sharable components (services). These components have well-defined platform-independent interfaces, which allow SOA-based systems to quickly and easily adapt to changing business conditions.

However, although there are good procedures for the design, development and management of Web services, there are scopes where Web service

DOI: 10.4018/978-1-4666-2089-6.ch005

adaptation is required. For instance, we may have services that would be suitable for the adaptation of the invoking client's specific context, service answers which should be adapted depending on the type of invoking device or services which are to return different answers depending on the specific client using it. In the past, we proposed a method for adapting services to the invoking device (Ortiz & Garcia de Prado, 2010a) as well as to adapt them to the client-specific context (Ortiz, & Garcia de Prado, 2010b); in this work, we will tackle their adaptation to the external context, which should be implemented appropriately, so that the loosely-coupled nature of web services is maintained. Previous approaches are good for the specific type of context dealt with –adapting to device and client-specific context– but are not prepared to deal with the external context, which requires of additional mechanisms in order to be able to capture the latter as well as detect what is relevant for the current service invocation.

In this regard, adapting services to context and current conditions might require the analysis of context information very often. Nevertheless, service-oriented architectures are not suitable for environments where it is necessary to continuously analyze the information flowing through the system, a key factor for an appropriate context-aware service implementation. This limitation may be solved by the joint use of Complex Event Processing (CEP) (Luckham, 2002) together with SOA. CEP can process and analyze large amounts of events and correlate them to detect critical or relevant information; in this scope event patterns are used to infer new more complex and meaningful events related to context.

However, most approaches implementing context-aware services do not use CEP or are not using it for this purpose, therefore having to continuously access a context server or manager.

Besides, requirements for service adaptation to context might change along the useful life of a service; since new relevant contexts might be taken into account or some older ones might be

discarded because they are not considered relevant any more. This leads to the fact that we need an approach which provides service adaptation in a completely decoupled way to facilitate service maintenance and evolution. In our previous approaches, Aspect-Oriented Programming (AOP) demonstrated to be a good alternative to decouple context adaptation from service implementation.

As a result of the facts described in previous paragraphs, in this work, we propose the use of CEP in conjunction with aspect-oriented adapters, to avoid services having to access external modules for their adaptation to context information and to ease their maintenance and evolution.

The rest of the chapter is organized as follows: Section 2 provides a short background on context-awareness, complex event processing and aspect-oriented programming. Then, Section 3 explains the envisaged architecture as well as provides an illustrating scenario to facilitate the proposal understanding. Afterwards, Section 4 outlines main related work. Finally, conclusions and future work are provided in Section 5.

BACKGROUND

In this section we will introduce the concept of context-awareness, complex event processing and aspect-oriented programming.

Context-Awareness

Dey et al.'s context definition in (Abowd et al., 1999) is specially well-known –page 3, section 2.2: "Context is any information that can be used to characterize the situation of an entity. An entity is a person, place, or object that is considered relevant to the interaction between a user and an application, including the user and applications themselves".

The term context-awareness supports the fact that the context information provided by the client, or taken from the environment, is properly used by the system so as to improve the quality of its; that is, using information such as location, social attributes and other information to foresee its necessities so that we can offer more personalized systems. Therefore, a system is context-aware if it uses the context to provide relevant information or services to the user, adapting the system behavior to the particular needs of a specific user.

A context-classification can be found at García de Prado and Ortiz (2011); in this work we will focus on the environmental context, which describes the environmental conditions of both user and services. Sensors or specific services are normally used in order to provide such kind of information as location, temperature, noise, social events, et cetera. This type of context will imply adapting the information sent to the client; for instance, if location is taken into account when searching a cinema, the result would be restricted to the current city, or when checking the playbill from a mobile device, it would be better to avoid film trailers.

Complex Event Processing

CEP (Ortiz & Garcia de Prado, 2010a) is a technology that provides a set of techniques to help discover complex events by analyzing and correlating other basic and complex events. A basic event occurs at a point in time, whereas a complex event can take place over a period of time, it is added from basic or other complex events and contains more semantic meaning. Therefore, CEP allows the detection of complex and meaningful events, known as situations, and inferring valuable knowledge for end users. For instance, let's suppose that we are looking for tourism activities in a city we are visiting; going to a museum is fine when is raining; however it is not the same that it is raining when you are going to visit the museum, than it is raining and public transports have gone on strike, when you are five kilometers away from the museum.

These events will help make decisions when necessary. Currently, the integration of Event-Driven Architecture (EDA) and SOA is known as Event-Driven SOA (ED-SOA) or SOA 2.0 (Sosinsky, 2011). SOA 2.0 will ensure that services do not only exchange messages between them, but also publish events and receive event notifications from others. For this purpose, an Enterprise Service Bus (ESB) will be necessary to process, enrich and route messages between services of different applications. Further information on the integration of CEP with SOA in other scenarios can be found at Boubeta, Ortiz, and Medina (2011).

Aspect-Oriented Programming

AOP arises due to problems detected in Object-Oriented Programming (OOP) (Elrad, Aksit, Kitzales, Lieberherr, & Ossher, 2001). OOP is supposed to permit the encapsulation and modularity of related data and methods which address a common goal. However, we may find it impossible to model several concerns into a unique and structured decomposition of units: these would be crosscutting concerns, which do not have a unique and logical decomposition of the code structure into separate functionalities. As a result of these, code is scattered and tangled all over our application.

AOP allows us to modularise crosscutting concerns encapsulating them into meaningful independent units called aspects. Afterwards, a method to weave the aspect code with the original one is applied. Further information on aspect-oriented techniques can be found at Elrad et al. (2001).

THE PROPOSAL IN A NUTSHELL

In this section we propose an architecture for adapting services to context automatically and we illustrate the proposal through an example scenario.

Figure 1. Architecture for context-aware services using CEP and AOP

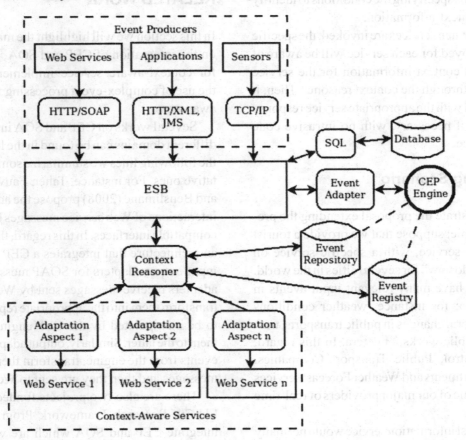

Proposed Architecture for Context-Aware Services

As we have previously mentioned, this work proposes the adaptation of services to context through the use of a CEP engine to detect basic and complex events (context) and through an aspect-oriented implementation of the adaptation code. For this purpose we have envisaged the architecture in Figure 1, which is described in the following paragraphs.

We propose a solution based on the integration of CEP and SOA. A CEP engine is the key element of the integration, which will facilitate the efficient detection of relevant situations in heterogeneous information systems.

We assume that events and/or patterns to be detected are already known and deployed in the CEP engine. We also assume that the right event producers have already been selected and plugged into the system. Event producers can be web services, applications and sensors. Some of these applications are Web applications that allow users to interact with information management systems. Sensors monitor the environment to capture information (temperature, rain, etc.) which is then transmitted to the system using the controller integrated into the mentioned sensors.

These events are then published in the ESB and processed by the context reasoner. Events are sent in parallel to the database management system for storage as well to event streams of the CEP engine. This engine will contain the defined event patterns specifying the conditions to identify relevant context information.

Finally, when services are invoked, the specific aspect deployed for each service will be aware of the relevant context information for the service in question through the context reasoner. Then, it will proceed with the appropriate service response adaptation, if necessary, with no intrusive code in the service.

Illustrating Scenario

Let's us illustrate the proposal extending the previous example: suppose that we provide a tourist information service, with a specific service on "what can I do now" for several cities in the world.

We may have many relevant input events in this scenario: for instance, weather conditions alerts, temporal changes in public transports, traffic jams, public works, et cetera. In this regard, Traffic Control, Public Transport Companies, Police Departments and Weather Forecast services might be some of our major providers of real-time information.

The tourist information service would normally collect all the possible activities in the city in question for today.

Let's imagine now that, from the events detected, we are aware that it is raining and public transports have gone on strike.

Bearing in mind these facts, among the multiple activities available a sunbath in the beach and climbing a mountain to reach a watch tower are discarded due to weather conditions.

Then a close-by museum could be suggested as a visiting alternative, but if it is five kilometers away (taking into account that public transports are not working), we could alternatively suggest to go to the nearby shopping mall. However, if we can also detect from the user-specific context that a car has been rented by the user for this vacation, then, the far-away museum is still a good alternative.

RELATED WORK

In this section we will highlight the main research on the integration of CEP and SOA, approaches for context-aware service implementation and the use of complex-event processing for context-awareness.

Several works on CEP and SOA integration in different domains can be found in the literature; in the following lines we summarize some representative ones. For instance, Taher, Fauvet, Dumas, and Benslimane (2008) propose the adaptation of interactions of Web service messages between incompatible interfaces. In this regard, they develop an architecture that integrates a CEP engine and input/output adapters for SOAP messages. Input adapters receive messages sent by Web services, transform them into the appropriate representation to be manipulated by the CEP engine and send them to the latter. Similarly, output adapters receive events from the engine, transform them to SOAP messages and then they are sent to Web services.

There are also two projects funded under the EU 7th Research Framework Programme that integrate CEP and SOA which are worth mentioning: MASTER and COMPAS. MASTER (Managing Assurance, Security and Trust for sERvices Project, 2011) provides an infrastructure that facilitates monitoring, enforcement, and auditing of security compliance and COMPAS (Compliance-driven Models, Languages, and Architectures for Services Project, 2011) designs and implements an architectural framework to ensure dynamic and on-going compliance of software services to business regulations and stated user service-requirements. In general, we can assert that integrating SOA and CEP is useful for several scenarios and architectures, but we did not find any work which integrated them for context-awareness.

Most of the work found in the context adaptation area specially focuses on the composition of different services depending on the specific context; for instance, Vukovic's dissertation (Vukovic,

2007). Another example is the paper from Pauty, Preuveeners, Rigole, and Berbers (2006), where they propose context-aware service development from several points of view; we are particularly interested in their context-aware services: they propose an ontology-based approach dependent on the proposed framework. Besides, the work from Keidl and Kemper (2004) consists of an approach for services to deal with client contextual information through a context framework. In their case, the context is always included in the client SOAP header as well as in service messages. This implies that not only services, but also clients have to process the context included in the header; however they do not explore how the client can deal with the received context. We expect to deal with external context too, without needing to deliver it through the SOAP message. Bucchiarone, Kazhamiakin, Cappiello, Di Nitto, and Mazza (2010) focus on the role of context in adaptation activities and describe a life-cycle for designing and developing adaptable service-based applications. They consider necessary to build contextual monitors and adaption mechanisms to detect context changes and trigger the subsequent actions. Furthermore, they propose rule engines as possible candidates for this purpose. However, implementations using rule engines are slower and less efficient in handling and receiving notifications, compared to those using CEP engines (Boubeta et al., 2011). Therefore, rule engines are not suitable for all the critical services in which a fast response is needed. A thorough analysis of context-awareness related work can be found in García de Prado and Ortiz (2011).

There are some approaches which use CEP for monitoring such as the one from Xu, Wolf, Stojanovic, and Happel (2010), where CEP is used in the Ambient Assisted Living (AAL) domain. They propose its use to detect events in AAL for being able to take real time actions. The paper from Li, Sehic, and Dustdar (2010) is also worth a special mention. They provide an adaptive approach to context provisioning and automatic generation of actions. The latter definitely bears similarities with our proposal, however we focus on non-intrusive service result adaptation rather than action taking.

To sum up, our proposal differs from others in benefiting from the advantages of the use of CEP and an aspect-oriented programming altogether with SOA to adapt services to context information in a decoupled way, where the context can be automatically detected through real time events.

FUTURE RESEARCH DIRECTIONS

In the future we expect to refine the architecture and build a prototype so as to prove its usefulness. We also plan to provide a user-friendly interface to define the context that should be taken into account, as well as a model-driven development for pattern and aspect code generation. Model-driven development allows us to focus on the essential aspects of the system, delaying the decision of which technology to use in the implementation for a later step. Models may be used at multiple phases of development, from the initial system specification to its testing and deployment. Each model will address one concern, regardless of the remaining issues involved in the system's development, thus allowing the separation of the final implementation technology from the business logic achieved by the system. Transformations between models and from models to code allow automated system development from the models themselves. As a consequence, Model-Driven Architecture aims to promote the roles of models in software development. MDA models are generally divided into three categories: Platform-Independent Models (PIM) representing the system without coupling it to any specific platform or language, Platform-Specific Models (PSM) express the system based on a specific platform, technology and programming languages, and finally, Code Layer provides the final application as code. A set of transformation rules may also be created in order to transform platform-independent models into platform-specific ones automatically and the latter into the final application code.

In this regard, we plan to continue our previous work providing a common syntax for the required adaptation description and these requirements should be included in the system models. In our previous work (Ortiz & Garcia de Prado, 2010a), we made use of a set of predefined stereotypes in order to mark the elements in the system model which should be adapted for different invoking devices. From this platform-independent model we followed a model-driven process until code generation; implementation details are out of the scope of this chapter and published at Ortiz & Garcia de Prado (2010a). In this regard, we plan to continue with the current stereotype definition, extending the stereotype set defined for device adaptation with an appropriate suite for context adaptation as well as for customization. However, it might be the case that adaptation to external context requires an extension of the proposal. In any case, we always aim to maintain a unified syntax and methodology for service adaptation.

CONCLUSION

In this chapter, we have presented an envisaged architecture for context-aware web services, where context is continuously monitored by a CEP engine and service adaptation to context is done through a non-intrusive aspect-oriented implementation. We therefore propose to be able to adapt web services in multiple scenarios and have discussed how current approaches propose to do it, which mostly modify the client-side implementation and do not use complex event processing mechanisms. We propose the adaptation to be done in the service-side, therefore saving client resources, as well as enabling the enlargement of the spectrum of prospective service users, facilitating context information through a real time observation thanks to a complex-event processing engine.

Besides, as already mentioned, aspect-oriented code for adaptation implementation will let us maintain the original main functionality service code completely encapsulated and separate from the adaptation code, facilitating maintenance of future changes in the adaptation requirements, as well as habilitating the chance of providing dynamic adaptations.

REFERENCES

Abowd, G. D., Dey, A. K., Brown, P. J., Davies, N., Smith, M., & Steggles, P. (1999). Towards a better understanding of context and context-awareness. In *1st International Symposium on Handheld and Ubiquitous Computing, Vol. 1707*, (pp. 304-307). Heidelberg, Germany: Springer-Verlag.

Boubeta, J., Ortiz, G., & Medina, I. (2011). *An approach of early disease detection using CEP and SOA. In 3rd International Conferences on Advanced Service Computing* (pp. 143–148). Italy: Xpert Publishing Services.

Bucchiarone, A., Kazhamiakin, R., Cappiello, C., Di Nitto, E., & Mazza, V. (2010). A context-driven adaptation process for service-based applications. In *2nd International Workshop on Principles of Engineering Service-Oriented Systems* (pp. 50-56). New York, NY: ACM.

Compliance-Driven Models, Languages, and Architectures for Services Project (COMPAS). (n.d.). Retrieved September 15, 2011, from http://www.compas-ict.eu/

Elrad, T., Aksit, M., Kitzales, G., Lieberherr, K., & Ossher, H. (2001). Discussing aspects of AOP. *Communications of the ACM, 44*(10), 33–38.

García de Prado, A., & Ortiz, G. (2011). *Context-aware services: A survey on current proposals. In 3rd International Conferences on Advanced Service Computing* (pp. 104–109). Italy: Xpert Publishing Services.

Keidl, M., & Kemper, A. (2004). Towards context-aware adaptable Web services. In *13th International World Wide Web conference on Alternate* (pp. 55-65). New York, NY: ACM.

Li, F., Sehic, S., & Dustdar, S. (2010). COPAL: An adaptive approach to context provisioning. In *6th International Conference on Wireless and Mobile Computing, Networking and Communications* (286-293). California: IEEE.

Luckham, D. (2002). *The power of events: An introduction to complex event processing in distributed enterprise systems*. Boston, MA: Addison-Wesley.

Managing Assurance, Security and Trust for sERvices Project (MASTER). (n.d.). Retrieved September 12, 2011, from http://www.master-fp7.eu/

Ortiz, G., & Garcia de Prado, A. (2010). Improving Device-Aware Web Services and their Mobile Clients through an Aspect-Oriented, Model-Driven Approach. *Information and Software Technology Journal, 52*(10), 1080–1093.

Ortiz, G., & Garcia de Prado, A. (2010). Web service adaptation: A unified approach versus multiple methodologies for different scenarios. In *5th International Conference on Internet and Web Applications and Services* (pp. 569-572). California: IEEE CS Press.

Pauty, J., Preuveeners, D., Rigole, P., & Berbers, Y. (2006). Research challenges in mobile and context-aware service development. In *Proceedings of Future Research Challenges in Software and Services* (pp. 141-148). Vienna, Austria

Sosinsky, B. (2011). *Cloud computing bible*. Indiana: Wiley.

Taher, Y., Fauvet, M., Dumas, M., & Benslimane, D. (2008). Using CEP technology to adapt messages exchanged by web services. In *17th International Conference on World Wide Web* (pp. 1231-1232). Beijing, China: ACM.

Vukovic, M. (2007). *Context-aware service composition. Technical Report*. Cambridge: University of Cambridge.

Xu, Y., Wolf, P., Stojanovic, N., & Happel, H. J. (2010). Semantic-based in the AAL domain. *Posters & Demos* In *9th International Semantic Web Conference* (pp. 9-12). Shanghai, China.

ADDITIONAL READING

W3C. (n.d.). *Simple object access protocol (SOAP)*. Retrieved October 22, 2011, from http://www.w3.org/TR/soap/

W3C. (n.d.). *Web services architecture*. Retrieved October 21, 2011, from http://www.w3.org/TR/ws-arch/

W3C. (n.d.). *Web services description language (WSDL)*. Retrieved October 25, 2011, from p://www.w3.org/TR/wsdl

Athanasopoulos, D., Zarras, A., Issarny, V., Pitoura, E., & Vassiliadis, P. (2008). CoWSAMI: Interface-aware context gathering in ambient intelligence environments. *Pervasive and Mobile Computing, 4*, 360–389.

Baldauf, M., Dustdar, S., & Rosenberg, F. (2007). A survey on context-aware systems. *International Journal of Ad Hoc and Ubiquitous Computing, 2*, 263–277.

Bardram, J. E. (2005). The Java context awareness framework (JCAF)–A service infrastructure and programming framework for context-aware applications. In Gellersen, H. W. (Eds.), *Pervasive Computing* (pp. 98–115). Berlin, Germany: Springer.

Cantera Fonseca, J. M., & Lewis, R. (2011). *W3C – Delivery context ontology*. Retrieved December 3, 2011, from http://www.w3.org/TR/dcontology/

Carton, A., Clarke, S., Senart, A., & Cahill, V. (2007). Aspect-oriented model-driven development for mobile context-aware computing. In *1st International Workshop on Software Engineering for Pervasive Computing Applications, Systems, and Environments* (pp. 5-5). Minneapolis, MN: IEEE.

Chaari, T., Laforest, F., & Celentano, A. (2004). *Design of context-aware applications based on web services.* Technical Report, Università Ca'Foscari di Venezia, Italy

Chen, G., & Kotz, D. (2000). *A survey of context-aware mobile computing research.* Hanover, NH: Dartmouth College.

Chen, H., Finin, T., & Joshi, A. (2003). An ontology for context-aware pervasive computing environments. *The Knowledge Engineering Review, 18,* 197–207.

Chen, I., Yang, S., & Zhang, J. (2006). Ubiquitous provision of context aware Web services. In *International Conference on Services Computing* (pp. 60-68). Chicago, IL: IEEE.

Clarke, S., & Baniassad, E. (2005). *Aspect-oriented analysis and design: The theme approach.* Addison-Wesley Professional.

De Almeida, D. R., Baptista, C. D., Da Silva, E. R., Campelo, C. E. C., De Figueiredo, H. F., & Lacerda, Y. A. (2006). A context-aware system based on service-oriented architecture. In *20th International Conference on Advanced Information Networking and Applications, Vol. 1.* (pp. 205-210). Vienna, Austria: IEEE.

Dey, A. K. (2001). Understanding and using context. *Personal and Ubiquitous Computing, 5,* 4–7.

Dey, A. K., Salber, D., & Abowd, G. D. (1999). *A context-based infrastructure for smart environments. Technical Report.* USA: Georgia Institute of Technology.

Dockhorn Costa, P., Ferreira Pires, L., van Sinderen, M. J., & Pereira Filho, J. G. (2004). *Towards a service platform for mobile context-aware applications* (pp. 48–61). Porto, Portugal: INSTICC Press.

Dorn, C., & Dustdar, S. (2006). Sharing hierarchical context for mobile web services. *Distributed and Parallel Databases, 21,* 85–111.

Grassi, V., & Sindico, A. (2007). Towards model driven design of service-based context-aware applications. In *International Workshop on Engineering of Software Services for Pervasive Environments in Conjunction with the 6th ESEC/FSE Joint Meeting – ESSPE* (pp. 69-74). Dubrovnik, Croatia: IEEE.

Gu, T., Pung, H. K., & Zhang, D. Q. (2005). A service-oriented middleware for building context-aware services. *Journal of Network and Computer Applications, 28,* 1–18.

Han, B., Jia, W., Shen, J., & Yuen, M.-C. (2005). Context-awareness in mobile web services. In Cao, J., Yang, L., Guo, M., & Lau, F. (Eds.), *Parallel and distributed processing and applications* (pp. 519–528). Berlin, Germany: Springer.

Held, A., Buchholz, S., Schill, A., & Schill, E. (2002). Modeling of context information for pervasive computing applications. In *the 6th World Multiconference on Systemics, Cybernetics and Informatics* (pp. 1-6). Orlando, FL: Citeseer.

Henricksen, K., Indulska, J., McFadden, T., & Balasubramaniam, S. (2005). Middleware for distributed context-aware systems. *International Symposium on Distributed Objects and Applications,* (pp. 846-863).

Indulska, J., Robinson, R., Rakotonirainy, A., & Henricksen, K. (2003). Experiences in using CC/PP in context-aware systems. In *4th International Conference on Mobile Data Management* (pp. 247–261). London, UK: Springer-Verlag.

Kapitsaki, G. M., Prezerakos, G. N., Tselikas, N. D., & Venieris, I. S. (2009). Context-aware service engineering: A survey. *Journal of Systems and Software, 82*, 1285–1297.

Kiczales, G., Lamping, J., Mendhekar, A., Maeda, C., Lopes, C., Loingtier, J.-M., & Irwin, J. (1997). Aspect-oriented programming. In *European Conference on Object-Oriented Programming* (pp. 220-242). Finland. Springer-Verlag.

Klein, C., Schmid, R., Leuxner, C., Sitou, W., & Spanfelner, B. (2008). A survey of context adaptation in autonomic computing. In *4th International Conference on Autonomic and Autonomous Systems* (pp. 106-111). Gosier, Guadeloupe: IEEE.

Korpipaa, P., Mantyjarvi, J., Kela, J., Keranen, H., & Malm, E.-J. (2003). Managing context information in mobile devices. *IEEE Pervasive Computing / IEEE Computer Society and IEEE Communications Society, 2*, 42–51.

Laakko, T., & Hiltunen, T. (2005). Adapting Web content to mobile user agents. *IEEE Internet Computing, 9*, 46–53.

Menkhaus, G. (2001). Architecture for client-independent Web-based applications. In *Technology of Object-Oriented Languages and Systems* (pp. 32–40). Zurich, Switzerland: IEEE.

Mohomed, I., Cai, J. C., Chavoshi, S., & de Lara, E. (2006). Context-aware interactive content adaptation". In *4th International Conference on Mobile Systems, Applications and Services* (pp. 42-45). Uppsala, Sweden: ACM.

Monfort, V., & Hammoudi, S. (2009). Towards adaptable SOA: Model driven development, context and aspect. In *International Joint Conference on Service-Oriented Computing* (pp. 175- 189). Heidelberg, Germany: Springer.

Osland, P. O., Viken, B., Solsvik, F., Nyngreen, G., Wedvik, J., & Myklbust, S. E. (2006). Enabling context-aware applications. In *Convergence in Services, Media and Networks*. Bordeaux, France: Springer.

Pashtan, A., Kollipara, S., & Pearce, M. (2003). Adapting content for wireless web services. *IEEE Internet Computing, 7*, 79–85.

Pashtan, A., Kollipara, S., & Pearce, M. (2003). Adapting content for wireless web services. *IEEE Internet Computing, 7*, 79–85.

Pedersen, P. E., & Ling, R. (2003). Modifying adoption research for mobile internet service adoption: Cross-disciplinary interactions. In *36th Annual Hawaii International Conference on System Sciences* (pp. 90-99). Los Alamitos, CA: IEEE.

Pokraev, S., Costa, P. D., Pereira Filho, J. G., Zuidweg, M., Koolwaaij, J. W., & Van Setten, M. (2003). *Context-aware services - State of the art. Telematica Instituut, Ericsson*. CTI.

Preuveneers, D., & Berbers, Y. (2005). *Adaptive context management using a component-based approach* (pp. 14–26). DAIS.

Prezerakos, G. N., Tselikas, N. D., & Cortese, G. (2007). Model-driven composition of context-aware web services using ContextUML and aspects. In *International Conference on Web Services* (pp. 320-329). Salt Lake City, UT: IEEE.

Sheng, Q. Z., & Benatallah, B. (2005). ContextUML: A UML-Based Modeling Language for Model-Driven Development of Context-Aware Web Services Development. In *International Conference on Mobile Business* (pp. 206-212). Sydney, Australia: IEEE.

Sheng, Q. Z., Pohlenz, S., Yu, J., Wong, H. S., Ngu, A. H. H., & Maamar, Z. (200). ContextServ: A platform for rapid and flexible development of context-aware Web services. In *31st International Conference on Software Engineering* (pp. 619-622). Vancouver, Canada: IEEE.

Song, Y. J., Lee, D. H., Yim, J. G., & Nam, T. Y. (2007). Privacy aware adaptable Web services using petri nets. In *International Conference on Convergence Information Technology* (pp. 1933-1938). Gyeongju-si, Korea: IEEE.

Strang, T., & Popien, C. (2004). A context modeling survey. In *Workshop on Advanced Context Modelling, Reasoning and Management – 6th International Conference on Ubiquitous Computing*. Nottingham-England.

Truong, H.-L., & Dustdar, S. (2009). A survey on context-aware web service systems. *International Journal of Web Information Systems, 5,* 5–31.

Truong, H.-L., Dustdar, S., Baggio, D., Corlosquet, S., Dorn, C., & Giuliani, G. … Yu, H. (2008). InContext: A pervasive and collaborative working environment for emerging team forms. *International Symposium on Applications and the Internet* (pp. 118-125). Turku, Finland: IEEE.

Truong, H.-L., Juszczyk, L., Manzoor, A., & Dustdar, S. (2007). ESCAPE – An adaptive framework for managing and providing context information in emergency situations. In Kortuem, G., Finney, J., Lea, R., & Sundramoorthy, V. (Eds.), *Smart sensing and context* (pp. 207–222). Berlin, Germany: Springer.

Vale, S., & Hammoudi, S. (2008). Model driven development of context-aware service oriented architecture. In *11th International Conference on Computational Science and Engineering - Workshops* (pp. 412-418). San Paulo, Brazil: IEEE.

Yau, S. S., & Karim, F. (2004). A context-sensitive middleware for dynamic integration of mobile devices with network infrastructures. *Journal of Parallel and Distributed Computing, 64,* 301–317.

Ying, X., & Fu-yuan, X. (2006). Research on context modeling based on ontology. In *International Conference on Computational Intelligence for Modelling Control and Automation and International Conference on Intelligent Agents Web Technologies and International Commerce* (pp. 188-188). Sydney, Australia: IEEE.

Zhang, D. (2007). Web content adaptation for mobile handheld devices. *Communications of the ACM, 50,* 75–79.

KEY TERMS AND DEFINITIONS

Aspect-Oriented Programming: A programming paradigm which complement object-oriented programming, in which transversal functions are isolated from the main program's business logic.

Complex-Event Processing: Consists of processing and identifying the most meaningful events within an information system, analyzing their impact, and taking subsequent actions in real time.

Enterprise Service Bus: Is a software architecture model used to facilitate interaction and communication between service-oriented applications.

Model-Driven Development: Is a software development methodology which focuses on creating models of the systems, leaving implementation technologies for a later stage.

Model-Driven Engineering: Is a software development methodology which focuses on creating domain models, rather than on the computing concepts.

Service-Oriented Architecture: Service-Oriented Architecture is an architectural style, based on services.

Web Service: Modular application that can be invoked through the Internet following some established standards.

ENDNOTE

[1] G. Ortiz acknowledges the support from Ministerio de Ciencia e Innovación (TIN2008-02985) and Fondo Europeo de Desarrollo Regional (FEDER) for presenting this work at WAS4FI'2011. The authors also thank the support from the University of Cádiz through the Plan Propio (PR2011-004) and from Ministerio de Ciencia e Innovación (TIN2011-27242). Last, but not least, we would like to specially thank Novayre (http://www.novayre.com/) managers for their fruitful feedback and discussions on CEP.

Section 3
Adaptation for Composition

Chapter 6
Service–Oriented Systems for Adaptive Management of Service Composition

Valeria Cardellini
University of Roma "Tor Vergata," Italy

Stefano Iannucci
University of Roma "Tor Vergata," Italy

Valerio Di Valerio
University of Roma "Tor Vergata," Italy

Francesco Lo Presti
University of Roma "Tor Vergata," Italy

ABSTRACT

Service Oriented Systems (SOSs) based on the SOA paradigm are becoming popular thanks to a widely deployed internetworking infrastructure. They are composed by a possibly large number of heterogeneous third-party subsystems and usually operate in a highly varying execution environment, that makes it challenging to provide applications with Quality of Service (QoS) guarantees. A well-established approach to face the heterogeneous and varying operating environment is to design a SOS as a runtime self-adaptable software system, so that a prospective enterprise willing to realize a SOA application can dynamically choose the component services that best fit its requirements and the environment in which the application operates. In this chapter, the authors first review some representative frameworks that have been proposed for SOSs able to adaptively manage a SOA application with QoS requirements. These frameworks are commonly architected as self-adaptive systems following the MAPE-K (Monitor, Analyze, Plan, Execute, and Knowledge) reference model for autonomic computing. The chapter organizes the review using a specific taxonomy for each MAPE-K phase, with the aim to classify the different strategies and mechanisms that can be applied. Even if a self-adaptive system requires every MAPE-K phase, the authors then focus on the Plan phase, which is the core of each adaptation framework, presenting both optimal and sub-optimal approaches that have been proposed to effectively face the adaptation task at runtime.

DOI: 10.4018/978-1-4666-2089-6.ch006

INTRODUCTION

As a case study of SOS for the adaptive management of service composition, we present the main features of a prototype that follows the MAPE-K reference model. We analyze through a set of experiments the different degrees of reliability achieved by a SOA application able or not to detect and adapt its behavior with respect to the churn of the services used to compose it. Our experimental results show that the SOA application managed by the SOS achieves a reliability improvement up to 20% with respect to its unmanaged counterpart.

In computer science, Service-Oriented Architecture (SOA) is now a mature reference paradigm for developing network accessible, service-based applications. The main goal of designing applications following the SOA paradigm is to achieve a better degree of interoperability with respect to legacy distributed applications, which are tied up by constraints, such as programming languages and specific protocols and technologies. SOA applications are built up by composing black-box services that can be discovered and invoked using standard protocols, therefore hiding possibly different technologies. The service composition is usually described by a workflow representing the actual business logic of the application, defining both the execution and data flow.

SOA applications have the clear advantage over legacy applications to be easily reused because they can be published as services in a standard registry, where other applications can discover them for further invocation. As a consequence, the focus in developing a SOA application is shifted to activities concerning the identification, selection, and composition of services offered by third parties rather than the classic in-house development.

Systems realized using the SOA paradigm take the name of Service Oriented Systems (SOSs). They benefit from the SOA flexibility as well as from the presence of a widely deployed internetworking infrastructure. The diffusion of systems deployed using the SOA paradigm is leading to the proliferation of service marketplaces (such as SAP Service Marketplace and Windows Azure Marketplace), where an enterprise can find every component needed to build its SOA applications. With an ever increasing number of service providers on the global market scene, it is becoming easy to find multiple providers implementing the same functionality with different quality levels, e.g., different providers can exhibit different response times or costs for services that present the same logic. Therefore, depending on the needs of the SOA application, it is possible to dynamically select the services that best fit its (possibly changing) requirements.

However, several problems arise when a SOA application, which is offered using third party services, needs to fulfill non-functional requirements, because existing services may disappear or their performance may quickly fluctuate over time, due to the highly varying execution environment. The SOA paradigm easily allows to replace services with equivalent ones, but this task could be very challenging for a human being, especially when several services must be replaced at the same time. Similarly, when the service composition logic needs to be partially or even entirely modified in order to account for changes in the functional requirements, it is hard to manually choose among several alternative workflows, considering also the non-functional requirements. In addition, the management complexity of SOSs rapidly grows as the number of services involved in the compositions increases. To tackle such complexity, to reduce management costs, and to provide better operativeness, a common and well-established approach is to design SOSs as runtime self-adaptable software systems (Salehie & Tahvildari, 2009), that is, software systems able to detect changes in the environment and to properly reconfigure themselves.

In the field of self-adaptable software systems, the main research branches that have been pursued regard the functional and non-functional requirements of SOA applications. In this chapter, we focus on non-functional requirements, expressed as Quality of Service (QoS) attributes of SOSs.

The adaptation of non-functional requirements can follow either the best effort or *QoS-constrained* strategy. The former aims to improve non-functional attributes (e.g., response time or reliability) of the overall SOA application without ensuring any kind of guarantee, while the latter aims to provide a SOA application with predictable QoS attributes. In the last years both approaches have been largely investigated, e.g., (Ezenwoye & Sadjadi, 2007; Michlmayr, Rosenberg, Leitner & Dustdar, 2010) for the best effort strategy and (Ardagna, & Pernici, 2007; Cardellini, Casalicchio, Grassi, Iannucci, Lo Presti & Mirandola, in press; Menascè, Casalicchio & Dubey, 2010) for the QoS-constrained strategy. Each solution has its own characteristics and peculiarities in the way it faces the self-adaptation. In particular, since in the context of SOA applications, the management, the control, and performance prediction of the QoS characteristics of the offered service have been identified as the most critical tasks as they ultimately determine how the system guarantees QoS levels, most of the above efforts have focused and mostly differ for the different strategies adopted for the aforementioned tasks. Nevertheless, despite their differences, all these approaches follow a more general framework, called MAPE-K.

MAPE-K (Kephart & Chess, 2003) is a conceptual guideline for realizing self-adaptable systems (Salehie et al., 2009) and is composed of four essential phases: Monitor, Analyze, Plan, and Execute. There is also a Knowledge layer that support all the phases. The model is based on a feedback-control loop, that detects changes in the execution environment, analyzes them, plans the necessary actions to maximize some utility function, and executes these actions. In literature, the same approach is also referred to as CADA (Dobson et al., 2006), which stands for Collect, Analyze, Design, and Act.

In this chapter we first present and classify the different frameworks for adaptive management of service composition. Since they can all be regarded as instances of the MAPE-K framework we present each phase of the MAPE-K loop and discuss how the self-adaptation frameworks for SOA applications, so far proposed, implement it.

We then concentrate on the adaptation strategies themselves. In particular, since we focus on fulfilling the non-functional requirements of the SOA application, we analyze the approaches for service selection. Given a service composition, the service selection's aim is to identify those component services that provide the best implementation of the needed functionalities in order to satisfy the QoS requirements of the SOA application. Although service selection is not the only adaptation mechanism, our presentation focuses on it because it is leveraged by most of the self-adaptation frameworks we consider in our review.

As case study of SOS for the adaptive management of service composition, we then present MOSES (Cardellini et al., in press). MOSES is a methodology and a software tool implementing it to support the QoS-driven adaptation of a service-oriented system and represents a working example of framework organized according to the MAPE-K loop.

We validate on a motivating scenario characterized by a varying operating environment the runtime adaptation features provided by MOSES. Specifically, we analyze through a set of experiments conducted using the MOSES prototype the different degrees of reliability achieved by a SOA application able or not to detect changes and adapt its behavior with respect to the component services churn, i.e., to the change in the set of component services due to joins, graceful leaves, and failures. Our experimental results show that the runtime adaptation carried out by MOSES is able to improve the SOA application reliability even in a highly varying operating environment.

The rest of the chapter is organized as follows. The section below introduces some basic terminol-

Figure 1. a) SOA reference model; b) SOA reference model with broker

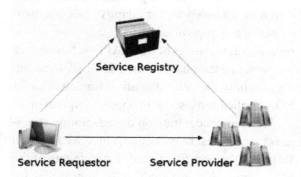
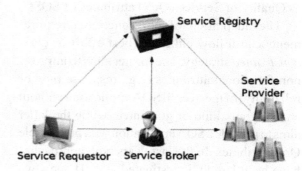

ogy used throughout the chapter. In the section after that we review the distinguishing features of the MAPE-K cycle and present our taxonomy for each specific MAPE-K phase. In the following two sections, we focus on the service selection approaches used in the Plan phase of MAPE-K, analyzing some representative formulations of optimization problems and heuristics. In the sixth section, we present our case study of adaptive SOS and analyze the experimental results. Finally, we present possible avenues for future work and conclude the chapter with some remarks.

SOA REFERENCE MODEL

Prior to analyze how to realize self-adaptable SOA applications, it is useful to introduce the SOA reference model, so to clarify the basic terminology used throughout the chapter.

The SOA reference model defines the interacting actors and their interaction modes. Looking over the SOA domain, the main actors are: the *service provider*, that offers a service, and the *service requestor*, that requests the service (in this chapter we will use service requestor and client interchangeably). To issue a service invocation, the service requestor has to know a service provider offering the needed functionality. To this end, the *service registry* holds information about existing services, which are published by service

providers themselves. Figure 1a illustrates the SOA reference model.

The above reference model is usually extended to include an intermediary entity. When the offered service is actually a service composition which adopts some adaptation mechanism, we refer to its provider as *service broker*. As shown in Figure 1b, the service broker is as an intermediary actor lying between the service requestors and the service providers, willing to offer to the requestors an added-value SOA application obtained by composing the services exposed by those providers.

As we will see in this chapter, the notion of service broker is crucial for a self-adaptive SOS: although the service requestor can be enhanced with some adaptation logic, a more consolidated approach is to place this logic at the service broker level.

A common implementation of the SOA reference model is realized by Web services. In this chapter we will therefore use service and Web service interchangeably.

MAPE-K: A CONTROL LOOP FOR SELF-ADAPTIVE FRAMEWORKS

MAPE-K is a reference model for realizing self-adaptable applications: the MAPE-K control loop uses an intelligent agent to perceive the surround-

Figure 2. MAPE-K control loop: adapted from (Kephart & Chess, 2003)

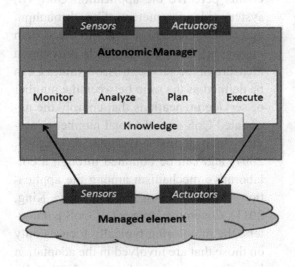

ing environment through sensors and uses the collected information to determine the actions that have to be performed on the environment itself.

In the context of SOA applications, the managed environment is constituted by (i) the workflow of activities concerning the invocation of external services and their orchestration, (ii) the external services, and (iii) the network interconnecting these activities with the service requestors and the service providers. The autonomic manager is constituted by software components for the different MAPE-K phases.

Figure 2 illustrates the MAPE-K control loop: the four steps of the autonomic manager, the managed element, the sensors, and the actuators. In the SOA context, the managed element is the SOA application, while the autonomic manager is a (possibly complex) software layer overlying the actual SOA application. While the application runs, the manager goes through the different MAPE-K steps:

1. **Monitor:** The application execution is monitored through sensors. In the SOA context, the sensors are implemented by means of probes over external services, with

the objective of detecting the actual values of the quality attributes such as response time, reliability, and availability.

2. **Analyze:** The Monitor phase output is taken as input by the Analyze phase, which usually performs statistical computation on the raw data collected by the preceding phase. The data analysis aims at determining whether some quality attribute has violated (or is going to violate) a previously specified internal policy, usually stored in the Knowledge layer. In the SOA domain, an internal policy can be the violation of a certain threshold for a quality attribute, e.g., for a given service the average response time measured over some interval exceeds the threshold established in the internal policy.

3. **Plan:** After the Analyze phase has detected some kind of violation of the internal policy, the Plan phase computes a new adaptation plan, possibly using the data elaborated by the Analyze phase with the support of the Knowledge layer. In the SOA context, the elaboration of a new adaptation plan can be the selection of different service providers implementing the needed functionalities. Alternatively, it can be an internal workflow re-arrangement so that the internal policy specifying the application requirements can be satisfied.

4. **Execute:** The new computed plan has to be executed by the SOA application controlled by the MAPE-K control loop. Such corrective actions are applied by means of actuators on the underlying SOA application. In the SOA domain, the corrective actions can be a different binding of functionalities to service providers, as well as an application re-deployment.

In the remainder of this chapter we will first describe the different phases of the MAPE-K loop intended for SOA applications; then, we will focus on the planning phase. For each MAPE phase we arranged a taxonomy to classify the different SOA frameworks that adopt the autonomic control loop to adaptively manage the service composition.

The questions driving the various taxonomies are based on the five Ws and one H concept (Hart, 2011).

- **What**: It identifies the relevant elements for each MAPE-K phase.
- **Where**: It characterizes where a certain phase can happen either at a logical or physical level.
- **When**: It classifies the temporal aspects that characterize each MAPE-K phase.
- **Who**: It identifies the entities involved in the execution of each MAPE-K phase.
- **How**: It describes how each MAPE-K phase can be implemented.

With respect to the five Ws and one H concept, we do not explicitly consider the Why question, because we assume that adaptation is the motivation that drives all the choices.

Monitor Taxonomy

Figure 3 illustrates the taxonomy of the Monitor phase.

- **What:** Monitoring usually targets the QoS parameters, i.e., the set of attributes that describe the performance of the SOA application, or the hardware/software resources that support its execution. For example, the attributes concerning the hardware resources can regard the CPU utilization or the amount of available memory, while those regarding the software resources can be the length of the backlog queues or the number of threads used by the application server. We can identify two different types of QoS parameters: (i) client-side parameters, like response time, availability, reliability, repu-

tation, and cost, which capture how the clients perceive the application QoS; (ii) system-side parameters, like throughput and cost, which are relevant to the system managers. Reputation, which provides a measure of the service trustworthiness, can be defined as the ratio between the number of service invocations that comply the negotiated QoS over the total number of service invocations (Ardagna & Pernici, 2007) and can be obtained through a collaborative mechanism among the application clients (Zheng, Ma, Lyu & King, 2011). Given the large set of QoS parameters, the monitoring typically focuses only on those that are involved in the adaptation loop. For example, in frameworks that dynamically adapt the amount of hardware resources used by the SOA application (Mirandola & Potena, 2011; Calinescu, Grunske, Kwiatkowska, Mirandola & Tamburrelli, 2011), the monitoring focuses on the hardware resources utilization in order to decide whether and when resize the CPU, memory, or disk. In other frameworks, that do not consider the hardware resource adaptation, other attributes are monitored, such as response time and reliability (Rouvoy et al., 2009; Menascé, Gomaa, Malek & Sousa, 2011; Bellucci, Cardellini, Di Valerio & Iannucci, 2010; Agarwal & Jalote, 2010; Ardagna, Baresi, Comai, Comuzzi & Pernici, 2011). Furthermore, the workload submitted to the SOA application can also be monitored, for example to derive some useful metric, like response time, from the gathered information. Examples of frameworks that monitor the workload include (Calinescu et al., 2011; Bellucci et al., 2010; Ardagna & Mirandola, 2010).
- **Where:** The monitored data can be collected at various different locations. A first approach is to collect the data at the client side

Figure 3. Monitor taxonomy

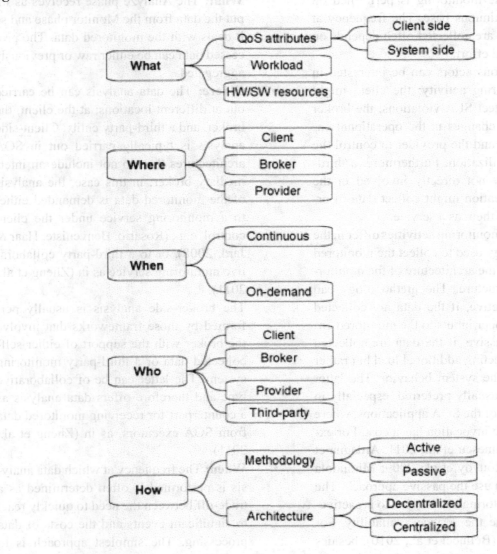

of the SOA application, like in (Rouvoy et al., 2009), where the client is responsible for detecting possible Service Level Agreements (SLA) violations. Another approach is to collect the data at the provider side, like the Amazon CloudWatch service: the service provider collects data for itself and makes them available to its clients. However, the most common solution adopted in the SOA context is to collect data on the service broker that manages the ad-

aptation of the SOA application, as done in (Mirandola et al., 2011; Calinescu et al., 2011; Menascé et al., 2011; Bellucci et al., 2010; Ardagna et al., 2011).

- **When:** The monitoring activity can be accomplished either continuously or on-demand. Although the latter seems to be a reasonable solution, for example the planning phase might choose to start a monitoring activity on a different perspective of the system, in all the frameworks we consider the monitoring is performed on a time-continuous base. The frequency at which data are collected often depends on the required effort.

- **Who:** Various actors can be interested in the monitoring activity: the client might want to detect SLA violations, the broker to identify changes in the operational environment, and the provider to control the resource utilization. Furthermore, a third-party entity not directly involved in the SOA application might collect data in order to offer them as a service.

- **How:** The monitoring activities differ in the methodology used to collect the monitored data and in the architecture of the monitoring infrastructure. The methodology can be either active, if the data are collected sending proper inputs to the monitored entities, or passive, if the data are collected without injecting additional load but rather observing the system behavior. The latter solution is usually preferred, especially in the context of the SOA applications, where each service invocation has a cost. For example, (Calinescu et al., 2011; Ardagna et al., 2011; Rouvoy et al., 2009; Mirandola et al., 2011) use the passive approach. The active monitoring can be used to proactively determine the service availability. For example in (Bellucci et al., 2010), besides using a passive approach, the framework periodically checks if the used services are available, in order to reduce the occurrence of a service failure during the invocation issued by a client.

- Finally, the monitoring activities can be performed by a single central entity or by a distributed sensors network.

Analyze Taxonomy

Figure 4 depicts the taxonomy for the Analyze phase of the MAPE-K loop.

- **What:** The Analyze phase receives as input the data from the Monitor phase and so it deals with the monitored data. The processed data can be either raw or previously aggregated.

- **Where:** The data analysis can be carried out at different locations: at the client, the broker, and a third-party entity. Client-side analysis is typically carried out in SOA architectures that do not include an intermediary broker; in this case, the analysis of the monitored data is demanded either to a monitoring service under the client control, e.g., (Rosario, Benveniste, Haar & Jard, 2008), or to a third-party collaborative monitoring service as in (Zheng et al., 2011).

  The broker-side analysis is usually performed by those frameworks that involve the broker with the support of either self-collected data or a third-party monitoring system. The latter can be of collaborative type and therefore offers data analysis as a counterpart for receiving monitored data from SOA executors, as in (Zheng et al., 2011).

- **When:** The frequency at which data analysis is performed is often determined as a trade-off between the need to quickly react to significant events and the costs of data processing. The simplest approach is to periodically analyze the data at fixed intervals (Bellucci et al., 2010). In the more sophisticated event-driven analysis, which is usually based on the concept of Continuous Query Processing (CQP), each monitored data is not only stored but might activate a trigger usually based on simple policies, like threshold violations (Calinescu et al., 2011). Event-driven analysis can also occur either after the execution of a specific service, a set of services, or even the whole workflow (Ardagna et al., 2011). The periodic and event-driven analysis approaches

Figure 4. Analyze taxonomy

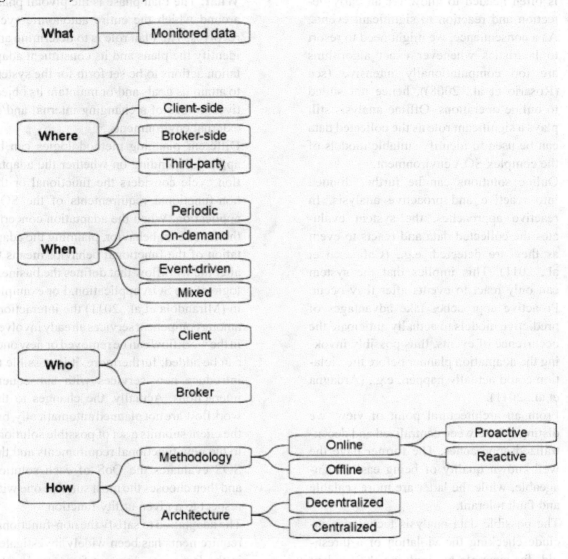

can be combined to obtain a periodic analysis coupled with an event-driven analysis for critical events detection (Calinescu et al., 2011). Finally, on-demand analysis can also be directly requested by a client, depending on its own analysis policies.

• **Who:** The actors interested in the Analyze phase coincide with those that will plan the adaptation actions, that is, the clients and the broker. A client may be interested in data analysis when it does not rely on

an external service broker, while a service broker is always interested in analyzing the monitored data.

• **How:** We distinguish between methodological and architectural issues regarding how the analysis can be accomplished.

• The Analyze policies can be roughly divided in two macro-categories: online and offline analysis. Since the SOS operations require the adaptation loop to quickly react to a changing environment, a fast analysis is often needed to allow for an early detection and reaction to significant events. As a consequence, we might need to resort to heuristics whenever exact algorithms are too computationally intensive (see (Rosario et al., 2008)), hence not suited to online operations. Offline analysis still plays a significant role as the collected data can be used to identify suitable models of the complex SOA environment.

- Online solutions can be further divided into reactive and proactive analysis. In reactive approaches, the system evaluates the collected data and reacts to event as they are detected, e.g., (Calinescu et al., 2011). This implies that the system can only react to events after they occur. Proactive approaches take advantages of predictive models to actually anticipate the occurrence of events, thus possibly invoking the adaptation planner before the violation could actually happen, e.g., (Ardagna et al., 2011).

- From an architectural point of view, we distinguish between centralized and decentralized approaches. The former have the well-known quality of being easily manageable, while the latter are more scalable and fault tolerant.

- The possible data analysis techniques include checking the violation of a threshold, for example by applying the Student t-test statistical significance to determine the probability of a QoS attribute to be violated (Mosincat, Binder, & Jazayeri, 2010), or creating an empirical distribution function that fits the actual QoS parameters distribution as in (Rosario et al., 2008).

Plan Taxonomy

The taxonomy of the Plan phase is shown in Figure 5.

- **What:** The Plan phase is the pivotal phase around which the entire autonomic cycle revolves. The Plan role is to determine and identify the plans and its constituent adaptation actions to be set forth for the system to attain its goals and/or maintain its objectives in face of a changing internal and/or external environments.

Different planning methodologies can be applied depending on whether the adaptation cycle considers the functional or the non-functional requirements of the SOA application. When the adaptation concerns the functional behavior, planning the adaptation of the functional behavior means to alter the workflow that defines the business logic of the SOA application. For example, in (Mirandola et al., 2011) the interactions among component services already involved in the workflow can be removed or new ones can be added; furthermore, it is possible to introduce new services with subsequent interactions. Actually, the changes to the workflow are not planned automatically, but the client submits a set of possible solutions to the new functional requirements and the SOS evaluates the QoS of each solution and then chooses the most suitable one with respect to a given utility function.

The adaptation to satisfy the non-functional requirements has been widely investigated in the last years. In most frameworks, the adaptive management is typically achieved by selecting at runtime the implementation corresponding to each functionality of the abstract composition from a set of candidates and leaving unchanged the composition logic. The overall methodology entails the discovery, identification, and selection of the actual services implementing the SOA application as to satisfy some non-functional requirements while optimizing a suitable utility function.

Figure 5. Plan taxonomy

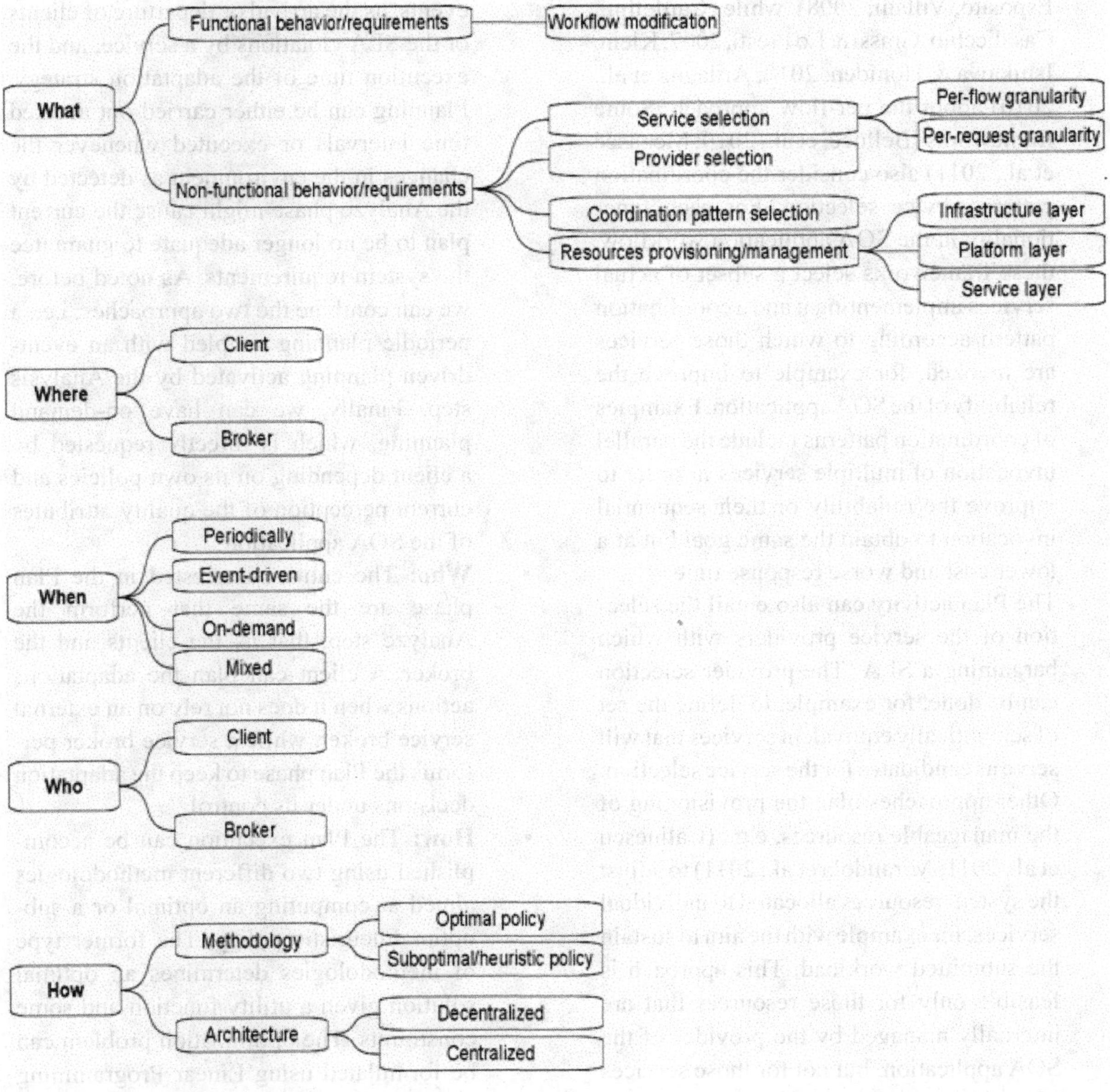

The service selection can be performed at two different granularity levels. With the *per-request* grain, the adaptation concerns a single request addressed to a composite service, and aims at making the system able to fulfill the QoS requirements of that specific request (e.g., minimize the cost of the SOA application), independently of the concurrent requests that may be addressed to the system. With the *per-flow grain*, the adaptation concerns an overall flow of requests, and aims at fulfilling the QoS requirements concerning the global properties of that flow, e.g., to minimize its average response time. Some proposals in the per-request case include (Ardagna et al., 2007;

Ardagna et al., 2011; Canfora, Di Penta, Esposito, Villani, 2008), while (Cardellini, Casalicchio, Grassi & Lo Presti, 2007; Klein, Ishikawa & Honiden, 2010; Ardagna et al., 2010) adopt the per-flow approach. Some frameworks (Bellucci et al., 2010; Menascé et al., 2011) also consider the coordination pattern service selection. For each functionality in the SOA application workflow, these frameworks select a subset of actual services implementing it and a coordination pattern according to which those services are invoked, for example to improve the reliability of the SOA application. Examples of coordination patterns include the parallel invocation of multiple services in order to improve the reliability or their sequential invocation to obtain the same goal but at a lower cost and worse response time.

The Plan activity can also entail the selection of the service providers with which bargaining a SLA. The provider selection can be done, for example, to define the set of semantically equivalent services that will serve as candidates for the service selection. Other approaches plan the provisioning of the manageable resources, e.g., (Calinescu et al., 2011; Mirandola et al., 2011) to adjust the system resources allocated to individual services, for example with the aim to sustain the submitted workload. This approach is feasible only for those resources that are internally managed by the provider of the SOA application, but not for those services offered by external providers.

- **Where:** The Plan phase is usually executed on the broker, and this is the solution adopted in almost all of the frameworks we consider. However, it is also possible to execute the planning on the client, like in (Rouvoy et al., 2009), in case of a brokerless architecture.
- **When:** Similarly to the Analyze phase, the Plan execution is determined by the trade-off between the need to react to significant events, as the arrival or departure of clients or the SLA violations by a service, and the execution time of the adaptation strategy. Planning can be either carried out at fixed time intervals or executed whenever the changes in the environment as detected by the Analyze phase might cause the current plan to be no longer adequate to guarantee the system requirements. As noted before, we can combine the two approaches, i.e., a periodic planning coupled with an event-driven planning activated by the Analysis step. Finally, we can have on-demand planning, which is directly requested by a client depending on its own policies and current perception of the quality attributes of the SOA application.
- **Who:** The entities interested in the Plan phase are the same that perform the Analyze step, that is, the clients and the broker. A client can plan the adaptations actions when it does not rely on an external service broker, while a service broker performs the Plan phase to keep the adaptation decisions under its control.
- **How:** The Plan execution can be accomplished using two different methodologies aimed at computing an optimal or a sub-optimal/heuristic policy. The former type of methodologies determines an optimal solution given a utility function and some constraints. The optimization problem can be formulated using Linear Programming (LP) as in (Cardellini et al., 2007; Klein et al., 2010), Integer Programming (IP) as in (Alrifai & Risse, 2009), or even Mixed Integer Linear Programming (MILP) as in (Ardagna et al., 2007). To overcome the computational complexity of optimal strategies, especially of integer formulations, the latter type of methodologies rely on heuristics that lead to suboptimal solutions but are faster to solve (Menascé et al.,

2011). As regards the planner architecture, it is centralized in most of the frameworks, although some decentralized approach exists, as in (Alrifai et al., 2009), where part of the computation is distributed across the network.

Execute Taxonomy

Figure 6 shows the taxonomy of the Execute phase of the MAPE-K loop.

- **What.** In this case, the question assumes a trivial meaning: what we are going to execute coincides with what we have planned in the previous step.
- **Where.** The adaptation plan can be executed at different layers, ranging from the highest business process layer to the lowest infrastructure layer. Starting from the latter, the adaptation actions can be run either on the internal infrastructure (Mirandola et al., 2011; Calinescu et al., 2011) or on an external infrastructure. By internal infrastructure we mean all those physical and virtual resources that are directly manageable by the SOA application provider, while with external infrastructure we intend every external physical or virtual resource used to improve or to replace any internal infrastructure. The actions available at the infrastructure layer include adding or removing physical or virtual machines, improving the network connections or the storage system.

  Going up through the abstraction layers, we find that adaptation can take place at the platform layer. The latter identifies every software needed to run the service we intend to adapt, thus ranging from the operating system to any application server (Calinescu et al., 2011). Changes on this layer involve everything that goes from kernel reconfiguration to application server tuning, but it does not involve any modification on services that take part in the business process. Such modifications belong to the service layer, where we can operate both service re-configuration and service tuning. Finally, at the business process layer, the adaptation actions involve the high-level logic of the business process (Bellucci et al., 2010; Menascè et al., 2011; Calinescu et al., 2011).

- **When.** Most of times the adaptation actions have to be carried out introducing the lowest possible delay into the business process execution. Depending on the adaptation actions, the adaptation may happen either at runtime or at deployment-time. Although it is possible to execute adaptation actions also at development-time or design-time, we do not consider them because we only focus on those solutions that do not require human intervention, being the latter a requirement for a truly autonomic system. We include in the deployment-time phase all those approaches that require a (even small) service interruption in order to apply the adaptation plan. All other approaches can be classified in the runtime case.

- **Who.** The entities involved in the actuation of the adaptation plan are the client, the broker, and the service provider.

  A client managing the entire service orchestration can apply by its own the adaptation actions previously computed in the planning phase. A broker can either apply its own computed adaptation plan or rely on some adaptation plan directly provided by the client, as in (Mirandola et al., 2011). Finally, the service provider can modify its behavior according to directives provided by the client or the broker. For example, it can receive an adaptation request issued by a broker that has detected a slowdown in the provider performance.

Figure 6. Execute taxonomy

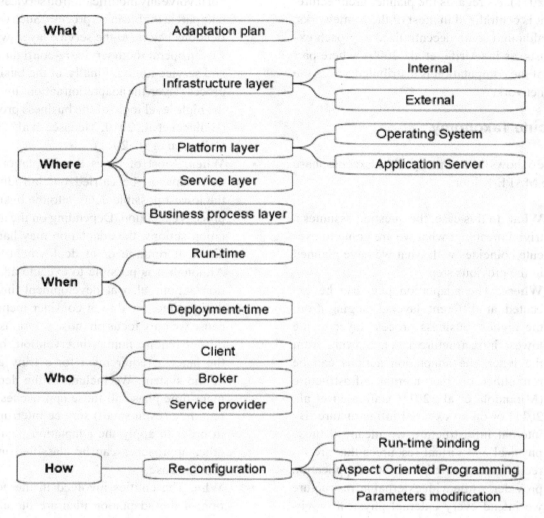

- **How.** The adaptation actions that can be taken are all part of a meta-branch called re-configuration. In particular, we have identified three possible mechanisms to execute the adaptation plan: runtime binding, Aspect Oriented Programming (AOP), and parameters modification.

  The runtime binding is the most leveraged approach, as it provides the SOA application with the ability to bind at runtime the invocation with the actual service according to the Plan decision. It is the most suited mechanism to implement service selection, coordination pattern selection or even a simple load balancing policy among functionally equivalent services.

  AOP can be used to inject code fragments (also known as sub-processes) into the SOA application itself, in order to have process segments changing at runtime (Leitner et al., 2010) or at deployment-time. This methodology is suited for both non-functional and functional adaptation as it can modify the functional as well as non-functional application behavior. The AOP methodology is based on the concepts of *aspect* (crosscutting concerns, which are turned off and on at design or runtime), *advises* (the actual implementation in terms of business logic of the aspects), *joinpoints* (points on the business process where advices can potentially be inserted), and *weaving* (the process of dynamically inserting advises in joinpoints).

- Finally, the parameters modification encompasses all those mechanisms that can be used to change some operative feature of the SOS.

Self-Adaptive Frameworks

As described in the previous subsections, each phase in the MAPE-K loop can be realized in several different ways. However, to design a consistent MAPE-K loop only a subset of the possible combinations is reasonable. For example, if the monitored data are analyzed on an event-driven basis, it is not appropriate to periodically execute the Plan phase. If a service broker monitors its hardware and software resources, it is not possible to plan a service selection for a service composition, unless the used Web services are all in-house, but it is an unreasonable scenario for a SOA application.

When we described the taxonomies of the MAPE loop phases, we referred to some existing frameworks for the self-adaptation of a SOA application. In this section, we analyze the overall mapping of these frameworks on those taxonomies. Specifically, we consider (Calinescu et al., 2011; Ardagna et al., 2011) among the cited frameworks, because they are the most documented; later in the chapter, we will analyze as a case study the MOSES framework (Cardellini et al., in press). In the remainder of this subsection we do not mention the *who* branch of the taxonomies, because it coincides with the service broker for both the frameworks.

Let us start with the Monitor phase. QoSMOS, which stands for QoS Management and Optimiza-

tion of Service-based systems (Calinescu et al., 2011), focuses on monitoring (*what*) the QoS attributes at the client side, the workload submitted to each service in the service composition, and the resources allocated to the in-house services. The monitoring is executed (*where*) at the broker side, (*when*) on a continuous basis, and (*how*) using a passive methodology.

Discorso, which stands for Distributed Information Systems for Coordinated Service-Oriented Interoperability (Ardagna et al., 2011), differs from QoSMOS only for the what branch of the monitor taxonomy, since it only monitors the QoS attributes at the client side. As discussed below, this slight difference in the Monitor phase affects the design of both the Plan and Execution phases of the MAPE-K loop for the two frameworks.

As regards the Analyze phase, both the frameworks perform (*what*) the analysis of the monitored data (*where*) at the broker side, (*how*) using an online methodology. The difference is in the timeliness: QoSMOS realize a reactive analysis, while Discorso a proactive one. However, this difference does not affect the design of the Plan and Execution phases, but only how the adaptation need is detected. Furthermore, the analysis is performed (*when*) both periodically and event-based for QoSMOS, and only event-based for Discorso.

The design of the Plan phase is affected by the differences in the monitoring. Although both the frameworks perform a non-functional adaptation, Discorso only plans (*what*) the service selection at the per-request granularity, while QoSMOS also the resource provisioning both at infrastructure and platform layers (this difference reflects the different kind of attributes that are monitored). The methodology used by the planning (*how*) is based on optimization models for both the frameworks and the computation is performed using a centralized architecture. In particular, Discorso uses an optimization problem formulated as MILP while QoSMOS an exhaustive research based on a Markovian model of the SOA application.

Eventually, the planning is executed (*where*) at the broker side and (*when*) with the same timeliness of the Analyze phase. Furthermore, QoSMOS performs an iteration of the MAPE-K loop also if a time interval has expired, even if no change is detected in the execution environment. Therefore, the planning phase is executed both periodically and event-based for QoSMOS, and only event-based for Discorso.

The design of the Execute phase is also affected by the design choices made in the previous MAPE-K steps. Indeed, the adaptation actions are executed (*where*) only on the business process layer for the Discorso framework, and also on the infrastructure and platform layers for QoSMOS. These actions are executed (*when*) at runtime, (*how*) using the runtime binding in both frameworks and the parameters modification only in QoSMOS.

SERVICE SELECTION

As previously observed, the Plan phase is the core of the autonomic control loop as it defines the self-adaptation logic. It is no surprise then that many research efforts on adaptive management of SOSs have focused on studying and developing planning strategies.

In the context of SOA applications, the most critical tasks of the planning phase have been identified with the ability to manage, control, and predict the QoS characteristics of the offered SOA applications (Papazoglou, Traverso, Dustdar & Leymann, 2007). Hence, most planning policies have addressed the issue of fulfilling non-functional requirements. Since SOA applications are built by composing loosely coupled services, which are easily replaceable at runtime with dynamic binding, most of the research efforts have focused on devising proper service selection and coordination pattern selection strategies.

In this section we review service selection strategies for SOA applications. In this respect,

we can clearly distinguish two broad classes of approaches, depending on whether we deal with the per-request or the per-flow granularity. Indeed, despite addressing similar issues, the two approaches significantly differ in the formulation of the optimization problem. In the first case, we have to deal with 0-1 problems, which are computationally complex, while in the second case we deal with probabilities, which lead to cheaper computations. We will focus on two representative solutions: (Ardagna et al., 2007) for the per-request approach and (Cardellini et al., 2007) for the per-flow approach. Since the optimal strategies for the per-request granularity are computationally expensive, many research efforts have focused on heuristics, which, albeit suboptimal, are computationally efficient; therefore, we will also review some representative examples in the next section.

In the following, we consider a broker that offers a SOA application P. We assume that the broker has negotiated SLAs with its clients and has the main task to fulfill these SLAs, while optimizing a suitable utility function and being constrained by the SLAs it has stipulated as a client with the providers of the services involved in the service composition. Depending on the utilization scenario, the utility function can optimize specific QoS attributes for different clients/service classes, e.g., minimizing the average response time, and/or the broker own utility, e.g., minimizing the overall cost paid by the broker to offer the SOA application. These different, and possibly conflicting, optimization goals can lead to a multi-objective optimization problem. This is usually tackled, e.g., (Ardagna et al., 2007; Cardellini et al., 2007), by considering a single objective function obtained by applying the Simple Additive Weighting (SAW) technique (Hwang & Yoon, 1981), which is the most widely used scalarization method. Following the SAW technique, the utility function can be defined as the weighted sum of the (normalized) QoS attributes.

We denote by S the set of abstract tasks belonging to the service composition P, where $S_i \in S$, $i = 1, \ldots, m$, represents a single task, being m the number of tasks composing P. A task is a functionality required by the SOA application and implemented by a set of services available in the marketplace. For each task S_i, we assume that the broker has identified a pool $I_i = \{cs_{ij}\}$ of concrete services implementing it. Figure 7a shows an example of workflow for a SOA application.

Per-Request Granularity

We first consider the per-request approach in (Ardagna et al., 2007). Let us focus, without loss of generality, on SLAs containing QoS constraints that refer to the following three attributes: (i) response time, defined as the interval of time elapsed from the service invocation to its completion; (ii) reliability, that is, the probability that the service completes its task when invoked; (iii) cost, which is the price charged for the service invocation. Furthermore, let us assume that this QoS model holds for SLAs stipulated by the broker with both its clients and service providers. In the per-

request approach, the broker tries to meet the QoS constraints specified in the SLA for each request, irrespective of whether it belongs to some flow generated by one or more clients.

The optimal service selection problem is then formulated as MILP problem. We denote with the vector $x = [x_1, \ldots, x_m]$ the optimal policy for a request to the SOA application, where each entry $x_i = [x_{ij}]$, $x_{ij} \in \{0, 1\}$, $i \in S$, $j \in I_i$, denotes the adaptation policy for task S_i and the constraint $\sum_{j \in Ii} x_{ij} = 1$ holds. That is, x_{ij} is the decision variable, which is equal to 1 if task S_i is implemented by service cs_{ij}, 0 otherwise. As an example, suppose that for the task S_i the broker has individuated 4 concrete services implementing it, namely cs_1, cs_2, cs_3 and cs_4. Assume that the per-request policy x determines that for a given request $x_i = [0, 0, 1, 0]$. It means that, according to this policy, for S_i the broker binds the request to cs_{i3}.

The fulfillment of the QoS constraints on a per-request basis means that the broker needs to take into account all the possible scenarios that might occur during the execution of the SOA application. To this end, the optimal strategy needs to consider all the possible execution paths that might

Figure 7. a) An example of workflow; b) Two different execution paths

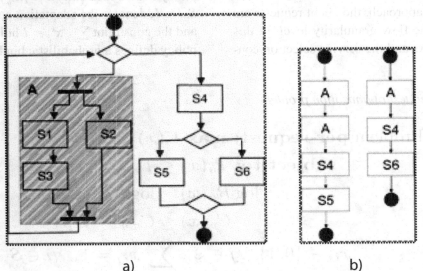

a)   b)

arise from the workflow of the SOA application (Ardagna et al., 2007). An execution path ep_n is a multiset of tasks $ep_n = \{S_1, S_2, \ldots, S_p\} \subseteq S$, such that S_1 and S_1 are respectively the initial and final tasks of the path and no pair S_i, $S_j \in ep_n$ belongs to alternative branches. An execution path does not contain any loop, because the loops are peeled, but it may contain parallel sequences. Loop peeling involves rewriting the loop as a sequence of branch conditions (the branch conditions that arise from loop peeling produce other execution paths, see the example in Figure 7b). In other words, the set of all the execution paths represents all the possible execution scenarios of a workflow.

Figure 8 shows a simplified version of the problem formulation for the per-request optimization, where x denotes the optimal service selection policy and $U(x)$ the broker utility function. We indicate with T_{max}, R_{min} and C_{max}, respectively the maximum response time, the minimum reliability, and the maximum cost that are allowed, i.e., the QoS constraints specified in the SLAs. On the other hand, $T_n(x)$, $R_n(x)$, and $C_n(x)$ denote the response time, reliability, and cost of the execution path ep_n under the selection policy x.

Per-Flow Granularity

In the per-flow approach, the client requests are considered at the flow granularity level. In this setting, the SLAs and the service selection con-cern the QoS and the behavior of the aggregated flow of requests generated by the clients. As a consequence, the constraints stated in the SLA do not make any provision on the QoS of each single request, but rather the SLA is concerned with the average value of the QoS attributes computed over the flow of requests generated by a given client.

To account for the existence of multiple concurrent requests made by the different clients, the per-flow approach in (Cardellini et al., 2007) requires to negotiate in the SLA the additional parameter L, which represents a bound on the amount of requests per unit of time a client can generate.

It is also assumed that there is a set K of service classes, with $k \in K$, for each service composition. Therefore, a client bargains its SLA with the broker referring to one of these service classes. Although this could seem a limitation, it actually is not, because the granularity level of the service classes may be arbitrarily fine and, at the finest level, each client could have its own service class.

The optimal service selection problem is then formulated as a LP problem, that is computationally lighter to solve than the MILP formulation of the per-request approach. For each class k, we denote with the vector $x^k = [x^k_1, \ldots, x^k_m]$ the optimal policy, where each entry $x^k_i = [x^k_{ij}]$, $0 \leq x_{ij} \leq 1$, $i \in S$, $j \in I_i$, denotes the adaptation policy for task S_i and the constraint $\sum_{j \in Ii} x^k_{ij} = 1$ holds. That is, the policy defines a probabilistic binding between S_i

Figure 8. Per-request optimization problem

$$\text{Problem } \mathbf{per\text{-}request: max } U(\boldsymbol{x})$$
$$\text{subject to: } T_n(\boldsymbol{x}) \leq T_{max} \quad \forall ep_n$$
$$\log R_n(\boldsymbol{x}) \geq \log R_{min} \quad \forall ep_n$$
$$C_n(\boldsymbol{x}) \leq C_{max} \quad \forall ep_n$$
$$x_{ij} \in \{0, 1\} \ \forall j \in \Im_i, \ \sum_{j \in \Im_i} x_{ij} = 1 \quad \forall i \in \mathcal{S}$$

and its implementation in I_i, whereby each entry x^k_{ij} of x^k_i denotes the probability that the class-k request will be bound to concrete service cs_{ij}. As an example, let us suppose that, as in the per-request case, the broker has individuated for the task S_i the same 4 concrete services implementing it, namely cs_1, cs_2, cs_3 and cs_4. Now assume that the per-flow service selection, for a given class k, determines $x^k = [0, 0.2, 0.5, 0.3]$. It means that, for a class-k request for S_i, the broker will bind cs_2 with probability 0.2, cs_3 with probability 0.5 and cs_4 with probability 0.3.

Figure 9 shows a simplified version of the optimization problem formulation. We indicate with T^k_{max}, R^k_{min} and C^k_{max}, respectively the maximum average response time, the minimum average reliability, and the maximum average cost, that correspond to the QoS constraints specified in the class-k SLA. $T^k(L, x)$, $R^k(L, x)$, and $C^k(L, x)$ are respectively the class-k response time, reliability, and cost, respectively, under the adaptation policy $x = [x^k]$ $k \in K$. Their expressions require the knowledge of V^k_i for each task S_i, that is the average number of times S_i is invoked by a class-k request. In particular, the second-last equation, where $L^k = \sum_u L^k_u$, is the aggregated service request rate of class-k clients (being u a client), ensures that the concrete services used in the SOA application will not be overloaded by the client requests, that is, the client requests will not exceed the volume of invocations l_{ij} agreed with each service provider.

A Brief Comparison between Per-Request and Per-Flow Granularity

The difference between the per-flow and the per-request approaches lies in the service selection policy: in the latter each task is bound to one and only one concrete service, while in the former each task is bound to a set of concrete services and at runtime one of them is probabilistically chosen. As a result, different concrete services can be used for implementing the same task in different executions of the service composition while the same adaptation plan holds. On the other hand, in the per-request approach the same concrete service is used for all similar requests until the same adaptation decision holds.

The study in (Cardellini, Di Valerio, Grassi, Iannucci & Lo Presti, 2011a) presents an experimental comparison between the two approaches, focusing on their impact on the SOS performance in term of service composition's response time. The results show that under a light request load the two approaches perform almost the same, but under a high request load the per-request approach

Figure 9. Per-flow optimization problem

$$\text{Problem } \textbf{per-flow: max } U(\boldsymbol{x})$$

$$\text{subject to: } T^k(L, \boldsymbol{x}) \leq T^k_{max} \quad \forall k \in K$$

$$\log R^k(L, \boldsymbol{x}) \geq \log R^k_{min} \quad \forall k \in K$$

$$C^k(L, \boldsymbol{x}) \leq C^k_{max} \quad \forall k \in K$$

$$\sum_{k \in K} x^k_{ij} V^k_{\alpha,i} L^k \leq l_{ij} \quad \forall j \in \Im_i, \forall i \in \mathcal{S}$$

$$x^k_{ij} \geq 0 \quad \forall j \in \Im_i, \quad \sum_{j \in \Im_i} x^k_{ij} = 1 \quad \forall i \in \mathcal{S}$$

exhibits scalability problems, while the per-flow approach performs much better. The motivation is as follows: in the per-request approach, all requests to a given task are resolved using the same concrete service until the same service selection solution holds. This works under light loads, but at higher loads the service capacity is eventually saturated and performance degrades. On the other hand, in the per-flow approach, the load is shared among multiple concrete services thanks to the probabilistic service selection without saturating any service thanks to the load constraints which prevent the services' overloading.

However, the main disadvantage of the per-flow approach is that the QoS levels are guaranteed on average for the overall flow; therefore, the performance of a single request is actually unpredictable. In (Cardellini, Di Valerio, Grassi, Iannucci & Lo Presti, 2011b) the interested reader can find a new service selection policy that combines the benefits of both approaches, i.e., the per-request guarantees and the per-flow probabilistic service selection, thus ensuring load balancing and overcoming the per-request scalability issues.

HEURISTICS

The high computational complexity of the optimal per-request service selection policies may limit their use for an online implementation. Various factors affect the time complexity of the service selection policies, among which the most important are the number of abstract tasks, the number of concrete services implementing each abstract task, and the number of QoS constraints that have to be considered. The service selection can be modeled as a Multi-choice Multidimensional Knapsack problem (MMKP), which is known to be NP-hard and therefore the time complexity in finding an exact solution is expected to be exponential (Martello & Toth, 1987). However, in a real-world scenario, the Plan component of the SOS must be able to determine in near real-

time the optimal service selection under possibly heavy load. To address this issue, many research efforts have proposed computationally efficient, albeit suboptimal, solutions to the service selection problem.

Since a MMKP problem can be formally expressed with an IP formulation, a common approach (Berbner et al., 2006; Klein, Ishikawa, & Honiden, 2010) is to relax the integer restriction on the variables of the IP problem, thus obtaining a LP problem that can be efficiently solved in polynomial time. The caveat is however that a solution to the relaxed problem does not necessarily solve the original problem. Therefore, solutions based on a LP formulation are more suited to address the selection problem at per-flow granularity level, where the QoS constraints are evaluated in the long-term and for a flow of requests, rather than the per-request granularity, where individual executions could violate the constraints.

The work in (Berbner et al., 2006) proposes an algorithm for finding a sub-optimal solution to the original IP problem by enumerating the solutions of the LP problem in a clever way, until the IP problem constraints are not violated. The authors show that the proposed heuristic is able to compute close to optimal solutions in a fraction of the time with respect to the exact MIP formulation, e.g., in case of a SOA application composed by 21 tasks, the heuristic reaches 98.83% of the objective function value of the optimal solution, but only needs 0.19% of the computation time to compute it.

On the other hand, the proposal in (Klein et al, 2010) does not try to fit the original IP problem, but rather to refine the LP solution so that it can be used to guarantee some QoS constraints for every execution of the SOA application, or at least for a large percentage (e.g., 99.9%) of the executions. The authors show that the proposed heuristic is able to provide less than 3% of deviation from the original IP solution.

Another approach to face the complexity of the IP formulation is to reduce the number of decision variables of the problem itself, as in (Alrifai et al., 2009). The authors first decompose each global QoS constraint into a set of m local constraints, so that each local constraint serves as a conservative upper bound such that the satisfaction of every local constraint guarantees the satisfaction of global constraints.

Then, they divide the quality range of each QoS attribute into a set of discrete quality levels and map each known concrete service to the appropriate quality level. This approach has two major benefits: first, it allows to distribute the computational effort among different nodes, because only independent local optimization problems have to be solved; secondly, since concrete services are replaced by quality levels, the size of the problem space is reduced. The authors show that their heuristic can achieve above 96% of optimality when compared to the results obtained by the global optimization approach. However, since QoS levels are discretized without considering potential correlations among different quality attributes, in scenarios with relatively strict constraints it is possible to incur in very restrictive decompositions of the global constraints, which therefore could not be satisfied by any concrete service even though a solution to the problem exists. A solution to the latter problem is presented in (Alrifai, Skoutas, & Risse, 2010), where the authors propose a different method for QoS level discretization: for each abstract task, skyline (dominant) concrete services are first determined. Subsequently, skyline concrete services are clustered using the k-means algorithm and, for each cluster, a virtual concrete service is created whose quality level is given by the worst quality attributes of the concrete services belonging to that cluster. Those virtual concrete services are then used to discretize QoS levels in a multidimensional fashion.

A completely different approach is proposed by (Canfora, Di Penta, Esposito, Villani, 2008), where a Genetic Algorithm (GA) is used to realize an enumeration of the optimization problem solutions. The search for the optimal solution starts with an initial population of individuals that are going to evolve over time: at each algorithm step individuals are evaluated using a fitness function and then selected through a selection operator. The higher is the fitness value of an individual, the more is likely that such an individual will be chosen for reproduction. The reproduction is obtained by applying crossover and mutation operators. The former produces an offspring recombining parent's genes, while the latter modifies one or more genes. The application of a GA in service selection maps a solution of the optimization problem to an individual, where each individual is composed by m genes and every gene represents a particular instance of concrete services. A different objective is pursued by (Wada et al., in press), which uses a GA for the service provisioning problem: in their work the individual is composed by several genes which do not represent a particular instance of concrete service, but the number of concrete services needed by a given abstract task to fulfill certain QoS constraints.

Finally, in (Yu, Zhang & Lin, 2007) the authors compare the MMKP problem solved through the branch-and-bound technique with several heuristics, based on either a combinatorial or a graph model. The proposed heuristics differ in the type of considered workflow structure, which can be either only sequential or more general (a sequential workflow contains neither conditional branches nor forks). Combinatorial heuristics for both sequential and general workflows are realized as a walk in the solution space: first, a concrete service is selected for each abstract task such that a quality attribute (possibly different for each abstract task) is locally maximized. If the obtained solution is feasible, then the second step tries to improve such a solution by both feasible and unfeasible upgrades, so that both local and global optima can be reached. The authors claim that in most cases (more than 98%), the heuristic finds a feasible solution at the first try, while the time complexity is a polynomial function. As regards general workflows, an additional heuristic is proposed, which tries to optimize only the execution route with the highest probability, while finding only feasible solutions for other routes.

Graph-based heuristics are based on the algorithm of single-source shortest paths in Directed Acyclic Graphs (DAG) (Cormen, Leiserson, Rivest, & Stein, 2001): a DAG is built up from the workflow by replacing every node representing a single abstract task with a set of nodes representing the concrete services implementing it and by adding edges between two concrete services if the abstract tasks they implement are connected. Loops, if any, are unfolded. The proposed heuristic limits the information held by each node: instead of maintaining the complete list of paths that meet the QoS constraints from the source to the node itself, only K paths are kept. The authors show that limiting the information to the K best paths leads to an optimality approximation greater than 90% even for small values of K, with a gain in terms of time and memory consumption of approximately 500%.

CASE STUDY: MOSES

As a representative case study of SOS that adaptively manages a SOA application adopting the MAPE-K model, we focus on MOSES (MOdel-based SElf-adaptation of SOA systems), which is a framework for the QoS-driven adaptation of a service-oriented system. Although MOSES is a particular instance of SOS, it is a fully functional prototype with a highly modular architecture that allows you to easily realize other solutions proposed in literature by replacing and/or adding a given component with another possible implementation realizing a different approach. For instance, the Plan phase in the original MOSES follows the per-flow approach, but we also implemented the per-request approach in (Ardagna et al., 2007) by replacing some MOSES components in order to perform the comparison presented in (Cardellini et al., 2011a). We will use the MOSES prototype to

validate the benefits of a SOS with self-adaptive features under a motivating scenario characterized by a varying operating environment, where component services appear and disappear.

For a comprehensive description of the methodology underpinning MOSES and the software tool that implements it, we refer the reader to (Cardellini et al., in press) and (Bellucci et al., 2010), respectively.

MOSES Architecture

The MOSES architecture represents an instantiation for the SOA environment of a self-adaptive software system, organized according to the MAPE-K loop and focused on the fulfillment of QoS requirements.

Figure 10 shows how the MOSES components are organized according to the MAPE-K control loop.

Monitor–Analyze Phases

The Monitor-Analyze subsystem comprises all those components that capture changes in the MOSES environment and, if they are relevant, modify at runtime the behavioral model and trigger a new adaptation plan. Specifically, the *QoS Monitor* is in charge of measuring and analyzing the QoS attributes of the concrete services used by MOSES to provide the SOA application. The *WS Monitor* periodically checks the availability of the concrete services. The *Execution Path Analyzer* is in charge of monitoring the variations of the usage profile. In case of the service selection at the per-flow granularity, it computes and updates for each abstract task S_i the expected number of times V^k_i that S_i is invoked by service class k. With respect to the Monitor taxonomy in Figure 3, these MOSES components monitor: (*what*) client-side, QoS attributes of services; (*where*) broker side; (*when*) on a continuous time basis; (*how*) using both active and passive methodologies in a centralized architecture. In particular, the *QoS*

Figure 10. MOSES architecture

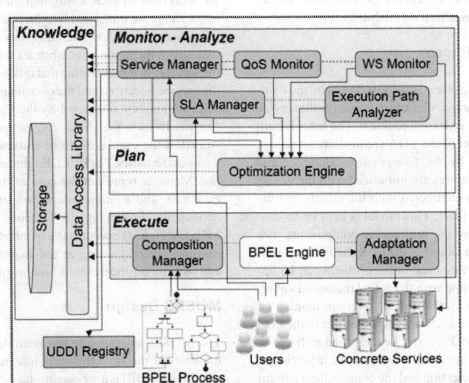

Monitor and the *Execution Path Analyzer* use a passive monitoring methodology by collecting the service invocation results, while the *WS Monitor* actively checks the services availability.

The Monitor-Analyze subsystem also includes the *Service Manager* and the *SLA Manager*, which are involved in the SLA negotiation processes where the broker acts as an intermediary. Indeed, the Service Manager is in charge of negotiating SLAs with the service providers and discovering candidate services offering the functionalities in the service composition, while the SLA Manager is responsible for the SLAs with the MOSES clients. In addition, the latter manages the client profiles, adding and removing them. We included these components in the Monitor-Analyze phases because they can invoke the Plan phase if new SLAs with clients or service providers are either stipulated or removed. Specifically, for each new SLA request, the SLA Manager performs an admis-

sion control to evaluate whether there are enough available resources to accept the incoming client, given the associated SLA and without violating already existing SLAs with other clients.

In MOSES the Analyze phase can be classified as follows on the basis of the taxonomy in Figure 4: (*where*) at the broker-side; (*when*) MOSES adopt all the approaches in Figure 4: the QoS Monitor analyzes periodically the QoS attributes of the concrete services, checking whether their measured values correspond to the stipulated one; the SLA Manager performs an on-demand analysis for client arrivals and departures, while the Service Manager and the WS Monitor adopt an event-driven analysis for discovering services and checking their availability, respectively; (*how*) the analysis is performed online with either proactive or reactive policies using a centralized architecture. In particular, the analysis is reactive for all the components except the QoS Monitor that can also use a proactive methodology.

Planning Phase

The planning phase is fully executed by the *Optimization Engine*, whose task is to solve the service selection optimization problem. The latter is built from a model of the SOA application workflow, instantiated by the *Composition Manager* and whose parameters are initialized with the values in the SLAs contracted with the clients and the service providers. This model is kept up-to-date at runtime by the monitoring components. For example, the values of the QoS attributes of each concrete service used in the problem can be updated at runtime with the actual measured values and the same holds for the average number of invocations to each task. With respect to the Plan taxonomy, MOSES can be classified as follows: (*what*) non-functional requirements, in particular the service selection and the coordination pattern selection. For sake of simplicity, we previously presented only the service selection problem; to account for the coordination pattern selection, the problem formulation is slightly more complicated as described in (Cardellini et al., in press). Eventually, (*where*) the Plan phase is executed at the broker on an event-driven basis, i.e., when the components in the Monitor–Analyze phases detect a relevant event to be addressed, and (*how*) the methodology adopted to plan the adaptation actions determines the service selection and pattern coordination relying on a centralized architecture.

Execution Phase

The execution phase is carried out by the *Composition Manager*, the *BPEL Engine*, and the *Adaptation Manager*. The *Composition Manager*, given a new service composition to be deployed as a BPEL process (OASIS, 2007), builds the workflow model that the *Optimization Engine* will use in the Plan phase. Furthermore, it modifies the workflow in such a way that all the service invocations are translated into invocations of the *Adaptation Manager*. The latter acts as a proxy that, given the name of an abstract task, invokes the service(s) implementing that task according to the service selection (and the coordination pattern selection) policy computed by the *Optimization Engine*. In turn, the *BPEL Engine* executes the workflow logic and is the front-end component to the client requests. The BPEL Engine and Adaptation Manager represent the core of the MOSES execution and runtime adaptation of the SOA application. Following the Execute taxonomy, MOSES: (*when*) executes the planned actions at runtime, (*where*) acting at the workflow level, and (*how*) using the dynamic binding mechanism.

MOSES Design

The MOSES architecture has been designed on the basis of the Java Business Integration (JBI) specification. JBI is a messaging-based pluggable architecture, whose components describe their capabilities through WSDL. Its major goal is to provide an architecture and an enabling framework that facilitates the dynamic composition and deployment of loosely coupled participating applications and service-oriented integration components. The key components of the JBI environment are: (i) the Service Engines (SEs) that enable pluggable business logic; (ii) the Binding Components (BCs) that enable pluggable external connectivity; (iii) the Normalized Message Router (NMR), which directs normalized messages from source to destination components according to specified policies.

As a JBI implementation, MOSES has been implemented within the open-source project *OpenESB* (ESB stands for Enterprise Service Bus), because it is an implementation and extension of the JBI standard. It implements JBI because it provides binding components, service engines, and the NMR; it extends JBI because it enables a set of distributed JBI instances to communicate as a single logical entity that can be managed through a centralized administrative interface. The GlassFish application server is the default runtime environment, although OpenESB can be integrated in several JEE application servers.

Figure 11 shows how the MOSES components are placed with respect to the JBI architecture: most of the components are executed by the JEE Service Engine, while the business process is executed by the BPEL Engine. The NMR works as a glue between the Service Engines and the Binding Components, having the ability to route messages between these sets of components.

The MOSES architecture is enriched by MDAL, which stands for MOSES Data Access Library. This library allows us to simplify the usage of the underlying Database layer by abstracting low-level queries with high-level methods.

Figure 12 shows the typical scenario in which a client issues a SOA request to MOSES. In the first step, the SOAP request is directed to the HTTP binding component. The received request is then forwarded to the NMR, which in turn routes it to the proper Service Engine, i.e., the BPEL Service

Engine. The latter is in charge of executing the required business process, after having performed some client authentication tasks, with the help of the Adaptation Manager when external invocations are needed.

The Adaptation Manager, differently from the other MOSES components, is not implemented as a JBI Service Unit. It is rather implemented as a standard Java class belonging to the application server classpath, and thus it is accessible by any application served by the application server itself. In particular, each invoke activity in the BPEL process, which should be executed by the BPEL Engine, is replaced by a call to the Adaptation Manager's entry method, whose tasks are: to read the most up-to-date service selection plan from the Database using the MDAL library, to invoke the concrete Web service(s), and finally to forward the Web service response to the BPEL Engine.

Once the business process ends its execution, the client response is put on the NMR, which in turn routes it to the HTTP BC, which finally delivers the message to the client.

Figure 11. MOSES architecture and the JBI environment

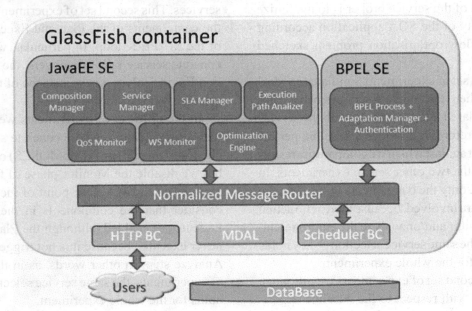

Figure 12. MOSES request-response cycle

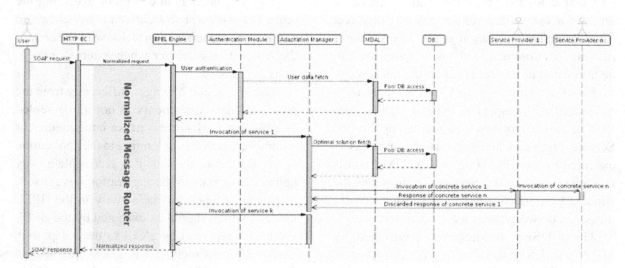

Experimental Results

In this section we illustrate the effectiveness of the adaptive management of service composition by analyzing a set of experimental results obtained with the MOSES prototype in controlled experiments. Specifically, we will study how MOSES is able to adapt its behavior with respect to the churn of the services it can use to offer the SOA application. In all the sets of experiments, the utility function of the service broker is to maximize the reliability of the SOA application according to the per-flow optimization problem sketched in Figure 9.

The first set of experiments simulates an ideal scenario, where the concrete services behave exactly as declared into their SLAs with the service broker. Therefore, it provides a baseline performance result against which we compare the results obtained in the two other sets of experiments. In this first set, only the components of the Execute subsystem are involved, because there is no actual need to monitor and/or analyze the environment. Therefore, the same service selection policy holds unchanged for the whole experiment.

In the second set of experiments we introduce some churn with respect to the baseline experi-

ment, by letting concrete services gracefully fail and recover over time. The failure/recovery model follows a two-state discrete Markov chain, with stationary probability distribution $\{p_{running}, p_{failed}\}=\{0.95, 0.05\}$, in which state changes can occur on average every 60 seconds. The gracefulness is given by the fact that the concrete services notify their state to MOSES, therefore allowing it to compute a new service selection policy including (excluding) the restored (failed) concrete services. This second set of experiments employs the components of the Plan and Execute phases of the MAPE-K loop. In particular, whenever a concrete service fails or recovers, the Optimization Engine solves a new instance of the service selection optimization problem.

In the third set of experiments we assume a real world scenario, where concrete services do not notify their clients (i.e., MOSES) of a failure, but we disable the Monitor phase of the control loop. From the MAPE-K point of view, we can consider that the components in the Plan and Execute are enabled, although the Plan phase is never executed because it is not triggered by the Analyze step. In other words, as in the first set of experiments, the same service selection policy holds for the whole experiment.

Finally, in the fourth set of experiments, we prove the effectiveness of the MAPE-K loop by activating the monitoring of the candidate concrete services performed by the WS Monitor component. The latter is configured to probe all the known concrete services every 5 seconds to find out what services are currently available. Whenever the WS Monitor finds that some service changed its state (going from running to failed or vice-versa), it sends a trigger to the Optimization Engine, which in turn computes the new service selection policy that will be applied by the Execute subsystem.

In each set, every experiment lasted 30 minutes and has been repeated twice, using a client request rate equal to 5 and 10 requests/seconds (in the following, referred to as *low* and *high* request rates) to show the behavioral differences that arise when MOSES is subject to different loads.

Experimental Setup

For all the sets of experiments, the testing environment consists of 3 Intel Xeon quadcore servers (2 Ghz/core) with 8 GB RAM each (nodes 1, 2, and 3), and 1 KVM virtual machine with 1 CPU and 1 GB RAM (node 4); a Gb Ethernet connects all the machines. The MOSES prototype is deployed as follows: node 1 hosts all the components of the Execute subsystem, node 2 the storage layer together with the candidate concrete services, and node 3 the components in the Monitor+Analyze and Plan subsystems. Finally, node 4 hosts the workload generator.

We consider the SOA application defined by the workflow in Figure 13, composed of 6 stateless tasks, and assume that 10 concrete services (with their respective SLAs) have been identified for abstract tasks S_1 and S_3, while 8 concrete services have been identified for any other task. Their respective SLA parameters, shown in Table

Figure 13. Workflow of the SOA application used in the experiments

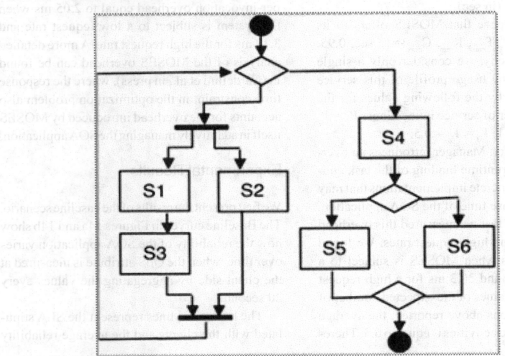

Table 1. SLA parameters for concrete services

cs	t_{ij}	r_{ij}	c_{ij}	cs	t_{ij}	r_{ij}	c_{ij}
$cs_{1[1,6]}$	2	0.995	6	$cs_{4[1,5]}$	0.5	0.995	1
$cs_{1[2,7]}$	1.8	0.99	6	$cs_{4[2,6]}$	0.5	0.99	0.8
$cs_{1[3,8]}$	2	0.99	5.5	$cs_{4[3,7]}$	1	0.995	0.8
$cs_{1[4,9]}$	3	0.995	4.5	$cs_{4[4,8]}$	1	0.95	0.6
$cs_{1[5,10]}$	4	0.99	3	$cs_{5[1,5]}$	1	0.995	3
$cs_{2[1,5]}$	1	0.995	2	$cs_{5[2,6]}$	2	0.99	2
$cs_{2[2,6]}$	2	0.995	1.8	$cs_{5[3,7]}$	3	0.99	1.5
$cs_{2[3,7]}$	1.8	0.99	1.8	$cs_{5[4,8]}$	4	0.95	1
$cs_{2[4,8]}$	3	0.99	1	$cs_{6[1,5]}$	1.8	0.99	1
$cs_{3[1,6]}$	1	0.995	5	$cs_{6[2,6]}$	2	0.995	0.8
$cs_{3[2,7]}$	1	0.99	4.5	$cs_{6[3,7]}$	3	0.99	0.6
$cs_{3[3,8]}$	2	0.99	4	$cs_{6[4,8]}$	4	0.95	0.4
$cs_{3[4,9]}$	4	0.95	2				
$cs_{3[5,10]}$	5	0.95	1				

1, differ in terms of cost c_{ij}, reliability r_{ij}, and response time t_{ij} (in sec).

We also suppose that MOSES offers to its clients the SLA $\{T_{max}, R_{min}, C_{max}\}=\{7$ sec, 0.95, 15$\}$. For simplicity, we consider only a single service class. The usage profile of this service classes is given by the following values for the expected number of service invocations: $V_1 = V_2 = V_3 = 1.5$, $V_4 = 1$, $V_5 = V_6 = 0.5$.

The Adaptation Manager introduces an overhead due to the runtime binding of the task endpoints to their concrete implementations that may affect the response time of the SOA application. In a preliminary test we measured this overhead under the low and high request rates. We found it to be 13.3 ms when MOSES is subject to a low request rate and 20.3 ms for a high request rate. Given the values of the expected number of service invocations above reported, the average number of invoke activities is equal to 6.5. There-

fore, the Adaptation Manager introduces a mean per-invocation overhead equal to 2.05 ms when the system is subject to a low request rate and 3.12 ms for the high request rate. A more detailed analysis of the MOSES overhead can be found in (Cardellini et al., in press), where the response time constraint in the optimization problem also accounts for the overhead introduced by MOSES itself in adaptively managing the SOA application.

Experimental Results

We first present the results of the baseline scenario. The Baseline curves in Figures 14a and 14b show how the reliability of the SOA application varies over time, when the QoS attribute is measured at the client-side by aggregating the values every 20 seconds.

The horizontal lines represent the SLA stipulated with the clients and the average reliability

Figure 14. a) Baseline reliability over time under low request rate; b) Baseline reliability over time under high request rate

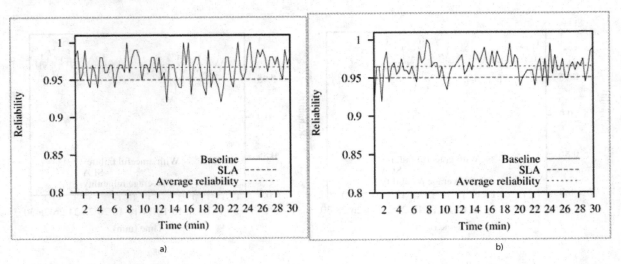

a)   b)

perceived by the clients over all the experiment duration. We can observe that the reliability fluctuates over time; most of the time it stays well above the SLA value, but occasionally it attains lower values. Nevertheless, as also shown in Table 2, where we report the average reliability of the baseline experiment along with the 95% confidence interval, MOSES is able to fulfill the reliability level agreed in the SLA.

In the second set of experiments we let the service providers gracefully fail, thus simulating, for instance, service programmed downtimes. The results in Figures 15a and 15b show how the reliability of the SOA application fluctuates over time; however, the average reliability is well above the agreed SLA.

The experimental values in Table 3 show that the average reliability, as well as the 95% confidence interval under the second scenario are perfectly comparable to those of the baseline experiment. Therefore, we can conclude that graceful leaves and joins do not affect the reliability performance since MOSES is able to adapt to the changed environment by re-computing the service selection policy.

Figures 16a and 16b show how the reliability of the SOA application varies over time when the concrete service providers exhibit the same churn rate of the second experiment, but without signaling their state to MOSES. The reliability levels fall down and the SLA stipulated by MOSES with its clients is no longer fulfilled. This experiment

Table 2. Average reliability and 95% confidence interval for the baseline experiment

	SLA	Average reliability	95% confidence interval
Low request rate	0.95	0.9664	0.0074
High request rate	0.95	0.9646	0.0054

Table 3. Average reliability and 95% confidence interval for the experiment with graceful failures

	SLA	Average reliability	95% confidence interval
Low request rate	0.95	0.9692	0.0071
High request rate	0.95	0.9659	0.0053

Figure 15. a) Reliability over time when services are subject to graceful failures under low request rate; b) Reliability over time when services are subject to graceful failures under high request rate

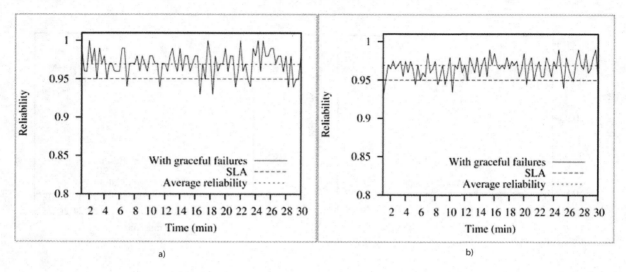

a)   b)

demonstrates that, if there are changes in the execution environment and no adaptation actions are taken to address these changes, the system is not able to satisfy the required QoS. It also points out that reliability levels are higher when the request rate is higher. The motivation is due to

the fact that the service selection policy binds each abstract task to a small subset of concrete services when the incoming request rate is low. On the other hand, with a higher request rate, the request load on any abstract task is balanced over a larger set of concrete services, depending on

Figure 16. a) Reliability over time when services are subject to failures, without WS Monitor under low request rate; b) Reliability over time when services are subject to failures, without WS Monitor under high request rate

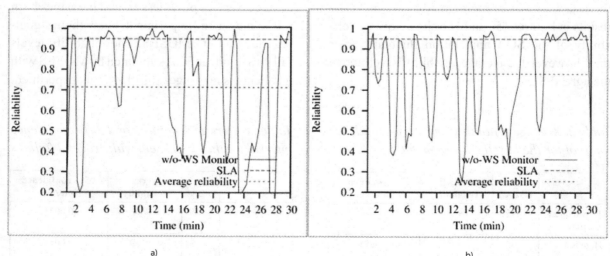

a)   b)

Table 4. Comparison of the average reliability and 95% confidence interval for the experiments with and without the WS monitor

	SLA	Average reliability	95% confidence interval
Low request rate without WS Monitor	0.95	0.7151	0.0187
Low request rate with WS Monitor	0.95	0.9101	0.0118
High request rate without WS Monitor	0.95	0.7798	0.0122
High request rate with WS Monitor	0.95	0.8974	0.0089

their capacity. Since we set the capacity of every concrete service to 10 req/sec, it is likely to have a single concrete service selected for any abstract task when the incoming request rate is equal to 5 req/sec, while it is likely to have two or more concrete services selected for any abstract task when the incoming request rate is 10 req/sec.

The objective of the last set of experiments is to show the improvement achieved thanks to the WS Monitor component.

Figures 17a and 17b show how the reliability of the SOA application varies over time when the service providers exhibit the same churn rate of the third experiment without signaling their

state to MOSES, but now with the WS Monitor enabled on MOSES.

As shown in Table 4, MOSES does not succeed in fulfilling the SLA stipulated with its clients, but the provided reliability has a significant improvement with respect to the results shown in Figures 16a and 16b, when the WS Monitor was disabled.

FUTURE RESEARCH DIRECTIONS

In this section, we briefly discuss some open challenges regarding the design of SOSs for the adaptive management of service composition that

Figure 17. a) Reliability over time when services are subject to failures, with WS Monitor under low request rate; b) Reliability over time when services are subject to failures, with WS Monitor under high request rate

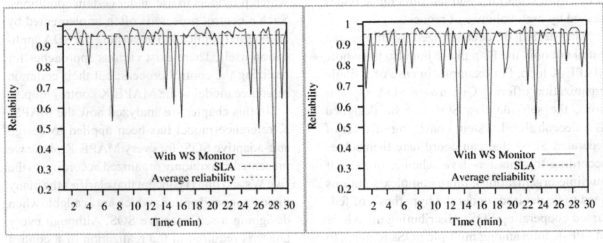

can be explored in future research. Some of these challenges directly stem from our own experience in designing and using the MOSES framework.

Using MOSES for our experimental evaluations, we found that a non–trivial issue is to adequately tune a quite large number of system parameters in the various software tools that we used to implement the MOSES prototype. Designing a self-tunable platform can greatly help the administrator of the service broker. For example, a self-adaptive tuning of the application server parameters according to the actual load of the SOA application can help to improve the resources utilization in the infrastructure layer, therefore allowing to reduce the number of required resources. More generally, future work can address the provisioning and management of the platform and infrastructure layers used by the SOS, also considering cross-cutting issues, for example regarding the SLAs.

Another challenging research issue is the development of decentralized approaches for the Plan phase. The optimization problems that are often used to define the adaptation plan can be computationally intensive applications that need to provide a solution in the shortest time possible, otherwise the service broker can incur in penalties due to the lack of SLA compliance. The centralized approaches that have been so far proposed may suffer from scalability and fault-tolerance issues caused by high volumes of requests.

The design of decentralized solutions can entail not only the Plan phase but also the whole MAPE-K loop. For example, in case of a single organization offering QoS-aware SOA applications, the self-adaptive SOS can be designed as a decentralized system consisting of a set of federated SOSs that can coordinate themselves according to a master-slave scheme. In case of multiple organizations, more complex solutions need to be devised: under the hypothesis of federated cooperating SOSs, distributing the whole MAPE-K loop among multiple SOSs requires to devise a distributed solution of the overall optimi-

zation problem. Analyzing the current literature, we noted that the case of several self-adaptive service-oriented systems under cooperating or non-cooperating scenarios is not yet satisfactorily covered and we believe that investigating how to cope with these issues is a timely and promising research indication.

CONCLUSION

The development of distributed applications has recently shifted from the classic in-house development to activities concerning the identification, selection, and composition of services offered by third party providers through a service marketplace and this shift is rapidly accelerating with the advent of Cloud computing. This new model, which is the basis of the SOA paradigm, increases the interoperability level of the applications, by forcing them to only use standard protocols for any activity. However, when QoS matters, SOA applications might suffer from their distributed nature because the QoS levels offered by service providers may quickly fluctuate over time, due to the highly varying execution environment. On the other hand, the dynamic composition of SOA applications can provide a solution to govern providers' QoS fluctuations by choosing at runtime which providers to use under certain conditions. Such a control process is often implemented by an external application governing the SOA application itself. There exist various approaches for realizing the control process, but their common reference model is the MAPE-K control loop.

In this chapter we analyzed how the MAPE-K reference model has been applied to design self-adaptive SOS; for every MAPE-K phase we presented a taxonomy organized according to the five Ws and one H concept that clarifies the many dimensions and options which are available when designing a self-adaptive SOS. Although every phase is required in the realization of a control process, we focused on the Plan phase because it is the core of the adaptation process; specifically, we analyzed how the SOS can self-adapt in order to satisfy some non-functional requirements. Most approaches in this research line address the adaptation by selecting the appropriate services that can be exploited during the SOA application execution or by properly managing the resource provisioning in such a way to meet the target QoS levels.

As a case study, we presented the MOSES framework, a fully functional prototype that realizes every phase of the MAPE-K model relying on a modular system architecture. We demonstrated how it is possible to improve the QoS of a SOA application that operates in a highly varying execution environment, where component services continuously appear and disappear. The experimental results showed that the execution of a SOA application managed by MOSES allows us to achieve a reliability improvement of 20% with respect to a service broker that does not fully exploit the MAPE-K architecture.

REFERENCES

Agarwal, V., & Jalote, P. (2010). From specification to adaptation: An integrated QoS-driven approach for dynamic adaptation of web service compositions. *In Proceedings of 2010 IEEE International Conference on Web Services (ICWS '10)* (pp. 275-282).

Alrifai, M., & Risse, T. (2009). Combining global optimization with local selection for efficient QoS-aware service composition. *In Proceedings of 18th International Conference on World Wide Web (WWW '09)* (pp. 881-890). ACM.

Alrifai, M., Skoutas, D., & Risse, T. (2010). Selecting skyline services for QoS-based Web service composition. *In Proceedings of 19th International Conference on World Wide Web (WWW '10)* (pp. 11-20). ACM.

Anselmi, J., Ardagna, D., & Cremonesi, P. (2007). A QoS-based selection approach of autonomic grid services. *In Proceedings of 2007 Workshop on Service-oriented Computing Performance: Aspects, Issues, and Approaches (SOCP '07)* (pp 1-8). ACM.

Ardagna, D., Baresi, L., Comai, S., Comuzzi, M., & Pernici, B. (2011). A service-based framework for flexible business processes. *IEEE Software*, *28*(2), 61–67.

Ardagna, D., & Mirandola, R. (2010). Per-flow optimal service selection for web services based processes. *Journal of Systems and Software*, *83*(8), 1512–1523.

Ardagna, D., & Pernici, B. (2007). Adaptive service composition in flexible processes. *IEEE Transactions on Software Engineering*, *33*(6), 369–384.

Bellucci, A., Cardellini, V., Di Valerio, V., & Iannucci, S. (2010) A scalable and highly available brokering service for SLA-based composite services. In *Proceedings of 2010 International Conference on Service-Oriented Computing (ICSOC '10)* (pp. 527–541). Springer.

Berbner, R., Spahn, M., Repp, N., Heckmann, O., & Steinmetz, R. (2006). Heuristics for QoS-aware Web service composition. *In Proceedings of IEEE International Conference on Web Services (ICWS '06)* (pp. 72-82).

Calinescu, R., Grunske, L., Kwiatkowska, M., Mirandola, R., & Tamburrelli, G. (2011). Dynamic QoS management and optimization in service-based systems. *IEEE Transactions on Software Engineering*, *37*(3), 387–409.

Canfora, G., Di Penta, M., Esposito, R., & Villani, M. L. (2008). A framework for QoS-aware binding and re-binding of composite Web services. *Journal of Systems and Software*, *81*, 1754–1769.

Cardellini, V., Casalicchio, E., Grassi, V., Iannucci, S., Lo Presti, F., & Mirandola, R. (in press). MOSES: A framework for QoS driven runtime adaptation of service-oriented systems. *IEEE Transactions on Software Engineering*, accepted for publication in June 2011.

Cardellini, V., Casalicchio, E., Grassi, V., & Lo Presti, F. (2007). Flow-based service selection for web service composition supporting multiple QoS classes. *In Proceedings of IEEE 2007 International Conference on Web Services* (pp. 743-750).

Cardellini, V., Di Valerio, V., Grassi, V., Iannucci, S., & Lo Presti, F. (2011). A performance comparison of QoS-driven service selection approaches. In *Proceedings of 4th European Conference Service Wave*. Springer.

Cardellini, V., Di Valerio, V., Grassi, V., Iannucci, S., & Lo Presti, F. (2011). A new approach to QoS driven service selection in service oriented architectures. *In Proceedings of IEEE 6th International Symposium on Service-Oriented System Engineering (SOSE '11)*.

Cormen, T. H., Leiserson, C. E., Rivest, R. L., & Stein, C. (2001). *Introduction to algorithms* (2nd ed.). MIT Press.

Dobson, S., Denazis, S., Fernandez, A., Gati, D., Gelenbe, E., Massacci, F., & Zambonelli, F. (2006). A survey of autonomic communications. *ACM Transactions in Autonomic and Adaptive Systems, 1*(2), 223–259.

Ezenwoye, O., & Sadjadi, S. M. (2007). RobustBPEL2: Transparent autonomization in business processes through dynamic proxies. In *Proceedings of 8th International Symposium on Autonomous Decentralized Systems (ISADS '07)* (pp. 17-24). IEEE Computer Society.

Hart, G. (2011). The five Ws of online help for tech writers. *TechWhirl*. Retrieved January 24, 2012, from http://techwhirl.com/columns/the-five-ws-of-online-help/

Hwang, C., & Yoon, K. (1981). *Multiple criteria decision making. Lecture Notes in Economics and Mathematical Systems*. Springer.

Kephart, J. O., & Chess, D. M. (2003). The vision of autonomic computing. *IEEE Computer, 36*(1), 41–50.

Klein, A., Ishikawa, F., & Honiden, S. (2010). Efficient QoS-aware service composition with a probabilistic service selection policy. *In Proceedings of 2010 International Conference on Service-Oriented Computing (ICSOC 2010)* (pp. 182-196). Springer.

Leitner, P., Wetzstein, B., Karastoyanova, D., Hummer, W., Dustdar, S., & Leymann, F. (2010). Preventing SLA violations in service compositions using aspect-based fragment substitution. In *Proceedings of 2010 International Conference on Service-Oriented Computing (ICSOC 2010)* (pp. 365-380). Springer.

Martello, S., & Toth, P. (1987). Algorithms for knapsack problems. *Annals in Discrete Mathematics, 31*, 70–79.

Menascè, D., Casalicchio, E., & Dubey, V. (2010). On optimal service selection in service oriented architectures. *Performance Evaluation, 67*(8), 659–675.

Menasce, D., Gomaa, H., Malek, S., & Sousa, J. (2011). SASSY: A framework for self-architecting service-oriented systems. *IEEE Software, 28*(6), 78–85.

Michlmayr, A., Rosenberg, F., Leitner, P., & Dustdar, S. (2010). End-to-end support for QoS-aware service selection, binding, and mediation in VRESCo. *IEEE Transactions in Service Computing, 3*(3), 193–205.

Mirandola, R., & Potena, P. (2011). A QoS-based framework for the adaptation of service-based systems. *Scalable Computing: Practice and Experience, 12*(1), 63–78.

Mosincat, A., Binder, W., & Jazayeri, M. (2010). Runtime adaptability through automated model evolution. *Proceedings of 14th IEEE International Enterprise Distributed Object Computing Conference (EDOC 2010)*, (pp. 217–226).

OASIS. (2007). *Web services business process execution language* (WSBPEL). Retrieved from http://www.oasis-open.org/committees/tc_home.php?wg_abbrev=wsbpel.

Papazoglou, M. P., Traverso, P., Dustdar, S., & Leymann, F. (2007). Service-oriented computing: State of the art and research challenges. *IEEE Computer*, *40*(1), 38–45.

Rosario, S., Benveniste, A., Haar, S., & Jard, C. (2008). Probabilistic QoS and soft contracts for transaction-based Web services orchestrations. *IEEE Transactions in Service Computing*, *1*(4), 187–200.

Rouvoy, R., Barone, P., Ding, Y., Eliassen, F., Hallsteinsen, S., & Lorenzo, J. (2009). MUSIC: Middleware support for self-adaptation in ubiquitous and service-oriented environments. In Cheng, B. H., Lemos, R., Giese, H., Inverardi, P., & Magee, J. (Eds.), *Software engineering for self-adaptive systems* (pp. 164–182). Springer-Verlag.

Salehie, M., & Tahvildari, L. (2009). Self-adaptive software: Landscape and research challenges. *ACM Transactions in Autonomic and Adaptive Systems*, *4*(2), 1–42.

Wada, H., Suzuki, J., Yamano, Y., & Oba, K. (in press). E³: Multi-objective genetic algorithms for SLA-aware service deployment optimization problem. *IEEE Transactions in Service Computing*.

Yu, T., Zhang, Y., & Lin, K. (2007). Efficient algorithms for Web services selection with end-to-end QoS constraints. *ACM Transactions in Web*, *1*(1).

Zheng, Z., Ma, H., Lyu, M. R., & King, I. (2011). QoS-Aware Web service recommendation by collaborative filtering. *IEEE Transactions in Service Computing*, *4*(2), 140–152.

KEY TERMS AND DEFINITIONS

MAPE-K: A reference model for architecting self-adaptive systems.

Quality of Service (QoS): The property of a service to provide predictable performance despite the availability of a limited set of resources.

Self-Adaptive: The capability of a system to autonomously change its behavior with respect to changes in itself and/or its surrounding environment.

Service Broker: An intermediate entity between users of SOA applications and candidate service providers. It offers a value-added service, possibly satisfying some QoS constraints.

Service Oriented Architecture (SOA): An architectural paradigm for building loosely-coupled network applications based on black-box software components named services. Such services can be easily composed to support dynamic and flexible applications.

Service Selection: Given a workflow, the ability to choose for each task in the workflow one or more specific service among a set of functionally equivalent implementations offered by service providers. The selection goal is to optimize some objective function (e.g., global utility) possibly subject to some constraints.

Workflow: A sequence of connected tasks and the related data flows representing the application logic.

Chapter 7
Mining Lifecycle Event Logs for Enhancing Service-Based Applications

Schahram Dustdar
Vienna University of Technology, Austria

Franco Maria Nardini
ISTI-CNR, Pisa, Italy

Philipp Leitner
Vienna University of Technology, Austria

Fabrizio Silvestri
ISTI-CNR, Pisa, Italy

Gabriele Tolomei
ISTI-CNR, Pisa, Italy

ABSTRACT

Service-Oriented Architectures (SOAs), and traditional enterprise systems in general, record a variety of events (e.g., messages being sent and received between service components) to proper log files, i.e., event logs. These files constitute a huge and valuable source of knowledge that may be extracted through data mining techniques. To this end, process mining is increasingly gaining interest across the SOA community. The goal of process mining is to build models without a priori knowledge, i.e., to discover structured process models derived from specific patterns that are present in actual traces of service executions recorded in event logs. However, in this work, the authors focus on detecting frequent sequential patterns, thus considering process mining as a specific instance of the more general sequential pattern mining problem. Furthermore, they apply two sequential pattern mining algorithms to a real event log provided by the Vienna Runtime Environment for Service-oriented Computing, i.e., VRESCo. The obtained results show that the authors are able to find services that are frequently invoked together within the same sequence. Such knowledge could be useful at design-time, when service-based application developers could be provided with service recommendation tools that are able to predict and thus to suggest next services that should be included in the current service composition.

DOI: 10.4018/978-1-4666-2089-6.ch007

INTRODUCTION

The vast majority of nowadays software-based systems, ranging from the simplest, i.e., small-scale, to the most complex, i.e., large-scale, record massive amounts of data in the form of logs. Such logs could either refer to the functioning of the system as well as keep trace of any possible software or human interaction with the system itself. For this reason, logs represent a valuable source of hidden knowledge that can be exploited in order to enhance the overall performances of any software-based system.

Well-known examples of systems that have started trying to improve their performances by analyzing event logs are surely Web Search Engines (SEs).

Roughly, SEs are increasingly exploiting past user behaviors recorded in query logs in order to better understand people search intents, thus, for providing users with better search experiences. Indeed, by accurately recognizing and predicting actual user information needs, SEs are now able to offer more sophisticated functionalities (e.g., query suggestion) as well as better relevant result sets in response to a specific query (e.g., query diversification).

Moreover, there are plenty of modern enterprise software systems that need to operate in highly dynamic and distributed environments in a standardized way. Such systems implement their business logic according to the Service-Oriented Architecture (SOA) principles, thus, assembling their business processes as the composition and orchestration of autonomous, protocol-independent, and distributed logic units, i.e., software services.

Service-based systems and applications (SBAs) require proper run-time environments where their composing services can be searched, bound, invoked, monitored and managed. Therefore, SBA's run-time support might keep track of what is going on during the whole application lifecycle by roughly recording all such events to log files, i.e., service event logs.

Analysis of such service event logs could reveal interesting patterns, which in turn might be exploited for improving the overall performances of SOA's run-time frameworks as well as supporting SBA designers during the whole application lifecycle.

The main contribution of this work concerns the application of data mining techniques to a real-life service event log collected by the VRESCo SOA run-time framework. Our aim is to analyze the historical events stored on VRESCo in order to discover software services that are frequently invoked and composed together, i.e., process mining.

Although traditional process mining refers to a set of techniques and methodologies whose aim is to distill a structured process description from a set of actual traces of executions recorded in event logs, here we treat it as an instance of the sequential pattern mining problem.

The remaining of the work is structured as follows. First, we start describing background concepts and past work that somehow concerns with service event log analysis. Section 1 describes the information collected by SOA lifecycle event logs, in particular focusing on the VRESCo run-time framework. In Section 2, we propose how VRESCo event log may be analyzed for approaching our research challenge. Therefore, Section 3 shows the experiments we conduct on a real VRESCo log data set. Finally, we summarize the contributions we provide in this work together with any further idea that could be better investigated as future work.

BACKGROUND AND RELATED WORK

In this work, we present a use case for event log mining in service-based systems. This idea bears some resemblance to the established idea of business activity management (BAM) (Kochar, 2005). BAM considers the event-driven governance of business processes, and is, hence, mostly a term from the business domain. Technically, BAM is enabled by monitoring runtime of services and their interactions within company SOAs. To this end, event-based monitoring approaches (Zeng, Lei, & Chang, 2007, Baresi, Guinea, Pistore, & Trainotti, 2009, Wetzstein, Strauch, & Leymann, 2009) produce a steady stream of low-level lifecycle events, similarly to the lifecycle events discussed in Section 1.2 and to the event logs produced by VRESCo. These low-level events need to be aggregated so that real business information can be gained from them. Existing techniques to do this include SLA aggregation (Unger, Leymann, & Scheibler, 2008) or event-based SLA monitoring (Sahai, Machiraju, Sayal, van Moorsel, & Casati, 2002, Michlmayr, Rosenberg, Leitner, & Dustdar, 2009). Related to the ideas of BAM is research work by (Mulo, Zdun, & Dustdar, 2008), which considers event-based monitoring of business compliance. Our research, specifically mining for invocation sequences that lead to failed service invocations, is complementary to BAM. While BAM is mostly concerned with discovering failures, our research can be used to identify or predict them in advance.

In literature, events emitted by service-based applications have found various other uses. For instance, (Michlmayr, Rosenberg, Leitner, & Dustdar, 2008b) uses eventing information (along with various other data sources) to generate visualizations of the past behavior and quality of Web services, mostly to ease management and selection of services for other uses. This is related to our work, which identifies services which have in the past been used together, mostly to suggest suitable services for new uses. (Zeng, Lingenfelder, Lei, & Chang, 2008, Leitner, Wetzstein, Rosenberg, Michlmayr, Dustdar, & Leymann, 2009) have used SOA events to generate predictions of SLA violations. This is done by training machine learning models from the collected event data, and using runtime event information as input to those models.

Finally, our research is related to the idea of process mining (van der Aalst, 2004, van der Aalst, Weijters, & Maruster, 2004, van der Aalst, Dongen, Günther, Rozinat, Verbeek, & Weijters, 2009). Generally speaking, process mining considers discovering structures (mostly business processes) from traces of earlier executions of information systems. This also includes making implicit processes (that people are subconsciously following) explicit, so that they can be optimized using the techniques of business process reengineering. Our work is different to process mining in the sense that we do not suggest new processes from event logs. Instead, we rather give recommendations which combinations of services have in the past been used together (indicating that it might make sense to use them in combination).

SOA LIFECYCLE EVENT LOGS

In the following, we will discuss SOA lifecycle event logs as they are used in this work. We then present the lifecycle events emitted by the VRESCo SOA runtime environment as a concrete example used in Section 2 and Section 3 of this work.

Lifecycle Events

Events and complex event processing (CEP) (Luckham, 2001) are frequently used tools to document and track the lifecycle of applications in various domains. For instance, in the business domain the idea of business activity monitoring (BAM) (Kochar, 2005) uses events to monitor business process performance. Analogously, technical implementations of business processes on top of SOAs (service compositions) are often monitored using CEP. To this end, many service composition engines can be configured to track their current state in event logs. For instance, the Apache ODE WS-BPEL engine triggers a rich model of execution events (http://ode.apache.org/

Figure 1. VRESCo event type classes

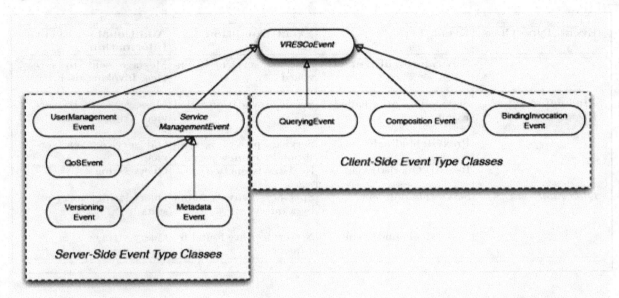

ode-execution-events.html). Similarly, service compositions implemented using Windows Workflow Foundation can use the .NET tracking service to persist event logs (http://msdn.microsoft.com/en-us/library/ms735887(v=vs.85).aspx). However, tracking system state via event logs in SOA is not confined to composition engines. For instance, The Vienna Runtime Environment for Service-Oriented Computing (VRESCo) (Michlmayr, Rosenberg, Leitner, & Dustdar, 2010) uses events to track not only service compositions, but all entities and interactions in a SOA (services, users, compositions, metadata and interactions).

In its most general form, an event log *E* consists of a sequence of *n* recorded events, i.e., $E = <e_1, e_2, ..., e_n>$. Each event e_i in *E* usually contains at least a unique identifier, an event timestamp, the publisher of the event (e.g., the BPEL engine), the subject of the event (e.g., the composition instance that triggered the event), and the event type. Depending on the concrete event type, more detailed information is available. This type-specific information cannot be described generally, i.e., it is different from event type to event type

as well as from system to system. In the following we describe the event types triggered by the VRESCo system as an example of the possibilities provided by event logs.

SOA Event Log: VRESCo

VRESCo is an experimental runtime environment developed at Vienna University of Technology. VRESCo is being developed under an open source license, and can be accessed via the project Web page (http://www.infosys.tuwien.ac.at/prototypes/VRESCo/). The project aims at solving some of the research problems identified in (Papazoglou, Traverso, Dustdar, & Leymann, 2007), e.g., dynamic selection of services based on Quality-of-Service (QoS), dynamic rebinding and service composition, service metadata and event-based services computing.

In the following we focus on the latter aspect. The foundations of event-based service-oriented computing have been discussed in (Michlmayr, Rosenberg, Leitner, & Dustdar, 2008a). In a nutshell, the goals of this earlier work were to track

Table 1. Client-triggered VRESCo events

Event Type Class	Event Type	Event Condition	Additional Event Information
BindingInvocation Event	ServiceInvokedEvent	Specific service is invoked	Message sent to service, Invoking user
	ServiceInvocationFailed Event	Service invocation failed	Message sent to service, Triggered fault
	ProxyRebindingEvent	Service proxy is (re-)bound to a new service	Old service, New service
QueryingEvent	RegistryQueriedEvent	Registry is queried	Query string
	ServiceFoundEvent	Specific service is found by a query	Query string, query results
	NoServiceFoundEvent	No services are found by a query	Query string

what is going on in a service-based application by constantly triggering events and using CEP to construct meaningful information from those events.

In a VRESCo system, events of various types are triggered. A simplified taxonomy of event type classes is depicted in Figure 1. As can be seen, events are triggered when services are queried, bound and invoked. Additionally, events indicate if the data or metadata about services changes (e.g., the QoS is changed, new operations are available). Each of the concrete event type classes (those with non-italic name) in turn contains a number of concrete event types that can be triggered. For full details on all events refer to (Michlmayr, Rosenberg, Leitner, & Dustdar, 2008a).

Events in VRESCo can be triggered either on client- or server-side. While events concerning metadata are triggered by the VRESCo server, all querying and invocation events are triggered by clients and only processed throughout the VRES-Co event engine. These client-triggered events are listed in more detail in Table 1. In the table, we provide the condition that triggers each event along with the event type and event type class of the event. All of these events provide the basic

information discussed above (sequence number, timestamp, etc.). In addition, events generally provide some type-specific additional information, which we also summarize in the table. For reasons of brevity, we have omitted composition events. Composition events in VRESCo are of comparable expressiveness as the events triggered by Apache ODE.

The VRESCo event engine stores triggered events in an event log. Therein, events are serialized as XML and can be accessed and analyzed via a RESTful service interface. In Figure 2, we provide an example event serialized to XML. Evidently, the event reflects a service invocation with a very simple input message (<order>) as payload.

LIFECYCLE EVENT LOG MINING

In this work, we are interested in exploring how event log collected by the VRESCo framework, i.e., service event log, could be harnessed for better supporting service-based applications during their whole lifecycle.

Figure 2. Serialized invocation event

```
<ServiceInvokedEvent
    xmlns="http://www.vitalab.tuwien.ac.at/vresco/usertypes">
  <Priority>0</Priority>
  <Publisher>guest</Publisher>
  <PublisherGroup>GuestGroup</PublisherGroup>
  <UserName>a007b09b-8c23-4fac-af30-0142a61f3795</UserName>
  <SeqNum>74006756-64f1-40cb-858e-565d4bc6a94c:24</SeqNum>
  <Timestamp>2010-11-09T09:58:49</Timestamp>
  <CurrentRevisionId>180</CurrentRevisionId>
  <CurrentRevisionWsdl>
      http://localhost:60000/AssemblingPlanningService?wsdl
  </CurrentRevisionWsdl>
  <FeatureName>GetPartFeature</FeatureName>
  <InvocationInfo>
    <service_input>
      <order><part1>text</part1></order>
    </service_input>
  </InvocationInfo>
</ServiceInvokedEvent>
```

Roughly, analysis of VRESCo event log data is finalized to the discovery of sequences of services that are frequently invoked together, thus, to detect processes, or part of those, as result of the compositions of highly co-invoked services.

This knowledge could be useful for improving the overall performances of the VRESCo run-time framework as well as supporting SBA designers during the whole application lifecycle. As an example, service-based application developers could be provided with service recommendation tools that are able to predict and, thus, to suggest next services that should be included in the current service composition at design-time.

Due to the huge amount of data collected in the VRESCo event log, data mining techniques represent a suitable approach for addressing our research challenge. In the following, we describe how processes may be mined from the VRESCo event log, namely how sequences of co-invoked services that frequently appear in the event log may be discovered and exploited.

Process Mining

According to van der Aalst *et al.* (van der Aalst, Weijters, & Maruster, 2004), the term process mining, also referred to as workflow mining, describes a set of techniques and methodologies whose aim is to distill a structured process description from a set of actual traces of executions recorded in event logs.

In our vision, a service log might be viewed as a database consisting of sequences of events that change with time, i.e., a time-series database (Han, & Kamber, 2006). Such kind of database records the valid time of each data set. For example, in a time-series database that records service invocation transactions, each transaction includes the unique identifier of the invoked service as well as an extra time-stamp attribute indicating when the event happened (Zhao, & Bhowmick, 2003).

Several kinds of patterns can be extracted from various types of time-series data. In this work, we are interested in finding sequences of services that are frequently invoked together in a specific order, i.e., sequential patterns (Agrawal, & Srikant, 1995).

Each process instance recorded on event logs might be expressed as an unrolled trace of invoked services. Thus, let $S = \{s_1, s_2, ..., s_m\}$ be a set of services and let $S_j \subseteq S$ be an itemset of services invoked at the same time (or within a small time window), i.e., $S_j = \{s_{j1}, s_{j2}, ..., s_{jk}\}$. Therefore, a process $p_j = <S'_1, S'_2, ..., S'_{|p|}>$ has a unique identifier and represents a sequence of service itemsets, chronologically-ordered according to their time-stamps. Globally, a process database is a sequence database $P = \{p_1, p_2, ..., p_n\}$ of executed and recorded processes.

Roughly, a sequential pattern is a sequence of service itemsets that occur frequently in P according to a specific order, i.e., appear as subsequence of a large percentage of sequences of P. More formally, a sequence $p' = <S'_1, S'_2, ..., S'_u>$ is a subsequence of $p'' = <S''_1, S''_2, ..., S''_v>$, i.e., $p' \ll p''$ if there exists integers $1 \leq i_1 < ... < i_u \leq u$, such that $S'_x \subseteq S''_{ix}$ for each $1 \leq x \leq u$.

Then we may define the support $supp(p')$ of a sequence of service itemsets p' as the proportion of processes in the database P that contains p' as its subsequence, that is:

```
supp(p') = |{p_j | p' << p_j}|/|P|.
```

Therefore, sequential pattern mining is the process of extracting certain sequential patterns whose support exceed a predefined minimal support threshold *min_supp*.

To this end, as a first approach we apply one of the more efficient sequence pattern mining algorithm to the VRESCo event log, namely *PrefixSpan* (Pei, Han, Mortazavi-Asl, & Pinto, 2001).

Furthermore, we extend our first approach in order to exploit the temporal information associated with each service invocation in a different way. Indeed, in traditional sequential pattern mining, event time-stamps are only used for establishing the chronological order between service invocations, i.e., for simply stating that service s_i is in-

voked before service s_j. However, observing that s_i and s_j are invoked really closed to each other, e.g., within 5 seconds, rather than noting that s_i and s_j are farther away from each other, e.g. 5 minutes, could lead to different conclusions. Thus, we apply another sequential pattern mining algorithm, which is able to deal with this issue, i.e., *MiSTA* (Giannotti, Nanni, Pedreschi, & Pinelli, 2006).

Finally, in Section 3, we describe the different results we obtain on the VRESCo event log when using the two approaches described above.

EXPERIMENTATION

In order to test our claim about finding frequent sequential patterns inside service event logs, we use a real-life log of events collected by the VRESCo runtime framework.

This event log consists of 89 transactions. Each transaction is in turn composed of several events according to the ones described in Table 1 (e.g., *ServiceInvokedEvent*, *ServiceInvocationFailedEvent*, etc.).

For the sake of our purposes, namely for discovering sequences of services that frequently are invoked together, we only consider the list of *ServiceInvokedEvent* for each transaction.

Firstly, we run the *PrefixSpan* algorithm (Pei, Han, Mortazavi-Asl, & Pinto, 2001) on the VRESCo data set. We use several thresholds on the minimum support of the sequential patterns to be extracted, ranging from 20% to 100%. However, the maximum support for frequent sequences found in our data set is 66%.

The following table shows the distribution of the lengths of extracted sequence patterns, i.e., the number of invoked services that are inside a frequent sequence. In particular, Table 2 (a), (b), and (c) show the results obtained by using a minimum support threshold of 25%, 50%, and 66%, respectively.

As one would expect, independently from the minimum support chosen, 2-length sequences are

Table 2. Statistics about the ground-truth data

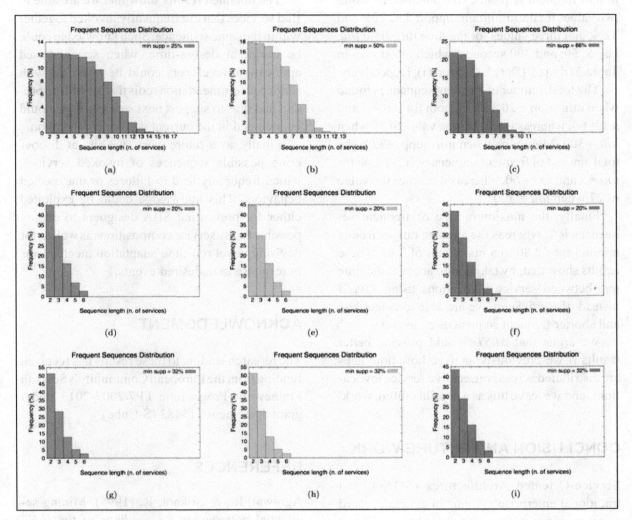

the most popular since for each *k*-length frequent sequences (*k > 2*) any *i*-length subsequence, i.e., $2 \leq i < k$, is also frequent by definition. Moreover, as the minimum support threshold increases, the maximum length of frequent sequences decreases as well from 17 to 11, and, also, most popular frequent sequences result to be globally shorter.

Finally, on average frequent sequences are composed of 5.86, 4.60, and 4.07 services for minimum support values of 25%, 50%, and 66%, respectively.

As a second step of our experimental phase, we also run the *MiSTA* algorithm (Giannotti, Nanni,

Pedreschi, & Pinelli, 2006) on the VRESCo event log. This algorithm differs from classical sequential pattern mining algorithms like *PrefixSpan* because it also takes care of the time gaps between consecutive items in a sequence. In other words, *MiSTA* extracts frequent sequences by considering not only the *minimum support* but also another parameter, i.e., *tau*, which basically represents a threshold on the time-gap between pairs of consecutive items.

In our experiments, we use several combinations of such two parameters, namely *min_supp* and *tau*. In the following, we describe the distribution of frequent sequence size obtained by using two values for the minimum support, i.e., 20% and 32%, and three values for the time threshold *tau*, i.e., 5, 60, and 300 seconds, which are shown in Table 2 (d), (e), (f), (g), (h), and (i), respectively.

The total number of frequent sequences found when min supp = 20% is 33, both for *tau* = 5 and *tau* = 60, whereas it reaches the value of 35 when *tau* = 300. Moreover, when min supp = 32% the total amount of frequent sequences is 20, both for *tau* = 5 and *tau* = 60, whereas it reaches the value of 27 when *tau* = 300.

Finally, the maximum size of frequent sequences is 7, whereas the average ranges from a minimum of 2.80 to a maximum of 3.07. These results show that, by taking into account the time gap between service invocations using *MiSTA* instead of *PrefixSpan*, we are able to detect less and shorter frequent sequences on average.

We argue that *MiSTA* could provide better results if we previously analyze how time gaps are distributed across consecutive service invocations, and we leave this as a possible future work.

CONCLUSION AND FUTURE WORK

Service-Oriented Architectures (SOAs), and traditional enterprise systems in general, record a variety of events (e.g., messages being sent and received between service components) to proper log files, i.e., event logs. These les constitute a huge and valuable source of knowledge that may be extracted through data mining techniques.

In this work, we focus on process mining as a specific instance of the more general sequential pattern mining problem. Basically, our aim is to detect frequent sequential patterns that might be present in actual traces of service executions recorded in event logs. To this end, we apply two sequential pattern mining algorithms to a real event log provided by the Vienna Runtime Environment for Service-oriented Computing, i.e., VRESCo.

The obtained results show that we are able to find services that are frequently invoked together within the same sequence. Such knowledge could be useful at design-time, when service-based application developers could be provided with service recommendation tools that are able to predict and thus to suggest next services that should be included in the current service composition.

Finally, as a future work, we aim at discovering possible sequences of invoked services, which frequently lead to failures or unexpected behaviors. This knowledge could be exploited either for preventing SBA designers to deploy possible faulty service compositions as well as for devising novel run-time adaptation mechanisms in response to undesired events.

ACKNOWLEDGMENT

The research leading to these results has received funding from the European Community's Seventh Framework Programme FP7/2007-2013 under grant agreement 215483 (S-Cube).

REFERENCES

Agrawal, R., & Srikant, R. (1995). Mining sequential patterns. *In Proceedings of the IEEE Conference on Data Engineering* (pp. 3-14).

Baresi, L., Guinea, S., Pistore, M., & Trainotti, M. (2009). Dynamo + Astro: An integrated approach for BPEL monitoring. In *Proceedings of the IEEE International Conference on Web Services* (pp. 230-237).

Giannotti, F., Nanni, M., Pedreschi, D., & Pinelli, F. (2006). Mining sequences with temporal annotations. In *Proceedings of the ACM Symposium on Applied Computing* (pp. 593-597).

Han, J., & Kamber, M. (Jim Gray, Series Editor). (2006). *Data mining: Concepts and techniques*. Morgan Kaufmann Publishers.

Kochar, H. (2005). *Business activity monitoring and business intelligence*. Retrieved from http://www.ebizq.net/topics/bam/features/6596.html

Leitner, P., Wetzstein, B., Rosenberg, F., Michlmayr, A., Dustdar, S., & Leymann, F. (2009). Runtime prediction of service level agreement violations for composite services. In *Proceedings of the Workshop on Non-Functional Properties and SLA Management in Service-Oriented Computing* (pp. 176-186).

Luckham, D. C. (2001). *The power of events: An introduction to complex event processing in distributed enterprise systems*. Addison-Wesley Longman Publishing Co., Inc.

Michlmayr, A., Rosenberg, F., Leitner, P., & Dustdar, S. (2008a). Advanced event processing and notifications in service runtime environments. In *Proceedings of the International Conference on Distributed Event-Based Systems* (pp. 115-125).

Michlmayr, A., Rosenberg, F., Leitner, P., & Dustdar, S. (2008b). Selective service provenance in the VRESCo runtime. *International Journal of Web Services Research, 7*(2), 65–86.

Michlmayr, A., Rosenberg, F., Leitner, P., & Dustdar, S. (2009). Comprehensive QoS monitoring of web services and event-based SLA violation detection. In *Proceedings of the International Workshop on Middleware for Service Oriented Computing* (pp. 1-6).

Michlmayr, A., Rosenberg, F., Leitner, P., & Dustdar, S. (2010). End-to-end support for QoS-aware service selection, binding, and mediation in VRESCo. *IEEE Transactions on Service Computing, 3*, 193–205.

Mulo, E., Zdun, U., & Dustdar, S. (2008). Monitoring web service event trails for business compliance. In *Proceedings of the IEEE International Conference on Service-Oriented Computing and Applications* (pp. 1-8).

Papazoglou, M. P., Traverso, P., Dustdar, S., & Leymann, F. (2007). Service-oriented computing: State of the art and research challenges. *IEEE Computer, 40*(11), 38–45.

Pei, J., Han, J., Mortazavi-Asl, B., & Pinto, H. (2001). Prefixspan: Mining sequential patterns efficiently by prefix-projected pattern growth. In *Proceedings of IEEE Conference on Data Engineering* (pp. 215-224).

Sahai, A., Machiraju, V., Sayal, M., van Moorsel, A. P. A., & Casati, F. (2002). Automated SLA monitoring for web services. In *Proceedings of the IFIP/IEEE International Workshop on Distributed Systems: Operations and Management* (pp. 28-41).

Unger, T., Leymann, F., Leymann, F., & Scheibler, T. (2008). Aggregation of service level agreements in the context of business processes. In *Proceedings of the IEEE Enterprise Distributed Object Conference* (pp. 43-52).

van der Aalst, W. (2004). Process mining: A research agenda. *Computers in Industry, 53*(3), 231–244.

van der Aalst, W., Dongen, B. F. V., Gunther, C., Rozinat, A., Verbeek, H. M. W., & Weijters, A. J. M. M. (2009). ProM: The process mining toolkit. *Industrial Engineering (American Institute of Industrial Engineers), 489*, 1–4.

van der Aalst, W., Weijters, T., & Maruster, L. (2004). Workflow mining: Discovering process models from event logs. *IEEE Transactions on Knowledge and Data Engineering, 16*(9), 1128–1142.

Wetzstein, B., Strauch, S., & Leymann, F. (2009). Measuring performance metrics of WS-BPEL service compositions. In *Proceedings of the International Conference on Networking and Services* (pp. 49-56).

Zeng, L., Lei, H., & Chang, H. (2007). Monitoring the QoS for web services. In *Proceedings of the International Conference on Service-Oriented Computing* (pp. 132-144).

Zeng, L., Lingenfelder, C., Lei, H., & Chang, H. (2008). Event-driven quality of service prediction. In *Proceedings of the International Conference on Service-Oriented Computing* (pp. 147-161).

Zhao, Q., & Bhowmick, S. S. (2003). *Sequential pattern matching: A survey*. Retrieved from http://cs.nju.edu.cn/zhouzh/zhouzh.files/course/dm/reading/reading04/zhao_techrep03.pdf

KEY TERMS AND DEFINITIONS

Process Mining: Extract hidden knowledge from SOA event logs.

Sequential Pattern Mining: The general problem of extracting specific sequential patterns from datasets.

SOA Event Log: Log file recording messages sent and received between SOA components (i.e., services).

SOA: Service-Oriented Architecture.

Workflow Mining: Discover structured patterns of service interactions from SOA event logs.

Chapter 8
From SOA to Pervasive Service Ecosystems:
An Approach Based on Semantic Web Technologies

Mirko Viroli
Università di Bologna, Italy

Graeme Stevenson
University of St Andrews, UK

Franco Zambonelli
Università di Modena e Reggio Emilia, Italy

Simon Dobson
University of St Andrews, UK

ABSTRACT

Emerging pervasive computing scenarios require open service frameworks promoting situated adaptive behaviors and supporting diversity in services and long-term ability to evolve. The authors argue that this calls for a nature-inspired approach in which pervasive services are modeled and deployed as autonomous individuals in an ecosystem of other services, data sources, and pervasive devices. They discuss how standard service-oriented architectures have to evolve to tackle the above issues, present a general architecture based on a shared spatial substrate mediating interactions of all the individual services of the pervasive computing system, and finally show that this architecture can be implemented relying primarily on standard W3C Semantic Web technologies, like RDF and SPARQL. A use case of adaptive pervasive displays for crowd steering applications is exploited as reference example.

INTRODUCTION

The ICT landscape, notably changed by the advent of ubiquitous wireless connectivity, is further reshaping due to the increasing deployment of pervasive computing technologies. Via RFID

tags and similar technologies, objects will carry a wide range of digital, self-describing information. Wireless sensor networks and camera networks will spread across our cities and buildings to monitor physical phenomena. Smartphones and other personal devices will increasingly sense and store

DOI: 10.4018/978-1-4666-2089-6.ch008

notable amounts of data related to our personal, social and professional activities, beyond feeding (and being fed by) the Web with spatial and social real-time information (Campbell et al., 2008).

This evolution is contributing to building integrated and dense infrastructures for the pervasive provisioning of general-purpose digital services. If all their components are able to opportunistically connect with each other, such infrastructures can be used to enrich existing services with the capability of autonomously adapting their behavior to the physical and social context in which they are invoked, and will also support innovative services for enhanced interactions with the surrounding physical and social worlds (Coleman, 2009).

Users will play an active role by contributing data and services and by making available their own sensing and actuating devices. This will make pervasive computing infrastructures as participatory and as capable of value co-creation as the Web (Spohrer et al., 2007), eventually acting as globally shared substrates to externalize, enhance, and make more valuable our physical and social intelligence.

We already face the commercial release of a variety of early pervasive services trying to exploit the possibilities opened by these new scenarios: GPS navigation systems providing real-time traffic information and updating routes accordingly, cooperative smartphones that inform us about the current positions of our friends, and augmented reality services that enrich what we see around with dynamically retrieved digital information (Ferscha and Vogl, 2010). However, the road towards the effective and systematic exploitation of these emerging scenarios calls for a radical rethinking of current service models and frameworks.

Elaborating on this problem, this chapter is organized as follows:

- In Section 2 we provide a background: starting from a case study of adaptive pervasive displays, we discuss the basic requirements of emergent pervasive com-

puting applications, namely situatedness, adaptation, and support for diversity and long-term evolution.

- In Sections 3-5 we present the main focus of the chapter: we propose how current SOA solutions are to be evolved to tackle those requirements, namely, by a deep rethinking inspired by nature and its mechanisms, promoting the idea of a "pervasive and shared spatial continuum" over which local individual interactions occur; and we present an innovative architecture for pervasive service ecosystems rooted in the concepts of "Live Semantic Annotations" (LSAs, representing interfaces of environment services) and "eco-laws" (global coordination rules enabling and regulating interactions). In Section 4 an implementation of the framework based on standard W3C technologies for the Semantic Web is discussed, namely, relying on RDF for supporting LSAs, and SPARQL for eco-laws; Section 5 presents a concrete example in the form of a crowd steering example.

- In Section 6 we discuss related works.

- Finally, in Section 7, we conclude by describing the future directions of the presented research.

BACKGROUND

As background for this chapter, we present the pervasive computing scenarios we intend to target, so as to emphasize the requirements they pose. We do this by means of a simple case study – representative of a larger class of emerging pervasive scenarios – which will be used to ground our arguments, sketch the requirements of future pervasive services, and ultimately discuss the proposed service framework.

It is a matter of fact that we are increasingly surrounded by digital displays: from those of wearable devices to wide wall-mounted displays pervading urban and working environments. Currently, the former interact with the environment and are affected by its contingencies in limited manners, while the latter are simply conceived as static information servers to show information in a manually-configured manner – e.g., cycling some pre-defined commercials or general interest news – independently of both the context in which they operate and of nearby users. However, such overall display infrastructures can be made more effective and advantageous for both users and information/service providers by becoming general, open, and adaptable information service infrastructures.

First, information should be displayed based on the current state of the surrounding physical and social environment. For instance, by exploiting information from sensors and from profiles of nearby users, a display sited within a museum could select an exhibition to advertise based on overlapping user interests. Also, actions could be coordinated among neighboring displays to enact different policies, e.g., to avoid irritating users with the same ads as they pass by, to combine adjacent displays for the purpose of presenting complex, multifaceted information, or to coordinate displays to steer people towards an exhibition. These examples express a general requirement for pervasive services:

- **Situatedness:** Pervasive services deal with spatially- and socially-situated activities of users, and should thus be able to interact with the surrounding physical and social world and adapt their behavior accordingly. The infrastructure itself, deeply embedded in the physical space, should effectively deal with spatial concepts and data.

Second, and complementary to the above, the display infrastructure and the services within should automatically adapt to their own modifications and contingencies in an automatic way without malfunctioning, and possibly take advantage of such modifications. Namely, when new devices are deployed, new information is injected, or new people arrive, a spontaneous re-distribution and re-shaping of the overall displayed information should take place. For instance: the route towards an exhibition could be automatically computed by self-organization so as to dynamically avoid overcrowded rooms or corridors, or alternative exhibitions could be selected if one has reached (or will shortly reach) capacity. In terms of a general requirement for decentralized and dynamic scenarios:

- **Adaptivity:** Pervasive services and infrastructures should inherently exhibit properties of autonomous adaptation and management, to survive contingencies without human intervention and at limited costs.

Third, the display infrastructure should enable users – other than display owners – to upload information and services to enrich the offerings available, or adapt the infrastructure to their own needs. For instance, users may continuously upload personal content (e.g., pictures and annotations related to the local environment) from their own devices to the infrastructure, both for better visualization and for increasing the overall local information offer. Similarly, a group of friends can exploit a public display by uploading software letting the display host a shared real-time map, visualizing what's happening nearby (which would also require opportunistic access to the existing environmental sensors and to any available user-provided sensors, to make the map alive and rich in real-time information). In general, one should enable users to act as "prosumers" – i.e., as both consumers and producers – of devices, data, and services. This will not only make environments meet the specific needs of any user (and capture the long tail of the market), but will also induce a process of value co-creation increasing the overall intrinsic value of the system and of its services (Vargo et al., 2008). If the mentioned real-time map accesses some sensors in unconventional ways to better detect situations around, this adds value both to such sensors and to all existing and future services requiring situation recognition. In terms of a general requirement:

- **Prosumption and Diversity:** The infrastructure should tolerate open models of service production and usage without limiting the number and classes of services provided, and rather taking advantage of the injection of new services by exploiting them to improve and integrate existing services whenever possible, and add further value to them.

Finally, besides short-term adaptation, in the longer-term any pervasive infrastructure will experience dramatic changes related to the technology being adopted, as well as in the kinds of services being deployed and in their patterns of usage. For instance, a display infrastructure will at some time integrate more sophisticated sensing means than we have today and will possibly integrate enriched actuators via which to attract user attention and interact with them. This can be the case of personal projection systems to make any physical object become a display, or of eyeglass displays for immersive perception and action. While this can open up the way for brand new classes and generations of services to be conceived and deployed, it also requires that such evolution can be gradually accommodated without harming the existing infrastructure and services. As a general requirement:

- **Eternity:** The infrastructure should tolerate long-term evolutions of structure, components, and usage patterns, to accommodate the changing needs of users and technological evolution without forcing significant and expensive re-engineering efforts to incorporate innovations and changes.

PERVASIVE SERVICE ECOSYSTEMS

From SOA to Nature-Inspired Pervasive Service Ecosystems

Can the above requirements be met by architecting pervasive service environments around standard service-oriented architectures (SOA)? To some extents, yes, but the final result would be a sort of scramble of current SOA methodology. Indeed, we believe the above requirements call for re-thinking some assumptions of SOA architecture, and evolving them with ideas and mechanisms proposed in the field of self-organizing computer systems, namely, relying on a nature-inspired approach as developed in the following.

Centralized SOA Solution

In general, SOA consider the inter-related activities of service components to be managed by various infrastructural (middleware) services such as: discovery services to help components find each other; context services to help components situate their activities; orchestration services to coordinate interactions according to specific application logics; and shared data-space services to support data-mediated interactions (Wells et al., 2008). To architect a pervasive display environment in such terms (Figure 1- top), one has to set up a middleware server in which to host all the necessary infrastructural services to support the various components of the scenario, i.e., displays, information and advertising services, user-provided services, sensing devices and personal devices.

Such components become aware of each other via the discovery service. However, in dynamic scenarios (users and devices coming and going), components are forced to continuously access (or be notified by) the discovery service to preserve up-to-date information—a computational and communication wasting activity. Also, since discovery and interactions among components have to rely on spatial information (i.e., a

Figure 1. Architecting pervasive service environments: Top) a solution with a centralized middleware server; Bottom) a solution relying on a distributed set of local middleware services

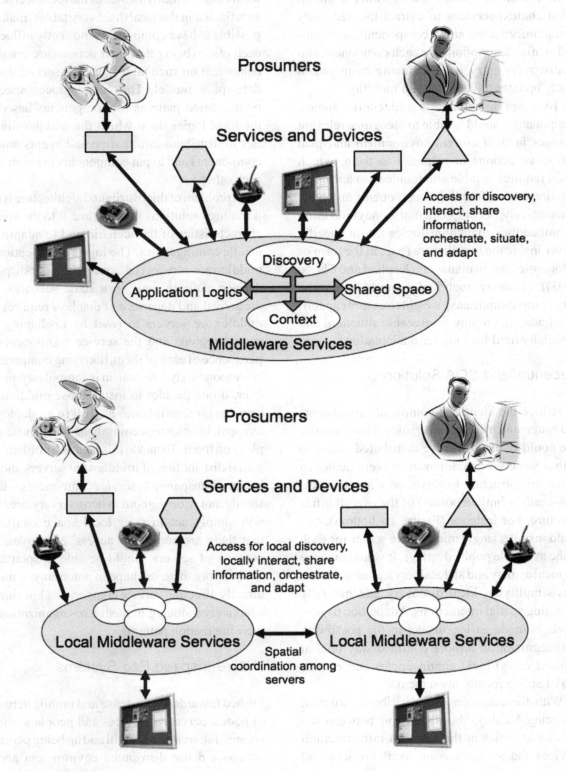

display is interested only in the users and sensors in its proximity), this requires either sophisticated context-services to extract the necessary spatial information about components, or to embed spatial descriptions for each component into its discovery entry, again inducing frequent and costly updates to keep up with mobility.

To adapt to situations and contingencies, components should be able to recognize relevant changes in their current environment and plan corrective actions in response to them, which again requires notable communication and computational costs for all the components involved. Alternatively, or complementary, one could think of embedding adaptation logics into a specific server inside the middleware (e.g., in the form of autonomic control managers (Kephart and Chess, 2003)). However, such logics would have to be very complex and heavyweight to ensure capability of adapting to any foreseeable situation, and especially hard for long-term adaptation.

Decentralized SOA Solution

To reduce the identified complexities and costs and better match the characteristics of the scenario, one could think of a more distributed solution, with a variety of middleware servers deployed in the infrastructure to serve, on a strictly local basis, only a limited portion of the overall infrastructure. For instance (Figure 1 - bottom), one could install a single middleware server for each of the available public displays. It would manage the local display and all local service components, thus simplifying local discovery and naturally enforcing spatial interactions. Adaptation to situations is made easier, thanks to the possibility of recognizing in a more confined way (and at reduced costs) local contingencies and events, and of acting locally upon them.

With the adoption of a distributed solution enforcing locality, the distinction between the logics and duties of the different infrastructural services fades: discovering local services and

devices implies discovering something about the local context; the dynamics of the local scenarios, as reflected in the local discovery tables, makes it possible to have components indirectly influence each other (being that their actions are possibly dependent on such tables), as in a sort of shared data-space model. This also induces specific orchestration patterns for components based on the local logics upon which the middleware relies to distribute information and events among components and to put components in touch with each other.

A problem of this distributed architecture is that it requires solutions both to tune it to the spatial characteristics of the scenario and to adaptively handle contingencies. The logics of allocation of middleware servers (i.e., one server per display) derives naturally only in a static scenario, but the arrival and departure of displays requires the middleware servers to react by re-shaping the spatial regions and the service components of pertinence of each of them, notifying components correspondingly. Dynamism is compulsory, moreover, if one decides to install those middleware services on smartphones as well (e.g., deployed as apps), in order to seemingly handle private displays on them. To tackle this general problem, the actual distribution of middleware servers should become transparent to service components—they should not worry about where servers are, but will simply act in their local space confident that there are servers to access. Moreover, the network of servers should be able to spontaneously re-organize its shape in autonomy, without directly affecting service components but simply adaptively inducing in them a re-organization of their interaction patterns.

Nature-Inspired Eco-Systems

Pushed towards a very dense and mobile network of nodes, pervasive devices and people's smartphones, the architecture will end up being perceivable as a dense distributed environment above which a very dynamic set of spatially-situated components discover, interact, and coordinate with each other. This is done in terms of much simplified logics, embedded into the unique (though highly distributed) infrastructural service, subsuming the roles of discovery, context, data-space, and orchestration services, and taking the form of a limited set of local rules embedded in the spatial substrate itself—deployed in each computational node. That is, we would end up with something that notably resembles the architecture of natural ecosystems: a set of spatially situated entities interacting according to a well-defined set of natural laws enforced by the spatial environment in which they situate, and adaptively self-organizing their interaction dynamics according to its the shape and structure.

Going further than architectural similarity, the natural metaphor can be adopted as the ground upon which to rely to inherently accommodate the requirements of pervasive service scenarios. Situatedness and spatiality are there by construction. Adaptation can be achieved because of the basic rules of the game: the dynamics of the ecosystem, as determined by the enactment of laws and by the shape of the environment, can spontaneously induce forms of adaptive self-organization beside the characteristics of the individual components. Accommodating new and diverse component species, even towards a long-term evolution, is obtained by making components party to the game in respect of its rules, and by letting the ecosystem dynamics evolve and re-shape in response to the appearance of such new species. This way, we can take advantage of the new interaction possibilities of such new services and of the additional value they bring, without requiring individual components or the infrastructure itself (i.e., its laws and structure) to be re-engineered (Jazayeri, 2005).

Indeed, nature-inspired solutions have already been extensively exploited in distributed computing (Babaoglu et al., 2006) for the implementation of specific adaptive algorithmic solutions or of specific adaptive services. Also, many initiatives – like those named upon digital/business service ecosystems (Ulieru and Grobbelaar, 2007) – recognize that the complexity of modern service systems is comparable to that of natural ones and requires innovative solutions also to effectively support diversity and value co-creation. Yet, the idea that natural metaphors can become the foundation on which to fully re-think the architecture of service systems is far from being metabolized.

A Reference Conceptual Architecture

The above discussion leads to the identification of a reference conceptual architecture for nature-inspired pervasive service ecosystems (see Figure 2).

The lowest level is the concrete physical and digital ground on which the ecosystem will be deployed, i.e., a dense infrastructure (ideally a continuum) of networked computing devices and information sources. At the top level, prosumers access the open service framework for using/consuming data or services, as well as for producing and deploying in the framework new services and new data components or for making new devices available. In our case study, they include the users passing by, the display owners, information providers, and the advertising companies interested in buying commercial slots. At both levels openness and its dynamics arise: new devices can join/leave the system at any time, and new users can interact with the framework and can deploy new services and data items on it. In our case study, we consider integration at any time of new displays and new sensors, and the presence of a continuous flow of new visualization services (e.g., commercial advertisers) and users, possibly having their own devices integrated in the overall infrastructure.

In between these two levels, lie the abstract computational components of the pervasive ecosystem architecture.

Figure 2. A conceptual architecture for pervasive service ecosystems

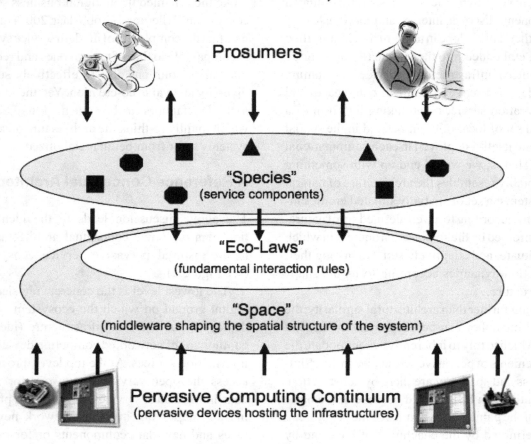

- **Species**: This level includes a variety of components, belonging to different "species" yet modeled and computationally rendered in a uniform way, representing the *individuals* (i.e., software agents) populating the ecosystem: physical and virtual devices of the pervasive infrastructure, digital and network resources of any kind, providers of persistent/temporary knowledge/data and contextual information, software services, or personal user agents. In our case study, we will have different software species to represent displays and their displaying service, the various kinds of sensors distributed around the environment and the data they express, software agents to act on behalf of users, display owners, and advertisers.

In general terms, an ecosystem is expected to be populated with a set of software agents physically deployed in the environment, situated in some portion of the ecosystem space, and dynamically joining/leaving it. The very occurrence of such agents is reified in our architecture in terms of so-called Live Semantic Annotations (LSAs), which play the role of ecosystem individuals. An LSA is a structured, semantically founded, and continuously updated annotation reflecting some relevant information for the coordination of an ecosystem, concerning events/ state/interface/goal of software agents—thus conceptually extending/embedding know concepts of service interface and behavior (as e.g., in WSDL and BPEL technologies). So, any entity, state, situation or event concerning an agent is manifested by it in the form of one or more LSAs.

- **Space:** This level gives shape to the spatial fabric supporting LSAs, namely, the spatial activities and interactions of agents. Given the spatial nature of pervasive services (as it is the case of information and advertising services in our case study), this level situates individuals in a specific portion of the space, so that their activities and interactions are directly dependent on their positions and on the shape of the surrounding space.

  Practically, the spatial structure of the ecosystem will be reified by a middleware substrate, deployed on top of the physical deployment context, supporting the execution and life cycle of individuals and their spatial interactions in each computational node of the network. From the viewpoint of such individuals, the middleware will have to provide them (via some API) with the possibility of advertising themselves by LSAs, accessing information about their local spatial context (including other nearby individuals) and detecting local events via a mechanism of LSA *bonding*—an LSA can bond to others, and an agent can access information expressed within those LSAs it is connected to by bonds. From the viewpoint of the underlying infrastructure, the middleware should provide for transparently absorbing dynamic changes and the arrival/departure of supporting devices, without affecting the perception of the spatial environment by individuals.

  Technologically, this can be realized by a network of active data-oriented and event-oriented localized services, spread across the nodes of the pervasive substrate, and accessible on a location-dependent basis by

individuals and devices. In the case study, for instance, one could think of assigning one such middleware service to each display and each smartphone, and have the various displays dynamically self-configure their spatial domain of competence accordingly to geographic and "line of sight" factors.

- **Eco-Laws:** The way in which individuals (whether service components, devices, or generic resources) live and interact is determined by the set of fundamental "eco-laws" regulating the ecosystem model. Enactment of eco-laws on individuals will typically affect and be affected by the local space and by the local individuals around. In our case study, eco-laws might provide for automatically and dynamically determining to display specific information on a screen as a sort of automatic reaction to specific environmental conditions, or support having two displays spontaneously aggregate and synchronize with each other in showing specific advertisements.

  An eco-law works as a sort of chemical law: it takes a set of reactant LSAs existing in the LSA-space, and substitutes it with a set of product LSAs—which could be placed either locally or in the neighborhood. Alternatively, an eco-law is a pattern of atomic transformations of groups of LSAs residing in the same locality, with an implicit/explicit scheduling policy and scope depending on the specific operational model. Such transformations can lead to: creation of new LSAs (e.g., representing composed services), deletion of existing LSAs (e.g., disposing of services no longer used), semantic manipulation of LSAs (e.g., changing a service state depending on extraction of some contextual information), creation/deletion of bonds (e.g., to connect two LSAs to make their agents interact), relocating/diffusing LSAs (e.g., to make the existence of a service be perceived in a region of space).

The proposed architecture represents a radically new perspective on modeling service systems and their infrastructures. An un-layered universe of components, all of which underlie the same model, living and interacting in the same spatial substrate, and obeying the same eco-laws—the latter being the only concept hardwired into the system, subsumes the typically multifaceted layers of SOA.

This rethinking is very important to ensure adaptation, diversity, and long-term evolution: no component, service or device is there to stay, everything can change and evolve, self-adapting over space and time, without undermining the overall structure and assumptions of the ecosystem. That is, by conceiving the middleware in terms of a simple spatial substrate in charge of enforcing only basic interaction rules, we have moved away from the infrastructure itself needing to adapt, and fully translated this as a property of the application level and of its dynamics.

Interactions between components, then, are based solely on the existence of a bond (or bonds) between their LSAs. Once established, all interaction is indirect, namely, by observing changes made to the structure and content of each partner's LSA. This embedding of core interaction principles within the environment represents a shift away from traditional coordination models, where interactions are externally shaped and executed.

The dynamics of the ecosystem will be determined by individuals acting based on their own goals/attitudes, yet being subject to the eco-laws for their interactions with others. Typical patterns that can be driven by such laws may include forms of adaptive self-organization (e.g., spontaneous service aggregation or service orchestration, where eco-laws play an active role in facilitating individuals to spontaneously interact and orchestrate with each other, also in dependence of current conditions), adaptive evolution (changing conditions reflected in changes in the way individuals in a locality are affected by the eco-laws) and of

decentralized control (to affect the ecosystem behavior by injecting new components into it).

In a sense, the pointwise character of services in standard SOA is replaced in our framework by a notion of service as the effect, triggered by some agents, of the overall ecosystem activity (including, e.g., the bonding together of some LSAs, the triggering of eco-laws that act on existing LSAs, the effect of other agents that are consequently activated, and so on).

A CONCRETE IMPLEMENTATION

Having introduced the proposed abstract architecture, we now analyze how it can be supported by existing concrete technologies. In particular, we will show that some technologies in the area of the Semantic Web community solidly match our problem domain. Here we first briefly overview our chosen technologies and their role in supporting the proposed architecture, and discuss perceived advantages over other candidate technologies, describe details of implementation of LSAs into RDF, show that the reasoning capabilities inherent to RDF provide one approach to realize the concept of semantic matching, and describe details of how eco-laws can be expressed into SPARQL.

The Resource Description Framework

The Resource Description Framework (RDF) (Miller and Manola, 2004) provides a formalization of a directed graph (with nodes representing resources and arcs representing properties). An RDF graph can be deconstructed to a set of *triples* $\langle s, p, o \rangle$, each asserting a relation, p, that holds between a subject, s and object, o. Subjects and relations in an RDF model are always resources (namely URIs[1], *namespace: string*) while objects may take the form of a resource or a literal value (a quoted string, possibly qualified by associated type information, e.g., using XML Schema datatypes).

RDF semantics are prescribed by two additional vocabularies, RDF Schema (RDFS) (Guha and Brickley, 2004) and the Web Ontology Language (OWL) (Krötzsch et al., 2009). RDFS provides a basic vocabulary for dividing RDF resources into classes, restricting the classes of resource a property may legally relate, and introduces *subClass* and *subProperty* properties to capture relations between classes and properties at different levels of abstraction. OWL provides a more expressive ontology language by, for example, supporting the expression of functional, transitive, symmetric, and inverse properties. Equivalent properties and classes may be declared, and cardinality restrictions allow constraints to be placed on the legal structure of class members. Off-the-shelf reasoners, e.g., Pellet (Sirin et al., 2007), can check the consistency of RDF models that use published vocabularies even if only partial data or partial ontology is available; this is desirable for a distributed scenario.

RDF is, in essence, a relational model for knowledge representation, which we use to model LSAs. We justify its selection over competing technologies by its two main advantages: domain-neutrality and natural support for data-distribution. RDF's domain-neutrality affords concurrent support for multiple applications across multiple domains, while its distributed data model supports seamlessly merging data from heterogeneous, distributed sources. Both benefits are a direct consequence of RDF's use of URIs to identify resources (i.e., giving triples unambiguous global

semantics). This can be contrasted with, say, traditional database schemata, whose terms and relations have no prescribed semantics, and XML Schema, which is concerned with the structure of a data hierarchy and not with capturing the relations between data elements. In addition, neither technology is predisposed to integrating data adhering to multiple schemata.

The RDFS vocabulary sufficiently models the LSA component of our architecture. In this respect, we consider OWL an added value technology that supports the expression of semantics compatible with but not core to our approach. We explore one such extension, semantic matching.

Suitable technologies for inspecting and updating RDF stores exist in the form of SPARQL (Seaborne and Harris, 2009) and SPARQL Update (Gearon and Schenk, 2009). SPARQL supports queries consisting of triple patterns, conjunctions, negations, disjunctions, and optional patterns, while SPARQL Update supports the conditional insertion and removal of triples from an RDF store. SPARQL provides a means of describing to which LSAs an eco-law should apply, while SPARQL Update supports the expression of manipulations those LSAs are subject to—in the following, when there is no risk of ambiguity, we shall refer to the SPARQL *framework* to mean these two languages and related tools.

RDF and the SPARQL framework, then, support the representation of distributed LSAs using terms from the most appropriate vocabularies for a particular environment, scenario, or set of ap-

Table 1.

```
ex:lsa1432
  museum:type museum:person ;
  museum:location loc:room131 ;
  museum:time "2011-05-31T12:45:39"^^xsd:dateTime ;
  foaf:age "20"^^xsd:integer ;
  ex:interest "music" ;
  ex:interest "sport" ;
  ex:interest "travelling" ;
```

Table 2.

```
:ProductDescription
  rdf:type owl:Class ;
  owl:equivalentClass
  [ rdf:type owl:Class ;
    owl:intersectionOf (
      [ rdf:type owl:Restriction ; owl:onProperty :height ; owl:hasValue :1METRE]
      [ rdf:type owl:Restriction ; owl:onProperty :productType ; owl:hasValue :Desk]
      [ rdf:type owl:Restriction ; owl:onProperty :colour ; owl:onClass :Blue ;
        owl:minQualifiedCardinality "1" ]
    )
  ] .
```

plications, with the resultant data straightforwardly integrated, inspected, and updated using standard tooling. In particular, RDF stores can be used as spaces of LSAs, installed in each node of the pervasive system, maintaining the LSAs injected there in the form of groups of triples. Query engines, supporting execution of SPARQL queries and updates, and reasoners (Sirin et al., 2007) (coupled with simple network agents providing relocation of LSAs) can be used to support scheduling and execution of eco-laws locally—and in particular, to support advanced matching abilities as described in the following sections.

Serialization of LSAs

The main principle behind the idea of using RDF to represent an LSA is to construct an RDF "packet", featuring a set of triples $\langle i, p, v \rangle$ with same subject i, the LSA-id, and a pair p, v per each assignment of a property p to a distinct value v. Equivalently, an LSA is hence modeled as an identifier i followed by an unordered list of multi-valued properties—namely, a semantic tuple. One such value could be the identifier of another LSA, by which we model bonds. Accordingly, we are able to represent LSA-identifiers as possible subjects (and objects) for RDF triples, properties as predicates (and objects), and values of primitive datatypes (numbers, strings, and so on) as objects, namely, serializing LSA-ids and

Table 3.

```
:ExampleDesk
  rdf:type :ProductDescription ;
  :height :100CM ;
  :productType :Desk ;
  :colour :MidnightBlue .
```

properties as URIs, and by mapping primitive data types to appropriate literal values (using XML Schema datatypes where appropriate). To illustrate, the RDF snippet (see Table 1, represented in Notation3 syntax (Berners-Lee and Connolly, 2011)) corresponding to the LSA of a user wandering the museum could be:

Semantic Matching

In addition to RDF's benefits as a data representation and exchange technology, the accompanying semantics provided by RDFS and OWL support vocabularies that define classes of resources, semantically-rich relations, and sets of restrictions on how both may legally be combined.

Application of these vocabularies to an RDF model may be verified for correctness by off-the-shelf reasoners, for example Pellet (Sirin et al., 2007), and inferences – such as the classification of resources – may be drawn. Indeed, standard OWL classification provides one approach to realizing semantic matching in the eco-law language. When two LSAs have to be matched, one can used relation <?A rdf:type ?B> using OWL semantics, which seeks for two LSAs – with id ?A and ?B – such that description of ?A satisfies the set of restrictions that describe ?B, an OWL Class description.

To illustrate, we discuss an example of a user in a shopping mall, interested in blue desks, 1 meter in height. In N3 notation, this description is constructed as shown in Table 2.

Consider also part of an LSA describing a desk's features of the kind (see Table 3) that differs in color and in its expression of height from the request. Assuming the vocabularies that define these terms also encode the knowledge that ex:MidnightBlue is of type ex:Blue, and that the term ex:1METRE is equivalent to ex:100CM, a reasoner can infer that the desk satisfies the description of Bob's interest.

This generalizes to other relations that a reasoner may dynamically compute. For example, the body of work relating to the semantic matching of web services defines many categories of match, including: *exact, plug-in, subsumes, intersection,* and *syntactic* (Bandara et al., 2008). Substituting rdf:type with terms from a vocabulary that describes these concepts, and introducing functions to compute such relations, supports their seamless integration into eco-laws.

The Eco-Law Language and its SPARQL Serialization

Eco-laws can be structured as chemical-resembling rules working on patterns of LSAs: they work by consuming a set of *reactant* LSAs based on left-hand side patterns and produce a set of *product* LSAs based on right-hand side patterns. They also obey a numeric transformation rate r written in the reaction arrow and representing a Markovian rate in a continuous-time Markov chain (CTMC) system. When not specified, this defaults to ∞, meaning the reaction is immediate.

The rate influences the scheduling policies—an eco-law with rate r is scheduled after an elapsed time following negative exponential distribution of probability with average time r time units.

A pattern is used to match an annotation, and is formed by a variable ?x that will hold the id of the annotation, and a sequence of filters used to control which annotations match—a pattern with an empty sequence of filters ?x:[ ] is shortened to ?x.

Filter clones ?x.D(/extends ?x.D) matches LSAs whose description exactly has(/includes) the property-value assignments of x—subsequent filters are then applied. Other filters constrain the values associated to a property in a point-wise manner: they take a term property on the left and a term property on the right. Case p = (v1,..,vn) matches those annotations in which property p is assigned *precisely* to values v1,..,vn, case p has (v1,..,vn) when p is assigned *at least* to values v1,..,vn, and p has-not (v1,..,vn) when p is assigned to *no* values in v1,..,vn. Variables identify properties on the left of an operator or lists of values/variables on the right. Besides the unconstrained variable ?x, which can match any value, we also allow syntax ?{x:f}, which can match any value v such that substituting ?x with v in formula f gives a Boolean expression evaluating to true. Formulas are generated out of terms (values and variables) using application-dependent or standard mathematical unary and binary operators.

Once LSAs are turned into RDF, it is natural to try to consider existing languages to query and manipulate RDF stores, like SPARQL, as possible target for the eco-law language. In particular, the premise of our translation is to convert an eco-law into two fragments: *(i)* a SPARQL query (or simply a *query*) playing the role of the eco-law reactant patterns, namely, checking for the existence of reactant LSAs (finding instantiations for all the variables in the left-hand side); *(ii)* a sequence of SPARQL Update statements (or simply *statements*), obtained by instantiating all variables bound in the previous SPARQL query,

Figure 3. Example translations: (top) [YOUNGEST] eco-law – of two fields with the same source, it retains ID of the older and content of the younger; (bottom) [BOND-PV] eco-law – bond based on a property-value combination on target

———— Eco-law [YOUNGEST] ————

```
?FIELD:[pump:source=(?L); pump:pump_time=(?T)]  +
?FIELD2:[clones ?FIELD.D; pump:pump_time=(?{T2: ?T2 > ?T}); pump:diff_time=(?DT)]
--->
?FIELD:[clones ?FIELD2.D]
```

———— Translation of [YOUNGEST] ————

```
1   SELECT DISTINCT * WHERE{
2     ?FIELD pump:source ?L .
3     FILTER NOT EXISTS {?FIELD pump:source ?o . FILTER (?o!=?L)}
4     ?FIELD pump:pump_time ?T .
5     FILTER NOT EXISTS {?FIELD pump:pump_time ?o .
6                       FILTER (?o!=?T)}
7     ?FIELD2 pump:pump_time ?T2 . FILTER (?T2 > ?T).
8     FILTER NOT EXISTS {?FIELD2 pump:pump_time ?o .
9                       FILTER (?o!=?T2)}
10    ?FIELD2 pump:diff_time ?DT .
11    FILTER NOT EXISTS {?FIELD2 pump:diff_time ?o .
12                      FILTER (?o!=?DT)}
13    FILTER NOT EXISTS {?FIELD2 ?p ?o .
14        FILTER(?p!=pump:pump_time) FILTER(?p!=pump:diff_time)
15        FILTER NOT EXISTS{?FIELD ?p ?o}}
16    FILTER NOT EXISTS {?FIELD ?p ?o .
17        FILTER(?p!=pump:pump_time) FILTER(?p!=pump:diff_time)
18        FILTER NOT EXISTS{?FIELD2 ?p ?o}}
19  }
20  REMOVE {!FIELD2 ?p ?o} WHERE {!FIELD2 ?p ?o}
21  INSERT {!FIELD2 ?p ?o} WHERE {!FIELD ?p ?o}
```

———— Eco-law [BOND-PV] ————

```
?TARGET:[?PROP has ?VALUES]  +
?SRC:[bond:request has (?BOND-REQ); ?B has-not (?TARGET)]   +
?BOND-REQ:[sapere:type has (bond:request_pv); bond:bond_prop=(?B);
           bond:target_prop=(?PROP); bond:target_value=?VALUES]
--->
?SRC:[?B has (?TARGET)]  +  ?BOND-REQ  +  ?TARGET
```

———— Translation of [BOND-PV] ————

```
1   SELECT DISTINCT * WHERE{
2     ?SRC bond:request ?BOND-REQ .
3     FILTER NOT EXISTS {?SRC ?B ?TARGET}
4     FILTER NOT EXISTS {?TARGET ?PROP ?o .
5         FILTER NOT EXISTS {?BOND-REQ bond:target_value ?o}}
6     ?BOND-REQ sapere:type bond:request_pv .
7     ?BOND-REQ bond:bond_prop ?B .
8     FILTER NOT EXISTS { ?BOND-REQ bond:bond_prop ?o.
9                       FILTER (?o!=?B) }
10    ?BOND-REQ bond:target_prop ?PROP .
11    FILTER NOT EXISTS { ?BOND-REQ bond:target_prop ?o.
12                      FILTER (?o!=?PROP) }
13  }
14  INSERT DATA {!SRC !B !TARGET .}
```

whose final effect is to update LSAs as prescribed by the eco-law.

Technically, we concretize eco-law variables as query variables of the form ?x, and write formulas f in the language of SPARQL FILTER and/or BIND constructs. We also introduce special notation (i.e., a parameter) !x in statements which is not part of SPARQL Update: the idea is that – before the statement is executed – !x is substituted with the value bound to former query variable ?x. Figure 3 provides two example translations, each composed of a query and a sequence of statements, for two eco-laws [YOUNGEST] and [BOND-PV]. Eco-law [YOUNGEST] is used to aggregate two LSAs, with id ?FIELD and ?FIELD2. The former is a cloned copy of an LSA source ?L, created at time ?T and then diffused in the network, the latter is a clone of the former, created at greater time ?T2 and later diffused at a different time ?DT: as a result, we only take ?FIELD (namely, ?FIELD2 is removed) though its content is cloned from that of ?FIELD2—namely, the resulting LSA retains the LSA-id of the older and content of the younger (such that new information overwrites old). Eco-law [BOND-PV] is used to create a bond from a source that specifies a property/value assignment that the target must include. It takes a ?SOURCE that is not already bound to a ?TARGET by property ?B, and that specifies via bond request an LSA of type request_pv describing that a bond has to be created using ?B towards an LSA with property ?PROP featuring values ?VALUES. The only result of applying this eco-law is that – after/ if one such LSA ?TARGET is found – ?SOURCE is bonded to ?TARGET by property ?B.

An eco-law is first translated into a single initial SELECT query, where each operation filter that occurs in the reactant pattern is turned into a WHERE clause that checks the necessary conditions. For instance, in [BOND-PV], line 2 handles "bond:request has (?BOND-REQ)" (triple ?SRC bond:request ?BOND-REQ should occur in the RDF store), line 3 handles "?B has-not (?TAR-GET)" (the triple should not exist), lines 4,5 handle "?PROP has ?VALUES" (there should be no value o assigned to bond:target_value in ?BOND-REQ that is not assigned to ?PROP in ?TARGET), line 6 handles "sapere:type has bond:request_pv" (similar to line 2), lines 7, 8, 9 handle "bond:bond_prop=(?B)" (the triple should exist but no other value should occur for the same property), and similarly lines 10, 11, 12—filter "bond:target_value=?VALUE" is already dealt with in lines 4, 5. Only one INSERT statement is needed, to add one RDF triple to the store.

The case of [YOUNGEST] is similar, but exposes tricky aspects related to the clones construct and filters. Line 7 shows that annotated variables generate additional filters, lines 13 – 18 handle cloning in the left-hand side (except for properties pump:pump_time and pump:diff_time, which are mentioned in filters, any triple with subject ?FIELD should exist in ?FIELD2 and vice-versa). Regarding update statements, triples where ?FIELD2 is the subject are first cleared and then reconstructed using those involving ?FIELD.

The full translation of eco-laws language into the SPARQL and SPARQL UPDATE dialects is not reported here for brevity.

ADAPTIVE DISPLAYS FOR CROWD STEERING APPLICATION

We consider a crowd steering scenario as a case study to exemplify the approach and show how it tackles some of the requirements discussed, namely, situatedness and adaptation. In this example we guide people towards events of interest in a complex, dynamic environment (semantically matching people's interests), avoiding obstacles such as crowded regions, and without any supervised approach, namely, in a self-organizing way. In particular, we consider a museum with a set of rooms connected by corridors, whose floor is covered with a network of computational devices (called sensor nodes). These devices exchange information based on proximity, sense the pres-

Figure 4. Eco-laws for universal generation of gradient data structures

```
──────────────────── Universal Eco-laws ────────────────────
[BOND-EXT]: Bond based on the target extending a whole description
?TARGET:[extends ?CONTENT.D]  +
?SRC:[bond:request has (?BOND-REQ)]   +
?BOND-REQ:[sapere:type has (bond:request_ext); bond:bond_prop=(?B); bond:content=(?CONTENT)]
--->
?SRC:[?B has (?TARGET)]  +  ?BOND-REQ  +  ?TARGET


[PUMP]: Creates a field from an LSA
?LSA:[pump:req_field_with_range=(?RNG); sapere:location=(?L); pump:pump_rate=(?RATE)]  +
?TIME:[sapere:type has (sapere:time); sapere:time=(?T)]
--?RATE-->
?LSA  +  ?TIME  +
?SRC:[extends ?LSA.D; pump:range=(?RNG); pump:pump_time=(?T); pump:distance=("0");
      sapere:type has (pump:field, pump:source); pump:req_field_with_range has-not (?RNG);
      pump:source=(?LSA); pump:source_loc=(?L); pump:prev_ann=(?LSA); pump:prev_loc=(?L)]


[DIFF]: A field diffuses a cloned version in a neighbouring space
?FIELD:[sapere:type has (pump:field); pump:distance=(?D); pump:slope=(pump:distance);
        sapere:location=(?L); pump:range=(?R); pump:diff_rate=(?RATE); pump:follow=()] +
?NEIGH:[sapere:type has (sapere:neighbour); sapere:neighbour_location=(?L1),
        pump:distance=(?{D1: ?D1<?R-?D})]
?TIME: [sapere:type has (sapere:time); sapere:time=(?T)]
--?RATE-->
?FIELD + ?NEIGH + ?TIME +
?CLONE:[clones ?FIELD.D; pump:distance=(?{D2: D2 is ?D+?D1}), pump:prev_ann=(?FIELD);
        pump:prev_loc=(?L); sapere:location=(?L1); pump:diff_time=(?T);
        sapere:type has-not (pump:source,pump:field); sapere:type has (pump:prefield)]


[PRE]: A pre-field becomes a field if it contextualisation property  is set
?PREF:[sapere:type has (pump:pre-field); pump:contextualising=()]
--->
?PREF:[sapere:type has-not (pump:pre-field); sapere:type has (pump:field)]


[NEWEST]: Of two fields, we keep the one with newest information
?FIELD:[sapere:type has (pump:field); pump:source=(?L); pump:pump_time=(?PT)]   +
?FIELD2:[sapere:type has (pump:field); pump:source=(?L);
         pump:pump_time=(?{PT2: ?PT2 < ?PT})]
--->
?FIELD


[SHORTEST]: Of two fields pumped at same time, keep one with shorter distance
?FIELD:[sapere:type has (pump:field); pump:source=(?L); pump:pump_time=(?PT);
        pump:distance=(?D)]  +
?FIELD2:[sapere:type has (pump:field); pump:source=(?L); pump:pump_time=(?PT);
         pump:distance=(?{D2: ?D2 > ?D})]
--->
?FIELD
```

ence of visitors, and hold information of various kinds of LSAs (e.g., about exhibits currently active in the museum). Visitors are equipped with a smartphone device that holds their preferences.

By interacting with sensor nodes, visitors can be guided towards rooms with targets matching their interests, via signs dynamically appearing on the smartphone.

General Eco-Laws

The only means by which an agent can get contextualised, such that it can gather information and decide how to act, is by the bonding mechanism—which allows an agent to read an LSA it did not inject itself. The agent typically cannot create those bonds, because it simply does not know which other LSAs are around – at least, initially – and which are pertinent. The typical situation is instead that some eco-law combines an agent's LSA with related ones forming its context, and accordingly creates a bond. Either such eco-laws act in an application-specific way based on the structure of the two LSAs, or some general mechanism has to be devised to let the agent manifest the intention of being bonded with LSAs having certain characteristics. One possible approach to bonding is shown by eco-law [BOND-EXT] presented in Figure 4, which combines a *source* LSA – exposing the description of a *target* – with the target itself, creating the bond. The owning agent can destroy bonds manually when there is need of doing so.

Such an eco-law assumes that the source defines a property bond:request_ext storing a bond towards an LSAs that describes all the aspects of the bonding request, which includes a reference to the source's property that will store the bond (bond:bond_prop), and most importantly a description of which LSAs can be a good target. The latter is in the form of another LSA (whose id is ?CONTENT) which the target should extend, namely, ?CONTENT defines all the property-value associations that the target should include.

The other eco-laws in Figure 4 are used to establish so-called computational fields (Mamei and Zambonelli, 2009; Viroli et al., 2011b; Beal and Bachrach, 2006; Viroli et al., 2011a; Pianini et al., 2011), a remarkable self-organization mechanism. A computational field is a data-structure distributed in a networked system based on spatial abstractions (distances, regions, and so

on). Examples of computational fields include: *gradients*, mapping each node to the minimum distance from a source; *paths*, mapping each node belonging to the optimal path from a source and a distance to a non-zero value; *partitions*, mapping each node to the nearer in a finite set of nodes; and so on—see the Proto initiative (MIT Proto, 2010; Bachrach et al., 2010). The gradient case, for instance, is a very important one in pervasive computing systems, for it makes a possibly large set of nodes that surround a single one (the gradient source) aware of its state (or parts of it), and aware also of how it can be reached efficiently (i.e., along an optimal path)—hence supporting long-distance interactions.

By eco-law [PUMP], a gradient data structure is eventually established out of one LSA (?SOURCE) featuring non-empty properties pump:req_field_with_range (storing the gradient horizon), pump:pump_rate (the gradient pumping rate), and pump:slope (the propagation dynamics). Altogether those eco-laws diffuse some *field* LSAs around, converging to a situation in which: *(i)* each node within the pump:range_distance_from_the_ source (computed by the estimated distance between nodes or on a step-by-step basis depending on the chosen slope) will carry one LSA of type sapere:field that clones the source; *(ii)* such an LSA has an updated pump:distance property (by following decreasing values of distance any agent can retrieve an optimal path towards the source); *(iii)* the overall structure is able to self-organize (namely, self-heal) to topological changes (Beal, 2009; Mamei and Zambonelli, 2009).

Eco-law [DIFF] continuously diffuses a field LSA in neighboring locations (one at a time), at rate pump:diff_rate, with increasing distance value depending on the estimated distance to the neighbor, and providing the overall distance does not escape the gradient range. Diffusion is realized by creating LSAs whose property sapere:location stores the identifier of a neighboring node: an underlying middleware service is in charge of

Table 4.

```
museum:sourcelsa1432
    sapere:type  (museum:exhibition) ;
    sapere:location (loc:room131) ;
    sapere:time ("2011-05-31T12:45:39"^^xsd:dateTime) ;
    pump:req_field_with_range ("1000"^^xsd:integer) ;
    pump:pump_rate ("1"^^xsd:integer) ; // once per minute
    pump:slope (pump:distance) ;        // proceeding based on distance
    pump:contextualising (pump:crowd) ;
    pump:decay_time ("60"^^xsd:integer) ; // in minutes
    museum:author (museum:michelangelo) ;
    museum:kind (museum:sculpture)
```

Table 5.

```
museum:crowdlsa1123
    sapere:type (museum:crowd) ;
    sapere:location (loc:sensor1231) ;
    sapere:time ("2011-05-30T11:00:00"^^xsd:dateTime) ;
    museum:crowdlevel ("1.0"^^xsd:decimal) ;
    museum:crowdfactor ("10.0"^^xsd:decimal)
```

Table 6.

```
museum:personlsa81
    sapere:type (museum:person) ;
    sapere:location (loc:room112) ;
    sapere:time ("2011-05-31T12:21:39"^^xsd:dateTime) ;
    bond:request (museum:req1211) ;
    user:profile (user:content99)

museum:req1211
    sapere:type (bond:request_wm) ;
    bond:bond_prop (museum:exhibitions) ;
    bond:local_prop (user:profile)

user:content99
    sapere:type (museum:exhibition) ;
    sapere:type (pump:field) ;
    sapere:author (museum:renaissance_sculptor)
```

relocating LSAs according to the content of this property.

Additionally, the contextual information about available neighboring nodes is reified by the middleware in terms of LSAs with property sapere:type set to sapere:neighbour, by which relocation is ultimately specified. Note that the diffused LSA is actually of type sapere:pre-field,

Table 7.

```
[PRE-CROWD]: A pre-field becomes a field after increasing its distance due to crowd
?PREF:[sapere:type has (pump:pre-field, museum:exhibition);
       pump:contextualising=(museum:crowd); pump:distance=(?D)]  +
?CROWD:[sapere:type has (museum:crowd); museum:crowdlevel=(?L),
        museum:crowdfactor=(?F)]
--->
?PREF:[sapere:type has-not (pump:pre-field); sapere:type has (pump:field);
       pump:distance=?D2: ?D2 is ?D+?L*?F]  +
?CROWD
```

Table 8.

```
museum:personlsa81
  sapere:type (museum:person) ;
  sapere:location (loc:room112) ;
  sapere:time ("2011-05-31T12:21:39"^^xsd:dateTime) ;
  museum:chosen_exhibition (museum:sourcelsa1432) ;
  bond:request (museum:req121)

museum:req1211
  sapere:type (bond:request_ext) ;
  bond:bond_prop (museum:field_to_follow) ;
  bond:content (museum:content100)

museum:content100
  sapere:type (museum:exhibition) ;
  sapere:type (pump:field) ;
  pump:source (museum:sourcelsa1432)
```

for it might need to be manipulated before being stored into one of type sapere:field.

Eco-law [PRE] implements the default manipulation behavior (activated if pump:contextualizing is empty): it stores the diffused LSA as it is—it needs an application specific eco-law to change this behavior, as we will develop next. Note that [PUMP, DIFF] keep creating new LSAs over time in the diffusion region; to remedy the inevitable divergence, [NEWEST] keeps the more recent field information in a node, while [SHORTEST] keep information of field LSAs with smaller distance from source.

LSAs

According to the proposed framework, all information exchanged, including agent representations, is encapsulated by LSAs, such as: (*i - source* LSAs) representing items or exhibits currently active; (*ii - field* LSAs) representing diffused copies of source LSAs and carrying an updated estimated distance from the source along the best path available; (*iii - pre-field* LSAs) temporary copies of field LSAs, used as intermediates to establish the final gradient; (*iv - user* LSAs) representing presence and state of a user (stored in their smartphone); (*v - crowd* LSAs) representing the presence of a crowded area by a sensor node. In particular, we rely on

Figure 5. A simulation run of the reference exposition (top-left, top-right, bottom-left, bottom-right): from random positions people move to 4 targets such that it will bond to the desired field, from which information on the directions to take can be observed and will be updated as it moves thanks to gradient automatic self-healing

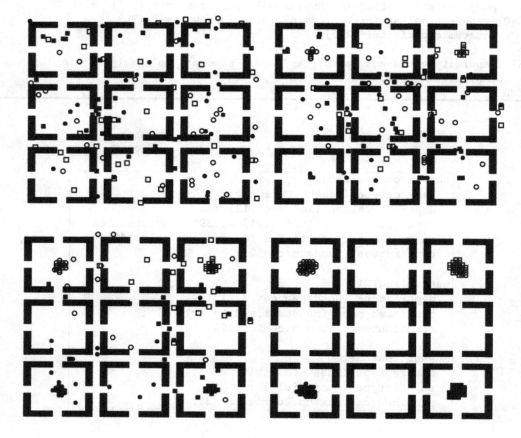

source LSAs of the kind describing an exposition of Michelangelo's sculpture (see Table 4).

A crowd LSA, generated in each sensor node takes the form where museum:crowdlevel set to 1.0 means that the sensor perceived the highest crowd, while crowd factor is a multiplication factor dictating how such a level should penalize a gradient. (see Table 5):

Finally, the LSAs of a user – seeking (field) exhibitions of any Renaissance's sculptor – is of the kind (see Table 6):

Note that this LSA will bond to field LSAs generated by museum:sourcelsa1432 above thanks to eco-law [BOND-WM]. Also, by the structure of source LSA we can expect eco-laws [PUMP,

DIFF-DST, YOUNGEST, SHORTEST, DECAY] to activate and support a stable gradient. However, a further application-dependent eco-law is needed since eco-law [PRE] is not effective here, for contextualisation is required to handle crowded areas. Table 7 shows one such eco-law, which increases the field LSA distance (i.e., a penalty) when the local crowd level is greater than 0.

When a user perceives exhibits and is bonded to field LSAs in its locality (by eco-law [BOND-EXT]), it will choose one such source to be steered to, and accordingly updates its LSA to such that it will bond to the desired field, from which information on the directions to take can be observed

Figure 6. Dark visitors occupy a central room: others move left to right by a longer, less crowded path circumventing the central room on top

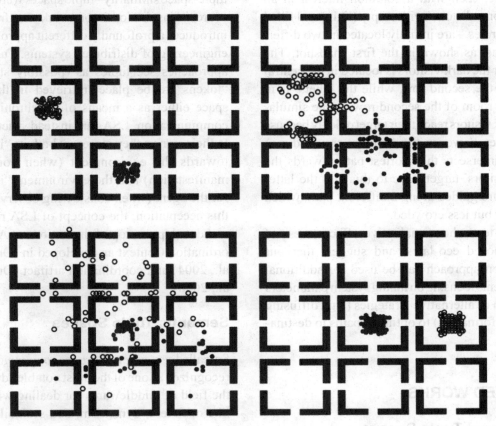

and will be updated as it moves thanks to gradient automatic self-healing (see Table 8).

Simulation

As a proof-of-concept for the proposed solution, we rely on simulations of the evolution of the population of LSAs. As such, once the initial state of LSAs and eco-laws is fixed, the evolution of a service ecosystem can be simulated using any available framework for CTMCs, like e.g., PRISM (University of Birmingham, 2007) (which also allows for stochastic model-checking), typically working via Stochastic Simulation Algorithms (SSA) based on (Gillespie, 1977).

We performed simulations conducted over an exposition of nine rooms connected via cor-

ridors. A first set of tests was aimed at evaluating the effectiveness of gradients in the process of steering to a destination, even in an averagely crowded situation. Snapshots of a simulation run are reported in Figure 5, where we consider four different targets located in the four rooms near environment edges. People (each having interest in one of the targets, chosen randomly) are initially distributed randomly throughout the museum, as shown in the first snapshot. They eventually reach the room in which the desired target is hosted, as shown in the last snapshot.

A second set of tests was aimed at verifying the management of overcrowding and, in particular, how the behavior of the ecosystem can dynamically and automatically become self-aware of crowding conditions and react accordingly.

Figure 6 shows another simulation run: two groups of people, each with a common interest in an exhibition – denoted with empty (light) and filled (dark) circles – are initially located in two different rooms, as shown in the first snapshot. The target for the dark visitors is located in the central room of the second row, while the others' is in the right room of the second row. In the simulation, dark visitors reach their target quickly because it is closer, however, the resultant crowded area formed intersects the shortest path towards the other visitors' target. Due to this jam the latter visitors are guided along a different path, which is longer but less crowded.

Both tests show qualitative effectiveness of the proposed eco-laws, and suggest that our simulation approach can be used for additional experiments focusing on tuning system parameters (factor k) or alternative strategies (e.g., diffusing crowd information) to optimize paths to destinations.

RELATED WORKS

Traditional Tuple Spaces

Interaction of agents in our framework is mediated by a space reifying and ruling interaction. This very idea has been proposed by the pioneer work in the Linda (Gelernter, 1985) tuple space model and its distributed implementations (Noble and Zlateva, 2001; Nielsen and Sørensen, 1993; Merrick and Wood, 2000; Atkinson, 2008). In Linda – which originated as a language for parallel computing but was later adopted as paradigm for distributed system coordination (Omicini and Viroli, 2011) – coordination is achieved by coordinated processes inserting tuples (records of primitive values) in the global shared space and retrieving (and removing) them based on templates (records possibly including wildcards). Retrieval is always blocking, though non-blocking versions are typically available in the above implementations.

Despite the evident LSA/tuple and LSA-space/tuple-space similarity – tuple spaces were indeed a source of inspiration for our work – our framework introduces a profoundly different approach to the engineering of distributed systems. Tuple space approaches see tuples as (possibly structured) "tokens" to be placed/retrieved in the shared space either as a means of synchronization or communication. LSAs are instead strictly bound to their owner: they represent both its "interface" towards the environment (when considering manifestation) and the environment "interface" for the agent (when considering observation). In this acceptation, the concept of LSA resembles and develops on top of the notions of Agent Co-ordination Context as developed in (Omicini et. al., 2004) and coordination artifact (Omicini et. al., 2006).

Semantic Tuple Spaces

So-called *semantic tuple space computing* has been recognized as one of the most notable advances in the field of middlewares for dealing with issues like openness, dynamism, and scalability—that are peculiar aspects of applications operating in open environments such as the Web. It basically amounts to augmenting tuple spaces with semantic representation and reasoning—an overview of some approaches is in Nixon et al., 2008, which we here briefly review and complete.

Triple space computing (TSC) (Fensel, 2004) provides an extension of tuple space computing with features of Semantic Web technology. In particular, this work proposes an extension of the classical flat data model adopted for tuples: it relies on the use of RDF to support applicability in the Semantic Web domain. This model is based on the assignment of URIs to tuples, which can be interlinked so as to form graphs. Moreover, tuples becomes RDF triples of a subject, a predicate and an object. Among the others, one of the main advantages of adopting Semantic Web technology lies in the possibility to provide a tuple space with more refined (semantic) matching algorithms than the usual template matching of Linda.

Born as an extension of TSC, Conceptual Spaces (CSpaces) is an independent initiative targeted at studying the applicability of semantic tuple space computing in scenarios other than Web, such as Ubiquitous Computing, Distributed Software Components, Enterprise Application Integration and so on. CSpaces features several components: a knowledge container, an organizational and a coordination model, a model for semantic interoperability, a security and trust model, a knowledge visualization model, and an architecture model. In particular tuples are records with exactly 7 fields, one of which being a logical formula expressed e.g. in Description Logics and representing the semantic content of the tuple. Other fields roughly resembles our synthetic properties and identifiers—for a thorough description of these components, the interested reader can refer to (Nixon et al., 2008).

Semantic Web Spaces (Tolksdorf et al., 2008; Nixon et al., 2008) has been devised as a middleware for the Semantic Web, where clients can exploit Semantic Web data to access and manipulate knowledge, so as to coordinate their activities. In particular, originally conceived as an extension of XMLSpaces – a tuple space platform supporting the exchange of XML documents – Semantic Web Spaces provides tuple spaces able to support the exchange of RDF triples (i.e., tuples), relying on RDFS reasoning capabilities as regards to matching.

The sTuples model (Khushraj et al., 2004; Nixon et al., 2008), developed by Nokia Research Center, is targeted at pervasive computing settings. There, given the heterogeneous and dynamic nature of pervasive environments, the combined adoption of Semantic Web and tuple spaces have been recognized as a viable solution not only to semantic interoperability issues, but also with respect to temporal and spatial decoupling, and synchronization. To this end, semantic tuples (based on JavaSpace object tuples) are provided

that extend data tuples, and tuple template matching is extended via a semantic matching mechanism on top of object-based matching. In addition, sTuples features agents residing in the space with the goal of performing user-centric services, such as tuple recommendation.

The RDFSwarms model in (Harasic et al., 2010) explores swarm approaches in semantic tuple spaces, combining self-organization aspects of tuple diffusion and manipulation with the semantic character of technologies like RDF, with the goal of optimizing the retrieval of tuples by semantic similarity.

A previous semantic tuple space approach of ours is presented in (Nardini et al., 2010), in which the TuCSoN tuple center model is extended with notions of semantic tuples and semantic templates, roughly corresponding to instance and classes in Description Logics, with a proposed tuple-like syntax used to retain simplicity of the approach. This work has been extended with concepts of fuzzy matching (Nardini et al., 2011).

Most of the above approaches limit tuples to just RDF triples, making it necessary to build complex graphs even to model simple individuals and concepts. One of the key features of our model, following the direction of (Nardini et al., 2010), is to consider a tuple as the overall description of an individual (e.g. as modeled in Description Logics), but inventing a language of tuples and of templates – namely, LSAs and eco-law patterns – that remains simple enough and does not expose the whole complexity of Description Logics—as e.g., in Conceptual Spaces. Differently from (Nardini et al., 2010), we address multi-valued properties and references to other individuals in a more natural and effective way, especially as far as translation to RDF is concerned.

Self-Organization in Tuple Spaces

As described in (Omicini and Viroli, 2011), applications of coordination models and languages – and especially space-based ones – are inevitably entering the realm of self-organization, where complexity of interactions becomes the key to make desired properties appear by emergence. Given the intrinsic difficulty of *designing emergence*, most approaches simply mimic nature-inspired techniques to organize and evolve tuples according to specified rules.

TOTA (Tuples On The Air) (Mamei and Zambonelli, 2009) is a tuple-based middleware supporting field-based coordination for pervasive computing applications. In TOTA each tuple, when inserted into a node of the network, is equipped with content (the tuple data), a diffusion rule (the policy by which the tuple has to be cloned and diffused around) and a maintenance rule (the policy whereby the tuple should evolve due to events or time elapsing).

Concerning TOTA, which is the model most similar to ours from the viewpoint of application domain, we observe that while our eco-laws are meant to be fixed for the application domain and apply to all LSAs (depending on semantic matching criteria), in TOTA each tuple is responsible for carrying its behavioral rules. So, while we call for specifying the evolution rules of tuples at design-time, when the application goals are identified, TOTA instead promotes a run-time approach: an agent defines diffusion behavior before injecting the tuple in the system. Embedding the behavior in the tuples, rather than in the space, make difficult and impractical the task of predicting overall ecosystem behavior in advance.

Finally, it is worth noting that the model presented here originates from previous work of ours (Viroli and Casadei, 2009; Viroli et al., 2011b; Viroli and Casadei, 2010), where a bio-chemical tuple space model is presented. There, tuples are associated with an *activity level*, which resembles chemical concentration and measures the extent to which the tuple can influence the state of system coordination—e.g., a tuple with low activity level would be rather inert, hence taking part in coordination with very low frequency. Chemical-like reactions, properly installed into the tuple space,

evolve activity level of tuples over time in the same way chemical concentration is evolved in chemical systems.

Other Semantic Rule-Based Approaches

The eco-law language bears a resemblance to other rule languages based on Semantic Web technologies, i.e., those designed (or bridged) to adhere to and operate over the RDF model.

A first category includes human-friendly languages designed primarily for readability, and localized to a particular piece of software. For example, Jena's rule language and associated inference engine (Carroll et al., 2004) supports manually specified rules, and is used within Jena to infer knowledge entailed by RDFS and OWL semantics. TRIPLE (Decker et al., 2005) is a proposed query and rule language for RDF, while N3 Logic (Berners-lee et al., 2008) provides a framework that extends N3 RDF syntax with support for rules. Beyond languages designed specifically to operate over the RDF model, general-purpose rule engines, such as Jess (Friedman-Hill, 2008), and Prova (Paschke and Schroder, 2007), have been successfully bridged to operate over RDF (O'Connor and Knublauch, 2005; Paschke and Schroder, 2007).

A second category is that of rule markup languages, which are heavily tailored towards the publication, interchange, and reuse of rules across software systems. There sit the Semantic Web Rule Language (SWRL) (Horrocks et al., 2004), an RDF-based language that combines a subset of features of OWL and the Rule Markup Language (RuleML) (Boley et al., 2001), and the REWERSE Rule Markup Language (Wagner et al., 2006), which extends SWRL with support for Object Constraint Language (Warmer and Kleppe, 1999). SPARQL Inferencing Notation (SPIN) (Knublauch et al., 2011) provides a vocabulary to represent SPARQL queries as RDF, and supports the execution of rules and object constraints over

RDF data models. Finally, the Rule Interchange Format (Kifer, 2008) is the product of an active W3C working group aiming to implement rule interchange between different rule languages in the Semantic Web.

Although a cosmetic correspondence between the structure of eco-laws and rules exists, differences in the goals and underlying semantics of each strongly differentiate them. In particular *(i)* eco-laws do not denote a logical inference, but a data transformation (that often modifies the law's reactants), *(ii)* working at the level of LSAs, eco-law operational semantics capture instructions to modify, create, delete, or connect "objects", rather that express the generation of new knowledge from the existence of combinations of individual "facts", *(iii)* the firing of an eco-law results in the transformation of a single pattern of LSAs matching the law's left-hand side; this can be juxtaposed with rule engines, where rule sets are usually evaluated as a batch, executing all matched patterns over all rules, finally *(iv)* eco-law scheduling is CMTC based, rather than priority based, which is typical of rule engines.

Points *(iii)* and *(iv)* additionally imply an entirely different methodology for working within the eco-law framework than with a rule engine. In a rule-based environment the rule set is typically evaluated immediately after new data is introduced or before the knowledge base is next queried, giving software agents the expectation that, *a)* the inference process with respect to the most recent input is complete, and *b)* in the absence of further input, the knowledge base remains static. Neither expectation holds within the eco-law framework, where software agents have no explicit control over the firing of eco-laws relative to the timing of its inspection of the environment, nor any expectation of knowledge stability within the LSA Space beyond the properties of LSAs that it directly governs.

Setting aside methodology and the semantics of execution, we note that parts of the eco-law semantics may be approximated by some of the rule languages described above. For example, a single LSA appearing on the left-hand side of an eco-law may be expressed in any rule languages as a conjunction of facts—one for each LSA property. Some rule languages (e.g., Jess) support the binding of new variables on the right-hand side of a rule, but this capability is not standard. The semantics of both the 'clones' and 'extends' operators are closely tied to the eco-law's "object oriented" view of the world—that is, both operate over knowledge that is implicitly declared by association to bound LSA identifiers. To the best of our knowledge, this precludes implementation of these operators in any the Semantic Web rule languages discussed above (e.g., Jena Rules and SWRL lack the capability to bind variables on the right-hand side of a rule, SWRL also does not support quantification necessary to operate over the set of properties associated with an LSA identifier). It appears possible to synthesize this functionality in the Jess language by using a combination of custom functions and procedural-style code within a rule, however this "algorithmic" approach to rule construction is non-standard.

Finally, we note that the existence of a formal translation from the eco-law language to SPARQL means that eco-laws may be executed against the majority of both open-source and proprietary RDF stores, using standard tooling.

CONCLUSION

In this chapter we presented a framework for pervasive service ecosystems, meant to overcome the limitations of standard SOA when dealing with situated and adaptive pervasive computing systems, along with an implementation schema based on standard W3C technologies for the Semantic Web, and an application case of crowd steering by public/private displays.

We believe that the main novelty of the proposed approach precisely lies in the interplay between eco-laws and LSAs: the former regulates the overall ecosystem by basic mechanisms of agent interaction via bonds and of spatial coordination (Viroli et al., 2011b); the latter regulates agent autonomy, controlling how a single agent is affected by the ecosystem and manifests to it. To this end, a key role is played by the liveness of LSAs, which is achieved by three fundamental mechanisms: *(i)* agents have responsibility for continuously updating the state of their LSAs over time; *(ii)* contextualization (seen as a middleware service) guarantees that information about the physical world promptly reflects in synthetic LSAs and properties; *(iii)* eco-laws enact continuous processes, evolving LSAs to reflect the overall ecosystem situation.

Concerning the use of W3C technologies, we remark that they come equipped with a set of reasoners and techniques we can adopt to devise analysis tools for pervasive ecosystems. The proposed translation also defines a reference implementation of an LSA-space based on an RDF-store coupled with a SPARQL interpreter. This does not mean that this is the preferred technological solution for the development of a middleware, but it provides a means to quickly prototype a correct-by-definition LSA-space implementation, and a reference to be compliant with in the case other solutions are considered. Finally, the approach described in this chapter paves the way for a deep connection with the use of existing/new OWL ontologies. They can be used not only to support OWL-based semantic matching, but also to declare the shape of valid LSAs, check/enact it, and enforce correctness of ecosystems developed on top of know LSAs and eco-laws.

Although necessarily early, we believe the experiments described in this chapter show some key properties of the proposed model: *(i)* expressiveness of the eco-law language in modeling basic interaction patterns up to sophisticated self-organization patterns; *(ii)* ability to compose universal and application-specific eco-laws; *(iii)* possibility of analyzing ecosystems – and the behavior of eco-laws therein – by simulation.

Future Works

The activities to be carried out in the next stages of this research include:

- To provide a formal operational model, grounding the proposed approach and giving semantics to the eco-law language.
- A methodology (or a coherent collection of methodology fragments) for the development of ecosystems will be developed, following early experiences in the context of the AOSE (agent-oriented software engineering) research field. In particular, the issue of application-independent versus application-specific eco-laws, and the problem of which application-independent eco-laws to provide to guide the basic aspects of ecosystem behavior, are to be studied in detail.
- Staying within the context of methodology, further exploration and deepening of the relationship between eco-law mediated interactions and traditional coordination technologies, with particular attention to BPEL, the business process model that describes interactions between web services.
- In order to work in a complete yet effective way, the methodology should be coupled with additional tools, including:
  - A fully-featured simulation framework for ecosystems, implementing in an efficient way the operational semantics of eco-laws.
  - A workbench for the formal analysis of static and behavioral properties of ecosystems, possibly reusing existing tools tackling fragments of the eco-law language.
  - Implementing prototype development tools, including editors and checkers.

ACKNOWLEDGMENT

This work has been supported by the EU FP7 project "SAPERE - Self-aware Pervasive Service Ecosystems" under contract No. 256873.

REFERENCES

Atkinson, A. K. (2008). Tupleware: A distributed tuple space for cluster computing. In *Proceedings of the 2008 Ninth International Conference on Parallel and Distributed Computing, Applications and Technologies*, (pp. 121–126). Washington, DC: IEEE Computer Society.

Babaoglu, O., Canright, G., Deutsch, A., Caro, G. A. D., Ducatelle, F., & Gambardella, L. M. (2006). Design patterns from biology for distributed computing. *ACM Transactions on Autonomous and Adaptive Systems, 1*(1), 26–66.

Bachrach, J., Beal, J., & McLurkin, J. (2010). Composable continuous space programs for robotic swarms. *Neural Computing & Applications, 19*(6), 825–847.

Bandara, A., Payne, T., Roure, D. D., Gibbins, N., & Lewis, T. (2008). *Semantic resource matching for pervasive environments: The approach and its evaluation*. Technical Report ECSTR-IAM08-001, School of Electronics and Computer Science, University of Southampton.

Beal, J. (2009). Flexible self-healing gradients. In S. Y. Shin & S. Ossowski (Eds.), *Proceedings of the 2009 ACM Symposium on Applied Computing (SAC)*, Honolulu, Hawaii, USA, March 9-12, 2009, (pp. 1197–1201). ACM.

Beal, J., & Bachrach, J. (2006). Infrastructure for engineered emergence on sensor/actuator networks. *IEEE Intelligent Systems, 21*(2), 10–19.

Berners-Lee, T., & Connolly, D. (2011). *Notation3 (N3): A readable RDF syntax*. W3C team submission, W3C. Retrieved from http://www.w3.org/TeamSubmission/n3/

Berners-Lee, T., Connolly, D., Kagal, L., Scharf, Y., & Hendler, J. (2008). N3logic: A logical framework for the world wide web. *Theory and Practice of Logic Programming, 8*, 249–269.

Boley, H., Tabet, S., & Wagner, G. (2001). Design rationale of RuleML: A markup language for semantic web rules. In *The Semantic Web Working Symposium*, (pp. 381–401).

Campbell, A. T., Eisenman, S. B., Lane, N. D., Miluzzo, E., Peterson, R. A., & Lu, H. (2008). The rise of people-centric sensing. *IEEE Internet Computing, 12*(4).

Carroll, J. J., Dickinson, I., Dollin, C., Reynolds, D., Seaborne, A., & Wilkinson, K. (2004). Jena: Implementing the Semantic Web recommendations. *In Proceedings of the 13th International World Wide Web Conference - Alternate Track Papers & Posters*, (pp. 74–83). New York, NY: ACM.

Coleman, B. (2009). Using sensor inputs to affect virtual and real environments. *IEEE Pervasive Computing / IEEE Computer Society and IEEE Communications Society, 8*(3), 16–23.

Decker, S., Sintek, M., Billig, A., Henze, N., Dolog, P., & Nejdl, W. … Zdun, U. (2005). *TRIPLE - An RDF rule language with context and use cases*. In Rule Languages for Interoperability.

Fensel, D. (2004). Triple-space computing: Semantic Web services based on persistent publication of information. In F. A. Aagesen, C. Anutariya, & V. Wuwongse (Eds.), *Intelligence in Communication Systems, IFIP International Conference, INTELLCOMM 2004, Proceedings, volume 3283 of Lecture Notes in Computer Science*, Bangkok, Thailand, (pp. 43–53). Springer.

Ferscha, A., & Vogl, S. (2010). Wearable displays – for everyone! *IEEE Pervasive Computing / IEEE Computer Society and IEEE Communications Society*, *9*(1), 7–10.

Friedman-Hill, E. (2008). *Jess, the rule engine for the Java platform*. Retrieved from http://www.jessrules.com/

Gearon, P., & Schenk, S. (Eds.). (2009). *SPARQL 1.1 update*. W3C working draft, W3C. Retrieved from http://www.w3.org/TR/2009/WD-sparql11-update-20091022/

Gelernter, D. (1985). Generative communication in Linda. *ACM Transactions on Programming Languages and Systems*, *7*(1), 80–112.

Gillespie, D. T. (1977). Exact stochastic simulation of coupled chemical reactions. *Journal of Physical Chemistry*, *81*(25), 2340–2361.

Guha, R. V., & Brickley, D. (2004). *RDF vocabulary description language 1.0: RDF schema*. W3C recommendation, W3C. Retrieved from http://www.w3.org/TR/2004/REC-rdf-schema-20040210/

Harasic, M., Augustin, A., Obermeier, P., & Tolksdorf, R. (2010). RDFSwarms: Self organized distributed RDF triple store. In *Proceedings of the 2010 ACM Symposium on Applied Computing, SAC '10*, (pp. 1339–1340). New York, NY: ACM.

Horrocks, I., Patel-Schneider, P. F., Boley, H., Tabet, S., Grosof, B., & Dean, M. (2004). *SWRL: A semantic web rule language combining OWL and RuleML*. Technical report, W3C Member Submission. Retrieved from http://www.w3.org/Submission/SWRL/

Jazayeri, M. (2005). Species evolve, individuals age. In *8th IEEE International Workshop on Principles of Software Evolution*, (pp. 3–12). Washington, DC.

Kephart, J. O., & Chess, D. M. (2003). The vision of autonomic computing. *IEEE Computer*, *36*(1), 41–50.

Khushraj, D., Lassila, O., & Finin, T. W. (2004). sTuples: Semantic tuple spaces. In *Proceedings of the 1st Annual International Conference on Mobile and Ubiquitous Systems: Networking and Services (MobiQuitous '04)*, (pp. 268–277). Boston, MA, USA.

Kifer, M. (2008). Rule interchange format: The framework. In *Web Reasoning and Rule Systems*. In *Lecture Notes in Computer Science* (*Vol. 5341*, pp. 1–11). Berlin, Germany: Springer.

Knublauch, H., Hendler, J. A., & Idehen, K. (2011). *SPIN: SPARQL inferencing notation*. W3C member submission, W3C. Retrieved from http://www.w3.org/Submission/2011/SUBM-spin-overview-20110222/

Krötzsch, M., Patel-Schneider, P. F., Rudolph, S., Hitzler, P., & Parsia, B. (Eds.). (2009). OWL 2 web ontology language primer. Technical report, W3C. Retrieved from http://www.w3.org/TR/2009/REC-owl2-primer-20091027/

Mamei, M., & Zambonelli, F. (2009). Programming pervasive and mobile computing applications: The TOTA approach. *ACM Transactions on Software Engineering and Methodology*, *18*(4).

Merrick, I., & Wood, A. (2000). Coordination with scopes. In *Proceedings of the 2000 ACM symposium on Applied computing - Volume 1, SAC '00*, (pp. 210–217). New York, NY: ACM.

Miller, E., & Manola, F. (Eds.). (2004). *RDF primer*. W3C recommendation, W3C. Retrieved from http://www.w3.org/TR/2004/REC-rdf-primer-20040210/

MIT. (2010). *MIT Proto*. Retrieved November 1, 2010, from http://proto.bbn.com/

Nardini, E., Omicini, A., & Viroli, M. (2011). *Description spaces with fuzziness*. In 26th Annual ACM Symposium on Applied Computing (SAC 2011), Tunghai University, TaiChung, Taiwan. ACM.

Nardini, E., Viroli, M., & Panzavolta, E. (2010). Coordination in open and dynamic environments with Tucson semantic tuple centres. In *Proceedings of the 25th Annual ACM Symposium on Applied Computing (SAC 2010)*, volume III, (pp. 2037–2044). Sierre, Switzerland: ACM.

Nielsen, B., & Sørensen, T. (1993). *Distributed programming with multiple tuple space Linda*. Aalborg University, Institute for Electronic Systems.

Nixon, L. J. B., Simperl, E., Krummenacher, R., & Martin-Recuerda, F. (2008). Tuplespace-based computing for the semantic web: A survey of the state-of-the-art. *The Knowledge Engineering Review, 23*(2), 181–212.

Noble, M. S., & Zlateva, S. (2001). Scientific computation with Javaspaces. In *Proceedings of the 9th International Conference on High-Performance Computing and Networking, HPCN Europe 2001*, (pp. 657–666). London, UK: Springer-Verlag.

O'Connor, M. J., & Knublauch, H. (2005). *Writing rules for the semantic web using SWRL and Jess*. In the Protege with Rules Workshop, held with 8th International Protege Conference.

Omicini, A., Ricci, A., & Viroli, M. (2005). RBAC for organisation and security in an agent coordination infrastructure. In *Electronic Notes in Theoretical Computer Science* (*Vol. 128*, pp. 65–85). Elsevier Science B.V.

Omicini, A., Ricci, A., & Viroli, M. (2006). Coordination artifacts as first-class abstractions for MAS engineering: State of the research. In *Software Engineering for Multi-Agent Systems, IV: Research Issues and Practical Applications, vol. 3914 di LNAI*, (pp. 71–90). Springer.

Omicini, A., & Viroli, M. (2011). Coordination models and languages: From parallel computing to self-organisation. *The Knowledge Engineering Review, 26*(1), 53–59.

Paschke, A., & Schroder, M. (2007). Inductive logic programming for bio-informatics in Prova. In *Proceedings of the 2nd Workshop on Data Mining in Bioinformatics at VLDB '07*.

Pianini, D., Montagna, S., & Viroli, M. (2011). A chemical inspired simulation framework for pervasive services ecosystems. In *Proceedings of the Federated Conference on Computer Science and Information Systems*, (pp. 675–682). Szczecin, Poland: IEEE Computer Society Press.

Seaborne, A., & Harris, S. (Eds.). (2009). *SPARQL 1.1 query*. W3C working draft, W3C. Retrieved from http://www.w3.org/TR/2009/WD-sparql11-query-20091022/

Sirin, E., Parsia, B., Grau, B. C., Kalyanpur, A., & Katz, Y. (2007). Pellet: A practical OWL-DL reasoner. *Web Semantics, 5*, 51–53.

Spohrer, J. C., Maglio, P. P., Bailey, J. H., & Gruhl, D. (2007). Steps toward a science of service systems. *IEEE Computer, 40*(1), 71–77.

Tolksdorf, R., Nixon, L. J. B., & Simperl, E. P. B. (2008). Towards a tuplespace-based middleware for the Semantic Web. *Web Intelligence and Agent Systems, 6*(3), 235–251.

Ulieru, M., & Grobbelaar, S. (June 2007). Engineering industrial ecosystems in a networked world. In *Proceedings of the 5th IEEE International Conference on Industrial Informatics*, (pp. 1–7). IEEE Press.

University of Birmingham. (2007). *The PRISM probabilistic model checker*. Retrieved from http://www.prismmodelchecker.org

Vargo, S. L., Maglio, P. P., & Akaka, M. A. (2008). On value and value co-creation: A service systems and service logic perspective. *European Management Journal*, *26*(3), 145–152.

Viroli, M., Beal, J., & Casadei, M. (2011a). Core operational semantics of Proto. *In Proceedings of the 26th Annual ACM Symposium on Applied Computing (SAC 2011), volume II: Artificial Intelligence & Agents, Information Systems, and Software Development*, (pp. 1325–1332).

Viroli, M., & Casadei, M. (2009). Biochemical tuple spaces for self-organising coordination. In *Proceedings of the 11th International Conference on Coordination Languages and Models, volume 5521 of LNCS*, (pp. 143–162). Lisbon, Portugal: Springer.

Viroli, M., & Casadei, M. (2010). Chemical-inspired self-composition of competing services. In *Proceedings of the 25th Annual ACM Symposium on Applied Computing (SAC 2010), volume III*, (pp. 2029–2036). Sierre, Switzerland: ACM.

Viroli, M., Casadei, M., Montagna, S., & Zambonelli, F. (2011b). Spatial coordination of pervasive services through chemical-inspired tuple spaces. *ACM Transactions on Autonomous and Adaptive Systems*, *6*(2), 14:1 – 14:24.

Wagner, G., Giurca, A., & Lukichev, S. (2006). A usable interchange format for rich syntax rules integrating OCL, RuleML and SWRL. In *Proceedings of the Workshop on Reasoning on the Web (RoW2006)*.

Warmer, J., & Kleppe, A. (1999). *The object constraint language: Precise modeling with UML*. Boston, MA: Addison-Wesley Longman Publishing Co., Inc.

Wells, G. C., Mueller, B., & Schulé, L. (2008). A tuple space web service for distributed programming - Simplifying distributed web services applications. In *Proceedings of the Fourth International Conference on Web Information Systems and Technologies* (WEBIST 2008), (pp. 93–100). INSTICC Press.

ADDITIONAL READING

Agha, G. (2008). Computing in pervasive cyberspace. *Communications of the ACM*, *51*(1), 68–70.

Androutsellis-Theotokis, S., & Spinellis, D. (2004). A survey of peer-to-peer content distribution technologies. *ACM Computing Surveys*, *36*(4), 335–371.

Banâtre, J.-P., & Le Métayer, D. (1993). Programming by multiset transformation. *Communications of the ACM*, *36*(1), 98–111.

Barros, A. P., & Dumas, M. (2006). The rise of web service ecosystems. *IT Professional*, *8*(5), 31–37.

Corkill, D. (1991). Blackboard systems. *Journal of AI Expert*, *9*(6), 40–47.

Dobson, S., Denazis, S., Fernández, A., Gaïti, D., Gelenbe, E., & Massacci, F. (2006). A survey of autonomic communications. *ACM Transactions on Autonomous and Adaptive Systems*, *1*(2), 223–259.

Gardelli, L., Viroli, M., Casadei, M., & Omicini, A. (2008). Designing self-organising environments with agents and artefacts: A simulation-driven approach. *International Journal of Agent-Oriented Software Engineering*, *2*(2), 171–195.

Gelernter, D., & Carriero, N. (1992). Coordination languages and their significance. *Communications of the ACM*, *35*(2), 97–107.

Huhns, M. N., & Singh, M. P. (2005). Service-oriented computing: Key concepts and principles. *IEEE Internet Computing*, *9*(1), 75–81.

Kalasapur, S., Kumar, M., & Shirazi, B. (2007). Dynamic service composition in pervasive computing. *IEEE Transactions on Parallel and Distributed Systems*, *18*(7), 907.

Omicini, A., Ricci, A., & Viroli, M. (2008). Artifacts in the A&A meta- model for multi-agent systems. *Autonomous Agents and Multi-Agent Systems*, *17*(3).

Prigogine, I., & Steingers, I. (1997). *The end of certainty: Time, chaos, and the new laws of nature*. Free Press.

Viroli, M., Holvoet, T., Ricci, A., Schelfthout, K., & Zambonelli, F. (2007). Infrastructures for the environment of multiagent systems. *Autonomous Agents and Multi-Agent Systems*, *14*(1), 49–60.

Viroli, M., & Zambonelli, F. (2010). A biochemical approach to adaptive service ecosystems. *Information Sciences*, *180*(10), 1876–1892.

Wegner, P. (1997). Why interaction is more powerful than algorithms. *Communications of the ACM*, *40*(5), 80–91.

Zambonelli, F., & Parunak, H. V. D. (2002). From design to intention: signs of a revolution. In *Proceedings of the First International Joint Conference on Autonomous Agents & Multiagent Systems, AAMAS 2002*, July 15-19, 2002, Bologna, Italy, (pp. 455–456). ACM.

KEY TERMS AND DEFINITIONS

Adaptivity: Possessing the ability to change behavior based on observed stimuli.

Autonomic: A characteristic of a computational resource or set of computational resources that can automatically adapt to certain types of environmental change without user intervention.

Eco-Law: A chemical-like global coordination rule that both enables and regulates interactions between agents within a pervasive ecosystem.

Live Semantic Annotation: A continuously updated, structured, formal representation of a portion of an agent's state, intended to support coordination.

Pervasive Ecosystem: The environment that results from the increased deployment and embedding of sensing technologies within everyday objects, designed to support general-purpose services that are based on opportunistic encounters between both static and highly mobile components.

Prosumer: A user, or agent that can potentially both contribute information to and consume information from their operating environment.

Situatedness: A property of a computation, action, or behavior that is influenced by the current state of the surrounding physical and social environment.

Spatial Substrate: A middleware-constructed, logical partition of space that abstracts from the physical network structure and is designed to support situated interactions between agents.

ENDNOTE

[1] Anonymous resources (sometimes referred to as blank nodes) designated with a locally-scoped identifier are also permitted by RDF, however we do not use them here.

Section 4
Dynamic Adaptation

Chapter 9
Flexible Coordination Techniques for Dynamic Cloud Service Collaboration

Gary Creaner
Dublin City University, Ireland

Claus Pahl
Dublin City University, Ireland

ABSTRACT

The provision of individual, but also composed services is central in cloud service provisioning. The authors describe a framework for the coordination of cloud services, based on a tuple-space architecture which uses an ontology to describe the services. Current techniques for service collaboration offer limited scope for flexibility. They are based on statically describing and compositing services. With the open nature of the web and cloud services, the need for a more flexible, dynamic approach to service coordination becomes evident. In order to support open communities of service providers, there should be the option for these providers to offer and withdraw their services to/from the community. For this to be realised, there needs to be a degree of self-organisation. The authors' techniques for coordination and service matching aim to achieve this through matching goal-oriented service requests with providers that advertise their offerings dynamically. Scalability of the solution is a particular concern that will be evaluated in detail.

INTRODUCTION

Service-oriented architecture (SOA) is an architectural style that allows for business processes to be implemented by integrating various services. These services can be thought of as software components. Cloud computing builds up on service architecture as the platform, providing cross-organisational, externally hosted services.

Most current SOA implementations use web services as the technology platform based on message passing, a service registry and static service

DOI: 10.4018/978-1-4666-2089-6.ch009

description respectively. This approach is rigid in that it requires services publish the details of their functionality and how to interact with them to a registry. This information must then be used by the requestor to bind to and invoke the service in the way in which the provider has published, usually using WS-BPEL. This is a property that does not meet the flexibility requirements of cloud computing, in particular if flexible service brokering and mediation is required where offered and requested cloud services are matched dynamically through a cloud brokering service. Intermediaries such as brokers that bundle and customise offerings in response to dynamic needs will become more important in the cloud domain in the near future. Currently, a cloud service user or broker would have to completely define what services are to be used, the order in which they would be used and how the input and output is passed from one service to another in order to implement a full business process.

Current approaches to service collaboration (Pahl, 2002) are web service orchestrations and choreographies like WS-BPEL (orchestration) and WS-CDL (choreography). Both require the services used to be specified prior to the execution of the process. This kind of static process specification does not lend itself to a dynamic, flexible approach in which provided cloud services could be used as part of a process without prior knowledge of the service.

In order to overcome the limitations described, a framework is needed allowing services to be chosen dynamically at run-time. Our framework introduces a coordination space for providers to collaborate their activities in order to fulfil requests. The coordination space consists of a tuple space where requestors can deposit their requests and providers can take on requests according to their capabilities (Doberkat et al., 1992; Li & Parashar, 2005; Pahl et al., 2011).

Ontologies can be used to add semantic descriptions to web services (Pahl, 2005; Pahl, 2007). There are ontologies available which of-

fer ways of describing services in terms of their functionality. These will be discussed and the way in which they could be used in the context of service matching will also be explored. Matching requested and provided web services is possible based on these ontological descriptions (Klusch et al., 2006; Sirin et al., 2003; Sycara et al., 2003; Nixon et al., 2007). However, these have not been integrated in a tuple space as their coordination platform. We integrate goal-based service matching into tuple space coordination in order to add flexibility and allow in-exact matches.

The proposed framework would change the service coordination model from a pull model to a push model, whereby requests are published to the coordination space and providers search for requests that they would be able to fulfil. This means that requestors would be able to focus more on the definition of their request rather than on the services that are provided to them.

The next section will introduce core technologies used and discuss related work. A use-case scenario will then be introduced. There, we will also discuss how a tuple space architecture could be used to implement a coordination space for web services. Afterwards, we will give some detail on how the matching of providers and requestors is performed. We discuss on the scalability tests which were performed on the architecture in order to evaluate such an approach. An evaluation of the work discussing possible limitations and ways of overcoming these limitations is also provided.

BACKGROUND

Tuple spaces are widely used to support coordination activities (Johannson & Fox, 2004; Li & Parashar, 2005; Nixon et al., 2007). We present their principles, an overview of the chosen platform, and some background regarding a semantic extension of tuple matching. We also review literature on service composition and coordination.

Coordination and Tuple Spaces

The tuple space architecture was introduced in (Gelernter, 1985) as a means of communication in distributed programming. Tuples are constructs which consist of a collection of actuals. Templates, used for matching, consist of a collection of formals or actuals, or a mixture of both. *out()* and *in()* are the two key operations proposed for Linda. The *out()* operation takes a tuple as input and adds the tuple to the tuple space. The *in()* operation takes a template as input and searches the tuple space for a tuple which matches the provided template, returns it to the process that called it and removes it from the tuple space blocking access to it by another process. There is also a *read()* operation which will return a tuple matching the template, but will not remove it from the tuple space. This allows more than one process to access the tuple. With both the *in()* and *read()* operations, the calling processes will block until a matching tuple is found. If no matching tuples are in the space when the calls are made, the processes will block until a matching tuple becomes available.

A prototype of our service request coordination architecture is based on the LighTS (Balzarotti et al., 2007) tuple space, which was designed as an open-source, lightweight, customisable tuple space framework. It provides support for the Linda operations described above and can also be easily extended or modified to change how the tuple space itself is implemented or how the matching is performed. We have added ontology-based matching and process-level coordination techniques.

The Semantic Web

The Semantic Web aims to give meaning to the web resources and describe the information provided in a machine interpretable way. The Resource Description Framework (RDF) is an XML based language used to create statements. These statements consist of a subject, predicate and object, or resource, property, and property value. The Web Ontology Language (OWL) is based on RDF. It provides constructs that can be used to aid reasoning about the ontologies. An application of OWL is OWL-S (Web Ontology Working Group, 2006), which is an OWL ontology to describe services in terms of functional and non-functional attributes. The non-functional description can include information such as the service name, and contact information of the provider. The functional description is used to describe the web service in terms of its inputs, outputs, preconditions and effects. OWL-S based matching of tuples containing service descriptions is our aim.

A number of techniques are used in our implementation. SWRL is a rule language for ontologies. The body and head of a rule consist of so-called atoms. Atoms can state that something is a member of a class, has a value for a certain property, is the same as or is different from something else. These atoms can be combined into atomlists. The atomlists can be used in the preconditions and effects part of the OWL-S service descriptions without the need for implication rules to be defined. SPARQL is a query language which can be used to implement queries on RDF graphs. It can be easily used to follow links between the various resources and provides SELECT, ASK, CONSTRUCT, and DESCRIBE queries. It also allows for WHERE clauses to be added to the queries. Jena is an open-source Java framework for programming with OWL and SWRL, which provides a programmatic interface to access the various technologies listed above. We combined LighTS and Jena in our implementation.

Service Composition and Coordination

The work on semantic service descriptions has continued to support the discovery and composition of services using ontologies (Klusch et al., 2006; Sirin et al., 2002; Sycara et al., 2003), allowing matching between requests and provided services taking a variety of concerns into account. Recently, dynamic composition, particularly as a result of failure occurring at runtime, has been addressed (Cavallaro & Di Nitto, 2008; Moser et al., 2008; Wang et al., 2009). Failure handling is not our primary concern, but enabling a marketplace where negotiations can be automated through dynamic ontology-based coordination. Küngas and Popova (2011) describe a step in this direction, where objects are the central artefacts that are processed by processes dynamically. We add an ontology-based technique here.

A TUPLE SPACE ARCHITECTURE FOR SERVICE COORDINATION

Use Case

As a use case to illustrate our work, we have chosen a case where a company would like to store data on their products in the cloud, but would also like this data validated before it is stored. In order to formulate this into a request, the company would need to specify in their request that they would need both actions to be carried out.

There are many cloud based storage solutions available currently - Amazon's simple storage server is an example. This is quickly becoming an attractive solution to companies for storage and sharing of their data. Some providers offer cloud-based data validation for companies wishing their data to be compliant with the relevant standards. If a company is looking to share data on their products with other companies then it must be ensured that the data is compliant with the industry standards, e.g. to ensure their data conforms to standards like GS1.

In this situation, a broker might take on the initial request and then involve other cloud providers to validate and then store the data.

Tuple Spaces for Service Coordination

In using a tuple space for service coordination, we suggested in (Pahl et al., 2011) that the tuples could consist of three fields:

- An object field, which would contain the input of the request, such as the *data* in our use case.
- A goal field which would contain a description of what should be achieved by processing this request, such as *validated(data) -> stored(data),* which means that only successfully validated data should be stored.
- Also an optional process field is included which would guide the choosing of services to complete the request, e.g. a conditional statement *if validate(data) then store(data)* that sequences validation and storage.

The tuple space is the central coordination component (Li & Parashar, 2005). Requestors deposit goal-based requests here (Andersson et al., 2005). Providers see if they can meet these requests. In doing so, they themselves can deposit further new requests into the tuple space. This allows the original goal to be broken into sub-goals and these to be deposited into the tuple space to be met by other services, forming a goal resolution process. In terms of the use case, this would involve a request tuple being created with the object field containing the data to be processed or perhaps a URI link to the data. The goal field would consist of an expression that data needs to be both validated and stored.

Service Coordination Architecture and Process

A service that provides any of the requested operations could chose to take on the processing of

Figure 1. Coordination and knowledge space architecture (Adapted from C. Pahl, V. Gacitua-Decar, K. Yapa Bandara, M. Wang. Ontology-based Composition and Matching for Dynamic Service Coordination. Workshop on Ontology, Models, Conceptualization and Epistemology in Social, Artificial and Natural Systems Workshop ONTOSE'2011, 2011)

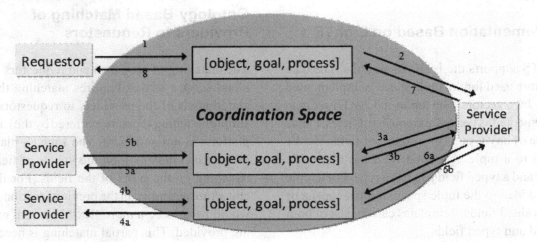

the request. It might then see if it can find another service that is able to fulfil parts of the task that it cannot fulfil. The service would then remove the tuple from the tuple space, blocking any other service from accessing it. This is a commitment to process the request and it should result in a completed tuple being entered in the tuple space later. Note, that in a negotiation process between cloud service users and providers, the handshake needs to be complete, i.e. the requestor would need to approve a provider. This would only require a simple coordination protocol (without significantly affecting the described tuple space functions) to be added and shall be neglected here.

Overall, the services involved in completing a request do not need to be specified prior to the request being formed. This method is a much more flexible approach than current approaches. As the services are picked dynamically at run time, this allows providers to join and leave the cloud market community as they wish. With other approaches like WS-BPEL, a service may be part of a BPEL process and the whole process could then fail if the service is no longer available. With the proposed method, a different service

that provides similar functionality could take on that part of the process and the request could still be completed. The diagram in Figure 1 explains this in more detail. The numbered arrows in the diagram show the sequence of events.

- The original request is entered into the tuple space (1), relating to the use case. This would be the request for the data to be validated and stored.
- The tuple is then taken by a broker service (2) which can coordinate the full request. This would require a validation service (3a) and, if necessary, storage (3b) - both deposited as two more detailed requests with storage and validation of the data as the respective goals.
- The validation service would retrieve the data validation tuple from the tuple space (4a). The storage service (5a) would then store this tuple from the tuple space and complete the request.
- Both would then put completed tuples back into the tuple space (4b), (5b).

- These would then be returned to the broker for the original requestor (6) to retrieve its completed request from the tuple space (7), (8).

Implementation Based on LighTS

LighTS supports the Linda operations. The data structure used for the tuple space is implemented using Java vectors. The tuples in LighTS are also implemented as vectors and consist of fields. Fields can be of any type. Any amount of fields can be added to a tuple. A valued field has a specific value and a typed field just has a type. For a tuple to be added to the tuple space, it must consist of only valued fields. Templates can consist of both valued and typed fields.

The *out()* method in this implementation takes a tuple as input, adds this tuple to the vector by calling its *addElement()* method. It then notifies any processes that are blocked to inform them that a new tuple has become available.

The *in()* method takes a template as its input. It compares the template to each element in the tuple space until it either finds a match or has tried every tuple and not found a match. If no match is found before the end of the tuple space operation, the process will be suspended in the while loop by calling a *wait()* inside a section of code that is synchronised on the tuple space. If a match is found, it will be assigned to the result tuple and this will cause the process to exit.

The matching in LighTS between a tuple and a template is performed by first checking if the tuple and template contain the same number of fields. If this is true, then the fields themselves are matched. For fields to match, the valued fields in the template must match the values in the tuple and the types of the typed fields in the templates must be of the same as the types of their corresponding tuple fields. The *in()* method removes the matching tuple from the tuple space.

The LighTS platform implements a strict form of matching that does not take flexibility regard-

ing parameter typing and effect specifications for services into account. We add ontology-based tuple matching - introduced below.

Ontology-Based Matching of Providers to Requestors

The matching of providers and requestors in the cloud service setting requires matching the declared goals of the providers to requestors. The simple matching semantics offered by the LighTS platform is not sufficient. The LighTS platform offers exact matching on the values of fields or matching on the types of the fields. For the architecture described in the previous section, there would need to be a more flexible partial matching provided. This partial matching is needed to allow a provider to determine if they can take on the request even if they cannot fully complete it and decompose the goal to involve other providers or if they can over-satisfy the requirements (Pahl & Zhu, 2006). More functionality must be added to the framework to enable providers to work out which part of the request they cannot fulfil. This will enable them to formulate a new request with a sub-goal which can be completed by another provider for the original request to be fully completed.

We used the OWL-S ontology to describe the services offered and their goals. OWL-S was also used to describe the request. OWL-S is based on the RDF format. The RDF format is a means of representing the resources in ontological format and the links between all the resources. It can be thought of as a graph or a collection of triples. The triples are composed of a subject, a predicate and an object. The subjects and objects are nodes in the graph and the predicate is the link between the nodes. For the given case study example,

```
validate(data) = GS1-compliant
```

or *[data, validate, GS1-compliant]* in triple notation, is a goal expressing the aim to have the subject *data* being *validated* (predicate) as *GS1-compliant* (object – the goal here).

OWL-S service descriptions can consist of non-functional properties, such as the name and contact information, but also describe the service in functional terms. The functional description is based on the inputs, outputs, preconditions and effects (IOPEs). It is this functional description that we use here to match the requestors and providers. SWRL expressions are used to define the effects of the services and the requested goal:

```
validated(data) -> stored(data)
```

In the implemented platform, the SWRL expressions in the effect descriptions are matched with each other. They are based on atomlists, which can be divided into atoms. Atoms can be thought of as representing ontology properties. The atomlists in the effect part of the OWL-S files can be thought of as describing the new state that the object will transition to when the service has completed.

The Jena platform offers a programmatic interface for interacting with RDF models using the Java interface, used for accessing and manipulating the ontology information (including SPARQL queries). This was used to extract the atomlists from the service and query descriptions. When these are extracted by the tuple space to see if they match, we attempt to match part of the query with the provider. If part of it matches, then the part that does not match is added - like *validate(data)* or *store(data)* - to a new tuple and this is added to the tuple space for another provider to take on this sub-goal. If this sub-goal can be completed by another service, then the original goal can be completed by the original provider service. Jena OWL-processing is used to determine which part of the goals match and also to build the goals from parts that do not match.

The completed tuples are removed from the tuple space by using a field to indicate whether it is completed or not and once the request is placed in the tuple space, the process that deposited it should try to match it again with the completed field set to true.

Scalability of the Tuple Space Architecture

One of the main concerns with such a coordination architecture is its scalability. How the platform will perform with varying numbers of providers and requestors, with differently sized tuples, and matching different data types needs to be looked at to demonstrate the applicability beyond toy examples.

Ideally, the tests would have to be carried out by providers making an *in()* call and waiting for a request to enter the tuple space. However, as *in()* calls are blocking, it would require the creation of a separate thread for each provider. As the aim of the scalability tests is to assess the time needed for the matching of requests to providers, the processing overhead that managing these threads would incur, would greatly skew the results obtained for large provider numbers. To overcome this, requests were first placed in the tuple space and then *in()* calls were made. Although this is opposite to the order which would be expected to occur, requests would not be removed from the tuple space until matched with a provider. It does not affect the results as the providers wait for a tuple to be introduced to the tuple space when no match is found and are woken when a new tuple becomes available. Access to the tuple space is synchronous, so the providers would be allowed access to the tuple space in an order similar to the way in which the requests are searched in order using this method.

The steps involved in carrying out the tests were:

1. Create an array of initialised tuples and rearrange their order within the array so that they are not searched for in the same order they were entered.

Figure 2. Performance evaluation results (different number of requests; different number of providers per request; differently sized tuples; matching different data types)

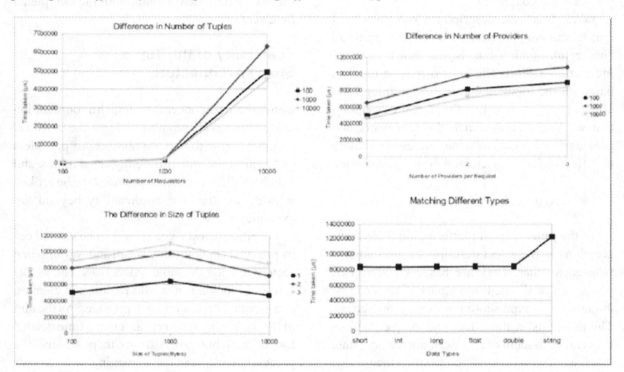

2. Insert the tuples into the tuple space using the *out()* operation.
3. Create an array of templates to match tuples and again rearrange the order.
4. Remove the matching tuples from the tuple space using the *in()* operation.

The time taken to perform the *in()* operations was measured to evaluate the scalability of using a tuple space architecture for service coordination.

The tuples consisted of 3 fields. The first was used for value-based matching and tests were run with this as an integer, a short, a long, a float, a double and a string. The second field was a byte array. This was only matched on type, not value and its size was varied between 100 bytes, 1000, bytes, and 10000 bytes. The third was a string that was value matched and was the same for each tuple. Tests were run with 100, 1000 and 10000 requesters and providers, then doubling

and tripling their respective numbers. Each test was run 10 times. Note, that we have displayed results as linear approximations for simplicity in Figure 2, although the actual functions might be non-linear.

As expected, the more tuples that were being matched, the longer the matching process took. The results in the graphs are taken from using integers as the matching type and the same number of providers as requestors. A typical example of such a graph from the data collected can be seen in Figure 2 (top left). The legend on the side indicates the size of tuples used for matching in the graphs.

The difference between the number of providers per request can be seen in Figure 2 (top right). The more providers are available per request, the longer the matching process takes. While there are more matching tuples per request, there are even more non-matching tuples per request and, therefore, more incorrect matches to check before finding a correct match. For the tests shown in the graph, the matching was done using short as the type, 10000 requests were matched. The legend on the side indicates the size of the byte array in the tuple.

Figure 2 (bottom left) shows the results of varying the size of the byte array in the tuple. The results are for a double valued field for matching and 10000 match requests. The numbers in the legend indicate the number of providers per request. The trend observed in this graph is unexpected, but can be explained through platform functions like garbage collection affecting the smaller inputs unduly.

The graph in Figure 2 (bottom right) illustrates the difference in using different types for matching. They all produce similar results except for strings, because the string used is much longer than the other types, but resembles more the ontology-based triple elements that we aim to simulate here. LighTS uses the default *matches()* methods of the data type to determine whether they match. For this graph, the time was taken from matching 10000 tuples with 3 providers per request and a byte array of 10000 bytes.

Overall, this demonstrates that the solution is scalable. In some situations, the performance is not linear anymore, but even the practically very high numbers still demonstrate acceptable performance.

Discussion of Ontology-Based Matching

To evaluate the platform for the concrete use case, we created two OWL-S description files for two services - one which would offer the service of validation of data and one which would offer storage of the data. To do this, we created a data ontology using OWL which included properties *locatedAt* and *isValidated*. The *locatedAt* property was a link between the resources *Data* and *Data-Location* and the *isValidated* property was a link

between the *Data* resource and a Boolean value to represent whether the data has been validated or not. Ontologies allow us to reason about described properties. This means that conclusions can be drawn about a resource's properties from other properties of the service resource. We created the properties that were needed for the services and requests and used the same properties to represent the same information for each.

For our implementation, the focus for the matching was put on the functional properties of the services. As explained previously, the effect of the services was expressed using SWRL expressions which consist of atomlists. The atomlists offer *first* and *rest* properties to describe what happens. For our implementation, we limited the services to only contain a *first* property. This means that each service must only offer one function. The request can have a *first* and a *rest* property. For the use case, the validation service's effect states that it changes the *isValidated* property changes from false to true. The storage service's effect states that it changes the *locatedAt* property changes from the input data's location to the location that will be returned. The request for validation and storage consists of an effect that specifies its *first* property should change *isValidated* from false to true and the *rest* indicates that *isLocated* should change from the input location to the output location.

When searching the tuple space for a provider to match the specified request, it first checks if they fully match. This means that the *first* property of the provider matches that of the request and that the request's *rest* property is empty. If this is not the case, then it checks if it is a partial match. This is true when the *first* properties match, but there is also a *rest* property in the request. If this is the case, a new goal model will be returned with the *first* property set to what the *rest* property of the original request was. This is then entered into the tuple space as a request to be met by a different provider. The provider then acts as a requestor and waits for the request to be returned to the tuple space with an indication of completion. If this is the case, the original provider can then remove the request tuple from the tuple space, blocking further access to it. It will then proceed to complete the request in the same manner in which it decided if it could meet the request.

FUTURE RESEARCH DIRECTIONS

These experimental executions realise a process that demonstrates the enhanced matching capabilities. However, we now discuss some implementation aspects, which demonstrate key difficulties in implementing a full-scale solution. The prototype currently does not allow for the case where a provider may provide a more complicated service that cannot be described by only a first property in its atomlist. However, the platform could be easily extended through more manipulation of the goal model before deciding how much of a match it is. Another current limitation of the model is that only the effect is considered when matching providers to requestors. It is assumed that for the input to all services needed, the process will be the same for the use case. However, some processes would need the output of one service to be the input of the next - validation is a requirement for storage. The OWL-S service descriptions contain resources that describe the inputs and outputs of their service and their types. This would have to be incorporated into a final model and some more work done in creating the subgoal request tuples and some more manipulation of the service descriptions in order to determine if the requests can be met. It would have to be ensured that one service can produce as its output the input needed by the next service to meet the sequencing constraint.

In terms of a cloud service brokerage or mediation solution, we have demonstrated the scalability of a flexible coordination model and the feasibility of ontology-based request matching. There are still areas for further investigation. Greater control over what providers are used to achieve the goal could be incorporated in the form of a

simple negotiation protocol - the process element of the request triples can serve this purpose here. As a basic solution, a ranking system for order of preference can be utilised. In the framework discussed in this chapter, the first matching service is the one to obtain the request. However, a negotiation process could be added whereby the matching services compete to see which one should be given the request. This could include the requestor specified control described above, but other properties could also be taken into consideration. If requestors are being charged for using services, the price of those services could be taken into account. Security characteristics of the web services are other non-functional properties that could influence this.

CONCLUSION

Current methods of service collaboration show limitations. We discussed limitations regarding the flexibility for the dynamic collaboration of the services involved in the process and introduced a framework for service collaboration that is suitable for cloud computing settings. A Linda tuple space model was implemented as a coordination space that service providers could use to advertise their capabilities. We have demonstrated the scalability of the solution through extensive tests. We also looked at the feasibility of an ontology-enhanced matching technique. We have focussed here on stateless coordination, as our aim was to explore advanced matching techniques. The original Linda coordination model was extended to include an ontology-based goal matching aspect, as the matching semantics used by the original model would not be sufficient. It has been shown that this is an effective way to offer flexible, dynamic collaboration of services where the providers have the freedom to advertise and withdraw their services when needed. Its ability to deal with a large number of providers and requesters working concurrently with a large number of differently typed and sized requests demonstrates the suitability of the approach for large multi-user service coordination environments such as cloud computing.

REFERENCES

Andersson, B., Bider, I., Johannesson, P., & Perjons, E. (2005). Towards a formal definition of goal-oriented business process patterns. *BPM Journal, 11*, 650–662.

Balzarotti, D., Costa, P., & Picco, G. P. (2007). The lights tuple space framework and its customization for context-aware applications. *Web Intelligence and Agent Systems, 5*(2), 215–231.

Cavallaro, L., & Di Nitto, E. (2008). An approach to adapt service requests to actual service interfaces. In *Proceedings of SEAMS Conference.*

Doberkat, E.-E., Franke, W., Gutenbeil, U., Hasselbring, W., Lammers, U., & Pahl, C. (1992). PROSET: A language for prototyping with sets. In *Proceedings Third International Workshop on Rapid System Prototyping* (pp. 235-248).

Gelernter, D. (1985). Generative communication in Linda. *ACM Transactions on Programming Languages and Systems, 7*(1), 80–112.

Johanson, B., & Fox, A. (2004). Extending Tuplespaces for coordination in interactive workspaces. *Journal of Systems and Software, 69*(3), 243–266.

Klusch, M., Fries, B., & Sycara, K. (2006). Automated semantic web service discovery with owlsmx. In *Proceedings of the Fifth International Joint Conference on Autonomous Agents and Multiagent Systems AAMAS '06,* (pp. 915–922). ACM.

Küngas, P., & Popova, V. (2011). Artifact-centric service interoperation. In *Estonian Information Society Yearbook 2010.* Estonian Department of State Information Systems.

Li, Z., & Parashar, M. (2005). Comet: A scalable coordination space for decentralized distributed environments. In *Proceedings of the Second International Workshop on Hot Topics in Peer-To-Peer Systems HOT-P2P,* (pp. 104-112). IEEE.

Moser, O., Rosenberg, F., & Dustdar, S. (2008). Non-intrusive monitoring and adaptation for WS-BPEL. In *Proceedings of the 17th International World Wide Web Conference (Web Engineering Track) WWW'08.*

Nixon, L., Antonechko, O., & Tolksdorf, R. (2007). Towards Semantic Tuplespace computing: The Semantic Web spaces system. In *Proceedings of the 2007 ACM Symposium on Applied Computing SAC'07,* (pp. 360-365). ACM.

Pahl, C. (2002). A formal composition and interaction model for a Web component platform. In *Proceedings ICALP'2002 Workshop on Formal Methods and Component Interaction, Electronic Notes on Computer Science ENTCS, 66*(4).

Pahl, C. (2005). Layered ontological modelling for Web service-oriented model-driven architecture. In *Proceedings European Conference on Model-Driven Architecture – Foundations and Applications ECMDA'2005, LNCS 3748* (pp. 88-102). Springer-Verlag.

Pahl, C. (2007). Semantic model-driven architecting of service-based software systems. *Information and Software Technology, 49*(8), 838–850.

Pahl, C., Gacitua-Decar, V., Wang, M. X., & Bandara, K. Y. (2011). A coordination space architecture for service collaboration and cooperation. In *Proceedings CAiSE Workshops* (pp. 366–377).

Pahl, C., & Zhu, Y. (2006). A semantical framework for the orchestration and choreography of web services. In *Proceedings of the International Workshop on Web Languages and Formal Methods (WLFM 2005). Electronic Notes in Theoretical Computer Science, 151*(2), 3–18.

Sirin, E., Hendler, J., & Parsia, B. (2003). Semi-automatic composition of web services using semantic descriptions. In *Proceedings Web Services: Modeling, Architecture and Infrastructure Workshop at ICEIS 2003* (pp. 17–24).

Sycara, K., Paolucci, M., Ankolekar, A., & Srinivasan, N. (2003). Automated discovery, interaction and composition of Semantic Web services. *Journal of Web Semantics, 1*, 27–46.

Wang, M., Yapa Bandara, K., & Pahl, C. (2009). Integrated constraint violation handling for dynamic service composition. In *Proceedings IEEE International Conference on Services Computing SCC 2009* (pp. 168-175).

Web Ontology Working Group. (2004). *OWL-S - semantic markup for Web services*. W3C. Retrieved 26 January, 2012, from http://www.w3.org/Submission/OWL-S/

ADDITIONAL READING

Alonso, G., Casati, F., Kuno, H., & Machiraju, V. (2004). *Web services - Concepts, architectures and applications*. Berlin, Germany: Springer-Verlag.

Ankolekar, A., Burstein, M., Hobbs, J. R., Lassila, O., Martin, D., & McDermott, D. ... Sycara, K. (2002). DAML-S: Web service description for the semantic web. In I. Horrocks & J. Hendler (Eds.), *Proceedings ISWC 2002, LNCS vol. 2342,* (pp. 279–348). Heidelberg, Germany: Springer-Verlag.

Arroyo, A., & Sicilia, M.-A. (2008). SOPHIE: Use case and evaluation. *Information and Software Technology, 50*(12), 1266–1280.

Baader, F., McGuiness, D., Nardi, D., & Schneider, P. P. (2003). *The description logic handbook*. Cambridge, UK: Cambridge University Press.

Brogi, A., & Popescu, R. (2006). Automated generation of BPEL adapters. In *Proceedings IC-SOC'06 LNCS 4294* (pp. 27-39). Springer-Verlag.

Buyya, R., Broberg, J., & Goscinski, A. (Eds.). (2011). *Cloud computing - Principles and paradigms*. Hoboken, NJ: Wiley.

Coalition, D. A. M. L.-S. (2002). DAML-S: Web services description for the Semantic Web. In *Proceedings First International Semantic Web Conference ISWC 2002, LNCS 2342* (pp. 279-291). Springer-Verlag.

Dingwall-Smith, A., & Finkelstein, A. (2007). Checking complex compositions of Web services against policy constraints. In *Proceedings 5th International Workshop on Modelling, Simulation, Verification and Validation of Enterprise Information Systems*.

Doberkat, E.-E., Franke, W., Gutenbeil, U., Hasselbring, W., Lammers, U., & Pahl, C. (1992). *PROSET - Prototyping with sets, language definition. Software-Engineering Memo 15*. Universität GH Essen.

Doberkat, E.-E., Hasselbring, W., & Pahl, C. (1996). Investigating strategies for cooperative planning of independent agents through prototype evaluation. In *Proceedings First International Conference on Coordination Models and Languages, LNCS 1061,* (pp. 416-419). Springer-Verlag.

Erl, T. (2005). *Service-oriented architecture – Concepts, technology and design*. Prentice Hall.

Gacitua-Decar, V., & Pahl, C. (2009). Automatic business process pattern matching for enterprise services design. In *Proceedings 4th International Workshop on Service- and Process-Oriented Software Engineering (SOPOSE-09)*. IEEE Press.

Hayes, B. (2008). Cloud computing. *Communications of the ACM, 51*(7), 9–11.

Lara, R., Stollberg, M., Polleres, A., Feier, C., Bussler, C., & Fensel, D. (2005). Web service modeling ontology. *Applied Ontology, 1*(1), 77–106.

NIST. (2003). *Process specification language (PSL) ontology - Current theories and extensions*. National Institute of Standards and Technology, USA. Retrieved 26 January, 2012, from http://www.mel.nist.gov/psl/ontology.html

Pahl, C. (2001). A Pi-calculus based framework for the composition and replacement of components. In *Proceedings Conference on Object-Oriented Programming, Systems, Languages, and Applications OOPSLA'2001 - Workshop on Specification and Verification of Component-Based Systems*. ACM Press.

Pahl, C. (2005). A conceptual architecture for semantic web services development and deployment. *International Journal of Web and Grid Services, 1*(3/4), 287–304.

Pahl, C. (2007). An ontology for software component description and matching. *International Journal on Software Tools for Technology Transfer, 9*(2), 169–178.

Pahl, C. (2010). Dynamic adaptive service architecture - Towards coordinated service composition. In *European Conference on Software Architecture ECSA'2010, LNCS*, (pp. 472-475). Springer-Verlag.

Pahl, C., Giesecke, S., & Hasselbring, W. (2009). Ontology-based modelling of architectural styles. *Information and Software Technology, 1*(12), 1739–1749.

Rao, J., & Su, X. (2004). A survey of automated Web service composition methods. In *Proceedings Intl. Workshop on Semantic Web Services and Web Process Composition 2004, LNCS 3387*, (pp. 43-54). Springer-Verlag.

Schaffert, S. (2004). *Xcerpt: A rule-based query and transformation language for the Web*. PhD Thesis, University of Munich.

Semantic Web Services Language (SWSL) Committee. (2006). *Semantic Web services framework (SWSF)*. Retrieved 26 January, 2012, from http://www.daml.org/services/swsf/1.0/

Tsai, W. T., Xiao, B., Chen, Y., & Paul, R. A. (2006). Consumer-centric service-oriented architecture: A new approach. In *Proceedings IEEE Workshop on Software Technologies for Future Embedded and Ubiquitous Systems, and Workshop on Collaborative Computing, Integration, and Assurance* (pp. 175-180).

Utschig-Utschig, C. (2008). *Architecting event-driven SOA: A primer*. Oracle. Retrieved 26 January, 2012, from http://www.oracle.com/technology/pub/articles/oraclesoa eventarch.html

Wang, M., Yapa Bandara, K., & Pahl, C. (2009). Integrated constraint violation handling for dynamic service composition. In *Proceedings IEEE International Conference on Services Computing SCC 2009* (pp. 168-175).

KEY TERMS AND DEFINITIONS

Cloud Broker: A mediator that matches service provider and requestor according to their needs and supports the negotiation of an agreement.

Cloud Service: A cloud service is a software service (typically a Web service) offered as part of a cloud platform (at SaaS, PaaS, or IaaS layer).

Coordination Space: An infrastructure that acts as a mediation tool between service requestors and service provider through the provision of standard operations to deposit and retrieve coordination data.

Dynamic Service Matching: Refers to the association of a provided service to a service request at runtime that satisfies the requirements of the requestor.

Semantic Service Description: Usually ontology-based annotation of services to cover functional and non-functional properties for automated processing.

Service Coordination: Refers to protocols, languages and tools that support the coordinated interaction between service users and service providers.

Tuple Space: The tuple space architecture is a means of communication in distributed programming that allows a flexible coordination of participants.

Chapter 10
A Framework for Situation–Aware Adaptation of Service–Based Applications

Ioannis Patiniotiakis
National Technical University of Athens, Greece

Yiannis Verginadis
National Technical University of Athens, Greece

Nikos Papageorgiou
National Technical University of Athens, Greece

Dimitris Apostolou
National Technical University of Athens, Greece

Gregoris Mentzas
National Technical University of Athens, Greece

ABSTRACT

This work presents Situation Action Networks, a new framework for modeling Service-Based Application adaptation triggered by interesting or critical situations. The framework is based on a goal model able to track at run time the fulfillment of goals. Situation Action Networks are tree-like hierarchical structures which enable goal decomposition into sub-goals and primitive actions in a recursive fashion which provides goal seeking execution plans, as a sequence of primitive actions. Situation Action Networks are dynamic and can evolve at runtime by using their inherent planning capabilities.

INTRODUCTION

Future Internet, an initiative emerged to bring together and interconnect services, objects and things of the real world to meet the changing global needs of business, is challenging the applications which need to consolidate various technologies such as Service-Oriented Architectures, Cloud Computing and Wireless Sensor Networks and

handle dynamic and continuous changes propagated though the different technology stacks. This poses the challenge of application adaptation, the ability to reconfigure applications so as to support continuous, unimpeded augmentation of services in response to changing environmental circumstances.

The notion of adaptation has been extensively studied in the computer science domain as it is

DOI: 10.4018/978-1-4666-2089-6.ch010

considered as one of the most desired functionalities of today's highly dynamic, distributed and ubiquitous environments in the service-oriented environment (Kazhamiakin et al, 2010). Adaptation, the process of modifying a system or application in order to satisfy new requirements and to fit new situations, can be performed either because monitoring has revealed a problem or because the application identifies possible optimizations or because its execution context has changed.

Our work focuses on the discovery of critical or interesting situations of the environment that are not ordinary – so called 'extraordinary' situations – and we employ event processing as a means to detect and reason about situations. In event-driven architectures, services generate, consume and exchange events asynchronously, following the pub-sub paradigm. Events which are relevant to specific Service Based Applications (SBAs) (Hielscher et al, 2009) can provide a means to discover extraordinary situations. Event processing, a paradigm of choice in many monitoring and reactive applications, enables events to be propagated, filtered aggregated and composed into mode complex events enabling detection of situations (Hinze et al, 2009). Our work aims to enhance the user's experience when interacting with an SBA by adapting the system behaviour to situations. In this work, we present specific requirements for situation-aware adaptivity and outline Situation Action Networks (SANs), a modeling and execution framework for recommending SBA adaptations in response to extraordinary situations.

REQUIREMENTS FOR SITUATION-AWARE ADAPTATION

To describe the requirements for situation-aware adaptation, we consider a crisis management scenario, which focuses on crisis situations related to a nuclear accident. Consider for example the case of a nuclear accident that caused radiation leakage and a grid of radiation sensors that monitors radiation levels in the area around the plant. The emergency plan prescribes that the Civil Protection Service subscribes to all sensors in a certain perimeter around the plant in order to detect the movement of the radioactive cloud. An extraordinary situation could be that in a short time after the accident, the wind increases and changes direction (e.g., North-West direction) while the weather forecast indicates that the wind direction will remain the same for the rest of the day. The ideal reaction to this situation, both in terms of cost and load processing, would be for the system to be subscribed at the right time only to events coming from sensors located south-east of the plant and are in a certain distance from it, which depends on the wind's velocity or other weather conditions like humidity. Based on the information gathered from radiation sensors, authorities expect that certain cities south-east of the plant will be affected and need to inform people in these areas to follow some precautions or evacuate the area. This is normally done by transmitting TV and Radio messages, however, in the extraordinary situation in which there is a power loss, a proper reaction would be to deploy police forces and inform people using manual means such as speakerphones.

By studying similar scenarios identified within the PLAY FP7 ICT project (www.play-project.eu), we summarize the following requirements for situation-aware adaptivity (Table 1).

SITUATION ACTION NETWORKS

To address the specific requirements for situation-aware adaptivity, we need a mechanism able to model desired, meaningful SBA reactions to extraordinary situations without predefining all possible details at design time. The approach presented in this work starts from powerful models to enforce the fulfillment of goals by SBAs. It assumes the adoption of a goal model able to track the fulfill-

Table 1. Requirements for situation-aware adaptivity

Requirement	Description
Situation Awareness	Situation awareness refers to the discovery of extraordinary situations. These situations are detected through the processing of the events generated both at the internal and external to the application environments. For example: the 'no measurements' situation occurs when no 'radiation measurement' events are received from measurement stations, probably due to electricity shortage.
Context checking and updating	This requirement ensures that the exchanged events and occurring situations are related to the application or service or process context, and furthermore using context to 'get the meaning' of events and situations. For example: weather information along with details of the detected nuclear accident could denote interesting/critical situations.
Planning reactions	The ability to recommend a change in the normal process to circumvent an extraordinary situation, for instance: to dispatch police forces in the affected cities and inform people using speakerphones in case of electricity black-out instead of using the mass media. It is expected that in several cases the reactions to take will not be known a priori or even at design time. The approach for event-driven adaptivity should be able to select the most suitable reaction at runtime, when the reactions need to be taken.
Adapting an SBA based on detected situations	This requirement is related to the analysis of the SBA and to the recommendations, based on situations, of appropriate adjustments to the service parameters and overall execution flow. For example, the Civil Protection Service should adapt to support informing people using manual means instead of using the mass media.
Finding relevant event sources at the right time	The ability to recommend subscription to event sources as a response to exceptional situations, e.g.,: detection of nuclear accident and north-west direction strong wind with the weather forecast indicating that it will continue for the rest of the day constitutes an interesting situation upon which an SBA should react and try to acquire meaningful information from a subset of all the possible event sources.

ment of goals at run time. We propose Situation Action Networks (SANs), a modeling framework that can be used for defining systems' reactions to extraordinary situations that can occur before the goal is fulfilled. In order to deal with the challenge of not having to model all possible reaction details at design time, we adopt the idea of hierarchal goal decomposition from Hierarchical Task Networks (HTNs), see e.g., (Nau et al, 2005) and Behavior Trees (BTs), see e.g., (Mehta, Ram, 2009). The main underpinning of SANs is to allow for high level definitions of goals, extraordinary situations and corresponding reactions at design time and to provide a reasoning mechanism that will be able to recommend at run time adapted reactions to detected extraordinary situations. SANs are tree structures whose nodes carry specific semantics used to model goal decompositions, enriched with flow control and planning capabilities. They provide a means to recursively decompose goals into subgoals, subgoals of subgoals, down to primitive actions. They furthermore provide plans for seeking and achieving the high-level goals. A plan is the order in which primitive actions should

be taken, and the way they should be combined, in order to fulfill a goal.

The simplest SAN possible is a two level tree with a parent (root) node and three child nodes, each of them having a distinguished role. Parent node models the Goal sought. The leftmost child node describes a situation that must occur, in order to start goal seeking. The middle child node requires that a specific condition is true before goal seeking starts, but after situation occurs. The rightmost child node specifies the action to be taken in order to fulfill the goal. Rightmost node can also be a subgoal node (or second-level goal) with its own three child nodes, or it can even be a construct joining several subgoals in sequence or in parallel. These possibilities will be presented in the following sections. The basic layout of a SAN is depicted in Figure 1.

Goal / Subgoal nodes model Goals and Sub-Goals that must be achieved and provide the means for Goal decomposition. Subgoal nodes are Goal nodes with a parent node. When a Goal is visited, the tree traversal immediately continues to its child nodes, from left-most to right-most. If all

Figure 1. Basic modeling primitives of SANs. (The black arrow indicates the order of visiting child nodes. Parent is visited first.)

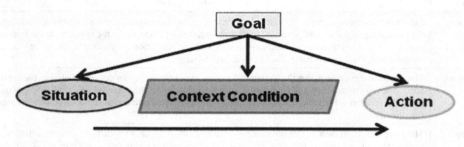

of child nodes are successful then the Goal is successful too. Situation nodes are leaf nodes with a Goal node as parent. They model extraordinary situations expressed as Complex Event Patterns (CEPATs) (Anicic et al, 2009). Context Condition nodes are leaf nodes, with a Goal parent. They express contextual conditions that must be true in order to perform an action. Action nodes are leaf nodes with a Goal as parent. They describe primitive tasks to be carried out, as soon as the node is visited (if the situation occurs and the contextual condition is true). Tasks must successfully complete or fail before SAN execution algorithm continues. Decorator nodes are inserted between a Goal node and an Action or Subgoal node, and carry behavioural specifications on how the subordinate Actions or Subgoals should be executed. Depending on the type of Decorator, SAN traversal can be modified (loop, condition, timer, exception handler and success or failure decorators) or interact with and influence contextual information (counter and condition decorators).

SAN execution is defined as the SAN tree traversal, i.e. visiting of SAN nodes one by one, and the execution of tasks associated to each one, using the parameters defined in the node. Therefore, SAN nodes are not mere structural elements of the trees, as ordinary tree nodes, but rather 'active' entities containing certain types of functionality and information. The traversal

pattern of SAN trees is similar to the 'depth-first in preorder' binary tree traversal algorithm, extended to support flow control, process logic and planning constructs. The order of depth-first preorder traversal is visiting the parent node first and then its (immediate) child nodes from left to right, i.e. parent node, left child, right child. If a child node has children it is also traversed using the same pattern.

SANs and their execution algorithm differ from binary trees and the 'depth-first in preorder' algorithm in that they use three child nodes (Situation, Context Condition and Action child nodes) rather than two as in binary trees. Therefore the traversal order is modified to include the middle child node and it becomes Parent / Goal node, Left / Situation child node, Middle / Context Condition node and Right / Action or Sub-goal node. A second difference is that SAN nodes are of different types, namely Goal/Subgoal nodes, Situation nodes, Context Condition nodes, Action nodes, Decorator nodes. Each class of nodes, apart from a name / identifier, it also requires that its instance nodes have some extra class-specific information; more specifically, the node execution parameters. SAN nodes are 'executable entities' meaning that when visited, during traversal, they carry out certain tasks. The node semantics contain task description and execution parameters. The task to be carried out varies among different node classes. It is also

Figure 2. SAN for recommending means of informing the public in case of nuclear contamination

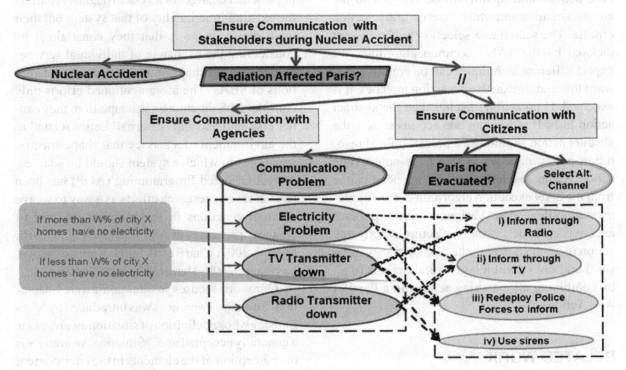

worth mentioning that SAN traversal freezes while a node task is been executed.

ILLUSTRATIVE EXAMPLE AND DISCUSSION

In this section we present a SAN usage example in the crisis scenario. The example (Figure 2) models extraordinary situations that may occur when aiming to inform the public about a nuclear emergency, such as electricity black-outs, damages to mass media or broadcast services, etc. The related SAN is a two-level tree where the first level checks whether it is necessary to monitor for extraordinary situations related to the primary goal which is to inform public about a nuclear emergency, whereas the second level monitors situations that might hamper the authorities' capability to inform the public and recommends alternative means of communication.

The example highlights the concept of situation abstraction whose purpose is to model generic situations which can be mapped to various real-world situations occurring at run-time. The blue ovals in the dashed box under abstract situation 'Inform Problem' are examples of situations that might be detected by the abstract situation. Additionally, the example includes abstract actions, leaf tree nodes which when visited they have to determine on-the-fly the task they should carry out, selecting it from a predetermined repository of actions called Action Pool. The green ovals in the second dashed box are the actions in the action pool associated to the related abstract action 'Inform'. The arrows connecting the possible situations to possible actions are a mere example. They are not a fixed or predetermined situation-to-action mapping. In fact, the mapping is decided at run-time based on the nature of the detected situation, the context metadata and an action search method needed for examining all action pool actions and identify those relevant to the current situation and which meet certain selection criteria. The search and selection method is not dictated by the SAN execution algorithm; we expect different techniques can be employed toward this end. If exactly one action matches, it is executed. If no action matches then the abstract action fails. If more than one actions match, the abstract action should use a predetermined resolution policy in order to select the appropriate action. Again, resolution policies are not dictated from the SAN execution algorithm but are implementation-dependent. Various resolution policies are envisaged such as ones selecting exactly one action (e.g., the one with the best similarity measure) and ones combining several actions (e.g., by combining all matching actions in a Parallel Any Action).

RELATED WORK

The main body of work related to service adaptation focuses (see e.g., Moser et al, 2008; Baresi et al, 2007; Siljee et al, 2005) on QoS parameters (e.g., response time, failure rates, availability) and infrastructure characteristics (e.g., load, bandwidth) which are monitored and adjustments are made if there are deviations from some expected values. These approaches follow the reactive approach to adaptation, i.e., the modification of the application takes place after the critical event happened or a problem occurred. There exist also proactive approaches such as the ones that systematically test services to uncover failures and deviations of the quality of services from the expected one. Existing approaches for testing SBAs mostly focus on testing during design time, which is similar to testing of traditional software systems (Gehlert et al, 2011) but there are also others like PROSA (Hielscher et al, 2008) that exploit online testing solutions, at run-time in order to proactively trigger adaptations. In the same direction, regression testing aims at check-

ing whether changes of a system negatively affect the existing functionality of that system but their main disadvantage is that they constrain it by considering the exchange of individual services as the only mechanism for performing adaptations of SBAs. The aforementioned efforts only consider QoS parameters in adaptation; they cannot take into account 'external' issues related to the environment of a service that shape specific situations, in which a system should be adapted. Aspect-Oriented Programming (AOP) has been used in several research efforts as a way to weave alternative actions in services that are part of business processes at run-time (see e.g., Charfi, Mezini, 2007; Charfi et al, 2009; Karastoyanova, Leymann, 2009; Hermosillo et al, 2010).

Our work focuses in situation-aware adaptation. Situation awareness was introduced by Mica Endsley whose definition of situation awareness is a generally accepted one: "Situation Awareness is the perception of the elements in the environment within a volume of time and space, the comprehension of their meaning, and the projection of their status in the near future" (Endsley, Connors, 2008; Endsley, 1995). Since these original works a lot of situation-related research has been carried out and has become a critical issue in domains in which there is the need to automatically and continuously identify and act on complex, often incomplete and unpredictable, dynamic situations; as a result, effective methods of situation recognition, prediction, reasoning, and control are required. Gartner considers event-driven SOA for situation-awareness one of five patterns in practicing SOA for the design of business applications (Natis, 2011).

Various situation representation approaches have been recently proposed, ranging from event-based approaches (Cardell-Oliver, Liu, 2010) to ontology-based ones. The SAWA approach (Kokar et al, 2009) is based on an upper ontology for situation awareness. The situation ontology by (Yau et al, 2005) incorporates situations as well as contexts and classifies situations into atomic and composite ones. In the context of event processing, situation is often defined as an event occurrence that might require a reaction (Adi, Etzion, 2004). The latter is the approach we follow in our work which we combine with a hierarchical decomposition technique to enable deriving relevant reactions to extraordinary situations, at run time.

DISCUSSION AND CONCLUSION

SANs provide a goal-driven approach to modeling and executing adaptivity in SBAs. They enable analyzing real-life problems by dividing them into high-level goals and a small set of sub-goals to be pursued in order to fulfill or implement the goals. Table 2 outlines how SANs address the requirements for situation-aware adaptivity presented in section 2.

We are currently developing an RDF-based language for translating the graphical models of SANs using a dedicated editor component. Also, their actual execution will be undertaken by a dedicated SAN execution engine that implements the appropriate algorithms for the traversal of the hierarchical structure of SANs. Currently SANs support built-in adaptation (Bucchiarone et al,

2009) of SBAs, i.e. possible adaptation configurations are fixed and known a priori (i.e. design time). In abstraction-based adaptation, adaptation needs are fixed, but the possible configurations in which adaptation is triggered, are not known a priori. Our future plans include the experimentation with search and selection mechanisms that will enable SANs to take advantage of the abstract actions and action pools and support abstraction-based adaptation. Finally, we plan to work on dynamic adaptation, where adaptation needs that may occur at runtime are not known at design time, by trying to match at run-time event semantics with situation and action semantics using semantic similarity approaches.

SANs can be considered as an ECA extension framework. Several well established approaches in the area of ECA based systems (Amit (Adi, Etzion, 2004), RuleCore (Seiriö, Berndtsson, 2005), Mars (May et al, 2005), XChange EQ (Bry, Eckert, 2007), etc.) have been consolidated as reliable solutions in the expert systems world. Our approach goes a step further by providing a hybrid view of ECA and planned based systems by exploiting their advantages. We introduce goal decomposition as a means of resolving extraordinary situations and introduce hierarchical structuring

Table 2. SAN support for situation-aware adaptivity requirements

Requirement	Description
Situation Awareness	SANs encompass Situation Awareness capabilities by using Complex Event Processing (CEP) which enable detection of situations through the processing of the events generated using complex event pattern detection.
Context checking and updating	SANs use contextual information in their Context Condition nodes, which check if Goal evaluation can continue.
Planning reactions	SANs provide a simple but flexible planning mechanism for coping with the lack of knowledge or uncertainty at design time. In the ill-defined points, SAN designers may use Abstract Action nodes, which will search for and choose the most suitable action, exactly the time it is needed, taking into consideration the current situation as well as the context. Effectively, Abstract Action nodes involve a planning step and then carry out the action chosen.
Adapting an SBA based on detected situations	SANs can be used for recommendation purposes because they can model both well-defined recommendation processes with a priori known recommended Actions, as well as less-concrete processes that include Abstract Actions instead of concrete ones. In such cases, Abstract Actions search in Action Pools containing Recommended Actions and ready-made recommendation-seeking SANs.
Finding relevant event sources at the right time	

of the goals sought and the behaviours exhibited. Thus we constitute a way to follow or predict the path of execution and address causality and maintenance issues. In addition the use of abstract situations and actions along with relevant search and selection methods and resolution policies that can be used, is considered as an additional step towards mitigating design efforts and bottlenecks that can be discovered in pure planning based frameworks (Ferreira H.M., Ferreira, D., 2006; Marrella, Mecella, 2011).

ACKNOWLEDGMENT

Research reported in this work has been partially funded by the European Commission under projects FP7 ICT 258659 (PLAY) and 262305 (REFLEX)

REFERENCES

Adi, A., & Etzion, O. (2004). Amit - The situation manager. *International Journal on Very Large Data Bases*, *13*(2), 177–203.

Anicic, D., Fodor, P., Stühmer, R., & Stojanovic, N. (2009). *Event-driven approach for logic-based complex event processing*. Paper presented at the 12th IEEE International Conference on Computational Science and Engineering, Washington DC, USA.

Baresi, L., Guinea, S., & Plebani, P. (2007). Policies and aspects for the supervision of BPEL processes. *Advanced Information Systems Engineering, LNCS, 4495*, 340–354.

Bry, F., & Eckert, M. (2007). *Rule-based composite event queries: The language XChange EQ and its semantics*. Paper presented at the International Conference on Web Reasoning and Rule Systems. Springer.

Bucchiarone, A., Cappiello, C., Di Nitto, E., Kazhamiakin, R., Mazza, V., & Pistore, M. (2009). *Design for adaptation of service-based applications: Main issues and requirements* (pp. 467–476). ICSOC/ServiceWave Workshops.

Cardell-Oliver, R., & Liu, W. (2010). Representation and recognition of situations in sensor networks. *IEEE Communications Magazine*, (March): 112–117.

Charfi, A., Dinkelaker, T., & Mezini, M. (2009). A plug-in architecture for self-adaptive web service compositions. In *Proceedings of the IEEE International Conference on Web Services (ICWS '09)*, (pp. 35–42). IEEE Computer Society.

Charfi, A., & Mezini, M. (2007). Ao4bpel: An aspect-oriented extension to BPEL. *World Wide Web (Bussum)*, *10*(3), 309–344.

Endsley, M. R., & Connors, E. S. (2008). Situation awareness: State of the art. *2008 Power and Energy Society Meeting* (pp. 1–4).

Endsley, R. (1995). Toward a theory of situation awareness in dynamic systems: Situation awareness. *Human Factors*, *37*, 32–64.

Ferreira, H. M., & Ferreira, D. (2006). An integrated life cycle for workflow management based on learning and planning. *International Journal of Cooperative Information Systems*, *15*(4), 485–505.

Gehlert, A., Metzger, A., Karastoyanova, D., Kazhamiakin, R., Pohl, K., Leymann, F., & Pistore, M. (2011). Integrating perfective and corrective adaptation of service-based applications. In S. Dustdar & F. Li (Eds.), *Service engineering: European research results book* (pp. 137-169). Springer. Hermosillo, G., Seinturier L., & Duchien, L (2010). Using complex event processing for dynamic business process adaptation. In *Proceedings of the IEEE SCC 2010*, (pp. 466–473).

Hielscher, J., Kazhamiakin, R., Metzger, A., & Pistore, M. (2008). A framework for proactive selfadaptation of service-based applications based on online testing. In the *Proceedings of the ServiceWave 2008*, (pp. 122-133).

Hielscher, J., Metzger, A., & Kazhamiakin, R. (2009). Taxonomy of adaptation principles and mechanisms. *S-Cube project, Deliverable # CD-JRA-1.2.2*, (pp. 39-56). Retrieved from http://www.s-cube-network.eu/

Hinze, A., Sachs, K., & Buchmann, A. (2009 July). *Event-based applications and enabling technologies*. Paper presented in DEBS 2009, July 6-9, Nashville, USA.

Karastoyanova, D., & Leymann, F. (2009). BPEL'n'aspects: Adapting service orchestration logic. In the *Proceedings of the IEEE International Conference on Web Services, ICWS 2009* (pp. 222–229).

Kazhamiakin, R., Benbernou, S., Baresi, L., Plebani, P., Uhlig, M., & Barais, O. (2010). Adaptation of service-based systems. *Service Research Challenges and Solutions for the Future Internet, LNCS, 6500*, 117–156.

Kokar, M. M., Matheus, C. J., & Baclawski, K. (2009). Ontology-based situation awareness. *Information Fusion, 10*, 83–98.

Marrella, A., & Mecella, M. (2011). *Continuous planning for solving business process adaptivity*. Paper presented at the 12th International Working Conference on Business Process Modeling, Development and Support, BPMDS 2011.

May, W., Alferes, J. J., & Amador, R. (2005). Active rules in the Semantic Web: Dealing with language heterogeneity. In the *Proceedings of International Conference on Rules and Rule Markup Languages for the Semantic Web* (pp. 30–44).

Mehta, M., & Ram, A. (2009). Runtime behavior adaptation for real-time interactive games. *IEEE Transactions on Computational Intelligence and AI in Games, 1*(3), 187–199.

Moser, O., Rosenberg, F., & Dustdar, S. (2008). Non-intrusive monitoring and service adaptation for WS-BPEL. In the *Proceedings of the International Conference on World Wide Web*, (pp. 815-824).

Natis, Y. V. (2011). *How to balance the business benefits and IT costs of SOA*. (Gartner Research, ID Number: G00209630).

Nau, D., Au, T. C., Ilghami, O., Kuter, U., Muñoz-Avila, H., & Murdock, J. W. (2005). Applications of SHOP and SHOP2. *IEEE Intelligent Systems, 20*(2).

Seiriö, M., & Berndtsson, M. (2005). Design and implementation of an ECA rule markup language. *LNCS, 3791*, 98–112.

Siljee, J., Bosloper, I., Nijhuis, J., & Hammer, D. (2005). DySOA: Making service systems self-adaptive. In the *Proceedings of the 3rd International Conference Service-Oriented Computing – ICSOC* (pp. 255–268).

Yau, S. S., Huang, D., Gong, H., & Davulcu, H. (2005). Situation-awareness for adaptive coordination in service-based systems. In the *Proceedings of the 2005 29th Annual International Computer Software and Applications Conference* (pp. 107–112).

KEY TERMS AND DEFINITIONS

Adaptation: Is a process of modifying Service-Based Aplications in order to satisfy new requirements and to fit new situations dictated by the environment on the basis of adaptation strategies designed by the system integrator [http://www.s-cube-network.eu/km/terms/a/adaptation].

Behavior Trees (BT): Is a technique and a formalism used in modeling the behaviour and logic of computer programmes. BTs have especially been proven as a technique in the field of Game AI. They enable logic/behaviour modularity, scalability and reuse.

Event-Driven Architecture (EDA): Is a software architecture pattern promoting the production, detection, consumption of, and reaction to events.

Goal Decomposition: Is the process of breaking a complex goal, which represents the solution to a complex problem, into simpler tasks. In this work, we consider a tree-like decomposition paradigm where a goal is analyzed into one or more sub-goals, which in turn can be further analyzed to other sub-goals or atomic tasks realizing the (sub-)goals.

Service-Based Application (SBA): Is an application comprised from a number of (possibly) independent services, available in a network. [http://www.s-cube-network.eu/km/terms/s/service-based-application].

Situation Action Network (SAN): Is an innovative modeling framework used for defining and implementing system reactions to situation changes. SAN encompasses situation awareness capabilities through the use of events, context detection and processing, and goal-based planning features.

Situation Awareness: Is the perception of the environmental elements with respect to time and/or space, the comprehension of their meaning, and the projection of their status after some variable has changed, such as time. In EDA applications situation awareness is achieved by exploiting incoming events.

Chapter 11
F-DRARE:
A Framework for Deterministic Runtime Adaptation of Cyber Physical Systems

Fahad Bin Tariq
University of Paderborn, Germany

Sandeep Korrapati
University of Paderborn, Germany

ABSTRACT

Modern systems are designed to have various non-functional attributes such as fault tolerance, robustness, et cetera. The ability of systems to adapt while being connected to a global network as in Cyber Physical Systems, presents new opportunities. Extra-functional qualities may be extended to nodes in the network that initially were devoid of them. It is inevitable that such vast global networks will consist of computationally constrained units. Extending such computationally constrained nodes with the ability to adapt is already a difficult challenge, which becomes more difficult when added with the constraint of timely behavior. In this chapter, the authors present an approach to tackle the issue of runtime adaptation on computationally constrained systems with real-time constraints. The focus is on systems with only a single general purpose processor, with the responsibility to run the system and application software. The authors introduce their framework towards this aim, followed by the architecture and a case study.

INTRODUCTION

Software is the most flexible entity on machines that employ programmable devices to carry out their tasks. The inherent flexibility in software instructions (due to their earlier form as punch cards and now in the form of voltage levels) translates into a degree of reusability for the machines or platforms on which they execute. By a mere change in software, the same platform can be used to fulfill different objectives. The desktop machines and handheld devices of today running

DOI: 10.4018/978-1-4666-2089-6.ch011

countless software on the same platform serve as an example. Further being connected to a global network such as the Internet allows users of these devices to access various software services to either increase their quality of experience or fulfill a timely need. To fully harness the possibilities provided by an inherently flexible entity such as software, changing the software while the system is operational, based on various parameters such as the current environment, new objectives etc. is necessary. The system is then said to have adapted during runtime to the environment or any changes in objectives. Some of the advantages of the ability to adapt during runtime are, the delaying of decisions from design time to runtime relying on more up-to-date context information resulting in higher decision accuracy, as well as the acquisition of new behavior to tackle new problems.

The pioneering work in runtime adaptation (a.k.a. runtime evolution, dynamic updates, online adjustment) in general may be attributed to the work done in Fabry (1976). In the area of embedded systems, the structure and behavior of a system are typically closed without any room for runtime adaptation. This is because safety and timeliness are the dominant qualities that govern system design in this domain. But due to the benefits that accompany the ability of a system to adapt, it was only a matter of time and recent years have shown an increased interest by the embedded systems community in harnessing the benefits associated with it. Runtime adaptation is the ability of a system to change its behavior and/or structure while remaining in a desirable state of operation. A desirable state of operation is a relative term depending on the domain of application. In a time-critical system a desirable state is where all deadlines are met whereas in a non-time-critical system a desirable state may be certain functional and/or QoS objectives.

Many reasons exist for having runtime adaptation as a characteristic property of the system. Along with an increase in system complexity as well as the complexity of the development process, the costs and efforts to maintain them have also increased. A system with the ability to adapt reduces maintenance costs by inherently supporting change during the runtime phase of the system lifecycle. Factors such as computational load and communication requirements may change overtime resulting in different overall resource requirements. Node failures in a distributed environment may require topological restructuring and load balancing such as the sharing of processing load or the creation of new connections. Systems with the ability to adapt enable them to acquire new properties in such scenarios, for example, fault tolerance.

The increasing complexity of embedded systems is due, but not limited, to the increasing quality and quantity of the resources involved. Multi-core processing units, sophisticated storage and communication devices are examples of the underlying platforms that some embedded systems are enjoying. Interestingly such resources are there in the first place due to increasing complexity brought onto the system by ever-increasing demands of more functionality (realized by software). Dividing the load in a distributed environment is one solution commonly practiced, but this results in a further requirement of managing the distributed resources. Having stated the above, increasing the connectivity of systems at various levels does give rise to potential benefits that have attracted a keen interest by both research and industry. New paradigms such as Cyber Physical Systems (Lee, 2008) and the Cyber Biosphere (Rammig, 2008) as well as concepts such as the Internet of Things aim to address these benefits. The Future Internet aims take standalone devices, autonomous systems, consumer electronics, vehicles etc. into the fold of the internet. From an adaptation perspective, being connected to a source of virtually un-limited resources, information and behavior opens up many possibilities. Behavior and qualities may be acquired by systems that were not present initially.

It is inevitable that the vast global network(s) mentioned above will consist of computationally constrained units. The concept of swarms consists of simple computational and communication units connected with similar units resulting in complex behavior (Dorigo & Birattari, 2007). Another example is of a group of communicating mobile robots called Bebots (Herbrechtsmeier, Witkowski, & Rückert, 2009). A Bebot at the individual level is a robot with a simple architecture but multiple Bebots communicate via an ad-hoc network and combine to execute complex behavior. Another more common example is a sensor network, which relies on very simple but large number of stationary sensing nodes, possibly distributed over a vast area to fulfill application specific tasks, such as the acquisition of environmental data. Extending such computationally constrained nodes with the ability to adapt is already a difficult challenge, which becomes more difficult when added with the constraint of timely behavior. This constraint stems from presence of the node in the real-time computation domain. The node must then guarantee all deadlines, as required by real-time systems, implying the need for deterministic adaptation.

In this chapter we present an approach to tackle the issue of runtime adaptation on computationally constrained systems with real-time constraints. Our focus is on systems with only a single general purpose processor, with the responsibility to run the system and application software. We introduce our Framework towards this aim, followed by the architecture and a case study.

BACKGROUND

The systems under focus in this chapter belong to the real-time and embedded domain. A real-time system consists of deadlines that have to be guaranteed under all circumstances. Every task is assigned a deadline that has to be met. Strategies are used to guarantee that no event effects the timely completion of all tasks. For example, strategies for resource usage are employed ensuring the absence of deadlocks. Well known scheduling strategies such as the Earliest Deadline First (EDF), Rata Monotonic scheduling etc. are used to ensure all tasks are schedulable with their Worst Case Execution Times (WCET). An embedded system, as the name suggests, is embedded within another larger system and usually has the task to aid the larger system in a specific task. Modern vehicles such as cars and airplanes are equipped with a large number of embedded devices to aid in aspects ranging from sensitive control to on-board entertainment. Embedded Systems typically lack the luxury of high quality and quantity of resources and due to reasons such as cost and weight, make-do with lighter ones.

Traditionally real-time embedded systems have been designed as standalone devices. Remaining standalone provides the surety of deterministic behavior, another critical requirement of this domain. Although with good reason, as already mentioned, remaining closed to any outside influence does limit and deny the system from reaching a more desirable state unforeseen during design time.

The term Cyber Physical Systems was coined around 2006 and one of its aim is to address the limitation above. According to the US National Science Foundation:

The term Cyber Physical Systems refers to the tight conjoining of and coordination between computational and physical resources. We envision that the cyber-physical systems of tomorrow will far exceed those of today in terms of adaptability, autonomy, efficiency, functionality, reliability, safety, and usability. (www.nsf.gov)

A system with a tight conjoining of and coordination between computational and physical resources is one which opens up and interacts with the environment. Further to exceed in qualities mentioned above, it must open up to a new level, as Lee (2008) states:

Unlike more traditional embedded systems, a full-fledged Cyber Physical System is typically designed as a network of interacting elements with physical input and output instead of as standalone devices.

The challenge is to provide such connectivity and the ability to adapt along with the domain specific requirements of deterministic timely behavior with as little as one processing unit as is the focus of chapter.

The introduction of this chapter already stated that the idea of runtime adaptation has been present with some variation as far back as the pioneering work done by Fabry (1976). Variation in naming such as, online update, runtime reconfiguration etc. exist, as well as the systems under consideration, to approaches for achieving adaptation. For instance, Fabry in the cited work provides the ability to change Abstract Data Types with the scope of the change present in the program code and realized by using privileged instructions. A good survey on these variations can be found in Vandewoude and Berbers (2002a). The same authors present their work on a Java-based component system SEESCOA (Vandewoude & Berbers, 2002b) that employs the adapt-at-once technique. Ritzau et al., also present a Java based approach where the Java Virtual machine (JVM) is extended (Ritzau & Andersson, 2000). This work is notable since it uses another approach to adaptation, namely the adapt-on-demand approach. We differ from these and similar approaches with respect to the timing of the adaptation by employing the timed phases to achieve determinism, a top priority in hard real-time systems. Another difference is the special focus on processing constrained systems.

The Flexible Resource Manager tries to optimize system behavior using a heuristic based on latest requirements in Hojenski and Oberthür (2006). This is achieved by toggling between a set of pre-defined profiles to reach the goal of resource optimization. Besides resource optimization, our work enables the acquisition of new behavior un-defined at system design time. Heavier adaptive platforms such as the Simplex Architecture (Sha, Rajkumar, & Gagliardi, 1995), besides having other differences, are not suited to the target embedded system in our focus.

In Andersson, de Lemos, Malek, and Weyns (2009), we find a reference model for adaptive systems which enables a qualitative evaluation of systems with the ability to reflect upon themselves, a necessary quality for self-adaptive systems. This is done by analyzing a system via the given reflection prism.

F-DRARE: FRAMEWORK FOR DETERMINISTIC RUNTIME ADAPTATION OF REALTIME EMBEDDED SYSTEMS

Problems to Some Approaches for Adaptation

Embedded systems are designed to have long life cycles such as modern vehicles or those running industrial systems. Once deployed, they may run for periods ranging from months to decades (Koopman, 1996). Embedded systems found within unmanned devices such as autonomous submarines or mobile robots (Herbrechtsmeier et al., 2009) play a major role in helping these devices fulfill their tasks. The target destination of these and similar devices may be remotely located and they may be left there for large periods of time. It is inevitable that they come across changes in their context. This may include changes to other components working with the embedded system such as hardware replacement due to a failure. System objectives and requirements may evolve over time with changes in the environment. QoS requirements may vary over time as well as resource consumption. As already emphasized, to cater to these changes, the systems need to adapt while maintaining a safe level of operation.

The ability of systems to adapt while being connected to a global network as in Cyber Physical Systems, presents new opportunities. Extra-functional qualities may be extended to nodes in the network that initially were devoid of them. Further, an open adaptable system that does not limit its adaptation to pre-defined and pre-containing states needs to be connected to one or more sources that may provide the necessary components to switch to the new state. Integrating the ability to adapt in a system becomes challenging when the system is computationally constrained. Moreover, the challenge increases when timely behavior is required due to real-time requirements. The system must guarantee all deadlines therefore a deterministic approach to adaptation becomes imperative. Hence the question of when to adapt must be addressed with real-time deadlines involved. In literature, two common techniques namely (a) adapt-at-once (e.g. Ritzau and Andersson, 2000) and (b) adapt-on-demand (e.g. Vandewoude and Berbers, 2002b), are found. In the former, all the required adaptation steps are scheduled in a single block. The duration of this block is not fixed and depends on the amount of adaptation. In the latter, adaptation takes place only when the functionality, to be directly affected by the adaptation, is accessed. In the first case, the duration of the adaptation is unpredictable, whereas in the second case, access times become unpredictable since an access may trigger adaptation. Both of these approaches are not suited to systems where timely execution of all tasks must be guaranteed. The inherent non-determinism in these approaches renders them unsuitable to the targeted domain.

Towards Inherent Adaptive Applications

The presence of computationally constrained systems in emerging paradigms such as the Internet of Things is inevitable. We propose a two step solution towards achieving our aim of extending computationally constrained nodes with the ability to adapt. In the first step, we propose to facilitate adaptation by having an application structure that is inherently adaptive. In this regards, we present our Behavioral model that provides structural recommendations for an application running on the target systems. The Behavioral model dictates how an application should be implemented and not what it implements. The resultant behavior consists of loosely coupled components that communicate indirectly. The components are developed independently and appear to each other and the underlying system as black boxes.

Following from Component Based Software Engineering (CBSE) principles, the components have a required and provided interface, where the former specifies the prerequisites of the component before it can fulfill its functionality. The provided interface then, manifests the different results the component produces on completing its function. The required interface consists of many entry points, as can be seen in Figure 1. Each entry point s_j represents an access point to the functionality a component has to offer. Hence, different entry points represent an access to different functionality of the component. Let the different functionality of a component C be denoted by F_C. The set of entry points of the component C is defined as:

$$EP_C = \{s \mid \exists C \in \hat{C}, \exists F_C \in N; \forall s : 1 \leq s \leq F_C\}$$

where N represents natural numbers and $\hat{C}$ is the set of all components.

A component may, for example, offer two services. A client wishing to access one of these must then provide any prerequisite data along with the associated entry state. Further, a component may combine two or more internal functionalities to fulfill a composite function. For example, a third service may be provided by combining the first two. From the clients' perspective, access to a simple or composite functionality of the component is transparent. An entry point triggers an atomic run that releases an exit index x_i

Figure 1. Component entry and exit points

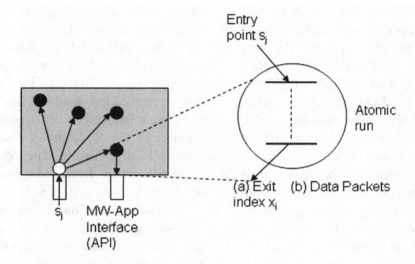

upon completion. An exit index denotes the state that the component is in after execution, from a set of possible and predefined states. Further, it also specifies the type of data produced by the component, if it has the ability to produce more than one type. The underlying system notifies other components about the generated exit index based on component connections present in the connection list. A connection is an association of an exit index of a component to an entry point of another component. The generation of an exit index is to inform other components that the generating component has finished execution and produced the necessary prerequisites for any connected component to start execution. Instead of actual point to point connections, the connection list is a mathematical relation between all the exit indices and their triggered entry points. An exit index may be associated with one or more entry points and vice versa, as given below:

$$CL = \{(x_i, s_j, o) \mid x_i \in XI_{Cl},$$
$$(s_j \in EP_{Ck} \vee s_j \in EP_{C\varphi}),$$
$$\forall C_k, C_l \in \hat{C}, \forall o \in N\}$$

where C_k and C_l are two components, XI_{Cl} is the set of exit indices of component C_l, whereas EP_{Ck} is the set of entry points of component C_k. $EP_{C\varphi}$ specifies that an exit index may possibly, not be associated with the entry point of any component. An exit index may also be associated with more than one entry point of the same csomponent; hence the ordering o specifies which entry point to choose at a given instance.

A component has meta-data that consists of platform independent and platform specific properties. The platform specific properties outline the compatibility of a component relative to specific platform, which may include the operating system and the processing unit. Each component also has a platform independent relative deadline, a platform specific worst case execution time and worst case memory usage. Besides these, pointers to the starting point of component code execution and communication interface are also provided. These are used by the underlying system to transfer execution control and send/receive data to/from the component via the Middleware-Application Interface (MW-App Interface) as shown in Figure 1.

Platform for Deterministic Adaptation

Once the behavior of the system has been captured in a desired structure, a supporting platform is needed that provides the mechanism for the behavior to execute and enable the system to adapt in a deterministic manner. Adaptation may include changes to the current behavior of the system realized as a composition of components, as well as addition of new behavior. This mechanism is provided by the underlying middleware. From the component perspective, the middleware acts as a component framework on top of which the components execute and communicate. The component framework is the middleware that separates the application components from the underlying operating system and other components, as well as enabling the current system to communicate with similar middlewares in a networked environment.

The middleware consists of two modes, the initialization mode and the running mode. In the initialization mode, the behavior, in the form of components, is deployed. Deploying the components consists of allocating resources such as memory space, registering the meta-data and linking the execution and communication interface pointers with the middleware. The connection list

is then used to register connections between the components.

Having mentioned the need for determinism as well as the drawbacks of the two approaches to adaptation namely adapt-at-once and adapt-on-demand, the middleware employs a highly deterministic approach called timed phases to achieve the intended objectives of behavioral execution and runtime adaptation. Since the target embedded systems have a constraint of only one processing unit, therefore the timed phases approach divides the processing time-line of the single processor into phases for computation, communication and adaptation, as shown in Figure 2.

After the components have been plugged in and connections registered, the middleware initializes the timed phases with the help of services offered by the underlying real-time operating system. The lengths of the computation, communication and adaptation phases, denoted by T_α, T_β and T_γ respectively, are determined based on the current application requirements and deployment scenario. For instance, the length of the adaptation phase will be different for a scenario with a high adaptive environment that from one with low frequency adaptation. The commencement of the timed phases signals the switch of the middleware to the running mode. Once the

Figure 2. Timed phases

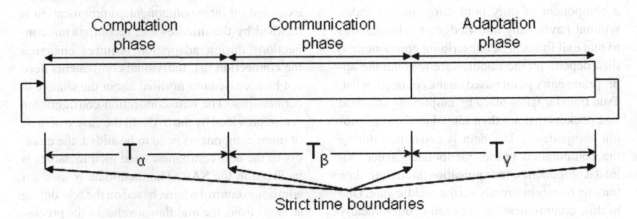

middleware enters the running mode, the three phase lengths cannot be changed for the complete duration of the system lifetime. In the running mode, the three phases are executed one after the other. The end of the adaptation phase triggers the start of another computation phase and the phases are repeated in cyclic manner.

During the computation phase the components execute their behavior depending upon the scheduling policy. The scheduling policy is fixed at design time, such as Earliest Deadline First (EDF) or Fixed Priority (FP). Once scheduled and released, a component receives an entry point to signal the desired functionality and a possible block of data registered under it in the middleware. This data may be required by the component to proceed with functionality it offers. Upon completion the component releases an exit index and any data generated as a result of the executed functionality. A component may have data that needs to persist for future reference, for example the average speed of a robot measured over a given duration. Such data is classified as the state information and is recorded by the middleware at the end of the computation phase.

In the communication phase the middleware delivers all necessary information to their target destinations via the communication protocol. The connection list is used to map the exit indices to entry points with an emulation of the publish-subscribe pattern. This is achieved by tasking a component of only publishing an exit index without having any knowledge of subscriptions to that exit index. The subscribing component(s) then depend on the middleware to route the appropriate entry point based on the connection list. Data transfer takes place by employing standard size packets that are then routed to the subscribing components. The data is consumed during the computation phase, mentioned earlier. All inter-component communication including data transfer occurs indirectly via the middleware. Due to this, communication between geographically distant nodes connected via a network appears transparent and similar to local communication to all components on these nodes.

The third and final phase is the adaptation phase. The middleware checks at the beginning of the phase for a Standard Adaptation Request (SAR). If none is found, soft real-time messages are exchanged for system diagnostics. An adaptation request may be triggered locally or remotely. A local request is sent from a component monitor responsible to reflect upon the system and ensure certain constraints are met. These constraints are dictated by the adaptation policy. An adaptation policy states the constraints under which the system must remain. If the constraints are found to be transgressed, action is taken to rectify the situation and bring the system back to a desired state. For example, the system may monitor on-board hardware for failures. This may be done by monitoring response time with a timeout implying failure. Upon a timeout, the component monitor may decide to rectify the situation by sending an adaptation request. Similarly, a remote request may be received from an external source, such as a human controller or a monitor in another node, in a networked system. If an adaptation request is found, the middleware initiates steps to successfully adapt. The type of the adaptation i.e. addition/removal of components and/or a reconfiguration of component connections is specified in the SAR. Since no direct connections exist and all inter-component communication is handled by the middleware, reconfiguring connections during adaptation requires changing the connection list. Individual components need not be accessed nor notified about the change in connections. The new connection configuration is also provided by the SAR. In the case where on or more components need to be added, the quantity of the new components and their metadata is included in the SAR. The meta-data is used for admission control where, based on the scheduling strategy used, the middleware checks the processor utilization to conclude whether the worst case timing and worst case memory requirements of existing and new components can be met. In case they are met, an approval is sent to the source of the request to complete the transfer by sending the components binaries.

Gupta in his work (GUPTA,1994) proved that determining appropriate constraints for the timing of an update is not decidable, in general. Following from this, the length of the adaptation phase cannot be fixed to a constant for all application scenarios. Although it remains constant throughout the system lifetime, the length assigned to it before system runtime must be determined case by case. To determine an appropriate value for T_y, parameters such as the expected adaptation frequency and application performance requirements must be taken into consideration.

Layered Architecture

The architecture of a system with application behavior in the form of components as described earlier, running on a component framework can be seen in Figure 3. The top layer consists of the application layer followed by the middleware layer below. The middleware is supported by a Real-Time Operating System (RTOS) to achieve low level functionality such as allocating storage space, garbage collection, scheduling, timer interrupt handling etc.. The RTOS is also responsible to act as an interface between the processing unit and software layers running above. The middleware does not access the RTOS directly but via the Operating System Adaptor Layer (OSAL) that typical RTOS method calls. These method calls are then implemented by a real RTOS. This approach renders the middleware independent of any specific RTOS. From the RTOS perspective, any RTOS implementing the OSAL can acquire the functionality of a component framework with deterministic adaptation.

In Figure 3, a system is a node in a network with each node having the same software architecture but with the possibility of a heterogeneous hardware platform, or it may even be a standalone system such as a single robot. A node may even have many application specific processing units but with only a single processing unit for the system software. Each node runs its own independent copy of the middleware but the application may be distributed on multiple nodes. Keeping with the idea of Cyber Physical Systems, these nodes may be connected to external networks

Figure 3. Architecture of a system in a network of single processor nodes

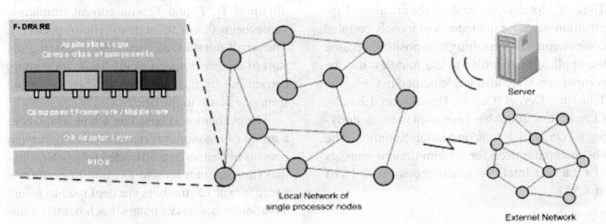

Figure 4. Bot 1 with SC replacing the VPU component due to hardware failure

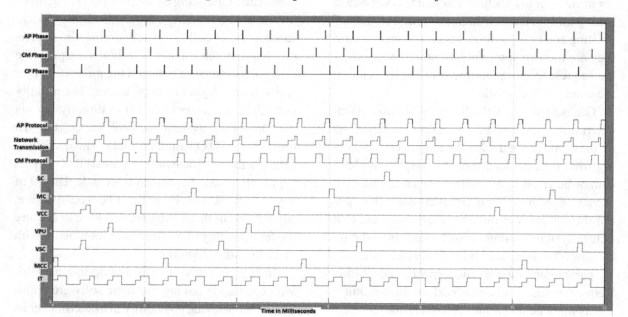

with or without the same architecture. The system is always connected to a component repository, also used for external monitoring. A node may send/receive an SAR and components to/from either the repository, other nodes in the local network or an external network.

Evaluation and Case Study

The middleware or component framework has been implemented using C++, as well as the OSAL. The behavioral model enabled the creation of application behavior in the form of loosely coupled components. The resulting composition became the application. Similar to the middleware, the components were also implemented in C++. The TrueTime Kernel (Cervin, Henriksson, Lincoln, Eker, & Rzn, 2003) has been used as the underlying RTOS, which runs on Matlab/Simulink. The host computer used for the simulations consists of a 2.8 Ghz Intel Pentium processor with 1 GB of RAM.

Simulation results of a case study with the granularity of time in milliseconds, is shown in Figure 4 and 5. The AP Phase, CM Phase and CP Phase stand for the adaptation, communication and computation phases respectively. The edges on the respective timelines indicate the start of that phase. The end of the computation phase is triggered by the start of the communication phase. Similarly the end of the communication phase is triggered by the start of the adaptation phase. The duration between the three edges correspond to the phase durations T_α, T_β and T_γ with current simulation values being 0.3ms, 0.2ms and 0.1ms respectively. The small duration of each edge triggering the start of the phase specifies the handover activity carried out by the middleware when switching from one phase to the next.

The evaluation is based on a scenario, where a group of autonomous remote land exploration bots (as in Bebots) are offloaded from a base station (Server) in a remote location to perform a specific task i.e. the bots are deployed to locate a particular species of plants. Each bot has similar component software to perform the task. In this case each bot will comprise of the following components

- **Video Sensor Component (VSC):** Drives the video sensor to capture visual data.
- **Visual Processing Unit Component (VPU):** Controls the application specific visual processing unit, designed to analyze the data captured by VSC.
- **Video Controller Component (VCC):** Examines the data received from VPU, to check if the target is located.
- **Motor Component (MC):** Directs the motors to move the bot to a specific location.
- **Main Controller Component (MCC):** The component responsible for (i) the coordination between the Bot and the Server and (ii) keeping track of the location of the bot.

The basic flow of the functionality is as follows: VSC captures the surroundings and passes them to VPU, which then processes this data and forwards it to VCC. VCC examines the processed data and informs the MCC if the target is located or not. If the target is located, MCC contacts the Server and transmits its co-ordinates. If the target is not located, it directs the MC to move the bot a specific location. During the search, the application specific visual processing unit of a bot (Bot 1) fails resulting in an interruption of the bots tasks. To overcome this situation, the bot enabled with the ability to adapt, sends an adaptation request to the server. The server acknowledges the adaptation by forwarding a "Substitute Component (SC)", to replace the VPU component rendered unnecessary due to the visual processing unit failure. The SC is responsible for compressing the data received from VSC and forwarding the compressed data to a neighbor bot (Bot 2), indicated by the server. Bot 2 is also forced to adapt by the server, such that its VPU can also process the obtained compressed data and return the resulting data back to Bot 1.

This scenario can be observed in the Figure 4, where after adaptation at 6ms, the VPU in Bot 1 does not execute but instead SC takes its place. The respective changes can also be observed in Bot 2 in Figure 5, where the frequency at which the VPU of Bot 2 is doubled. This is due to the

Figure 5. Bot 2, with an enhanced VPU to process external requests

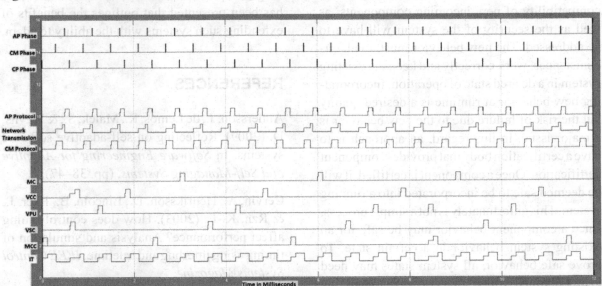

increase in load brought on to Bot 2 by requiring it to process visual data from both bots. In this scenario, by transferring some workload of a faulty bot to a neighbor, the bot acquired the quality of fault tolerance. This increased the system functionality time of the bot with faulty hardware and enabled it to continue operating.

FUTURE RESEARCH DIRECTIONS

In this chapter, we have seen that in the Future internet, the Internet of Things will be an integral part. The scope of services offered by web services will increase due to their access to objects that are tightly conjoined with the physical environment. From the 'Things' perspective, paradigms such as Cyber Physical Systems will enable them to open up and connect to the global network. This will provide access to unlimited services that open up possibilities that are also very vast. Systems will adapt to changing scenarios and will have the ability to import new behavior and as a result portray qualities initially absent. Since safety and time critical embedded systems will also be part of the Internet of Things, access to new services and the import of new behavior will need to be strictly scrutinized. Important issues such as the compatibility of new incoming components, as well as the security of the system will have to be addressed. The new behavior must, in all circumstances, work correctly and keep the existing system in a desired state of operation. Incorporating new behavior at runtime is a desired quality but the risk of failure due to the new behavior is a major issue. In this regard, an approach is to have a certification body that provides component certification. Once a component is certified, it will be deemed safe to be incorporated into a running system. This unfortunately is not a simple process, since a component behavior may be safe for an existing system behavior in a certain state. To prove safe behavior, all system states may need to be examined, which for a system in a changing environment, is not a simple process. Approaches such as online model checking are being used to overcome the state space explosion problem in such cases.

CONCLUSION

With the concept of Cyber Physical Systems changing the stance from closed to open and connected embedded systems, the potential to harness new abilities such as the acquisition of system qualities as well as functionality not present at design time, becomes a possibility. To achieve this, systems in the real-time domain must have the ability to adapt while simultaneously fulfilling their timing guarantees. It is inevitable that the vast global network will consist of nodes with processing constraints, making adaptation a challenge. In this chapter we have presented our framework F-DRARE, which works towards providing recommendations to produce inherently adaptive software applications via the behavioral model. The framework also provides an underlying support mechanism to achieve deterministic runtime adaptation for the targeted systems, thus taking a step towards meeting the above mentioned challenge. To provide proof of concept, a case study has been presented that outlines the benefits of extending such systems with the ability to adapt.

REFERENCES

Andersson, J., de Lemos, R., Malek, S., & Weyns, D. (2009). Reflecting on self-adaptive software systems. In *Software Engineering for Adaptive and Self-Managing Systems*, (pp. 38–47).

Cervin, A., Henriksson, D., Lincoln, B., Eker, J., & Rzn, K.-E. (2003). How does control timing affect performance? Analysis and simulation of timing using jitterbug and truetime. *IEEE Control Systems Magazine*.

Dorigo, M., & Birattari, M. (2007). Swarm intelligence. *Scholarpedia*, *2*(9), 1462.

Fabry, R. S. (1976). *How to design systems in which modules can be changed on the fly*. In Intl. Conf. on Software Engineering.

Gupta, D. (1994). *On-line software version change*. Doctoral Thesis.

Herbrechtsmeier, S., Witkowski, U., & Rückert, U. (2009). Bebot: A modular mobile miniature robot platform supporting hardware reconfiguration and multi-standard communication. In *Progress in Robotics, Communications in Computer and Information Science, Proceedings of the FIRA RoboWorld Congress 2009*, Vol. 44, (pp. 346–356). Incheon, Korea: Springer.

Hojenski, K., & Oberthür, S. (2006). *Towards self optimizing distributed resource management*. In Selbstorganisierende, Adaptive, Kontextsensitive verteilte Systeme (SAKS 06), Kassel, Germany.

Ibm (2006). An architectural blueprint for autonomic computing. *Quality, 36*(June), 34.

Koopman, P. (1996). Embedded system design issues (the rest of the story). In *Proceedings of the 1996 International Conference on Computer Design, VLSI in Computers and Processors*, ICCD '96, (p. 310). Washington, DC: IEEE Computer Society.

Lee, E. A. (2008). *Cyber physical systems: Design challenges*. In International Symposium on Object/Component/Service-Oriented Real-Time Distributed Computing (ISORC). Invited Paper.

Rammig, F. J. (2008). Cyber biosphere for future embedded systems. In *Proceedings of the 6th IFIP WG 10.2 International Workshop on Software Technologies for Embedded and Ubiquitous Systems, SEUS '08*, (pp. 245–255). Berlin, Germany: Springer-Verlag.

Ritzau, T., & Andersson, J. (2000). *Dynamic deployment of java applications*. In Java for Embedded Systems Workshop.

Sha, L., Rajkumar, R., & Gagliardi, M. (1995). Evolving dependable real-time systems. In *IEEE Aerospace Applications Conference*, (pp. 335–346).

US National Science Foundation. (n.d.). *Cyber-physical systems*. Retrieved from http://www.nsf.gov/funding/pgm_summ.jsp?pims_id=503286

Vandewoude, Y., & Berbers, Y. (2002a). An overview and assessment of dynamic update methods for component-oriented embedded systems. In *Proceedings of The International Conference on Software Engineering Research and Practice*, Las Vegas, USA.

Vandewoude, Y., & Berbers, Y. (2002b). Run-time evolution for embedded component-oriented systems. In *Proceedings of the International Conference on Software Maintenance*, (pp. 242–245). IEEE Computer Society.

KEY TERMS AND DEFINITIONS

Cyber Physical Systems: Tight conjoining and interaction of systems with the physical or external. Unlike embedded systems, these systems are open to external interaction allowing the possibility of runtime manipulation.

Embedded System: A system, usually, with limited resources due to it being embedded into an environment or another system. Traditionally, it is closed to any runtime manipulation.

Middleware: A layer separating two layers in a horizontally partitioned system. Typically provides services to the layer above and uses services of the layer beneath.

Real Time System: A system where the correctness of a computation is not only dependent on the resulting value but also on its time of arrival.

All tasks have deadlines that have to be met for the system to functions correctly.

Reflection: The ability of a system to monitor itself and reason for change possibly resulting in adaptation.

Runtime Adaptation: The ability to change the structure or behavior during the execution of a system.

Software Component: An independently developed and deployable black-box with well defined interfaces.

Section 5
Device–Based Future Internet Adaptation

Chapter 12
Addressing Device-Based Adaptation of Services:
A Model Driven Web Service Oriented Development Approach

Achilleas P. Achilleos
University of Cyprus, Cyprus

Kun Yang
University of Essex, UK

George A. Papadopoulos
University of Cyprus, Cyprus

ABSTRACT

The rapid growth of the mobile devices market and the increasing requirements of mobile users augment the need to develop Web Service clients that could be deployed and run on both mobile and desktop devices. Different developers attempt to address this heterogeneity requirement and provide solutions that simplify and automate the development of device-aware services. This chapter proposes a Model-Driven Web Service oriented approach, which allows designing and automatically generating mobile and desktop-based clients that are able to invoke ubiquitously Web Services from different devices. This is further enabled via the Web Services Description Language that allows generating the required proxy classes, which support the communication with platform-specific clients. The applicability and efficiency of the approach is demonstrated via the design and development of a device-aware Web Service prototype.

DOI: 10.4018/978-1-4666-2089-6.ch012

INTRODUCTION

Mobile devices have obtained great prominence in the marketplace (Bartolomeo et al., 2006) and mobile users requirements have significantly increased in terms of running mobile services on these devices (Kapitsaki et al., 2009). The continuous development of existing technologies (e.g. J2ME, C#) and the introduction of brand new technologies (e.g. Android) raises new requirements and imposes new restrictions when developing service-clients (Daniel Dern, 2010). Consequently, an all-important constraint arises, which is principally associated with the interface limitations and restrictions imposed when developing platform-specific service clients for invoking and utilising Web Services from different devices.

During the early days of computing, the development of complete desktop-based applications was the main focus of developers. With the advent of Web Services the focus shifted to the development of services designed to be accessible from resource-rich (i.e. desktop, laptop) devices. Nowadays, the rapid and continuous growth of mobile devices hardware and software technologies shifted the focus towards mobile computing. Thus, the necessity arises to design Web Services in a flexible way because of the requirement to invoke them from different types of devices; i.e. mobile and stationary. This prerequisite perplexes the development of platform-specific service clients (running on different mobile devices) mainly because of interface limitations and restrictions; e.g. screen size, resource-constraints, processing power.

In this chapter we concentrate on the formulation of a model-driven approach, which attempts to exploit also the benefits of the Web Services technology. The key point is the separation of the development of the service clients from the implementation of the functionality of the Web Services. This offers a flexible, modular and abstract approach, which simplifies and accelerates the development of device-aware Web Services. The term device-aware Web Services refers to the development of both the service clients and the server-side functionality (i.e. Web Service). Hence, such an approach automates and speeds up development for the following categories of devices (Ortiz and Prado, 2009):

- **Resource-Rich Devices:** These refer to powerful desktop and laptop devices that do not impose restrictions in terms of processing power, memory, screen size, etc.
- **Resource-Competent Devices:** An intermediate category of devices that are not as powerful as the above but have higher computing resources than mobile devices and smartphones; e.g. Netbooks, IPad, Kindle.
- **Resource-Constrained Devices:** Devices such as smartphones and mobile phones that have inferior computational power, memory, interface capabilities, etc. Also, they support a restrictive set of Application Programming Interfaces (APIs).

In order to accomplish this objective, the Presentation Modelling Language (PML) is defined that allows designing and automating the implementation of service clients for the above categories of devices. Moreover, the Web Services Description Language (WSDL) is exploited since it allows designing and automatically generating the required device-specific proxy classes for each service client, which support communication with the Web Service. In this way, we allow users to design Web Service clients in the form of graphical user interfaces (GUIs) and collections of communication endpoints capable of exchanging messages (W3C, 2001) with implemented Web Service(s). Both definitions are specified in the form of graphical models that are transformed to different platform-specific implementations and deployed on the corresponding devices to enable access to the Web Service(s). Thus, an experienced developer only requires to implement the main functionality of the Web Service (at the server-side) in one of the many possible implementations; e.g. Java, .NET.

In this work, the BookStore Web Service is manually implemented in Java. This service enables the user of a mobile or desktop device to search and retrieve information on specific books. Following, it enables the user to provide his personal and payment details to complete the purchase of the book. The service clients of this prototype device-aware Web Service are designed in the form of a single platform-independent GUI model that is subsequently transformed to various target implementation technologies (e.g. C#, Android, J2ME). In addition, the communication endpoints of the clients with the Web Service are defined in the form of a WSDL model. In particular, the model describes in an abstract form the operations and parameters of the methods implemented in the Web Service. Hence, both the PML and WSDL models are transformed to the corresponding implementation technologies to enable the communication with the Web Service. Note that the transformation of GUI models is accomplished using the code generators defined in this work, while the transformation of WSDL models is achieved via the use of existing platform-specific code generators.

The rest of the chapter is structured as follows: The following section presents related work, which motivates the research steps undertaken in this work to extend the current state of the art on device-aware Web Service development. The third section introduces the architecture of the Model-Driven Web Service oriented approach proposed in this research work. Following, an initial requirement analysis of the GUI modelling domain is performed, the PML is defined in the form of an Eclipse Modelling Framework (EMF) (EMF, 2011) metamodel and the necessary domain-specific constraints are defined and imposed onto the PML. The fifth section introduces the PML code generation process and the

platform-specific code generator tools defined and used in this work. It also presents example code generation scripts and template definitions for the Android implementation technology, in order to showcase how code generators are developed for the different target implementations. The following section demonstrates the design and implementation of the BookStore device-aware Web Service prototype. Finally, conclusions and plans for extension of this research work are presented in the final section.

BACKGROUND

The development of GUIs is a difficult and essential task in software development. In particular, the development overheads are largely increased while developing the same software service for miscellaneous platforms that have different requirements and impose different restrictions (Jelinek and Slavik, 2004). This applies explicitly to mobile services since the complexity of implementing GUIs is increased due to the advanced user-service interaction and the heterogeneity requirement. Thus, the capability must be provided to define GUIs in an abstract manner, which can support the advanced interaction of the user with the software application (Sauer et al., 2006), (Heines and Schedlbauer, 2007). Moreover, generation of different implementations from the same GUI models should be feasible in order to enable the invocation of Web Services from different mobile devices. In conclusion, the MDD approach should provide the capability to generate the implementation that enables communication with the implemented Web Service(s). Thus, the developer would only require implementing the main functionality of the Web Service in a single programming language or using an existing Web Service.

One initial research work on GUI modelling focuses on the design of the structure of the user interface using presentation diagrams and its behaviour with hierarchical statechart diagrams (Sauer et al., 2006). This design step is performed using the developed GuiBuilder modelling tool that supports also the transformation of the models to the corresponding Java-based code. Also, the GuiBuilder supports the simulation of the modelled behaviour being generated. The main objective though of this work is to develop a tool that supports the model-driven development of graphical multimedia user interfaces. As a result the approach does not deal with the development of complete applications but sticks simply to the development of Java-based GUIs for the multimedia domain. The authors do state that in future work the attempt will be to demonstrate the flexibility of the transformation approach by tailoring the generator function to other implementations; i.e. addressing application heterogeneity.

Link et al. (2008) concentrate also on the aspect of user interaction by proposing a simple, tool-supported approach for the model-driven development of graphical user interfaces for miscellaneous target platforms. The goal is to define GUI features of the application via modelling and transforming these features to source code. In particular, explicit transformation rules are defined that allow transforming platform-independent models (PIMs) to platform-specific models (PSMs). Then additional transformation rules (i.e. code generators) are defined that support the transformation of PSMs to GUI-specific source code. This provides an increased automation in software development but solely for the development of the GUIs of the application.

Balagtas-Fernandez and Hussmann (2008) take the above research work a step further since they address the development of fully functional software applications for mobile platforms; by developing PIMs of an application. Their main goal is to provide the capability to non-expert users to design specialised mobile applications with ease. In particular, the authors state that: it still takes a large amount of skill and familiarity with different APIs to create a simple mobile application. Thus,

developers need to consider the different API restrictions imposed on mobile applications such as device limitations (e.g. memory, screen size, power consumption) and finally, even setting up the different development environments remains still a complex task. Hence, a modelling tool named Mobile Applications (MobiA) modeller is developed, which allows designing mobile applications that could be transformed to the corresponding platform-specific code. Note that the development of transformation tools is considered as future work and thus no documented results are reported on the capability of addressing heterogeneity. Also the approach does not exploit the potential of the Web Services technology, which means that the functionality of the application is implemented on the actual device. Thus a great burden is enforced on resource-constrained devices and interoperability still remains an open issue.

The work performed by Dunkel and Bruns (2007) also attempts to provide a simple and flexible approach for developing mobile applications. The authors acknowledge that despite significant progress in the development of mobile applications, there is still a lot of space for improvements by employing code generation and declarative approaches. Hence, a model-driven approach is presented that allows modelling the user interface of the client and the service workflow in the form of graphical models. From these models the XML-based descriptions are generated as XForms code. The XForms W3C standard was specifically selected due to its close correlation with the Mobile Information Device Profile (MIDP) of J2ME. Hence, it allows mapping XForm elements to MIDP elements and generating the corresponding source code; e.g. service-client J2ME code. This discloses that the approach is tailored to the J2ME technology, although it can be extended by defining additional code generation tools for addressing different mobile implementation technologies. Moreover, as the authors state, a drawback of the approach is that miscellaneous Unified Modelling Language (UML) (OMG UML, 2007) tools must be integrated and used that do not fully support metamodelling and provide proprietary and not yet stable code generation tools.

Ortiz et al. (2009) state that device diversity and their non-stop use in everyday life activities reveals the necessity to access Web Services from these mobile devices. The main objective of their approach is to adapt the result of the Web Service invocation in accordance to the type of the client's device. Thus, they propose a server-side approach that allows developers to extend the implemented service through aspect-oriented development, so as to enable the adaptation of the result depending on the client device. Note that the Web Service code is not directly affected but rather an aspect is developed that intercepts the invocation of the service operation and adapts it according to the type of device it detects. The approach suffers though from three main issues: (i) the necessity arises to implement on the client-side the functionality that allows detecting the type of the device that invokes

the Web Service, (ii) it increases response time since the aspect code must process and adapt the result in accordance to the content of the Simple Object Access Protocol (SOAP) header and (iii) it does not consider the implementation of platform-specific service clients (i.e. GUIs); authors state that GUI restrictions imposed by mobile platforms increase the complexity of developing clients (Ortiz & Prado, 2009).

MODEL-DRIVEN WEB SERVICE ORIENTED ARCHITECTURE

The proposed approach combines the Model Driven Architecture (MDA) paradigm (Kleppe et al., 2003; Singh and Sood, 2009) and Web Services technology in an attempt to exploit their potentials and overcome their limitations. Figure 1 presents the architecture of the MDD approach that comprises the client-side and the service-side.

Figure 1. Model-driven Web service oriented architecture

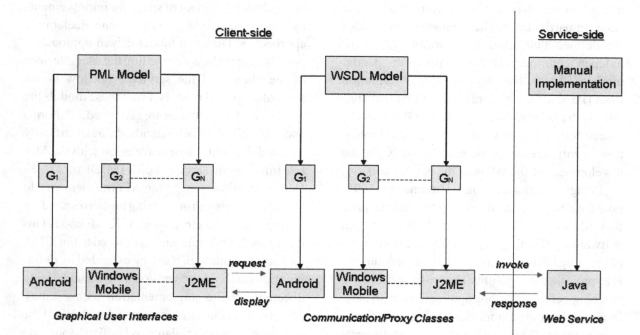

The client-side refers to the graphical user interfaces deployed on the mobile or desktop device, which allow the user to interact with the service by exchanging the necessary information. In order to accomplish this interaction the required communication classes (i.e. proxy classes) are used that act as the client-side connection endpoints. These end-points allow invoking Web Service(s) operations and retrieving responses through the exchange of SOAP messages.

Both the GUIs and the communication classes are automatically generated from the abstract models (i.e. PML, WSDL); as shown in Figure 1. In particular, different code generators (G1, G2, ..., GN) are defined in this work that allow transforming the PML model to different target implementations; e.g. Android, Windows Mobile. Also, existing code generation tools are utilised that support the transformation of the WSDL model to platform-specific implementations. For instance, in the case of the Android platform, the Android GUI classes utilise the Android proxy classes to invoke the Web Service, receive the appropriate response and display the information on the corresponding Android mobile device. The aforesaid communication method described for the Android platform is valid for the rest of the implementation technologies.

On the service-side the Web Service functionality is the only part that requires to be implemented manually by developers. The service functionality is coded though in one implementation technology (in this case the implementation is Java-based) and can be consumed using the capabilities of the Web Services technology by different clients. These clients do not need to be implemented using the same implementation platform (i.e. Java) but can be coded in different target implementations. This is possible since the communication is performed using SOAP, which is a simple protocol specification for exchanging XML-based structured information in computer networks. It also relies on Remote Procedure Call (RPC) and HyperText Transfer Protocol (HTTP) protocols for connec-

tion negotiation and message transmission. Thus, a service-client implemented in .NET or C# (i.e. Windows mobile) is able to communicate with the Java-based Web Service deployed and executed on a GlassFish Axis Web Server. This enables as a result interoperability, which is a widely-accepted and proven characteristic of Web Services (Kapitsaki et al., 2008), between the different platforms and simplifies and enables the rapid development of fully functional device-aware Web Services.

THE PRESENTATION MODELLING FRAMEWORK

Requirement Analysis

Service heterogeneity refers to the capability to deploy the same software service (i.e. application) on different devices. In this work service heterogeneity is satisfied via a model-driven, Web Service oriented approach that allows designing the different artefacts of the application in the form of models. Therefore, from the models (i.e. GUI, WSDL) the source code is generated for different platform-specific implementations. As aforesaid the implementation includes the service-client GUIs and the proxy classes that enable the communication with the Web Service. In particular, the generation of the source code that implements the graphical user interfaces for the client-side is very important. This aspect is fundamental due to the difficulties imposed on developers when implementing GUIs, due to the restrictions and limitations that each technology imposes. Thus, by automating the implementation of GUIs for the service-clients the development of the complete device-aware Web Service is simplified and expedited.

In addition to service heterogeneity the interaction of the user with mobile services should be simplified by providing easy-to-use and highly-capable graphical user interfaces. Due to user's mobility and the diversity of devices that need to run mobile services, the requirement arises to design GUIs in an abstract manner that allows generating the different implementation for this assortment of devices. This ensures as a result that there is no compromise in terms of developing GUIs and thus the interaction of the user with the service remains quite straightforward but still of the highest quality.

To gratify these requirements it is imperative to provide a flexible and extensible model-driven approach that allows designing GUIs and generating the implementation code using model-to-text transformations. Hence, the Presentation Modelling Language must include abstract concepts that can be mapped using the necessary transformation rules to different implementations. For example, the top element component for implementing GUIs in Java is provided either using the *javax.swing. JFrame* or the *java.awt.Frame* implementation classes. Similarly, the *javax.microedition.lcdui. Display* class is the top-level component of the J2ME technology, the *android.app.Activity* class is the top-level of the Android technology and the *System.Windows.Forms.Form* class is the top level of the Windows Desktop and Mobile technologies. Thus, we define a modelling element of the PML that represents in an abstract form any of the above top level components without considering the final implementation technology. Furthermore, we define abstract properties for this element that can be mapped using transformation rules to the respective graphical properties of each implementation technology.

Apart from the aforementioned components, the most important and widely used components of the implementation technologies are identified and included in the form of abstract modelling elements in the PML metamodel. In particular, the platform-specific components selected, are the ones that represent equivalent/comparable graphical concepts in all the implementation technologies. For instance, the *java.awt.Label*, the *javax. microedition.lcdui.StringItem* and the *android. widget.TextView* classes serve a similar purpose,

since they all represent a component capable of displaying a single-line of read-only text. Another example is the graphical component that serves the task of editing a single line of input text, which is implemented in the Java technology via the *java. awt.TextField* or *javax.swing.JTextField* class, in the J2ME technology via the *javax.microedition. lcdui.TextField* class and in the Android technology platform via the *android.widget.EditText* class. Thus (considering all cases) the abstract representation of the platform-specific graphical components is deducted and defined accordingly in the PML. Moreover, an additional requirement is captured in the PML definition that refers to the capability to represent the relationships between displays, containers and secondary components.

Finally the capability is provided to define different graphical properties for each of the above components. The different restrictions and limitations imposed by the different platforms call for a flexible and extensible approach when defining graphical properties. This provides the capability to extend the PML definition and introduce new properties, which may be added in any of the implementation technologies addressed in this work. The only prerequisite is that the transformation of these properties to implementation code is supported by the transformation rules defined within the code generators. Also the coherency of the PML definition (in terms of the many different properties that can be defined) is preserved by imposing and enforcing the necessary Object Constraint Language (OCL) (OMG OCL, 2006) rules. These OCL constraints ensure that only the permitted graphical properties can be specified in the PML model definition.

Presentation Modelling Language

The requirements analysis presented in the previous subsection drives the derivation and definition of the GUI concepts in the Presentation Modelling Language. In this work the PML is defined in the form of an EMF-based metamodel using the

Figure 2. EMF metamodel definition of the presentation modelling language

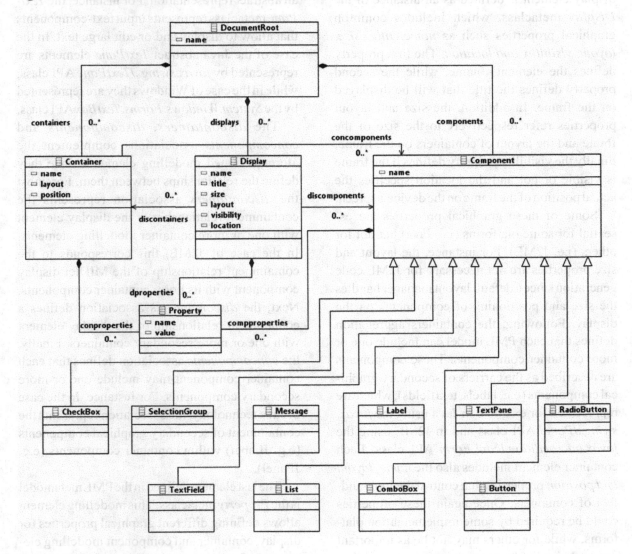

Graphical Modelling Framework (GMF) Ecore diagram tool included in the MDD environment presented in our previous work (Achilleos et al., 2007; Achilleos et al., 2008). Figure 2 illustrates the PML metamodel that defines the modelling elements, associations and properties that support the design of PML models; i.e. abstract notions of graphical user interfaces.

The top-level modelling element defines the PML model and is specified in the PML definition using the *DocumentRoot* metaclass. From the root

metaclass aggregations are defined that represent the containment relationships with the rest of the modelling elements of the GUI model. Initially, the displays aggregation showcases that each PML model may contain different displays (i.e. screen of a mobile device). In order to reduce though the complexity of a PML model an OCL constraint is defined that restricts the definition to a single display within each model. This improves also the comprehension of a PML model and avoids designing large and complex PML models. Each display element is defined as an instance of the *Display* metaclass, which includes common graphical properties such as *name, title, size, layout, visibility and location*. The first property defines the element's name, while the second property defines the title that will be displayed on the frame. In addition, the size and layout properties refer respectively to the size of the frame and the layout of containers on the frame. Finally the visibility property defines if the frame is visible or not and the location specifies the actual position of the frame on the device's screen.

Some of these graphical properties are essential for some platforms (i.e. Java) but not for others (i.e. J2ME). For instance, the layout and size properties are not necessary for J2ME code generation since a default layout manager handles the size and positioning of components on the display. Following, the containers aggregation defines that each PML model can include one or more container components. These components are described as the carriers of secondary graphical components (e.g. labels, textfields), which are represented for example in Java using the *javax.swing.JPanel* API class and in J2ME using the *javax.microedition.lcdui.Form* API class. Each container element includes also the *name, layout and position* properties that control the look-and-feel of containers. Once again these properties could be required by some implementation platforms, while for others may not be as important due to the use of layout managers.

Apart from the single display and its containers, the PML definition includes also miscellaneous important graphical components that are common and widely-used in all implementation platforms. Foremost the *Component* abstract metaclass defines the superclass of the subclasses: *Message, Label, Button, TextPane, RadioButton, ComboBox, CheckBox, TextField, List and SelectionGroup*. By creating instances of these metaclasses the designer is able to model different secondary graphical components (e.g. *Android TextView, J2ME StringItem, Java JLabel*) using

an abstract representation. For instance, the *TextPane* metaclass represents input text-components that allow to display and/or edit large text. In the case of the Java abstract *TextPane* elements are represented by *javax.swing.JTextPane* API class, while in the case of Windows they are represented by the *System.Windows.Forms.TextBox* API class.

The *discontainers, discomponents* and *concomponents* associations complement the aforementioned modelling elements since they define the relationships between them. Foremost the *discontainers* association represents the containment relationship of the display element with one or more container modelling elements. In the case of J2ME, this corresponds to the containment relationship of the MIDlet display component with its Form container components. Next, the *discomponents* association defines a containment relationship of the display element with one or more secondary containers. Finally, the *concomponents* association defines that each container component may include one or more secondary components. For instance, in the case of Java technology, the association represents the containment of secondary graphical components (e.g. JLabel) within container components (e.g. JPanel).

The last element defined in the PML metamodel is the *Property* metaclass. This modelling element allows defining different graphical properties for display, container and component modelling elements. In fact, the aggregation associations named *dproperties, conproperties* and *compproperties* define clearly that each of the aforesaid modelling elements may contain one or more graphical properties defined as an instance of the *Property* metaclass. These properties are defined using the *name* attribute in the form of keywords and can be parsed via the transformation rules defined in the code generators. Furthermore, using a single OCL constraint we are able to ensure that the designer will be permitted to define keywords (i.e. graphical properties) that are supported in the current version of the PML. This provides the flexibility and extensibility to add/remove new properties by adding/removing keywords to this OCL rule. Finally the *value* attribute defines the value of the *Property* element, which may represent (for example) the actual text that will appear on a label.

Presentation Modelling Language Constraints Definition

The definition of the PML as an EMF-metamodel allows the design PML models that represent graphical user interfaces. It is not possible to ensure the design of coherent PML models via the metamodel definition. Thus, it is important to define the domain-specific modelling rules that restrict the definition of PML models to valid graphical user interfaces. This provides a complete and coherent PML definition and allows generating the corresponding Presentation Modelling Framework (PMF), using the capabilities of the generic MDD environment (Achilleos et al., 2007; Achilleos et al., 2008). The PMF comprises a modelling editor with drag-and-drop capabilities that permits the design and validation of PML models.

From the complete set of OCL rules imposed to the PML the following two are selected to showcase their importance and reveal also how the flexibility and extensibility of the PML is preserved. The primary OCL constraint is imposed onto the *Display* metaclass in order to restrict the definition of the container's position property in accordance to the layout property of the display. In particular, the constraint defines that in the case that the layout property is set as *"default"* the position property of the associated containers should be defined using the following values: (i) *CENTER*, (ii) *EAST*, (iii) *WEST*, (iv) *NORTH* and (v) *SOUTH*. For instance, in the case of the Java platform the *"default"* value defines that the corresponding *BorderLayout* API class should be generated and used. This class permits plac-

ing the display's containers in one of the above positions; e.g. CENTER. Furthermore, the *"else"* conditional statement specifies that the position property should be defined as an *Integer* since the current layout refers to the *GridLayout* API class. The integer indicates as a result the index number that reveals the position of the container. Note that in the current version of the PML only the *BorderLayout* and *GridLayout* managers are supported for the design and transformation of GUI models to Java-based code.

```
context Display
inv: if self.layout = 'default'
then self.discontainers→forAll(con:
Container | con.position = 'CENTER')
or self.discontainers→forAll(con:
Container | con.position = 'EAST')
or self.discontainers→forAll(con:
Container | con.position = 'WEST')
or self.discontainers→forAll(con:
Container | con.position = 'NORTH')
or self.discontainers→forAll(con:
Container | con.position = 'SOUTH')
else self.discontainers→forAll(con:
Container | con.position.toInteger().
oclIsTypeOf(Integer))
endif
```

The second OCL constraint presented in this work showcases the importance of OCL rules and reveals also how the flexibility and extensibility of the PML is preserved. This domain rule defines the keywords that are currently supported by the PML and can be defined as graphical properties of the PML elements. In the case the designer attempts to assign a non-supported property to any modelling element then a constraint violation is raised that reveals the design error. In this way the capability is provided to extend the PML definition simply by adding new keywords to the following OCL constraint. Thus, the flexibility and extensibility of the PML is preserved, providing also the capability to address the miscellaneous graphical requirements and restrictions that different platform-specific implementations impose. The definition of OCL constraints completes the PML definition and enables the design and validation of PML models.

```
context Property
inv:Property.allInstances()→forAll(p:
Property | p.name = 'text' or p.name
= 'title' or p.name =
'message' or p.name = 'rows' or
p.name = 'columns' or p.name = 'line-
Wrap' or p.name =
'stringArray' or p.name = 'command')
```

PLATFORM-SPECIFIC CODE GENERATORS DEFINITION

In order to support the transformation of PML models to the necessary platform-specific implementations it is required to define precise transformation rules that compose the code generators. The definition of precise transformation rules is imperative, in order to ensure the correctness of the operational semantics of the generated implementation. Therefore, apart from the necessity to design precise PML models it is required to exploit a widely-used MDD approach that simplifies and aids the definition of coherent platform-specific code generators. Moreover, existing WSDL code generation tools are utilised in this work to generate the service-client proxy classes that enable communication of the service clients with the Web Service.

Presentation Modelling Language Code Generation

The part of the Web Service stubs generation is not addressed in the current work. In the literature existing works on generation from WSDL descriptions exist and are employed in this work. WSDL,

serving as the specification descriptor language for WSs, offers an abstract layer depicting the service functionality. Clients that wish to consume specific WSs rely on this WSDL specification in order to discover the operations supported, the input arguments needed and the expected response messages. WSDL provides a generic description independently of the network protocols that can be adopted for communication purposes. WSDL code generators can be found in Java WS frameworks, such as the Novell exteNd Director Development environment and the Axis2 Service Archive Generator Wizard offering the wsdl2java tool. .NET offers its own custom wsdl code generation tool. In the proposed framework the two latter tools have been employed along with the J2ME generator that forms part of the Sun Java Wireless Toolkit for CLDC. However, since no such tool is available for the Android platform, in the current stage of the presented work the WS communication classes were developed manually. Further discussion on code generators for WSs is not included in the current work, which focuses on the applicability of the presentation code generation tools on multi-platform environments. However it should be noted that in the framework of MDE some works exploit WS models and introduce tools for model transformation procedures. For further information on such issues the reader can refer to relevant publications (Kapitsaki et al., 2009, Gronmo et al., 2004, Sheng et al., 2005).

In terms of the presentation layer, the code generation process allows transforming PML models to the appropriate platform-specific code. A set of generators targeting various platforms of stationary and mobile devices have been implemented: Java, J2ME, Android, Windows Mobile and Windows Desktop. In this subsection the Android specific code generator is described in order to showcase the flexibility of the code generation approach. To keep the chapter comprehensive and due to space limitations it is not possible to describe the whole generators set.

Figure 3. The PML code generation process

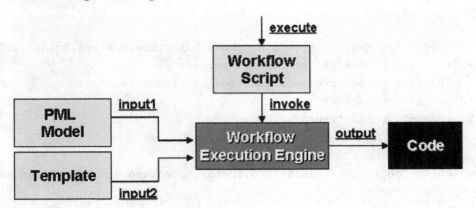

The MDD environment (Achilleos et al., 2007; Achilleos et al., 2008) proposed in previous work features the openArchitectureWare (oAW) software tool. oAW is a MDA generator framework implemented in Java, which supports explicitly the definition of model-to-text transformation rules. It includes the Xpand template language, a template text-editor and the workflow execution engine. Also it features additional languages, namely Check and Xtend, which include their individual text-editors. Foremost, the Xpand template language supports the definition of advanced code generators in the form of templates that capture the transformation rules and control the output document generation; e.g. XML, Java, C#, HTML. These templates are defined using the Xpand text-editor and include references to extension functions defined using the Xtend language. Extension functions are considered as utility functions (i.e. similarly to Java utility functions) that support the definition of well-formulated generators and improve the structure of the generated code. Moreover, the Check language supports the definition of additional constraints using a proprietary language. Finally the workflow execution engine drives the code generation in accordance to the defined templates.

Figure 3 illustrates the code generation process that is driven by the workflow engine. The executable workflow script presented in Listing 1 allows delegating calls to the necessary Java-based classes of the oAW component. It creates an "XmiParser" component and calls the "org. openarchitectureware.emf.XmiReader" that allows loading and parsing the model into memory. In fact, the PML model ("WebServiceClients. pres") is serialised in the form of XML-Metadata Interchange (XMI) format. The metamodel defined in this work is referenced also in the script, so as to be able to recognise, parse and load elements, associations and properties defined in the PML model; i.e. making them accessible at runtime. Following, the important *"Generator"* component is defined, by referencing the *"org. openarchitectureware.xpand2.Generator"* class. Also the flag *skipOnErrors= "true"* allows terminating code generation if errors are detected in the template definition. Moreover, the component defines that the input PML model is an instance of an EMF-based metamodel (i.e. PML metamodel) and that the template definition is based on the PML metamodel.

The most important artefact in the workflow script is the template definition, which describes the rules for transforming the PML model to the corresponding code. Listing 2 presents a sample part of the Android template definition that allows demonstrating how code generation is achieved.

Listing 1. PML code generation workflow script

```
1. <workflow>
2. <component id="xmiParser" class="org.openarchitectureware.emf.XmiReader">
3. <modelFile value="models/WebServiceClients.pres"/>
4. <metaModelPackage value="presentation.PresentationPackage"/>
5. <outputSlot value="model"/>
6. <firstElementOnly value="true"/>
7. </component>
............
10. <component id="generator" class="org.openarchitectureware.xpand2.Generator"
11. skipOnErrors="true">
12. <metaModel id= "mm" class="org.openarchitectureware.type.emf.EmfMetaModel">
13. <metaModelPackage value="presentation.PresentationPackage"/>
14. </metaModel>
15. <expand value="templates::AndroidPresentation::Root FOR model"/>
............
18. </component>
19. </workflow>
```

Listing 2. Part of the Android template definition

```
1.  <<EXTENSION templates::AndroidPresentation>>
2.  <<DEFINE Root FOR presentation::DocumentRoot>>
.....
30. <<REM>>Starts iteration and creates a View for each container.<<ENDREM>>
31. <<FOREACH this.discontainers AS discon->>
32. public View <<discon.name+"View">>(){
33. this.setTitle(<<discon.conproperties.select(e|e.name.contains("title")).
         value.first()>>);
34. <<discon.name>> = new TableLayout(this);
35. <<REM>>Create the respective components contained in each View.<<ENDREM>>
36. <<FOREACH discon.concomponents AS concomp->>
37. <<IF concomp.metaType.name.matches("presentation::Label")->>
38. <<concomp.name>> = new TextView(this);
39. <<concomp.name>>.setText(<<concomp.compproperties.select
             (e|e.name.contains("text")).value.first()>>);
40. <<ELSEIF concomp.metaType.name.matches("presentation::TextField")->>
41. <<concomp.name>> = new EditText(this);
    .....
71. <<REM>>Ends the loop associated with the components collection.<<ENDREM>>
72. <<ENDFOREACH>>
73. <<REM>>Ends the loop associated with the containers collection.<<ENDREM>>
74. <<ENDFOREACH>>
```

The main part of the sample generator presented in this work is included in lines 31-74. This part is repeated for all display containers of the model enabling access to the graphical properties of the containers and the secondary components associated to them. For instance, line 34 illustrates how we can generate an Android *TableLayout* object and set accordingly its name in accordance to the name of the current container in the iteration, i.e. << *discon:name* >>. The iteration through the collection of secondary components associated with each container is performed in lines 36-72. Depending on the type of element read and parsed (indicated by the properties of *concomp*) the respective object is generated. For instance a *TextView* object is generated for each *Label* element as indicated in lines 37-39, where the keyword *"text"* used at line 39 provides the capability to set the text on the label to the value parsed from the *Label* element definition. The list of conditional statements allows reading, parsing and generating other types of secondary components using the same reasoning. An equivalent approach was followed for defining the templates that support the transformation of the models to the other four platform-specific implementations; e.g. Java, J2ME, Windows Mobile and Desktop.

Web Service Description Language Code Generation

In the previous subsection the code generation process was explained, which allows transforming PML models and generating the service clients. This subsection introduces briefly the transformation of WSDL models (see Figure 4) to the corresponding proxy classes that support the communication with the Web Service. The WSDL serves as a common specification language for the Web Services domain, which allows defining the Web Service functionality using abstract models. Therefore, different implementation technologies have developed their own code generation tools that allow transforming these abstract WSDL models to the respective implementation classes that permit to invoke and retrieve responses from the Web Service. In this work we exploit existing WSDL code generation tools (e.g. *Axis2 wsdl2java* tool, *.NET wsdl* tool) and refrain from applying a similar code generation process such as the one described in the previous subsection. Details on the implementation of the WSDL code generation tools are out of the scope of this work.

Figure 4. The BookStore Web service description language model

BookStoreWebServiceService			
BookStoreWebService			
http://194.42.16.116:808...			

🔘 BookStoreWebService		
⚙ getBookDetails		
▷ input	🗗 parameters	ⓔ getBookDetails
◁ output	🗗 parameters	ⓔ getBookDetailsResponse
⚙ setBookOrderDetails		
▷ input	🗗 parameters	ⓔ setBookOrderDetails
◁ output	🗗 parameters	ⓔ setBookOrderDetailsResponse
⚙ setCustomerOrderDetails		
▷ input	🗗 parameters	ⓔ setCustomerOrderDetails
◁ output	🗗 parameters	ⓔ setCustomerOrderDetailsResponse
⚙ confirmTransaction		
▷ input	🗗 parameters	ⓔ confirmTransaction
◁ output	🗗 parameters	ⓔ confirmTransactionResponse

THE BOOKSTORE WEBSERVICE PROTOTYPE

The prototype is a *BookStore* Web Service that allows a user to search, find and purchase books. In particular, the user enters the necessary information on the book (i.e. book title) and invokes through a button generated event the function "getBookDetails" of the Web Service; see Figure 4. This function accepts as input parameter the title of the book and returns as output parameter the details of the book (e.g. book description, book price). The user is then able to purchase the book by invoking the "setBookOrderDetails" operation of the Web Service that stores the necessary details of the book order into the database. The next two screens allow the user to enter personal and payment information to confirm the transaction. This is performed by invoking the corresponding functions of the Web Service through user-generated events, which allow performing the necessary operations. The final screen displays to the user details on the purchase and the user may continue shopping or choose to terminate the application. Note that the functionality of the *BookStore* Web Service is implemented manually and utilises Java Open Database Connectivity (ODBC) that allows accessing database management systems (DBMS) and querying and retrieving data from the database. Moreover, different service-clients are generated by transforming automatically the PML model to different implementations and the WSDL model to proxy classes that enable communication with the Web Service.

Figure 4 presents the WSDL model that represents the abstract functionality of the *BookStore* Web Service. This model is defined using the Eclipse WSDL modelling editor plug-in integrated in the MDD environment used in this work. The model defines the abstract functions of the Web Service and their input and output parameters. As aforementioned, the necessary proxy classes are automatically generated from the WSDL model using existing code generation tools. These classes enable the communication with the Web Service by allowing the invocation of the implemented operations using the SOAP protocol, which allows exchanging messages represented as structured XML-based information. In particular, connection negotiation and message transmission are performed through the network using the RPC and HTTP protocols. In this work the functionality of the Web Service is implemented in Java and it is deployed and executed on a GlassFish Axis web server. Consequently, the different service-clients (e.g. Android, Windows mobile, and J2ME) generated from the PML model are able to invoke and utilise the functionality of the Web Service using the corresponding proxy classes.

Figure 5 illustrates the designed PML model that represents the GUIs of the service clients and its actually an instance of the *DocumentRoot* metaclass. The model defines at the center an instance of the *Display* metaclass, which is the main screen of the service. The display element is associated with four different container components that represent the different views of the service during its execution. They are defined as instances of the *Container* metaclass. The primary container (i.e. *searchForBooks*) is associated with secondary components that represent the GUI components that allow searching for a book by entering the title and invoking the corresponding Web Service operation. The second container (i.e. *proceedToShipping*) is the GUI view that includes the graphical components that allow displaying details of the book in case it is available. At this stage the user is able to invoke the Web Service function, which allows storing the information of the book into the database as part of the order details. The user is then presented with the third container (i.e. *customerDetails*), which allows entering personal and shipping information. Following, the user-generated event invokes the service function that stores this information in the database as additional order details. Finally

Figure 5. The bookstore presentation modelling language model

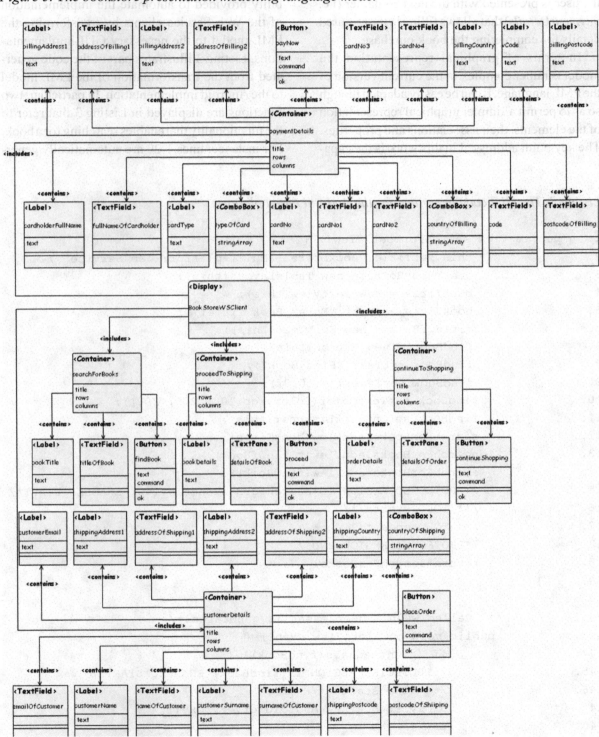

the user is presented with the next container (i.e. *paymentDetails*) that allows filling in the required details for completing the book purchase.

In terms of graphical representation the model is rather complex in the current version of the PML language. It can be easily adapted though so as to permit a simpler graphical representation of the elements, their associations and properties. The key point addressed in this work is the capa-

bility provided to automate the implementation of the Web Service clients by transforming the PML model to the necessary GUI implementations. Listing 3 illustrates part of the code generated from the transformation of the PML model to the Android implementation. In particular, two functions are displayed in Listing 3 that refer to the functionality that enables searching for a book. For instance, lines 1-20 are automatically gener-

Listing 3. The GUI code generated for the Android target platform

```
1.      public View searchForBooksView() {
2.              this.setTitle("BookStore - Multi-platform Web Service");
3.              searchForBooks = new TableLayout(this);
4.              bookTitle = new TextView(this);
5.              bookTitle.setText("Enter Book Title:");
6.              titleOfBook = new EditText(this);
7.              findBook = new Button(this);
8.              findBook.setText("Find Book");
9.              findBook.setTextSize(10.0f);
10.             findBook.setTextColor(Color.rgb(100, 200, 200));
11.             findBook.setOnClickListener(this);
12.             searchForBooks.addView(bookTitle);
13.             searchForBooks.addView(titleOfBook);
14.             searchForBooks.addView(findBook);
15.             /*PROTECTED REGION ID(searchForBooksAddToView) ENABLED START*/
16.             /** TODO starts */
17.             /** TODO ends */
18.             /*PROTECTED REGION END*/
19.             return searchForBooks;
20.      }
 .....
442.          /**  Called when a user event is generated.*/
443.          public void onClick(View event) {
444.                  if (event.equals(findBook)) {
445.                  /*PROTECTED REGION ID(findBook) ENABLED START*/
446.                  /** TODO starts */
447.                  proxy_stub = new AndroidServerProxy();
448.                  try {
449.                  _book_Details =
      proxy_stub.getBookDetails(titleOfBook.getText().toString());
          .....
```

Figure 6. The bookstore Web service deployed on different platforms

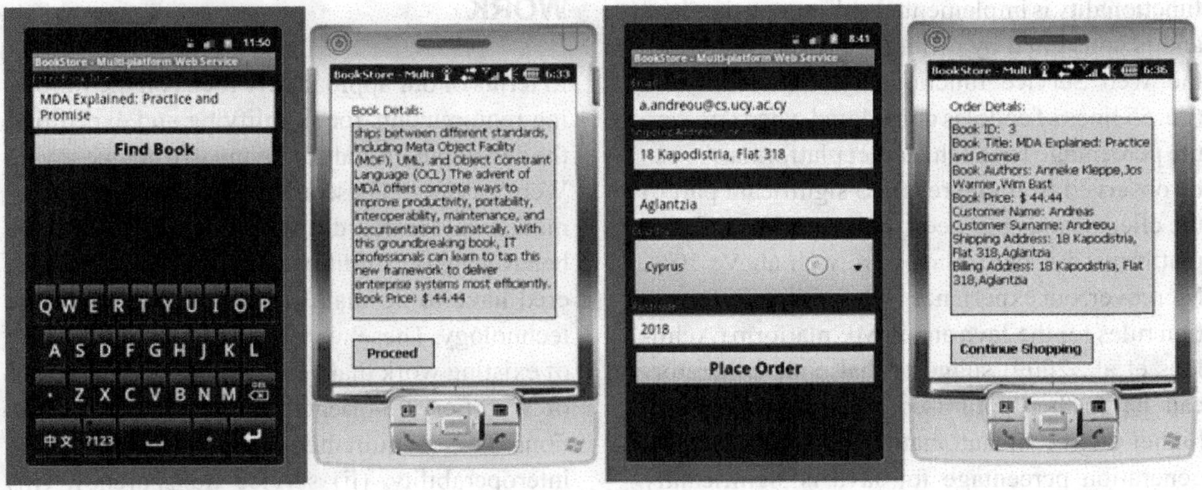

ated via the execution of the transformation rules defined in lines 30-74 of Listing 2. These rules are applied on the *Container, Label, TextField and Button* elements of the *searchForBooks* container illustrated in Figure 5. The developer must implement manually a few lines of code (i.e. protected TODO branches), which handle adding components on the container and invoking the appropriate Web Service function (lines 445-449) using the proxy classes generated from the WSDL model. Therefore, the implementation effort is significantly reduced since a large percentage of the GUI code is generated from the PML model. Equivalent transformation rules are defined and applied for generating the GUI implementation for Java, J2ME, Windows Mobile and Desktop platforms. Therefore Web Service heterogeneity is achieved via the automatic generation of the service-clients GUI implementation for miscellaneous platforms.

Figure 6 demonstrates screenshots captured during the use of the *BookStore* Web Service on mobile clients deployed on the Android and Windows Mobile platforms. The screens for searching for a book, displaying the results and filling out the information for purchasing the book are displayed in the figure. Alternated screenshots capture different steps during the execution of the service on these platforms. Moreover, a brief evaluation of our approach using the LoC software metric is performed. Our attempt is to showcase the reduction of the coding effort when developing the *BookStore* Web Service for the platforms presented in our case study.

Table 1 presents the results obtained by comparing the code generated from the models (i.e. PML, WSDL) against the full implementation code for each platform-specific service client. It

Table 1. Evaluation results on the model-driven, Web Service-oriented approach

LoC Metric (per platform)	Generated Code	Overall Code	Generated/ Overall (%)
Java	189	334	56.59
J2ME	267	369	72.39
Android	244	361	67.59
Windows Mobile	360	481	74.84
Windows Desktop	360	475	70.3
All Platforms	1420	2020	70.3

is important to point out that the Web Service functionality is implemented only once using Java and is consumed by different clients. Therefore, the Web Service functionality implementation (i.e. 55 lines of code) is considered when deriving the percentage for all the target platforms. As can be observed from the results a significant part of the clients' code has been generated for different platforms; i.e. percentages are well above 50%. Moreover, our experience in defining transformation rules for the Java and J2ME platform (Achilleos et al., 2009) suggests that code generators can be further optimised in order to achieve higher-degree of automation. For instance, the generation percentage for Java is significantly lower since the code for placing components on containers must be manually implemented. In all other platforms a default layout manager handles placing components on the container. Thus, for those platforms it is only necessary to add the components to the container. Finally, the number of platforms considered in this work showcases the flexibility and applicability of the transformation method so as to be applied successfully to other platforms; e.g. Nokia Symbian OS, Apple iOS, BlackBerry RIM.

COMPARISON WITH EXISTING WORK

In terms of our approach we focus on the following requirements for simplifying and expediting the development and deployment of device-aware Web Services. These are: (i) the degree of automation in service development and (ii) device heterogeneity. Additional requirements considered have to do mainly with the Web Services technology. These were extracted from the study of existing work that deals with the development of Web Service-oriented device-aware applications. These requirements are namely: (i) service interoperability, (ii) service transparency, (iii) service consistency, (iv) code duplicity and (v) user-awareness (Ortiz & Prado, 2009). Table 2 illustrates a comparison with existing work, which focuses on two development aspects. At first, research work focuses on model-driven development of graphical user interfaces, so as to simplify and accelerate the development of complete mobile applications. More recent research work focuses on simplifying and automating the development of device-aware Web Services using either model-driven and/or aspect-oriented approaches.

The initial research effort conducted by Sauer et al. (2006) addresses the model-driven devel-

Table 2. Comparative analysis of MDD approaches for device-aware Web services

	Main requirements		Web Service Requirements				
	Development Automation	Heterogeneity	Interoperability	Service-side Transparency	Service Consistency	Non-duplicity	User-awareness
Sauer et al.	*M/H*	*M/H*	*NA*	*NA*	*NA*	*NA*	*NA*
Link et al.	*H*	*H*	*NA*	*NA*	*NA*	*NA*	*NA*
Balagtas & Hussmann	*L*	*L*	*NA*	*NA*	*NA*	*NA*	*NA*
Dunkel & Bruns	*H*	*H*	*H*	+	+	*x*	*x*
Ortiz et al.	*M*	*H*	*VH*	+	*x*	+	*x*
Our approach	*VH*	*VH*	*VH*	+	+	*x*	*x*
	L: Low, M: Medium, H: High, VH: Very High *NA: Not Applicable, +: Satisfied, x: Not Satisfied*						

opment of GUIs in an attempt to simplify the development of multimedia applications. The authors have build a prototype GUI modelling tool (i.e. GuiBuilder) that allows to design the structure of a multimedia user interface using presentation diagrams and its behaviour with hierarchical statechart diagrams. This initial work demonstrates the potential of modelling multimedia GUIs and generating automatically the Java SWT implementation for the multimedia application. The approach though does not reveal how transformation rules can be tailored, so as to address the heterogeneity requirement. Also, the modelling tool is manually implemented using the Plug-in Development Toolkit (PDT) and the Graphical Editor Framework (GEF) of Eclipse. In this work we claim that a model-driven development approach should allow generating the modelling tools being used. Thus, a fully integrated MDD environment is preferred that provides the capability to generate the modelling tools and allows to easily define transformation rules that target different implementations. Moreover, such an approach allows extending/modifying the modelling language and regenerating its modelling tool. Finally this approach does not deal with the Web Services technology.

A similar approach is defined by Link et al. (2008) that concentrates on the aspect of the interaction of the user with the application. Their objective is to define GUIs in the form of models and transform these models into source code; i.e. targeting miscellaneous platforms. The proposed MDD approach defines in fact two UML profiles that support the model-driven development of GUIs and specifies transformation rules using the Query/View/Transformation (QVT) standard. Hence, the approach complies largely with the MDA paradigm and provides as a result general applicability and flexibility in terms of modelling and definition of transformation rules. Therefore, the degree of automation in software generation is considerably high and the capability is also provided to easily define transformation rules for

miscellaneous platforms. The only predicament is that UML tools do not satisfactorily support metamodelling and do not provide highly-competent and stable code generation tools. Once again the approach tackles merely the development of GUIs, although it can be tailored to address also the development of complete Web Service-based applications.

The approach proposed by Balagtas-Fernandez and Hussmann (2008) considers the model-driven development of fully functional mobile applications rather than just the GUIs of the application. This preliminary research work developed an initial modelling prototype tool that allows defining a user interface model that describes the GUIs, a navigation model that defines how the mobile application navigates from one screen to the next and the information retrieval model that helps in showing how information is exchanged between models. The development of the necessary transformations rules is not a main focus of this work. Authors do state though that in future work the objective is to provide rules that transform the graphical models to XML-based models and then to code. Consequently, the merits of the approach in terms of development automation and application heterogeneity are still to be proven. Moreover, the approach examines the development of complete applications that run on the mobile device, which is not highly-suitable for resource-constrained mobile devices.

Dunkel and Bruns (2007) declare that a powerful architecture is indispensable for applying model-driven development of mobile applications and achieving automation and heterogeneity. The authors propose the BAMOS platform that comprises different architectural components: (i) Service Provider - offers implemented services (i.e. Web Services) to other systems, (ii) Service Broker - acts as the mediator between Service Providers and Adhoc Clients and (iii) Adhoc Client - software component running on a mobile device. Hence, the BAMOS architecture provides the necessary interoperability and allows an Adhoc Client to use different services; e.g. Web Services. The approach provides a Domain Specific Language (DSL) (Dunkel & Burns, 2009) defined as a UML profile (similar to a metamodel) for developing mobile applications based on BAMOS. The defined models describe the Adhoc client (i.e. GUIs) and the service work flow specification that can be transformed to XForms code. Subsequently, the XForms representation can be transformed to J2ME code due to its strong correlation with MIDP. Thus the approach is bound to the J2ME implementation and the BAMOS platform, although it can be adapted to target other platforms.

The architecture of the approach, i.e. being Web Service oriented, allows evaluating the approach against the Web Service requirements. First the approach satisfies service-side transparency because the Web Service does not need to implement complex code, which allows detecting from which device the service is invoked. A simple option will be to duplicate methods in the Web Service and thus each client may invoke a different method according to the device that the client is deployed. This implies though that some code is duplicated in the Web Service implementation. Also service consistency is preserved since the generated service implementation is consistent with the original service definition; i.e. no additional code needs to be inserted at the service-side. In addition, the approach does not consider user-awareness, which means that the user is not able to intervene and adapt the service response in accordance to his/her preferences; e.g. displaying fewer output information.

One of the most competent approaches (especially in terms of satisfying Web Service requirements) is the model-driven, aspect oriented approach proposed by Ortiz et al. (2009). The authors describe different techniques for adapting Web Services for different devices and choose from these alternatives the model-driven, aspect-oriented technique. This technique allows adding an optional tag in the SOAP message header so as to adapt the results in accordance to

each device. The technique is characterised by service transparency and non-duplicity of code at the service-side. It does not satisfy though service consistency since the SOAP header is modified and through the adaptation imposed by the aspect-code handler the service returns different results with the same input parameters. Also, the approach cannot be adapted to address user-awareness since the adaptation functionality is hard-coded in the application. Non-satisfied Web Service requirements can be addressed in this approach using one of the proposed techniques (Ortiz et al., 2009). In terms of development automation and service heterogeneity the approach allows generating Web Service skeletons for the main functionality and service-side aspect-oriented code that enables device-specific adaptation. Therefore, the approach reduces significantly the coding effort but does not support the automatic development of client-side GUIs for different platforms. In addition, the approach targets Java and J2ME implementation technologies and does not attest as to the flexibility in adapting code generation for additional platforms.

In contrast to the aforementioned approaches our proposed method provides a fully extensible MDD approach that provides high-degree of automation in developing device-aware Web Services. The proposed approach automates the development of the GUIs and the Web Service proxy classes for different target implementations. Moreover, we have illustrated the extensibility of our approach in terms of adding new graphical features to the PML and also the efficiency provided in defining transformation rules for different implementations. In addition, via the BookStore Web Service prototype we have demonstrated that it is possible through our approach to address heterogeneity. Finally the proposed approach satisfies half of the Web Service requirements, since non-duplicity and user-awareness are not achieved. We also argue that duplicating some code in the Web Service implementation is a small price to pay for achieving adaptation based on the device. To further clarify this point, advanced-adaptation might be required in cases where it might be essential to show less information on a mobile device; e.g. due to resource limitations. Thus the best option would be to duplicate some methods at the service-side, which would return less amount of information. Concluding, user-awareness is an essential requirement that can be considered in future work.

CONCLUSION

In this work, a Model-Driven framework has been presented that automates the development of device-aware Web Services. The proposed approach allows modelling GUIs using the notation of the Presentation Modelling Language, whereas the key contribution refers to the transformation of PML models to functional code targeting different platforms encountered on mobile and stationary devices. The code generators proposed have been implemented using a set of tools provided by the openArchitectureWare modelling component of the generic MDD environment. Regarding the communication of the client with the Web Service existing code generation tools (e.g. *Axis2 wsdl2java* tool, *.NET wsdl* tool) that support the transformation of WSDL models to corresponding proxy classes have been used.

The developed prototype showcased the applicability and efficiency of the proposed Model-Driven Web Service oriented framework. The efficiency of the approach has been discussed on the basis of the prototype and the results derived using the LoC metric. The proposed Model-Driven Web Service oriented framework consisting of the PML, WSDL and the code generators revealed the capability to address heterogeneity. In particular, the approach enables developers to automatically generate the required source code of Web Service client applications that allow invoking services from different platforms. An interesting extension of this work is to consider the preferences

of the user when adapting the Web Service. For instance, a user might want to receive full details of a book even while using a resource-constrained device. Another user might be satisfied simply by receiving in the response message the book's title and price.

REFERENCES

W3C. (2001). *Web services description language (WSDL) specification* v1.1.

Achilleos, A., Georgalas, N., & Yang, K. (2007). An open source domain-specific tools framework to support model driven development of OSS. In *ECMDA-FA, Lecture Notes in Computer Science, Vol. 4530* (pp. 1 – 16).

Achilleos, A., Yang, K., & Georgalas, N. (2008). A model-driven approach to generate service creation environments. In *Proceedings of the IEEE Globecom, Global Telecommunications Conference* (pp. 1 – 6).

Achilleos, A., Yang, K., & Georgalas, N. (2010). Context modelling and a context-aware framework for pervasive service creation: A model-driven approach. *Elsevier Journal on Pervasive and Mobile Computing, Context Modelling. Reasoning and Management, 6*(2), 281–296.

Balagtas-Fernandez, F. T., & Hussmann, H. (2008). Model-driven development of mobile applications. In *Proceedings of the 23rd IEEE/ACM International Conference on Automated Software Engineering*, (pp. 509-512).

Bartolomeo, G., Blefari-Melazzi, N., Cortese, G., Friday, A., Prezerakos, G., Walker, R., & Salsano, S. (2006). SMS: Simplifying Mobile Services - For users and service providers. In *Proceedings of the Advanced International Conference on Telecommunications and International Conference on Internet and Web Applications and Services*, (p. 209).

Dern, D. (2010). Cross-platform smartphone apps still difficult. *IEEE Spectrum*, 2010.

Dunkel, J., & Bruns, R. (2007). Model-driven architecture for mobile applications. In *Proceedings of the 10th international conference on Business information systems*, (pp. 464-477).

Eclipse Foundation Incorporation. (2011). *Eclipse modelling framework*. EMF.

Evermann, J., & Wand, Y. (2005). Toward formalizing domain modelling semantics in language syntax. *IEEE Transactions on Software Engineering, 31*(1), 21–37.

Gronmo, R., Skogan, D., Solheim, I., & Oldevik, J. (2004). Model-driven Web services development. In *IEEE International Conference on e-Technology, e-Commerce and e-Service*, (pp. 42-45). IEEE Press.

Heines, J. M., & Schedlbauer, M. J. (2007). Teaching object-oriented concepts through GUI programming. In *Proceedings of the 11th Workshop on Pedagogies and Tools - Teaching and Learning Object Oriented Concepts*.

Jelinek, J., & Slavik, P. (2004). GUI generation from annotated source code. *In Proceedings of the 3rd Annual Conference on Task Models and Diagrams*, (pp. 129-136).

Kapitsaki, G. M., Kateros, D. A., Prezerakos, G. N., & Venieris, I. S. (2009). Model-driven development of composite context-aware Web applications. *Elsevier Journal Information and Software Technology, 51*(8), 1244–1260.

Kapitsaki, G. M., Kateros, D. A., Prezerakos, G. N., & Venieris, I. S. (2009). Model-driven development of composite context-aware web applications. *Information and Software Technology, 51*(8), 1244–1260.

Kapitsaki, G. M., Kateros, D. A., & Venieris, I. S. (2008). Architecture for provision of context-aware web applications based on Web services. In *IEEE 19th International Symposium on Personal, Indoor and Mobile Radio Communications*, (pp. 1-5).

Kleppe, A. G., Warmer, J., & Bast, W. (2003). *MDA explained: The model driven architecture: Practice and promise*. Boston, MA: Addison-Wesley Longman Publishing Co.

Link, S., Schuster, T., Hoyer, P., & Abeck, S. (2008). Focusing graphical user interfaces in model-driven software development. In *Proceedings of the First International Conference on Advances in Computer-Human Interaction*, (pp. 3-8). IEEE Computer Society.

Object Management Group. (2006). *Object constraint language (OCL) specification* v.2.0.

Object Management Group. (2007). *Unified modelling language (UML) specification* v.2.1.2.

Ortiz, G., & Prado, A. G. (2009). Adapting Web services for multiple devices: A model-driven, aspect-oriented approach. In *Proceedings of the IEEE Congress on Services*, (pp. 754-761).

Ortiz, G., & Prado, A. G. (2009). Mobile-aware Web services. In *International Conference on Mobile Ubiquitous Computing, Systems, Services and Technologies*, (pp. 65-70).

Sauer, S., Drksen, M., Gebel, A., & Hannwacker, D. (2006). *GUIbuilder: A tool for model-driven development of multimedia user interfaces*.

Serral, E., Valderas, P., & Pelechano, V. (2010). Towards the model-driven development of context-aware pervasive systems. *Elsevier Journal on Pervasive and Mobile Computing, Context Modelling. Reasoning and Management, 6*(2), 254–280.

Sheng, Q. Z., & Benatallah, B. (2005). ContextUML: A UML-based modeling language for model-driven development of context-aware web services. In *International Conference on Mobile Business*, (pp. 206-212). IEEE Computer Society Press.

Singh, Y., & Sood, M. (2009). Model driven architecture: A perspective. In *IEEE International Advance Computing Conference*, (pp. 1644-1652).

KEY WORDS AND DEFINITIONS

Code Generation: Defines the process that enables the transformation of a model to the corresponding implementation code, which can be readily executed on a specific platform.

Metamodelling: The process that guides the definition of a metamodel, which describes the elements, properties and relationships of a particular modelling domain; i.e. domain specific language.

Mobile Services: Define software services that can be accessed and used through mobile or wireless networks from any type of device; smartphone, laptop, etc.

Model-Driven Development: A software development methodology that focuses on the design and implementation of software applications at an abstract platform-independent level.

Service Development: Defines the systematic procedure that includes the phases of requirement analysis, design, implementation and deployment of a software service.

Services Adaptation: Refers to the capability of the software service to be accessible and adapt its behaviour in accordance to the type of mobile client from which it is executed and the context information.

Web Services: Software systems designed to support interoperable computer interaction over a network. They are implemented as application programming interfaces (API) or Web APIs accessed in a standardized way using the XML, SOAP, WSDL and UDDI open standards over an Internet protocol backbone.

Chapter 13
A Service-Based Approach to Connect Context-Aware Platforms and Adaptable Android for Mobile Users

Valérie Monfort
SOIE, Tunisia

Sihem Cherif
SOIE, Tunisia

Rym Chaabani
ISIG, Tunisia

ABSTRACT

Many companies include in their Information Systems (IS) several communicating heterogeneous middleware according to their technical needs. The need is the same when IS require the use of context aware platforms for different aims. Moreover, users may be mobile and would like receiving and send services with their PDAs that emphasize further the need to Android based human man interface. In this chapter, the authors show how they extend Android to make it adaptable and interoperable. They also present how we communicate between different heterogeneous context-aware platforms as WComp and OpenORB by using Android and Web Services. The usefulness of the proposed approach is demonstrated through a concrete case study.

INTRODUCTION

Economical context influences companies and their Information System (IS). Companies acquire other competitors or develop new business skills, delocalize the whole or a part of their organization.

Moreover they are faced to powerful competitors, and they have to shortly develop new products that fit to customer needs. New functional needs are not the only changes to take into account by the architects because technologies are constantly moving forward which impacts seriously architectures. It is the reason why architectures have to

DOI: 10.4018/978-1-4666-2089-6.ch013

be flexible enough to take into account changes and to reduce impacts that are costly in terms of time and resources.

Service Oriented Architecture (SOA) offers a great flexibility to IS. Each application owns interfaces masking the implementation details. Applications are seen as black boxes independently connected to each other as Enterprise Application Integration (EAI) bus with its adapters (connecting the bus to the applications). However, this integration solution does not allow connecting heterogeneous applications or infrastructures as distant IS.

Web services (O'Reilly, 2005), (Ferrara, 2004), (Staab & vander & Benjamins, 2003) represent the cheapest and simplest solution to resolve this problem. They offer interoperability because they are based on standards as XML (XML, 210) and allow loose coupling. We proposed aspects-based solutions to gain in terms of simplicity and flexibility without re-deploying code with a non intrusive manner (Hmida & Tomaz & Monfort, 2006), (Tomaz & Hmida & Monfort, 2006). We based our more recent approach on extended BPEL (Business Process Execution Language) and temporized automatons (Alur & Drill, 1994) (Hennicker & Knapp, 2007), that we prototyped by providing client, and server adaptability. Moreover, these are also used to manage contextual data coming from different equipments as supervision infrastructure for instance. Current middleware (EAI and ESB as Enterprise Service Bus) are not fitted to deal with these kinds of information such as sending alarms and taking decision. Context adaptation (Sanchez-Loro, 2008), (Addison-Wesley, 1995) platforms such as WCOMP (Tigli & Lavirotte & Rey & Hourdin & Cheung-Foo-Wo & Callegari & Riveill, 2009), OpenORB (Cheung-Foo-Wo & Riveill & Tigli, 2009), Aura (Garlan & Siewiorek & Smailagic & Steenkiste, 2002), Cortex (Biegel & Cahill,2004) and OpenCom (Cheung-Foo-Wo & Riveill & Tigli, 2009)aim to manage contextual data.

On top of all, users are most of the time mobile and they want to access specific and fitted services according to their profile and their location with push and pull manners. Unfortunately, Human Man Interface platforms as Android do not allow adaptability. Concretely, Android (Burnette, 2009) is one of the most famous environments used for PDA. The Android platform uses many different technologies. Some of them are new, and some have been seen before in other settings such as: i) Location awareness, through inexpensive GPS devices, ii) Handheld accelerometers, such as those found on the Nintendo Wii remote, iii) Mashups, often combining maps with other information. Several popular Android programs use these concepts to create a more compelling and relevant experience for the user. For example, the Locale application can adapt the settings on the user's phone based on where he is.

Introducing such platforms in IS shows some problems as: i) Interoperability between context aware platforms as WComp and OpenORB, ii) Interoperability with other applications and other middleware, iii) using Human Man Interface that communicates with any platform by message sending, iv) making current Human Man Interface technologies such as Android adaptable according to context, v) processes are supported by all platforms. In this chapter we propose an Aspects and Web Services approach to make Android adaptable according to context and to communicate between Android, WComp and OpenORB. This chapter is structured as followed. Firstly, we present main technologies we used in our research work. Secondly, we present a case study. Thirdly, we show how we introduce aspects in Android. Fourthly, we propose to add aspects in Android code to increase adaptability. In the Fifth section we show how to bridge the gap between heterogeneous platforms as Android, WComp and OpenORB. Then, we present related works, future works. Then, we conclude. First of all, let us describe now the main technologies we use.

Figure 1. Web service approach

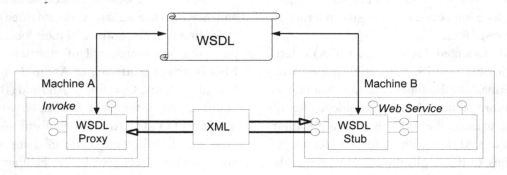

BASIC CONCEPTS

Web Services

Web services (OMG, 1989), (Staab & vander & Benjamins, 2003), (Tidwell, 2000) like any other middleware technology, aim to provide mechanisms to bridge heterogeneous platforms, allowing data to flow across various programs. The Web services technology looks very similar to what most middleware technologies looks like. Consequently, each Web service possesses an Interface Definition Language, namely WSDL (Web Service Description Language), which is responsible for the message payload, itself described with the equally famous protocol SOAP (Simple Object Access Protocol), while data structures are explained by XML (eXtended Modeling language) (Cheung-Foo-Wo & Riveill & Tigli, 2009). Very often, Web services are stored in UDDI (Universal Description Discovery and Integration) registry. In fact, the winning card of this technology is not its mechanism but rather the standards upon which it is built. Indeed, each of these standards is not only open to everyone but, since all of them are based on XML, it is pretty easy to implement these standards for most platforms and languages. For this reason, Web services are highly interoperable and do not rely on the underlying platform they are built on, unlike many ORPC. According to a vast majority of industrial leaders, Web services are the best fitted technology for implementing SOA (Zimmerli, 2009), (Bell, 2010).

Web services provide a minimalist mechanism to interconnect different applications. But one fundamental point is the importance of the WSDL being the exact interface of the system. As noted previously, most of ORPCs take a great care of hiding the message layer details from the developer. This approach breaks down when the applications involved do not lay on the same middleware infrastructure, and when interoperability becomes a major concern, Traditional ORPC fails to achieve this properly. With Web services, the message contract (WSDL) is the central meeting point which connects applications. The WSDL contract constitutes the design view upon which developers can generate both client and server sides (proxy and stub), as can be seen in Figure 1.

WS-BPEL is a Web services orchestration language. An orchestration specifies an executable process that involves message exchange with other systems. For example, the message exchange sequences are controlled by the orchestration designer. WS-BPEL provides a language for the specification of Executable and Abstract business processes. By doing so, it extends the WS interaction model and enables it to support business transactions.

Mule ESB

Mule ESB is a lightweight Java-based Enterprise Service Bus (ESB) and integration platform. It allows developers to connect applications together quickly and easily, enabling them to exchange data.

Figure 2. Message flow

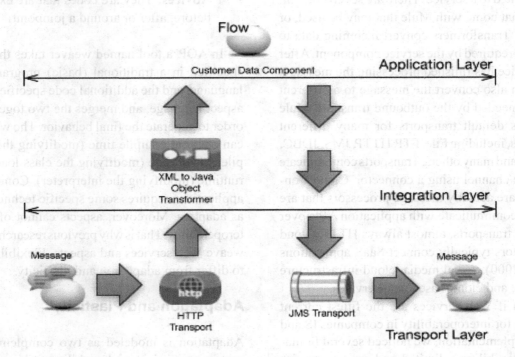

Mule ESB enables easy integration of existing systems, regardless of the different technologies that the applications use, including JMS, Web Services, JDBC, HTTP, etc.

The key advantage of an ESB is that it allows different applications to communicate with each other by acting as a transit system for processing data exchange between applications within the enterprise or across the Internet. Mule ESB includes powerful capabilities that include:

- Service creation, hosting expose and host reusable services, using Mule ESB as a lightweight service container.
- Service mediation shield services from message formats and protocols, separate business logic from messaging, and enable location-independent service calls.
- Message routing routes, filters, aggregates, and re-sequences messages based on content and rules.

- Data transformation is a mechanism to encapsulate data in a transport protocol because these data are shared and exchanged and their format is heterogeneous.

As shown with Figure 2 Mule architecture splits up into following layers: the application layer, the integration layer, and the transport layer. A service component is a class, Web service, or another application that contains the business logic to plug into the Mule service bus. It is possible to use any existing Java class, Spring Bean, a Cloud Connector, or create a new component. The Mule configuration file allows configuring all the needed elements in Mule instance. Message Processors are the basic building blocks in Mule and components, routers, filters; transformers are all message processors. Inbound routers specify how messages are routed to a service, while outbound routers specify how messages are routed after the service has finished processing them. Filters specify conditions that must be met for a message to be routed to a service. There are several default filters that come with Mule that may be used, or created. Transformers convert incoming data to the type required by the service component. After the service has finished processing the message, they can also convert the message to a different type as needed by the outbound transport. Mule provides default transports for many different channels, including File, FTP, HTTP, JMS, JDBC, Quartz, and many others. Transports communicate with the channel using a connector. Cloud Connectors are actually message processors that are used to communicate with application APIs over existing transports, almost always HTTP. Cloud Connectors typically connect SaaS applications (SaaS, 2000), social media, cloud infrastructure services, and cloud-based data services.

Even if Web services are the fittest current solution for interoperability in companies IS and SOA implementation, we noticed several limitations. Flexibility is limited and any change involves to redeploy services. For this reason we used Aspect Oriented Programming (AOP) to increase flexibility of SOA.

Aspects

Aspect Oriented Programming (AOP) is viewed as an answer to improve Web services flexibility. AOP (Kiczales & Lamping & Maeda & Lopes, 1997) , (Verheecke & Cibran & Jonckers, 2003), (Charfi & Mezini, 2004) is a paradigm that enables the modularization of crosscutting concerns into single units called aspects, which are modular units of crosscutting implementation.

Aspect-oriented languages are implemented over a set of definitions:

- **Joinpoints:** They denote the locations in the program that are affected by a particular crosscutting concern.
- **Pointcuts:** They specify a collection of conditional joinpoints.
- **Advices:** They are codes that are executed before, after or around a joinpoint.

In AOP, a tool named weaver takes the code specified in a traditional (basic) programming language, and the additional code specified in an aspect language, and merges the two together in order to generate the final behavior. The weaving can occur at compile time (modifying the compiler), load time (modifying the class loader) or runtime (modifying the interpreter). Connecting applications requires some specific technologies as adapters. Moreover, aspects cannot offer interoperability. That is why previous research works weave Web services and aspects. Flexibility has to differ from adaptation and plasticity.

Adaptation and Plasticity

Adaptation is modeled as two complementary system properties: i) adaptability, and ii) adaptivity. Adaptability is the capacity of the system to allow users to customize their system from a predefined set of parameters. Adaptivity is the capacity of the system to perform adaptation automatically without deliberate action from the user's part. Whether adaptation is performed on human requests or automatically, the design space for adaptation includes three additional orthogonal axes.

- **The Adaptation Target:** This axis denotes the entities for which adaptation is intended: adaptation to users, adaptation to the environment, and adaptation to the physical characteristics of the system. The physical characteristics of a system can be refined in terms of interactional devices (e.g., mouse, keyboard, screen, video cameras), computational facilities (e.g., memory and processing power), and communicational facilities (e.g., bandwidth rate of the communication channels with other computing facilities).

- **The Adaptation Means:** This axis denotes the components of the system involved in adaptation. Typically, the system task model, the rendering techniques, and the help subsystems, may be modified to adapt to the targeted entities. The system task model is the system implementation of the user task model specified by human factor specialists. The rendering techniques denote the observable presentation and behavior of the system. The help subsystems include help about the system and help about the task domain.

- **The Adaptation Temporal Dimension:** Adaptation may be static (i.e., effective between sessions) and/or dynamic (i.e., occurring at run time).

The term "plasticity" is inspired from the property of materials that expand and contract under natural constraints without breaking, thus preserving continuous usage. By analogy, plasticity is the capacity of a user interface to withstand variations of both the system physical characteristics and the environment while preserving usability. In addition, a plastic user interface is specified once to serve multiple sources of variations, thus minimizing development and maintenance costs. Plasticity may be static and/or dynamic. It may be achieved automatically and/or manually. Within the design space of adaptation, plasticity is characterized in the following way:

- Along the target axis, plasticity is concerned with the variations of the system physical characteristics and/or the environment. Therefore, it does not cover adaptation to users' variations.

- Along the means axis, plasticity involves the modification of the system task model and/or of the rendering techniques.

- The temporal and automaticity axis are left opened.

Technically, plasticity requires software portability. However, platform independent code execution is not a sufficient condition. Virtual toolkits, such as the Java abstract machine, offer very limited mechanisms for the automatic reconfiguration of a user interface in response to variations of interactional devices. All of the current tools for developing user interfaces embed an implicit model of a single class of target computers (typically, a keyboard, a mouse and at least a 640x480 color screen).

As a result, the rendering and responsiveness of a Java applet may be satisfactory on the developer's workstation but not necessarily usable for a remote Internet user. Experience shows that portability does not guarantee usability continuity. In addition, the iterative nature of the user interface development process, as well as code maintenance, makes it difficult to maintain consistency between the multiple target versions.

The user profile (Hancock & Toma & Ellison, 2007) covers broad aspects such as its cognitive and social environment, which determine its intentions during a session of research. The construction of the profile reflects a process that allows to instantiate its representation from various sources. This process, generally implicit, is based on an inference process on the user's context and preferences via his behavior during the use of: i) An access system to information requests, ii) A Web browser and, iii) Other e-mail applications tools. The evolution of the profiles indicates their adaptation to the variation of the users' interests they describe, and consequently, the variation of their services and information needs in time.

Mobility (Schilit & Theimer, 1994), user's profiles, are context elements that impact on adaptability. The term context (Dey, 2001) is defined as any information that can be used to characterize the situation of an entity. An entity is a person, place or object that is considered relevant to the interaction between a user and an application, including the user and application themselves (Dey & Abowd, 2000) . Some examples of con-

Table 1. Main characteristics of the context adaptation platforms

Criteria		WComp	OpenORB
Architecture	Centralized	X	
	Decentralized		X
Service		X	X
Events management		X	
Object/Component	Object		X
	Component	X	
Re configuration	Reflexion		X
	Assembling	X	
Configuration file	.dll	X	
	.jar		X
Interoperability		X	X
Adaptability approach	MOP		X
	Weaving	X	
	Generation	X	

text include location, company policy, resource availability, hardware and software environment, physical environment, user identity and the goals of the user.

Context-Aware Platforms

There are many Context-aware platforms that are mostly research works and are considered as middleware. Platforms classification allows us defining two great groups once based on Java (.Jar files) as OpenOrb and the other based on .Net (.dll files) such as WComp (Table 1). OpenOrb and Wcomp are representative of these two groups. They are all based on services for interoperability but adaptability techniques change. For instance, OpenOrb is based on reflexion and MOP, WComp uses dynamic components reconfiguration.

OpenORB (Cheung-Foo-Wo & Riveill & Tigli, 2009) is an adaptable and reflexive middleware. OpenORB provides a Java implementation of the OMG CORBA 2.4.2 specification including following services as: Concurrency Control Service, Event Service, Interoperable Naming Service, Notification Service, Persistent State Service, Property Service, Time Service, Trading Service,

and Transaction Service. OpenORB combines all CORBA features with implementation specific extensions, with the aim of being the most powerful and complete CORBA implementation in Java.

WComp (Tigli & Lavirotte & Rey & Hourdin & Cheung-Foo-Wo & Callegari & Riveill, 2009) is a prototyping "development" environment for context-aware applications. The WComp Architecture is organized around Containers and Designers paradigms. The purpose of the Containers is to take into account system services required by Components of an assembly during runtime: instantiation, destruction of software Components and Connectors. The purpose of the Designers allows configuring assemblies of through Containers. To promote adaptation to context WComp uses Aspect Assembly paradigm and dynamic reconfiguration of components.

Wcomp is an embedded platform used in industrial systems and smart houses; whereas OpenOrb is used as a middleware in Information System to connect applications such as ESB and EAI. Based on Services and aspects they allow both interoperability and aspects. These two platforms are used in the followings case studies to illustrate our approach.

CASE STUDY 1

Description

A person owns a PDA and walks in the street. This person subscribed to different service provider's access to different services dynamically provided according to location but also according to the person's desire or goal. Some other services in a SaaS (SaaS, 2000) manner are also offered to the person according to his profile: sex, age, profession, handicapped or not. Moreover, the person can precise the distance between him and the services. For instance, the person subscribed to bank services. He walks in the street and the vocal system asks for him: "Do you want to find a bank," the person can answer "yes." The system can propose the closest bank and indicates the way to go to the bank. The person can ask for another bank one kilometer around. The system proposes to him other banks and asks him what kind of operations he wants to do. The person can ask for an ATM, and the system can indicate the ATM of the selected bank does not work; the person has to choose another proposed bank. Moreover, the HMI adapts itself according to the profile of the person. For instance, for a girl the Interface will be in pink, for a boy in blue. If the person is blind, the vocal interface will be switched on. The person can ask to dynamically change the color or the display mode. This person may use his PDA to manage the different devices in his smart house and he can switch on the light, TV. remotely. Moreover, this person works in a company that manages different devices and he has to administrate the equipments. The equipments send information to a middleware that sends information to a database or if there is a problem the user receives a message on his PDA else on his TV screen if the PDA is switched off.

Proposed Architecture

WComp is the middleware used in the Smart House where services are embedded. OpenORB is used in the company as a middleware to collect information and alarms from the equipments to send them in a data base and/or on the user's PDA. WComp, OpenORB and Android have to communicate even if they are not based on the same technologies. We use Sharp-Develop software to implement the case study. So, we can solve the interoperability problem between platforms to connect the three platforms: Open ORB, Android and Wcomp using Web services. Each user reaches this gateway with his account. So, the main process is as followed: i) To adapt the Human Man Interface according to location and profile, ii) to show the alarms via OpenORB, iii) to recover the messages of alarms via user's PDA, iv) to send the alarms from PDA via WCOMP in the Smart House, iv) if PDA is off OpenORB sends the messages on the TV screen. Communication and interoperability is allowed by Web Services (cf. Figure 3).

Android side architecture (cf. Figure 4) proposes to embed Android on the PDA. Android dynamically adapts presentation. It allows asking for services, and sending location and user ID (step 1) to an identification gateway (step 2) that identifies and authenticates the user to know his profile (step 3). Then, profile information are sent to Android that adapt the HMI(step 4) and the system looks for the fitted available services (step

Figure 3. General architecture

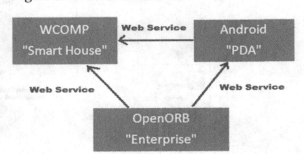

Figure 4. Android side architecture

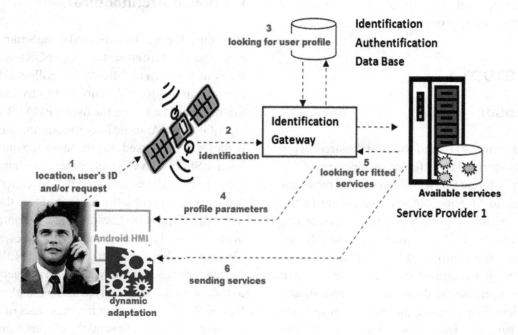

Figure 5. SCA modeling

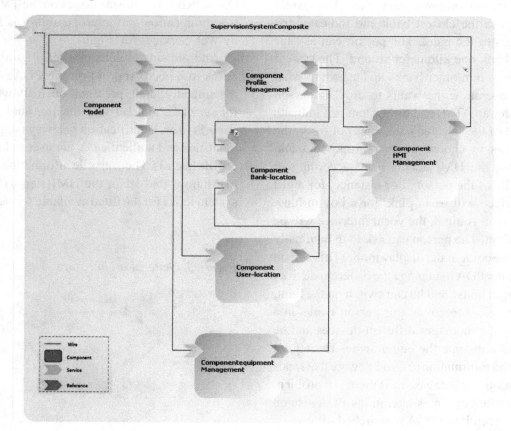

Figure 6. Communications between platforms

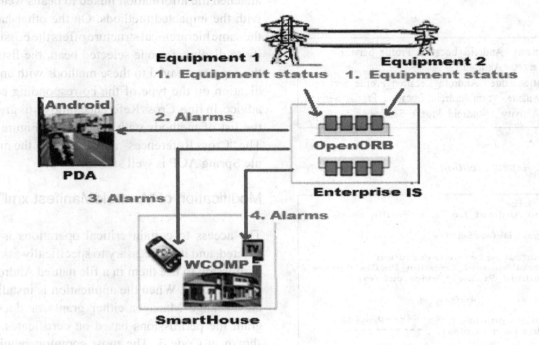

5) that are sent to the user via Android (step 6). So services are sent on a pulled or pushed manner.

Figure 5 shows the services according to SCA formalism (The Edwards, 2011). It presents the set of services for mobility associated to a user's profile to find a bank and ATM. HMI offers services and is adapted according to location and profile.

Figure 6 shows the different equipments of the company sending messages to the OpenORB middleware in the Information System (IS) of the company (step1). It collects messages and according to the status of the message, it sends critical messages to the user on his PDA (step 2) via Android platform. The user may be mobile as walking in the street or be static in his house. So the alarms are sent to his PDA in the Smart House (step 3). If the PDA is off, alarms are sent from OpenORB via Wcomp that sends the alarms via TV screen if it is switched on. The following sections show the different step to implement interoperability and the results of this implementation.

Android Adaptability Prototype 1

Android Project Files

Each Android project includes three main files as: i) Main.XML that manages interface components, ii) AndroidManifest.XML that contains the set of references used to execute Android application, iii) Active.java that is used to start Android.

Android Project Creation

As proposed in Code 1, the name of the project is "Android_Location_Profil_Services" with the characteristics of the created project.

Creation of the "Before" Aspect

Before the method "onCreate" (Code 2) an aspect is created that displays the following message: "Provide available services please:." Line 2 shows the aspect "BeforeService." Line 3 contains a "pointcut" that intercepts the method of

Code 1. Characteristics of the Android created project

```
Project name:  Android_Location_Profile_Service
Build Target:   Android 1.6
Application name:  Android_Location_Profile_Service
Package name:   com.Android_Location_Profile_Service
Create Activity:   Android_Profile_Service
```

Code 2. Aspect creation

```
1.  package
    com.Android_Location_Profile_Service ;

2.  aspect BeforeService {

3.  pointcut aspbefore ():execution
    (*com.Android_Location_Profile_Service.
    Android_Profile_Service.onCreate (..));

4.  before () : aspbefore (){

System.out.println ("**********Provide
available services please : **********");
```

the class "Android_Profil_Service" from "com.Android_Location_Profil_Service" package.

The extension of the Spring IDE plug-in includes Spring IDE AOP Extension. Spring IDE AOP offers the Bean Cross References view that allows watching the various aspects weaved to one bean. This view owns a hierarchical structure to display all the various aspects as well as the contained code advice. Then, for each of them, is attached the information linked to beans weaved with the impacted methods. On the other hand, the same hierarchical structure offers the possibility to display, for one selected bean, the lists of the aspects weaved to these methods with an indication on the type of the corresponding code advice. In fine, Cross References allows us giving the list of methods with aspects (cf. Figure 7). The "Cross References" make sure that the module Spring AOP is well started.

Modification of "AndroidManifest.xml"

The access to certain critical operations is restricted, and it is necessary to specifically ask for permission to use them in a file named AndroidManifest.xml. When the application is installed, the Package Manager either grants or doesn't grant the permissions based on certificates. As shown in Code 3. The most common required permissions are:

- **INTERNET:** Access the Internet.
- **ACCESS_COARSE_LOCATION:** Use a coarse location provider such as cell towers or WIFI.
- **ACCESS_FINE_LOCATION:** Use a more accurate location provider such as GPS.

Figure 7. Cross references

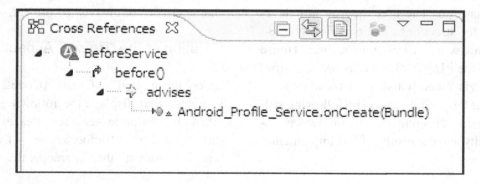

Code 3. AndroidManifest.xml

```
1.  <uses-permission
2.  android:name="android.permission.ACCESS_COARSE_LOCATION">
3.  </usespermission>
4.  <uses-permission
5.  android:name="android.permission.ACCESS_FINE_LOCATION">
6.  </usespermission>
7.  <uses-permission android:name="android.permission.INTERNET">
8.  </usespermission>
```

Using XML tags in AndroidManifest.xml allows restricting who can start an activity, start or bind a service, broadcast intents to a receiver, or access the data in a content provider. So, we add these lines to "AndroidManifest.xml" before the XML tag <application>. The system uses this permission before running the application. Lines 1 to 3 allows an application accessing to a secondary location (as WIFI for instance). Lines 4 to 6 allow an application to access the fitted site (as GPS). Lines 7 and 8 allow an application accessing to Internet.

Modification of "main.xml"

« main.xml » is an Android XML file. Android is optimized for mobile devices with limited memory. The Eclipse plug-in invokes the Android resource compiler, to adapt, and to preprocess the XML into a compressed binary format. This format, with the original XML text, is stored on the device. Line 1 code 4 offers to create a component "TextView" called "Location." From this component, the text "Location." Line 2 proposes a component "EditText" in the Android interface. The text area "Edit text" is used to fill up the coordinates to select users.

Android uses XML files for the Layout of widgets. In our example, the Android for Eclipse plug-in generates a main.xml file for the layout. This file owns the XML based definitions of the different widgets and their containers.

Creation of the Classes: "Profile," "Service,"" Location"

We would like creating three data bases as: profile. db, service.db and location.db. Profile.d includes a "profile" table that shows five attributes: id-profile, name, sex, job, and age. Service.db contains a "service" table that includes five other attributes: id-service, service-name, description, location and distance. Location.db includes a "location table that includes three attributes as: id-location, longitude, altitude (Code 4). We add in the title bar the identifier of the person during application loading application (cf. Figure 8).

Creation of the First Interface

From Code 5, we get information concerning the user (e.g. name, sex, age) and the system joins this information to a message called "Hello." The system looks for services (Code 6) corresponding to "Cherif Sihem" profile in the database as shown in Code 7. This method adds a new person to the database. The message "Do you want a service?" is displayed to the user. We aim to get data from profile.db database and to use them in the Android application. For instance, we insert, in the text id-profile of the Android activity, the id-profile of the profile.db database.

Code 4. Main.xml

```
1.    <TextView android:textColor="#000000"
      android:layout_width="wrap_content"
      android:id="@+id/position" android:text="Position"
      android:layout_height="wrap_content">
      </TextView>

2.    <EditText android:layout_width="100dip"
      android:text=" "
      android:id="@+id/editposition"
      android:gravity="center"
      android:layout_height="50dip"
      android:layout_marginLeft="60dip" >

3.    </EditText>

4.    <EditText android:layout_width="100dip"
      android:text=" "
      android:id="@+id/editposition1"
      android:gravity="center"
      android:layout_height="50dip"
      android:layout_marginLeft="10dip" >

5.    </EditText>
```

Figure 8. General interface

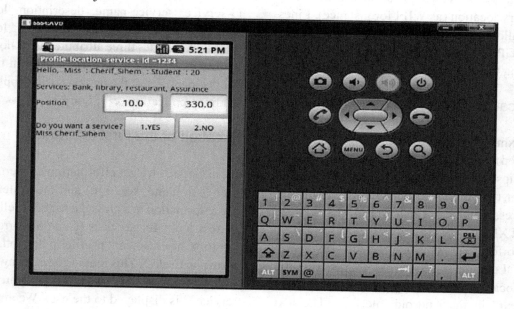

Experimentation Results

The user is detected with a GPS system. The services are displayed according to his profile and his location. The system detects Sihem is a girl without any handicap but she asks for vocal assistance (cf. Figure 9). So, it proposes her a list of services on her screen. To get the list, she selects "1.YES" then a list of services is chosen. We only displayed the left part of the PDA screen.

Code 5. Interface building

```
1   String id_profile= cursor.getString(1);
2   String Name= cursor.getString(2);
3   String Sexe = cursor.getString(3);

4   builder.append(Sexe).append(" : ");
5   builder.append(Name).append(" : ");
6   builder.append(Age).append("\n ");

// Display on the screen

7   setTitle( "Profile_location_service: id
    ="+id_profile);
8   bonjour.setText("Hello, "+builder);
```

Code 6. Profile linked to service

```
TextView service_by_profile= ( TextView)
findViewById(R.id.Services_by_profile);
service_by_profile.setText("Services: Bank,
library, restaurant, Assurance");
```

Code 7. Identification of the user and profiling

```
1   profil = new EventsData(this);
try {
2   addEvent("1234","Cherif_Sihem","Miss",
    "Student","20");

3   Cursor cursor = getEventsprofil();
4   showEventsprofil(cursor);
```

She says "Insurance" and the system proposes her several possibilities (cf. Figure 10) as: BIAT, STB, BNA with the distance according to her location. She chooses BIAT Company. She decided also to change the color of the screen.

Figure 9. Proposed services according to location

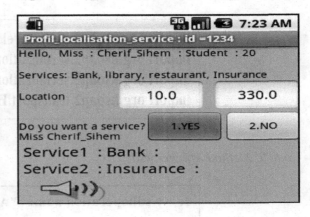

Figure 10. Proposing services with the distance

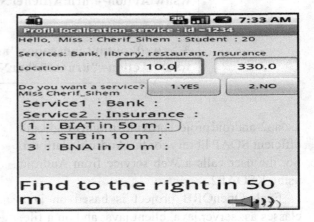

After presenting the introduction of aspects in Android code to get adaptability, we illustrate now to illustrate interoperability between platforms.

Interoperability Implementation

Parameterization

This initialization of the system requires several steps shown as follows. To call the Web services on Android, we use KSOAP2 (cf. Code 8) (ksoap2-android-ensemble-2.4-jar-with-dependencies. jar). Then we start Apache Axis2 server. So our application is executed in Web mode. The

Code 8. Using KSOAP2

```
import org.ksoap2.SoapEnvelope;
import org.ksoap2.serialization.SoapObject;
import org.ksoap2.serialization.SoapSerializationEnvelope;
import org.ksoap2.transport.HttpTransportSE;
```

Code 9. Method Afficher.wsdl

```
1.  <wsdl:operation name="AfficherNormal">

2.  < wsdl:input message="ns:AfficherNormalRequest"
wsaw:Action="urn:AfficherNormal" />

3.  <wsdl:output message="ns:AfficherNormalResponse"
wsaw:Action="urn:AfficherNormalResponse" />
```

ksoap2-android project provides a lightweight and efficient SOAP library for the Android platform. So, the user calls a Web service from Android using KSOAP2.

Each OpenORB project is based on java classes as: server.java, client.java, and on a file. Then, the goal of the OpenORB server is to provide objects (corresponding to the implementation) to the clients, to receive the requests. This operation includes 3 stages: i) Initialization of the ORB, ii) Activation of the POA (the POA - Portable Object Adapter - is an object adapter that allows managing several CORBA objects) and iii) End of the execution of the ORB.

Then come the steps of the creation of the OpenORB client. The goal of the client is to reach the distant object and to call upon the methods suggested by this object. This operation proceeds in 3 steps: i) initialization of the ORB, ii) invocate the distant method and iii) obtaining a generic reference towards the distant object (starting from the IOR). Then, a basic method is created to display a simulator to generate alarms com-

ing from equipments (alarms normally coming from the equipments). We aim now to transform OpenORB classes into Web Services. Then we shall call these services in an Android project. For instance, we call the service "AfficherNormal."

Then we create a method to display alarms called Afficher.wsdl (Code 9). We create Web services, by using as source code the Java classes of the "Enterprise" application we created before, as shown from line 1 to 3.

Then we modify the activity of Android Gateway (Code 10). Line 1 allows using the dynamic project Web "Ent" that contains Web services. Line 2, allows defining the Web services method. Line 3, allows declaring a SOAP action. Line 4, of code 10, defines the relative path of the Web service, to do so, it is necessary to use IP address "192.168.1.2" with port 8080 instead of local host.

Then, Change "AndroidManifest.xml" We add the line 1, (Code 11), "AndroidManifest.xml" before the tag XML < application > that allows an application to get Internet.

Code 10. Activity modification of Android "portal"

```
1. private  String NAMESPACE = "http://Ent";
2. private   String METHOD_NAME = "AfficherNormal";

3. private   String SOAP_ACTION = NAMESPACE + METHOD_NAME;
// NAMESPACE + method name

4. private static final   String URL =
"http://192.168.1.2:8080/Entreprise/services/EntImpl?wsdl";
```

Code 11. Change "AndroidManifest.xml"

```
1.      <uses-permission
android:name="android.permission.INTERNET">
</usespermission>
```

When the tag <uses….INTENET> is added it is possible to access to the Android application via Internet and Web Services.

Results: Getting Connection with Enterprise Portal and Android to Receive Alarms

Figure 11 represents the user interface that allows reaching the portal and controlling the status of the equipments. With "Show Message" button, the user can retrieve the messages coming from the enterprise middleware with the Web Services via Android.

WComp and OpenORB Connection

The Wcomp modeling tool allows us showing the set of components. We show through a Human Man Interface, how a user can receive messages from a company via a TV screen or PDA. Wcomp in any application is as an assembly of components encapsulated in a composite service. Line 1 (Code 12) shows invocation of a method named "AfficherNormal."

Line 2 allows attributing the "results"of the method "AfficherNormal. We invoke OpenORB methods with Web services. With SharpDevelop, we create a new "web service proxy» that includes parameters such as the location of Web Service "WSDL URL" and the name of the workspace.

The simulation of alarms coming in the Smart House, either on the PDA or on the TV Screen is illustrated as followed. The process is design with the WComp design tool (cg. Figure 12). The link (step 1) with the user interface allows activating "button 1" (assembly) and the component "entreprise31" defining the entry methods, the events management associated to components. It allows getting back the OpenORB project. If radio Button called "radiobutton 1" has the status "check," then the PDA is switched on and the message is shown on the PDA, and if radio Button "radiobutton 1" is in a state "not check," then the PDA is switched off and the message will be shown on the TV. The link (step 2) represents the assembly between

Figure 11. Android interface showing company gateway and alarms

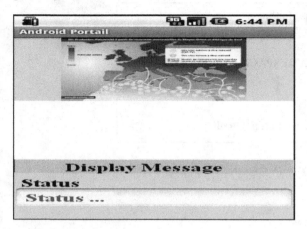

the component "Enterprise" and the component "EventToggler." The component "EventToggler" changes the status of component "radiobutton 1" (step 3) to change the status of "check." The link (step 4) represents the assembly enter the component "radiobutton 1" and the component "PDA." The component PDA feigns a PDA (step5) of an intelligent house which allows showing messages. The Web services intervene and allow specifying the event to be produced and to be shown in a Textbox «PDA.» The «EventToggler» component changes the status of the «PDA» and «TV» components with its specific evenemential methods. I mean to change the status "checked"

into "not checked" status and vice versa (step 6). The component «SOAP proxy» is a Web Service. The component "PDA" is a textbox showing the PDA interface. The "TV" (step 7) component is textbox representing the TV interface.

Case Study 2: Searching Interoperability between ESB, Context-Aware Platforms and Adaptable Android

Case Study 2 Description

A company manages a set of electrical equipments 24h/24h. It owns an Information System that receives and performs data coming from equipments and other kinds of information (clients, employees, etc). Sensors included in the equipments send messages that are routed via Mule ESB. There are three kinds of possible messages such as: normal, maintenance required, and imminent danger. An application linked to the middleware sorts each message per severity. Messages are stored in an alarm file per day and the bus sends messages via maintenance operator interface to take decision. If operator is on call, he receives messages either via his PDA equipped with Android platform, either on the TV screen if it is on. If no device is on, a message is sent to the operator's manager. They both have a smart house. The operator's

Code 12. Displaying service description

```
1. public AfficherNormalResponse AfficherNormal() {

2. object[] results = this.Invoke("AfficherNormal", new object[0]);

3. att_AfficherNormal = ((AfficherNormalResponse)(results[0]));

4. this.FireAfficherNormalMethodEvent(att_AfficherNormal);

5. return ((AfficherNormalResponse)(results[0]));
```

Figure 12. WComp modeling for alarms routing

house is equipped with WComp middleware. The manager's house owns Open Orb. So, when message is coming WComp detects devices that are on. If message indicates an imminent danger a vocal message is sent. Message is sent via his laptop, after that, via his PDA, then via Android interfaces, and finally, via his TV screen. If no device is on message is stored in an alarm file in the operator's smart house who can read this

file afterwards when one of these devices are on. Then message is routed to Open Orb via manager's home.

Proposed Architecture

WComp is the middleware offering embedded Web services found in the Smart house. Mule is used in the company as a middleware to collect information and alarms from the equipments to send them on the user's PDA. WComp, Mule and Android have to communicate even if they are not based on the same technologies. We use Sharp-Develop software to implement the case study. So, we can solve the problem of interoperability between platforms, and we can connect them with Web services. Figure 13 shows the different equipments of the company sending messages to the Mule middleware in the Information System (IS) of the company (step1). It collects messages and according to the status of the message, it sends critical messages to the user on his PDA (step 2) via Android platform. The user may be mobile as walking in the street or he may be in his house, so the alarms are sent to his PDA in the Smart House (step 3). If the PDA is off, alarms are sent from Mule via WComp that sends the alarms via TV screen if it is switched on.

Figure 14 presents SCA models and the services offered to .receive alarms according to the availability and the location of the operator or the manager

BPMN (BPMN,2011) (cf. Figure 15) is the standardized formalism used to model Process. The BPMN process shows the activties of the equipments, the operator and the manager. The equipments generate alarms that are stored and sent to the operator and to the manager if the operator is not available.

We aim to propose now a solution: i) to bridge WComp to process and, ii) to demonstrate interoperability with heterogeneous platforms as Mule, Open Orb, Android and WComp.

Figure 13. Communications between platforms

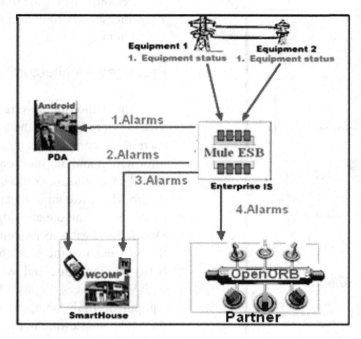

Figure 14. SCA model

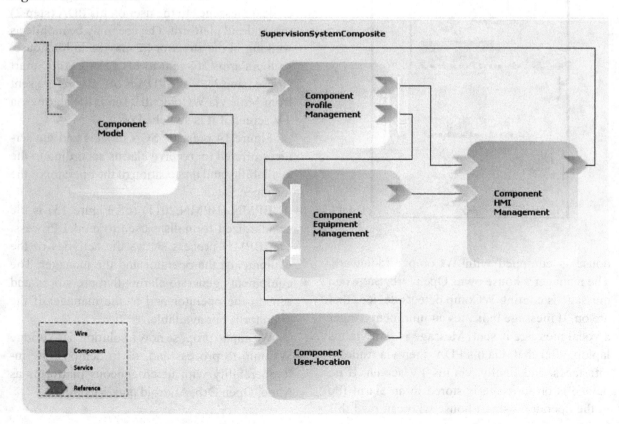

Figure 15. BPMN process

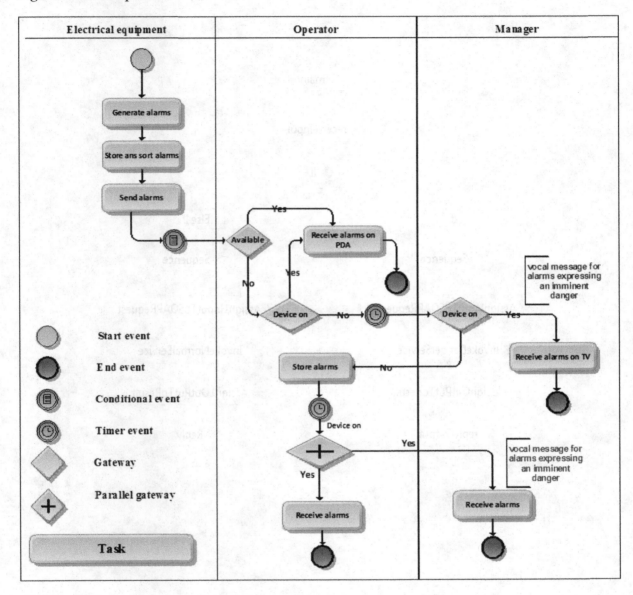

Adding Process to Wcomp

The three first steps include environment configuration. BPEL plug-in is added to Eclipse environment (cf. Figure 16) and then, Tomcat Apache is installed with ODE orchestration services engine. The step 3 allows creating a BPEL project including a BPEL extension file, a WSDL file that describes the file and an XML file for service deployment in the orchestration engine. Process is divided into two sequences according to received messages. With "if" service entry is tested. If true "danger" service is invoked. Else, service entry is tested and "normal" service is invoked. As output process, each sequence generates its own message. This message is provided by invoked service. This service owns "messaged" operation that acts as followed: if the process in-

Figure 16. BPEL with ODE orchestration service engine

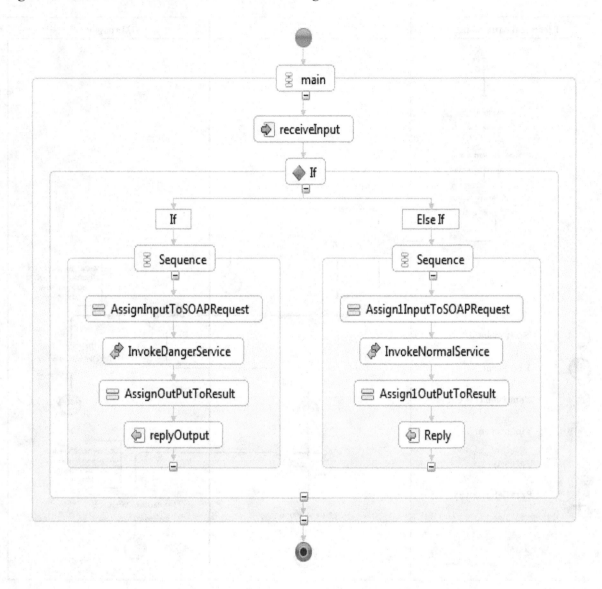

put is "danger" message so its output will be the message "system is in danger. Code 13 shows a part of WSDL description of the "danger" service. Line 1 presents the service name. Line 3 shows IP address and code 14 indicates 8087 port of the orchestration engine (ODE). Let us present now generated WSDL (cf. Figure 17).

To execute the process via orchestration engine ODE we need deployment file called deploy.xml (code15). Line 3 shows the service Provider. The Line 4 shows the BPEL process. Line 7 and 10 implement service invocation.

Last step consists in invoking BPEL process in WComp.

Code 13. Danger expression with WSDL

```
1 <wsdl:service name="Danger"
2 <wsdl:port name="DangerHttpSoap11Endpoint"
binding="ns:DangerSoap11Binding">
3  <soap:address
location="http://192.168.1.2:8087/DangerProj/services/
Danger.DangerHttpSoap11Endpoint/" />
4 </wsdl:port>
5 </wsdl:service>
```

Code 14. Process invocation with an URL

```
1 public BusinessProcessService() {
2 this.Url =
"http://localhost:8087/ode/processes/
Business Process"; }
                                    Port

                    Process
```

Figure 17. WSDL process

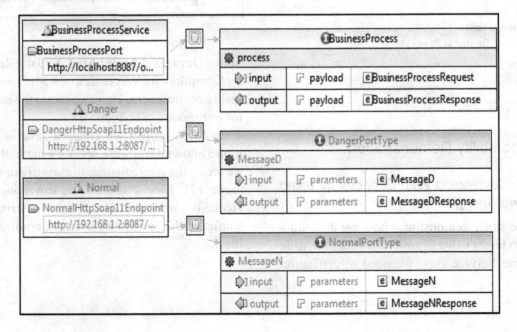

Code 15. Deploy.xml file

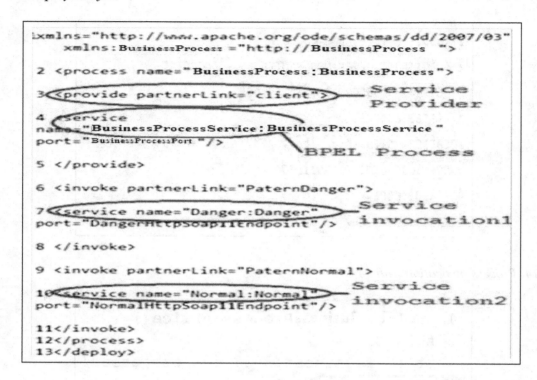

```
1 xmlns="http://www.apache.org/ode/schemas/dd/2007/03"
      xmlns:BusinessProcess ="http://BusinessProcess ">

2 <process name="BusinessProcess:BusinessProcess">

3 <provide partnerLink="client">                    Service
                                                     Provider
4 <service
  name="BusinessProcessService:BusinessProcessService"
  port="BusinessProcessPort"/>
                                                  BPEL Process
5 </provide>

6 <invoke partnerLink="PaternDanger">

7 <service name="Danger:Danger"               Service
  port="DangerHttpSoap11Endpoint"/>          invocation1

8 </invoke>

9 <invoke partnerLink="PaternNormal">

10 <service name="Normal:Normal"              Service
   port="NormalHttpSoap11Endpoint"/>        invocation2

11</invoke>
12</process>
13</deploy>
```

Figure 18. Service proxy creation for WComp process

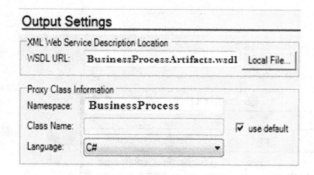

Interoperability Demonstration

Step 1: Developing Web Services by using Mule and Spring

The case study demonstrates how we develop a Web Service by using Spring with CXF and Mule Enterprise Service Bus. We need to configure:

Code 16. Interface ServiceESB.java

```
1.  package org.mule.components.simple;
2.  public interface ServiceESB
3.  { public String service(String service); }
```

Spring (Java IDE), Mule ESB, CXF Jars (Required for Compilation). We create a new Mule project in spring environment. Then, we create the interface for our service (ServiceESB).

In Mule project we create a Java interface. Line 3 allows declaring « service » method. Then, we create the implementation class of our service (code 17). Line 2 allows implementing "ServiceESB" interface that returns a string. We configure the service by creating configuration files.

Code 17. Creation of ComponentServiceESB.java

```
1.   import
     org.mule.component.simple.LogComponent;
2.   public class  ComponentServiceESB extends
     LogComponent implements ServiceESB
3.   {public String service (String service) {
4.   return service; } }
```

Code 18. Creation of ComponentServiceESB.java

```
1 <service name=" ComponentServiceESB ">
2 <component class="org.mule. ComponentServiceESB
"/>
3 </service>
```

Code 19. Spring Configuration file

```
1.   <bean id="ServiceESB" class="org.mule.
     ComponentServiceESB"
     scope="singleton">
2.   </bean>
```

To configure the service, you add a <service> element to your Mule XML configuration file and provide the name attribute. Line 1 presents the service (code 18).

Spring configuration consists in at least one bean definition, but typically there will be more than one bean definition. When using XML-based configuration, these beans are configured as <bean/> elements inside a top-level <beans/> element. These bean definitions (code 19) correspond to the actual objects that make up the application.

To expose the service as a web service, the cxf endpoint is added. The endpoint would be defined in the Mule configuration file as shown in code 20.

We can receive a SOAP service via an inbound-endpoint. To invoke the component as a SOAP request, we can open a browser and type the following in the address bar shown in code 21.

Step 2: Service Invocation of the Step 1 (Mule) Service in Wcomp

Service is invoked in WComp with WSDL URL (cf. Figure 19).

Concerning the full scenario (cf. Figure 20) of the service invocation and BPEL invocation we start scenario by activating enterprise service proxy (step1). The service displays (step2) in the « TestBox » component the « danger » message sent via mule ESB. Step 3 shows message sending to «BusinessProcessService » SOAP Proxy. This component performs received message and reformulates it with « le system is in danger status » then, it sends it to TV Component (step 4). Display mode is simulated (step 5) on a « TextBox » component. Then final modified message is sent by using « TextToSpeech » component (step 6).

Code 20. Adding tags to mule-configure xml

```
1.   <spring:beans>
2.   <spring:import resource="Context.xml" />
3.   </spring:beans>
4.   <model name="services">
5.   <service name=" ComponentServiceESB ">
6.   <inbound>
7.   <cxf:inbound-endpoint
8.   address="http://localhost:65082/services/
     ComponentServiceESB" />
9.   </inbound>
10.  <component>
11.  <spring-object bean=" ComponentServiceESB"
     />
12.  </component>
```

Code 21. To invoke the component as a SOAP request

```
1.   http://localhost:65082/services/ComponentServiceESB
     ?wsdl
```

Figure 19. Creation of service proxy in Wcomp

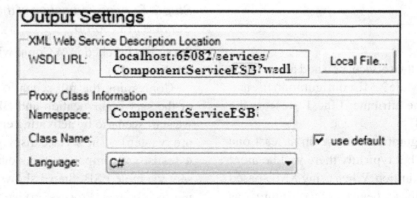

Code 22. Invocation of service with URL

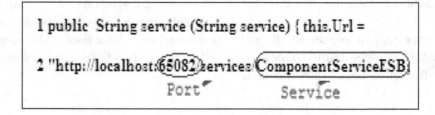

Figure 20. Scenario in WComp

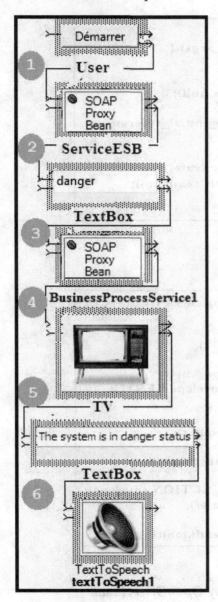

Code 23. Module entreprise.idl

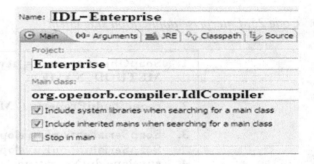

```
module Alarm {

    interface Alarm {

        String DispalyAlarm();
    };
};
```

OpenORB Adaptability Prototype

Entreprise.idl

The role of a server is to put a set of objects available to clients. To be able to reach these objects, the clients must be able to know all the methods

Figure 21. Compilation of entreprise.idl

Name: **IDL-Enterprise**

Main | Arguments | JRE | Classpath | Source

Project:
Enterprise

Main class:
org.openorb.compiler.IdlCompiler

☑ Include system libraries when searching for a main class
☑ Include inherited mains when searching for a main class
☐ Stop in main

upon which they can call on these objects. This is made through "contracts" defined by means of the Interface Definition Language (IDL). The language IDL allows expressing the cooperation between the Providers and the users of services by separating the interface of the implementation (code 23).

Server implementation: OpenORB Server

Then it is the OpenORB server (Code 24). The goal of the server is to provide objects (corresponding to the implementation) to the clients, to receive the requests. This operation proceeds in 3 stages: i) Initialization of the ORB, ii) Activation of the POA (the POA - Portable Object Adapter - is an object adapter that allows managing several CORBA objects), iii) End of the execution of the ORB.

Code 24. Enterprise application side server

```
1.  public class Server {
2.  public static void main(String[] args) {
3.  try {
4.  org.omg.CORBA.ORB orb =
    org.omg.CORBA.ORB.init(args,null);
5.  POA rootPOA =
    POAHelper.narrow(orb.resolve_initial_references(
    "RootPOA"));
6.  monEntrprise = new EntImpl();
7.  rootPOA.the_POAManager().activate();
8.  System.out.println(«The server is ready...»);
9.  orb.run();
```

Code 25. Enterprise application side client

```
1.  SoapObject request = new SoapObject(NAMESPACE,
    METHOD_NAME);

2.  request.addProperty ("Message","");

3.  SoapSerializationEnvelope envelope = new
    SoapSerializationEnvelope(SoapEnvelope.VER11);
4.  envelope.dotNet = true;

5.  envelope.setOutputSoapObject (request);

6.  HttpTransportSE androidHttpTransport = new
    HttpTransportSE(URL);
7.  androidHttpTransport.call(SOAP_ACTION,envelope);
8.  Object result = envelope.getResponse();

9.  System.out.println("Result : " + result.toString());
```

Client implementation: OpenORB Client

Next, we illustrate the creation of the OpenORB client (cf. Code 25). The goal of the customer is to reach the distant object and to call upon the methods suggested by this object. Its operation proceeds in 3 steps: i) Initialization of the ORB, ii) Invocate the distant method and iii) Obtaining a generic reference towards the distant object (starting from the IOR).

Display OpenORB Result

Figure 22. Display OpenORB result

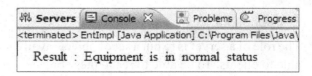

328

Code 26. Danger equipment number

```
1. private void  Test1() {
2. TextView t = (TextView) findViewById(R.id.text1);
3.for (int i=0; i<10; i++)

4. { if (METHOD_NAME=="Danger")

5. t.setText(result1.toString()+ i );
6. t.setBackgroundColor(Color.RED);}}}
```

Figure 23. General Android interface

Figure 25. Android interface showing a danger alarm

Figure 24. Android interface showing equipement in normal status

Android Adaptability Prototype 2

Figure 23 represents the user interface that allows controlling the status of the system. This user can receive this message Equipment is in normal status (cf. Figure 24), and can retrieve the messages coming from the enterprise with the Web Services via Android (Figure 25).

RELATED WORKS

Many research works focus on context-aware adaptability with different approach as platforms(Schilit & Theimer,1994), (Sanchez-Loro, 2008) , model engineering, and HMI (I-Ching, 2011), with actors dedicated to plasticity and that take into account a limited range of context elements such as screen size, language… The problem found in the approach is the difficulty in capturing and processing the contextual data. The Rainbow project (Hennicker & Knapp, 2007) promotes a reusable infrastructure with dynamic adaptation on runtime. With HMI adaptation it becomes difficult to retrieve information as parameters and data with this approach. Other research works mix mobile agents and aspects (Biegel & Cahill, 2004) for a simple HMI plasticity problem resolution but do not base on improved context adaptation platform. Interoperability with Android is allowed with Web Services. Other works such as (I-Ching, 2011) propose a Multi-layer Context Framework (MCF) that consists of context sensor layer, context information layer, context service layer, context representation layer, mobile device layer, and context-aware mobile Web 2.0 application layer. The technological approach is simplified because it is based on REST Web services to provide interoperability. However, the demonstration of interoperability with adaptability remains limited compared to our chapter. Here we used different context-aware platforms, addressed to different aims (embedded systems or information systems), and Android to demonstrate also the adaptability and interoperability with HMI. To do so, we extended Android with aspects, WCOMP with processes. We benefit reflexion and dynamic re configuration for adaptability.

CONCLUSION

Mobility coupled with the development of a wide variety of access devices has engendered new requirements for HMI such as the ability to be adapted to different contexts of use. Moreover, with the apparition of attractive and flexible platforms such as Android, HMI development offers a new opportunity to propose to the users multi functions and services including business, M-learning, usual life. Even if we proved Android adaptability and platforms interoperability, this approach presents some limitations as it remains a prototype with test cases. We would like to develop a concrete system with context adaption plate forms and data bases in SaaS and Cloud environment. We also would like to assess performances of such approach and improve it from a security viewpoint. Moreover, a full context aware approach requires interoperability between platforms to support adaptability. Even if Web Services are the fitted solution to support interoperability, nevertheless it remains the challenge for companies.

REFERENCES

W3.org. (2010). *XML 1.0 specification*. Retrieved August 22, 2010, from http://www.w3.org/TR/REC-xml

Alur, R., & Dill, D. L. (1994). A theory of timed automata. *Theoretical Computer Science, 126*(2), 183–235.

Bell, M. (2010). *SOA modeling patterns for service-oriented discovery and analysis* (p. 390). Wiley & Sons.

Biegel, G., & Cahill, V. (2004). A framework for developing mobile, context-aware applications. *Proceedings of the 2nd IEEE Conference on Pervasive Computing and Communication*, (pp. 361–365). Retrieved from http://cortex.di.fc.ul.pt/

Burnette, E. (2009). *Hello, Android, 2nd ed.: The pragmatic programmers bookshelf*. ISBN -10: 1-934356-49-2

Charfi, A., & Mezini, M. (2004). Aspect-oriented Web service composition with AO4BPEL. In *Proceedings of the 2nd European Conference on Web Services (ECOWS), volume 3250 of LNCS,* (pp. 168–182). Springer.

Cheung-Foo-Wo, D., Riveill, M., & Tigli, J. (2009). *Adaptation dynamique par tissage d'aspects d'assemblage.* Thèse I3S, Nice Sophia Antipolis.

Dey, A. K. (2001). Understanding and using context. *Personal and Ubiquitous Computing, 5*(1), 4–7.

Dey, A. K., & Abowd, G. D. (2000). *Towards a better understanding of context and context-awareness.* ACM Conference on Human Factors in Computer Systems (CHI 2000), The Hague, Netherlands, April 2000.

Edwards, M. (2011). *Service component architecture.* OASIS. Retrieved 7 April 2011, from http://oasis-opencsa.org/sca

Ferrara, A. (2004). Web services: A process algebra approach. In *ICSOC '04: Proceedings of the 2nd International Conference on Service Oriented Computing,* (pp. 242–251). New York, NY: ACM Press.

Gamma, E., Helm, R., Johnson, R., & Vlissides, J. (1995). *Elements of reusable object-oriented software.* Addison-Wesley Publishing Company.

Garlan, D., Siewiorek, D. P., Smailagic, A., & Steenkiste, P. (2002). Aura: Toward distraction free pervasive computing. *IEEE Pervasive Computing / IEEE Computer Society and IEEE Communications Society, 1*(2).

Hancock, J. T., Toma, C., & Ellison, N. (2007). The truth about lying in online dating profiles. *Proceedings of the ACM Conference on Human Factors in Computing Systems (CHI 2007),* ACM, (pp. 449–452).

Hennicker, R., & Knapp, A. (2007). Activity-driven synthesis of state machines. In M. D. Dwyer & A. Lopes (Eds.), *Proceedings 10th International Conference Fundamental Approaches to Software Engineering (FASE'07), volume 4422 of LNCS,* (pp. 87-101). Berlin, Germany: Springer.

Hmida, M. B., Tomaz, R. F., & Monfort, V. (2006). Applying aop concepts to increase web services flexibility. *Journal of Digital Information Management, 4*(1), 37–43.

I-Ching, H. (2011). An architecture of mobile Web 2.0 context-aware applications in ubiquitous Web. *Journal of Software, 6*(4).

Kiczales, G., Lamping, J., Maeda, C., & Lopes, C. (1997). Aspect-oriented programming. In *Proceedings European Conference on Object-Oriented Programming, volume 1241,* (pp. 220–242). Berlin, Germany: Springer-Verlag.

Monfort, V. (2010). *The benefits of SaaS.* Retrieved from http://www.computerworld.com/action/article.do?command=view ArticleBasic&articleId=107276

O'Reilly, T. (2005) *What is Web 2.0?* Retrieved July 12, 2010, from http://www.oreillynet.com/pub/a/oreilly/tim/news/2005/09/30/what-is-web-20.html

OMG. (2011). *BPMN 2.0.* Retrieved from http://www.omg.org/spec/BPMN/2.0/

OMG. (1989). Retrieved from Omg.org

Sanchez-Loro, X. E. (2008). *Ubiquitous web access: Collaborative optimization and dynamic content negotiation.* In International Conference on Multimedia and Ubiquitous Engineering.

Schilit, B. N., & Theimer, M. M. (1994). Disseminating active map information to mobile hosts. *IEEE Network, 8*(5), 22–32.

Staab, S., vander Aalst, W., & Benjamins, V. R. (2003). Web services: Been there, done that? *IEEE Intelligent Systems*, *18*(1), 72–85.

Tidwell, D. (2000). *Web services: The web's next revolution*.

Tigli, J. Y., Lavirotte, S., Rey, G., Hourdin, V., Cheung-Foo-Wo, D., Callegari, E., & Riveill, M. (2009). WComp middleware for ubiquitous computing: Aspects and composite event-based web services. *Annals of Telecommunications, 64*(3-4), 197. ISSN 0003-4347

Tomaz, R. F., Hmida, M. B., & Monfort, V. (2006). Concrete solutions for web services adaptability using policies and aspects. *The International Journal of Cooperative Information Systems, 15*(3), 415–438.

Verheecke, B., Cibran, M., & Jonckers, V. (2003). AOP for dynamic configuration and management of web services. In *Proceedings of the International Conference on Web Services Europe, vol. 2853.*

Zimmerli, B. (2009). *Business benefits of SOA.* University of Applied Science of Northwestern Switzerland, School of Business, 11 November 2009.

Chapter 14
Adaptive Future Internet Applications:
Opportunities and Challenges for Adaptive Web Services Technology

Clarissa Cassales Marquezan
The Ruhr Institute for Software Technology, Paluno, University of Duisburg-Essen, Germany

Vegard Engen
IT Innovation Centre, University of Southampton, UK

Andreas Metzger
The Ruhr Institute for Software Technology, Paluno, University of Duisburg-Essen, Germany

Michael Boniface
IT Innovation Centre, University of Southampton, UK

Klaus Pohl
The Ruhr Institute for Software Technology, Paluno, University of Duisburg-Essen, Germany

Stephen C. Phillips
IT Innovation Centre, University of Southampton, UK

Zlatko Zlatev
IT Innovation Centre, University of Southampton, UK

ABSTRACT

Adaptive capabilities are essential to guarantee the proper execution of Web services and service-oriented applications once dynamic changes are not exceptions but the rule. The importance of adaptive capabilities significantly increases in the context of Future Internet (FI) applications will have to autonomously adapt to changes on service provisioning, availability of things and content, computing resources, and network connectivity. Current solutions for adaptive Web services and adaptive service-based applications will be challenged in such a setting because they fall short to support essential characteristics of FI applications. This chapter analyzes and justifies the need for the transition from adaptive Web services and service-based applications to adaptive FI applications. Based on two real-world use cases from multimedia and logistics, the authors examine where current solutions fall short to properly address the adaptive needs of FI applications. They propose future research challenges that should be considered in adaptive FI applications.

DOI: 10.4018/978-1-4666-2089-6.ch014

INTRODUCTION

Adaptive capabilities are essential to guarantee the proper execution of Web services and service-oriented applications once dynamic changes are not exceptions but the rule. The importance of adaptive capabilities significantly increases in the context of Future Internet (FI) applications. As it will be described in this chapter, applications in this context will have to autonomously adapt to changes on availability of things and content, computing resources, and network connectivity in addition to changes in service provisioning as faced in Service-Oriented Systems. The unprecedented level of heterogeneity and dynamic changes of FI applications will demand a transition from adaptive Web Services and service-oriented systems to adaptive FI applications.

Four major pillars constitute the FI: the Internet of Services (IoS, e.g., software services based on third-party services), the Internet of Things (IoT, e.g., smart sensors and devices), the Internet of Content (IoC, e.g., video streams and online games) and the Network of the Future (NoF, e.g., ubiquitous connectivity). These pillars will all converge into an integrated environment (Domingue et al., 2011). It is expected that – to a large extent – FI applications will thus be composed of third-party offerings deployed on federated service delivery platforms through different cloud delivery models, such as Infrastructure as a Service (IaaS), Platform as a Service (PaaS) and Software as a Service (SaaS) (Armbrust et al., 2010).

Ultimately, this means that loosely-coupled Internet services will form a comprehensive base for developing value-added applications in an agile way (Metzger & Di Nitto, 2013, forthcoming). This is unlike traditional application development, which uses computing resources and software components under local administrative control. To maintain their quality of service, FI applications therefore need to dynamically and autonomously adapt to an unprecedented level of changes of heterogeneous entities that may occur during runtime.

Problem Statement

Over the past decade a wealth of technologies for engineering adaptive Web-based services and service-oriented systems has emerged. Those technologies offer significant advancements for what concerns furnishing applications with self-adaptive capabilities. Still, those solutions focus on isolated pillars of the FI. For example, many solutions consider software services (i.e., IoS) but fall short of integrating things (i.e., IoT) yet, the IoT amplifies the level of heterogeneity and changes on available resources and data.

Contribution

In this chapter, we review trends and current solutions for adaptive Web services and service-oriented applications. Based on real-world use cases from multimedia applications, as well as transport & logistics, we examine the transition from adaptive Web services to adaptive capabilities for FI applications. We demonstrate that FI applications promise full integration and combination of real, physical world services, business objectives and ICT services. This means a shift from considering adaptation only on the ICT level (and business level, as some initiatives already show), i.e., such as service-oriented applications, to extending this concept to unprecedented levels. The first use case explores how adaptation of IoC and IoS should be considered in FI multimedia applications. The second use case demonstrates the importance of combining IoT, IoS, and business objectives for the success of FI transport & logistics applications. Finally, we conclude proposing relevant research challenges that remain to be addressed.

In the next two sections we first describe the major facts and topics that are relevant for the purpose of this chapter. We start with the introduction of how research and ideas related to Web-services, service-oriented applications, adaptation and Future Internet evolved over the past years and got connected to each other. After this, we present an overview of technical solutions specifically developed for adaptation of Web services and service-oriented applications. The fourth section presents the use cases and describes their scope and adaptation needs. Then, we discuss the challenges faced in those use cases to advance from adaptive service-oriented applications to adaptive FI applications.

THE ROAD FROM ADAPTIVE WEB SERVICES TO ADAPTIVE FUTURE INTERNET APPLICATIONS

The goal of this section is to show the evolution of ideas starting from the development of Web services and service-based applications, passing through the design of adaptive solutions and arriving at the definition of FI applications and the discussion about the need for adaptive characteristics in FI applications. This section is organized

in three parts which address, respectively, each one of the ideas mentioned before.

Web Services and Service-Based Applications

Web services technology (e.g., building on standards such as WS-BPEL, WSDL, SOAP, WS-Transaction, WS-Coordination, WS-Policy) and the Service Oriented Architecture (SOA) are increasingly adopted by practitioners for building highly dynamic and distributed applications. Such service-based applications (also known as composed services, service-based systems, or Web services-based applications) are typically realized by composing individual Web services. Fundamental changes related to how software is developed, deployed, and maintained (Di Nitto, Ghezzi, Metzger, Papazoglou, & Pohl, 2008) emerge with the use of Web services and service-orientation. Software services separate ownership, maintenance and operation from the use of the software. Service users do not need to acquire, deploy and run the individual piece of software, because they can access the functionality of that software remotely through the service's interface, as illustrated in Figure 1. Ownership, maintenance and operation of the software remains with the

Figure 1. Service-based applications and the involved stakeholders

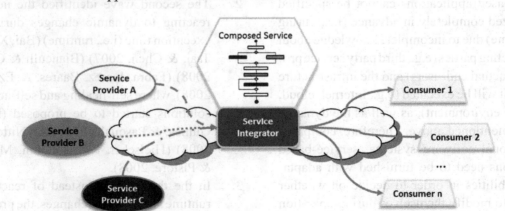

service provider, and can thus be performed by third-parties (Di Nitto et al., 2008).

In a simplified way, it is possible to say that there are three major stakeholder roles involved in service-based applications using third-party services as illustrated in Figure 1. The first one is the service provider who owns the Web services. The second one is the service integrator who is responsible for invoking and composing the third-party services. The third one is the entity that consumes the composed services provided by the service integrator. Figure 1 also depicts the composed service (represented by a workflow) provided by the service integrator. In this example one can observe that the Web services from service providers "A", "B" and "C" are composed and exposed to the consumer as atomic and self-contained applications. The resulting environment of service-based applications is extremely heterogeneous, decentralized and subject to highly dynamic changes such as the availability of the third party services, changes on the code of the third-party services, and network connectivity among the stakeholders (Papazoglou, Pohl, Parkin, & Metzger, 2010) (Qureshi & Perini, 2010).

Adaptive Web Services and Service-Based Applications

Service-based applications cannot be specified and realized completely in advance (i.e., during design-time) due to incomplete knowledge about the interacting parties (e.g., third party service providers or actual end-users) and the infrastructure in which it will be executed (e.g., Internet, cloud, pervasive environment), as well as the dynamic changes mentioned above. Therefore, compared to traditional software systems, service-based applications need to be furnished with adaptation capabilities in order to decide on whether and how to modify themselves during operation (i.e., during run-time). Adaptive capabilities are essential features to guarantee the proper execu-

tion of service-based applications, once dynamic changes are not exceptions but the normal behavior imposed on these applications. Over the past years, many efforts have been made towards adaptive Web services and service-based applications. Based on the analysis of the literature (Papazoglou et al., 2010) (Mancioppi, 2011), Figure 2 depicts an illustrative and simplified time-line summarizing some of the main groups of efforts especially related to service-oriented applications. This time-line is not an extensive and exhaustive description of the field: it aims at capturing and illustrating some keywords associated with adaptive Web Services and service-based applications with the focus more on the technical level rather than on the business level.

Reviewing the literature in the field, we had been able to map three major waves of research efforts:

1. The first wave addressed adaptive Web services through the use of more exible and adaptive composition engines (e.g., BPEL engines) (Jang, Choi, & Zhao, 2003) (Charfi & Mezini, 2004) (Patel, Supekar, & Lee, 2004) (Zhou, Tang, & He, 2005) (Siljee, Bosloper, Nijhuis, & Hammer, 2005) (Chae, Dasgupta, Kumar, Mittal, & Srivastava, 2006) (Dong, Yu, & Zhang, 2006) (Ardagna & Pernici, 2007).

2. The second wave identified the need for reacting to dynamic changes during the execution time (i.e., runtime) (Bai, Xu, Dai, Tsai, & Chen, 2007) (Bianculli & Ghezzi, 2008) (Fabra, lvarez, Baares, & Ezpeleta, 2008), where self-healing and self-adapting solutions started to be proposed (Baresi, Guinea, & Pasquale, 2007) (Di Nitto et al., 2008) (Hielscher, Kazhamiakin, Metzger, & Pistore, 2008).

3. In the third wave, instead of reacting to runtime and dynamic changes, the proposed solutions started to focus on preventive and proactive adaptation (Psaier, Juszczyk,

Figure 2. Illustrative and simplified time-line of keywords related to technical solutions found in the literature associated with service-based systems and adaptation

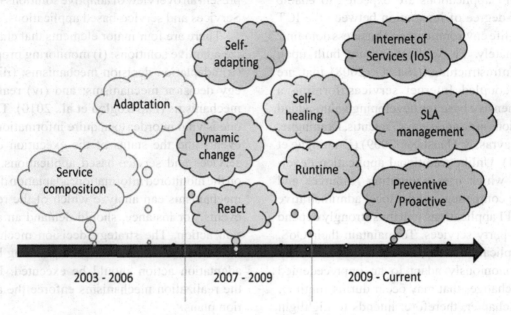

Skopik, Schall, & Dustdar, 2010) (Dranidis, Metzger, & Kourtesis, 2010). Service Level Agreements (SLA) and the stipulated QoS objectives regulate the relationship among the stakeholders, and the management of SLAs became an important research topic towards providing adaptive service-based applications (Di Modica, Tomarchio, & Vita, 2009) (Zheng & Lyu, 2010). In addition, the emergence of the Internet of Services (IoS) (Corradi, Lodolo, Monti, & Pasini, 2008) (Spillner, Winkler, Reichert, Cardoso, & Schill, 2009) broadened and intensified the need for adaptive service-based applications in a third-party environment (Qureshi & Perini, 2010) (Mos et al., 2009) (Brenner, Atkinson, Hummel, & Stoll, 2007).

Indeed, the need for adaptation will become significantly more important in the context of the FI. A clear trend indicates that future service-based applications will be increasingly composed of third party services that are accessible over the

Internet (Domingue et al., 2011). FI application context, nevertheless, also involves more elements that contribute to an even more dynamic and heterogeneous environment.

Adaptive Future Internet Applications

One of the main characteristics of the Future Internet is the convergence among areas: IoS, IoT (e.g., sensors and smartphones), IoC (e.g., video streams and online games), and the Network of the Future (NoF, which involves cloud infrastructures and ubiquitous network connectivity). Future Internet applications will be able to explore and combine those different areas. Service technologies will play a key role in enabling the relationship among those areas. For example, the information associated with sensors of the IoT will become accessible globally so that their functionalities can be discovered and accessed over the Internet (in fact, proposals in this direction have already been made (Spiess et al., 2009) (Guinard, Trifa,

Karnouskos, Spiess, & Savio, 2010) (Shelby, 2010)). FI applications are expected to enable a higher degree of integration between the ICT and real-life environments and business domains.

Ultimately, FI Applications are built upon the FI Infrastructures (ISTAG, 2008) that are loosely-coupled Internet services forming a comprehensive base for developing value-added applications in an agile way (Tselentis, Domingue, Galis, Gavras, & Hausheer, 2009) (Domingue et al., 2011). Unlike traditional application development, which uses computing resources and software components under local administrative control, FI applications will thus strongly depend on third-party services. To maintain their QoS, those applications therefore need to dynamically and autonomously adapt to an unprecedented level of changes that may occur during runtime.

This chapter, therefore, intends to highlight the importance of properly engineering adaptive FI applications having in mind the new scenario and conditions present in FI Infrastructures. In the next section we present a brief overview of current adaptive solutions applied in Web services and service-based applications. Two case studies of adaptive FI Applications in different domains are discussed and we argue why the current adaptive solutions need to be extended and enhanced in order to properly provide adaptation characteristics for such case studies.

OVERVIEW ON SOLUTIONS FOR ADAPTIVE WEB SERVICES AND SERVICE BASED APPLICATIONS

The literature associated with adaptive Web services and Service-based applications is very diverse. In some cases, the word adaptation is not employed; however, the effects of the actions proposed by these solutions are the same as the ones expected from adaptive solutions, i.e., healing, reconfiguration, and adjustment in face of changes in the Web services or service-based applications. The intention of this section is to present an overview of adaptive solutions for Web Services and service-based applications.

There are four major elements that characterize adaptive solutions: (i) monitoring properties; (ii) adaptation decision mechanisms; (iii) strategy decision mechanisms; and (iv) realization mechanisms (Papazoglou et al., 2010). The first one is vital in order to acquire information about events and the status of the execution of Web services and service-based applications. Based on the monitored information, adaptation decision mechanisms can analyze which of the reported events, for instance, should demand an adaptation action. The strategy decision mechanisms are associated with the task of planning how an adaptation action should be executed. Finally, the realization mechanisms enforce the adaptation plans.

The literature shows that some proposals focus on the combination of all these elements (Mannava & Ramesh, 2011) (Sheng, Benatallah, Maamar, & Ngu, 2009), the combination of few of them (Brogi & Popescu, 2006) (Mosincat & Binder, 2011), or on one element in specific (Bianculli, Jurca, Binder, Ghezzi, & Faltings, 2007) (Ivanovi´c, Treiber, Carro, & Dustdar, 2010). In addition, there are proposals that focus on particular perspectives such as time and layer when the adaptation activities are executed and also how centralized or decentralized they are. In this section we present an overview on works addressing these different foci on adaptive Web services and service-based applications.

Solutions proposed in (Sheng et al., 2009) (Mannava & Ramesh, 2011) (Psaier et al., 2010) (Erradi & Maheshwari, 2008) (Gui, De Florio, Sun, & Blondia, 2011) (Pernici & Rosati, 2007) share, in a high level, the same adaptive characteristics, i.e., these proposals are able to monitor, analyze, plan and execute actions related to adaptation of Web services or service-based applications. The scope of the adaptive solution can be similar or vary significantly from one proposal to another.

For example, proposals use context information as an asset of the adaptive solution. Nevertheless, the same proposals focus on different abstraction levels of adaptation, i.e., for instance, Sheng et al. target the adaptation of the workflow model (Sheng et al., 2009) while Erradi and Maheshwari focus on adapting the running instance of a composition (Erradi & Maheshwari, 2008). Different from the previously mentioned, the proposals in (Psaier et al., 2010) and (Pernici & Rosati, 2007) do not use context information but are both related to repair and model the "misbehavior" in Web services compositions.

There are also proposals that focus on different adaptation activities. For instance, the work presented in (Mosincat & Binder, 2011) is mostly focused on monitoring and analysis phases of adaptation, providing monitoring of process and service performance and ensuring maintenance of process performance through automated detection of service failures and SLA violations, diagnosis, and repair. In (Hepner, Baird, & Gamble, 2009) the focus is on formally specifying reconfiguration of BPEL workflows based on dynamic web service changes. The other work in (Ivanović et al., 2010) focuses on the analysis phase of adaptation. Such a solution addresses the automatic derivation of dynamic, continuous-time models of behavior of service orchestrations to assure that the specified QoS levels are met.

Examples of proposals focused on the time perspective of adaptation actions are listed as follows. Dranidis et al. describe a novel approach for just-in-time testing of the behavior of conversational services which allows potential failures to be detected shortly before the execution of services (Dranidis et al., 2010), thus enabling the service compositions to be adapted pro-actively. In (Leitner et al., 2010), SLA violations on service-based applications are predicted using regression models which have been trained based on monitoring information from past process instances. In (Ivanovic, Carro, & Hermenegildo, 2010), solutions are proposed for quality assur-

ance of service-based applications execution and quality prediction techniques to support proactive adaptation.

In addition, there are some trends exploring the cross-layer approach for executing adaptation activities. For instance, Baresi et al. (Baresi, Guinea, Pistore, & Trainotti, 2009) propose a monitoring framework that enables the integration of a wide range of events into more complex properties. The authors created an extended recursive model of monitored properties and capabilities to correlate and aggregate a variety of events from independent sources which enabled cross-layer service-based applications monitoring. In (Wetzstein et al., 2009) a cross-layer monitoring solution is also proposed. The purpose of this work is to define an integrated framework for runtime monitoring and analysis of the performance of WS-BPEL processes in a cross-layer setting based on machine learning. In (Popescu, Staikopoulos, Liu, Brogi, & Clarke, 2010) a cross-layer adaptation methodology is proposed. This solution attempts to enhance and semi-automate the adaptation in multi-layer applications by combining templates (which are specially target to deal with behavior adaptation issues) and taxonomies of adaptation issues (which are intended to support the semi-automated discovery and selection of cross-layer adaptation templates). Finally, (Kertesz, Kecskemeti, & Brandic, 2009) address the problem of renegotiating SLAs across the SOA layers in order to adapt to changes that might lead to SLA violations.

Despite of the fact that Web services and service-based applications are technologies by nature associated with distributed environments, we cannot take for granted that solutions developed for those technologies are decentralized. For instance, in (Yau, Huang, & Zhu, 2007) a virtual machine-based architecture is defined for the execution, monitoring and control of workflows in service-based systems. The model adopted by Yau et al. includes centralized entities reasoning based on distributed information. The work described in (El Falou, Bouzid, Mouaddib, & Vidal, 2010) does not address adaption directly but focuses on the planning phase of services compositions. The authors propose an iterative and hierarchical solution for planning Web services composition which helps to reduce the computational load for defining a composition plan. In (Tang & Xu, 2006), the authors create an adaptive model of service composition which is based on policy-driven and multi-agent negotiation. Although it is not explicitly claimed by the authors, in theory, the model proposed would allow their services to interact in a totally decentralized fashion. The decentralized model used by the authors considers decentralized decision based on distributed information.

As briey discussed above, there are many different perspectives and solutions proposed for adaptive Web services and service-oriented applications. In summary, the main focus of the current solutions addressing adaptation are still related to the ICT aspects of the services, some integration between business objectives and technical level (mainly in respect to monitoring and predicting), and some integration with the underlying computational infrastructure supporting the ICT services. To move from adaptive service-oriented applications to FI applications, the current techniques will have to be extended in order to accommodate the upcoming requirements of the applications.

FI APPLICATION DOMAINS

In this section we introduce two use case scenarios from different application domains to motivate the need for extending and integrating existing service adaptation techniques in order to properly design adaptive FI applications. The first use case is related to multimedia applications and the second is related to business applications for transport & logistics.

Multimedia Applications

Multimedia applications are typically highly interactive and especially challenging when it comes to provision their stable performance and adequate user experience. These challenges are due to the complexities in estimating the software performance on a given hardware infrastructure and also due to the varied behavior of the users resulting in varied and difficult to assess workloads. The SaaS paradigm gives multimedia application providers the capability to reach an increasingly large number of users and also enables users to use the applications as a utility rather than having to unnecessarily invest in infrastructure and software. In addition, such a paradigm is able to better deal with provisioning challenges of applications once auto-scaling techniques can be used by the providers in order to compensate the changes of the application demands.

These challenges of multimedia application can be addressed by the means of adaptive environments used to operate the applications provided. Research in the IRMOS (IRMOS, 2011) and BonFIRE (BonFIRE, 2011) projects address these challenges. For instance, the IRMOS project addresses the challenges in an IoC scenario that explores an interactive real-time Application as a Service. In this example, SaaS providers encounter challenges in providing soft real-time multimedia applications with guaranteed (probabilistic) QoS. Examples of such applications include interactive and collaborative film post-production, virtual and augmented reality within the engineering design process, and interactive online eLearning environments. Consider the post-production scenario, for example, in which resources are needed on short notice to host a session with many users located in different countries working on a film. Compute, storage and networking resources need to be selected to ensure the QoS to the users, who will be streamed a video and will interact with it by, for example, pausing, rewinding, or editing frames. One Key Performance Indicator (KPI) of such an application is whether frames are dropped, which should have certain QoS guarantees.

The IRMOS and BonFIRE Solutions

The IRMOS project has developed a toolbox of techniques that allow applications with soft real-time requirements to be planned and executed on virtualized service oriented infrastructure operated by third-party service providers. In the case of the IoC scenario, there is a need for well-defined SLAs that have guaranteed QoS. The IRMOS toolbox provides an adaptive environment of tools for negotiating, monitoring and managing SLAs and applications.

One of the main components in the IRMOS toolbox is the Performance Estimation Service (PES), as seen in Figure 3, which encapsulates a methodology for the SaaS provisioning planning. The PES is used for planning the deployment of the SaaS application in terms of resources that need to be reserved, as well as during the operation of the application to adapt its provisioning in response to critical events. A critical event could be, for example, the observation of KPI deterioration below the agreed level, or observing a deviation from the expected application workload that may compromise the agreed QoS.

During SLA negotiation, the PES estimates the required resources for a particular application based on the predicted performance of an application model on some given resources (according to availability by an IaaS provider). Details on an example model for the e-Learning application mentioned above can be found in (Cucinotta et al., 2010). The predicted performance is evaluated against the QoS terms set in the SLA with an objective function that encapsulates the business objectives of the SaaS provider. This is typically a function that evaluates the maximum profit for the SaaS provider, based on the expected income for running the application, minus the infrastructure costs and any penalties for not fulfilling the QoS. The IRMOS toolbox includes

global and local optimization algorithms to determine the best resources according to the defined objective function, supported by a framework of caching execution results of application models and objective functions to speed up this process.

Once the SLA is agreed upon, the application is deployed and run. To guarantee the agreed QoS, a performance feedback loop is implemented that facilitates reactive and proactive types of application provisioning adaptation via a Performance Feedback Service (PFS). During the application operation, KPI metrics are logged and fed back to the PFS. These observed metrics are compared against the agreed ones and in the event of deviation the resources are scaled according to predefined rules.

The work on predicting application performance in IRMOS has been continued in the Bon-FIRE project (BonFIRE, 2011), which offers a multi-site testbed of heterogeneous cloud resources for experimentation on the FI. One of the main foci of the work continued in BonFIRE is to address the challenges of predicting application performance for QoS estimation based on the descriptions of resources offered by IaaS providers.

Today, IaaS QoS offerings are expressed in low level terms (i.e., machine level, CPU speed, disk space, etc), whilst their customers, typically application users, are often interested in application-level parameters because the application is what gives the customer the value (e.g. CFD simulation or video rendering). Therefore, the gap between the terms the Infrastructure provider offers and what the users really demand is large, resulting in a complex relationship between application performance and resource parameters. The complexity of this relationship is increased for applications deployed across federated clouds where even low-level resource descriptions may differ due to lack of standardization.

IaaS resources should ideally be described in a uniform and descriptive manner which can be fruitful for predicting application performance. The Dwarf taxonomy introduced in (Cavallo, Di

Figure 3. IRMOS solution for IoC scenario in multimedia application domain

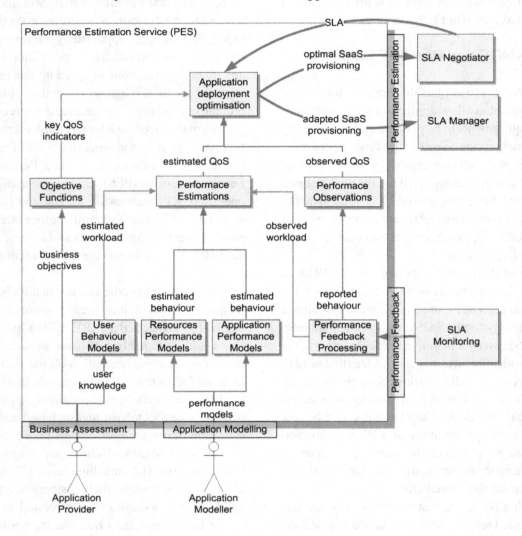

Penta, & Canfora, 2010) is one alternative, which currently comprises 13 classes of computational benchmarks (Asanovic et al., 2009). A Dwarf benchmark is defined as "an algorithmic method that captures a pattern of computation and communication" (Asanovic et al., 2006). Ultimately, we could imagine each IaaS provider describing the performance of their resources in terms of a standard set of benchmark scores (such as Dwarfs) and even agreeing on SLAs in those terms. Alternatively, a PaaS provider may measure the performance of many IaaS providers, adding to one of many possible services that could be offered.

Initial findings in (Phillips, Engen, & Papay, 2011) indicate that scores on Dwarf benchmarks show promise as a means of describing computing resources in the cloud, demonstrating that they can discriminate between different compute resources even when the IaaS provider labels them the same. Furthermore, the initial findings in (Phillips et al., 2011) show different Dwarfs correlate more strongly with different applications, indicating that they can be useful in predicting application performance. Moreover, expression of IaaS parameters in this way can simplify the creation of application-level QoS that can be easily understood by users, as well as improving robustness and adaptability to QoS changes by making it easier to determine suitable resources to deploy from different IaaS providers.

Transport and Logistics Applications

The Transport & Logistics (T&L) domain is a global industry which represented 13.8% of the global GDP and 10-15 % of the final product costs according to the communication of the European Commission in 2006 (Commission of the European Communities, 2006). In addition to its economical relevance, the T&L domain produces environmental impacts and, in 2005, this industry was responsible for 14.3% of the world's greenhouse gas emissions (World Resources Institute, 2010). Despite to the achieved improvements in this domain, there are still major obstacles to be overcome in order to optimize the execution of T&L processes and enable a more efficient and sustainable industry. Examples of such obstacles are: (i) limited visibility on the T&L processes and critical events, i.e., during the transportation of the goods the involved partners have only a partial knowledge of what is actually happening; (ii) closed logistics supply chains which reduces the inter-organizational information exchange and collaboration; and (iii) the T&L processes are still highly dependent on manual intervention (Metzger & Marquezan, 2011). Different projects tackle different angles of these problems (eFreight, 2010) (FREIGHTWISE, 2006). One example is the FInest project that investigates the employment of FI areas in order to design and develop T&L FIApps.

The FInest Solution

Figure 4 illustrates the solutions envisioned by FInest. The front end layer of the FInest platform provides users with role specifc, secure, ubiquitous access from different devices to information concerning the operation of the transport and logistics network. The back end layer of the FInest platform provides access to, and integration with, legacy systems, third party services and any IoT devices that may provide information during the transport lifecycle. Legacy system integration is facilitated by service-oriented technology, e.g., by exposing features of legacy systems as services or by offering access to legacy systems via the SaaS (Mietzner, Metzger, Leymann, & Pohl, 2009). The core layer of the FInest platform is composed of independent transport and logistics modules (E-Contracting, Event Processing, Transport Planning) integrated through the Business Collaboration Module. The independent service modules are cloud-based applications that provide essential capabilities for the shipment of goods.

The FInest modules are realized by leveraging FI services based on the IoT and IoS currently under development through the European Union's Future Internet Public Private Partnership (FI PPP) program. The following list describes the FI technologies of primary importance for implementing the FInest Platform. Most of these are addressed within the FI-WARE project, which aim at developing the FI Core Platform within the FI PPP program (www.fi-ware.eu):

- Infrastructure, methodology, and tools for cloud-based platform and application development, including an infrastructure for deploying the FInest Platform and its components on public or private clouds along with methodology and tool support for developing additional end-user services for individual transport and logistics stakeholders.

Figure 4. FInest solution for T&L application domain integrating IoS, Cloud, and IoT

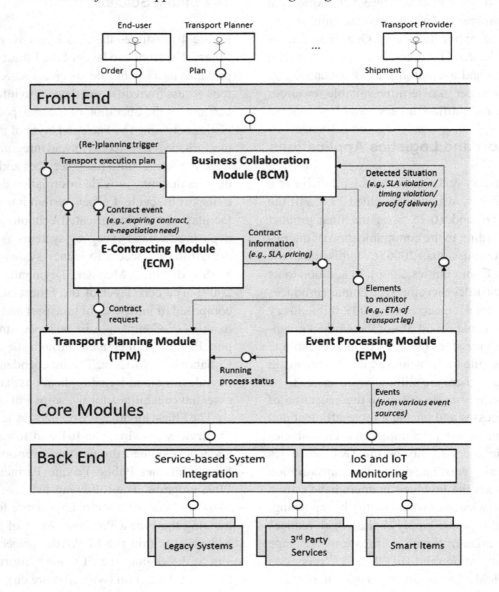

- Language and tool support for the IoS, including a service description language that covers both technical and business requirements along with integrated tool support for the provisioning, management, and consumption of services; this shall be used for realizing the back-end layer of the FInest platform and for managing the interaction of the FInest core modules.

- Access to real-world data from the IoT, enabling the integration and technical handling of real-world data obtained from sensor networks for real-time monitoring and tracking during the execution phase of transport and logistics processes.

- Facilities for data and event processing in the Internet of Contents, allowing to process huge amounts of data to retrieve insights into relevant scenarios, as well as analyzing real-time event data to quickly determine relevant situations and instantly trigger actions.

Adaptation Needs of FI applications for T&L

Three scenarios were identified by the FInest project and one is related to the process of exporting goods from Turkey to the United Kingdom (UK). In this scenario, a supply chain composed of material supplier, truck carrier, sea carrier, warehouse, and material assembly, is formed. The proper support for the end-to-end visibility of such supply chain is provided by FInest platform through the use of IoT and IoS. In this section, we present what are the adaptation requirements that need to be considered in such scenario. For example, suppose that the vessel of the sea carrier has sensors and cameras for monitoring the status of the transported material. For the end-to-end visibility of the supply chain it is necessary to keep the availability of information about the material status. In the situation of damages on some sensors the information received by the application is not complete, i.e., part of the monitored area is not covered any more. The option to adapt to this change of the environment would be to change the source of the information from sensor to camera in the monitored area. In a first instance, one can think that the service substitution technique traditionally employed in Web services and service-oriented application would suffice. For example, instead of using a service that provides information coming from sensors, the system would discover and substitute the "current failed service" for another. This raises the question of how to detect that the service associated with the sensor information has failed. The service itself is available and sending data, but the problem is that the data is not the one expected by the application.

The notion of service failure might also be reevaluated and might open opportunities for exploring the cross-cutting aspects of adaptation.

For example, the service composition layer might not be able to recognize a failure, but this might also require the intervention of the business layer in the monitoring process. Current monitoring cross-layer solutions could be the start point. The combination of information coming from the sensors, services compositions, and business layer might advance the design of cross-cutting aspects adaptation support.

Another issue in this scenario is the need for a decentralized monitoring process. Current decentralized monitoring techniques, as discussed in the previous section, could help, for instance, to support the distributed information monitoring need in this scenario. Nevertheless, the current decentralized solutions for adapting service-based applications would not provide the required support in said scenario because they are not able to operate in a federated third-party environment. Suppose that each player in the supply chain of this scenario is an ICT service integrator itself. For example, the truck carrier would compose its own services and offer it to the supply chain as a unique service. The federation of the parties' services would form the supply chain. In this case, a centralized entity integrating the services of each one of the parties would not be able to directly execute decentralized adaptations along the infrastructure of the parties because it would not have access to the infrastructure of each party. Thus, decentralized negotiations must be considered in order to adapt to changes in the services of this scenario.

Remarks

In contrast to current service-based applications, FI applications will (i) continue to increase the scale and heterogeneity of involved parties, and (ii) provide a much stronger connection between real-life elements and the business connected by the application. Thus, the environment of FI applications tends to be much more dynamic and heterogeneous than the ones which service-based applications are subjected to. The techniques and models of adaptive service-based applications may be considered as the baseline for adaptive FI applications; nevertheless, enhancements are needed to properly engineer and execute adaptation in the dynamic and heterogeneous FI applications environment.

REQUIREMENTS AND CHALLENGES TO ENABLE TRULY ADAPTIVE FI APPLICATIONS

One key enabler for adaptive FI applications will be the ability to have a seamless and consistent way of monitoring, detecting and predicting critical events for the different areas of the FI and thus for the types of services offered. As an example, consider that an IoT-based RFID-sensor that would track packages within a warehouse fails. Seamless monitoring would allow switching to video data and video analysis to track those packages. Further, due to the very large scale of FI applications, this requires significant progress towards decentralized and highly dispersed facilities for monitoring, detecting and predicting critical events. On the other hand, the high volume of data from different sources (such as services, things or media items) may provide refined approaches towards detecting and predicting critical events; e.g., by correlating trends from those various sources or applying more powerful complex event processing facilities.

Detection

As indicated previously, many practical applications will have "soft" QoS requirements. This means that the decision whether QoS expectations have been violated is not a clear cut one but needs to rely on objective functions (such as the one introduced from the point of view of the provider in IRMOS). In addition, utility functions that assess the "severity" of the violation from the

point of view of the end-user need to be taken into account for assessing whether a monitoring event indicates a critical event. This means that the notion of Quality of Experience (QoE) needs to be considered during detection. When talking about QoE, the role of the context in which an application executes will have an additional impact; for instance, users traveling in an airplane might not necessarily expect to have broadband access to their services and thus would be satisfied with much less connectivity.

Prediction

The prediction of critical events (such as deviations in the QoS of constituent services or SLA violations of service-oriented systems or multimedia applications) will always have a margin for error. Thus, in order to decide whether a proactive adaptation decision should be based on the prediction of a critical event, metrics and tools need to be in place in order to assess the accuracy of such a prediction. The availability of a wider range of data sources in the FI may provide an additional level of accuracy, as predictions can be based on increasingly more frequent information. For example, one could correlate trends from those various sources or apply more powerful complex event processing facilities. However, how to exploit this in an integrated and coordinated way and how to accommodate potential uncertainties in the data on which predictions are based (e.g., reliability of sensor readings) are still an open question.

In addition, the highly dynamic setting of FI applications will make it difficult to select the best and most suitable prediction technique during design time. As discussed before, benchmarking application behavior to better predict infrastructure properties is quite challenging particularly since there is currently no uniform way of describing resource offerings in the cloud. This is a challenge that is currently investigated in the BonFIRE project. However, it is only one piece of the puzzle in order to achieve scalable and dynamic prediction of application performance. For example, dynamic approaches to adapting the prediction models based on operative data could be an interesting research direction.

Finally, predicted problems may be "contextualized" in order to better understand the criticality of the forecast event. Here, QoE considerations again may play an important role. In addition, cost models become important in order to balance the costs of not taking an adaptation vs. the cost of doing so and thereby being able to quantify the risk involved in both these decisions. As an example, the cost of the predicted violation might be smaller than the penalty to be paid for an SLA violation. Such a critical event could then be safely ignored.

Cross-Cutting Aspects

The capacity of dealing with aspects that cut across different areas and layers of the FI is a characteristic that is not entirely covered by current strategies. Existing solutions, such as the ones developed in the EU Network of Excellence S-Cube (Papazoglou et al., 2010), focus on cross-layer aspects of the service-oriented architecture only (i.e., on the service infrastructure, service composition, and business process layers). However, applications are envisioned to encompass all areas of the FI (e.g., IoS, IoC) in an integrated fashion so that IT systems and business can be tightly integrated into the physical world (Domingue et al., 2011).

One question related to cross-cutting is that of where cross-layer/-area adaptation starts The idea of different areas of FI is not mature enough. In fact, there are many discussions about what exactly the FI is. However, there is at least a common sense that the future will see a convergence among the many areas on current isolated development, such as IoS and IoT. The convergence of different types of networks already started and will be the basis for the NoF. Adaptation strategies, for instance, are being developed in each one of the fields. But when it comes to the FI context, one is faced with the problem of drawing the limits among cross-layer and cross-area adaptation actions. For instance: Is the disruption of network connectivity a problem to be solved only by the NoF in the FI Platform layer, or should the FI application be able to decide which kind of connectivity adaptation would be more suitable for the application scope? This simple question opens up many opportunities for investigating revolutionary designs and methodologies devoted to create adaptive FI applications.

Decentralization

Existing solutions typically employ a central entity for gathering information from distributed sources and for taking decisions. This leads to at least two critical problems: (i) in a third-party service provider environment, the central entity will only have limited access to information about the external service provider (for example, nothing can be known about the invocation load of the external service); (ii) a central entity will present classical problems like single point of failure, lack of scalability, and bottlenecks which will not be acceptable once the scale of the FI includes not only traditional devices (e.g., PCs, notebooks, smartphones) but also sensors, RFIDs, or any kind of device that can be endowed with network communication features. There are solutions that employ hierarchical strategies to gather and analyze the information, which reduces the impact of centralization. Nevertheless, these solutions tend to ignore the restrictions imposed by the third-party environment when executing the actions associated with adaptation (i.e., monitoring, analyzing, planning, and executing). Nevertheless, the question of how many decentralized adaptive decision-making processes can be really used remains. This question is also very much related to the role of humans in the design of decentralized adaptive FI applications. Maybe autonomic decisions might be designed based on decentralized models, but human-in-the-loop decisions might not be designed solely based on fully decentralized models.

Boundaries

Given the strong interaction of FI applications with the real world, one has to decide where to draw the boundary between normal application logic and adaptation. One of the important changes that will be introduced by FI applications is the strong connection with the physical world through the use of IoT technology. The ICT services will be merged with real world services. For example, one type of logistics services is the door-to-door shipment of goods. When a person contracts a shipment through a logistics FI application, the ICT services will help the business owner to execute such logistics services (combining IoS and IoT). This merge of ICT systems and services involves the real world will create boundary issues related to adaptation. For instance: Might we consider the change on a dispatching truck executed by a transport & logistics IT system already an adaptation? What is the actual system (entity) that is being adapted? If only the business process changes (but not the underlying IT System), is this adaptation? These are questions that emerge from this deep relationship of ICT systems and real world and that need to be better investigated.

Remarks

The discussion above tried to capture, based on concrete scenario problems, questions that need to be understood and answered in order to engineer truly adaptive FI Applications. The challenges and requirements discussed in this section are not an exhaustive and closed list. We discussed some aspects of adaptation, i.e., detection, prediction, cross-cutting and decentralization, and identified the gaps that current solutions proposed to address but fail to properly tackle.

CONCLUSION

There are many questions to be answered, and for each question new ones emerge. Despite all the uncertainties surrounding FI applications, there is at least one certain and incontestable fact: FI applications will have to be engineered explicitly considering adaptation aspects and dynamically adapt to an unprecedented level of changes that may occur during runtime.

In this chapter, we discussed the need of re-thinking and designing FI applications taking into account aspects beyond the ones considered by current adaptive Web services and service-based applications. To enable adaptive FI applications, it is clear that a seamless and consistent way of monitoring, detecting and predicting critical events, dealing with cross-cutting aspects, decentralization, and boundaries between application logic and adaptation needs is required.

ACKNOWLEDGMENT

The research leading to these results has received funding from the European Community's 7th Framework Programme FP7/2007-2013 under grant agreements 214777 (IRMOS), 215483 (S-Cube), 257386 (BonFIRE), 285248 (FI-WARE) and 285598 (FInest).

REFERENCES

Ardagna, D., & Pernici, B. (2007, June). Adaptive service composition in flexible processes. *IEEE Transactions on Software Engineering, 33*(6), 369–384. doi:10.1109/TSE.2007.1011

Armbrust, M., Fox, A., Griffith, R., Joseph, A. D., Katz, R., & Konwinski, A. (2010, April). A view of cloud computing. *Communications of the ACM, 53*, 50–58. doi:10.1145/1721654.1721672

Asanovic, K., Bodik, R., Catanzaro, B. C., Gebis, J. J., Husbands, P., Keutzer, K., et al. (2006). *The landscape of parallel computing research: A view from Berkeley.* (Electrical Engineering and Computer Sciences, University of California at Berkeley UCB/EECS-2006-183.)

Asanovic, K., Bodik, R., Demmel, J., Keaveny, T., Keutzer, K., & Kubiatowicz, J. (2009, October). A view of the parallel computing landscape. *Communications of the ACM, 52*, 56–67. doi:10.1145/1562764.1562783

Bai, X., Xu, D., Dai, G., Tsai, W., & Chen, Y. (2007). Dynamic reconfigurable testing of service-oriented architecture. In *Proceedings of the 31st Annual International Computer Software and Applications Conference (COMPSAC).*

Baresi, L., Guinea, S., & Pasquale, L. (2007). Self-healing BPEL processes with Dynamo and the JBoss rule engine. In *Proceedings of the ES-SPE '07 - International Workshop on Engineering of Software Services for Pervasive Environments -In Conjunction with the 6th ESEC/FSE Joint Meeting* (pp. 11-20).

Baresi, L., Guinea, S., Pistore, M., & Trainotti, M. (2009, july). Dynamo + Astro: An Integrated Approach for BPEL Monitoring. In *Proceesings of the IEEE International Conference on Web Services, ICWS 2009* (pp. 230 -237).

Bianculli, D., & Ghezzi, C. (2008). SAVVY-WS at a glance: Supporting verifiable dynamic service compositions. In *Automated Engineering of Autonomous and Run-Time Evolving Systems (ARAMIS 2008),* Co-located with ASE 2008, L'Aquila, Italy.

Bianculli, D., Jurca, R., Binder, W., Ghezzi, C., & Faltings, B. (2007). Automated dynamic maintenance of composite services based on service reputation. In Krmer, B., Lin, K.-J., & Narasimhan, P. (Eds.), *Service-Oriented Computing ICSOC 2007* (*Vol. 4749*, pp. 449–455). Berlin, Germany: Springer. doi:10.1007/978-3-540-74974-5_42

BonFIRE. (2011). *EC FP7-ICT BonFIRE Project.* Retrieved October 2011 from http://www.bonfire-project.eu/

Brenner, D., Atkinson, C., Hummel, O., & Stoll, D. (2007). Strategies for the run-time testing of third party web services. In *Proceedings of the IEEE International Conference on Service-Oriented Computing and Applications* (pp. 114–121). Washington, DC: IEEE Computer Society.

Brogi, A., & Popescu, R. (2006). Automated generation of BPEL adapters. In Dan, A., & Lamersdorf, W. (Eds.), *Service-Oriented Computing ICSOC 2006* (*Vol. 4294*, pp. 27–39). Berlin, Germany: Springer. doi:10.1007/11948148_3

Cavallo, B., Di Penta, M., & Canfora, G. (2010). An empirical comparison of methods to support QoS-aware service selection. In *Proceedings of the 2nd International Workshop on Principles of Engineering Service-Oriented Systems* (pp. 64–70). New York, NY: ACM.

Chae, G., Dasgupta, K., Kumar, A., Mittal, S., & Srivastava, B. (2006). Adaptation in Web service composition and execution. In *Proceedings of the ICWS 2006: 2006 IEEE International Conference on Web Services* (pp. 549-557).

Charfi, A., & Mezini, M. (2004). Aspect-oriented web service composition with AO4BPEL. *Lecture Notes in Computer Science, 3250*, 168–182. doi:10.1007/978-3-540-30209-4_13

Commission of the European Communities. (2006, June). *Freight transport logistics in Europe.* Retrieved October 2011 from http://europa.eu/legislation summaries/environment/tackling climate change/l24456 en.htm

Corradi, A., Lodolo, E., Monti, S., & Pasini, S. (2008, July). A user-centric composition model for the Internet of Services. In *Proceedings IEEE Symposium on Computers and Communications, ISCC 2008* (p. 110). Washington, DC: IEEE Computer Society.

Cucinotta, T., Checconi, F., Kousiouris, G., Kyriazis, D., Varvarigou, T., Mazzetti, A., et al. (2010, December). Virtualised e-learning with real-time guarantees on the IRMOS platform. In *Proceedings. IEEE International Conference on Service-Oriented Computing and Applications (SOCA)*, (pp. 1-8). Washington, DC: IEEE Computer Society.

Di Modica, G., Tomarchio, O., & Vita, L. (2009). Dynamic SLAs management in service oriented environments. *Journal of Systems and Software*, *82*(5), 759–771. doi:10.1016/j.jss.2008.11.010

Di Nitto, E., Ghezzi, C., Metzger, A., Papazoglou, M., & Pohl, K. (2008). A journey to highly dynamic, self-adaptive service-based applications. *Automated Software Engineering*, *15*(3-4), 313–341. doi:10.1007/s10515-008-0032-x

Domingue, J., Galis, A., Gavras, A., Zahariadis, T., Lambert, D., & Cleary, F. (2011). *The future Internet. Future Internet Assembly 2011: Achievements and Technological Promises* (*Vol. 6656*). Heidelberg, Germany: Springer.

Dong, W.-L., Yu, H., & Zhang, Y.-B. (2006). Testing BPEL-based Web service composition using high-level Petri nets. In *EDOC '06: Proceedings of the 10th IEEE International Enterprise Distributed Object Computing Conference*. IEEE Computer Society.

Dranidis, D., Metzger, A., & Kourtesis, D. (2010). Enabling proactive adaptation through just-in-time testing of conversational services. In Di Nitto, E., & Yahyapour, R. (Eds.), *Towards a Service-Based Internet* (*Vol. 6481*, pp. 63–75). Berlin, Germany: Springer. doi:10.1007/978-3-642-17694-4_6

eFreight. (2010, January). *e-FREIGHT is an integrated project within the EU's 7th Framework programme*. Retrieved October 2011 from http://www.efreightproject.eu/

El Falou, M., Bouzid, M., Mouaddib, A.-I., & Vidal, T. (2010, July). A distributed planning approach for web services composition. In *Proceedings of the IEEE International Conference on Web Services (ICWS), 2010* (pp. 337-344).

Erradi, A., & Maheshwari, P. (2008). Dynamic binding framework for adaptive web services. In *Proceedings of the 3rd International Conference on Internet and Web Applications and Services, ICIW 2008* (pp. 162-167).

Fabra, J. lvarez, P., Baares, J., & Ezpeleta, J. (2008). Runtime protocol binding: Flexible service integration by means of exible service interactions. In *Proceedings of the 2008 IEEE International Conference on Services Computing, SCC 2008* (Vol. 1, pp. 291-298).

FREIGHTWISE. (2006, November). *FREIGHTWISE - Management framework for intelligent intermodal transport*. Retrieved October 2011 from http://freightwise.info/cms/

Gui, N. B. C., De Florio, V. B., Sun, H. B., & Blondia, C. B. (2011). Toward architecture-based context-aware deployment and adaptation. *Journal of Systems and Software*, *84*(2), 185–197. doi:10.1016/j.jss.2010.09.017

Guinard, D., Trifa, V., Karnouskos, S., Spiess, P., & Savio, D. (2010). Interacting with the SOA-based internet of things: Discovery, query, selection, and on-demand provisioning of web services. *IEEE Transactions on Services Computing*, *3*, 223–235. doi:10.1109/TSC.2010.3

Hepner, M., Baird, R., & Gamble, R. (2009). Dynamically changing workows of web services. In *Proceedings of the SERVICES 2009 -5th 2009 World Congress on Services* (p. 422-429).

Hielscher, J., Kazhamiakin, R., Metzger, A., & Pistore, M. (2008, 10-13 December). A framework for proactive self-adaptation of service-based applications based on online testing. In Servicewave 2008. Springer. doi:10.1007/978-3-540-89897-9_11

IRMOS. (2011). *EC FP7-ICT IRMOS Project.* Retrieved October 2011 from http://www.irmosproject.eu/ Service Management.aspx

ISTAG. (2008, January). FP7 ICT Advisory Group -Working Group on "Future Internet infrastructure". *ISTAG Report.* Retrieved October 2011 from ftp://ftp.cordis.europa.eu/pub/ist/docs/future-internet-istag en.pdf

Ivanovic, D., Carro, M., & Hermenegildo, M. (2010, July). Towards data-aware QoS-driven adaptation for service orchestrations. In *Proceedings of the IEEE International Conference on Web Services (ICWS), 2010* (pp. 107 -114).

Ivanovic, D., Treiber, M., Carro, M., & Dustdar, S. (2010). Building dynamic models of service compositions with simulation of provision resources. In Parsons, J., Saeki, M., Shoval, P., Woo, C., & Wand, Y. (Eds.), *Proceeding of Conceptual Modeling ER 2010* (*Vol. 6412*, pp. 288–301). Berlin, Germany: Springer. doi:10.1007/978-3-642-16373-9_21

Jang, J., Choi, Y., & Zhao, J. (2003). Adaptive workow management with open kernel framework based on web services. In *Proceedings of the International Conference on Web Services (ICWS), 2003* (p. 124-130).

Kertesz, A., Kecskemeti, G., & Brandic, I. (2009). An SLA-based resource virtualization approach for on-demand service provision. In *Proceedings of the 3rd International Workshop on Virtualization Technologies in Distributed Computing* (pp. 27–34). New York, NY: ACM.

Leitner, P., Wetzstein, B., Karastoyanova, D., Hummer, W., Dustdar, S., & Leymann, F. (2010). Preventing SLA violations in service compositions using aspect-based fragment substitution. In Maglio, P., Weske, M., Yang, J., & Fantinato, M. (Eds.), *Service-Oriented Computing* (*Vol. 6470*, pp. 365–380). Berlin, Germany: Springer. doi:10.1007/978-3-642-17358-5_25

Mancioppi, M. (Ed.). (2011, November). *Consolidated and updated state of the art report on service-based applications.* Deliverable CD-IA-1.1.7 of S-Cube Project. Retrieved October 2011 from http://www.s-cube-network.eu/results/deliverables/wp-ia-1.1/CD-IA-1.1.7-Consolidated%20and%20updated%20state%20of%20the%20art%20report%20on%20Service-Based.pdf/at_download/file

Mannava, V., & Ramesh, T. (2011). A novel event based autonomic design pattern for management of web services. *Communications in Computer and Information Science, 198 CCIS*, (pp. 142-151).

Metzger, A., & Di Nitto, E. (2013, forthcoming). Addressing highly dynamic changes in service-oriented systems: Towards agile evolution and adaptation. In Wang, X., Ali, N., Ramos, I., & Vidgen, R. (Eds.), *Agile and lean service-oriented development: Foundations, theory and practice.* Hershey, PA: IGI Global.

Metzger, A., & Marquezan, C. C. (2011, October). Future Internet apps: The next wave of adaptive service-oriented systems? In *Proceedings 4th European Conference Towards a Service-Based Internet, ServiceWave2011* (Vol. 6994, pp. 230-241). Heidelberg, Germany: Springer.

Mietzner, R., Metzger, A., Leymann, F., & Pohl, K. (2009, May). Variability modeling to support customization and deployment of multi-tenant-aware software as a service applications. In *ICSE workshop on Principles of Engineering Service Oriented Systems* (pp. 18–25). PESOS. doi:10.1109/PESOS.2009.5068815

Mos, A., Pedrinaci, C., Rey, G. A., Gomez, J. M., Liu, D., Vaudaux-Ruth, G., et al. (2009). Multi-level monitoring and analysis of web-scale service based applications. In *Proceedings of the 2009 International Conference on Service-Oriented Computing* (pp. 269–282). Berlin, Germany: Springer-Verlag.

Mosincat, A., & Binder, W. (2011). Automated maintenance of service compositions with SLA violation detection and dynamic binding. *International Journal on Software Tools for Technology Transfer*, *13*(2), 167–179. doi:10.1007/s10009-010-0181-7

Papazoglou, M., Pohl, K., Parkin, M., & Metzger, A. (Eds.). (2010). *Service research challenges and solutions for the future internet: Towards mechanisms and methods for engineering, managing, and adapting service-based systems*. Springer.

Patel, C., Supekar, K., & Lee, Y. (2004). Provisioning resilient, adaptive web services-based workow: A semantic modeling approach. In *Proceedings IEEE International Conference on Web Services* (pp. 480-487).

Pernici, B., & Rosati, A. M. (2007, November). Automatic learning of repair strategies for web services. In *Proceedings of the Fifth European Conference on Web Services, ECOWS '07* (pp. 119 -128).

Phillips, S. C., Engen, V., & Papay, J. (2011). Snow white clouds and the seven dwarfs. In *2011 IEEE Third International Conference on Cloud Computing Technology and Science (CloudCom)*, (pp. 738 -745).

Popescu, R., Staikopoulos, A., Liu, P., Brogi, A., & Clarke, S. (2010). Taxonomy-driven adaptation of multi-layer applications using templates. In *Proceedings of the 2010 Fourth IEEE International Conference on Self-Adaptive and Self-Organizing Systems* (pp. 213–222). Washington, DC: IEEE Computer Society.

Psaier, H., Juszczyk, L., Skopik, F., Schall, D., & Dustdar, S. (2010). Runtime behavior monitoring and self-adaptation in service-oriented systems. In *Proceedings -2010 4th IEEE International Conference on Self-Adaptive and Self-Organizing Systems, SASO 2010* (pp. 164-173).

Qureshi, N. A., & Perini, A. (2010). Requirements engineering for adaptive service based applications. In *Proceedings of the 2010 18th IEEE International Requirements Engineering Conference* (pp. 108–111). Washington, DC: IEEE Computer Society.

Shelby, Z. (2010, December). Embedded web services. *IEEE Wireless Communications*, *17*(6), 52–57. doi:10.1109/MWC.2010.5675778

Sheng, Q., Benatallah, B., Maamar, Z., & Ngu, A. (2009). Configurable composition and adaptive provisioning of Web services. *IEEE Transactions on Services Computing*, *2*(1), 34–49. doi:10.1109/TSC.2009.1

Siljee, J., Bosloper, I., Nijhuis, J., & Hammer, D. (2005). DySOA: Making service systems self-adaptive. *Lecture Notes in Computer Science*, *3826 LNCS*, (pp. 255-268).

Spiess, P., Karnouskos, S., Guinard, D., Savio, D., Baecker, O., Souza, L. M. S. d., et al. (2009). SOA-based integration of the internet of things in enterprise services. In *Proceedings of the 2009 IEEE International Conference on Web Services* (pp. 968–975). Washington, DC: IEEE Computer Society.

Spillner, J., Winkler, M., Reichert, S., Cardoso, J., & Schill, A. (2009). Distributed contracting and monitoring in the internet of services. In *Proceedings of the 9th IFIP WG 6.1 International Conference on Distributed Applications and Interoperable Systems* (pp. 129–142). Berlin, Germany: Springer-Verlag.

Tang, J.-F., & Xu, X.-L. (2006). An adaptive model of service composition based on policy driven and multi-agent negotiation. In *Proceedings of the 2006 International Conference on Machine Learning and Cybernetics* (Vol. 2006, pp. 113-118).

Tselentis, G., Domingue, J., Galis, A., Gavras, A., & Hausheer, D. (2009). *Towards the future internet: A European research perspective*. IOS Press.

Wetzstein, B., Leitner, P., Rosenberg, F., Brandic, I., Leymann, F., & Dustdar, S. (2009). Monitoring and analyzing inuential factors of business process performance. In *Proceedings of the 13th IEEE International Enterprise Distributed Object Computing Conference (EDOC09), Auckland, New Zealand*.

World Resources Institute. (2010, October). *Citywide transportation greenhouse gas emissions inventories: A review of selected methodologies*. Retrieved October 2011 from http://www.wri.org/publication/citywide-transportation-greenhouse-gas-emissions-inventories

Yau, S., Huang, D., & Zhu, L. (2007). An approach to adaptive distributed execution monitoring for workows in service-based systems. In *Proceedings of the International Computer Software and Applications Conference* (Vol. 2, pp. 211-216).

Zheng, Z., & Lyu, M. (2010). An adaptive QoS-aware fault tolerance strategy for web services. *Empirical Software Engineering, 15*(4), 323–345. doi:10.1007/s10664-009-9126-8

Zhou, B., Tang, J.-F., & He, Z.-J. (2005). An adaptive model of virtual enterprise based on dynamic web service composition. In *Proceedings of the Fifth International Conference on Computer and Information Technology, CIT 2005* (Vol. 2005, pp. 284-289).

KEY TERMS AND DEFINITIONS

Adaptation: Adaptation is a process of modifying service-based applications in order to satisfy new requirements and to fit new situations dictated by the environment on the basis of Adaptation Strategies designed by the system integrator.

Cross-Cutting: Related to the capacity of dealing with aspects that cut across different areas and layers of the FI applications.

Detection: Identification of situations that could lead to problems in the service-based application execution.

Future Internet Applications: Applications that will use the combination of Internet of Services (IoS), Internet of Content (IoC), Internet of Things (IoT) and Network of the Future (NoF).

Prediction: The ability to predict the future quality of services belonging to a service-oriented system.

Service-Based Application: A Service-based Application is composed by a number of possibly independent services, available in a network, which perform the desired functionalities of the architecture.

Third-Party Services: Services that are not owned by service-based application.

354

Compilation of References

Abowd, G. D., Dey, A. K., Brown, P. J., Davies, N., Smith, M., & Steggles, P. (1999). Towards a better understanding of context and context-awareness. In *1st International Symposium on Handheld and Ubiquitous Computing, Vol. 1707*, (pp. 304-307). Heidelberg, Germany: Springer-Verlag.

Achilleos, A., Georgalas, N., & Yang, K. (2007). An open source domain-specific tools framework to support model driven development of OSS. In *ECMDA-FA, Lecture Notes in Computer Science, Vol. 4530* (pp. 1 – 16).

Achilleos, A., Yang, K., & Georgalas, N. (2008). A model-driven approach to generate service creation environments. In *Proceedings of the IEEE Globecom, Global Telecommunications Conference* (pp. 1 – 6).

Achilleos, A., Yang, K., & Georgalas, N. (2010). Context modelling and a context-aware framework for pervasive service creation: A model-driven approach. *Elsevier Journal on Pervasive and Mobile Computing, Context Modelling. Reasoning and Management, 6*(2), 281–296.

Adi, A., & Etzion, O. (2004). Amit - The situation manager. *International Journal on Very Large Data Bases, 13*(2), 177–203.

Agarwal, V., & Jalote, P. (2010). From specification to adaptation: An integrated QoS-driven approach for dynamic adaptation of web service compositions. *In Proceedings of 2010 IEEE International Conference on Web Services (ICWS '10)* (pp. 275-282).

Aggarwal, R., Verma, K., Miller, J., & Milnor, W. (2004). Constraint driven web service composition in METEOR-S. In *Proceedings of SCC'04*, (pp. 23–30). IEEE Computer Society.

Agrawal, R., & Srikant, R. (1995). Mining sequential patterns. *In Proceedings of the IEEE Conference on Data Engineering* (pp. 3-14).

Allen, A., & Garlan, D. (1997). A formal basis for architectural connection. *ACM Transactions on Software Engineering and Methodology, 6*(3), 213–249.

Alrifai, M., & Risse, T. (2009). Combining global optimization with local selection for efficient QoS-aware service composition. *In Proceedings of 18th International Conference on World Wide Web (WWW '09)* (pp. 881-890). ACM.

Alrifai, M., Skoutas, D., & Risse, T. (2010). Selecting skyline services for QoS-based Web service composition. *In Proceedings of 19th International Conference on World Wide Web (WWW '10)* (pp. 11-20). ACM.

Alur, R., & Dill, D. L. (1994). A theory of timed automata. *Theoretical Computer Science, 126*(2), 183–235.

Andersson, J., de Lemos, R., Malek, S., & Weyns, D. (2009). Reflecting on self-adaptive software systems. In *Software Engineering for Adaptive and Self-Managing Systems*, (pp. 38–47).

Andersson, B., Bider, I., Johannesson, P., & Perjons, E. (2005). Towards a formal definition of goal-oriented business process patterns. *BPM Journal, 11*, 650–662.

Andrews, T., et al. (2005). *Business process execution language for web services (WSBPEL)*. BEA Systems, IBM, Microsoft, SAP AG, and Siebel Systems, 2005.

Anicic, D., Fodor, P., Stühmer, R., & Stojanovic, N. (2009). *Event-driven approach for logic-based complex event processing*. Paper presented at the 12th IEEE International Conference on Computational Science and Engineering, Washington DC, USA.

Anselmi, J., Ardagna, D., & Cremonesi, P. (2007). A QoS-based selection approach of autonomic grid services. *In Proceedings of 2007 Workshop on Service-oriented Computing Performance: Aspects, Issues, and Approaches (SOCP '07)* (pp 1-8). ACM.

Ardagna, D., Baresi, L., Comai, S., Comuzzi, M., & Pernici, B. (2011). A service-based framework for flexible business processes. *IEEE Software, 28*(2), 61–67.

Ardagna, D., & Mirandola, R. (2010). Per-flow optimal service selection for web services based processes. *Journal of Systems and Software, 83*(8), 1512–1523.

Ardagna, D., & Pernici, B. (2007). Adaptive service composition in flexible processes. *IEEE Transactions on Software Engineering, 33*(6), 369–384.

Armbrust, M., Fox, A., Griffith, R., Joseph, A. D., Katz, R., & Konwinski, A. (2010, April). A view of cloud computing. *Communications of the ACM, 53*, 50–58. doi:10.1145/1721654.1721672

Arnold, A. (1994). *Finite transition systems. International Series in Computer Science*. Prentice-Hall.

Arsanjani, A., Zhang, L.-J., Ellis, M., Allam, A., & Channabasavaiah, K. (2007). S3: A service-oriented reference architecture. *IEEE IT Professional, 9*, 10–17.

Asanovic, K., Bodik, R., Catanzaro, B. C., Gebis, J. J., Husbands, P., Keutzer, K., et al. (2006). *The landscape of parallel computing research: A view from Berkeley.* (Electrical Engineering and Computer Sciences, University of California at Berkeley UCB/EECS-2006-183.)

Asanovic, K., Bodik, R., Demmel, J., Keaveny, T., Keutzer, K., & Kubiatowicz, J. (2009, October). A view of the parallel computing landscape. *Communications of the ACM, 52*, 56–67. doi:10.1145/1562764.1562783

Athanasopoulos, G., Tsalgatidou, A., & Pantazoglou, M. (2006). Interoperability among heterogeneous services. In *InteRNational Conference on Services Computing* (pp. 174-181). IEEE Computer Society Press.

Atkinson, A. K. (2008). Tupleware: A distributed tuple space for cluster computing. In *Proceedings of the 2008 Ninth International Conference on Parallel and Distributed Computing, Applications and Technologies*, (pp. 121–126). Washington, DC: IEEE Computer Society.

Autili, M., Benedetto, P. D., & Inverardi, P. (2009). Context-aware adaptive services: The PLASTIC approach. In *Proceedings of FASE '09, volume 5503 of Lecture Notes in Computer Science*, (pp. 124–139). Springer.

Autili, M., Benedetto, P. D., Inverardi, P., & Mancinelli, F. (2008). *Chameleon Project*. SEA group.

Autili, M., Inverardi, P., Navarra, A., & Tivoli, M. (2007). SYNTHESIS: A tool for automatically assembling correct and distributed component-based systems. In *Proceedings of ICSE, 07*, 784–787.

Babaoglu, O., Canright, G., Deutsch, A., Caro, G. A. D., Ducatelle, F., & Gambardella, L. M. (2006). Design patterns from biology for distributed computing. *ACM Transactions on Autonomous and Adaptive Systems, 1*(1), 26–66.

Bachrach, J., Beal, J., & McLurkin, J. (2010). Composable continuous space programs for robotic swarms. *Neural Computing & Applications, 19*(6), 825–847.

Bai, X., Xie, J., Chen, B., & Xiao, S. (2007). DRESR: Dynamic routing in enterprise service bus. In *IEEE International Conference on E-Business Engineering*, (pp. 528-531). Los Alamitos, CA: IEEE Computer Society. Retrieved from http://doi.ieeecomputersociety.org/10.1109/ICEBE.2007.102

Bai, X., Xu, D., Dai, G., Tsai, W., & Chen, Y. (2007). Dynamic reconfigurable testing of service-oriented architecture. In *Proceedings of the 31st Annual International Computer Software and Applications Conference (COMPSAC)*.

Balagtas-Fernandez, F. T., & Hussmann, H. (2008). Model-driven development of mobile applications. In *Proceedings of the 23rd IEEE/ACM International Conference on Automated Software Engineering*, (pp. 509-512).

Balzarotti, D., Costa, P., & Picco, G. P. (2007). The lights tuple space framework and its customization for context-aware applications. *Web Intelligence and Agent Systems, 5*(2), 215–231.

Bandara, A., Payne, T., Roure, D. D., Gibbins, N., & Lewis, T. (2008). *Semantic resource matching for pervasive environments: The approach and its evaluation*. Technical Report ECSTR-IAM08-001, School of Electronics and Computer Science, University of Southampton.

Baresi, L., Guinea, S., & Pasquale, L. (2007). Self-healing BPEL processes with Dynamo and the JBoss rule engine. In *Proceedings of the ESSPE '07 -International Workshop on Engineering of Software Services for Pervasive Environments -In Conjunction with the 6th ESEC/FSE Joint Meeting* (pp. 11-20).

Baresi, L., Guinea, S., Pistore, M., & Trainotti, M. (2009). Dynamo + Astro: An integrated approach for BPEL monitoring. In *Proceedings of the IEEE International Conference on Web Services* (pp. 230-237).

Baresi, L., Guinea, S., Pistore, M., & Trainotti, M. (2009). Dynamo + Astro: An integrated approach for BPEL monitoring. In *Proceedings of ICWS*, *09*, 230–237.

Baresi, L., Guinea, S., & Plebani, P. (2007). Policies and aspects for the supervision of BPEL processes. *Advanced Information Systems Engineering, LNCS, 4495*, 340–354.

Barros, A., Dumas, M., & Oaks, P. (2006). Standards for Web service choreography and orchestration: Status and perspectives. In Bussler, C. (Eds.), *Business Process Management Workshops* (Vol. 3812, pp. 61–74). Lecture Notes in Computer Science Berlin, Germany: Springer-Verlag.

Bartolomeo, G., Blefari-Melazzi, N., Cortese, G., Friday, A., Prezerakos, G., Walker, R., & Salsano, S. (2006). SMS: Simplifying Mobile Services - For users and service providers. In *Proceedings of the Advanced International Conference on Telecommunications and International Conference on Internet and Web Applications and Services*, (p. 209).

Bastide, R., Sy, O., Navarre, D., & Palanque, P. A. (2000). A formal specification of the CORBA event service. In *Proceedings of FMOODS*, *00*, 371–396.

Basu, S., & Bultan, T. (2011). Choreography conformance via synchronizability. In *WWW'11* (pp. 795-804). ACM Press.

Basu, S., Bultan, T., & Ouderni, M. (2012). Deciding choreography realizability. In *POPL'12* (pp. 191-202). ACM Press.

Beal, J. (2009). Flexible self-healing gradients. In S. Y. Shin & S. Ossowski (Eds.), *Proceedings of the 2009 ACM Symposium on Applied Computing (SAC)*, Honolulu, Hawaii, USA, March 9-12, 2009, (pp. 1197–1201). ACM.

Beal, J., & Bachrach, J. (2006). Infrastructure for engineered emergence on sensor/actuator networks. *IEEE Intelligent Systems, 21*(2), 10–19.

Bell, M. (2010). *SOA modeling patterns for service-oriented discovery and analysis* (p. 390). Wiley & Sons.

Bellucci, A., Cardellini, V., Di Valerio, V., & Iannucci, S. (2010) A scalable and highly available brokering service for SLA-based composite services. In *Proceedings of 2010 International Conference on Service-Oriented Computing (ICSOC '10)* (pp. 527–541). Springer.

Benatallah, B., Hacid, M., Rey, C., & Toumani, F. (2003). Request rewriting-based web service discovery. In *Proceedings of ISWC'03, volume 2870 of Lecture Notes in Computer Science*, (pp. 242–257). Springer.

Berbner, R., Spahn, M., Repp, N., Heckmann, O., & Steinmetz, R. (2006). Heuristics for QoS-aware Web service composition. *In Proceedings of IEEE International Conference on Web Services (ICWS '06)* (pp. 72-82).

Berners-Lee, T., & Connolly, D. (2011). *Notation3 (N3): A readable RDF syntax*. W3C team submission, W3C. Retrieved from http://www.w3.org/TeamSubmission/n3/

Berners-Lee, T., Connolly, D., Kagal, L., Scharf, Y., & Hendler, J. (2008). N3logic: A logical framework for the world wide web. *Theory and Practice of Logic Programming, 8*, 249–269.

Bianculli, D., & Ghezzi, C. (2008). SAVVY-WS at a glance: Supporting verifiable dynamic service compositions. In *Automated Engineering of Autonomous and Run-Time Evolving Systems (ARAMIS 2008)*, Co-located with ASE 2008, L'Aquila, Italy.

Bianculli, D., Jurca, R., Binder, W., Ghezzi, C., & Faltings, B. (2007). Automated dynamic maintenance of composite services based on service reputation. In Krmer, B., Lin, K.-J., & Narasimhan, P. (Eds.), *Service-Oriented Computing ICSOC 2007* (Vol. 4749, pp. 449–455). Berlin, Germany: Springer. doi:10.1007/978-3-540-74974-5_42

Biegel, G., & Cahill, V. (2004). A framework for developing mobile, context-aware applications. *Proceedings of the 2nd IEEE Conference on Pervasive Computing and Communication*, (pp. 361–365). Retrieved from http://cortex.di.fc.ul.pt/

Black, A. (1987). Distribution and abstract types in Emerald. *IEEE Transactions on Software Engineering, 13*(1), 65–76.

Boley, H., Tabet, S., & Wagner, G. (2001). Design rationale of RuleML: A markup language for semantic web rules. In *The Semantic Web Working Symposium*, (pp. 381–401).

Bolton, F. (2001). *Pure Corba*. SAMS Publishing.

BonFIRE. (2011). *EC FP7-ICT BonFIRE Project*. Retrieved October 2011 from http://www.bonfire-project.eu/

Bordeaux, L., Salaun, G., Berardi, D., & Mecella, M. (2004). When are two Web services compatible? In *Proceedings of TES'04, volume 3324 of Lecture Notes in Computer Science*, (pp. 15–28). Springer.

Boreale, M., De Nicola, R., & Pugliese, R. (2002). Trace and testing equivalence on asynchronous processes. *Information and Computation, 172*(2), 139–164.

Boubeta, J., Ortiz, G., & Medina, I. (2011). *An approach of early disease detection using CEP and SOA. In 3rd International Conferences on Advanced Service Computing* (pp. 143–148). Italy: Xpert Publishing Services.

Bouquet, P., Giunchiglia, F., van Harmelen, F., Serafini, L., & Stuckenschmidt, H. (2004). Contextualizing ontologies. *Journal of Web Semantics, 1*(4), 325–343.

Bracciali, A., Brogi, A., & Canal, C. (2005). A formal approach to component adaptation. *Journal of Systems and Software, 74*(1), 45–54.

Bravetti, M., & Zavattaro, G. (2006). *Towards a unifying theory for choreography conformance and contract compliance*. Technical report. Retrieved from http://cs.unibo.it/~bravetti/html/techreports.

Bravetti, M., & Zavattaro, G. (2007a). Towards a unifying theory for choreography conformance and contract compliance. In *SC'06, volume 4829 of LNCS*, (pp. 34–50).

Bravetti, M., & Zavattaro, G. (2007b). Contract based multi-party service composition. In *FSEN'07, volume 4767 of LNCS*, (pp. 207–222).

Bravetti, M., & Zavattaro, G. (2007c). A theory for strong service compliance. In *Coordination'07, volume 4467 of LNCS*, (pp. 96-112).

Bravetti, M., & Zavattaro, G. (2008). *Contract compliance and choreography conformance in the presence of message queues*. Technical report. Retrieved from http://cs.unibo.it/~bravetti/html/techreports

Bravetti, M., & Zavattaro, G. (2009). Contract compliance and choreography conformance in the presence of message queues. *Proceedings WS-FM'08, volume 5387 of LNCS*, (pp. 37-54).

Bravetti, M., & Zavattaro, G. (2009). A theory of contracts for strong service compliance. *JouRNal of Mathematical Structures in Computer Science, 19*(3), 601–638.

Brenner, D., Atkinson, C., Hummel, O., & Stoll, D. (2007). Strategies for the run-time testing of third party web services. In *Proceedings of the IEEE International Conference on Service-Oriented Computing and Applications* (pp. 114–121). Washington, DC: IEEE Computer Society.

Broens, T., Pokraev, S., van Sinderen, M., Koolwaaij, J., & Costa, P. (2004). Context-aware, ontology-based service discovery. In *Proceedings of EUSAI'04, volume 3295 of Lecture Notes in Computer Science*, (pp. 72–83). Springer.

Brogi, A., & Popescu, R. (2006). Automated generation of BPEL adapters. In *Proceedings of ICSOC'06, volume 4294 of Lecture Notes in Computer Science*, (pp. 27–39). Springer.

Brogi, A., Corfini, S., & Popescu, R. (2008). Semantics-based composition-oriented discovery of Web services. *ACM Transactions on Internet Technology, 8*(4), 19:1–19:39.

Brogi, A., & Popescu, R. (2006). Automated generation of BPEL adapters. In Dan, A., & Lamersdorf, W. (Eds.), *Service-Oriented Computing ICSOC 2006 (Vol. 4294*, pp. 27–39). Berlin, Germany: Springer. doi:10.1007/11948148_3

Bry, F., & Eckert, M. (2007). *Rule-based composite event queries: The language XChange EQ and its semantics*. Paper presented at the International Conference on Web Reasoning and Rule Systems. Springer.

Bryant, R. (1986). Graph-based algorithms for Boolean function manipulation. *IEEE Transactions on Computers, 35*(8), 677–691.

Bucchiarone, A., Kazhamiakin, R., Cappiello, C., Di Nitto, E., & Mazza, V. (2010). A context-driven adaptation process for service-based applications. In *2nd International Workshop on Principles of Engineering Service-Oriented Systems* (pp. 50-56). New York, NY: ACM.

Bucchiarone, A., Cappiello, C., Di Nitto, E., Kazhamiakin, R., Mazza, V., & Pistore, M. (2009). *Design for adaptation of service-based applications: Main issues and requirements* (pp. 467–476). ICSOC/ServiceWave Workshops.

Burnette, E. (2009). *Hello, Android, 2nd ed.: The pragmatic programmers bookshelf.* ISBN-10: 1-934356-49-2

Burton-Jones, A., Storey, V., Sugumaran, V., & Purao, S. (2003). A heuristic-based methodology for semantic augmentation of user queries on the Web. In *Proceedings of ER'03, volume 2813 of Lecture Notes in Computer Science*, (pp. 476–489). Springer.

Buscemi, M. G., & Montanari, U. (2011). QoS negotiation in service composition. *Journal of Logic and Algebraic Programming*, *80*(1), 13–24.

Busi, N., Gorrieri, R., Guidi, C., Lucchi, R., & Zavattaro, G. (2005). Choreography and orchestration: A synergic approach for system design. In *ICSOC'05, volume 3826 of LNCS*, (pp. 228-240).

Calinescu, R., Grunske, L., Kwiatkowska, M., Mirandola, R., & Tamburrelli, G. (2011). Dynamic QoS management and optimization in service-based systems. *IEEE Transactions on Software Engineering*, *37*(3), 387–409.

Cámara, J., Martín, J., Salaün, G., Cubo, J., Ouederni, M., Canal, C., & Pimentel, E. (2009). ITACA: An integrated toolbox for the automatic composition and adaptation of web services. In *Proceedings of ICSE*, *09*, 627–630.

Campbell, A. T., Eisenman, S. B., Lane, N. D., Miluzzo, E., Peterson, R. A., & Lu, H. (2008). The rise of people-centric sensing. *IEEE Internet Computing*, *12*(4).

Canal, C., Murillo, J., & Poizat, P. (2006). Software adaptation. *L'Objet Special Issue on Coordination and Adaptation Techniques for Software Entities*, *12*(1), 9–31.

Canal, C., Poizat, P., & Salaün, G. (2008). Model-based adaptation of behavioural mismatching components. *IEEE Transactions on Software Engineering*, *34*(4), 546–563.

Canfora, G., Di Penta, M., Esposito, R., & Villani, M. L. (2008). A framework for QoS-aware binding and re-binding of composite Web services. *Journal of Systems and Software*, *81*, 1754–1769.

Carbone, M., Honda, K., & Yoshida, N. (2007). Structured communication-centred programming for web services. In *ESOP'07, volume 4421 of LNCS*, (pp. 2-17).

Cardellini, V., Casalicchio, E., Grassi, V., & Lo Presti, F. (2007). Flow-based service selection for web service composition supporting multiple QoS classes. *In Proceedings of IEEE 2007 International Conference on Web Services* (pp. 743-750).

Cardellini, V., Casalicchio, E., Grassi, V., Iannucci, S., Lo Presti, F., & Mirandola, R. (in press). MOSES: A framework for QoS driven runtime adaptation of service-oriented systems. *IEEE Transactions on Software Engineering*, accepted for publication in June 2011.

Cardellini, V., Di Valerio, V., Grassi, V., Iannucci, S., & Lo Presti, F. (2011). A new approach to QoS driven service selection in service oriented architectures. *In Proceedings of IEEE 6th International Symposium on Service-Oriented System Engineering (SOSE '11)*.

Cardellini, V., Di Valerio, V., Grassi, V., Iannucci, S., & Lo Presti, F. (2011). A performance comparison of QoS-driven service selection approaches. In *Proceedings of 4th European Conference Service Wave*. Springer.

Cardell-Oliver, R., & Liu, W. (2010). Representation and recognition of situations in sensor networks. *IEEE Communications Magazine*, (March): 112–117.

Carpineti, S., Castagna, G., Laneve, C., & Padovani, L. (2006). A formal account of contracts for Web services. In *WS-FM'06, volume 4184 of LNCS*, (pp. 148-162).

Carroll, J. J., Dickinson, I., Dollin, C., Reynolds, D., Seaborne, A., & Wilkinson, K. (2004). Jena: Implementing the Semantic Web recommendations. *In Proceedings of the 13th International World Wide Web Conference - Alternate Track Papers & Posters*, (pp. 74–83). New York, NY: ACM.

Castagna, G., Dezani-Ciancaglini, M., & Padovani, L. (2011). On global types and multi-party sessions. In *FMOODS/FORTE'11, volume 6722 of LNCS*, (pp. 1-28).

Castagna, G., Gesbert, N., & Padovani, L. (2008). A theory of contracts for web services. In *POPL'08*, (pp. 261-272). ACM Press.

Castellani, I., & Hennessy, M. (1998). Testing theories for asynchronous languages. In *FSTTCS'98, volume 1530 of LNCS*, (pp. 90-101).

Cavallaro, L., & Di Nitto, E. (2008). An approach to adapt service requests to actual service interfaces. In *Proceedings of SEAMS Conference*.

Cavallo, B., Di Penta, M., & Canfora, G. (2010). An empirical comparison of methods to support QoS-aware service selection. In *Proceedings of the 2nd International Workshop on Principles of Engineering Service-Oriented Systems* (pp. 64–70). New York, NY: ACM.

Cervin, A., Henriksson, D., Lincoln, B., Eker, J., & Rzn, K.-E. (2003). How does control timing affect performance? Analysis and simulation of timing using jitterbug and truetime. *IEEE Control Systems Magazine*.

Chae, G., Dasgupta, K., Kumar, A., Mittal, S., & Srivastava, B. (2006). Adaptation in Web service composition and execution. In *Proceedings of the ICWS 2006: 2006 IEEE International Conference on Web Services* (pp. 549-557).

Chang, S. H., La, H. J., Bae, J. S., Jeon, W. Y., & Kim, S. D. (2007). Design of a dynamic composition handler for ESB-based services. In *IEEE International Conference on e-Business Engineering, ICEBE 2007* (pp. 287–294).

Chappel, D. A. (2004). *Enterprise service bus*. O'Reilly, 2004.

Chappell, D. (2004). *Enterprise service bus: Theory in practice*. O'Reilly Media.

Charfi, A., & Mezini, M. (2004). Aspect-oriented Web service composition with AO4BPEL. In *Proceedings of the 2nd European Conference on Web Services (ECOWS), volume 3250 of LNCS,* (pp. 168–182). Springer.

Charfi, A., Dinkelaker, T., & Mezini, M. (2009). A plug-in architecture for self-adaptive web service compositions. In *Proceedings of the IEEE International Conference on Web Services (ICWS '09)*, (pp. 35–42). IEEE Computer Society.

Charfi, A., & Mezini, M. (2004). Aspect-oriented web service composition with AO4BPEL. *Lecture Notes in Computer Science, 3250*, 168–182. doi:10.1007/978-3-540-30209-4_13

Charfi, A., & Mezini, M. (2007). Ao4bpel: An aspect-oriented extension to BPEL. *World Wide Web (Bussum), 10*(3), 309–344.

Chen, L., & Chen, H. (2008). Efficient type checking for a subclass of regular expression types. In *InteRNational Conference for Young Computer Scientists* (pp. 1647-1652). IEEE Computer Society Press.

Chen, H., Finin, T., & Joshi, A. (2003). An intelligent broker for context-aware systems. In *Proceedings of UbiComp, 03*, 183–184.

Cheung-Foo-Wo, D., Riveill, M., & Tigli, J. (2009). *Adaptation dynamique par tissage d'aspects d'assemblage*. Thèse I3S, Nice Sophia Antipolis.

Coleman, B. (2009). Using sensor inputs to affect virtual and real environments. *IEEE Pervasive Computing/IEEE Computer Society and IEEE Communications Society, 8*(3), 16–23.

Commission of the European Communities. (2006, June). *Freight transport logistics in Europe*. Retrieved October 2011 from http://europa.eu/legislation summaries/environment/tackling climate change/l24456 en.htm

Compliance-Driven Models, Languages, and Architectures for Services Project (COMPAS). (n.d.). Retrieved September 15, 2011, from http://www.compas-ict.eu/

Cormen, T. H., Leiserson, C. E., Rivest, R. L., & Stein, C. (2001). *Introduction to algorithms* (2nd ed.). MIT Press.

Corradi, A., Lodolo, E., Monti, S., & Pasini, S. (2008, July). A user-centric composition model for the Internet of Services. In *Proceedings IEEE Symposium on Computers and Communications, ISCC 2008* (p. 110). Washington, DC: IEEE Computer Society.

Cubo, J., & Pimentel, E. (2011). DAMASCo: A framework for the automatic composition of component-based and service-oriented architectures. In *Proceedings of ECSA'11, volume 6903 of Lecture Notes in Computer Science*, (pp. 388–404). Springer.

Cubo, J., Pimentel, E., Salaün, G., & Canal, C. (2010). Handling data-based concurrency in context-aware service protocols. In *Proceedings of FOCLASA'10, volume 30 of Electronic Proceeding in Theoretical Computer Science*, (pp. 62–77).

Cubo, J., Salaün, G., Cámara, J., Canal, C., & Pimentel, E. (2007). Context-based adaptation of component behavioural interfaces. In *Proceedings of COORDINATION'07, volume 4467 of Lecture Notes in Computer Science*, (pp. 305–323). Springer.

Cubo, J., Salaün, G., Canal, C., Pimentel, E., & Poizat, P. (2007b). A model-based approach to the verification and adaptation of WF/.NET components. In *Proceedings of FACS'07, volume 215 of Electronic Notes in Theoretical Computer Science*, (pp. 39–55). Elsevier.

Cubo, J., Sama, M., Raimondi, F., & Rosenblum, D. (2009). A model to design and verify context-aware adaptive service composition. In *Proceedings of SCC'09*, (pp. 184–191). IEEE Computer Society.

Cubo, J., Canal, C., & Pimentel, E. (2011). Model-based dependable composition of self-adaptive systems. *Informatica*, *35*, 51–62.

Cucinotta, T., Checconi, F., Kousiouris, G., Kyriazis, D., Varvarigou, T., Mazzetti, A., et al. (2010, December). Virtualised e-learning with real-time guarantees on the IRMOS platform. In *Proceedings. IEEE International Conference on Service-Oriented Computing and Applications (SOCA)*, (pp. 1-8). Washington, DC: IEEE Computer Society.

Dargie, W. (Ed.). (2009). *Context-aware computing and self-managing systems*. CRC Press.

Davis, J. (2009). *Open source SOA* (1st ed.). Manning Publications.

de Alfaro, L., & Henzinger, T. A. (2001). Interface automata. In *Proceedings of ESEC/FSE'01*, (pp. 109–120). ACM Press.

De Nicola, R. (1887). Extensional equivalences for transition systems. *Acta Informatica*, *24*(2), 211–237.

De Nicola, R., & Hennessy, M. (1984). Testing equivalences for processes. *Theoretical Computer Science*, *34*, 83–133.

Decker, G., Kopp, O., Leymann, F., & Weske, M. (2007). BPEL4Chor: Extending BPEL for modeling choreographies. In *IEEE 2007 International Conference on Web Services (ICWS)*. IEEE Computer Society.

Decker, S., Sintek, M., Billig, A., Henze, N., Dolog, P., & Nejdl, W. ... Zdun, U. (2005). *TRIPLE - An RDF rule language with context and use cases*. In Rule Languages for Interoperability.

Delgado, J. (2012). Bridging provider-centric and user-centric social networks. In Cruz-Cunha, M. (Eds.), *Handbook of research on business social networking: Organizational, managerial, and technological dimensions* (pp. 63–83). Hershey, PA: IGI Global.

Dern, D. (2010). Cross-platform smartphone apps still difficult. *IEEE Spectrum*, 2010.

Dey, A. K., & Abowd, G. D. (2000). *Towards a better understanding of context and context-awareness*. ACM Conference on Human Factors in Computer Systems (CHI 2000), The Hague, Netherlands, April 2000.

Dey, A., & Abowd, G. (2000). Towards a better understanding of context and context-awareness. In *Proceedings of Workshop on the What, Who, Where, When and How of Context-Awareness*, (pp. 304–307).

Dey, A. K. (2001). Understanding and using context. *Personal and Ubiquitous Computing*, *5*(1), 4–7.

Di Modica, G., Tomarchio, O., & Vita, L. (2009). Dynamic SLAs management in service oriented environments. *Journal of Systems and Software*, *82*(5), 759–771. doi:10.1016/j.jss.2008.11.010

Di Nitto, E., Ghezzi, C., Metzger, A., Papazoglou, M., & Pohl, K. (2008). A journey to highly dynamic, self-adaptive service-based applications. *Automated Software Engineering*, *15*(3-4), 313–341. doi:10.1007/s10515-008-0032-x

Diaz, G., & Rodriguez, I. (2009). Automatically deriving choreography-conforming systems of services. In *IEEE InteRNational Conference on Services Computing* (pp. 9-16). IEEE Computer Society Press.

Dietz, J. (2006). *Enterprise ontology: TheoRY and methodology*. Berlin, Germany: Springer-Verlag.

Doberkat, E.-E., Franke, W., Gutenbeil, U., Hasselbring, W., Lammers, U., & Pahl, C. (1992). PROSET: A language for prototyping with sets. In *Proceedings Third International Workshop on Rapid System Prototyping* (pp. 235-248).

Dobson, S., Denazis, S., Fernandez, A., Gati, D., Gelenbe, E., Massacci, F., & Zambonelli, F. (2006). A survey of autonomic communications. *ACM Transactions in Autonomic and Adaptive Systems, 1*(2), 223–259.

Domingue, J., Galis, A., Gavras, A., Zahariadis, T., Lambert, D., & Cleary, F. (2011). *The future Internet. Future Internet Assembly 2011: Achievements and Technological Promises (Vol. 6656)*. Heidelberg, Germany: Springer.

Dong, W.-L., Yu, H., & Zhang, Y.-B. (2006). Testing BPEL-based Web service composition using high-level Petri nets. In *EDOC '06: Proceedings of the 10th IEEE International Enterprise Distributed Object Computing Conference*. IEEE Computer Society.

Dorigo, M., & Birattari, M. (2007). Swarm intelligence. *Scholarpedia, 2*(9), 1462.

Dranidis, D., Metzger, A., & Kourtesis, D. (2010). Enabling proactive adaptation through just-in-time testing of conversational services. In Di Nitto, E., & Yahyapour, R. (Eds.), *Towards a Service-Based Internet (Vol. 6481,* pp. 63–75). Berlin, Germany: Springer. doi:10.1007/978-3-642-17694-4_6

Drools Fusion. (2010). Retrieved from http://www.jboss.org/drools/drools-fusion.html

Dumas, M., Spork, M., & Wang, K. (2006). Adapt or perish: Algebra and visual notation for service interface adaptation. In *Proceedings of BPM'06, volume 4102 of Lecture Notes in Computer Science,* (pp. 65–80). Springer.

Dunkel, J., & Bruns, R. (2007). Model-driven architecture for mobile applications. In *Proceedings of the 10th international conference on Business information systems,* (pp. 464-477).

Earl, T. (2005). *Service-oriented architecture: Concepts, technology, and design.* Upper Saddle River, NJ: Prentice Hall PTR.

Earl, T. (2007). *SOA: Principles of service design.* Upper Saddle River, NJ: Prentice Hall PTR.

Eclipse Foundation Incorporation. (2011). *Eclipse modelling framework.* EMF.

Edwards, M. (2011). *Service component architecture.* OASIS. Retrieved 7 April 2011, from http://oasis-opencsa.org/sca

eFreight. (2010, January). *e-FREIGHT is an integrated project within the EU's 7th Framework programme.* Retrieved October 2011 from http://www.efreightproject.eu/

El Falou, M., Bouzid, M., Mouaddib, A.-I., & Vidal, T. (2010, July). A distributed planning approach for web services composition. In *Proceedings of the IEEE International Conference on Web Services (ICWS), 2010* (pp. 337 -344).

Elgammal, A., Turetken, O., van den Heuvel, W., & Papazoglou, M. (2011). On the formal specification of regulatory compliance: A comparative analysis. In Maximilien, E. (Eds.), *Service-Oriented Computing (Vol. 6568,* pp. 27–38). Lecture Notes in Computer Science Berlin, Germany: Springer.

Elrad, T., Aksit, M., Kitzales, G., Lieberherr, K., & Ossher, H. (2001). Discussing aspects of AOP. *Communications of the ACM, 44*(10), 33–38.

Endsley, M. R., & Connors, E. S. (2008). Situation awareness: State of the art. *2008 Power and Energy Society Meeting* (pp. 1–4).

Endsley, R. (1995). Toward a theory of situation awareness in dynamic systems: Situation awareness. *Human Factors, 37,* 32–64.

Erenkrantz, J., Gorlick, M., Suryanarayana, G., & Taylor, R. (2007). From representations to computations: The evolution of web architectures. In *6th Joint Meeting of the European Software Engineering Conference and the ACM SIGSOFT Symposium on the Foundations of Software Engineering* (pp. 255-264). ACM Press.

Erl, T. (2005). *Service-oriented architecture (SOA): Concepts, technology, and design.* Prentice Hall.

Erl, T. (2009). *SOA design patterns* (1st ed.). Prentice Hall PTR.

Erl, T., Karmarkar, A., Walmsley, P., Haas, H., Yalcinalp, L. U., & Liu, K. (2008). *Web service contract design and versioning for SOA* (1st ed.). Prentice Hall.

Erradi, A., & Maheshwari, P. (2008). Dynamic binding framework for adaptive web services. In *Proceedings of the 3rd International Conference on Internet and Web Applications and Services, ICIW 2008* (pp. 162-167).

Evermann, J., & Wand, Y. (2005). Toward formalizing domain modelling semantics in language syntax. *IEEE Transactions on Software Engineering, 31*(1), 21–37.

Ezenwoye, O., & Sadjadi, S. M. (2007). RobustBPEL2: Transparent autonomization in business processes through dynamic proxies. In *Proceedings of 8th International Symposium on Autonomous Decentralized Systems (ISADS '07)* (pp. 17-24). IEEE Computer Society.

Fabra, J. lvarez, P., Baares, J., & Ezpeleta, J. (2008). Runtime protocol binding: Flexible service integration by means of exible service interactions. In *Proceedings of the 2008 IEEE International Conference on Services Computing, SCC 2008* (Vol. 1, pp. 291-298).

Fabry, R. S. (1976). *How to design systems in which modules can be changed on the fly.* In Intl. Conf. on Software Engineering.

Fang, R., Chen, Y., Fong, L., Lam, L., Frank, D., Vignola, C., & Du, N. (2007). A version-aware approach for web service client application. In *10th IFIP/IEEE International Symposium on Integrated Network Management, IM'07* (pp. 401–409).

Fensel, D. (2004). Triple-space computing: Semantic Web services based on persistent publication of information. In F. A. Aagesen, C. Anutariya, & V. Wuwongse (Eds.), *Intelligence in Communication Systems, IFIP International Conference, INTELLCOMM 2004, Proceedings, volume 3283 of Lecture Notes in Computer Science*, Bangkok, Thailand, (pp. 43–53). Springer.

Ferguson, D. (2010). *The internet service bus. On the Move to Meaningful Internet Systems 2007: CoopIS* (p. 5). DOA, ODBASE, GADA, and IS.

Ferrara, A. (2004). Web services: A process algebra approach. In *ICSOC '04: Proceedings of the 2nd International Conference on Service Oriented Computing,* (pp. 242–251). New York, NY: ACM Press.

Ferreira, H. M., & Ferreira, D. (2006). An integrated life cycle for workflow management based on learning and planning. *International Journal of Cooperative Information Systems, 15*(4), 485–505.

Ferscha, A., & Vogl, S. (2010). Wearable displays – for everyone! *IEEE Pervasive Computing / IEEE Computer Society and IEEE Communications Society, 9*(1), 7–10.

Fiadeiro, J. L., & Lopes, A. (2010). A model for dynamic reconfiguration in service-oriented architectures. In *Proceedings of ECSA'10, volume 6285 of Lecture Notes in Computer Science,* (pp. 70–85). Springer.

Fielding, R. (2000). *Architectural styles and the design of network-based software architectures.* Unpublished doctoral dissertation, University of California at Irvine, Irvine, California.

Filman, R. E., Elrad, T., Clarke, S., & Aksit, M. (2004). *Aspect-oriented software development.* Addison-Wesley.

Formica, A. (2007). Similarity of XML-schema elements: A structural and information content approach. *The Computer Journal, 51*(2), 240–254.

Foster, H., Uchitel, S., & Kramer, J. (2006). LTSA-WS: A tool for model-based verification of web service compositions and choreography. In *Proceedings of ICSE, 06*, 771–774.

Fournet, C., Hoare, C. A. R., Rajamani, S. K., & Rehof, J. (2004). Stuck-free conformance. In *CAV'04, volume 3114 of LNCS,* (pp. 242-254).

Frantz, R. Z. (n.d.). *Guaraná DSL.* Retrieved June 26, 2011, from http://www.tdg-seville.info/rzfrantz/Guaran%C3%A1+DSL

FREIGHTWISE. (2006, November). *FREIGHTWISE - Management framework for intelligent intermodal transport.* Retrieved October 2011 from http://freightwise.info/cms/

Friedman-Hill, E. (2008). *Jess, the rule engine for the Java platform.* Retrieved from http://www.jessrules.com/

Fu, X., Bultan, T., & Su, J. (2004). Analysis of interacting BPEL web services. In *Proceedings of WWW, 04*, 621–630.

Fu, X., Bultan, T., & Su, J. (2004). Conversation protocols: A formalism for specification and verification of reactive electronic services. *Theoretical Computer Science, 328*(1-2), 19–37.

Fu, X., Bultan, T., & Su, J. (2005). Synchronizability of conversations among Web services. *IEEE Transactions on Software Engineering, 31*(12), 1042–1055.

Gamma, E., Helm, R., Johnson, R., & Vlissides, J. (1995). *Elements of reusable object-oriented software*. Addison-Wesley Publishing Company.

García de Prado, A., & Ortiz, G. (2011). *Context-aware services: A survey on current proposals. In 3rd International Conferences on Advanced Service Computing* (pp. 104–109). Italy: Xpert Publishing Services.

Garlan, D., Siewiorek, D. P., Smailagic, A., & Steenkiste, P. (2002). Aura: Toward distraction free pervasive computing. *IEEE Pervasive Computing / IEEE Computer Society and IEEE Communications Society, 1*(2).

Gaspari, M., & Zavattaro, G. (1999). A process algebraic specification of the new asynchronous CORBA messaging service. In *Proceedings of ECOOP '99, volume 1628 of Lecture Notes in Computer Science*, (pp. 495–518).

Gearon, P., & Schenk, S. (Eds.). (2009). *SPARQL 1.1 update*. W3C working draft, W3C. Retrieved from http://www.w3.org/TR/2009/WD-sparql11-update-20091022/

Gehlert, A., Metzger, A., Karastoyanova, D., Kazhamiakin, R., Pohl, K., Leymann, F., & Pistore, M. (2011). Integrating perfective and corrective adaptation of service-based applications. In S. Dustdar & F. Li (Eds.), *Service engineering: European research results book* (pp. 137-169). Springer. Hermosillo, G., Seinturier L., & Duchien, L (2010). Using complex event processing for dynamic business process adaptation. In *Proceedings of the IEEE SCC 2010*, (pp. 466–473).

Gelernter, D. (1985). Generative communication in Linda. *ACM Transactions on Programming Languages and Systems, 7*(1), 80–112.

Gelernter, D. (1985). Generative communication in Linda. *ACM Transactions on Programming Languages and Systems, 7*(1), 80–112.

Giannotti, F., Nanni, M., Pedreschi, D., & Pinelli, F. (2006). Mining sequences with temporal annotations. In *Proceedings of the ACM Symposium on Applied Computing* (pp. 593-597).

Gillespie, D. T. (1977). Exact stochastic simulation of coupled chemical reactions. *Journal of Physical Chemistry, 81*(25), 2340–2361.

González, L. (2011, October 18). *Plataforma ESB adaptativa para sistemas basados en servicios* (Master's Thesis). PEDECIBA Informática | Instituto de Computación – Facultad de Ingeniería – Universidad de la República.

González, L., & Ruggia, R. (2010). Towards dynamic adaptation within an ESB-based service infrastructure layer. In *Proceedings of the 3rd International Workshop on Monitoring, Adaptation and Beyond, MONA '10* (pp. 40–47). New York, NY: ACM. doi:10.1145/1929566.1929572

González, L., & Ruggia, R. (2011a). *Addressing the dynamics of services contracts through an adaptive ESB infrastructure*. Presented at the 1st International Workshop on Adaptive Services for the Future Internet, Poznan-Poland.

González, L., & Ruggia, R. (2011b). *Addressing QoS issues in service based systems through an adaptive ESB infrastructure*. Presented at the 6th Middleware for Service Oriented Computing Workshop, Lisboa-Portugal.

Gronmo, R., Skogan, D., Solheim, I., & Oldevik, J. (2004). Model-driven Web services development. In *IEEE International Conference on e-Technology, e-Commerce and e-Service*, (pp. 42-45). IEEE Press.

Guha, R. V., & Brickley, D. (2004). *RDF vocabulary description language 1.0: RDF schema*. W3C recommendation, W3C. Retrieved from http://www.w3.org/TR/2004/REC-rdf-schema-20040210/

Gui, N. B. C., De Florio, V. B., Sun, H. B., & Blondia, C. B. (2011). Toward architecture-based context-aware deployment and adaptation. *Journal of Systems and Software, 84*(2), 185–197. doi:10.1016/j.jss.2010.09.017

Guinard, D., Trifa, V., Karnouskos, S., Spiess, P., & Savio, D. (2010). Interacting with the SOA-based internet of things: Discovery, query, selection, and on-demand provisioning of web services. *IEEE Transactions on Services Computing, 3*, 223–235. doi:10.1109/TSC.2010.3

Gupta, D. (1994). *On-line software version change*. Doctoral Thesis.

Hameurlain, N. (2007). Flexible behavioural compatibility and substitutability for component protocols: A formal specification. In *Proceedings of SEFM, 07*, 391–400.

Han, J., & Kamber, M. (Jim Gray, Series Editor). (2006). *Data mining: Concepts and techniques*. Morgan Kaufmann Publishers.

Hancock, J. T., Toma, C., & Ellison, N. (2007). The truth about lying in online dating profiles. *Proceedings of the ACM Conference on Human Factors in Computing Systems (CHI 2007)*, ACM, (pp. 449–452).

Han, W., Shi, X., & Chen, R. (2008). Process-context aware matchmaking for web service composition. *Journal of Network and Computer Applications, 31*(4), 559–576.

Harasic, M., Augustin, A., Obermeier, P., & Tolksdorf, R. (2010). RDFSwarms: Self organized distributed RDF triple store. In *Proceedings of the 2010 ACM Symposium on Applied Computing, SAC '10*, (pp. 1339–1340). New York, NY: ACM.

Hart, G. (2011). The five Ws of online help for tech writers. *TechWhirl*. Retrieved January 24, 2012, from http://techwhirl.com/columns/the-five-ws-of-online-help/

Heckel, R. (2008). Architectural transformations: From legacy to three-tier and services. *Software Evolution, 2008*, 139–170.

Heines, J. M., & Schedlbauer, M. J. (2007). Teaching object-oriented concepts through GUI programming. In *Proceedings of the 11th Workshop on Pedagogies and Tools - Teaching and Learning Object Oriented Concepts*.

Hennessy, M., & Lin, H. (1995). Symbolic bisimulations. *Theoretical Computer Science, 138*(2), 353–389.

Hennicker, R., & Knapp, A. (2007). Activity-driven synthesis of state machines. In M. D. Dwyer & A. Lopes (Eds.), *Proceedings 10th International Conference Fundamental Approaches to Software Engineering (FASE '07), volume 4422 of LNCS*, (pp. 87-101). Berlin, Germany: Springer.

Hepner, M., Baird, R., & Gamble, R. (2009). Dynamically changing workows of web services. In *Proceedings of the SERVICES 2009 -5th 2009 World Congress on Services* (p. 422-429).

Hérault, C., Thomas, G., & Fourier, U. J. (2005). Mediation and enterprise service bus: A position paper. *Proceedings of the First International Workshop on Mediation in Semantic Web Services*. Retrieved from http://citeseerx.ist.psu.edu/viewdoc/summary?doi=10.1.1.142.7416

Herbrechtsmeier, S., Witkowski, U., & Rüuckert, U. (2009). Bebot: A modular mobile miniature robot platform supporting hardware reconfiguration and multi-standard communication. In *Progress in Robotics, Communications in Computer and Information Science, Proceedings of the FIRA RoboWorld Congress 2009*, Vol.44, (pp. 346–356). Incheon, Korea: Springer.

Hielscher, J., Kazhamiakin, R., Metzger, A., & Pistore, M. (2008). A framework for proactive selfadaptation of service-based applications based on online testing. In the *Proceedings of the ServiceWave 2008*, (pp. 122-133).

Hielscher, J., Metzger, A., & Kazhamiakin, R. (2009). Taxonomy of adaptation principles and mechanisms. *S-Cube project, Deliverable # CD-JRA-1.2.2*, (pp. 39-56). Retrieved from http://www.s-cube-network.eu/

Hinze, A., Sachs, K., & Buchmann, A. (2009 July). *Event-based applications and enabling technologies*. Paper presented in DEBS 2009, July 6-9, Nashville, USA.

Hmida, M. B., Tomaz, R. F., & Monfort, V. (2006). Applying aop concepts to increase web services flexibility. *Journal of Digital Information Management, 4*(1), 37–43.

Hoare, T. (1985). *Communicating sequential processes*. Prentice-Hall.

Hofstede, A. H. M. T., Aalst, W. M. P. V. D., Adams, M., & Russell, N. (2009). *Modern business process automation: YAWL and its support environment* (1st ed.). Springer.

Hohpe, G., & Woolf, B. (2003). *Enterprise integration patterns: Designing, building, and deploying messaging solutions*. Addison-Wesley Professional.

Hojenski, K., & Oberthür, S. (2006). *Towards self optimizing distributed resource management*. In Selbstorganisierende, Adaptive, Kontextsensitive verteilte Systeme (SAKS 06), Kassel, Germany.

Holdener, A. III. (2008). *Ajax: The definitive guide*. Sebastopol, CA: O'Reilly Media, Inc.

Hong, J., Suh, E., & Kim, S. (2009). Context-aware systems: A literature review and classification. *Expert Systems with Applications, 36*, 8509–8522.

Horrocks, I., Patel-Schneider, P. F., Boley, H., Tabet, S., Grosof, B., & Dean, M. (2004). *SWRL: A semantic web rule language combining OWL and RuleML*. Technical report, W3C Member Submission. Retrieved from http://www.w3. org/Submission/SWRL/

Hosoya, H., & Pierce, B. (2002). Regular expression pattern matching for XML. *Journal of Functional Programming, 13*(6), 961–1004.

Hutchison, B., Schmidt, M., Wolfson, D., & Stockton, M. (2005, July 26). *SOA programming model for implementing Web services, Part 4: An introduction to the IBM enterprise service bus*. CT316. Retrieved June 26, 2011, from http://www.ibm.com/developerworks/library/ws-soa-progmodel4/

Hwang, C., & Yoon, K. (1981). *Multiple criteria decision making. Lecture Notes in Economics and Mathematical Systems*. Springer.

Ibm (2006). An architectural blueprint for autonomic computing. *Quality, 36*(June), 34.

I-Ching, H. (2011). An architecture of mobile Web 2.0 context-aware applications in ubiquitous Web. *Journal of Software, 6*(4).

Idrissi, Y. E. B. E., Ajhoun, R., & Idrissi, M. J. (2010). Multicriteria-based decision for services discovery and selection. *Smart Innovation. Systems and Technologies, 6*, 41–51.

Inverardi, P., & Tivoli, M. (2003). Deadlock-free software architectures for COM /DCOM applications. *Journal of Systems and Software, 65*(3), 173–183.

IRMOS. (2011). *EC FP7-ICT IRMOS Project*. Retrieved October 2011 from http://www.irmosproject.eu/ Service Management.aspx

ISTAG. (2008, January). FP7 ICT Advisory Group -Working Group on "Future Internet infrastructure". *ISTAG Report*. Retrieved October 2011 from ftp://ftp. cordis.europa.eu/pub/ist/docs/ future-internet-istag en.pdf

Ivanovic, D., Carro, M., & Hermenegildo, M. (2010, July). Towards data-aware QoS-driven adaptation for service orchestrations. In *Proceedings of the IEEE International Conference on Web Services (ICWS), 2010* (pp. 107-114).

Ivanovic, D., Treiber, M., Carro, M., & Dustdar, S. (2010). Building dynamic models of service compositions with simulation of provision resources. In Parsons, J., Saeki, M., Shoval, P., Woo, C., & Wand, Y. (Eds.), *Proceeding of Conceptual Modeling ER 2010 (Vol. 6412*, pp. 288–301). Berlin, Germany: Springer. doi:10.1007/978-3-642-16373-9_21

Jang, J., Choi, Y., & Zhao, J. (2003). Adaptive workow management with open kernel framework based on web services. In *Proceedings of the International Conference on Web Services (ICWS), 2003* (p. 124-130).

Jazayeri, M. (2005). Species evolve, individuals age. In *8th IEEE International Workshop on Principles of Software Evolution*, (pp. 3–12). Washington, DC.

JBoss Community. (2010). *JBossESB*. Retrieved from http://www.jboss.org/jbossesb/

Jelinek, J., & Slavik, P. (2004). GUI generation from annotated source code. *In Proceedings of the 3rd Annual Conference on Task Models and Diagrams*, (pp. 129-136).

Jensen, M., Meyer, C., Somorovsky, J., & Schwenk, J. (2011). On the effectiveness of XML schema validation for countering XML signature wrapping attacks. In *InteRNational Workshop on Securing Services on the Cloud* (pp. 7–13). IEEE Computer Society Press.

Jeong, B., Lee, D., Cho, H., & Lee, J. (2008). A novel method for measuring semantic similarity for XML schema matching. *Expert Systems with Applications, 34*, 1651–1658.

Johanson, B., & Fox, A. (2004). Extending Tuplespaces for coordination in interactive workspaces. *Journal of Systems and Software, 69*(3), 243–266.

Jongtaveesataporn, A., & Takada, S. (2010). Enhancing enterprise service bus capability for load balancing. *WSEAS Transactions on Computers, 9*, 299–308.

Juric, M., & Pant, K. (2008). *Business process driven SOA using BPMN and BPEL: From business process modeling to orchestration and service oriented architecture*. Birmingham, UK: Packt Publishing.

Kapitsaki, G. M., Kateros, D. A., & Venieris, I. S. (2008). Architecture for provision of context-aware web applications based on Web services. In *IEEE 19th International Symposium on Personal, Indoor and Mobile Radio Communications*, (pp. 1-5).

Kapitsaki, G. M., Kateros, D. A., Prezerakos, G. N., & Venieris, I. S. (2009). Model-driven development of composite context-aware Web applications. *Elsevier Journal Information and Software Technology, 51*(8), 1244–1260.

Karastoyanova, D., & Leymann, F. (2009). BPEL'n'aspects: Adapting service orchestration logic. In the *Proceedings of the IEEE International Conference on Web Services, ICWS 2009* (pp. 222–229).

Kazhamiakin, R., Benbernou, S., Baresi, L., Plebani, P., Uhlig, M., & Barais, O. (2010). Adaptation of service-based systems. *Service Research Challenges and Solutions for the Future Internet, LNCS, 6500*, 117–156.

Keidl, M., & Kemper, A. (2004). Towards context-aware adaptable Web services. In *13th International World Wide Web conference on Alternate* (pp. 55-65). New York, NY: ACM.

Keller, U., Lara, R., Lausen, H., Polleres, A., & Fensel, D. (2005). Automatic location of services. In *Proceedings of ESWC'05, volume 3532 of Lecture Notes in Computer Science*, (pp. 1–16). Springer.

Kephart, J. O., & Chess, D. M. (2003). The vision of autonomic computing. *IEEE Computer, 36*(1), 41–50.

Kertesz, A., Kecskemeti, G., & Brandic, I. (2009). An SLA-based resource virtualization approach for on-demand service provision. In *Proceedings of the 3rd International Workshop on Virtualization Technologies in Distributed Computing* (pp. 27–34). New York, NY: ACM.

Khadka, R. (2011). Model-driven development of service compositions for enterprise interoperability. In van Sinderen, M., & Johnson, P. (Eds.), *Lecture Notes in Business Information Processing, 76* (pp. 177–190). Berlin, Germany: Springer.

Khushraj, D., Lassila, O., & Finin, T. W. (2004). sTuples: Semantic tuple spaces. In *Proceedings of the 1st Annual International Conference on Mobile and Ubiquitous Systems: Networking and Services (MobiQuitous'04)*, (pp. 268–277). Boston, MA, USA.

Kiczales, G., Lamping, J., Maeda, C., & Lopes, C. (1997). Aspect-oriented programming. In *Proceedings European Conference on Object-Oriented Programming, volume 1241*, (pp. 220–242). Berlin, Germany: Springer-Verlag.

Kifer, M. (2008). Rule interchange format: The framework. In *Web Reasoning and Rule Systems*. In *Lecture Notes in Computer Science* (*Vol. 5341*, pp. 1–11). Berlin, Germany: Springer.

Kim, D., & Shen, W. (2007). An approach to evaluating structural pattern conformance of UML models. In *ACM Symposium on Applied Computing* (pp. 1404-1408). ACM Press.

Klein, A., Ishikawa, F., & Honiden, S. (2010). Efficient QoS-aware service composition with a probabilistic service selection policy. *In Proceedings of 2010 International Conference on Service-Oriented Computing (ICSOC 2010)* (pp. 182-196). Springer.

Kleppe, A. G., Warmer, J., & Bast, W. (2003). *MDA explained: The model driven architecture: Practice and promise*. Boston, MA: Addison-Wesley Longman Publishing Co.

Klusch, M., Fries, B., & Sycara, K. (2006). Automated semantic web service discovery with owls-mx. In *Proceedings of the Fifth International Joint Conference on Autonomous Agents and Multiagent Systems AAMAS '06*, (pp. 915–922). ACM.

Klusch, M., Fries, B., & Sycara, K. (2006). Automated Semantic Web service discovery with OWLS-MX. In *Proceedings of AAMAS, 06*, 915–922.

Knublauch, H., Hendler, J. A., & Idehen, K. (2011). *SPIN: SPARQL inferencing notation*. W3C member submission, W3C. Retrieved from http://www.w3.org/Submission/2011/SUBM-spin-overview-20110222/

Kochar, H. (2005). *Business activity monitoring and business intelligence*. Retrieved from http://www.ebizq.net/topics/bam/features/6596.html

Kokar, M. M., Matheus, C. J., & Baclawski, K. (2009). Ontology-based situation awareness. *Information Fusion, 10*, 83–98.

Kokash, N., & Arbab, F. (2009). Formal behavioral modeling and compliance analysis for service-oriented systems. In Boer, F., Bonsangue, M., & Madelaine, E. (Eds.), *Formal Methods for Components and Objects* (*Vol. 5751*, pp. 21–41). Lecture Notes In Computer Science Berlin, Germany: Springer-Verlag.

Koopman, P. (1996). Embedded system design issues (the rest of the story). In *Proceedings of the 1996 International Conference on Computer Design, VLSI in Computers and Processors*, ICCD '96, (p. 310). Washington, DC: IEEE Computer Society.

Kouadri, S., & Hirsbrunner, B. (2003). Towards a context-based service composition framework. In. *Proceedings of ICWS, 03*, 42–45.

Krötzsch, M., Patel-Schneider, P. F., Rudolph, S., Hitzler, P., & Parsia, B. (Eds.). (2009). OWL 2 web ontology language primer. Technical report, W3C. Retrieved from http://www.w3.org/TR/2009/REC-owl2-primer-20091027/

Kruchten, P. (2003). *The rational unified process: An introduction*. New York, NY: Addison Wesley.

Küngas, P., & Popova, V. (2011). Artifact-centric service interoperation. In *Estonian Information Society Yearbook 2010*. Estonian Department of State Information Systems.

La, H., Bae, J., Chang, S., & Kim, S. (2007). Practical methods for adapting services using enterprise service bus. *Proceedings of the 7th International Conference on Web Engineering*, (pp. 53–58).

Laitkorpi, M., Selonen, P., & Systa, T. (2009). Towards a model-driven process for designing ReSTful Web services. In *IEEE InteRNational Conference on Web Services* (pp. 173-180). IEEE Computer Society Press.

Lanese, I., Guidi, C., Montesi, F., & Zavattaro, G. (2008). Bridging the gap between interaction- and process-oriented choreographies. In *SEFM'08*, (pp. 323-332).

Laneve, C., & Padovani, L. (2007). The must preorder revisited - An algebraic theory for web services contracts. In *Concur '07*. In *LNCS* (*Vol. 4703*, pp. 212–225). Springer.

Lapadula, A., Pugliese, R., & Tiezzi, F. (2007). Calculus for orchestration of web services. In *ESOP '07, volume 4421 of LNCS*, (pp. 33-47).

Läufer, K., Baumgartner, G., & Russo, V. (2000). Safe structural conformance for Java. *The Computer Journal, 43*(6), 469–481.

Lausen, H., Polleres, A., & Roman, D. (2006). *Web service modeling ontology (WSMO)*. W3C Member Submission.

Lee, E. A. (2008). *Cyber physical systems: Design challenges*. In International Symposium on Object/Component/Service-Oriented Real-Time Distributed Computing (ISORC). Invited Paper.

Leitner, P., Michlmayr, A., Rosenberg, F., & Dustdar, S. (2008). End-to-end versioning support for Web services. In *2008 IEEE International Conference on Services Computing* (pp. 59-66). Honolulu, HI, USA. doi:10.1109/SCC.2008.21

Leitner, P., Wetzstein, B., Karastoyanova, D., Hummer, W., Dustdar, S., & Leymann, F. (2010). Preventing SLA violations in service compositions using aspect-based fragment substitution. In *Proceedings of 2010 International Conference on Service-Oriented Computing (ICSOC 2010)* (pp. 365-380). Springer.

Leitner, P., Wetzstein, B., Rosenberg, F., Michlmayr, A., Dustdar, S., & Leymann, F. (2009). Runtime prediction of service level agreement violations for composite services. In *Proceedings of the Workshop on Non-Functional Properties and SLA Management in Service-Oriented Computing* (pp. 176-186).

Leitner, P., Wetzstein, B., Karastoyanova, D., Hummer, W., Dustdar, S., & Leymann, F. (2010). Preventing SLA violations in service compositions using aspect-based fragment substitution. In Maglio, P., Weske, M., Yang, J., & Fantinato, M. (Eds.), *Service-Oriented Computing* (*Vol. 6470*, pp. 365–380). Berlin, Germany: Springer. doi:10.1007/978-3-642-17358-5_25

Li, F., Sehic, S., & Dustdar, S. (2010). COPAL: An adaptive approach to context provisioning. In *6th International Conference on Wireless and Mobile Computing, Networking and Communications* (286-293). California: IEEE.

Li, Z., & Parashar, M. (2005). Comet: A scalable coordination space for decentralized distributed environments. In *Proceedings of the Second International Workshop on Hot Topics in Peer-To-Peer Systems HOT-P2P*, (pp. 104-112). IEEE.

Li, L., & Horrocks, I. (2003). A software framework for matchmaking based on Semantic Web technology. In *Proceedings of WWW, 03*, 331–339.

Lin, K. J., & Chang, S. H. (2009). A service accountability framework for QoS service management and engineering. *Information Systems and e-Business Management, 7*(4), 429–446.

Lin, K., Panahi, M., & Zhang, Y. (2007). The design of an intelligent accountability architecture. In *Proceedings of the IEEE International Conference on e-Business Engineering, ICEBE '07* (pp. 157–164). Washington, DC: IEEE Computer Society. Retrieved from http://dx.doi.org/10.1109/ICEBE.2007.145

Link, S., Schuster, T., Hoyer, P., & Abeck, S. (2008). Focusing graphical user interfaces in model-driven software development. In *Proceedings of the First International Conference on Advances in Computer-Human Interaction,* (pp. 3-8). IEEE Computer Society.

López, M., Qayyum, Z., Cuesta, C. E., Marcos, E., & Oquendo, F. (2008). Representing service-oriented architectural models using pi-AD. In *Proceedings of ECSA'08, volume 5292 of Lecture Notes in Computer Science,* (pp. 273–280). Springer.

Loutas, N., Peristeras, V., & Tarabanis, K. (2011). Towards a reference service model for the Web of services. *Data & Knowledge Engineering, 70*, 753–774.

Luckham, D. (2002). *The power of events: An introduction to complex event processing in distributed enterprise systems.* Boston, MA: Addison-Wesley.

Luckham, D. C. (2001). *The power of events: An introduction to complex event processing in distributed enterprise systems.* Addison-Wesley Longman Publishing Co., Inc.

Luo, N., Yan, J., Liu, M., & Yang, S. (2006). Towards context-aware composition of Web services. In *Proceedings of GCC'06,* (pp. 494–499). IEEE Computer Society.

Magee, J., Kramer, J., & Giannakopoulou, D. (1999). Behaviour analysis of software architectures. In *Proceedings of WICSA, 99*, 35–49.

Mamei, M., & Zambonelli, F. (2009). Programming pervasive and mobile computing applications: The TOTA approach. *ACM Transactions on Software Engineering and Methodology, 18*(4).

Managing Assurance, Security and Trust for sERvices Project (MASTER). (n.d.). Retrieved September 12, 2011, from http://www.master-fp7.eu/

Mancioppi, M. (Ed.). (2011, November). *Consolidated and updated state of the art report on service-based applications.* Deliverable CD-IA-1.1.7 of S-Cube Project. Retrieved October 2011 from http://www.s-cube-network.eu/results/deliverables/wp-ia-1.1/CD-IA-1.1.7-Consolidated%20and%20updated%20state%20of%20the%20art%20report%20on%20Service-Based.pdf/at_download/file

Mannava, V., & Ramesh, T. (2011). A novel event based autonomic design pattern for management of web services. *Communications in Computer and Information Science, 198 CCIS,* (pp. 142-151).

Marrella, A., & Mecella, M. (2011). *Continuous planning for solving business process adaptivity.* Paper presented at the 12th International Working Conference on Business Process Modeling, Development and Support, BPMDS 2011.

Martello, S., & Toth, P. (1987). Algorithms for knapsack problems. *Annals in Discrete Mathematics, 31*, 70–79.

Masternak, T., Psiuk, M., Radziszowski, D., Szydlo, T., Szymacha, R., Zielinski, K., & Zmuda, D. (2010). ESB-modern SOA infrastructure. In Ambroszkiewicz, S. (Ed.), *SOA infrastructure tools: Concepts and methods.* Poznan University of Economics Press.

Mateescu, R., Poizat, P., & Salaün, G. (2008). Adaptation of service protocols using process algebra and on-the-fly reduction techniques. In *Proceedings of ICSOC'08, volume 5364 of Lecture Notes in Computer Science,* (pp. 84–99). Springer.

May, W., Alferes, J. J., & Amador, R. (2005). Active rules in the Semantic Web: Dealing with language heterogeneity. In the *Proceedings of International Conference on Rules and Rule Markup Languages for the Semantic Web* (pp. 30–44).

Mehta, M., & Ram, A. (2009). Runtime behavior adaptation for real-time interactive games. *IEEE Transactions on Computational Intelligence and AI in Games, 1*(3), 187–199.

Menascè, D., Casalicchio, E., & Dubey, V. (2010). On optimal service selection in service oriented architectures. *Performance Evaluation, 67*(8), 659–675.

Menasce, D., Gomaa, H., Malek, S., & Sousa, J. (2011). SASSY: A framework for self-architecting service-oriented systems. *IEEE Software, 28*(6), 78–85.

Merrick, I., & Wood, A. (2000). Coordination with scopes. In *Proceedings of the 2000 ACM symposium on Applied computing - Volume 1*, SAC '00, (pp. 210–217). New York, NY: ACM.

Metzger, A., & Marquezan, C. C. (2011, October). Future Internet apps: The next wave of adaptive service-oriented systems? In *Proceedings 4th European Conference Towards a Service-Based Internet, ServiceWave2011* (Vol. 6994, pp. 230-241). Heidelberg, Germany: Springer.

Metzger, A., & Di Nitto, E. (2013, forthcoming). Addressing highly dynamic changes in service-oriented systems: Towards agile evolution and adaptation. In Wang, X., Ali, N., Ramos, I., & Vidgen, R. (Eds.), *Agile and lean service-oriented development: Foundations, theory and practice*. Hershey, PA: IGI Global.

Metzger, A., & Pohl, K. (2009). Towards the next generation of service-based systems: The S-Cube research framework. In *Advanced Information. Systems Engineering*, 11–16. Retrieved from http://dx.doi.org/10.1007/978-3-642-02144-2_6

Meyer, B. (1988). *Object-oriented software construction*. Prentice-Hall, 1988.

Meyer, B. (2000). *Object-oriented software construction* (2nd ed.). Upper Saddle River, NJ: Prentice Hall.

Michlmayr, A., Rosenberg, F., Leitner, P., & Dustdar, S. (2008a). Advanced event processing and notifications in service runtime environments. In *Proceedings of the International Conference on Distributed Event-Based Systems* (pp. 115-125).

Michlmayr, A., Rosenberg, F., Leitner, P., & Dustdar, S. (2009). Comprehensive QoS monitoring of web services and event-based SLA violation detection. In *Proceedings of the International Workshop on Middleware for Service Oriented Computing* (pp. 1-6).

Michlmayr, A., Rosenberg, F., Leitner, P., & Dustdar, S. (2008b). Selective service provenance in the VRESCo runtime. *International Journal of Web Services Research, 7*(2), 65–86.

Michlmayr, A., Rosenberg, F., Leitner, P., & Dustdar, S. (2010). End-to-end support for QoS-aware service selection, binding, and mediation in VRESCo. *IEEE Transactions in Service Computing, 3*(3), 193–205.

Microsoft. (2009). *The. NET framework*. Microsoft Corporation. Retrieved September 23, 2010, from http://www.microsoft.com/net

Microsoft. (2010). *BizTalk ESB toolkit*. Retrieved from http://msdn.microsoft.com/en-us/biztalk/dd876606

Microsoft. (2010). *COM: Component object model*. Microsoft Corporation. Retrieved October 10, 2011, from http://www.microsoft.com/com

Mietzner, R., Metzger, A., Leymann, F., & Pohl, K. (2009, May). Variability modeling to support customization and deployment of multi-tenant-aware software as a service applications. In *ICSE workshop on Principles of Engineering Service Oriented Systems* (pp. 18–25). PESOS. doi:10.1109/PESOS.2009.5068815

Miller, E., & Manola, F. (Eds.). (2004). *RDF primer*. W3C recommendation, W3C. Retrieved from http://www.w3.org/TR/2004/REC-rdf-primer-20040210/

Milner, R. (1980). Lecture Notes in Computer Science: *Vol. 2. Calculus of communicating systems*. Springer.

Milner, R. (1989). *Communication and concurrency*. Prentice-Hall.

Mirandola, R., & Potena, P. (2011). A QoS-based framework for the adaptation of service-based systems. *Scalable Computing: Practice and Experience, 12*(1), 63–78.

MIT. (2010). *MIT Proto*. Retrieved November 1, 2010, from http://proto.bbn.com/

Mokhtar, S., Fournier, D., Georgantas, N., & Issarny, V. (2006). Context-aware service composition in pervasive computing environments. In *Proceedings of RISE'05, volume 3943 of Lecture Notes in Computer Science*, (pp. 129–144). Springer.

Monfort, V. (2010). *The benefits of SaaS.* Retrieved from http://www.computerworld.com/action/article.do?command=view ArticleBasic&articleId=107276

Mos, A., Pedrinaci, C., Rey, G. A., Gomez, J. M., Liu, D., Vaudaux-Ruth, G., et al. (2009). Multi-level monitoring and analysis of web-scale service based applications. In *Proceedings of the 2009 International Conference on Service-Oriented Computing* (pp. 269–282). Berlin, Germany: Springer-Verlag.

Moser, O., Rosenberg, F., & Dustdar, S. (2008). Non-intrusive monitoring and service adaptation for WS-BPEL. In the *Proceedings of the International Conference on World Wide Web,* (pp. 815-824).

Mosincat, A., Binder, W., & Jazayeri, M. (2010). Run-time adaptability through automated model evolution. *Proceedings of 14th IEEE International Enterprise Distributed Object Computing Conference (EDOC 2010),* (pp. 217–226).

Mosincat, A., & Binder, W. (2011). Automated maintenance of service compositions with SLA violation detection and dynamic binding. *International Journal on Software Tools for Technology Transfer, 13*(2), 167–179. doi:10.1007/s10009-010-0181-7

Mulo, E., Zdun, U., & Dustdar, S. (2008). Monitoring web service event trails for business compliance. In *Proceedings of the IEEE International Conference on Service-Oriented Computing and Applications* (pp. 1-8).

Mykkänen, J., & Tuomainen, M. (2008). An evaluation and selection framework for interoperability standards. *Information and Software Technology, 50,* 176–197.

Nardini, E., Omicini, A., & Viroli, M. (2011). *Description spaces with fuzziness.* In 26th Annual ACM Symposium on Applied Computing (SAC 2011), Tunghai University, TaiChung, Taiwan. ACM.

Nardini, E., Viroli, M., & Panzavolta, E. (2010). Coordination in open and dynamic environments with Tucson semantic tuple centres. In *Proceedings of the 25th Annual ACM Symposium on Applied Computing (SAC 2010),* volume III, (pp. 2037–2044). Sierre, Switzerland: ACM.

Natis, Y. V. (2011). *How to balance the business benefits and IT costs of SOA.* (Gartner Research, ID Number: G00209630).

Nau, D., Au, T. C., Ilghami, O., Kuter, U., Muñoz-Avila, H., & Murdock, J. W. (2005). Applications of SHOP and SHOP2. *IEEE Intelligent Systems, 20*(2).

Nezhad, H. R. M., Benatallah, B., Martens, A., Curbera, F., & Casati, F. (2007). Semi-automated adaptation of service interactions. In *Proceedings of WWW'07.* ACM Press.

Nicoara, A., & Alonso, G. (2005). *PROSE - A middleware platform for dynamic adaptation.* Demo presented at AOSD'05.

Nielsen, B., & Sørensen, T. (1993). *Distributed programming with multiple tuple space Linda.* Aalborg University, Institute for Electronic Systems.

Nierstrasz, O., Denker, M., & Renggli, L. (2009). Model-centric, context-aware software adaptation. In *Software Engineering for Self-Adaptive Systems.* In *Lecture Notes in Computer Science* (Vol. 5525, pp. 28–145). Springer.

Nixon, L., Antonechko, O., & Tolksdorf, R. (2007). Towards Semantic Tuplespace computing: The Semantic Web spaces system. In *Proceedings of the 2007 ACM Symposium on Applied Computing SAC'07,* (pp. 360-365). ACM.

Nixon, L. J. B., Simperl, E., Krummenacher, R., & Martin-Recuerda, F. (2008). Tuplespace-based computing for the semantic web: A survey of the state-of-the-art. *The Knowledge Engineering Review, 23*(2), 181–212.

Noble, M. S., & Zlateva, S. (2001). Scientific computation with Javaspaces. In *Proceedings of the 9th International Conference on High-Performance Computing and Networking, HPCN Europe 2001,* (pp. 657–666). London, UK: Springer-Verlag.

O'Connor, M. J., & Knublauch, H. (2005). *Writing rules for the semantic web using SWRL and Jess.* In the Protege with Rules Workshop, held with 8th International Protege Conference.

O'Reilly, T. (2005) *What is Web 2.0?* Retrieved July 12, 2010, from http://www.oreillynet.com/pub/a/oreilly/tim/news/2005/09/30/what-is-web-20.html

OASIS. (2007). *Web services business process execution language* (WSBPEL). Retrieved from http://www.oasis-open.org/committees/tc_home.php?wg_abbrev=wsbpel.

OASIS. (2007). *Web services business process execution language version 2.0*. Retrieved from http://docs.oasis-open.org/wsbpel/2.0/wsbpel-v2.0.pdf

Object Management Group. (2006). *Object constraint language (OCL) specification* v.2.0.

Object Management Group. (2007). *Unified modelling language (UML) specification* v.2.1.2.

Oliva, G., Hatori, F., Leite, L., & Gerosa, M. (2011). *Web services choreographies adaptation: A systematic review*. Technical Report No: RT-MAC-2011-02. Retrieved October 30, 2011, from http://hal.inria.fr/inria-00585829/

OMG. (1989). Retrieved from Omg.org

OMG. (2011). *BPMN 2.0*. Retrieved from http://www.omg.org/spec/BPMN/2.0/

Omicini, A., Ricci, A., & Viroli, M. (2006). Coordination artifacts as first-class abstractions for MAS engineering: State of the research. In *Software Engineering for Multi-Agent Systems, IV: Research Issues and Practical Applications, vol. 3914 di LNAI*, (pp. 71–90). Springer.

Omicini, A., Ricci, A., & Viroli, M. (2005). RBAC for organisation and security in an agent coordination infrastructure. In *Electronic Notes in Theoretical Computer Science* (*Vol. 128*, pp. 65–85). Elsevier Science B.V.

Omicini, A., & Viroli, M. (2011). Coordination models and languages: From parallel computing to self-organisation. *The Knowledge Engineering Review*, *26*(1), 53–59.

Ortiz, G., & Garcia de Prado, A. (2010). Web service adaptation: A unified approach versus multiple methodologies for different scenarios. In *5th International Conference on Internet and Web Applications and Services* (pp. 569-572). California: IEEE CS Press.

Ortiz, G., & Prado, A. G. (2009). Adapting Web services for multiple devices: A model-driven, aspect-oriented approach. In *Proceedings of the IEEE Congress on Services*, (pp. 754-761).

Ortiz, G., & Prado, A. G. (2009). Mobile-aware Web services. In *International Conference on Mobile Ubiquitous Computing, Systems, Services and Technologies*, (pp. 65-70).

Ortiz, G., & Garcia de Prado, A. (2010). Improving Device-Aware Web Services and their Mobile Clients through an Aspect-Oriented, Model-Driven Approach. *Information and Software Technology Journal*, *52*(10), 1080–1093.

Overdick, H. (2007). The resource-oriented architecture. In *IEEE Congress on Services* (pp. 340-347). IEEE Computer Society Press.

Padovani, L. (2011). Fair subtyping for multi-party session types. In *Coordination'11*. In *LNCS* (*Vol. 6721*, pp. 127–141). Springer.

Pahl, C. (2002). A formal composition and interaction model for a Web component platform. In *Proceedings ICALP'2002 Workshop on Formal Methods and Component Interaction, Electronic Notes on Computer Science ENTCS*, *66*(4).

Pahl, C. (2005). Layered ontological modelling for Web service-oriented model-driven architecture. In *Proceedings European Conference on Model-Driven Architecture – Foundations and Applications ECMDA'2005, LNCS 3748* (pp. 88-102). Springer-Verlag.

Pahl, C., Gacitua-Decar, V., Wang, M. X., & Bandara, K. Y. (2011). A coordination space architecture for service collaboration and cooperation. In *Proceedings CAiSE Workshops* (pp. 366–377).

Pahl, C. (2007). Semantic model-driven architecting of service-based software systems. *Information and Software Technology*, *49*(8), 838–850.

Pahl, C., & Zhu, Y. (2006). A semantical framework for the orchestration and choreography of web services. In *Proceedings of the International Workshop on Web Languages and Formal Methods (WLFM 2005)*. *Electronic Notes in Theoretical Computer Science*, *151*(2), 3–18.

Panahi, M., & Lin, K. 0001, Y. Z., Chang, S., Zhang, J., & Varela, L. (2008). The LLAMA middleware support for accountable service-oriented architecture. In *ICSOC* (pp. 180-194).

Paolucci, M., Kawamura, T., Payne, T., & Sycara, K. (2002). Semantic matching of Web services capabilities. In *Proceedings of ISWC'02, volume 2342 of Lecture Notes in Computer Science*, (pp. 333–347). Springer.

Papageorgiou, A., et al. (2009). Bridging the gaps towards structured mobile SOA. In *InteRNational Conference on Advances in Mobile Computing & Multimedia* (pp. 288-294). ACM Press.

Papazoglou, M. P. (2008). The challenges of service evolution. In *Proceedings of the 20th International Conference on Advanced Information Systems Engineering, CAiSE '08* (pp. 1–15). Berlin, Germany: Springer-Verlag. Retrieved from http://dx.doi.org/10.1007/978-3-540-69534-9_1

Papazoglou, M. (2007). *Web services: Principles and technology* (1st ed.). Prentice Hall.

Papazoglou, M. P., Traverso, P., Dustdar, S., & Leymann, F. (2007). Service-oriented computing: State of the art and research challenges. *IEEE Computer, 40*(1), 38–45.

Papazoglou, M., Pohl, K., Parkin, M., & Metzger, A. (2010). *Service research challenges and solutions for the future internet: Towards mechanisms and methods for engineering, managing, and adapting service-based systems* (*Vol. 6500*). New York, NY: Springer-Verlag Inc.

Papazoglou, P., Traverso, P., Dustdar, S., & Leymann, F. (2008). Service-oriented computing: A research roadmap. *InteRNational JouRNal of Cooperative Information Systems, 17*(2), 223–255.

Paschke, A., & Schroder, M. (2007). Inductive logic programming for bio-informatics in Prova. In *Proceedings of the 2nd Workshop on Data Mining in Bioinformatics at VLDB'07*.

Patel, C., Supekar, K., & Lee, Y. (2004). Provisioning resilient, adaptive web services-based workow: A semantic modeling approach. In *Proceedings IEEE International Conference on Web Services* (pp. 480-487).

Patil, A., Oundhakar, S., Sheth, A., & Verma, K. (2004). METEOR-S Web service annotation framework. In *Proceedings of WWW, 04*, 553–562.

Pautasso, C., & Wilde, E. (2009). Why is the web loosely coupled? A multi-faceted metric for service design. In *InteRNational Conference on World Wide Web* (pp. 911-920). ACM Press.

Pautasso, C., Zimmermann, O., & Leymann, F. (2008). Restful web services vs. "big"' web services: Making the right architectural decision. In *InteRNational Conference on World Wide Web* (pp. 805-814). ACM Press.

Pauty, J., Preuveeners, D., Rigole, P., & Berbers, Y. (2006). Research challenges in mobile and context-aware service development. In *Proceedings of Future Research Challenges in Software and Services* (pp. 141-148). Vienna, Austria

Pei, J., Han, J., Mortazavi-Asl, B., & Pinto, H. (2001). Prefixspan: Mining sequential patterns efficiently by prefix-projected pattern growth. In *Proceedings of IEEE Conference on Data Engineering* (pp. 215-224).

Perepletchikov, M., Ryan, C., Frampton, K., & Tari, Z. (2007). Coupling metrics for predicting maintainability in service-oriented designs. In *Australian Software Engineering Conference* (pp. 329-340). IEEE Computer Society Press.

Pernici, B., & Rosati, A. M. (2007, November). Automatic learning of repair strategies for web services. In *Proceedings of the Fifth European Conference on Web Services, ECOWS '07* (pp. 119 -128).

Phillips, S. C., Engen, V., & Papay, J. (2011). Snow white clouds and the seven dwarfs. In *2011 IEEE Third International Conference on Cloud Computing Technology and Science (CloudCom),* (pp. 738 -745).

Pianini, D., Montagna, S., & Viroli, M. (2011). A chemical inspired simulation framework for pervasive services ecosystems. In *Proceedings of the Federated Conference on Computer Science and Information Systems,* (pp. 675–682). Szczecin, Poland: IEEE Computer Society Press.

Popescu, R., Staikopoulos, A., Liu, P., Brogi, A., & Clarke, S. (2010). Taxonomy-driven adaptation of multi-layer applications using templates. In *Proceedings of the 2010 Fourth IEEE International Conference on Self-Adaptive and Self-Organizing Systems* (pp. 213–222). Washington, DC: IEEE Computer Society.

Prandi, D., & Quaglia, P. (2007). Stochastic COWS. In *ICSOC'07, volume 4749 of LNCS,* (pp. 245-256).

Psaier, H., Juszczyk, L., Skopik, F., Schall, D., & Dustdar, S. (2010). Runtime behavior monitoring and self-adaptation in service-oriented systems. In *Proceedings -2010 4th IEEE International Conference on Self-Adaptive and Self-Organizing Systems, SASO 2010* (pp. 164-173).

Qureshi, N. A., & Perini, A. (2010). Requirements engineering for adaptive service based applications. In *Proceedings of the 2010 18th IEEE International Requirements Engineering Conference* (pp. 108–111). Washington, DC: IEEE Computer Society.

Rademakers, T., & Dirksen, J. (2008). *Open-source ESBs in action: Example implementations in mule and service mix* (1st ed.). Manning Publications.

Rajamani, S. K., & Rehof, J. (2002). Conformance checking for models of asynchronous message passing software. In *CAV'02, volume 2404 of LNCS*, (pp. 166-179).

Rajesh, A., & Srivatsa, S. (2010). XML schema matching – Using structural information. *InteRNational JouRNal of Computer Applications, 8*(2), 34–41.

Rammig, F. J. (2008). Cyber biosphere for future embedded systems. In *Proceedings of the 6th IFIP WG 10.2 International Workshop on Software Technologies for Embedded and Ubiquitous Systems, SEUS '08*, (pp. 245–255). Berlin, Germany: Springer-Verlag.

Rensink, A., & Vogler, W. (2007). Fair testing. *Information and Computation, 205*(2), 125–198.

Ritzau, T., & Andersson, J. (2000). *Dynamic deployment of java applications.* In Java for Embedded Systems Workshop.

Rosario, S., Benveniste, A., Haar, S., & Jard, C. (2008). Probabilistic QoS and soft contracts for transaction-based Web services orchestrations. *IEEE Transactions in Service Computing, 1*(4), 187–200.

Ross, A., Rhodes, D., & Hastings, D. (2008). Defining changeability: Reconciling flexibility, adaptability, scalability, modifiability, and robustness for maintaining system lifecycle value. *Systems Engineering, 11*(3), 246–262.

Rouvoy, R., Barone, P., Ding, Y., Eliassen, F., Hallsteinsen, S., & Lorenzo, J. (2009). MUSIC: Middleware support for self-adaptation in ubiquitous and service-oriented environments. In Cheng, B. H., Lemos, R., Giese, H., Inverardi, P., & Magee, J. (Eds.), *Software engineering for self-adaptive systems* (pp. 164–182). Springer-Verlag.

Sahai, A., Machiraju, V., Sayal, M., van Moorsel, A. P. A., & Casati, F. (2002). Automated SLA monitoring for web services. In *Proceedings of the IFIP/IEEE International Workshop on Distributed Systems: Operations and Management* (pp. 28-41).

Salaün, G. (2008). Generation of service wrapper protocols from choreography specifications. In *Proceedings of SEFM, 08*, 313–322.

Salaun, G., Bultan, T., & Roohi, N. (2011). Realizability of choreographies using process algebra encodings. *IEEE Transactions on Services Computing, 99*, 1.

Salber, D., Dey, A., & Abowd, G. (1999). The context toolkit: Aiding the development of context-enabled applications. In *Proceedings of CHI'99*, (pp. 434–441). ACM Press.

Salehie, M., & Tahvildari, L. (2009). Self-adaptive software: Landscape and research challenges. *ACM Transactions in Autonomic and Adaptive Systems, 4*(2), 1–42.

Sanchez-Loro, X. E. (2008). *Ubiquitous web access: Collaborative optimization and dynamic content negotiation.* In International Conference on Multimedia and Ubiquitous Engineering.

Sauer, S., Drksen, M., Gebel, A., & Hannwacker, D. (2006). *GUIbuilder: A tool for model-driven development of multimedia user interfaces.*

Scheibler, T., & Leymann, F. (2008). A framework for executable enterprise application integration patterns. In *Enterprise Interoperability III* (pp. 485-497). Retrieved from http://dx.doi.org/10.1007/978-1-84800-221-0_38

Scheibler, T., Mietzner, R., & Leymann, F. (2008). EAI as a service - Combining the power of executable EAI patterns and SaaS. In *12th International IEEE Enterprise Distributed Object Computing Conference, EDOC '08.* (pp. 107-116). doi:10.1109/EDOC.2008.21

Schilit, B. N., & Theimer, M. M. (1994). Disseminating active map information to mobile hosts. *IEEE Network, 8*(5), 22–32.

Schilit, B., Adams, N., & Want, R. (1994). Context-aware computing applications. In *Proceedings of WMCSA, 94*, 85–90.

Schmidt, M., Hutchison, B., Lambros, P., & Phippen, R. (2005). The enterprise service bus: Making service-oriented architecture real. *IBM Systems Journal, 44*(4), 781–797. doi:10.1147/sj.444.0781

Scribner, K. (2007). *Microsoft Windows workflow foundation: Step by step*. Microsoft Press.

Seaborne, A., & Harris, S. (Eds.). (2009). *SPARQL 1.1 query*. W3C working draft, W3C. Retrieved from http://www.w3.org/TR/2009/WD-sparql11-query-20091022/

Seiriö, M., & Berndtsson, M. (2005). Design and implementation of an ECA rule markup language. *LNCS, 3791*, 98–112.

Serral, E., Valderas, P., & Pelechano, V. (2010). Towards the model-driven development of context-aware pervasive systems. *Elsevier Journal on Pervasive and Mobile Computing, Context Modelling. Reasoning and Management, 6*(2), 254–280.

Sha, L., Rajkumar, R., & Gagliardi, M. (1995). Evolving dependable real-time systems. In *IEEE Aerospace Applications Conference*, (pp. 335–346).

Sharp, J. (2007). *Microsoft Windows communication foundation: Step by step*. Microsoft Press.

Shelby, Z. (2010, December). Embedded web services. *IEEE Wireless Communications, 17*(6), 52–57. doi:10.1109/MWC.2010.5675778

Sheng, Q. Z., & Benatallah, B. (2005). ContextUML: A UML-based modeling language for model-driven development of context-aware web services. In *International Conference on Mobile Business*, (pp. 206-212). IEEE Computer Society Press.

Sheng, Q., Benatallah, B., Maamar, Z., Dumas, M., & Ngu, A. H. (2009). Configurable composition and adaptive provisioning of Web services. *IEEE Transactions on Services Computing, 2*(1), 34–49.

Siljee, J., Bosloper, I., Nijhuis, J., & Hammer, D. (2005). DySOA: Making service systems self-adaptive. *Lecture Notes in Computer Science, 3826 LNCS*, (pp. 255-268).

Simon, R. (2010). JBoss drools fusion. *Módulo de Taller - InCo - FING - UdelaR*. Retrieved August 7, 2011, from http://www.fing.edu.uy/~lauragon/tesis/mt-2010-drools-fusion.pdf

Singh, Y., & Sood, M. (2009). Model driven architecture: A perspective. In *IEEE International Advance Computing Conference*, (pp. 1644-1652).

Sirin, E., Hendler, J., & Parsia, B. (2003). Semi-automatic composition of web services using semantic descriptions. In *Proceedings Web Services: Modeling, Architecture and Infrastructure Workshop at ICEIS 2003* (pp. 17–24).

Sirin, E., Parsia, B., Grau, B. C., Kalyanpur, A., & Katz, Y. (2007). Pellet: A practical OWL-DL reasoner. *Web Semantics, 5*, 51–53.

Sleiman, H. A., Sultán, A. W., Frantz, R. Z., & Corchuelo, R. (n.d.). *Towards automatic code generation for EAI solutions using DSL tools*.

Sosinsky, B. (2011). *Cloud computing bible*. Indiana: Wiley.

Spanoudakis, G., Mahbub, K., & Zisman, A. (2007). A platform for context aware runtime Web service discovery. In *Proceedings of ICWS, 07*, 233–240.

Spiess, P., Karnouskos, S., Guinard, D., Savio, D., Baecker, O., Souza, L. M. S. d., et al. (2009). SOA-based integration of the internet of things in enterprise services. In *Proceedings of the 2009 IEEE International Conference on Web Services* (pp. 968–975). Washington, DC: IEEE Computer Society.

Spillner, J., Winkler, M., Reichert, S., Cardoso, J., & Schill, A. (2009). Distributed contracting and monitoring in the internet of services. In *Proceedings of the 9th IFIP WG 6.1 International Conference on Distributed Applications and Interoperable Systems* (pp. 129–142). Berlin, Germany: Springer-Verlag.

Spohrer, J. C., Maglio, P. P., Bailey, J. H., & Gruhl, D. (2007). Steps toward a science of service systems. *IEEE Computer, 40*(1), 71–77.

Staab, S., vander Aalst, W., & Benjamins, V. R. (2003). Web services: Been there, done that? *IEEE Intelligent Systems, 18*(1), 72–85.

Sun Microsystems. (2003). *Java 2 platform enterprise edition specification*, v1.4. Final release, 11/24/03, Nov.

Sycara, K., Paolucci, M., Ankolekar, A., & Srinivasan, N. (2003). Automated discovery, interaction and composition of Semantic Web services. *Journal of Web Semantics*, *1*, 27–46.

Taher, Y., Fauvet, M., Dumas, M., & Benslimane, D. (2008). Using CEP technology to adapt messages exchanged by web services. In *17th International Conference on World Wide Web* (pp. 1231-1232). Beijing, China: ACM.

Tang, J.-F., & Xu, X.-L. (2006). An adaptive model of service composition based on policy driven and multi-agent negotiation. In *Proceedings of the 2006 International Conference on Machine Learning and Cybernetics* (Vol. 2006, pp. 113-118).

Taylor, R., Medvidovic, N., & Oreizy, P. (2009). Architectural styles for runtime software adaptation. In *Joint Working IEEE/IFIP Conference on Software Architecture* (pp. 171-180). IEEE Computer Society Press.

Tidwell, D. (2000). *Web services: The web's next revolution*.

Tigli, J. Y., Lavirotte, S., Rey, G., Hourdin, V., Cheung-Foo-Wo, D., Callegari, E., & Riveill, M. (2009). WComp middleware for ubiquitous computing: Aspects and composite event-based web services. *Annals of Telecommunications, 64*(3-4), 197. ISSN 0003-4347

Tolk, A. (2006). What comes after the Semantic Web - PADS implications for the dynamic Web. In *20th Workshop on Principles of Advanced and Distributed Simulation* (pp. 55-62). IEEE Computer Society Press.

Tolksdorf, R., Nixon, L. J. B., & Simperl, E. P. B. (2008). Towards a tuplespace-based middleware for the Semantic Web. *Web Intelligence and Agent Systems, 6*(3), 235–251.

Tomaz, R. F., Hmida, M. B., & Monfort, V. (2006). Concrete solutions for web services adaptability using policies and aspects. *The International Journal of Cooperative Information Systems, 15*(3), 415–438.

Tselentis, G., Domingue, J., Galis, A., Gavras, A., & Hausheer, D. (2009). *Towards the future internet: A European research perspective*. IOS Press.

Ulieru, M., & Grobbelaar, S. (June 2007). Engineering industrial ecosystems in a networked world. In *Proceedings of the 5th IEEE International Conference on Industrial Informatics*, (pp. 1–7). IEEE Press.

Unger, T., Leymann, F., Leymann, F., & Scheibler, T. (2008). Aggregation of service level agreements in the context of business processes. In *Proceedings of the IEEE Enterprise Distributed Object Conference* (pp. 43-52).

University of Birmingham. (2007). *The PRISM probabilistic model checker*. Retrieved from http://www.prismmodelchecker.org

US National Science Foundation. (n.d.). *Cyber-physical systems*. Retrieved from http://www.nsf.gov/funding/pgm_summ.jsp?pims_id=503286

van der Aalst, W. (1999). Process-oriented architectures for electronic commerce and interorganizational workflow. *Information Systems, 24*(8), 639–671.

van der Aalst, W. (2004). Process mining: A research agenda. *Computers in Industry, 53*(3), 231–244.

van der Aalst, W. M. P., Lohmann, N., Massuthe, P., Stahl, C., & Wolf, K. (2010). Multiparty contracts: Agreeing and implementing interorganizaitonal processes. *The Computer Journal, 53*(1), 90–106.

van der Aalst, W., Dongen, B. F. V., Gunther, C., Rozinat, A., Verbeek, H. M. W., & Weijters, A. J. M. M. (2009). ProM: The process mining toolkit. *Industrial Engineering (American Institute of Industrial Engineers), 489*, 1–4.

van der Aalst, W., & ter Hofstede, A. (2005). YAWL: Yet another workflow language. *Information Systems, 30*(4), 245–275.

van der Aalst, W., Weijters, T., & Maruster, L. (2004). Workflow mining: Discovering process models from event logs. *IEEE Transactions on Knowledge and Data Engineering, 16*(9), 1128–1142.

Vandewoude, Y., & Berbers, Y. (2002a). An overview and assessment of dynamic update methods for component-oriented embedded systems. In *Proceedings of The International Conference on Software Engineering Research and Practice*, Las Vegas, USA.

Vandewoude, Y., & Berbers, Y. (2002b). Run-time evolution for embedded component-oriented systems. In *Proceedings of the International Conference on Software Maintenance*, (pp. 242–245). IEEE Computer Society.

Vargo, S. L., Maglio, P. P., & Akaka, M. A. (2008). On value and value co-creation: A service systems and service logic perspective. *European Management Journal, 26*(3), 145–152.

Vergara, S., & Beceiro, J. (2010). Acceso a datos y servicios de la Web a través de un ESB. *Reporte Taller de Sistemas de Información 3 - InCo - FING - UdelaR.* Retrieved August 7, 2011, from http://www.fing.edu.uy/~lauragon/tesis/tsi3-2010-web-esb.pdf

Verheecke, B., Cibran, M., & Jonckers, V. (2003). AOP for dynamic configuration and management of web services. In *Proceedings of the International Conference on Web Services Europe, vol. 2853.*

Viroli, M., & Casadei, M. (2009). Biochemical tuple spaces for self-organising coordination. In *Proceedings of the 11th International Conference on Coordination Languages and Models, volume 5521 of LNCS,* (pp. 143–162). Lisbon, Portugal: Springer.

Viroli, M., & Casadei, M. (2010). Chemical-inspired self-composition of competing services. In *Proceedings of the 25th Annual ACM Symposium on Applied Computing (SAC 2010), volume III,* (pp. 2029–2036). Sierre, Switzerland: ACM.

Viroli, M., Beal, J., & Casadei, M. (2011a). Core operational semantics of Proto. *In Proceedings of the 26th Annual ACM Symposium on Applied Computing (SAC 2011), volume II: Artificial Intelligence & Agents, Information Systems, and Software Development,* (pp. 1325–1332).

Viroli, M., Casadei, M., Montagna, S., & Zambonelli, F. (2011b). Spatial coordination of pervasive services through chemical-inspired tuple spaces. *ACM Transactions on Autonomous and Adaptive Systems, 6*(2), 14:1 – 14:24.

Vukovic, M. (2007). *Context-aware service composition. Technical Report.* Cambridge: University of Cambridge.

W3.org. (2010). *XML 1.0 specification.* Retrieved August 22, 2010, from http://www.w3.org/TR/REC-xml

W3C. (2001). *Web services description language (WSDL) specification* v1.1.

W3C. (2005). *Web services choreography description language.* Retrieved from http://www.w3.org/TR/2005/CR-ws-cdl-10-20051109/

Wada, H., Suzuki, J., Yamano, Y., & Oba, K. (in press). E^3: Multi-objective genetic algorithms for SLA-aware service deployment optimization problem. *IEEE Transactions in Service Computing.*

Wagner, G., Giurca, A., & Lukichev, S. (2006). A usable interchange format for rich syntax rules integrating OCL, RuleML and SWRL. In *Proceedings of the Workshop on Reasoning on the Web (RoW2006).*

Wang, M., Yapa Bandara, K., & Pahl, C. (2009). Integrated constraint violation handling for dynamic service composition. In *Proceedings IEEE International Conference on Services Computing SCC 2009* (pp. 168-175).

Wang, L., & Krishnan, P. (2006). A framework for checking behavioral compatibility for component selection. In *Proceedings of ASWEC, 06,* 49–60.

Wang, Z., Elbaum, S., & Rosenblum, D. S. (2007). Automated generation of context-aware tests. In *Proceedings of ICSE, 07,* 406–415.

Warmer, J., & Kleppe, A. (1999). *The object constraint language: Precise modeling with UML.* Boston, MA: Addison-Wesley Longman Publishing Co., Inc.

Web Ontology Working Group. (2004). *OWL-S - semantic markup for Web services.* W3C. Retrieved 26 January, 2012, from http://www.w3.org/Submission/OWL-S/

Wells, G. C., Mueller, B., & Schulé, L. (2008). A tuple space web service for distributed programming - Simplifying distributed web services applications. In *Proceedings of the Fourth International Conference on Web Information Systems and Technologies* (WEBIST 2008), (pp. 93–100). INSTICC Press.

Wetzstein, B., Leitner, P., Rosenberg, F., Brandic, I., Leymann, F., & Dustdar, S. (2009). Monitoring and analyzing inuential factors of business process performance. In *Proceedings of the 13th IEEE International Enterprise Distributed Object Computing Conference (EDOC09), Auckland, New Zealand.*

Wetzstein, B., Strauch, S., & Leymann, F. (2009). Measuring performance metrics of WS-BPEL service compositions. In *Proceedings of the International Conference on Networking and Services* (pp. 49-56).

World Resources Institute. (2010, October). *Citywide transportation greenhouse gas emissions inventories: A review of selected methodologies.* Retrieved October 2011 from http://www.wri.org/publication/citywide-transportation-greenhouse-gas-emissions-inventories

Wu, B., Liu, S., & Wu, L. (2008). Dynamic reliable service routing in enterprise service bus. In *Proceedings of the 2008 IEEE Asia-Pacific Services Computing Conference* (pp. 349–354). Washington, DC: IEEE Computer Society. doi:10.1109/APSCC.2008.145

Wylie, H., & Lambros, P. (2009, March 10). *Enterprise connectivity patterns: Implementing integration solutions with IBM's enterprise service bus products.* CT316. Retrieved August 28, 2010, from http://www.ibm.com/developerworks/library/ws-enterpriseconnectivitypatterns/index.html

Xu, Y., Wolf, P., Stojanovic, N., & Happel, H. J. (2010). Semantic-based in the AAL domain. *Posters & Demos* In *9th International Semantic Web Conference* (pp. 9-12). Shanghai, China.

Yan Fang, R., Ru, F., Zhong, T., Eoin, L., Harini, S., Banks, T., & He, L. (2006, May 30). *Cache mediation pattern specification: An overview.* CT316. Retrieved July 21, 2010, from http://www.ibm.com/developerworks/webservices/library/ws-soa-cachemed/

Yau, S. S., Huang, D., Gong, H., & Davulcu, H. (2005). Situation-awareness for adaptive coordination in service-based systems. In the *Proceedings of the 2005 29th Annual International Computer Software and Applications Conference* (pp. 107–112).

Yau, S., Huang, D., & Zhu, L. (2007). An approach to adaptive distributed execution monitoring for workows in service-based systems. In *Proceedings of the International Computer Software and Applications Conference* (Vol. 2, pp. 211-216).

Yellin, D. M., & Strom, D. E. (1997). Protocol specifications and components adaptors. *ACM Transactions on Programming Languages and Systems, 19*(2), 292–333.

Yu, T., Zhang, Y., & Lin, K. (2007). Efficient algorithms for Web services selection with end-to-end QoS constraints. *ACM Transactions in Web, 1*(1).

Yuan, H., Choi, S. W., & Kim, S. D. (2008). A practical monitoring framework for ESB-based services. In *Proceedings of the 2008 IEEE Congress on Services Part II* (pp. 49–56). Washington, DC: IEEE Computer Society. doi:10.1109/SERVICES-2.2008.5

Zapletal, M. (2008). Deriving business service interfaces in windows workflow from UMM transactions. In *Proceedings of ICSOC '08, volume 5364 of Lecture Notes in Computer Science,* (pp. 498–504). Springer.

Zapletal, M., van der Aalst, W., Russell, N., Liegl, P., & Werthner, H. (2009). An analysis of Windows workflow's control-flow expressiveness. In *Proceedings of ECOWS, 09,* 200–209.

Zeng, L., Lei, H., & Chang, H. (2007). Monitoring the QoS for web services. In *Proceedings of the International Conference on Service-Oriented Computing* (pp. 132-144).

Zeng, L., Lingenfelder, C., Lei, H., & Chang, H. (2008). Event-driven quality of service prediction. In *Proceedings of the International Conference on Service-Oriented Computing* (pp. 147-161).

Zhao, Q., & Bhowmick, S. S. (2003). *Sequential pattern matching: A survey.* Retrieved from http://cs.nju.edu.cn/zhouzh/zhouzh.files/course/dm/reading/reading04/zhao_techrep03.pdf

Zheng, Z., & Lyu, M. (2010). An adaptive QoS-aware fault tolerance strategy for web services. *Empirical Software Engineering, 15*(4), 323–345. doi:10.1007/s10664-009-9126-8

Zheng, Z., Ma, H., Lyu, M. R., & King, I. (2011). QoS-Aware Web service recommendation by collaborative filtering. *IEEE Transactions in Service Computing, 4*(2), 140–152.

Zhou, B., Tang, J.-F., & He, Z.-J. (2005). An adaptive model of virtual enterprise based on dynamic web service composition. In *Proceedings of the Fifth International Conference on Computer and Information Technology, CIT 2005* (Vol. 2005, pp. 284-289).

Zielinski, K., Szydło, T., Szymacha, R., Kosinski, J., Kosinska, J., Jarzab, M., & Mickiewicza, A. (2011). Adaptive SOA solution stack. *IEEE Transactions on Services Computing, 99*(1).

Zimmerli, B. (2009). *Business benefits of SOA.* University of Applied Science of Northwestern Switzerland, School of Business, 11 November 2009.

Ziyaeva, G., Choi, E., & Min, D. (2008). Content-based intelligent routing and message processing in enterprise service bus. In *International Conference on Hybrid Information Technology,* (pp. 245-249). Los Alamitos, CA: IEEE Computer Society. Retrieved from http://doi. ieeecomputersociety.org/10.1109/ICHIT.2008.267

Zongyan, Q., Xiangpeng, Z., Chao, C., & Hongli, Y. (2007). Towards the theoretical foundation of choreography. In *WWW'07*, (pp. 973–982). ACM Press.

Zou, J., Pavlovski, C. J., & Wang, Y. (2008). A disclosure framework for service accountability in SOA. In *IEEE International Conference on e-Business Engineering, ICEBE'08* (pp. 437–442).

Zyp, K. (Ed.). (2010). *A JSON media type for describing the structure and meaning of JSON documents.* Internet Engineering Task Force. Retrieved October 30, 2011, from http://tools.ietf.org/html/draft-zyp-json-schema-03

About the Contributors

Guadalupe Ortiz completed her PhD in Computer Science at the University of Extremadura (Spain) in 2007. Since graduating in 2001 and for the following eight years, she worked as an Assistant Professor as well as a research engineer at the University of Extremadura's Computer Science Department. In 2009 she joined the University of Cádiz as Professor in the Department of Computer Science. She has published numerous peer-reviewed papers in international journals, workshops, and conferences. She has been a member of various programme and organization committees of scientific workshops and conferences over the last years and acts as a reviewer for several journals. Her research interests embrace aspect-oriented techniques as a way to improve Web service development in various fields, with an emphasis on model-driven extra-functional properties and quality of service, as well as service context-awareness and their adaptation to mobile devices.

Javier Cubo completed his PhD in Computer Science at the University of Málaga (Spain) in 2010. He has worked both in academia and industry, including The State University of New York (SUNY) (2002-2003), Andalusian Centre of Innovation, Information Technology, and Communications (CITIC) (2004-2006), and Department of Computer Science of University of Málaga (2003, 2006-onwards – as research associate). He has been awarded with two grants: Researcher "Torres Quevedo" Program, Science and Innovation Spanish Ministry and European social Fund (2004-2006), and PhD student - Doctoral Fellowship, Science and Innovation Spanish Ministry (2006-2010), while he has worked collaborating in teaching tasks. He has also got two scholarships as visiting research PhD student at University College London (2008), and as postdoctoral at University of Pisa (2011). His research is focused on the development of formal models in software engineering, specifically in the paradigms of service-oriented computing, cloud computing and component-based software development, applied to context-aware and self-adaptive systems, service composition and reusing in mobile and pervasive systems, and dynamic reconfiguration. He has participated in numerous research projects (national, and international, such as NSF and FP7) and conferences, has published in journals and international workshops and conferences, and has been member of PC and OC, as well as reviewer of several scientific workshops and conferences over the last years.

* * *

Achilleas P. Achilleos received his PhD from the School of Computer Science and Electronic Engineering at the University of Essex, co-funded by the UK Engineering and Physical Sciences Research Council (EPSRC) and British Telecom (BT). During the last year of his PhD he was also working as a part-time researcher at BT. He received his M.Sc. with distinction from the same department and a B.Sc. with excellence from the Budapest University of Technology and Economics in Hungary. Currently he is working as a post-doctoral researcher at the Software Engineering and Internet Technologies lab, where he participated in the last few years in EU FP6, FP7 and AAL projects such as MUSIC, COIN, and CVN. His research interests include ubiquitous computing, service-oriented computing, Web Services, mobile computing, and model-driven development. He has published his research work in internationally refereed journals and conferences and as book chapters. He served also as a TPC member and referee in various conferences related to his research area. He is a member of the IEEE Computer Society and Cyprus Scientific and Technical Chamber (ETEK).

Dimitris Apostolou is Senior Researcher at ICCS and an Assistant Professor in the Informatics Department of the University of Piraeus. He holds a PhD on Knowledge Management and Decision Support from NTUA, an MSc in IT with distinction from University College London, UK, an MSc in Chemical Engineering from New Jersey Institute of Technology, USA, and a Diploma Degree in Chemical Engineering from NTUA. He has an extensive experience as a management consultant, has coordinated two and participated in more than fifteen IST projects. In the past he has participated in research and consulting projects in the areas of geographical information systems, data warehousing and OLAP applications, business process modeling, as well as projects dealing with the technical analysis of energy and environmental systems.

Michael Boniface is the Technical Director of the IT Innovation Centre. He joined IT Innovation in 2000 after several years at Nortel Networks developing infrastructure to support telecommunications interoperability. His roles at IT Innovation include technical strategy of RTD across IT Innovation's project portfolio, technical leadership, and business development. He has over 10 years' experience of RTD into innovative distributed systems for science and industry using technologies such as Semantic Web, Grid, and service-oriented architectures. He leads IT Innovation's contribution to the Future Internet initiative through Expert Groups including leadership of the FIA socio-economic working group. Michael provides architecture and business modelling direction in RTD projects including project coordinator EC EXPERIMEDIA, scientific leadership in EC TEFIS, leadership of sustainability activities in EC BonFIRE, and socio-economic impact assessment of Future Internet technologies in EC SESERV and Network of Excellence EINS. Michael has a BEng in Multimedia Communications.

Juan Boubeta-Puig has worked as an Assistant Professor in the Department of Computer Science of the University of Cádiz (Spain) since 2009 where he received his degree on Computer Science in 2010. He is currently doing his PhD and his research focuses on Web service compositions (WS-BPEL), the integration of complex event processing into event-driven service-oriented architectures and the model-driven development of advanced user interfaces. Despite his relatively short research career, he has published several papers in international and national conferences and a national journal. He is a researcher of the UCASE Software Engineering Research Group and he has participated as a researcher in a project funded by the University of Cádiz Research Promotion Plan.

Mario Bravetti, PhD in 2012, is Associate Professor at the Computer Science department of the University of Bologna, Italy. He is member of the FOCUS (Foundations of Component-based Ubiquitous Systems) team which is part of the INRIA Sophia Antipolis □ Méditerranée research center. He is co-author of more than 60 publications in international conferences, journals, and books. He is co-founder and member of the steering committee of the international workshop on Web Services and Formal Methods (currently at its 9th edition). He has been: organizer/program committee chair of several international conferences and events (such as Concurrency Theory – CONCUR and the meeting on the 25th anniversary of Process Algebra), guest editor for numerous proceeding volumes and special issues of international journals, invited speaker/lecturer at several international conferences (such as the International Conference on Quantitative Evaluation of SysTems – QEST) and PhD schools.

Valeria Cardellini is Assistant Professor in the Department of Computer Science, Systems and Production of the University of Roma "Tor Vergata," Italy. She received her PhD degree in Computer Science in 2001 and her Laurea degree in Computer Engineering in 1997, both from the University of Roma "Tor Vergata." She was a visiting researcher at IBM T.J. Watson Research Center in 1999. Her research interests are in the field of distributed computing systems, with special emphasis on large-scale systems and services based on Internet and the Web. On these subjects she has co-authored around 60 papers in international journals, book chapters, and conference proceedings. She has been co-chair of AAA-IDEA 2009, has served as a member of program and organizing committees of international conferences on Web and performance analysis areas, and serves as frequent reviewer for various international journals. She is a member of ACM and IEEE.

Rim Chaabani got her Master of Science in Intelligent Information system in Kairouan. She learnt context aware platforms such as Wcomp and she introduced process and orchestration in WComp. She teaches at the Institute of Computer and Management of Kairouan. She got certification in CCNA1 and CCNA2 « NETWORKING BASICS » in CISCO Systems networking academy.

Sihem Cherif is a PhD student, SOIE Laboratory in Tunisia. She is starting a career as a scientist and has already published in several famous conferences. She works on context aware platforms and interoperability. She teaches at the Institute of Mathematics and Computer Science of Kairouan.

Gary Creaner received a Bachelor in Computer Applications degree from Dublin City University. Recently, he also graduated with an M.Sc. in Software Engineering from Dublin City University. Gary's interests lie in service engineering and software architecture. As part of his research, he has investigated coordination mechanisms for service and cloud architectures.

José C. Delgado is an Associate Professor at the Computer Science and Engineering Department of the Instituto Superior Técnico (Lisbon Technical University), in Lisbon, Portugal, where he earned the Ph.D. degree in 1988. He lectures courses in the areas of Computer Architecture, Information Technology and Service Engineering. He has performed several management roles in his faculty, namely Director of the Taguspark campus, near Lisbon, and Coordinator of the B.Sc. and M.Sc. in Computer Science and Engineering at that campus. He has been the coordinator of and researcher in several research projects, both national and European. As an author, his publications include one book, several book chapters, and more than 40 papers in international refereed conferences and journals.

Valerio Di Valerio is a second-year Ph.D. student in Computer Engineering in the Computer Science, Systems and Production Department at the University of Roma "Tor Vergata," Italy. His research interests are in the field of distributed computing systems, with special emphasis on modeling and performance evaluation.

Simon Dobson became Professor of Computer Science at the University of St Andrews in 2009. His main research interest is in software design and analysis, especially in developing the mathematical models, novel programming languages, and techniques for building adaptive sensor-driven systems. This research is vital for fields like environmental sensing, where Simon's work is helping to build systems that can respond to changes the phenomena they are observing. Adaptive sensing techniques can also be applied to observe and influence networks, smart buildings, and even financial instruments. Simon is a Chartered Fellow of the British Computer Society and a Chartered Engineer.

Schahram Dustdar is Full Professor of Computer Science with a focus on Internet Technologies heading the Distributed Systems Group, Vienna University of Technology (TU Wien). He is also Honorary Professor of Information Systems at the Department of Computing Science at the University of Groningen (RuG), The Netherlands. He is Chair of the IFIP Working Group 6.4 on Internet Applications Engineering and a founding member of the Scientific Academy of service Technology.

Vegard Engen is a Research Engineer at the IT Innovation Centre, currently working on European projects in the areas of service oriented architectures, risk management, and web science. Recent research focuses on service level agreements and quality of service, resource provisioning and adaptation for interactive future internet applications, and proactive risk management in online communities. With a background in artificial intelligence, Vegard has researched and delivered machine learning solutions applied to a range of real-world problems ranging from network based intrusion detection to medical diagnosis. He has also worked in the field of population based simulations with a focus on social influence models. Vegard has a PhD in Computer Science and has a keen interest in natural computation, especially nature inspired search and optimisation algorithms in distributed environments.

Alfonso García de Prado received his degree on Computer Engineering at the University of Extremadura (Spain) in 2007 and is currently doing his PhD at the University of Cádiz (Spain), where he is working as an Assistant Professor. His previous work in the industry – Atos Origin, MSL and CSIC, among others– has provided him with a great experience on system development, analysis, and architectures. His research focuses on the use of model-driven development and aspect-oriented programming as a way to provide context-awareness and device adaptation for web services. He has published several papers in various IEEE conferences and an international journal. He has also participated as a researcher in a project financed by the University of Extremadura and Santander Bank and he recently joined to UCASE Software Engineering Research Group.

Stefano Iannucci is a third-year Ph.D. student in Computer Engineering in the Computer Science, Systems and Production Department at the University of Roma "Tor Vergata," Italy. His research interests are in the fields of adaptive and self-managed service oriented systems and Cloud computing.

Sandeep Korrapati is pursuing a Master in Computer Science at the University of Paderborn, Germany since October 2010. His area of specialization for his masters is Embedded Systems. He obtained his Bachelor's degree in Computer Science from Vellore Institute of Technology University, India, in May 2008. After his Bachelor's degree, he worked as Assistant Systems Engineer at Tata Consultancy Services Ltd., India for 2 years. He has been working and researching with Fahad Bin Tariq since April 2011, assisting in research and development of modules related to the research work. Sandeep's areas of interests include cyber physical systems, and hardware software co-design.

Laura González is Computer Engineer (University of the Republic, Uruguay) and she holds a Master degree in Computer Science (PEDECIBA). She is Assistant Professor at the Computer Science Department of the University of the Republic of Uruguay, where she lectures on Enterprise Application Platforms, Information Systems and Middleware. Since 2004 she has worked in consulting, research projects, and teaching activities at this department. Her research interests include middleware technologies, enterprise application integration, interoperability, service oriented computing, e-government and digital inclusion. She is currently working on her PhD thesis, in the area of adaptive service platforms.

Philipp Leitner has a Ph.D. in Business Informatics from Vienna University of Technology. He is currently a Postdoctoral Researcher at the Distributed Systems Group at the same university. Philipp's research is focused on middleware for distributed systems, especially for SOAP-based and RESTful Web services.

Francesco Lo Presti is an Associate Professor in the Department of Computer Science, Systems and Production of the University of Roma "Tor Vergata," Italy. He received the Laurea degree in Electrical Engineering and the Doctorate degree in Computer Science from the University of Roma "Tor Vergata," Italy, in 1993 and 1997, respectively. His research interests include measurements, modeling and performance evaluation of computer and communications networks. He has more than 50 publications in international conferences and journals. He has served as a program member of international conferences on networking and performance areas, and serves as reviewer for various international journals.

Clarissa Cassales Marquezan is a Postdoctoral Researcher of the "Adaptive Software and Services" research group at Paluno (The Ruhr Institute for Software Technology) of the University of Duisburg-Essen. Since 2011, she is work package leader of the FI PPP use case project FInest contributing to the design of cloud-based solutions for the Transport and Logistics domain. She has over 10 years of experience on research, design and implementation of distributed and network systems using, for example, technologies associated with Policy-Based Management, Service-Oriented Architectures, P2P, and Self-* properties. Her current research interesting includes adaptive service-oriented systems with the focus on decentralization and cross-cutting aspects of such systems with networks and services management. Clarissa received her Ph.D. in Computer Science in 2010 from the Federal University of Rio Grande do Sul (UFRGS), Brazil.

Inmaculada Medina-Bulo received her PhD in Computer Science at the University of Seville (Spain). She has been a Professor in the Department of Computer Science of the University of Cádiz (Spain) since 1995. She held the post of Department Secretary in 1997 and has been a member of the Council of the School of Engineering (ESI) as well as a Socrates/Erasmus Program Coordinator for several years. From July 2010 to July 2011 she was appointed Degree Coordinator for the Computer Science Studies and a member of the Board of the ESI. Her research was supported by research stays at the USA, the UK and Germany. She has served in program and organizing committees at different conferences. She has published numerous papers in international journals and conferences. She is the main researcher of the UCASE Software Engineering Research Group and she has two project funded by the Spanish Ministry and the University of Cádiz Research Promotion Plan.

Gregoris Mentzas is Professor of Information Management at the School of Electrical and Computer Engineering of the National Technical University of Athens (NTUA) and Director of the Information Management Unit (IMU) of ICCS. He currently serves as Director of the division of Industrial Electric Devices and Decision Systems while during 2006-2009 he served in the Board of Directors of ICCS. His research concerns e-service technologies, social computing, e-government and knowledge management. He has coordinated or participated in more than 40 international projects funded by the European Commission and other funding bodies. He is an Associate Editor in five scientific journals and was Program Committee member in more than 55 international conferences like WWW, IEEE RE, ECAI, DEXA, AAAI Symposia, IFIP eGOV, PRO-VE, IDT, and ESWC among others. Prof. Mentzas has (co-) authored or edited 4 books on Semantic Web applications and knowledge management and published more than 200 papers in international peer-reviewed journals and conferences.

Andreas Metzger is Senior Researcher and leader of the "Adaptive Software and Services" research area at Paluno (the Ruhr Institute for Software Technology), at the University of Duisburg-Essen. Since 2008, he is activity and work package leader of S-Cube, the European Network of Excellence on software, services & systems, and member of the network's management board. Since 2011, he is the technical coordinator of the EU FI PPP use case project FInest. His current research interests include software engineering and service-based systems engineering, focusing on online quality prediction for adaptive systems. Here, Andreas investigates novel techniques that allow anticipating and proactively responding to imminent software failures. He has co-authored over 40 papers, articles and book chapters and acted as member of the program committee for numerous international events.

Valerie Monfort is an Assistant Professor in Paris 1 Panthéon Sorbonne, working also in Tunisia where she created a research team. She teaches: Information System changes via performance, Mobile Information Systems, SOA based distributed architectures, project management, methodology, et cetera. She wrote several books in French to disseminate Web service technology. She also wrote several papers about Web service and adaptability. She worked more than twenty years in the industry as an international consultant working for big companies as: IBM, Airbus, DEXIA, BNP, Carrefour, and MMA.

Franco Maria Nardini is currently a Research Fellow at Scuola Normale Superiore in Pisa, Italy and a Research Associate at ISTI-CNR in Pisa, Italy. He received his Ph.D. degree from the Department of Information Engineering of the University of Pisa in 2011 after discussing his thesis "Query Log Mining to Enhance User Experience in Search Engines." His research interests are mainly focused on Information Retrieval and Web Data Mining. His work is focused on developing techniques for extracting and exploiting valuable knowledge from the behavior of Web search engine users, and on the usage of those techniques within efficient and effective solutions to increase the user experience in Web search engines. He is author of more than 15 papers published on the major conferences and journals of information retrieval.

Claus Pahl is a Senior Lecturer at Dublin City University, School of Computing. His main research area is Software and Systems Engineering. He has been working on software engineering technologies, where he has investigated software service technologies including semantic services and architectures. Specific interests include service process architectures and architectural patterns, model-driven service engineering, and service integration architectures. He has published more than 200 papers. He has been an invited speaker and an invited panelist at conferences and workshops in the area of service engineering.

George A. Papadopoulos holds the (tenured) rank of Professor of Software Engineering in the Department of Computer Science, University of Cyprus. His research interests include middleware platforms, context-aware management systems, component-based systems, mobile computing, e-health, e-learning, open and distance learning, adaptive and distributed systems, service oriented computing and cooperative systems. He has published over 150 papers as book chapters or in internationally refereed journals and conferences and he serves in the Editorial Board of 7 international journals. Professor Papadopoulos is a recipient of a 1995 ERCIM, HCM scholarship award. He has been involved or is currently participating, as coordinator or partner, in over 50 internationally and nationally funded projects with a personal funding of more than 7 MEUR. He is the Director of the Software Engineering and Internet Technologies (SEIT) Laboratory (http://www.cs.ucy.ac.cy/seit).

Nikos Papageorgiou is Researcher at ICCS. He holds Diploma degree in Electrical and Computer Engineering from the National Technical University of Athens, Greece, and MSc degree in Engineering-Economic Systems. His Diploma Thesis was in the area of programming distributed systems using CORBA and his MSc degree was on innovation evaluation using a groupware platform. He has an extensive experience in software engineering, especially in enterprise resource planning (ERP) systems. He has worked as analyst and developer and as ICT consultant in various firms. His research interests include software engineering, knowledge management, Semantic Web, ontology-based modelling, and collaboration services.

Ioannis Patiniotakis is Researcher at ICCS. He holds Diploma degree in Electrical and Computer Engineering from the National Technical University of Athens, Greece, and MSc degree in Engineering-Economic Systems. His Diploma Thesis was in the area of programming distributed systems using CORBA and his MSc degree was on the evaluation of Groupware Systems. He has an extensive experience in software engineering, especially in analysis and development of web-based information systems. He has worked as analyst and developer and as ICT consultant in various firms. His research interests include software engineering, knowledge management, Semantic Web, service adaptation, e-government, and e-commerce.

Stephen C Phillips is a Project Manager and Senior Research Engineer at the IT Innovation Centre. Through national and European projects Stephen has spent over seven years working in the area of service oriented architectures with a special focus on management systems and service level agreements.

Stephen's current work with major broadcasters and archives in the PrestoPRIME project is complemented by his experience of designing service management systems for companies in the aerospace, automotive and pharmaceutical industries. Stephen has a background in chemistry and mathematics and a PhD in computational chemistry.

Ernesto Pimentel holds the BSc and MSc degrees in Mathematics (1988), and the PhD degree in Computer Science (1993). He is full Professor at the University of Malaga since 2003. His research activity is focused on methodologies for the development of software components and services, the application of formal methods to software engineering, including topics such as models for concurrency, component-based software development, and adaptation and composition of software services. Most of his work has been published in more than 30 international journals and almost 100 conferences and workshops.

Klaus Pohl is a full Professor for Software Systems Engineering at the University of Duisburg-Essen, adjunct professor at the University of Limerick, Ireland and director of Paluno (the Ruhr Institute for Software Technology) of the University of Duisburg-Essen (UDE), Germany. From 2005 to 2007 he acted as the founding scientific director of Lero, the Irish Software Engineering Research Centre. He is network coordinator of S-Cube, vice-chair of the Steering Committee of NESSI, member of its executive board, and Steering Committee member of the German Innovation-Alliance SPES 2020. Klaus received his Ph.D. and habilitation from RWTH Aachen. His research interests are requirements engineering, service-based systems engineering, software quality assurance, and software product lines. He has co-authored over 150 peer-reviewed papers and acted as member of the program committee for numerous national and international events. As a consultant he supports industry and public organizations to improve the requirements engineering processes.

Raul Ruggia is Computer Engineer (University of the Republic, Uruguay) and received his Ph.D. in Computer Science from the University of Paris VI (France). He works as Professor at the Computer Science Department of the University of the Republic of Uruguay, where he lectures on Information Systems, supervises graduate students, and directs research activities on middleware, data quality management, and data warehousing. He has also supervised technological projects on e-Government and telecommunications domains joint with Uruguayan government agencies.

Fabrizio Silvestri is currently a Researcher at ISTI-CNR in Pisa, Italy. He received his Ph.D. from the Computer Science Department of the University of Pisa in 2004. His research interests are mainly focused on Web information retrieval with particular focus on efficiency related problems like caching, collection partitioning, and distributed IR in general. In his professional activities Fabrizio Silvestri is member of the program committee of many of the most important conferences in IR as well as organizer and, member of the steering committee, of the workshop Large Scale and Distributed Systems for Information Retrieval (LSDS-IR). Recently, Fabrizio Silvestri has been appointed as Work-Package leader and Activity leader of the EU Network of Excellence project S-Cube. He is author of more than 60 publications in highly relevant venues spanning from distributed and parallel computing to IR and data mining related conferences.

Graeme Stevenson is a PhD candidate at the University of St Andrews in the United Kingdom. His research interests include middleware for smart spaces, sensor network based situation recognition within smart spaces, programming languages, approaches to programming over semi-structured data models, ontologies, reasoning, and the Semantic Web. Stevenson has an MPhil in Computer Science from the University of Strathclyde, UK.

Fahad Bin Tariq completed his undergraduate degree in 2003 in Computer Science at Muhammad Ali Jinnah University in Karachi, Pakistan. Thereafter he went to RWTH-Aachen in Germany to successfully complete his Master of Science degree in the area of Software Systems Engineering. In 2007 he was awarded a scholarship from the International Graduate School of the University of Paderborn to pursue a PhD degree at the Department of Distributed Embedded Systems. He is interested in emerging trends such as the Internet of Things and their potential in enabling systems to adapt during runtime, thereby acquiring potentially unlimited new behaviour as well as desirable system qualities.

Gabriele Tolomei is currently a Postdoctoral Research Fellow at the Data-Intensive and SCalable Information Systems Lab at the "Ca' Foscari" University of Venice, Italy. He also collaborates with the High Performance Computing Lab of the ISTI-CNR in Pisa, Italy, as a Research Associate. He received his Ph.D. degree in Computer Science from the "Ca' Foscari" University of Venice in 2011, and both his M.Sc. and B.Sc. degrees in Computer Science from the University of Pisa, Italy in 2005 and 2002, respectively. His research interests include information retrieval, machine learning, data mining, and natural language processing topics. In particular, he obtained remarkable results in Web Search and Web Mining. He is author of more than 10 papers published on relevant international conferences and journals.

Yiannis Verginadis is Senior Researcher at ICCS. He holds Diploma and Doctoral degrees in Electrical and Computer Engineering from the National Technical University of Athens, Greece. His Diploma Thesis was in the area of collaboration and workflow management systems over IP, using browser and client server architectures and his PhD degree was on Inter-organizational Workflow Management Systems. He has an extensive experience in management of information systems, software engineering, workflow management, electronic government, and electronic commerce, and he participated in more than ten IST projects. His research interests include management information systems, software engineering, workflow management, service adaptation, electronic government, and electronic commerce.

Mirko Viroli is Associate Professor at the DEIS, Department of Electronics, Informatics and Systems of the Alma Mater Studiorum–Università di Bologna, Italy. He is an expert in computational models, in the areas of agent-based systems, coordination infrastructures, self-organising systems, and pervasive computing. He has written over 150 articles on such topics, of which more than 30 on international refereed journals. He was Program Chair of the 2008 and 2009 ACM Symposium on Applied Computing (SAC), he is member of the Editorial Board of *The Knowledge Engineering Review* journal, and leader of the Bologna Unit of the FP7 STREP project "SAPERE - Self-Aware Pervasive Service Ecosystems."

Kun Yang received his PhD from University College London (UCL), UK and is currently a full Professor in the School of Computer Science and Electronic Engineering (CSEE), UEssex, UK. Prior to this post, he worked at UCL on several EU research projects such as FP4 FAIN, MANTRIP, FP5

CONTEXT. His main research interests include mobile wireless networks, IP network management, pervasive service engineering and cloud computing, in which he has more than 20 years' experience and has published 150+ papers. He was/is a general chair, TPC chair of many IEEE conferences. He serves on the editorial boards of both IEEE and non-IEEE journals. He has managed many research projects as the PI (Principal Investigator) such as UK EPSRC project PANDA and PAL, and EU project EVANS, etc. The ongoing joint research projects he is currently involved in includes: UK project PAL (5 partners), EU FP7 projects GEYSERS (an IP project), MANTYCHORE (a STREP project), PURSUIT (a STREP project), etc.

Franco Zambonelli is full Professor of Computer Science at the University of Modena and Reggio Emilia. He got his PhD in Computer Science and Engineering from the University of Bologna in 1997. His research interests include: pervasive computing, multi-agent systems, self-adaptive, and self-organizing computing. He has published over 70 papers in peer-reviews journals, and has been invited speaker at many conferences and workshops. He is the co-Editor in Chief of the ACM *Transactions on Autonomous and Adaptive Systems,* and he is in the Editorial Board of the Elsevier *Journal of Pervasive and Mobile Computing,* of the *BCS Computer Journal,* and of the *Journal of Agent-Oriented Software Engineering,* and he is in the Steering Committee of the IEEE SASO Conference. He has been scientific manager of the EU FP6 Project CASCADAS and is currently coordinator of the EU FP7 Project SAPERE. He is a senior member of ACM and IEEE.

Gianluigi Zavattaro, PhD in 2000, is Associate Professor since 2005 at the Computer Science department of the University of Bologna, Italy. He is co-author of more than 100 publications in international conferences and journals. He has been chair of the program committee of conferences like CONCUR (International Conference on Concurrency Theory), COORDINATION (International Conference on Coordination Models and Languages), and ECOWS (IEEE European Conference on Web Services) and invited speaker at conferences like FORTE (International Conference on Formal Techniques for Networked and Distributed Systems) and TGC (International Symposium on Trustworthy Global Computing). He is member of the IFIP Working Group 6.1 "Architectures and Protocols for Distributed Systems" and of the "Journal of Software (JSW)."

Zlatko Zlatev is a Research Engineer at the IT Innovation Centre. After spending a number of years in the industry as a Senior Developer, designing and developing data warehousing solutions and business workflows solutions, he developed interests in the fields of machine learning and data mining. In January 2007, he joined the IT Innovation Centre at the University of Southampton where he has worked on a wide range of large scale collaborative projects, contributing in the areas of systems performance modelling for engineering of service oriented infrastructures, statistical modelling and prediction of natural phenomena, software solutions for archiving of digital data for the media and oil and gas industry, communication architectures and information management solutions for the domain of large scale natural disasters management. Zlatko has an MSc in Computing Machines and Technologies and an MSc (Dist.) in Machine Learning and Data Mining.

Index